CHASING
THE
FOUR WINDS

The Incredible True Story of a 45-Year
Professional Flying Career Filled with
Adventure and Danger

Mike Stock

ASPEN RIDGE PRESS
Sellersburg, Indiana

Cover design by Laurie Schutza
Text design by www.tothepointsolutions.com

Photos: All photographs are from the Stock family collection or in the public domain, unless otherwise noted.

Front cover: Four aircraft that figured prominently in my flying career as a bush pilot, test pilot, and combat pilot. *From upper left clockwise:* DeHavilland DHC-6 Beaver (photo by Mark Stadsklev); Northrop T-38 Talon (U.S. Navy photo); Bell UH-1B Iroquois (U.S. Navy photo); and Piasecki PA-97 Heli-Stat (photo courtesy Piasecki Aircraft Corporation).

So that you will better know your husband,
father and grandfather. I dedicate this book to Barbara,
Brian, Ashley, Julie, and their children.

Contents

Preface

MANY PILOTS HAVE MORE FLIGHT HOURS IN THEIR LOGBOOKS OR have flown more models of aircraft. Other pilots have survived more hair-raising encounters. But few pilots have had the diversity of flying experience that has been my good fortune.

Because of my unique aviation career, the thought crossed my mind that maybe my children, grandchildren, and extended family might like to ride along as copilot, to vicariously share in some of the memorable adventures I accumulated in over a half century of professional flying. And so, I started writing.

Supported by reference documents, logbooks, diaries, photographs, and other materials that I had saved, I was able to reconstruct my life in an organized and comprehensive manner, which would have been impossible from memory alone. As I relived my successes and failures, the good times and the bad, I alternately laughed and cried, struggled anew, and basked once more in fleeting glory. It has been more than a sentimental journey—it has been the trip of a lifetime!

In 2004, when I started this project, my intent was to write a traditional one-volume memoir. But it soon became apparent that it would be necessary to publish multiple volumes to tell the whole story without creating a monster book of awkward proportions. So, I wrote and published a three-volume series, titled *The Reluctant Aviator*, that chronicled my life as well as my aviation career. It was intended primarily for family and friends.

After publishing volume Three, however, I decided to condense the three books into one so I could share my story with a wider audience of fellow pilots and aviation enthusiasts. It was a much harder task than I ever imagined. Cutting approximately one half of the original manuscript was a painful process. In the end, I chose to eliminate virtually all reference to my family, to my childhood, and to periods of my aviation career that did not involve much flying, like the two years I was assigned to the *USS*

Raleigh LPD-1 as the Air Officer, and the three years I served as the Executive Officer of the Naval ROTC Unit at Purdue University. My intent was to retain a narrative that focused on my days in the cockpit. Hopefully, I didn't throw out some of the wheat with the chaff.

Additionally, for marketing reasons and to avoid confusion, I decided to retitle the combined book to *Chasing the Four Winds*, which I think is appropriate because I was always looking for the next flying challenge no matter where it led—a wanderlust that was never satisfied.

All of the events recounted in this book are true and happened as I have described them. I feel compelled to make this statement because some readers might think my many diverse flight experiences and narrow escapes could not have possibly happened to one pilot. But they did. That I have been fortunate and lucky goes without saying. The only poetic license was used in the dialogue between me and various protagonists. Most is contrived to represent what might have been said at that particular moment, except in certain cases where I can remember exactly what was said.

If *Chasing the Four Winds* had been constructed entirely from memory, there would be good reason to doubt the accuracy of this account. Although my memory was useful to connect and maintain continuity, and in some cases vital to the story itself, it was backed up by a mountain of reference material that I had religiously saved. When writing a memoir, it is good to have been a packrat. I had kept most things pertaining to my naval career, such as official and unofficial records and documents, flight logbooks, photographs, and memorabilia. My wife and my mother had saved over one hundred letters that I had written during Navy flight training, Vietnam, and at various other times. I was a prolific photographer in Vietnam and Alaska, and these images brought those periods of my life into sharper focus. Many times during my research, I said to myself, "Boy, I had forgotten that." Or, I came across evidence to suggest that some stories I had been telling for years did not occur exactly as I had remembered. Although a memoir is never as thoroughly researched and documented as a biography or historical treatise, I am satisfied that this book is factual and devoid of embellishment.

Normally, I am not a diary writer. Keeping a diary requires commitment and discipline, and at the end of a long day, I would much rather read a good book. That being said, there were two times during my aviation career when I did keep a diary: during my combat tour in Vietnam and the six summer seasons I flew in Alaska. I am so glad that I did because those two periods were central to my aviation story. Having my diaries to fall back on was both a blessing and a curse. On the one hand, I was able to faithfully reconstruct events that otherwise would have been fuzzy or forgotten altogether. On the other hand, it was often painful to relive the stressful times and my tussles with the Grim Reaper.

Whenever possible, I have used real names, except to deliberately avoid assassinating anyone's character or besmirching their good name. However, we all encounter people that impact our lives in a negative manner and sometimes their role must be told to provide a fuller understanding of events. In these few cases, I have changed their names or identified them only by job title or position to protect them and their families from embarrassment.

Throughout the book, I offer my opinions and judgments about events as I saw them. I take full responsibility for these comments and make no apologies, even though some readers may reach a different conclusion.

One author recommended the removal of as many personal pronouns as possible from a memoir. I have tried to follow his advice, but this is, after all, my memoir, so at times my prose may take on a bragging or cocky tone. My hope is that my braggadocio is tempered by an equal part of humility.

Acknowledgments

THERE ARE MANY PEOPLE WHO DESERVE MY APPRECIATION FOR THEIR contributions directly or indirectly to this book, but none more so than my wife, Barbara. Now I know why authors thank their spouses—spouses have to be so incredibly tolerant of being constantly ignored and tuned-out during the creative process. So, I thank Barbara for being so understanding and patient during the long hours I spent locked away in my study, staring at my computer screen, hoping for inspiration. As she has told family and friends over the years, "My job is to keep him fed and watered."

I wish to thank Laurie Schutza (lschutza@gmail.com) who designed the striking front and back covers of this book. Her creative genius never ceases to amaze me.

To my editor, Mary Jo Zazueta (www.tothepointsolutions.com) I owe a huge debt of gratitude. She did a fantastic job on proofing, editing, interior design, and placement of photos within the manuscript. She was such a pleasure to work with. The finished product you hold in your hands is in large measure a tribute to her skills and experience in the publishing business.

Finally, I wish to thank my parents, family, and all of my teachers, coaches, Boy Scout leaders, friends, flight instructors, bosses, chief pilots, coworkers, fellow pilots, and crewmembers who have directly or indirectly guided and shaped the most enjoyable aviation career a man could ask for.

Introduction

ASIDE FROM A FEW PERSONAL DETAILS THROWN IN TO PROVIDE A more complete picture, this book is first and foremost a memoir that details my long professional flying career. As stated in the Preface, there are many pilots who have more flight hours, who have flown more models of aircraft, who have survived more catastrophic situations, and who have garnered more fame and accolades. Many *combat pilots* have participated in heroic missions at greater risk to their lives; many *test pilots* have made greater contributions to the advancement of human flight; and many *bush pilots* have pushed the limits of their aircraft further and exhibited much greater skill. But few pilots have had the privilege of taking to the skies as a combat pilot, a test pilot, and a bush pilot.

What makes my aviation career unique is the breadth of my piloting experience, ranging from supersonic jets to airships, in almost every facet of the aviation industry where pilots are employed: military aviator, combat pilot, airline pilot, test pilot, corporate pilot, charter pilot, bush pilot, ferry pilot, air tour pilot, flight instructor—as the cliché goes: "Been there, done that."

Most of my jobs were the result of careful planning and effort on my part, others involved luck and serendipity. No matter what type of aircraft I was flying or what job I was doing at the time, I loved every minute. Not once did I ever get up in the morning and say, "Damn, I have to go flying today." Flying was never work, never drudgery. How many people can truthfully say that about their chosen career path?

Given what little you know about my flying background thus far, you might think that I wanted to be a pilot from the time I could walk. That I grew up building and flying model airplanes and reading aviation books and flying magazines. That I hung around the local airport as a teenager, washing airplanes to pay for flying lessons and soloed an airplane on my sixteenth birthday (the youngest allowed by the FAA). You would be wrong on all accounts!

Like most young people graduating high school, I didn't have any clear direction to my life or a well-thought-out career objective. The closest thing I had to a goal was a lukewarm desire to be a naval officer. Where that desire sprang from, I do not remember. Maybe it was a movie I had seen or a book I had read. I do know that my Uncle Harry had some influence. He was a retired chief petty officer with close to thirty years of active duty service. I never tired of listening to his stories of shipboard life in the early days of the Navy, and his combat service aboard destroyers in the Pacific during World War II. I listened with rapt attention as he spoke of the day his ship was hit by a Japanese kamikaze in the latter days of the war, which killed eleven of his shipmates. He showed me a piece from the enemy aircraft that he had kept as a war souvenir.

As I expressed increasing interest in joining the Navy, my uncle encouraged me to get a college education and go in as an officer. He said that officers had it much better than enlisted men.

After narrowly missing a chance to go to the Naval Academy, I enrolled halfheartedly at the University of Buffalo. Two semesters later, I dropped out, disillusioned and aimless. After working for a year, I decided to give college another try and entered Penn State, where I enrolled in Naval ROTC as a Contract (non-scholarship) student. My dream of becoming a naval officer was rekindled; not to fly, but to be a surface officer on ships.

One day, during the spring term of my sophomore year at Penn State, as I was passing through the student union in my Navy ROTC uniform, a Navy recruiter was set up in an alcove off the main hallway. As I passed by, the petty officer said, "Do you have a few minutes? How would you like to take the aptitude test to be a Navy pilot?"

"Yes, I have time, but I am not really interested in being a pilot. I want to be a surface officer," I stated emphatically.

"What do you have to lose? And, besides, if you pass, the results are good forever—you'll never have to retake the test in case you change your mind somewhere down the road," he replied. "It will only take about forty minutes. What do you say?"

I decided to do it. After I finished the exam, he immediately graded my paper. "Congratulations, Mike. You passed," he said, offering his hand. He reached for a legal-sized green logbook and entered the date, my name, and my test scores. "There, if you ever change your mind, your scores are a matter of record." I was proud that I had passed, but gave it no more thought.

In 1963, eight months later and midway through fall term of my junior year, I came to the realization that my goal of becoming a naval officer was slipping away due to poor academic performance, and it was nobody's fault except my own. I reached the conclusion that if I didn't take some drastic action, I would never amount to anything.

The only option for me to become a commissioned naval officer without a college degree was to be accepted into the Naval Aviation Cadet Program (NAVCAD). This program required two years of college—I had three and one half years of college, of which I could probably squeeze out two years' worth of transferable credit. The kicker was that I had to be a pilot. Faced with the choice of being a slacker and underachiever for the rest of my life or becoming a naval officer, I decided to try being a pilot. It turned out to be a life-changing decision that gave birth to a fifty-three-year professional flying career, as satisfying as it was long.

The United States Navy gave me the chance to be a pilot, gave me the best training in the world, and gave direction to my life's work. I am extremely grateful to the Navy for the gift of flight and very proud to have been a naval aviator for twenty years. There is seldom a day that goes by without a conscious thought about the Navy. It was such a large part of my life and it continues to influence my daily activities. Naval service was the seminal event of my existence—it defines who I am.

In my everyday life out of the cockpit, I have always been somewhat cautious and conservative in selecting activities in which to participate. Anything that seemed risky was quickly ruled out. For example, I don't ride motorcycles, sky dive, bungee jump, kayak white-water rivers, or engage in other extreme sports. In the air, I am a different person, like Clark Kent and his alter-ego Superman. Not that I do daredevil stunts or that I disregard acceptable norms—just the opposite. I am very safety conscious while flying. Yet there is a part of me that is willing to participate in flight activities that would cause other pilots to wince. I do this probably because I feel that I can safely control the outcome—the master of the machine. As you read various stories in this book, you might be tempted to exclaim, "My, god! What was he thinking?" There is a dichotomy between my behavior on the ground and in the air that even I can't fully explain.

I will be the first to admit that I have lived a charmed life. I have survived two helicopter crashes, the in-flight breakup and crash of an experimental heavy-lift aircraft, three engine failures in single-engine aircraft, over four hundred combat missions, a near collision with an aircraft carrier at night, and the collapse of a two-story scaffolding. To say that my guardian angel has been working overtime would be an understatement. Sometimes it was my skill that saved the day, but mostly it just wasn't my time to go.

Let's begin the story, shall we?

CHASING
THE
FOUR WINDS

Chapter 1

Ground Flyer

AFTER RETURNING HOME IN DECEMBER 1963, FROM A LESS-THAN-stellar academic performance at Penn State, I did what any young man who has just bombed out of college and did not have a job would do—I bought a new car. The sporty Corvair Monza Spyder was the first car I had ever owned. Never mind that my parents never purchased brand-new cars—why saddle yourself with a secondhand rattletrap when you can drive around town looking so cool, albeit in return for a monthly payment? Now, I really needed to find employment.

Again through Dad's connections, I got a laborer's job working for Nelson Rendell, a local building contractor and family friend. He was a great guy to work for: patient, a good teacher, and always cheerful with a great sense of humor bordering on playfulness. It was fun going to work and I learned a lot about carpentry and other construction skills.

In the meantime, I anxiously checked the mailbox each day, hoping to hear from the Navy stating that I had been accepted into the Naval Aviation Cadet (NAVCAD) program. In the first week of March 1964, I received a phone call that fundamentally changed my life for the better. Commander Hollenbach, the Aviation Officer Procurement Officer at Naval Air Station Willow Grove called to congratulate me on being selected for Navy flight training. After being rejected by the Naval Academy and an uninspiring performance at two universities, I was being given a new chance. I was determined to make the most of it.

Indoc

A dull screech of the main tires and a slight bump signaled the arrival of an Eastern Airlines Electra at Pensacola Municipal Airport. It was Sunday, April 8, 1964, a little past 1:00 p.m., when the journey from my old life in New York to a new start in Florida began. As I emerged from the airplane and walked down the air-stairs to the tarmac, I could barely contain my glee and heightened sense of anticipation at what lay ahead. My arrival in Pensacola was 405 years after Don Tristan de Luna and two thousand soldiers entered Pensacola Bay in 1559 to establish the first white settlement in North America. There was another similarity: de Luna and his men were met by hostile savages from indigenous Indian tribes—and an unfriendly band of Marine drill instructors awaited my arrival.

Having been advised to pack lightly, with a small suitcase in hand, I headed to the curb to hail a taxi. As I settled in the backseat, the driver, a friendly African American man, asked, "Where to?"

"U.S. Naval School Pre-Flight at NAS Pensacola," I replied.

He nodded knowingly. "I'm taking you to the wolves. Those Marine DIs are always looking for fresh meat."

"Yes, so I've heard," I said bravely.

Glancing at me in the rearview mirror, he solemnly delivered more good news. "Well, down here, we is getting into the hot and humid time of the year. You'll find out soon enough when you are running the O course with one of them Marines screaming in your face." With a final, "Good luck to ya, man," he dropped me off in front of a large brick building with several large, white, wooden pillars guarding the entrance.

As I opened the door onto the quarterdeck, I saw a Marine DI sitting behind a desk about twenty feet away. I gave him a copy of my orders and he checked my name off on a clipboard. Pointing to my left, he directed me to a large squad-bay at the end of a long passageway.

"Find a rack and a locker to put your gear in," he said. "Chow formation will be at 1715." His instructions were delivered with no hint of a smile or other human reaction to meeting a new comrade-in-arms— maybe that's because I wasn't his comrade. I was just another new puke who had to be broken of his civilian ways.

After claiming a top rack in the corner and unpacking my suitcase, I met a few other members of Class 15-64. Two of the guys were from my neck of the woods: Jim Williams from Cleveland, Ohio, and Pete Schult from Scotia, New York. They were NAVCADs like me. Another fella was an AOC from Texas, a term I was not familiar with. John Shuft explained that AOC stood for Aviation Officer Candidate and that AOCs already had bachelor's degrees. Whereas NAVCADs would not be commissioned until they received their wings, AOCs were commissioned as ensigns in four months after completing Pre-Flight.

As we stood around talking, we happened to glance down the passageway, where we had a good view of the Marine DI sitting at his desk on the quarterdeck. A new candidate had just walked in. The new guy was standing in front of the desk, dressed in a tank-top, Bermuda shorts, and flip-flops, with golf clubs over his left shoulder and a portable TV in his right hand. Suspecting that a memorable scene was about to unfold, I said to my new classmates, "Watch this." As the Marine looked up from his desk and took in the totality of the disaster standing in front of him, he exploded. He leaped to his feet and leaned forward so that the rim of his Smokey-Bear hat was poking the candidate in the forehead.

"Who in the hell are you?" he screamed. "Do you think you are checking into a country club? The only thing you forgot was your tennis racquet, you maggot."

The poor guy was in a state of shock. He was trying to speak, but nothing was coming out. He took a deep breath and set his clubs and TV down. Wrong move!

"Get that shit off my quarterdeck, mister!" The DI shouted with such force, it nearly blew the candidate backward. Pointing to the entrance door, he snapped, "Deposit your crap out there and come back in and try this again."

It wasn't entirely this man's fault for getting off on the wrong foot. His recruiter didn't do a good job of preparing him for this moment. On the other hand, this guy was also clueless about the military and, perhaps, too caught up in the idea of being "an officer and a gentleman." Or maybe he spent too much time reading the promotional brochures from the Pensacola Chamber of Commerce touting a sportsman's paradise with white-sand beaches and a beautiful Southern belle on each arm.

This poor fellow lasted until the following morning, when he DOR'ed, which means Drop on Request. A candidate could DOR anytime during Pre-Flight without incurring a penalty. After beginning flight training, a NAVCAD who voluntarily DOR'ed or was washed out of the program was sent to the fleet to serve a total of two years active duty as an enlisted man—a powerful incentive to study hard and apply oneself.

At 0500 the next morning, the lights in the squad-bay suddenly came on and someone in an authoritarian voice shouted, "Ladies, you have five minutes to get dressed and fall-in in front of the building!" I leaped out of bed, almost forgetting that I was in the top rack. I hurriedly pulled on my clothes and stumbled outside with the rest of my classmates.

Standing in front of us in the early morning light was a different DI from the one who checked us in the previous day. He was of medium height, very muscular, wearing an impeccable uniform, and standing ramrod straight. "Good morning, my name is Staff Sargent Mikitis. I will be your drill instructor during the time you are assigned to the Indoctrination Battalion or INDOC as we call it around here," he bellowed. "My job is to make military men out of you civilian pukes. I am not your friend."

He then spent a few minutes pushing and pulling us into three rows of the formation he wanted whenever we were told to "fall-in." Satisfied with the results, he proceeded to give us additional rules and instructions. "If you are in the squad-bay and I tell you to fall-in, you have exactly thirty seconds to be lined up here, on this sidewalk. If the man in front of you is slow, don't go around him, *GO OVER HIM*."

From that moment on, there was a paralyzing fear of falling in the passageway and being trampled to death by those behind you. It was also a good thing that the screen door leading to the sidewalk swung outward, as we nearly tore it off its hinges during each stampede. His draconian order had the desired effect—we were always lined up at attention in less than thirty seconds. Abject fear, as we found out in the days to come, was the primary motivator behind everything we did.

"When I ask you a question that demands a yes or no answer, you are to respond: 'Sir, yes, sir.' or 'Sir, no, sir.' Do you understand?"

A few guys responded with a meek, "Yes, sir."

"Were you morons listening to me? I want to hear everyone in unison. Do you understand me?" he shouted, as, spittle showered the guys in the first rank.

"Sir, yes sir," we all responded.

"I can't hear you."

"Sir, yes sir!" we screamed at the top of our lungs—another lesson learned.

Staff Sargent Mikitis then rattled off more rules of behavior to be observed during INDOC, including: "No walking. You will either be marching in formation or double-timing (running). You will begin and end everything you say with 'sir.' You shall salute all officers on foot or in their cars. There will be no whistling or chewing gum. When passing a member of the cadre in a passageway, you shall flatten yourself against the wall, at attention, until that person passes, while appropriately greeting him, like 'Sir, good morning, sir.' And there will be no *skylarking* (a catch-all term for unmilitary-like bearing and behavior).

"Beginning tomorrow morning, and each day thereafter, you will have five minutes after reveille to fall-in, right here, in PT gear. Do you understand me?"

"Sir, yes sir."

"Are there any questions?" he asked, not expecting any. A candidate would be a fool to ask a question and risk being singled out and humiliated.

"Sir, no sir!" we shouted at the top of our lungs.

With that, we marched off to begin our first full day in the United States Navy.

After making our racks, cleaning up the squad-bay, shaving and showering, and eating chow, we marched over to Clothing Issue where we were given our INDOC uniform: one set of baggy, ill-fitting, olive-drab coveralls, which everyone called "poopy suits"; a pair of leather *boondock-ers* (ankle high work shoes made of the stiffest, coarsest cowhide known to man); and a Marine utility cover with a permanent "50 mission crush." We also received five sets of underwear and socks and a set of rain gear, which consisted of a smelly, oily poncho. With the exception of the new boondockers, underwear, and socks, everything else looked like it had been in continuous use since the Spanish-American War.

After our clothing issue, we returned to the squad-bay and packed up every item we had brought with us, including our suitcase, and mailed them back home. The only things we could keep were our shaving kits and wallets. Perhaps this severing of all ties with our former lives was more symbolic than necessary, but it did put us on notice as to who was running the railroad—talk about "owing your soul to the company store" as the old Tennessee Ford ballad laments. The standard refrain from all boot camps past came to mind: "If the military wanted you to have a wife, they would have issued you one."

Our next stop was the base barber, where we received a *buzz-job*, the traditional haircut given to all new military recruits. Faster than shearing time on an Australian sheep ranch, we looked like concentration camp survivors in less than one minute flat. In our poopy suits and shaved heads, we resembled escapees from the Gulag.

Everything about INDOC was carefully constructed and orchestrated to achieve a specific purpose. For example, consider the boondockers, which were purposefully designed to be big and clunky in order to swiftly kill any candidate who was trampled during the rush to fall-in on the sidewalk. This natural selection process weeded out the weak and unco-ordinated. After one week of continuous wear, the slovenly poopy suits, which did not come by their name accidentally, served as an object lesson of how not to look and smell in uniform—they also identified us to the rest of the base community as being poor slobs worthy of pity. Having a DI constantly screaming in our face made us respond in an obedient and unquestioning manner to every command—and made us wonder if Marines really did eat their young. Learning the intricacies of close order drill and manual of arms on the *grinder* (large asphalt area where we marched with M-1 rifles) taught us the value of working together as a team—and how hot those poopy suits were in the blazing sun.

After a long day that began at 0500, a day that consisted of PT and marching and more PT and more marching, interrupted only by chow and a classroom lecture thrown in here and there, we were exhausted and ready for sleep—the only time we weren't being harassed by a DI.

At 2155, the bugle call *tattoo* was played over the PA system signaling that it was five minutes before Taps and lights out. One disadvantage of a top bunk was crawling up into it when your body was rebelling against any physical exertion. But the coma that followed was worth the effort.

Thankfully, after ten days, INDOC was over! We went back to Clothing Issue, where we were given five sets of wash khaki uniforms, web belts, brass belt buckles, black uniform shoes, fore and aft garrison covers, and a heavy foul-weather jacket. We were also fitted for dress blue, khaki, and white uniforms, which were issued at a later date. We happily returned our poopy suits, to be washed for the next group of candidates. As I remember, we stood them in the corner, at attention, without the need for a hanger.

Naval Aviation Cadet Michael J. Stock. This photo was taken at the beginning of flight training at Pensacola, Florida. April 1964. *(U.S. Navy photo)*

Although we had gotten over the first hurdle of INDOC, fifteen more weeks of Pre-Flight lay ahead: thirteen weeks of academic, military, and physical training; one week of survival training; and one week as a cadet officer, putting into practice what we had learned and observed about leadership—and, finally, graduation day. Then we would be sent to Naval Auxiliary Air Station Saufley Field, where we would get our hands on an airplane for the first time and begin to learn our craft as a pilot.

Even though he proved over and over that "he was not our friend," Staff Sargent Mikitis had done his job well. He had taken a motley group of civilian recruits and turned us into a reasonable facsimile of a military unit. Sadly, he was killed in action the following year in Vietnam.

Batt One

In our new khaki uniforms, we marched over to join Battalion One. The Cadet Regiment was comprised of Battalions One, Two, and Three, with each battalion containing five classes like ours (one class graduated each week while a new one entered INDOC). We were handed off to our new drill instructor, Staff Sargent Howard, who would take us all the way from Pre-Flight to graduation fifteen weeks later.

Most of the older DIs were combat veterans, as evidenced by the rows of ribbons for bravery hanging on their chests. Staff Sargent Howard was a Korean War veteran with eighteen years in the Corps. His leadership style was more low-key than that of Mikitis. He was soft-spoken, fair-minded, not in your face, and less given to over-the-top theatrics. Just the same, he was not one to cross. His "no bullshit" demeanor and steely look of determination was enough to gain compliance without the need to scream and holler.

Our new home in Batt One was just around the corner from INDOC. Our living space was on the second floor of a large red-brick building that had been constructed during World War II. Two cadets were assigned to a room, that contained a bunk bed, two dressers, a study table and two chairs, one large electric fan, a large walk-in closet, two large floor-to-ceiling windows, and highly polished terrazzo floors. It was roomy and well lighted, but, unfortunately, not air conditioned, which made for some steamy nights despite the mighty efforts of the electric fan. There was a large community head just down the passageway.

My roommate was Dan Merkle from Georgia. He was an OCAN, a navigator in training. Dan was a short, humorous guy with blonde hair and a stocky build—we got along famously and enjoyed many a laugh over our shared predicament at the mercy of the Navy and Marine cadre.

As usual, I claimed the top bunk, which had the unintended benefit of making it easier to eliminate *Irish pennants*, little pieces of white sheet that could hang below the spring frame when the sheet was tucked under the mattress. If the room inspector saw any of these little white flags sticking below the mattress frame, he would give you demerits. Since the top of our bunk had to be taut enough to bounce a quarter, it took some time and effort to tuck the sheet under the mattress without leaving any Irish pennants. By having a top rack, I was able to lie on Dan's bunk (obviously, before he made his bed) to do this time-intensive task. Dan, on the other hand, had to lie on the floor under his rack to do the same.

Room inspections became a way of life—daily inspections by a cadet officer and periodic Room Locker Personnel (RLP) inspections by Staff Sargent Howard. In addition to our bunks, the inspector looked for dust on the furniture, windowsills, and on the deck; proper stowage of clothing and towels; wastebasket empty—in short, everything in its place and squared away. Since our underwear, socks, handkerchiefs, and other required articles of clothing had to be arranged in our dresser in a precise order and folded to a prescribed size, all cadets resorted to using a *static display*, meaning that our drawers became museum showpieces that once setup were never touched and, therefore, did not have to be fussed with each morning. We simply acquired additional clothing to actually wear and kept it in our closet, where the rules were less stringent. Even the lid on a shoe polish can had to be affixed in a specific way—to this day, I still replace the shoe polish lid in the same manner. Every morning before leaving for classes, Dan and I would spray Pledge on the deck and polish the terrazzo to a high gleam, and then give the room one last check for articles adrift, turn off the lights and the fan, and head to morning formation.

The Daily Grind

The Monday through Friday routine began at 0500 with reveille. Five minutes later, we formed-up in our PT gear, ready for calisthenics, followed by a three-mile formation run along the seawall. Twenty-five minutes was allotted to shave and shower and get dressed in our wash khaki uniforms, and we had thirty minutes to make our bunk and get the room ready for inspection. Next was breakfast in the Cadet Mess across the street. For breakfast and the evening meals we were usually allowed to straggle individually, while we typically marched in formation to lunch.

At 0745 we again formed-up on the sidewalk, with our book bags containing textbooks and study materials. At this time, our class leader gave us an outline of the day's activities and passed out pertinent information. Randomly, Staff Sargent Howard would show up to conduct a quick inspection of our uniforms, with emphasis on spit-shined shoes and polished brass belt buckles—we even had to polish the back of the buckle. If he found any discrepancies, in addition to an ass-chewing, the offender received a certain number of demerits. After all of that was completed, our class leader called us to attention and then gave the command, "Up book bags. Up." On hearing the first part of the command, in unison, we reached down and grabbed the handle of our book bags with our left hands. On the second "Up," we lifted the bag and straightened back to standing at attention. It was then "Right face" and "Forward march" and we marched to the classroom building two blocks away in time for our first class at 0800.

The cadre selected a cadet from each class to be the Class Leader based on leadership potential displayed during INDOC. Our class leader was Larry Gardiner, a former enlisted "white hat" from the fleet. Larry proved to be an effective and well-liked leader—smart, organized, and tough when he had to be, but still one of the guys. Being class leader meant a lot more work on top of a demanding curriculum. I don't know if we ever thanked him for his efforts. So, Larry, if you happen to read this book, "Thank you, sir!"

We normally had all of our classroom lectures in the morning, while the afternoons were devoted to physical training and marching. The only variation occurred on Friday mornings, when the whole Cadet Regiment formed up on the parade field for graduation ceremonies, which included a Pass in Review in front of admirals and other high-ranking officers and dignitaries.

After the evening meal, we had free time until 1930, when we had to be in our rooms, sitting at our table, studying for two hours. If you were caught out of your chair, you received demerits. Tattoo was at 2155 and Taps (lights out) and in bed was at 2200. Many a night, Dan and I were in bed before Taps, thankful to have survived another day in paradise.

After our fifth week of Pre-Flight, cadets who were demerit-free for the week prior were granted liberty every Saturday from 1000 to 2400 and on Sunday from 1200 to 1900. Those who wished to go off base would have to obtain a blue liberty card with their name on it from the duty office, and surrender it when they returned from liberty.

Those cadets who had committed infractions during the week, in addition to having their liberty cards "pulled," marched their demerits off on the grinder every Saturday afternoon, with a rifle on their shoulder—one hour for every five demerits. This intimate time spent with your rifle was called Extra Military Instruction (EMI). The military has such innocuous sounding names for hardship and misery. The most that could be marched off on a Saturday was ten demerits. If a cadet had more than ten demerits, the excess carried over to the following Saturday. Fortunately, I only received a total of five demerits during Pre-Flight—for leaving my shaving kit *adrift* (out of place). I clearly remember marching off the demerits in the hot sun.

On Sunday morning, we marched to a mandatory church service: either Catholic mass or Protestant service. Other denominations and non-believers could attend either service, but they had to go to one. Most cadets had a positive view of church service because it was one of the few air-conditioned buildings on base and there were no screaming DIs to be found—further proof that drill instructors were not only heartless, but godless too.

Nearly everything we did between breakfast and dinner, Monday through Friday, was graded by our watchful Navy and Marine instructors. Every day was "game day" and we had to put our best foot forward if we wanted to graduate from Pre-Flight and go on to become naval aviators. *Academic training* included: Naval Orientation (history, traditions and customs, and military etiquette), Mathematics review through calculus, Navigation, Engines, Aerodynamics, Leadership, Meteorology, Physics, and Counter-Insurgency Operations. *Physical training* included: swimming (timed one-mile swims in swimsuits and while fully clothed in flight suit, boots, and flight helmets; underwater swims; treading water for thirty minutes while fully clothed; escaping from a submerged cockpit *Delbert Dunker*; and escaping from a parachute harness while being dragged through water), timed shuttle and distance runs, obstacle course, gymnastics (trampoline, high bar, horse, parallel bars, and tumbling), parachute landing falls, and survival training for downed airmen. *Military training* included: Close-order marching and Manual of arms, Room Locker Personnel inspections, watch standing, and cadet leadership positions. There was a lot to learn and the pace was quick. "Up book bags. Up."

My scholastic achievement in the last three years of high school and at the University of Buffalo and Penn State suffered due to a lack of drive and self-motivation. Pre-Flight was an entirely different matter, where I thrived on the structure, discipline, tidiness, and established routine of Navy life. The suddenness of the turn-around surprised even me. In keeping with my nature of setting goals, I set a goal of finishing number one in my Pre-Flight class, which would be based on the final grades in academic, military, and physical training. Consequently, I applied a full-court press by foregoing liberty on the weekends in favor of working on my studies and physical fitness or preparing my uniform and shoes for inspection. I ran the obstacle course and the one-and-a-half-mile timed run in the sand over and over to improve my strength and endurance and, ultimately, my times or swam a mile in the pool to increase my speed and stamina. Many an hour was spent studying and reviewing classroom assignments and working to get ahead. If the old saying "all work and no play makes Johnny a dull boy" was true, then I must have been very dull, indeed. About the only luxury I allowed myself was attending the base movie on Friday or Saturday night for ten cents or reading an occasional book from the library. In fact, by week six, I had spent a grand total of two dollars on myself.

Red Badge

To recognize cadet achievement, Pre-Flight awarded three different colored badges to be worn over the right pocket of the uniform shirt to signify high grades in Academic, Military, or Physical Training. If a cadet excelled in one of the three areas, he was authorized to wear a *Blue badge*; in two areas a *Red badge*; and in all three areas a *White badge*. Inscribed on the colored badges were abbreviations for the areas in which a cadet qualified: Acad, Mil, or PT. Badges were handed out at the end of week six and twelve.

As a result of my efforts, I wrote home to my parents at the end of the sixth week that I was number one in academics in my class and had gotten a perfect score on the trampoline, which constituted one-half of the gymnastics grade, which, in turn, was one-half of the overall PT grade. So, as a consequence, I was awarded a Red badge with "Acad and PT" on it. At the end of week twelve, I managed to hang on to the Red badge, but try as I might, I fell a little short of the required Military grade. Consequently, I never got a White badge. It would have been a significant accomplishment because there were only two White badges in the entire cadet regiment.

By week fourteen, we had survived many tests and exams in the classroom, the obstacle course and the Delbert Dunker, and over ninety room inspections. Now we would have to survive three days in the wild with no food or other comforts.

Snakes and Flying Squirrels

Survival week began with lectures and demonstrations concerning the techniques that should be used by downed airmen to keep body and soul together until rescued. The instructors outlined general survival methods and then narrowed the discussion to specific terrain and climate conditions, such as artic, desert, jungle, and water. There were also lectures on escape and evasion behind enemy lines. These presentations were all interesting, and the only stress we were under was trying to stay awake in class while keeping our stomachs from rumbling until lunch or dinner.

Now it was time to put what we had learned to the test in the semitropical jungle of Eglin Air Force Base located fifty miles to the east of Pensacola. At 0430 on Thursday morning, Class 15-64 was eating breakfast at an enlisted mess at Sherman Field, the only chow hall open that early. One half hour later, we were on a grey Navy bus heading to Eglin Air Force Base. Most of the sleepy group was trying to get a little extra shut-eye, but not me—I was thinking about the poisonous snakes that were awaiting our arrival in the jungles of Eglin.

During one of our survival lectures, the instructor had told us about the four types of poisonous snakes indigenous to the United States: rattlesnakes, water moccasin, copperhead, and the coral snake. He cheerfully added that all four could be found in Eglin. In a letter to my parents the week prior, I wrote: "It all sounds like fun except for the snakes out there. The other week they caught a rattlesnake that was absolutely huge and coral snakes are quite plentiful. The idea of running around there just doesn't strike me as being too safe. They claim that not many cadets are bitten! Some consolation, huh?" For the first four or five hours in the field, I moved slowly and watched carefully where I placed each step. After that, as I grew more tired, thirsty, and hungry, I didn't give a damn about snakes—bring 'em on!

Over the next three days, the Navy survival instructors taught us how to construct shelters out of palm leaves, how to build and light fires, where to look for water and how to purify it, and how to prepare and cook food that was procured. Since the area had hosted a new cadet class each week for years, the animal, bird, and fish populations were in serious danger of becoming extinct—worse than the aftermath of Sherman's March to the Sea. So, like all Navy survival training I attended later in my career, the instructors brought in one sacrificial rabbit to feed the multitude, except there was no Biblical miracle this time. In addition to a mouthful of rabbit stew, they showed us how to construct a small smoke chamber to make rabbit jerky.

Yes, we were hungry and exhausted, but there were no quizzes or examinations, so all we had to do was survive the three days in the field and we would be able to check off the last remaining requirement (aside from cadet officer week) before graduation. Basically, all we had to do was to exist for three days and we would be home-free.

With that mindset, we boarded the bus Sunday morning in a triumphal mood as we lowered our weary bodies into the seats for the return trip to Pensacola. Then a pernicious rumor began to circulate around the bus that we had failed survival and that we would have to repeat the field exercise next week. Apparently, our class leader had been given the bad news. Well, even in our short time in the military, we knew that rumors were a way of life and that most of them were unfounded. So, we were sort of dismissive of this report, saying, "They wouldn't do that. How can you fail survival? Fail what? There was nothing to fail. We didn't do any more or any less than thousands of cadets before us." We knew there were many ways to fail at Pre-Flight, but survival was not one of them. Nonetheless, a bit of gloom settled over our band of brothers. We would just have to wait and see what transpired. When we got back to Pensacola, we were told that the Training Officer wanted to meet with us at 0900 the next day.

At the appointed hour on Monday morning, we were assembled in the auditorium. After being called to attention, Commander Morgan, dressed in a crisp summer white uniform, strode to the podium. Getting to the point, he said, "My survival instructors have informed me that some of you did not perform up to the standards we require during the field exercise at Eglin. Those who failed will be held back one week and will have to repeat the Eglin phase of training." There was no further explanation. We were not told what we had done wrong. So, the rumor was true. Now, we waited for the next shoe to drop. He proceeded to read off the names, in alphabetical order, of the ten individuals who had failed. "… Keller, Kier, Shult, Stock …" I don't remember hearing the rest. "Those of you I called, remain behind. The rest of you are dismissed."

We were soon branded "The Terrible Ten," the first class in the history of Pre-Flight to fail survival. We were later told by the staff that we were singled out because we "had a bad attitude." We looked at one another and were perplexed as to how they arrived at that determination. I still don't understand it. My opinion is that the field exercise had taken on the reputation of being one that had to be tolerated, but not one that required much effort. The staff wanted to change that perception and the best way to do that was to fail a few cadets. Within an hour, we were the talk of the cadet regiment. The Terrible Ten was the first and the last group to fail—I would say they achieved their objective.

At zero-dark-thirty the next Thursday morning, we were on the same grey bus heading to Eglin. By this time, we had gotten over our shock, anger, and disbelief, and we were determined to make the best of it and hold our heads up high. The ten of us were separated from the rest of Class 16-64 and assigned an outstanding survival instructor, who knew his stuff and demonstrated great interpersonal skills. At no point did he treat us like a bunch of losers who deserved to be ridden hard. To the contrary, he taught us an amazing variety of survival skills in a friendly and non-condescending manner.

One specific thing I remember about this instructor was his unbelievable skill with a slingshot. We saw him kill two flying squirrels in mid-air with a single ball-bearing shot to the head. When I commented about his headshots, he replied modestly, "I don't want to spoil the meat." On another occasion, as we were crossing a small stream, he killed a water moccasin bearing down on us in an aggressive manner—again with a headshot. He also killed a rabbit. We ate well.

Graduation

When our second field trip ended, we all agreed that we had learned a great deal and that it had been worthwhile. The only downside was that we did not graduate with our original class, with whom we had so closely bonded over fourteen weeks.

During Cadet Officer Week, I served as the Cadet Regimental Supply Officer, a "three-bar man," referring to the three small gold bars I wore on my uniform. As I write this, I can't remember what my duties were, but I did enjoy talking informally to the new guys going through INDOC, answering their questions, and trying to alleviate some of the unknowns for them.

Finally, after seventeen weeks, I graduated from Pre-Flight. Due to inclement weather, the graduation parade was cancelled in favor of an indoor ceremony, which was not nearly as impressive. Of the original thirty-three guys who started back in April, twenty-eight graduated, the rest having failed to meet prescribed standards. I just missed my goal of finishing number one in my original class, 15-64. Two one-hundreds of a point separated my final grade from Steve Kelso, who finished number one. Steve, who hailed from Yakima, Washington, and attended Dartmouth for three years, DOR'ed shortly after arriving at Saufley Field, surprising all of his classmates. Both Steve and I were awarded the Outstanding Student Award, the only two so recognized from our original class.

Pre-Flight marked a turn-around in my life—or maybe I had finally grown up. Whatever the reason, I was in the best mental and physical condition of my life, which set the stage for future success.

Chapter 2

Cleared for Takeoff

THERE WERE MANY TIMES DURING PRE-FLIGHT WHEN THE ROAR OF A jet going overhead caused us to look skyward and lust for the day when we would be up there and in control of that sleek machine. On Tuesday and Wednesday mornings, at 0830, the Blue Angels would take to the Pensacola skies to practice their routines for an upcoming weekend airshow. Even inside the classroom, we could hear the rumble as the Blues lit the afterburners on their F-11 jet fighters and streaked down the runway for takeoff. If we happened to be outside in between classes, we would marvel at the precision and beauty of their signature diamond formation as they flew over the air station at treetop level. We fantasized that one day one of us might be a Blue Angel pilot and perform before millions of awestruck spectators. Watching an endless variety of Navy aircraft fly overhead each day during Pre-Flight served to motivate and keep us focused on our ultimate goal of one day wearing the wings of a naval aviator. With our successful completion of Pre-Flight, we were one step closer to realizing our dream.

First Solo

We wasted no time moving to our new home at Naval Auxiliary Air Station Saufley Field, located twelve miles northwest of NAS Pensacola. I reported to Training Squadron One (VT-1) on August 6, the same day of graduation from Pre-Flight. This phase of the program was called Primary Flight Training and was scheduled to last five weeks, but in my case, it took eight weeks due to a backlog caused by bad flying weather.

The air station was named after Lieutenant Junior Grade Richard C. Saufley, Naval Aviator #14, who was killed in 1916 while attempting to set an endurance record. The field was built during World War II, along with a number of other naval training bases in the Pensacola area to handle the large influx of pilot trainees—61,658 naval aviators were trained between 1942 and 1945.

As I walked down the passageway to my new room in the cadet barracks, I noticed that a few rooms had the remnant of a black necktie hung on the outside of the door. "What's with the neckties?" I asked a passing cadet.

"Oh, after you solo, your buddies cut off your tie. I guess it's a tradition that goes back a long time," he said.

"Did they get your tie already?" I inquired.

"Yep, I soloed two days ago," he responded with a big smile. "It was great feeling."

"Congratulations," I said. "Man, I can't wait. Is the T-34 fun to fly?"

"It's a blast, especially when there's no instructor in the backseat critiquing and grading everything you do," he said enthusiastically. "I am sure you can appreciate that just coming from the world of the Marine drill instructor."

"Do I ever," I groaned.

"Oh, there is one other part of the solo tradition that I may as well tell you about," he said. "After the first solo, you have to give your instructor a bottle of his favorite booze."

"No problem. That's a small price to pay. Hey, thanks for the info. I better get my gear stowed before chow. See you around."

As would be the case for the reminder of flight training, students were divided into *Morning Wing* or *Afternoon Wing* for flying. Assignment to Morning Wing, for example, meant that you flew in the morning and went to ground school in the afternoon. This was done to maximize limited aircraft and instructor resources. At Saufley, I was assigned to Afternoon Wing and attended ground school in the morning. As it turned, this was the better draw because many of the early-morning flights were cancelled due to ground fog that often rolled in from nearby Perdido Bay.

The pace of both flight and ground training was just as intense as Pre-Flight and required the same degree of constant effort to keep from being washed out of the flight program. But there were differences too, that made life a little more normal. Cadets weren't as regimented as before. After morning muster formation, we were allowed to straggle to chow, to ground school, and to the flight line—gone was the requirement to march as a group. We still had to make our racks and keep our rooms squared away, but we didn't have daily room inspections. More onus was placed on individual responsibility, just like it would be in the fleet. In other words, it was like being on a college campus, except we wore uniforms or flight suits, and we said "Yes, sir" and "No, sir."

Academics were also different in that the classes were aimed at enhancing our skills as pilots and, in particular, flying the T-34 Mentor, our primary flight trainer.

Shortly before my first flight, I was told to report to Flight Gear Issue where I was given two orange flight suits; a pair of leather flight gloves; a flight helmet; and, best of all, a leather flight jacket and a white silk scarf. (We wore the boondockers issued during INDOC as our flight boots—we would be issued real flight boots later.) Wow! I now could pretend to be a Navy pilot with the best of them. The sight of my flight suit and helmet hanging next to my uniforms in my room locker was a constant source of pride and a reminder of my purpose in being there.

Lieutenant Mander was my first flight instructor. Like most flight instructors, he had a flying tour in the fleet before reporting to Pensacola. As I recall, he flew the P-5M, a large-hulled seaplane used in anti-submarine operations. He was soft-spoken, friendly, and approachable; and most important, he was a good instructor. Many of the basic habits I have used to guide my flying over the years can be traced to him.

Besides looking good in our new flight suits and leather jackets, there were more substantive training requirements that had to be mastered before our first flight. One was the blindfolded cockpit check. At Saufley, like at other training bases, there were five or six mock-ups available to students called *cockpit trainers*. These devices were an exact replica of a specific aircraft cockpit, complete with all instruments, levers, and switches in their correct positions. Many of the switches and levers moved in the proper manner. Instruments, on the other hand, were simply blanks with a fixed reading. These training aids, forerunners of the modern-day flight simulators, were used to practice checklists for the various phases of flight as well as for rehearsing emergency procedures. With blindfolds in place, we were required to touch or point to each cockpit component as directed by the instructor, with no errors.

Another helpful training aid was a set of detailed flight procedures for each aircraft published in a booklet called Flight Training Instructions (FTI). Everything a student was expected to know and perform during any syllabus flight was spelled out step-by-step in a comprehensive and understandable fashion. Before any given flight, a student was expected to know the procedures contained in the FTI down pat.

So, after successfully completing the blindfold cockpit check, committing the FTI to memory, practicing cockpit procedures over and over in the static trainer, and completing ground classes, I was finally ready for my first instructional flight with Lieutenant Mander.

In the civilian world, beginning flight students normally start in a simple aircraft with fixed landing gear and propeller and very rudimentary instruments. The military does not have the same luxury of starting out slow because there is so much knowledge and skills that must be imparted in a relatively short period of training. Over the course of fourteen months, a Navy flight student goes from first solo to acrobatic, instrument, cross-country flight day

Beechcraft T-34 Mentor. The first airplane I flew at Pensacola. *(U.S. Navy photo)*

and night; formation; aircraft carrier qualification landings; and advanced tactical flight in four different aircraft while accumulating less than 250 total flight hours. It is a whirlwind experience designed to separate the men from the boys.

The T-34, manufactured by Beechcraft, was a fairly complex tandem-seat, low-wing airplane equipped with retractable landing gear, controllable pitch propeller, and a six-cylinder 225-horse power engine. The T-34 was modeled after the highly successful civilian model, the Beechcraft Bonanza.

Any aircraft with retractable landing gear poses a whole new level of risk for pilots. The system used to lower the gear can malfunction, which can result in one or more of the wheels failing to extend, thereby necessitating an emergency landing, which will cause damage to the aircraft and perhaps injury to crewmembers. Or even worse from the standpoint of the pilot's ego, he may forget to lower the gear prior to landing.

There is an old saw in aviation that states: "There are those who have landed gear up and those who will." (In a later chapter, I describe my close encounter with this theory.) There are also many jokes and stories that go along with this oversight; like: "How did the Marine pilot know he landed gear up?" "It took full power to taxi back to the flight line." (I am sure if a Marine were telling the story, it would be a Navy pilot in the spotlight.) And there is the true story of two FAA inspectors who were out getting some proficiency flight time and landed gear up at their home airport. When the fire trucks and emergency vehicles arrived within minutes, the firemen were surprised to see that the FAA was already at the scene of the accident. "How did you guys get here so fast?" they asked. The embarrassed and humbled inspectors quipped, "We flew in."

So, resplendent in my orange flight and brown-leather flight jacket, I reported to Lieutenant Mander for my first flight on September 2. After going through the checklist and starting the engine, I haltingly called ground control for permission to taxi to the active runway. The next task to master was trying to taxi in a straight line with a castering nosewheel that required the judicious use of brakes at slow speeds. It wasn't pretty—the only time I was on the yellow centerline was when I crossed it from one side of the taxiway to the other. But, with a little help and coaching from my instructor, I managed to get to the runway.

The takeoff was the easiest part of the whole flight. After being cleared for takeoff, release the brakes, advance to full throttle, and at about fifty knots apply a little aft stick, and the airplane flies itself off the runway. *Holy cow! I did it all by myself! I am really doing the flying.* Although I had never controlled a surface vessel, I was slowly beginning to think that being a pilot had to be better than being a ship driver.

Following a climb to a safe altitude, Mander showed me how to fly straight and level and to make gentle, level turns. All of that didn't seem too difficult, and I was beginning to get a little overconfident. Then we descended into the traffic pattern at Out Lying Field (OLF) Canal for some touch and go landings (OLFs were Navy-owned paved airports spread throughout the training area located along the Gulf Coast west of Pensacola and east of Mobile Bay. These fields did not have air traffic control towers, but were manned by a Navy fire truck during daylight hours.)

After three circuits of the landing pattern, my morale went from thinking this was easy to doubting I would ever master landings. There were so many details to keep track of: completion of the landing checklist, proper position of the prop lever, lower the flaps, maintain the proper airspeed, check that the oil pressure and temperature were within limits, fly a prescribed path over the ground while accounting for wind drift, keep track of the fuel gages, and—oh, yes—don't forget to lower the landing gear. Some observers of the aviation scene say that any landing you can walk away from is a *good* landing; while others say if you can reuse the airplane, it's a *very good* landing. All I can say about these runway judges is that their level of expectation is really low, or I made the best landings ever recorded by a Naval Aviation Cadet.

On our return to Saufley, my instructor introduced an entirely new way to enter the traffic pattern. The "break" was flown at traffic-pattern altitude of 1,000 feet above the ground, at cruise airspeed of 120 knots, and directly over the runway in the direction of the landing. When arriving at the midpoint of the runway, I was to abruptly roll into a 60 to 70 degree angle of bank to the left, while simultaneously retarding the throttle to idle, shoving the prop lever full forward, and lowering the landing gear at 110 knots—"Chop, Prop, 110, Drop" was a memory aid used to teach the proper sequence of cockpit actions. The break was used on the aircraft carrier to provide proper spacing downwind for a formation of returning aircraft. So, why not practice it right from the beginning of training?

Over the next eleven flights, Lieutenant Mander patiently refined my basic flying skills and honed my landings. He was a pleasure to fly with and I appreciated his great introduction to naval aviation and the world of flying.

My twelfth flight was a check flight with another instructor, to determine if I was safe for solo. After completing two touch-and-go landings at OLF Silverhill and on downwind for the third, Lieutenant Riley said, "Stock, make this a full-stop landing."

On landing, Riley told me to taxi off the runway to the parking apron. As I brought the airplane to a stop, I could hear him in the backseat unfastening his seatbelt and shoulder harness. After getting out on the left wing and securing the rear cockpit, he stuck his head into my cockpit.

"Well, Stock, do you think you can do this?" he asked with a smile.

"Yes, sir, I believe I can."

"Okay, I want you to make two touch and go's and a full-stop." As he stepped off the wing, he called over his shoulder, "Oh, by the way, don't forget to come back to pick me up."

As I advanced the throttle for takeoff, I did so with a mixture of nervousness and excitement. Would I really be able to remember and then execute all of the necessary steps to make a safe landing? By the time I turned downwind, all of my study, the time spent in the cockpit procedures trainer, and the skills ingrained after seventeen hours with a flight instructor kicked in to produce a smooth rhythm. Manipulation of the flight controls and management of the cockpit became automatic. After making an acceptable first landing, all of the pre-solo jitters disappeared. I still couldn't believe I was actually in the airplane all by myself. By the time I stopped to pick up Lieutenant Riley, I was ecstatic. A pilot's first solo flight is an experience that he or she will never forget. As I write this account fifty-four years later, I clearly remember the joy of that moment.

Before the formalities of cutting my tie and passing a bottle of whiskey to my instructor could occur, I had to make a solo flight that originated and terminated at Saufley Field. So, later that same day, I took off and headed to the practice area to review some air maneuvers and to do some more touch and go's. Since my morning flight with Lieutenant Riley, a solid overcast had blanketed the area. It was one of those homogeneous cloud layers that defied precise determination of the altitude of the base of the clouds. As I was climbing to the prescribed altitude for transit to the practice area, I inadvertently flew into the bottom of the clouds.

Up to this point in flight training, I had not been introduced to basic instrument flying. Furthermore, the T-34 did not have the instrumentation required for instrument flight. Consequently, Lieutenant Mander emphatically warned that I was never to fly into a cloud. He implied that bad things would happen if I did, but he did not elaborate exactly what those bad things were; nor did he tell me what to do if it happened. As the clouds enveloped the airplane, I experienced real panic for the first time in my short flying career. Not knowing what to do, but fearing the worst, I abruptly pushed forward on the control stick. This created negative Gs, something else I had never experienced. As my body was forced against the shoulder harness straps in an attempt to eject me through the top of the canopy, I wondered if this was one of those bad things he was talking about. Fortunately, I quickly popped out of the bottom of the cloud. I was so shaken by the experience that I cut my flight short and returned to Saufley.

Jets or Props

After cutting my tie, my flight instructor pinned a single gold bar with a small anchor in the middle above the left pocket of my uniform shirt to signify I had soloed. It was a proud moment, and now everyone could see I had taken the first major step toward winning the coveted "Wings of Gold."

Next, acrobatic flight was introduced: spins, wing-overs, rolls, barrel rolls, loops, and Immelmann turns. I did them because I had to, but I never felt really comfortable. On my second solo flight, I climbed to 6,000 feet so I could safely practice what I had learned. Wing-overs and rolls turned out okay, so I moved on to loops. At the top of my first loop, I stalled out and flopped over on my back. I froze, not knowing what to do. Eventually, I managed to right the airplane, but not before giving myself a good scare. On my next instructional flight, I told Lieutenant Mander what had happened, but he wasn't sure what I had done wrong, so he told me to do one. The same thing happened, and he knew exactly what I had done wrong. "You're not pulling enough G to get over the top," he said. "You need an initial pull of 3.5 to 4 Gs." That's all it took. I never had trouble with loops from then on.

About the time I entered flight training, the Navy was engaged in a national billboard campaign that featured a handsome Navy pilot, resplendent in his flight suit, G-suit, and fancy flight helmet; with his oxygen mask hanging off at a jaunty angle, standing in front of an F-4 Phantom, a top-of-the-line fighter. The huge caption across the top of the billboard proclaimed *Fly Your Own Jet*. There was nothing subtle about the message and the promotional campaign was successful in drawing young men to naval aviation—second only to *Top Gun* with Tom Cruise two decades later. So, it is little wonder that I too wanted to fly jets.

Between sexy advertising and the Blue Angels, every virile male who entered Navy flight training wanted to fly jets. In fact, we were surprised to learn that Navy pilots also flew propeller driven airplanes of various kinds and helicopters.

The training pipeline leading to Navy wings had several forks in the road. The first occurred at the end of Primary at Saufley: Jets or props. Each student was graded on each ground school class and every flight with an instructor. All of these grades were combined to produce an overall grade for Primary. At the end of each week, the graduating students for that week were ranked from top to bottom according to their combined grade. Each student was asked for his first choice: Jets or props. Since most students wanted jets, only those near the top of the ranking got their first choice. I had good enough grades to fly jets, but I had soured on that idea since arriving in Pensacola.

It was not a snap decision, but one that evolved over a period of several months. The Naval Safety Center published a widely circulated document titled *The Weekly Summary*. Once a week, this publication summarized all of the aircraft accidents that had occurred in the Navy and Marine Corps for that week. It listed the model aircraft, the number of fatalities and serious injuries, and the extent of damage to the aircraft. As I continued to read *The Weekly Summary*, I noticed a disturbing pattern. The chances of being killed in a jet were far greater than any other type of aircraft. For example, during an eight-month cruise aboard the carrier *USS Enterprise*, eight jet pilots and four jet navigators were killed in accidents. Eventually, the constant drumbeat of jet-pilot fatalities convinced me I wanted no part of that business. It was a decision I never regretted.

So, I chose props and moved to another air station located close to Pensacola, Naval Auxiliary Air Station Whiting Field, to start Basic Flight Training in the T-28 Trojan. My goal was to attend multi-engine training in Corpus Christi, Texas, after finishing at Whiting, which would prepare me for an eventual career as an airline pilot.

My plans would change one more time before getting my wings.

Flying the Mighty Trojan

Walking across the parking apron toward our assigned airplane, for my first flight in the T-28, the instructor reminded me how much right rudder I would have to apply on takeoff to counteract torque of the big radial engine. No problem, I thought. *How bad could it really be? After all, three more degrees of right rudder trim were added for takeoff over what was used on the T-34. And, my success at Saufley meant I was a better than average "stick." Bring it on.*

As I smoothly advanced the throttle to fifty-six inches of manifold pressure, the aircraft immediately began a swerve to the left. "Right rudder! Right rudder!" the instructor screamed through my helmet. I couldn't believe how much force I was having to apply with my right leg. I could feel him on the pedals applying additional right rudder. Finally, we were tracking more or less straight down the runway. As we climbed away from the field, he was still fuming, "You idiot. Maybe the next time you will pay attention to what I tell you."

It was not a very auspicious beginning in a new aircraft with a new instructor. Among other lessons, the debacle injected a needed dose of humility into my swagger.

Located twenty miles northeast of Pensacola, Whiting Field, like so many naval air stations in the area, was constructed during the World War II build-up. The base consisted of two full-sized airfields: North Field and South Field, each with its own control tower. Training Squadron Two (VT-2) occupied North Field and Training Squadron Three (VT-3) was at South Field. It was like having two distinct naval air stations within the same perimeter fence. Each squadron had identical missions, and since I was assigned to VT-2, my only connection to South Field was through some of my Pre-Flight classmates who had been assigned to VT-3.

Like at Saufley, I was assigned to the afternoon wing, which meant going to ground school every morning, Monday through Friday. The subjects were the same as before, but more advanced in scope. And, two new classes were introduced: Aircraft Recognition and Morse Code. The purpose of the first course was to teach us how to differentiate enemy aircraft (Soviet Union) from U.S./Allied aircraft. Although some photos of real aircraft were used, the majority of the class was taught using black silhouettes of front and side views projected on a screen—just like they did during World War II. *Hey, if it was good enough for the "big rebellion," it'll be okay twenty years later.* Another dinosaur left over from another age was learning Morse code. Back during the War, many radio transmissions were sent using Morse code, but by 1964, aircraft radio technology had moved on. We had not. So, we were required to send and receive so many words per minute. I will say that our instructor did a good job because I can still remember many of the letters today—you just never know when this skill might come in handy.

On the flying side, the curriculum was divided into five stages: TPA (transition, precision, and acrobatics), BI (basic instrument), RI (radio instrument), Night, and Formation. Ideally, a student would complete all five stages in five months and accumulate one hundred hours of flight time in the T-28, split between dual (with an instructor) and solo hours.

North American T-28 Trojan. I flew most of my fixed-wing training in this powerful airplane, including carrier landings. *(U.S. Navy photo)*

The T-28 Trojan, built by North American Aviation, was first introduced into the Naval Air Training Command in 1953 to gradually replace the SNJ (Navy version of the T-6 Texan). Since the Navy was moving away from tail-wheel equipped aircraft, it needed a trainer with a nose wheel and it also needed a trainer with a larger engine and more speed.

The new aircraft looked like a T-34 on steroids. It was huge. A T-34 could easily fit under the wing of a T-28. With a 1,425-horsepower radial engine with a two-stage supercharger, the T-28 had over six times the power of the T-34. Maximum speed went from 170 in the T-34 to 285 knots. The T-28 had a service ceiling of 39,000 feet and a rate of climb of four thousand feet per minute. Its performance was akin to a World War II fighter in terms of maneuverability and rate of roll. In fact, it was used by many air forces around the world as a fighter-bomber. Once a student coming from Saufley, with a grand total of thirty-two flight hours, got used to flying such a large, powerful machine, it was a blast to fly. In a letter to my parents shortly after soloing the T-28, with only twelve hours in the airplane, I gushed: "It's like going from a riding lawnmower to a fast race car."

We flew two different variants of the T-28: the *B model* and the *C model*. The only noticeable difference was the shortened prop and tailhook on the C model, which was used for carrier landings. Otherwise, they both flew the same.

There were two types of flight instructors that students hated: screamers and control-riders. The first type berated students for the slightest error while screaming obscenities and other condescending terms of endearment. Some even resorted to reaching forward to whack students on their helmets with a kneeboard.

Although control-riders did not verbally abuse students, their methods were equally damaging to student learning. No matter what maneuver a student was attempting, from the simplest to the most difficult, the instructor in the backseat was on the flight controls, exerting pressure and movement that could be readily felt by the student. Under these conditions, the student could not separate what he was doing from what the instructor did. A student learns best by making mistakes and then applying the correct blend of flight control input the next time. I had one instructor who was so bad that I discreetly took my hands and feet completely off the controls for one whole maneuver. At the end, he critiqued all of the mistakes that had been made—his mistakes! Probably had he known what I had just done, he would have turned into a screamer as well.

Lieutenant Junior Grade John Ellis was my first instructor in the T-28. He was a spitting image of Clark Gable: tall, with jet black hair and a pencil-thin mustache. He was one of several instructors to be sent right back to the training command after receiving his wings due to a shortage of fleet openings. John Ellis was also a *SCREAMER!* He was the nicest guy outside of the airplane, but once he stepped into the rear cockpit, he began to scream and berate me even before I had a chance to make a mistake. As we walked out to the airplane, he might put his arm around my shoulder, call me by my first name, and be as pleasant and approachable as can be. However, once he strapped himself in the rear cockpit, it was Katie-bar-the-door. I felt like looking over my shoulder to see if another instructor had taken his place.

I remember coming back from one flight where I couldn't seem to do anything right—at least in his eyes. After touching down on landing, he hollered over the intercom, "Stock, you didn't land, YOU CRASHED!" I was so demoralized, I thought he would give me a "down," which was an unsatisfactory grade for the flight. Depending on the circumstances of the flight and whether there was a surplus of students in the pipeline at the time, one down could mean dismissal from the flight program, so it was a much-feared consequence. As I dejectedly climbed down from the front cockpit, he was waiting for me on the ground, where he put his arm around my shoulder and said, "Mike, that was a great flight." I was stunned—and confused.

Years later, I had another opportunity to fly with John when he checked me out in the SNJ at the Kalamazoo Air Museum in Michigan. I expected the same treatment from the backseat, but he remained as delightful in the air as he was on the ground. So, I realized that in the Navy, John was a screamer only because he thought a gruff demeanor produced the best naval aviators.

Flight training was not without risk. From time to time, we would get distressing news that instructors and students had been killed in aircraft accidents. I remember listening to a fellow cadet relating his experience of being involved in a midair collision earlier in the day. He managed to bail out, but his instructor was not able to get out and died in the crash. The other crew managed to safely land their crippled airplane. Luckily, I did not lose any friends or classmates during flight training. That record, unfortunately, would not hold once I reached the fleet.

The only scare I had during my time at Whiting Field occurred on a day navigation hop to Meridian, Mississippi, as part of a four-plane solo formation flight. After takeoff from a refueling stop and shortly after leveling at 9,500 feet, my engine quit running—not very long, but long enough for me to depress the microphone to alert my instructor. All that came out of my panic-stricken mouth was a long pronounced unintelligible squeal. The instructor in the chase airplane didn't help any when he said, "Who's the whimpering baby on the radio?" By that time, my engine was purring normally again. Maybe it had swallowed some water in the fuel, who knows? I will say that I was a little nervous on the way back to Whiting, half expecting my engine to crap out any minute.

A few students who thought they were God's gift to aviation, would brag about some of stunts they pulled while on solo flights, like doing snap rolls, hammerhead stalls, simulated strafing runs on cars and trucks on the highway, and dog-fighting with their friends. It was a sure way to end your naval flying career if caught and, perhaps, your life, so I was not inclined to follow suit. The only thing I tried a couple times was flying inverted, but I never felt comfortable hanging upside down in the straps and feeling like I was about to crash through the top of the canopy. Not that I followed every single rule later in my career, but I generally did not stray too far from the flagpole.

Under the Bag

After completing TPA Stage, I moved to BI, and a whole new world of solely flying by reference to cockpit instruments—or what was called "blind flying" in the early days of aviation. In BI, the instructor and student switch seats because the rear seat was fitted with an accordion-style canvas hood that could be pulled forward to enclose the entire rear cockpit. The "bag," as it was called, did not allow the student to cheat by looking outside. It was like being in a dark cave with a trickle of light filtering in around the edges of the bag.

In BI, a student learns how to fly basic maneuvers using the flight instruments: altimeter, airspeed indicator, vertical speed indicator, attitude indicator, and turn needle and balance ball. After a few flights, a student

The accordion-style hood, called "the bag," that encapsulated an instrument student so he couldn't cheat by peeking out. *(U.S. Navy photo)*

is able to perform straight and level flight, level turns, gentle climbs and descents, and airspeed and configuration changes—all the maneuvers necessary to fly from point A to B.

Before a student's first flight in the airplane, he had to endure a number of sessions in the *blue box*, which was the name given to a boxy contraption made of plywood and painted blue that somewhat resembled an airplane minus the engine and propeller, wings, and tail. Inside the cockpit were a stick, rudder pedals, throttle, and basic flight and navigation instruments that looked similar but not exactly like the equipment found in the T-28 or any other aircraft. After strapping himself in the seat, the student was encapsulated in the cockpit by a canopy-like cover that slid forward. Students communicated with an enlisted instructor positioned on the outside of the device via a headset and intercom system. It was officially called a *Link Trainer* after its inventor, Edwin Link. The Link Trainer was little changed from when it was first introduced to flyers in World War II, further proving that if it was good enough for the "Greatest Generation" it could still be of service two decades later. In many ways, I felt like I was trapped in a World War II time-warp during my flight training.

The purpose of the Link Trainer was to teach instrument-scanning techniques, checklists, and procedures. Unlike modern-day high-end flight simulators, which are designed to fly exactly like the aircraft they replicate, the blue boxes did not fly anything like a real aircraft. They could be maneuvered in pitch, roll, and yaw, but the movements were jerky and not well integrated. For example, when the rudder pedals were pushed, nothing happened for a second or two, then with a great deal of hissing from the bowels of the machine, it finally began to move. So, in essence, students had to learn how to fly—maybe a better term would be *operate*—an entirely new machine. Aside from that, the trainer served its purpose to prepare students for BI and RI in an airplane at a fraction of the cost of doing all instrument training in a real aircraft.

Commander Guy P. Bordelon, USN, CO of VT-2, presenting me with the Student of the Week award. March 1965. *(U.S. Navy photo)*

I enjoyed flying in the blue box and under the bag in the T-28, in "splendid isolation," and did well enough to be selected as VT-2's Student of the Week for March 15, 1965, chosen from a group of 412 students, for having the highest combined ground school and flight grades. The CO of VT-2, Commander Guy P. Bordelon, presented the award to me in his office. I was honored not only to receive the award, but also to meet and talk with Bordelon, the only Navy ace and only night ace from any branch of service during the Korean War.

Formation Flight

We flew two solo cross-country flights at night—if you would call twenty airplanes in a single file about a quarter mile apart, following an instructor in the lead, as being "solo cross-country." Following the white taillight of the T-28 ahead reminded me of a bunch of circus elephants walking around an arena trunk-to-tail.

With BI, RI, and Night stages completed, I moved into a realm of flying that is foreign to civilian pilot training. The ability to fly in close formation with other aircraft is a necessary skill for military pilots. It is almost as important as learning to take off and land. Beginning with a two-plane *section* with an instructor in each aircraft, the student then progresses to flying solo under the careful eye of an instructor flying in a chase airplane. Finally, flying in a four-plane *division* is introduced, first with an instructor and then solo. It was a little bit intimidating at first to be so close to another aircraft, but once you get the hang of detecting and controlling relative motion between two airplanes, formation flying was actually fun.

Another maneuver we performed with two airplanes was called *tail chase*, which simulated a dog-fighting technique where you closed on your adversary from the six o'clock position and matched his evasive movements until you had him in your gun-sight. I frankly had a little trouble keeping on the tail of the other airplane as it climbed, dove, and turned aggressively. Maybe it was good that I decided not to be a fighter pilot.

It was during formation stage when I received the only unsatisfactory flight or "down"; and I got it before ever leaving the ground. I was the number four aircraft in a four-plane solo flight, and we were lined up in the run-up area going through our pre-takeoff checklists. The chase instructor pulled into the line next to me and noticed that the battery door on the left side of my aircraft was open and hanging down. Because I couldn't takeoff in that condition, he directed me to taxi back to parking to have a mechanic close it. After doing that, I rejoined the group and flew the flight, just slightly behind schedule. When we returned to Whiting, he gave me a down for improper pre-flight inspection. I didn't think it was fair, but there was nothing I could do. There was no way I could have missed this door hanging down. I think a mechanic had closed it, but forgot to screw the fasteners tight and it opened from the vibration of taxiing. Fortunately, the infraction did not rise to the level that required me to appear before a Student Pilot Disposition Board, which everyone called a "Speedy Board." And, therefore, I was not in danger of being washed out of the flight program.

One Thousand Feet Low

The exact reasons for my decision to fly helicopters have long been forgotten. Maybe it was the ride I took as a passenger in a Navy helicopter back in October, or perhaps I thought it would make me more marketable being able to fly both fixed and rotary-wing aircraft after I left the Navy. Whatever the reasoning, my decision would have a profound effect on the direction of my future naval career and, to a lesser extent, on life after the Navy. I have never once regretted my decision.

At the time I volunteered for helicopters, there was a developing shortage of Navy helicopter pilots and, as a consequence, a number of my friends were ordered to helicopters despite their strong objections. They went kicking and screaming to Ellyson Field Naval Auxiliary Air Station, the home of helicopter training. However, all of them became true believers after a few flights, attesting to the allure of flying these amazing machines.

After completing Formation Stage, those students going to helicopters were sent to VT-6, also based at Whiting North Field, for an advanced course in radio instruments. It was here when I made a serious flying error that could have resulted in being bounced from the flight program.

On my final flight in VT-6, the check instructor told me to plan and file an IFR (Instrument Flight Rules) flight from Whiting Field to Maxwell AFB in Montgomery, Alabama, and return. I made an instrument takeoff under the bag from Whiting, climbed to the cruising altitude assigned by Air Traffic Control (ATC), and correctly navigated to my destination. Everything was going great. I was on top of my game and I thought I had this checkride nailed. ATC cleared me for a VOR instrument approach to Maxwell, and I descended and leveled at the initial altitude depicted on the approach plate clipped to my kneeboard. After flying several minutes at this altitude, the instructor said in a very stern voice: "Stock, pop your bag."

"Yes, sir." I reached up and unsnapped the hood, which then retracted behind me.

"Look out. Do you see anything strange?"

As I peered over the canopy rail, I noticed immediately that we were flying just above the treetops. "Looks like we're a little low, sir," I responded meekly.

"A little low?" he thundered. "You are exactly one thousand feet low."

Somehow, I had misread my altimeter.

"I've got the aircraft," he stated in a disgusted tone of voice, as he moved the stick in a rapid circular motion, signifying that he was now flying.

He started a climb and abruptly turned back in the direction of Whiting. He didn't utter another word on the thirty-minute return flight. He didn't have to elaborate just how serious my error was. Had we been in the clouds and the trees just a bit taller, the two of us would have been incinerated in the ensuing fireball. Knowing I had just earned a down, I felt pretty miserable and was kicking myself for making such a stupid mistake. The instructor gave me the silent treatment, and I was left to stew in my own juices. I began to envision that my once promising flying career had come to an end. I had never felt lower.

As we got within twenty miles of Whiting, the weather dramatically changed from the forecast. The field was surrounded by angry-looking thunderstorms punctuated by numerous lightning flashes, and the aircraft was engulfed in very heavy rain. The instructor threw me a lifeline. "Stock, if you can successfully make an ADF approach under these weather conditions, I won't give you a down." Although I knew that ADF was the most difficult approach to do, I eagerly accepted the opportunity to redeem myself. The pressure was on. Somehow, I managed to pull it off.

The Big Boat

Having dodged a bullet on my last flight at Whiting Field, I moved back to Saufley for carrier training in VT-5, the next challenge standing in the way of wearing *Wings of Gold*.

While I was going through Primary in the T-34 seven months earlier, I was in awe of the cadets in the mess hall and in the barracks who wore double gold bars on their uniforms, signifying that they were *carrier qualified* and had landed solo on an aircraft carrier. It was like rubbing shoulders with rock stars. I wondered if I had what it took to follow in their footsteps. I was on the threshold of finding out.

Unlike other phases of training, we only received one day of ground school. I don't remember everything that was said that day in the classroom, but I do recall a few of the salient points.

Since we would be *deck launching* under our own power in the T-28, rather than being catapulted into the air, it was critical that we assumed the takeoff attitude at a precise time in the takeoff roll. The classroom instructor said, "When you reach the forward elevator in the flight deck, I want you to haul back on the stick. Whatever you do at that point, *do not look at the airspeed indicator* because it will be so slow that it will scare the hell out of you. Trust me, you will have enough flying speed before reaching the end of the ship." The other reassuring tidbit he threw out that day concerned what to do in case of engine failure right after takeoff. "Try to turn left or right before hitting the water, otherwise, the carrier will run right over you because it takes several miles to stop that big boat. If you manage to do that, the helicopter will pick you up."

Got it! Alrighty now, I guess I'm ready for that "big boat." Well, not so fast, big fella. The Navy wants you to practice doing a lot of simulated carrier landings on a runway that is not pitching and rolling. These practice sessions were called Field Carrier Landing Practice (FCLP). For one solid week before flying to the carrier, we flew two FCLP flights per day, for a total of twelve: three with an instructor and the remainder solo. We flew these practice sessions at OLF Barin Field, another airfield built during World War II, when it was an active naval air station. An outline of a carrier flight deck was painted on the runway and a visual guidance system, called a Mirror Optical Landing System, was installed to provide proper glidepath information to the pilot—the visual image seen by the pilot was called "the ball." The mirror system had been used for years aboard carriers, but had been replaced by the Fresnel Optical Landing System, which gave a slightly different visual presentation to the pilot, but in principle worked the same way. When installed aboard the carrier, the glide path indication to the pilot was gyro-stabilized to account for the pitch and roll of the ship. Each FCLP session was manned by an Landing Signals Officer (LSO), just like on the carrier. His job was to provide line-up and glide-path guidance to supplement the optical system. He also provided the "cut signal" when the pilot was required to rapidly reduce the throttle to idle just before touchdown and he also gave the wave-off signal if the approach became too dangerous to continue.

After doing seventy-two FCLP landings, the pattern, approach, and landing on the simulated carrier deck became second nature—we were now ready for the real deal!

The next day we would be going to the carrier. I slept very little that night. I arrived at Barin Field at 0630 for 0730 launch. The weather gods, however, were not cooperating, so we sat in the ready room hour after hour, waiting for the clouds to part. In the meantime, I got more wound up and tense by the minute. Finally, at 1030, we were told to man our aircraft.

The formation consisted of four students flying solo with an instructor pilot flying chase in a fifth airplane. Takeoff and join-up went off without a hitch. After reaching our cruising altitude, the instructor told us to set cruise power, which was 2,000 prop RPM and twenty-four inches of manifold pressure (MAP). I did that, but immediately began to fall back out of my number four position in the formation. I added throttle up to the maximum allowable MAP of twenty-seven inches to no avail—the three aircraft ahead were slowly pulling away. This was not good. I racked my brain trying to determine what was wrong, but came up empty. Well, I had to do something quick. So, I advanced the prop to 2,200 RPM, so that I could use more throttle without damaging the engine. After doing that, I was able to catch up and remain in proper position. But I now had a new problem: instructors would often get behind a student's aircraft and look through their propeller arc into the student's arc. If the student's prop appeared to strobe, then his RPM did not match that of the instructor's and the student could expect to have his ass chewed. While I was waiting for the verbal assault, which never came, I wondered anew what had gone wrong.

Thirty minutes later, the formation arrived overhead the USS Lexington (CVS-16), a World War II Essex-class aircraft carrier, as it sailed in the Gulf of Mexico off Pensacola. We immediately entered into an orbit called the Delta Pattern. It was then when I noticed what my power problem was—the huge cowl flaps on each side of the engine, used for cooling, were fully open, causing a lot of additional drag. Upon taking the runway for takeoff from Barin, normal procedure called for retracting the cowl flaps to the trail position (just barely open), but I missed this important step because of my frayed nerves. I missed another opportunity to catch my mistake on level-off when the cowl flaps should have been fully closed. Once I closed the flaps, I could finally reduce the RPM back to 2,000. Great, now I could concentrate on the main event.

Next, the formation was given *Signal Charlie*, which meant we were to descend to the landing pattern, evenly spaced in single file, on the downwind leg of the traffic pattern. The plan called for the first two approaches to be touch-and-go landings, so we could get the feel of the process before attempting an arrested landing with the tailhook. Between waiting three extra hours before takeoff and my oversight of the cowl flaps, I was now stretched tighter than a piano wire. Consequently, I overshot the landing centerline both times and had to be waved-off before I collided with the island superstructure—I never did do a touch and go!

On my third time downwind, the LSO told me over the radio, "Lower your hook, son. It's now or never!" I reached up with my left hand and pushed the hook-shaped lever at the top of the instrument panel to the down position. Shortly, I heard a reassuring clunk as the tailhook locked into place. Abeam the end of the ship, I lowered full flaps, reduced the throttle, and began a gentle descending left turn back toward the carrier. After crossing the ship's wake, I gradually rolled the wings level to line up with the centerline of the angled deck. Damn that ship looked too small to land on! About that time, I spotted the "ball" in the optical system and called it to the LSO, who responded, "Roger ball." Now it was a matter of maintaining three parameters within narrowly prescribed limits as I rapidly approached the fantail of the ship: approach airspeed, alignment with the centerline of landing area, and keeping a centered "ball." As I got closer to the moment of truth, the ship seemed much larger. Airspeed, line-up, ball. Getting close now. Airspeed, line-up, ball. I was about to cross over the fantail as I looked for the cut signal. There it was—chop the throttle and hold the pitch attitude constant. Wham! I hit hard on the flight deck, just the way we were supposed to. If you tried to grease it on (called "spotting the deck"), your tailhook was likely to miss the cables. As soon as the wheels touched, I went to full throttle so I could take off in case the tailhook failed to snag a wire (this is called a "bolter"). Not this time—the hook engaged a cable. My body was thrust forward into the shoulder harness as my airplane rapidly decelerated to a stop in less than three hundred feet. I reduced the throttle to idle and took a deep breath.

However, before I could pat myself on the back, a guy in a yellow jersey gave the hook-up signal and directed me to the right to line up with the centerline of the axial deck of the carrier for takeoff. I quickly completed my takeoff checklist and gave a thumbs-up to the Catapult Officer, who signaled me to go to full throttle while holding the brakes. When he and I were satisfied that the engine was producing full power, I saluted him and he dropped his right arm and pointed to the bow of the ship. This was my signal to release the brakes and go roaring off down the flight deck toward the "pointy end." There was the forward elevator, haul back on the stick, and almost immediately I was airborne. I raised the gear and the flaps and turned downwind for another landing.

I will never forget the less than encouraging words of the LSO as I flew downwind after blowing the first two attempts at a landing. But, when it counted, I finally got my act together. I made six acceptable "traps" into the arresting cables stretched across the flight deck. I was a carrier pilot! I was so giddy, I don't remember a single thing about the flight back to Barin Field, but presumably I remembered my cowl flaps.

Upon landing and befitting my accomplishment, I traded my single gold bar for the double gold bars of a carrier-qualified pilot. Landing aboard the "Lex" was one of the high points of my long flying career, and that day will forever be etched in my memory.

Until about 1967, every individual who wore the wings of a naval aviator, had to qualify during flight training by making six arrested landings in a fixed-wing aircraft aboard an aircraft carrier. In a move to save taxpayers a few dollars, after 1967, students who chose to fly non-carrier-based aircraft or helicopters did not have to meet this test—a misguided move, in my opinion. The special skill and training required to make a carrier landing has long differentiated naval aviators from pilots in other branches of the service. I was thankful I was trained before this change, and have always been proud of the fact that I am carrier qualified.

Chapter 3

Wings of Gold

THE LAST STOP ON MY JOURNEY TO EARNING NAVY WINGS WAS
Helicopter Training Squadron Eight (HT-8) at Auxiliary Landing Field Ellyson Field, located about fifteen miles to the east of
Naval Air Station Pensacola. At Ellyson, I would become an "unrestricted
naval aviator," which is what helicopter pilots called themselves because
they were qualified and certified to fly both fixed and rotary-wing aircraft;
while jet pilots could only fly "stiff-wing" machines. Naturally, the friendly
rivalry between helo drivers and jet jockeys cut both ways. They had a
number of pithy maxims to describe their contempt for their rotary-wing
brethren: "Helicopters are not meant to fly, they simply beat the air into
submission," "Helicopters are nothing more than thousands of parts flying
in close formation, all intent on self-destruction," and my favorite, "If the
wings are traveling faster than the fuselage, it's probably a helicopter and
therefore unsafe."

Learning to Hover

Settling into the now familiar pattern of attending ground school for
half of the day and flying the other half, I set about in earnest to learn
the ins and outs of helicopter aviation. The only differences were: I had
a single room in the Bachelor Officer's Quarters (BOQ), had no morning muster, and had unrestricted liberty. Apparently, we cadets were close
enough to being commissioned that the Navy could start giving us a few
perks that officers enjoyed.

In basic helicopter training, which included solo flying, we flew the Bell
TH-13, a two-place, skid-mounted light helicopter with a large bubble in
front that looked much like the med-evac helicopters used on the TV
series *MASH*. This stage of training was devoted to learning to control the
helicopter during very basic flight maneuvers, such as hovering, air taxi,
various hover patterns, normal takeoffs and landings, steep approaches,

Bell TH-13 helicopter. The first helicopter I flew and also the type that I crashed in July 1965 (shown here is the Bell Model 47, the civilian version of the TH-13).

Sikorsky H-34 was the helicopter used for advanced training. I also flew this helicopter four years later in a ferry squadron, VRF-32

and running landings. Aside from a few minor differences, flying a helicopter above forty knots was similar to flying airplanes—so that was the easy part. Below forty knots, flying a helicopter was a whole new ball game—and this end of the flight envelope was the focus in the H-13.

For advanced training, we flew the large Sikorsky H-34, which was still being used operationally by both the Navy and the Marine Corps. In the H-34, we learned the finer points of helicopter flying such as BI, RI, formation, night flight, external loads, running and confined-area landings, and using the rescue hoist.

But, first things first. I had to learn how to hover, a task far harder than it looked. On my first flight in the H-13, my instructor flew from Ellyson to Site 4, one of several large grass fields in the Pensacola area used strictly for helicopter training. As we sat on the ground in the middle of the large field, my instructor turned to me and said, "Mike, I am going to teach you to hover by giving you one flight control at a time. Then, after you have gained some familiarity with each, we'll combine them and you can take a stab at all three. Are you ready to give it a try?"

"Yes, sir," I said eagerly, while thinking it simply can't be that difficult.

My instructor lifted the helicopter into a steady hover five feet off the ground. "Okay, I'm going to give you the rudder pedals first." The rudder pedals were used for directional control, i.e., where the nose of the helicopter is pointed.

"Do you see the windsock in the middle of the field, over there?"

"Yes, sir."

"Use the pedals to keep the nose pointed toward the windsock. I'll control the cyclic and collective. All right, you have the pedals."

"I have the pedals," I said as I carefully placed my feet on the two rudder pedals on the floor in front of me.

As he moved the collective up, the nose moved right, so I had to apply a little left rudder to bring the nose back to the windsock and vice versa when he lowered the collective. After five minutes, I was able to control the pedals; in fact, it was easy.

"All right, I've got the pedals back. No problem there. Next, I will give you the collective. I will retain control of the pedals and cyclic. The collective is used to control the up and down motion of the helicopter. You have the collective."

"I have the collective." He had me move the helicopter up five feet and then back down several times. Piece of cake. This was easier than the pedals.

"Now, I'm going to move the nose left and right, which, you will notice, requires a slight adjustment of the collective in order to maintain a constant hover height above the ground."

I discovered that if he applied left rudder, I needed to apply a little up collective, and down collective if he moved the nose to the right. After five minutes, I had the collective down, or so I thought.

"Okay, Mike, let's put the collective and pedals together. Keep it pointed at the windsock and five feet above the ground."

For the next five minutes, I played around with the collective and pedals. Again, everything seemed straightforward and relatively easy.

"Good job. Now it's time for the most difficult of the three controls, the cyclic. As you know from ground school, the cyclic, much like the stick in a fixed-wing aircraft, controls pitch and roll. So, I've got the pedals and collective, you have the cyclic."

"I've got the cyclic." No sooner had I uttered those words when the helicopter began to slowly move forward. I immediately applied some aft cyclic, but nothing happened as the machine continued to move forward. Well, I must need more aft cyclic. Due to an inherent lag between cyclic movement and helicopter reaction, both inputs took effect at about the same time. Now we were moving backward at a rapid clip. I countered with a whole bunch of forward cyclic—and things began to unravel quickly.

"I have the cyclic," the instructor said calmly—having been down this road a time or two. "It takes very small cyclic movements. You were just over-controlling, a common mistake for beginners. Let's try it again."

With beads of sweat running down my cheeks (all four), I struggled to get the hang of the cyclic. My oscillations were getting smaller and I could go longer before the instructor had to intervene—*but damn, this was hard.*

Too soon, or so it seemed, the instructor said, "Okay, Mike. Let's see how you do with all three controls."

I knew it was coming. *Do I have to? If most helicopters fly with a copilot, why can't I just handle the rudder pedals and the collective?* "You have all the controls. Just try to keep it within the boundary of this hundred-acre field."

Ten seconds after my taking over all controls, the helicopter was lurching wildly in pitch, roll, and yaw—in other words, I was completely and hopelessly OUT OF CONTROL! We would have crashed right then and there, giving the onsite Navy crash crew something to relieve their constant boredom. Mercifully, my instructor took control and effortlessly regained the upper-hand in the fight with gravity.

In mock dismay, he said that he hadn't even given me the throttle yet on the end of the collective. *Yikes! Why didn't I go jets when I had the chance? I'll take my chances getting run over by an aircraft carrier.*

Like all things, practice makes perfect. Over the next few flights, my hovering skills improved rapidly and I was able to solo on my twelfth flight, right on schedule.

Fateful Meeting at Breakfast

While I was struggling to master the intricacies of hovering, a recent graduate of Fairhope High School was working as a waitress at an Alabama restaurant sixty miles west of Pensacola, to earn money for college. The intersection of our two lives was written by fate—we just didn't know it yet.

Two days after my third flight in the Bell TH-13, my friend and Pre-Flight classmate, Jim Williams, and I decided to go a nurses' party in

Mobile. It was Saturday, July 16. The three nursing schools in the large city on the western shore of Mobile Bay provided a seemingly unlimited number of attractive southern belles who were not bashful when it came to dating Pensacola flight students.

Jim was a real mover when it came to meeting girls. I, on the other hand, could have been described as being backward when it came to the opposite sex. I was the type of guy who, after spending ten minutes building up his courage to ask a girl to dance, was beaten out at the last minute by a more aggressive guy. So, I was not too keen about going with Jim, but Jim persisted, and I went against my better judgment.

The party was being held in a nice apartment complex, complete with a lighted swimming pool in the courtyard. Sure enough, shortly after the party started, everyone had paired off and disappeared. I was the only one left in the living room. I knew this was going to happen and I was furious with myself for letting Jim talk me into coming. Since Jim had the wheels, I was stuck. So, for the next six hours, I had to content myself with playing records on the stereo, swimming in the pool, and bemoaning my sorry state of affairs.

By the time Jim finally showed up, about 0615, I was in a foul mood. On the way back to Pensacola, we decided to stop for breakfast at the Spanish Fort Restaurant at the top of the causeway on the eastern shore of Mobile Bay. As we took our seat, I noticed a really cute waitress who was waiting on another table. I asked our waitress for her coworker's name. She told me it was Barbara. Stepping totally out of character, I said boldly, "Would you please ask Barbara to come over to our table when she gets a chance?"

When Barbara came over to our table several minutes later, I said, "Pardon me, this may sound a bit forward, but I would like a date with you." I think even Jim was taken aback at the directness of my advance. Barbara was mildly put off by my aggressiveness, but not enough to immediately pour cold water on my ardor. She figured we were flight students from Pensacola, by our haircuts, and that I was using my standard pickup line.

"I tell you what, here's my phone number. You can give me a call," she replied a little hesitantly.

"Thank you. I will call you," I said. I was shocked by my audacity, but pleased with the outcome.

"Well, I better get back to work," Barbara said. As she headed toward the kitchen, she told herself that I wasn't serious and probably would not follow through, especially because it would be a long-distance call.

That evening, much to her surprise, I phoned Barbara. We agreed to meet at her house one week later, on Sunday afternoon, after she finished her shift at the restaurant.

The following Sunday, I drove to Barbara's house in Daphne, Alabama, located on the eastern shore of Mobile Bay, five miles south of the Spanish Fort Restaurant. It was a bit uncomfortable for both of us since we had talked all of thirty seconds at the restaurant. She didn't know me, I didn't know her, and here I was already meeting her parents, brothers and sisters, and the family dog. I enjoyed meeting her family, especially talking with her older brother, Jim, who was a lieutenant in the surface Navy. But as I drove back to Pensacola that night, I realized Barbara and I didn't know each other much better because there had been no opportunity to talk privately. There was, however, enough of a spark to propel our budding romance forward. We began to date two times per week, once on the weekend and once during the week, until I got my wings in October.

Our courtship led to a marriage that has endured for fifty-three years, as this book goes to the printer.

Pieces Flying Everywhere

By the time of my seventh solo in the H-13, I was feeling good about my abilities as a helicopter pilot—in fact, I was a bit cocky. After the humbling nature of the first several flights, when hovering seemed well beyond my grasp, I now felt I was the master of this amazing machine. I was having a blast! It was so much fun to fly. There was so much more you could do with a helicopter compared with an airplane—and you could legally fly low and slow.

One of the fun maneuvers we practiced was running landings on the grass fields of the practice sites. These landings simulated a technique that helicopters could use when there was insufficient power to hover for a vertical landing. The skid landing gear on the bottom of the H-13 resembled the two runners on a horse-drawn sleigh. As long as the pilot touched down in a level attitude with no sideward drift, it was not dangerous and the helicopter would slowly come to a stop due to ground friction.

One of the operating rules, when doing running landings at the practice sites, was that takeoffs had to be commenced from the first third of the field. This meant that upon completion of a running landing, the pilot had to lift into a hover, turn 180 degrees, and taxi downwind to a takeoff point in the first third of the field. Once the takeoff point was reached, the pilot would then make another 180-degree hover turn into the wind for takeoff.

Instructors, on the other hand, to save the time of having to come to a complete stop before making the 180-degree turn, would slow to about five knots, pull the nose up, kick left rudder, turn to the takeoff heading, and commence the takeoff—all in one smooth motion. It was so cool to watch, and it further demonstrated how maneuverable a helicopter was and how much fun they were to fly. My instructor told me not to do the *instructor turn*—but he never told me the consequences if I tried it on a solo flight. All he said was I should come to a complete stop and then do a pedal turn to the takeoff direction.

On my seventh solo flight, I was at Site 4, practicing normal takeoffs and landings and the various hover patterns. I was feeling especially good about my piloting skills. All of my maneuvers were spot-on. I decided to do a running landing. In keeping with the restriction on taking off from the first third of the field, I lifted the helicopter into a hover, turned 180 degrees, and began air taxiing downwind to the takeoff point. Because I felt on top of my game, I decided to do an instructor turn for the first time, even though I had been warned several times not to do one.

Mimicking my instructor, I slowed to about five knots, pulled the nose up, and kicked in left rudder. So far, so good. After turning about 45 degrees to the left, I detected in my peripheral vision that the helicopter was beginning to descend. I immediately pulled up collective, but it did not arrest the descent. With forward momentum still carrying me downwind, the left rear skid contacted the ground first, which caused the helicopter to pitch forward onto the forward part of the left skid followed by right skid ground contact. Time stood still. Because the motion was fairly gentle, I thought my blunder might turn out okay. But because I was turned 45 degrees to the path over the ground, the helicopter pivoted suddenly about the right skid and rolled over. The rotor blades contacted the ground and broke off with pieces flying in every direction. The main transmission directly behind the cockpit broke loose and the tail rotor contacted the ground, causing the tail boom to separate from the rest of the aircraft. It was violent, disorienting, and frightening. It was definitely one of those *Oh, shit!* moments.

In a matter of seconds, it was over. The cockpit structure came to rest on its right side and it was time to extricate myself before it caught on fire. Since we always flew with both doors removed, it was one less thing to worry about. From my position in the left pilot's seat, I released my seat belt and fell past the sandbags strapped into the right seat for ballast, and onto the ground, still inside of the cockpit. In my dazed frame of mind, I spent a number of precious seconds unsuccessfully trying to squeeze between the right door opening and the ground, a space of about five inches. After my head cleared a little, I stood on the ground and thrust the upper part of my body straight up out of the left door opening and prepared to hoist myself out. Just then, I noticed the huge yellow crash truck pulling up to the wreckage. Positioned on top of the truck was a sailor dressed in his fireproof suit manning a large nozzle ready to hose me and the helicopter with fire-retardant foam in the event we suddenly caught on fire.

The crash crew helped me out of the helicopter and asked if I was okay. Other than a bruised ego, I was fine. Soon a Navy ambulance arrived to transport me to the base dispensary, where I was checked over by a doctor, who grounded me for two days as a precaution.

After being released from the clinic, writing out a complete statement of my version of the events, and being interviewed by the HT-8 Safety Officer, I went to my room in the BOQ. Bad news travels fast, so by the time I got to my room, the entire base and my friends knew of my inappropriate landing. In fact, the ribbing began immediately. From then on, I was called "crash"—not exactly the sobriquet you want to be known as among the guys.

The crash occurred early on a Friday afternoon, and I needed to relax and unwind. I called Barbara to see if she was available for a date. She was, thank goodness, because I needed someone to cheer me up.

Site 4 was on the way to Daphne, so I planned to visit the crash site, if I could. As I was leaving the BOQ, Jim Williams asked if he could follow me in his car over to Site 4. I said sure. When we got there, the wreckage was within one hundred yards of a side road and we were able to drive up close to it. There was a lone sailor guarding the crash site; we asked if we could come inside the fence to look at the wreck. He said it was okay. When we got closer to the guard, we could tell he was not a happy camper. He had the unfortunate job of having to guard the wreckage all night; a tent and camping gear were near where he was standing.

"I had a hot date tonight, and now I have to guard this goddamn mess because of some stupid idiot flight student," he fumed, kicking a dirt furrow made by one of my skids. "You don't know him, do you?"

I glanced at Jim. "No, I don't." Had I confessed, I am positive he would have bludgeoned me to death with the billy club hanging from his belt.

On Monday morning, I was told to report to the base commander's office in my dress blue uniform. I knew I was in trouble. At the appointed time, I was ushered into the spacious, well-appointed office of Captain George L. Bliss, USN. He was seated behind a large wooden desk; and Major Blades, USMC, the chief flight instructor, was seated on a couch off to the right. I entered smartly and squared-off in front of the Captain's desk.

"Aviation Cadet Stock reporting as ordered, sir," I said nervously while standing at rigid attention.

"Stock, because of your inexcusable actions and willful disregard of policies and procedures that caused the destruction of one of my helicopters last Friday, I fully intended to hang you. I wanted to throw you out of the flight program and make an example out of you."

I swallowed hard and avoided making direct eye contact with one very angry Navy captain. He paused to let his words sink in while drumming a pencil on his desk. The tap, tap, tap felt like Chinese water torture.

"Well, I'm not going to do that. You know why?" Before I could decide if he wanted an answer, he continued, "Because Major Blades went to bat for you. He told me that you have a pretty good record over the last sixteen months of training."

I felt like I had suddenly been jerked back from the edge of a precipice. I took my first breath.

"But, if you screw up the *slightest* militarily, academically, or flight-wise from now on, I will throw you out so fast it will make your head spin. You'll be chipping paint on some rust-bucket in the fleet before you can pack your seabag. You understand me, mister?"

"Yes, sir!"

"Dismissed," he barked.

I did an about-face and marched out of his office—one relieved, but thoroughly chastened, young man. The added pressure of having to maintain a perfect record in an already tough program would put me to the test during the final two months of training.

Soon after this episode, I learned I had gotten my first choice of duty after leaving Pensacola: Helicopter Combat Support Squadron Four (HC-4) based at Naval Air Station Lakehurst, New Jersey. Now all I had to do was keep my nose clean and graduate.

Ensign Stock

Eighteen months and thirteen days after my arrival in Pensacola, I realized my dream when Captain Bliss pinned Navy Wings of Gold on my crisp, white uniform shirt. Just moments before, I had taken the oath of office as an Ensign in the United States Navy Reserve. Captain Bliss is the same officer who wanted to throw me out of the flight program two months earlier. Thankfully, he did not mention that occasion, but I am sure he recognized my smiling face. Come to think of it, maybe he didn't recognize me because I was not smiling when we last met—nor was he.

In a letter that he sent to my parents, dated November 5, 1965, he wrote: "You can take justifiable pride in your son's accomplishment. Naval flight training is difficult and competitive. The successful completion of the Navy flight syllabus requires ability, perseverance, courage, and hard work. The United States Navy is proud to add his name to the illustrious list of naval aviators."

In light of my dismal performances at the University of Buffalo and Penn State University, I was glad I could finally deliver some good news to my parents, who were unwavering in their support during those wayward times.

Captain Bliss, USN, presenting my Navy Wings of Gold several minutes after I was commissioned as an Ensign in the United States Navy. October 22, 1965 *(U.S. Navy photo)*

Thirty minutes after receiving my wings, I hopped in my car and drove to Mobile Airport, where I boarded a Southern Airways flight to Jackson, Mississippi. My destination was the FAA office across the street from the terminal. I was still wearing my white Navy uniform with wings that identified me as a Navy pilot.

Under an FAA regulation titled "military competency," any military aviator is entitled to a Commercial Pilot Certificate by simply passing a fifty-question multiple-choice test on Federal Aviation Regulations. The thinking was that military flight training far surpasses civilian training, so there was no reason to force military pilots to meet civilian standards and pass a flight check. The one area that was different concerned operating rules, hence the test on regulations.

The reason for the hurry to obtain my civilian license was my desire to take Barbara up for a flight in a civilian airplane before I left for my next duty station in a few days.

I passed the test, received my pilot's certificate, and boarded a return flight to Mobile. By 2:00 p.m. that same afternoon, I was at the Fairhope Airport located six miles south of Daphne to get checked out in a four-seat Cessna 172, so I could take Barbara, who was waiting in the car, for a ride. *This shouldn't take long*, I thought. *After all, I am a Navy pilot and I can fly anything, including the box it came in.*

The owner of the airport, who would fly with me, confirmed what I was already thinking—this would be a slam-dunk for the dashing aviator in the white uniform. Well, it didn't turn out that way—not even close.

During flight training in the T-34 and T-28, students were not exposed to landing in strong crosswinds because another runway more aligned with the wind could always be used or, if the winds got too high, solo operations were cancelled. So, when I showed up at Fairhope Airport that afternoon, I didn't realize I was not adept at crosswind landings

The airport had a single north-south paved runway and the windsock was standing straight out 90 degrees to the runway. If I did notice the windsock taxiing to the runway, it didn't register because I had never paid much attention to them in the past—didn't need to. I attempted to land three times and I wasn't even close to getting the airplane straightened out. It was bugging the hell out of me, too. I just couldn't figure out what I was doing wrong. Finally, he took the controls and made a final landing. I was crestfallen and deeply embarrassed. He let me down gently by graciously saying, "The winds are pretty strong today. Why don't you come back tomorrow and try again?"

After returning to Barbara's house, I found a room to myself and re-played the flight in my mind. After much thought, I realized what I had been doing wrong.

The next morning, I returned to the airport, and with the windsock in the same 90-degree position, I made three very nice crosswind land-ings—although not before eating a slice of humble pie, which makes all of us better people—even better pilots.

That afternoon, I took Barbara for a ride. Actually, I was surprised she was willing to go up with me after the fiasco of the previous day.

Chapter 4

Crash Number Two

I N THE DISTANCE, LOOMING ABOVE THE TREES, WAS AN ENORMOUS building. What was it? By my calculations, Naval Air Station Lakehurst was another six miles ahead on the left, too far for me to see from here. Having left my parent's house early that morning, it had been a very long day on the road. Since crossing the Delaware River into New Jersey at Philadelphia two hours ago, I had been driving on a quiet two-lane highway that snaked its way through the pine forests of southern Jersey. Other than the occasional small town, there was nothing to break the monotony of the flat countryside dotted with thousands of conifers. Maybe fatigue was causing me to hallucinate.

As I approached the main gate of the base, I had my first close-up view of left behind relics from the days when giant behemoths patrolled the world's oceans from above. Just ahead, three of the largest hangars I had ever seen stood guard over a rich history of mankind's involvement with *ships of the air*. The largest of the three was obviously the building I had seen from a distance because it was twice the size of other two.

I learned later that this enormous structure was Hangar One, which was built in 1921 to house the large, rigid airships built for the U.S. Navy during the 1920s and early 1930s. *USS Shenandoah, USS Los Angeles, USS Akron,* and *USS Macon* were actually commissioned vessels with a commanding officer, executive officer, and a crew of eighty-nine officers and men. The *Akron* and the *Macon*, at 785 feet long, were the largest airships ever used by the Navy. Some called them "aircraft carriers" because they each carried four F9C Sparrow Hawk bi-plane fighters that were launched and recovered from a trapeze that hung beneath the airship.

Hangar One was 966 feet long, 350 feet wide, and 224 feet high and could accommodate the *Akron* and the *Macon* at the same time. It was rumored that low clouds would sometimes form inside the hangar if the big doors on each end were open. Hangar One, a Registered Historical

Landmark, is still being used today by the Navy for purposes unrelated to lighter-than-air vehicles, but it stands ready to answer the call should the military ever decide to bring back *ships of the air.*

The German airships Graf Zeppelin and Hindenburg also used Hangar One during their transatlantic passenger flights from Europe, thus making NAS Lakehurst the first international airport in the United States. On May 6, 1937, the doors of Hangar One were opened in anticipation of providing overnight refuge for the Hindenburg, which was scheduled to tie up at the mooring circle three hundred yards to the west. The Hindenburg's well-publicized arrival ended in disaster when the giant airship caught fire on its landing approach and crashed, killing thirteen passengers, twenty-two crewmembers, and one ground handler.

Forty-nine years later, I would experience an airship disaster of my own at Lakehurst, very close to where the Hindenburg went down.

Naval Air Station Lakehurst

HC-4, my new squadron, was located in the north half of Hangar Three, while HC-2 occupied the southern half. Office and shop spaces were contained within two-story wings that ran the entire length of the hangar, while the hangar deck itself, formerly a storage area for blimps, was used to park approximately fifteen helicopters for each squadron.

HC-4 provided helicopter detachments to non-carrier ships of the Atlantic Fleet, including icebreakers operating in the Arctic and Antarctic oceans. The missions flown by sea-going detachments included hauling cargo, mail, and personnel; ship gunfire spotting; radar calibration; hydrographic surveys; photographic flights; ice reconnaissance; and mine countermeasures. HC-2, the other squadron that shared Hangar Three, provided detachments to aircraft carriers.

With a blue base sticker on my windshield that signified I was an officer and thus required a salute from the Marine guard, I drove my loaded Chevelle station wagon toward the HC-4 duty office in Hangar Three, to begin my career as a Navy helicopter pilot—perhaps, the only newly minted bachelor naval aviator driving a station wagon.

After getting my orders stamped by the Squadron Duty Officer (SDO), I checked into my second-floor room in the BOQ, which was nicely appointed with period furniture from World War II. At least I shared a bathroom with my neighbor in the next room and not a community head.

The date was November 17, 1965. Ensign Michael J. Stock, United States Navy Reserve at your service!

Over the next several months, half of The Terrible Ten, who had failed survival in our Pre-Flight class, also reported to HC-4: Jim Williams, Pete

Shult, Bill Keller, and Larry Kier. It was good to know I would be serving with them for the next three and a half years, especially if we ever had to endure a real survival experience, given our "advanced" training at Eglin AFB.

The squadron wardroom numbered about seventy-five officers, and all of them were great guys—the best group I ever had the privilege of serving with during my twenty-year naval career. Most of the lieutenant commanders had been World War II pilots who had been recalled for Korea, but because of their broken service between the wars, they had been passed over for commander. They were crusty and irreverent, with plenty of sea stories of the good old days. One had flown carrier strike missions against Tokyo Harbor and another was forced to bail out of a F6F Hellcat. The latter was Bull Dawson, who had played college football for the University of Nebraska and didn't get his nickname because he looked like a wallflower.

The ready-room, in addition to where we held our all-officers meetings each morning, was also where we congregated during free time, ate lunch, played ping-pong, and used to unwind. It was the scene of many laughs, good times, and camaraderie.

Having a large hangar deck meant that the helicopters from both squadrons could be accommodated easily, with plenty of room to maneuver individual aircraft to and from the flight line. One problem, though,

NAS Lakehurst, New Jersey. The monstrous building in the background is Hangar One. Hangar Three, the smallest of the three hangars, was home to my squadron, HC-4. The lead helicopter is a Sikorsky H-19 and the other two helicopters are Kaman UH-2s. *(U.S. Navy photo)*

with having so much unused cavernous space above the helicopters was the presence of pigeons—lots of pigeons. The droppings from these birds was not only a continual royal pain to clean up, but was very corrosive if left on the helicopter's rotor blades and fuselages. The Navy tried all types of schemes to scare the birds away, to no avail. Short of using poison, we were stuck with these pests.

One day, during a squadron personnel inspection in white uniforms, I was standing in ranks directly behind an officer who was standing in the line of fire. A great dump of gooey yellow-green slime hit the edge of his hat and slowly dripped onto his right shoulder, spreading down the back of his sparkling white uniform. It was one of life's moments when you felt great empathy for the victim, but had to smile at the same time.

Although I was assigned a couple minor ground jobs during my eighteen months in the squadron, the primary job for us *nuggets* (new naval aviators) was to gain more helicopter flight hours so we could be assigned to sea-going detachments. Since we had flown the H-13 in the training command, the nuggets were quickly checked out in the single seat and two-seat models and turned loose to build hours. The only "real" mission I flew in the H-13 was to drop a wreath in the Delaware River on Memorial Day.

Toms River Sandpit

Straight ahead looked bleak. A number of small, tree-studded ravines ran perpendicular to our direction of flight. As our helicopter plummeted to earth, it looked like we were going to impact in the midst of these ugly surface scars. I braced myself for impact.

Pete Nelson, three enlisted aircrew who were along to log hours required for flight pay, and I had lifted off from NAS Lakehurst in a UH-2B helicopter forty-five minutes earlier. It was my third instructional flight in the aircraft; Pete was the instructor pilot.

After performing several touch and go's at the air station, we departed the landing pattern and flew to a large uninhabited area near Toms River, located about eight miles east, to practice emergency fuel approaches that simulated how a pilot could safely land the helicopter if the automatic fuel control system were to fail. This was my first exposure to the tricky business of manually controlling the amount of fuel flowing into the jet engine. One careless move could burn up a half-million-dollar engine.

Using a base altitude of one thousand feet above the ground to simulate a runway, I made three landing approaches using the emergency system. Upon completion of the third run, Pete took control of the helicopter and then made another emergency approach to a base altitude of five hundred

Kaman UH-2B helicopter. My second helicopter crash occurred in this model of aircraft on March 11, 1966 in the Toms River, New Jersey area. *(U.S. Navy photo)*

feet. As he was climbing out after terminating his approach and passing seven hundred feet, he instructed me to switch back to normal fuel. As ordered, I reached up to an overhead panel and moved a large toggle switch from the "Emergency" to the "Normal" position. Before allowing me to make the change in switch position, Pete was required to rotate the range control (throttle) on the collective from the flight idle position to the normal "Fly" position. He failed to do that. Consequently, when I moved the switch to the normal position, the jet engine powering the main rotors immediately decelerated to idle thrust. The effect on the helicopter was the same as if the engine had failed completely.

At that point, it was too late to restore fuel to the engine before ground contact. Our only hope of avoiding a potentially fatal crash was to enter autorotation—an unpowered emergency descent, that if handled expertly, would allow the pilot to glide the helicopter to a survivable touchdown. To enter autorotation, the pilot must immediately lower the collective to the full down position. Otherwise, main rotor RPM will rapidly decrease to the point where the pilot will lose total control of the helicopter.

Being new to the helicopter, I didn't know what was happening. I looked over at Pete, and he had a confused look on his face. Things were rapidly spiraling out of control; we would be on the ground one way or another in about five seconds. I realized we were losing rotor RPM and descending rapidly toward some unpleasant-looking terrain straight ahead. We were losing RPM because Pete had failed to fully lower the collective, but I did not know that at the time. The rotor was passing 84 percent the last time I glanced at the gauge—we were close to losing total control of events.

At the last possible instant, Pete dove into a sandpit off to the right. We crashed hard, ripping off the right main landing gear and the tail wheel, wrinkling the fuselage from stem to stern, and overstressing nearly every component on the helicopter. The damage was so great that the Navy ended up scrapping the aircraft as being uneconomical to repair.

Amazingly, the aircraft remained upright and none of the four main rotor blades hit the ground on impact. Not having been trained for this situation, I instinctively applied the rotor brake to bring the rotors to a stop and quickly exited the aircraft.

Incredibly, all of us were uninjured except for a few minor cuts and bruises. There was fuel leaking from the aircraft, but the sand was absorbing it and there was no fire. As the five of us congregated alongside the battered helicopter, we were smiling and congratulating ourselves on a miraculous escape.

Then we realized that things happened so fast, we were unable to get out a mayday transmission, so no one knew we were down. Pete assigned one of the crewmen to remain with the wreckage, while the rest of us walked about a quarter mile down a dirt access path to a paved road. There was a house on the corner, which we approached, hoping to use their telephone. There was a large sign on the front door saying that the house was quarantined due to infectious disease. What are the odds of the only house within walking distance being under quarantine? However, I am not sure any person would have opened their door to four men standing there in orange suits anyway. They might have feared we were extra-terrestrials from a faraway galaxy, or worse, prison escapees.

So, we walked back to the road. The first passing car picked up our motley group and returned us to the base. The first stop was the base clinic to be poked and probed by the medical folks to make sure we were physically okay. Then the fun began—written statements, interviews by everybody and his brother, and a little finger pointing. Fortunately, I was not the pilot in command and I was not flying at the time of the accident, so I didn't have to answer the tough questions. However, this event did serve to reinforce the nickname that I gained after my first crash in Pensacola. Two years and two crashes—I hoped future years would be kinder.

First Cruise

After volunteering for every new detachment being formed to go aboard ship, I was finally assigned to a short two-week cruise to the Caribbean aboard the *USS Francis Marion* (APA-249) flying a Sikorsky H-19, a

Approaching to land on the flight deck of the USS Francis Marion (APA-249). June 1966. (U.S. Navy photo)

vintage helicopter from the Korean War. Our primary mission was to provide helicopter transportation services for the Commander Amphibious Forces Atlantic Fleet, Vice Admiral William Mack, who would be using the Francis Marion as his flagship.

A month before the cruise began, the squadron arranged for some deck time on a Navy icebreaker transiting off the coast of New Jersey, so that us newbie pilots could make our first shipboard landings in a helicopter. I was again teamed up with Pete Nelson as the instructor, and hoped for a better outcome than the last time I flew with him.

We headed out to sea to find the ship on my third flight in the H-19. As we passed over the New Jersey coastline, we radioed the ship to report "feet wet," meaning we were over water. The ship picked us up on radar and vectored us to their location. The ship soon appeared as a distant speck on the horizon, getting larger as we closed the distance. Painted on the flight deck was a landing circle and two line-up stripes, one for an approach from the starboard side of the ship and the other for a port approach. Ideally, the ship would try to place the *wind-over-deck* (the wind that resulted from combining the natural wind with the relative wind caused by the ship's speed) along one of the line-up stripes.

On our arrival at the ship, conditions were just about perfect for my first non-aviation shipboard landing: the skies were clear and sunny, the seas were fairly calm, and the winds were light. "Winds are port twenty degrees. You have a green deck," the ship's air controller said.

This meant that the wind-over-deck was coming from 20 degrees off the port bow and we were cleared to commence our landing. The final approach was started at about three hundred feet above the water and sixty knots and a quarter mile from the ship with the helicopter aligned with the line-up stripe. From that point, it was just like landing to a specific spot on a runway except this spot was constantly moving forward. I made eleven landings and was pronounced qualified, but as with all new skills, I had much to learn about shipboard operations.

On June 12, 1966, Bob Reitmeyer, the detachment officer-in-charge (OIC), and I flew an H-19 from Lakehurst to the naval base at Norfolk, Virginia, to join the ship. Since there were zero navigation radios onboard our aircraft, we used pilotage (flying by reference to ground landmarks) to stay on course. Actually, we followed railroad tracks most of the way. On arrival, we were able to fly directly aboard the *Francis Marion* tied up to a pier on the base. We were soon reunited with Bill Foley and the rest of the crew who had traveled by truck.

Like most *non-aviation ships* (non-aircraft carriers) of the day, the *Francis Marion* had a small landing platform on the fantail large enough to accommodate a single helicopter. Since there was no hangar to protect it from weather exposure and highly corrosive salt air, the helicopter was simply lashed down on deck and covered with tarpaulins when not in use. All maintenance and inspections were performed by detachment personnel in the open; sometimes on a pitching and rolling flight deck. It was a potentially hazardous operating environment for the aircrew and deck crew.

The two-week cruise was pleasant and mostly uneventful. Admiral Mack was friendly and unassuming, and we were able to deliver him on schedule to other ships in the taskforce and to conferences ashore. The only thing out of the ordinary occurred late one afternoon when a wooden Navy minesweeper that was tied up two berths from the *Francis Marion* caught fire in the port of San Juan, Puerto Rico. Our helicopter flew two round-trips to the Naval Air Station at Roosevelt Roads, located on the northwest corner of the island of Puerto Rico, to pick up firefighting foam. In the end, our contribution and the efforts of Navy firefighters were in vain because the ship capsized during the night.

Second Cruise

At the height of the Cold War the U.S. knew that Washington, D.C. would likely be destroyed if nuclear war with the Soviet Union were to occur. To enable the President and civilian and military leaders to continue to direct the war efforts, three alternate command centers were set up with elaborate communication systems: one underground at a secret location in the Virginia countryside, one airborne command post, and another one aboard a Navy ship at sea.

The floating command post consisted of two ships that shared the duty on a rotating basis: *USS Northampton* (CC1) and *USS Wright* (CC2). HC-4 had a permanent helicopter detachment assigned to support these two ships with a UH-2B helicopter. The on-duty ship ranged up and down the East Coast of the United States, but seldom more than one hundred miles from the mainland. Every two weeks the detachment *cross-decked* to the other command ship as it began its two-week tour of duty.

USS Wright (CC2), one of the two floating presidential command ships. Note the UH-2B helicopter belonging to HC-4 on the flight deck. The *Wright* was converted from a Saipan-class aircraft carrier. *(U.S. Navy photo)*

Apparently tired of hearing my constant drumbeat of "Put me in coach" when I volunteered for every cruise that came along, the operations officer assigned me to the *Northampton-Wright* detachment for the months of October and November 1966. Since this was a two-pilot detachment, I did not have to share flying with another copilot, like I had on my first cruise. The Detachment OIC for the last month of the cruise was Lieutenant Dennis Frederickson, a tall, taciturn, likeable officer, who went on to serve in the Minnesota Senate for thirty years after he left active duty.

Typical detachment missions involved the transport of personnel, cargo, and mail to and from the duty ship to military bases ashore. Although these flights were boring and routine, it was still exciting for me to be flying helicopters from ships at sea—to be part of the fleet, where time-honored naval traditions and customs were practiced and observed every day. To someone who had never been to sea and breathed in the distinctive aroma of salt air or felt the motion of a ship tossed by stormy oceans, it was hard to explain the lure and fascination of being aboard ship. I had chosen the right military service—flying was icing on the cake.

During one stint aboard the *USS Wright*, the ship sailed up the Chesapeake Bay and anchored off the U.S. Naval Academy at Annapolis. While there, I was involved in an incident that could have ended in disaster.

We were tasked to transport an admiral from the *Wright* to the Pentagon helicopter pad on the west side of the building. Normally, the heliport did not see a lot of activity, so the tower allowed visiting helicopters to shut down on the pad itself. This time, however, they were expecting a high-ranking officer, so they asked us to park on the lawn adjacent to the pad. After dropping off the admiral, I lifted the helicopter into a hover and slid it sideways onto the lawn and lowered the collective to land. As the weight was gradually being transferred to the landing gear, the helicopter suddenly lurched and rolled to the right as the right main landing gear broke through the sod and fell into a subterranean void that had been created by a hidden water flow. Reacting on sheer instinct, I jerked up on the collective and wobbled back into the air averting a disaster that would surely have been featured on the television evening news; and not to mention that the offices of the Secretary of Defense and the Chairman of the Joint Chiefs of Staff overlooked the site where our helicopter would have beat itself to death. I had already checked that box in Pensacola, so I was relieved I did not have to reprise it again.

Multi-Engine Driver

In less than two years, I had morphed from a "Reluctant Aviator" to an "Eager Aviator." My normal day job didn't come close to satisfying my insatiable need to fly, so I expanded to nights, weekends, and holidays. I simply couldn't get enough of it—addicted as surely as those who struggle with cigarettes, alcohol, or drugs. It didn't matter what kind of aircraft, if it got off the ground, I wanted to try it. My dad observed that there would come a time when I wouldn't feel like I had to fly every day. He was right, of course, but it was many years before that became a reality.

The paltry fifteen to twenty hours per month of helicopter flying I was getting in HC-4 was only an appetizer, so I went to all of the tenant commands on base who owned and flew aircraft—the Naval Air Technical Training Center (NATTC), the Naval Air Reserve Unit (NARU), a Navy experimental Catapult and Arresting Gear Site, an Army maintenance depot for helicopters, an Army flight detachment, and the naval air station itself—offering my services to fly as copilot almost anytime they needed me. As it turned out, they were always looking for pilots because many military aviators only flew so they could draw flight pay. Once they

Beechcraft C-45 (Beech 18 civilian model). I accumulated 246 flight hours in this model aircraft during my short time at NAS Lakehurst. *(U.S. Navy photo)*

flew the required fours each month, they weren't that motivated, especially after normal working hours or on the weekends. As a consequence, I flew helicopters, multi-engine airplanes, and jets. I was like the proverbial kid in the candy shop.

I wasted no time getting started. Exactly one week after reporting for duty with HC-4, I flew my first flight with NATTC in their C-45, a small twin-engine tail-wheel equipped airplane, better known in the civilian world as the Beech 18. In less than six months, I was promoted to aircraft commander.

Since NATTC, NARU, and NAS Lakehurst each had a C-45, I was able to schedule a flight anytime I wanted. It was like having a personal aircraft with my name painted on the side. In the fifteen months I was stationed at Lakehurst, I logged 246 hours in the C-45 alone. Some of the flights had a specific purpose, like transporting personnel on official Navy business or picking up urgently needed parts for HC-4; while other flights were simply to build time—what some would call "boring holes in the sky."

There was many a time when I would go to the large United States map on the wall at Base Ops to find a military airfield that sounded interesting within 250 miles of Lakehurst. I would fly to that airport, refuel, have lunch or a snack, and fly back to Lakehurst while logging four hours of multi-engine time in my logbook. Not only did I gain multi-engine experience, but I also received lots of exposure to all kinds of flying conditions—instrument approaches in minimum weather, icing, thunderstorms, and night flights in IFR weather conditions—that I would not have been exposed to flying helicopters in HC-4. Along the way, about fifteen of my squadron mates flew as my copilot and were thus able to gain new aviation insight as well.

Among the official business missions was flying the air station parachute club on weekend skydiving drops. After removing the aft entrance door, I would take five or six jumpers to 12,500 feet, which would give them one minute of free-fall. They offered numerous times to give me lessons and equipment so that I could jump for free. But I never bought into the idea of jumping out of a perfectly good airplane.

Another task I was given was to fly the Navy jet pilots attending the Catapult and Arresting Gear School at NATTC, so they could get their four hours a month for flight pay. I had been warned that jet pilots aren't used to using the rudders pedals because engines on a jet are mounted on the centerline of the airplane, thus causing negligible yaw. Since the C-45 required constant attention to the rudders, especially on landing and taxi, it was good advice, but like all warnings, sometimes they are best remembered after seeing the results firsthand.

One day, a jet jock in the copilot's seat made a very hard landing which caused the aircraft to bounce back into the air about fifteen feet. No problem, any decent pilot could handle this by adding a touch of power to cushion the second landing—except, the airplane simultaneously cocked 45 degrees to the right. Touching down in a skid of this magnitude would have sheared off the landing gear. I grabbed the controls and shoved both throttles to the firewall and hoped for the best. Somehow, I managed to dodge a bullet—one of hundreds that missed me during my long flying career.

On another occasion, I was flying as copilot for the Army Flight Detachment in a C-47 (DC-3). Our mission was to fly the commanding general from nearby Fort Monmouth to Washington, D.C. for an important dinner engagement later that evening. The pilot-in-command was a Department of the Army civilian pilot. This was my first encounter with a civilian flying for the military, but then I was a newbie and had a lot to learn. He was dressed in a coat and tie and he took one look at my greasy orange Navy flight suit (flying helicopters and grease go together) and pronounced that Army aviators wore their class A uniform, not a flight suit, when flying VIPs. I replied that no one had told me that important detail and it was too late for me to change, so we went out to the aircraft to get ready for the general's arrival.

To complete the bizarre picture, we were flying a C-47 on loan to the Army from the FAA, with agency markings and paint scheme. The most imaginative novelist couldn't have created a more diverse cast of characters—civilian pilot in a suit, Navy copilot in orange, flying an FAA aircraft, and transporting an Army two-star general. Come to think of it, the scene would have blended perfectly into the movie Catch-22.

Soon the general's helicopter landed next to our airplane and he and his entourage boarded. Accompanying the general were two brigadier generals and two full colonels. I had never been in the company of so much brass. I wondered if they would notice my orange flight suit.

After takeoff, the weather deteriorated in the D.C. area, to the point that we couldn't land. After conferring with the general, we decided to land at Philadelphia International Airport and go from there. After landing, all of us—passengers and crew—were standing in a small circle in the middle of the terminal trying to decide how best to salvage their dinner engagement. Should we fly them to another airport where they could rent a car or should they take a train from Philadelphia? I noticed this one brigadier general eyeballing me rather closely, in particular my nametag. Would he chew me out for wearing a flight suit? Finally, he said, "You mean to tell me, you're an ensign?" I don't know whether he had never seen an ensign before, or if he was astonished that an ensign would be flying as copilot on his airplane—the flight suit was never mentioned.

FAA Flight Instructor

Not content with all the military flying, I joined nearby McGuire AFB Aero Club to work toward a FAA flight instructor certificate. After obtaining my rating in 1966, I worked with a couple flight students on their private pilot licenses at McGuire.

About that time, I also joined the Lakehurst Flying Club, which had recently returned to service a T-34 that club members had painstakingly restored. Since I was the only flight instructor in a club with few members, it was like having my own private airplane at a very reasonable cost—$6.50 per flight hour, which included fuel.

One of my first assignments as the club instructor was to check out members who met the minimum flight experience requirements for the T-34. One of these candidates was my neighbor in Pinehurst Estates, Lieutenant Junior Grade John Wilson, who had nearly finished the flight program before being washed out on his final instrument check in Corpus Christie. Because he had flown the T-34 at Saufley, it would be a simple checkout. All I had to do was familiarize John with the differences between a military flight pattern and a civilian one.

I took him to a nearby non-towered airport to practice a few touch and go's. I was flying from the rear seat. "John, civilians extend the downwind leg instead of beginning a turn abeam the intended point of landing," I intoned into John's headset.

"Oh, I see," said John.

"Civilians make all turns perpendicular from the downwind to the base leg and from base to final," I droned on in my best instructor voice.

As we approached the end of the runway, only about one hundred feet in the air, John squeezed the intercom button and inquired casually, "When do civilians lower their landing gear?"

I was absolutely stunned. I was just a few seconds from making a gear-up landing and severely damaging the newly restored airplane. Fortunately, because John had flown the airplane before, he saved me from making "my gear-up landing." It was another humbling moment.

Shortly after joining the Lakehurst Flying Club, I decided to fly Barbara down to Fairhope to see her family. This was Barbara's first ride in the T-34, so I had to familiarize her with the rear cockpit before takeoff. In place of a back cushion, there was a standard Navy back-type parachute. After helping her fasten her shoulder harness and lap belt and showing her how to talk to me over the intercom using the headset, I grabbed the parachute from the front seat out of habit and strapped it on nice and tight while standing on the wing. Barbara was watching all of this very carefully, but said nothing at the time. After landing for fuel at the next stop, she asked why I hadn't strapped her into a parachute in Lakehurst. Trying to be funny, I said, "I didn't think you would be able to get out of the airplane in an emergency and there was no sense in us both going down with aircraft." She was not amused.

In terms of advancing my aviation knowledge and flight experience, my tour of duty at Lakehurst had been more that I could have asked for. In a span of fifteen months, I was able to fly seven new aircraft, logged 253 helicopter hours, 262 multi-engine hours, 222 hours in civilian aircraft, went on two short cruises to the fleet, was promoted to aircraft commander in the H-2 helicopter, and received my FAA flight instructor certificate. On top of it all, I was promoted to Lieutenant Junior Grade on December 1, 1966. I was flying high and ready for the next adventure.

Chapter 5

Vietnam Beckons

B Y 1966, UNDER THE DIRECTION OF FOUR PRESIDENTS, THE UNITED States had a long history of military involvement in Vietnam. In September 1950, President Harry Truman authorized the formation of a Military Advisory Assistance Group (MAAG) Indochina to assist France during their war against the communist forces led by Ho Chi Minh. After a major defeat of French forces at Dien Bien Phu in May 1954, and the subsequent Geneva Accords several months later, Vietnam was partitioned at the 17th parallel into two countries: a Communist-controlled government in the north and a democratic government in the south. As a consequence, President Eisenhower shifted the principal military focus in Indochina to supporting the Republic of South Vietnam led by President Ngo Dinh Diem.

Under the direction of President John F. Kennedy, the level of United States support grew from providing military advice and assistance to the government of South Vietnam to furnishing operational support to the South Vietnamese armed forces. After Lyndon Johnson became President, the war effort intensified dramatically. In April 1965, he signed National Security Action Memorandum 328 which authorized the introduction of combat troops into South Vietnam. From this point, the role of the United States shifted from advisory and support of South Vietnamese forces to direct combat operations. Starting with 128 men in 1950, the total number of United States military personnel engaged in South Vietnam rose to 11,000 by 1962—and then increased dramatically to 276,000 in 1966, with a peak of 543,400 in June 1969.

Back in 1950, among the initial 128 men, was a small contingent of U.S. Navy advisors. As the overall efforts of the United States intensified in South Vietnam, from 1950 to 1966, so did the level of naval involvement, ranging from aircraft carrier battle groups in the Tonkin Gulf to maritime surveillance and interdiction along the coastline of North and

South Vietnam, to the efforts of the so-called Brown Water Navy of the Mekong Delta, the latter forming the genesis of my war experience.

To understand the mission of the Brown Water Navy, one must begin with a basic appreciation of the geography of the Delta area of South Vietnam. This vast sea-level area, located west and southwest of Saigon and comprising nearly one quarter of the country, is crisscrossed by four major rivers—all flowing from the mighty Mekong River that begins in Tibet—and numerous tributaries and manmade canals. Denied the use of traditional transportation methods by air and land, the enemy forces seeking to overthrow the legitimate government of South Vietnam in Saigon had a ready-made solution to their transportation requirements: the natural and manmade waterways of the Delta.

Thus, the basic mission of the Brown Water Navy, which was composed of U.S. and South Vietnamese naval forces, was to intercept and destroy enemy Vietcong forces and supplies plying the navigable waters. On the U.S. side, the principal weapon used was a fast, shallow-draft, thirty-one-foot boat called a Patrol Boat River (PBR). Armed to the teeth, manned by a crew of four, and operating in pairs, these fearless marauders, like their World War II counterparts in PT boats, were highly successful in slowing the amount of enemy supplies that reached the Delta from the Ho Chi Minh Trail, the name given to the crude and tortuous unpaved route that stretched from North Vietnam through the neutral countries of Laos and Cambodia.

No matter how well-armed, courageous, and bold these intrepid sailors on PBRs were, they were vulnerable to Vietcong ambushes, often with devastating results. To mitigate the threat, Commander Naval Forces Vietnam (COMNAVFORV) requested dedicated air support in the form of helicopter gunships. Initially, U.S. Army Aviation units were tasked, and, although they did a good job, it was not feasible for the long haul because these gunships were desperately needed to support Army combat operations, and it was felt that gunships flown by U.S. naval flight crews would result in better coordination since "they both spoke the same language."

Due to the fact the U.S. Navy had never flown helicopter gunships and had no such aircraft in its inventory, the new mission presented major obstacles and a steep learning curve. But, in keeping with naval tradition when presented with an order, the naval aviation establishment said, "Aye, aye, sir" and marched off to war.

Helicopter Combat Support Squadron ONE (HC-1), a helicopter utility squadron based in San Diego, California, immediately formed four detachments and sent them to Vietnam, where the U.S. Army provided surplus Huey helicopter gunships and a quick training course on how to be a gunship pilot. Already in motion, however, was a permanent replacement for the HC-1 detachments in the form of a brand-new Navy squadron: Helicopter Attack (Light) Squadron Three (HAL-3) to be established in Vietnam on April 1, 1967.

In November 1966, an All-Navy message was sent to all U.S. naval units ashore and afloat requesting volunteers for this new gunslinger outfit. Heeding the siren call, I raised my hand.

Fort Benning

My offer to volunteer was not a snap judgment made against the backdrop of swirling patriotism, like the long lines that formed at military recruiting stations around the country following the attack on Pearl Harbor. It was more the culmination of intrigue and excitement that had been building over several months.

I had always been curious and interested in world events; reading the newspaper and watching the national news on TV was a regular part of my life. I can remember very clearly as a young boy sitting on the back steps of our home during the summer of 1950, reading the *Buffalo Evening News* as it chronicled, day-by-day, the ebb and flow of the Korean War. Likewise, I had been closely following the build-up of U.S. forces in Vietnam during 1965 and 1966, particularly the Navy's role in the air war over North Vietnam. Being a helicopter pilot, I was also keenly interested in the "helicopter war" being waged in South Vietnam that brought unmatched tactical surprise and mobility to the battlefield.

A tenant command at Naval Air Station Lakehurst during this period was a U.S. Army Flight Detachment. Several of the pilots assigned to the Detachment had already served one tour of duty in Vietnam. One day, our squadron training officer invited one of these Vietnam veterans to speak at an all-officer meeting held in the ready-room. I don't remember his name or his face, but I distinctly remember being riveted by the retelling of his exploits as a helicopter gunship pilot. There had been rumors in prior months that the Navy was soon to get into the gunship business in the Mekong Delta, so his message resonated and filled me with eagerness and a thirst for adventure.

So, when I read the All-Navy message asking for volunteers, I was primed and receptive to its entreaty. What I did next was not the smartest move for a recently married man—I volunteered without consulting my wife. You can imagine Barbara's reaction when I got home that evening and told her what I had done.

"How was your day at work, honey?"

"Oh, a pretty routine day, boring really, but I did volunteer for Vietnam."

"You did what?"

Through the screaming and crying she managed to blurt out, "How could you be so selfish? Don't you love me?"

I did my best to reassure her that it was very unlikely that I would be chosen from the large number of Navy helicopter pilots worldwide, who would surely volunteer for such a glamorous assignment. Furthermore, I told her that thirteen pilots from the HC-4 signed up and they couldn't take nearly that many without leaving the squadron grossly undermanned. My chances of being selected were slim indeed—I actually believed that, and so did Barbara after much persuasion. But guess what? On February 28, 1967, I received my official orders to Vietnam. In fact, all thirteen of my squadron mates were chosen—so much for my cool assessment of the odds. I would have training stops in Fort Benning, Georgia, and Coronado, California, before leaving the country.

The next several weeks were a blur. I had to disengage from my duties at the squadron and complete a multi-page departure checklist; arrange for a moving company to pack up and transport our household goods, some to storage and the remainder to Fairhope, Alabama, where Barbara would stay with her parents; get my will and financial affairs in order; clean our apartment in base housing sufficiently to pass inspection; turn over my responsibilities at the Flying Club; ensure our car was ready for a long road trip; and say goodbye to all of our friends. It was a time of great anticipation for me and elevated melancholy for Barbara. I was busy with a myriad of details, while she was alone day after day in our apartment, able to stew over the upcoming separation. It was not a happy time for our young marriage, and I give a lot of credit to Barbara for not bolting for the door.

On March 23, with our station wagon packed to overflowing, Barbara and I left Lakehurst for Fairhope, Alabama, and an uncertain future. After getting her settled at her parent's home at 800 Edwards Avenue, I embarked on a two-month journey that would ultimately place me in harm's way—first stop, Fort Benning, just outside of Columbus, Georgia.

The first sight a newcomer to Fort Benning notices upon driving through the front gate is a number of tall jump towers where students going through airborne training practice descending under a fully deployed parachute. Little did I know my youngest daughter would win her Army jump wings there thirty-nine years later. In addition to the Airborne School, Fort Benning is the home of the Infantry School and other important active-duty Army units and commands. It is the largest training installation in the Army.

What was a Navy guy doing at Fort Benning? You recall that the Navy did not have any helicopter gunships or pilots trained to fly them, but the Army did. So, all ninety-two volunteers, like myself, who were selected in the Navy dragnet, were sent to the 181st Aviation Company in groups of about twenty for a ten-flight-hour transition course to learn to fly the Bell H-1 "Huey" helicopter, followed by five flight hours on the gun range learning to fire rockets and machine guns.

The real question was: was the Army ready for the Navy—a bunch of lost-looking souls in strange uniforms; speaking a foreign language that included terms such as *decks, bulkheads, scuttlebutts, gedunk,* and *smoking lamps*; and possessing an irreverent attitude for hallowed Army customs and traditions. As a case in point was the crest for the Infantry School, which was in the shape of a Medieval knight's shield with a bayonet pointing upward to their motto "Follow Me." A devious pilot in the first group to be trained (I was in the second group) custom-designed a shield to herald the Navy's arrival. It prominently featured an extended middle finger pointing upward to the words "After You." Mercifully, no where on the emblem did it say U.S. Navy, otherwise, I suspect the Army would have found a new use for those tall towers.

Although Fort Benning was only a four-hour drive northeast from Fairhope, I decided to drive up on Saturday, so I would have Sunday to get acclimated, learn my way around, and be fully rested for the start of training on Monday. Checking in at Bachelor Officer Quarters (BOQ), I was told by the desk clerk that I would be sharing a room with another Navy officer. Normally, I value solitude and would have preferred a private room, but having a roommate who wears the same uniform might not be so bad while staying in Army country.

I knocked on the door to my room and shifted my suitcase to my left hand. A smallish guy, about five feet six, with brown eyes, closely cropped dark hair, and wearing Bermuda shorts and a polo shirt opened the door.

"Hi, my name is Mike Stock," I said, as I extended my hand. "I'm your new roommate."

"Nice to meet you, Mike. I'm Tom Gilliam," he said as he stepped back into the room, allowing me to enter.

"When did you arrive, Tom?"

"Oh, about three hours ago. I don't know about you, but it was quite an ordeal to find this place. Starting at the main gate, nobody seemed to know what to do with a naval officer reporting for duty."

"Yeah, I got the same run-around. Hopefully, our training is better organized than the check-in process," I commiserated.

I placed my suitcase on the empty bed and looked around at our spartan accommodations—a small desk and chair, an open closet with a few rusted coat hangers, two windows with dusty white venetian blinds, and a small bathroom at one end of the room that we shared with two other officers in an adjoining room. It was comforting to know that the Army didn't live any better than the Navy. I guess the same civil servant who flunked out of design school decorated and furnished the BOQ rooms for all military services.

"Tom, what squadron did you come from?"

"Oh, I'm new. Right out of the training command. Got my wings three weeks ago. How about you?"

"Well, I came from HC-4 in Lakehurst. I received my wings about eighteen months ago."

"Mike, it's nice to be bunking with someone who has some fleet experience. What did you fly in Lakehurst?"

"I started out flying the H-13, then made my first cruise in the H-19, and recently I was made an aircraft commander in the UH-2B."

Tom seemed to appreciate my "vast" naval experience, and I relished not being the new guy for once. We hit it off immediately. He was quiet and unassuming, friendly, a fellow Catholic; and being from Ohio, not too far from my neck of the woods in western New York. We formed a close friendship that would last throughout our stateside training and our introduction to combat flying with the Army in South Vietnam.

At 0800 Monday morning, we were seated in a classroom at Lawson Army Airfield, anxious to begin our transition to the Huey. A stocky Army Major stood behind the lectern. "Good morning, gentlemen. I'm Major Joe Berry, the Operations Officer. I would like to be the first to welcome you to the 181st Aviation Company." He glanced around the room as he paused to take measure of the assembled group dressed in short-sleeve khaki uniforms—a sharp contrast to his highly starched and pressed green utility uniform and spit-shined black boots. "We don't have much water around here, but we will do our best to make you feel comfortable. I suppose we could set up a lawn sprinkler and let you guys run through it during class breaks," he said, obviously pleased with his attempt to provide a little levity. But we weren't buying it—too early in the day for Navy jokes.

"Gentlemen, judging from the course critiques submitted by the first group that finished last week, we delivered the training that the Navy desired. To be honest, there were a few areas that needed improvement and, hopefully, we have corrected those problems. I am confident that when you leave here in three weeks, you will be competent Huey pilots and feel fairly comfortable in the machine. However, with only five hours allotted for the gun range, you certainly won't be proficient in firing rockets, machine guns, and tactics. In-country on-the-job-training will provide the finishing touches to your gunship-pilot résumé. But, I can assure you, our instructors will do their very best to provide a quality training experience. The Vietnam conflict requires a team effort to defeat a determined and resourceful enemy, and we welcome our Navy brothers to the fray.

"Speaking of our instructor pilots, most of them have already completed one combat tour in Vietnam, and a few have two tours under their belt. So, I encourage you to pick their brains. Your mission may be slightly different from the Army's, but gunship tactics should be similar in both arenas.

"The plan for the rest of today is to get you ready to fly your first flight tomorrow morning. You will be issued flight gear, given your instructor assignments, and go over a preflight inspection of the H-1. The Monday-through-Friday routine will be to fly in the mornings and go to ground school in the afternoons. We will not be flying on Sundays, and will only fly on Saturday if we get behind due to weather. Are there any questions?"

Seeing no hands, Major Berry said, "Okay, gentlemen. Thank you for your attention, and welcome again to Army aviation. At this point, I'll turn things over to Captain Harbough, who will take you through the rest of your day."

After lunch, the instructor-student assignments were posted on the bulletin board outside of the classroom. I was paired with another lieutenant junior grade by the name of Mike Louy; the two of us were assigned to fly with Chief Warrant Officer 3 Wade Kern, who happened to be somewhat of a celebrity in the company. When John Wayne and a movie production company came to Fort Benning several months earlier to film *The Green Berets*, Wade had a three-word speaking part as he sat in the cockpit of his helicopter.

Mike Louy, who I had just met the day before, was from a Helicopter Anti-Submarine Warfare squadron based in Quonset Point, Rhode Island. He had been in the fleet about the same length of time as I; maybe that's why we were paired together. At any rate, he seemed like a good guy to fly with—always smiling, laughing, and cracking jokes.

The next morning, Mike and I reported to the flight briefing room at the airfield at 0630 to meet our new instructor and to plan the morning's flight activities. Wade Kern was a country boy from the deep South, with an accent and demeanor to match. I was certain that if it had not been specified by Army regulations to wear military-issued flight gear, he would be wearing a Stetson, blue jeans, and cowboy boots—maybe even some spurs. He had a swagger that matched his two combat tours in Vietnam. He was direct and a bit gruff—a no-nonsense, take-no-prisoners sort of a fellow. Mike looked at me with a half-smile and I thought, *This could be a rather interesting few days.*

After the conclusion of the flight brief, the three of us strolled out to the flight line and to our assigned UH-1D helicopter. Mike and I flipped a coin to see who would fly first and I won the toss. I did my best imitation of a proper pre-flight inspection of a Huey as Wade tagged along, suggesting additional items to check based on personal experience. He climbed into the left front seat where the instructor sat, I strapped into the right front seat, and Mike got into the rear of the aircraft and sat in a forward-facing jump-seat positioned between the two front seats.

Ever since day one at Pensacola, as a brand-new flight student, it was drilled into me and every aspiring naval aviator to *always use a checklist.* You used a checklist to start the engine, one before takeoff, after takeoff, cruise, one before landing—even emergency procedures had checklists. A pilot didn't do anything without a checklist, and you didn't dare memorize one because you couldn't trust your memory. In naval aviation, it was the equivalent of the Holy Grail. So, after fastening my seat belt and shoulder harness, I dutifully reached into a leg pocket of my flight suit and pulled out the checklist for a UH-1D helicopter.

Wade bellowed, "What's that?"

"Uhh, it's the checklist," I replied confidently.

"I can see that, you moron! Do you suppose during a mortar attack on the airfield you will have time to read that damn thing?" Not waiting for an answer, he dropped a bombshell, "Put that thing away. I want you to memorize it."

Whoa! That's as close to blasphemy as it gets in naval aviation, I thought.

Then, Wade really outdid himself. He reached into his flight suit and pulled out a big Cuban cigar, lit it, and growled, "Now, let's get this damn thing cranked up. Daylight's a wastin'."

Wait, wait, I protested silently. *What about the other cardinal rule about no smoking within fifty feet of an aircraft?* I glanced back at Mike. He wore the same half smile he had back in the briefing room.

Reluctantly, I put the official checklist back into my flight suit and, with Wade's coaching, somehow managed to start the machine and bring the rotors up to flying RPM. My mind was still reeling from being deprived of my checklist, like a child whose binky is taken away. I was jerked back to reality by Wade's gruff voice. "Well, son. What are you waiting for? Lift this thing into a hover and move it over there," pointing with his cigar toward the runway as smoke from the tip curled toward the top of cockpit.

Will I ever be able to please this guy? I wondered. I changed my mind—this was not going to be an interesting three weeks. It was going to be a long three weeks, if I made it.

After the awkward beginning, life did get better. Flying the Huey was pure joy. It was sweet, nimble, graceful, and easy to fly—the best helicopter I had ever flown! Mike and I both came to appreciate, trust, and, even love our instructor. Despite his rough edges and crusty demeanor, Wade was a fabulous instructor who taught us many things that would not only save our lives later in Vietnam, but made us better pilots throughout our flying careers. There were several helicopter-flying techniques he taught me that I have passed on to my students over the years. To say Wade Kern had a profound impact on me is to understate the obvious. By the luck of the draw, we got the best flight instructor at Fort Benning.

Mike and I alternated doing the flying; we would generally switch seats about mid-morning when we came back to refuel. Whether flying or observing from the jump seat, we sat at the master's knee as Wade took the Huey to the very edge of the flight envelope, performing maneuvers the Navy would never dream of doing because of the risk to man and machine. We performed full touchdown auto rotations, both day and night, until we became so proficient that we knew, without any doubt, we could land the helicopter safely if the engine was ever shot out by enemy fire. We practiced over and over how to regain control after encountering dangerously low rotor RPM, simulating what often happened in Vietnam following a heavily-loaded takeoff.

Perhaps the most dangerous flying we did, but also the most exhilarating and fun, was what the Army referred to as *low-level flight*," another name was *contour flying*. The idea is to conform to the terrain by flying the helicopter as low as you possibly can without hitting a tree, large boulder, or a building; or flying into the ground or water—all while traveling at the Huey's top speed of about 144 miles per hour. Believe me, the first time I dropped down on a narrow, winding river that snaked its way across the backcountry of the military reservation, it was an eye-opener. Flying five feet above the water, well below the tops of the trees that lined each bank, at a speed that made my peripheral vision a blur, was exceedingly stressful and adrenaline-pumping—wow, what fun—like the rush a skilled kayaker experiences while hurtling down the chute of Class V rapids. The Navy called dangerously low flying just for the thrill of it *flat-hatting* and it was a sure way to end an officer's career—either in a flaming wreck or by court-martial. But here, it was legal and a necessary skill for a combat helicopter pilot to minimize his chances of being shot down by enemy ground fire.

While dispensing life-saving tips from his customary left seat, Wade also interjected a number of colloquial "Kern-isms." His favorite was "Pull pitch and let her eat." Mike and I knew that *pull pitch* meant to pull up on the collective control lever of the helicopter, but we never did figure out what *let her eat* meant. Invariably, while hovering at the end of the runway, ready for takeoff, Wade would proclaim loudly, "Pull pitch and let her eat!" On the gun range, as we were boring in on the target and getting ready to loosen a load of rockets, he would shout gleefully, "Pull pitch and let her eat!" I admit the phrase had a nice ring to it, but I never could assimilate it into my flying vocabulary.

Another of his favorites, but this one was saved only for a rocket run, was "Stick in their ear" which he would repeat excitedly several times in quick succession. So, between "Pull pitch and let her eat" and "Stick in their ear," firing runs on the gun range featured a verbal onslaught that would surely awaken the comatose. I got so caught up in Wade's enthusiasm that I didn't care where my rockets hit. Yeehaw!

You can imagine how hard it was to sit in the classroom each afternoon, learning the parts of the T-53 Lycoming jet engine and other obscure details of the Huey helicopter after a heart-pumping, adrenaline-flowing, airborne symphony in the morning—Wade Kern, conducting! But, somehow, I managed to stay awake most of the time and absorb enough to pass the written exam at the end.

Following a jog after class, dinner, and a little evening study, I had no trouble falling asleep—"Pull pitch and let her eat!"

After ten flight hours learning to fly the H-1 helicopter and four hours on the gun range under the tutelage of Chief Warrant Officer Wade Kern, it was time to fly without him. On my last flight to the gun range, I flew as aircraft commander with my roommate, Tom Gilliam, as my copilot. It felt good to be on my own, and also a little intimidating. As I shut down the helicopter for the final time at Lawson Army Airfield, I was technically a qualified combat pilot in the Huey—as it turned out, there was much to learn!

I will be forever grateful to the Army. They had gone all out for us, taught us everything they knew about flying the Huey, and prepared us well for the dark days ahead. And, thanks to good flying weather and an aggressive training schedule, we finished our instruction four days early. I looked forward to spending those extra days with Barbara before I had to depart for Vietnam.

Naval Amphibious Base Coronado

The four-hour drive to Fairhope afforded ample opportunity to reflect on the current state of my affairs. I was being drawn inexorably to a place of great danger, like a lemming to the edge of the abyss. Gone was the euphoria that surrounded volunteering and being selected for a risky assignment on a foreign shore. Those halcyon days were replaced with two competing realities: I would soon be separated from my young wife, who embodied dreams of family and home, a lovely person who I might never see again—and a lingering sense of embarking on a grand adventure. The pure joy I had experienced flying the Huey added to the contradiction. The heavy burden started to fade as my thoughts drifted to being in Barbara's arms again in a few more miles.

My twelve days in Alabama slipped by too quickly as I took care of last-minute details before shipping off to war. Barbara and I did manage to get away for several days, to visit my grandparents in central Florida, but it was hard to totally relax. The impending separation was wearing on both of us. Gloom descended on those last few hours, like thick fog rolling in off the Maine coast.

The day we had been dreading finally arrived. Saturday, April 29, 1967, was a beautiful, sunny day in Fairhope—the azaleas and magnolias were in full bloom and spring flowers offered a colorful panorama to please the senses. Before departing for the Mobile Airport, the two of us stood arm-in-arm

A sad and emotional moment when I said goodbye to Barbara before leaving for Vietnam. I did not think that I would ever see her again. April 29, 1967.

in the backyard for a photo; Barbara in a pretty, two-piece suit and I in my service dress khaki uniform. It was a sad moment, not only because we were saying goodbye, but because I had an overwhelming feeling that I would never see her again. I am normally an upbeat, positive-thinking person—not that day! Obviously, I did not share my foreboding with Barbara, although I desperately wanted to. Like a doomed couple inside an airliner falling out of control to earth, holding each other tightly during those last terrifying moments, I wanted to hold Barbara close and tell her how much I loved her and how much I regretted not being able to ever see her again. As my airplane took off and flew over the Gulf of Mexico, heading westward, I looked out the window, hoping to catch a glimpse of the azure water, but copious tears obscured my vision. It was a lonely, empty feeling—one I shall never forget.

As the airliner winged its way west, I was charting new territory. My westernmost penetration of our great country, up to this point, had been Jackson, Mississippi, on the day I received my FAA pilot's certificate. I was glad to have a window seat that afforded me a commanding view of the changing landscape below. Until we were west of Dallas, Texas, the scenery didn't look much different from the eastern United States, but then the change was dramatic when treeless, semi-desert, flat terrain gave way to the majestic and rugged Rocky Mountains. The sheer beauty that was unfolding below me gave my sagging spirits a much-needed lift.

You might say that I was *California dreamin'* because I immediately became infatuated with San Diego and the Southern California lifestyle. Enveloped by cool temperatures, low humidity, and sunny skies, San Diego was a composite of old Spanish charm, with its slow but measured pace; and a modern, free-spirited whirlwind epitomized by surfers, Beach Boys music, outdoor enthusiasts, and gorgeous tans on parts of the body not normally exposed to the sun (at least not east of the Mississippi).

I went to my first Mexican restaurant and threw down my first margarita, and then a second. Free from training activities on the weekend, I attended a bull fight just across the border in Tijuana, Mexico, and went to the world-famous San Diego Zoo. I was so smitten, that I wrote to Barbara gushing, "I really do feel that out here, somewhere, we are going to stay, build our home, and raise our family!" Well, maybe, but first there was a little matter called Vietnam that had to be dealt with.

I was, after all, in Southern California to attend a three-week training course on Counter-Insurgency, Self-Protection, and Survival. Those three ominous-sounding words must have been selected for their maximum shock value—nothing coy about the nature of this course. *Ugh, I think I will have another margarita!*

The first week of training was held at the Naval Amphibious Base Coronado. located on a narrow strip of land between the Pacific Ocean and San Diego Bay. The base provided operations, training, and support for naval amphibious and special warfare units of the Pacific Fleet. It was, perhaps, most famous for being the place where Navy SEALs received their initial rigorous BUD/S training and went through the much-publicized Hell Week.

We attended class for eight hours each day, Monday through Friday. Some of the classes were interesting and well-presented, while others were not. It was a long five days. We had classes on Vietnamese customs and culture, the geography of North and South Vietnam, and a basic introduction to the Vietnamese language. It was the type of information that any first-time traveler to a foreign country would want to know. But, that's where the similarity to the average tourist ended. We also had classes on the origin and objectives of the Vietnam War and the role the U.S. Navy was playing and classes on knowing your enemy and how to survive in a combat zone. We were constantly reminded that U.S. forces were in South Vietnam to assist that country in its fight against Communist forces seeking to overthrow a legitimately elected government. We were not there for personal gain and we should never act like occupiers or conquerors.

We were issued green, heavy-cotton, two-piece fatigue uniforms that were hot to wear, even in the mild temperatures of Southern California.

Our instructors told us not to wear white undershirts because they could be spotted easily by an enemy sniper. *Yikes! What am I getting myself into? My recruiter never mentioned anything about snipers.*

Marine Corps Base Camp Pendleton

After a weekend savoring more San Diego delights, we boarded a gray Navy bus early Monday morning for a one-hour ride north to the large, sprawling Marine base at Camp Pendleton, for a five-day course on self-protection.

The first two days were spent in the classroom for a series of mind-numbing lectures on every weapon known to man, with the possible exception of a rock-flinging catapult. All of these monologues were delivered in excruciating detail by NCOs using the time-tested Marine techniques of in-your-face, short words, and brute force. Having spent sixteen weeks in Pensacola at the beginning of flight training under the "gentle" auspices of Marine Drill Instructors, I was used to their instructional methods, which offered no subtle nuance or thought-provoking metaphor. For other Navy students in my class, who were not pilots, this was their first contact with hard-core, real Marines. It was not your average college classroom.

On the third, fourth, and fifth days, we marched five miles early each morning to Edson Range, where we personally fired all of the weapons discussed in the classroom, with the exception of the .50 caliber machine guns. We took turns firing the M-1 carbine, the M-14 and M-16 rifles, the M-60 machine gun, the M-79 grenade launcher, and the .38 and .45 caliber pistols. We watched a fire-power demonstration of the .50 caliber machine gun, which was truly awe-inspiring for its destructive power. It made me wince at the thought of what it could do to a thin-skinned helicopter. No wonder this machine gun had seen continuous service since its introduction way back in World War I.

On our last day at the firing range, before returning to the Amphib Base in San Diego, we all threw a live hand grenade. Each of us had watched soldiers and Marines throwing grenades in combat footage of World War II and Korea—grab the grenade in one hand, pull the pin with the other, heave it mightily toward the enemy position, and wait for the explosion four to five seconds later. Contrary to urban legend and John Wayne movies, you don't pull the pin with your teeth.

It seemed easy enough, but for the Marine instructors overseeing this phase of training, it was a potential nightmare. What if a clumsy student dropped the grenade into the throwing pit after pulling the pin? The instructors warned us that it had happened. We were told that if we accidentally dropped the grenade, we were to dive out of the way of the instructor, who would be frantically trying to grab the live grenade and toss it over the protective wall of the pit before it exploded. You couldn't have paid me enough to be one of those Marine instructors. Needless to say, when it was my turn, I tightly held on to the grenade as I pulled the pin, and then quickly threw it.

During my time with the Marines, I began to have second thoughts about my grand Vietnam adventure, as evidenced by a letter I sent to Barbara in which I wrote, "If I knew what I know now, I would not have volunteered for this program, mainly, because I am going to be away from you."

Remote Training—Warner Springs

Two weeks of training down, one more to go. The Navy had saved the worst for last—the training most of us feared: SERE School, which stood for Survival, Evasion, Resistance, and Escape. As pilots and aircrew members, going through Navy survival school was a familiar requirement. I had completed several such schools during my three years active duty. But SERE had a reputation as being the most physically and mentally challenging of them all, a reputation that was undoubtedly part legend, part rumor, and part fact; scary nonetheless.

Ready or not, very early on Tuesday morning, we were loaded onto a— you guess the color—Navy bus and transported into the rolling foothills northeast of San Diego to a large, desolate training area. At 3,200 feet elevation, you would expect the daytime temperatures to be cooler there than along the coast in San Diego, but that was not the case. It was hot during the day and very cold at night—a perfect combination to ensure maximum misery.

As the military does at every survival school, our orders were stamped "government quarters and messing available" when we checked in at Warner Springs. Technically, I suppose, a lean-to made of sticks and moss qualified as government-furnished quarters and a few wild berries and grasshoppers fulfilled the meals part. I mention this because I want to impress upon you that your tax dollars are being well spent.

We started out, as usual, in the classroom with a series of lectures concerning each phase of training we would encounter during SERE. Three days were allotted to Survival, one half day to Evasion, and two and one-half days to Resistance and Escape, commonly called the POW Compound. After noon chow, consisting of C-rations, the last government meal provided during training, and a few more lectures in the afternoon, we were turned loose to begin the survival phase.

Under the direction of expert survival instructors, we learned and practiced the basic skills necessary to keep body and soul together until rescue: shelter building, fire starting, water and food procurement, and land navigation. Conquering the first three was not an issue, but food was another matter. Any potential meal of substance, whether it crawled, swam, ran, or flew had long been consumed by previous classes. That left edible vegetation and insects, neither of which were appealing or energy-producing. Consequently, we became more tired and listless as the days dragged on—exactly the physical condition the Navy was striving for to make the Evasion and POW phases more realistic and challenging.

The Evasion phase attempted to recreate a scenario that might occur when an aircrew, that had been shot down, was forced to move to a location more favorable for helicopter rescue; all the while having to evade capture by the enemy forces searching for them. We assembled at one end of a large treeless field about three hundred yards wide and a mile long, where we received our mission: remaining within the field boundaries, evade capture by "enemy soldiers" while working our way to the rescue point at the other end. There were some bushes and a few small rises and ditches to conceal movement, but the terrain definitely favored being captured, which was to be the ultimate fate of every student. We were only given five hours for this exercise, at which time all of us would find ourselves in a simulated POW camp; so the only incentive to avoid capture, beyond personal pride, was to prolong being inserted into the notorious POW compound earlier than required.

I decided the best way to avoid capture would be to slowly low-crawl using whatever terrain features I could find. After about one hour, the instructors posing as enemy soldiers began sweeping the field, hollering, and firing blanks into the air. Whenever they found an "imperial Yankee dog," they would unceremoniously jerk the prisoner to his feet at gunpoint and haul him off to a waiting truck. Have you ever tried to crawl on your stomach for one mile over less than perfect terrain? It was painful and slow going. Since my fate was preordained anyway, I began to lessen my misery by getting off my stomach and taking more chances with a higher profile. Sure enough, about two hours into the evasion phase, I was staring at two black combat boots inches from my face as a rifle barrel was jabbed into my ribs. Just as it would for someone who was captured by a real enemy, my tidy and comfortable world was about to suffer an abrupt change of fortune.

As I sat blindfolded in the back of a truck with other captured students, waiting to be transported to the POW compound, genuine fear and apprehension descended upon my tired, hungry, and thirsty body as I contemplated what was coming next. I had heard that the camp instructors used an interrogation technique called *water-boarding*, where the victim was strapped to a board head down and an undershirt is clasped tightly over his face while water is slowly poured over the shirt. The person cannot breathe and feels as though he is being suffocated. Once the individual becomes unconscious due to lack of oxygen, his tormentors remove the shirt and he is allowed to recover on his own. But, from the victim's point of view, a person would experience exactly what it would be like to actually die from suffocation or drowning. This barbarous method is highly effective in getting a person to talk, especially if employed multiple times on the same individual. (Since then, water-boarding has been denounced in the western world as being torture and inhumane.) At Warner Springs, so the rumor went, there would be a Navy doctor present to ensure that you weren't accidentally killed. *Oh, wonderful, I was so relieved.* Luckily, the week I went through the training, they had temporarily suspended water-boarding. We did not know this at the time, so you can imagine how fearful I was sitting there in the truck.

My other big fear was being crammed into a small box just big enough to accommodate my contorted body. I had always been claustrophobic to the point of panic if my body was constrained by something or someone physically touching me, like being in a narrow-diameter pipe or under a big pile of boys playing football. The rumor was that everyone would be placed into a box, so I was concerned if I could mentally handle it.

We also knew that we would be slapped around and physically abused during our forty-eight hours of captivity. I reasoned that at least they couldn't deliberately kill or maim me, but beyond that I wasn't sure. To say that I was stressed going into the POW phase was a gross understatement of my state of mind, and, of course, my present physical and mental conditions were precisely where the Navy wanted them. How else could they begin to create the atmosphere of an actual POW camp in forty-eight hours?

The actions and performance of American military personnel taken prisoner during the Korean War represents a sad chapter in the long military history of the United States. Of the 7,245 U.S. POWs, nearly forty percent died in captivity. Although torture and brutal treatment, malnourishment, and unsanitary living conditions accounted for the deaths of some POWs, the vast majority died because they simply gave up. They lost faith in themselves, their fellow prisoners, and their country. They reached the point where they no longer had the will to live. The POWs called this condition *give-up-itis*, and they could tell immediately when someone contracted this fatal "disease" because they could see it in their eyes. They would usually die within two days, even though they might be as healthy as anyone else in the camp.

To better equip future prisoners of war to survive the rigors of captivity and ultimately to be repatriated, the Department of Defense unveiled a set of guidelines in 1955 called the Code of Conduct:

1. I am an American, fighting in the forces which guard my country and our way of life. I am prepared to give my life in their defense.

2. I will never surrender of my own free will. If in command I will never surrender those under my command while they still have the means to resist.

3. If I am captured I will continue to resist by all means available. I will make every effort to escape and aid others to escape. I will accept neither parole nor special favors from the enemy.

4. If I become a prisoner of war, I will keep faith with my fellow prisoners. I will give no information nor take part in any action which might be harmful to my comrades. If I am senior I will take command. If not, I will obey the lawful orders of those appointed over me and will back them up in every way.

5. When questioned, should I become a prisoner of war, I am required to give name, rank, service number, and date of birth. I will evade answering further questions to the utmost of my ability. I will make no oral or written statements disloyal to my country and its allies or harmful to their cause.

6. I will never forget that I am an American, responsible for my actions, and dedicated to the principles which made my country free. I will trust in my God and in the United States of America.

Since 1955, the Code of Conduct has indeed helped hundreds of American POWs overcome seemingly unbearable adversity during long months of captivity. Perhaps the real heroes of the Vietnam War were the American POWs who came home with honor despite being subjected to brutal torture and deprivation. Of course, this footnote of history was written several years after I went through SERE training in 1967.

Warner Springs was not my first introduction to the Code of Conduct. I had attended numerous classes on the Code during flight training and afterward. So, as the truck passed into the barbed-wire enclosure of the POW compound, with guard towers on the four corners, I knew what the Code expected of me. Basically, it boiled down to three things: only give name, rank, service number, and date of birth when being interrogated; if senior, take command; and attempt to escape. The Code, however, did not lessen my apprehension.

Those of us who were captured early, milled around in a group inside the compound awaiting the rest of the evaders to join us. When all thirty members of the class were present, we were ordered into a formation of ten across, three rows deep. During the survival phase, we memorized the seniority ranking of all class members, so we lined up according to rank and seniority. Standing in front of us was a beefy guy with stumps for arms, a long Fu Manchu mustache, a mean-looking scowl on his face, and red stars on his green uniform.

"Welcome to the People's Republic of Narwa," he said with a slight smile. "My name is Comrade Disciplinarian and I am the Camp Commandant."

That's an odd name, I thought. *And it probably doesn't bode well for us in the coming hours.*

"Although you have been captured while trying to overthrow our democratic government, you will be well treated as prisoners of war provided you obey the camp rules," he intoned, as he surveyed the bedraggled group standing before him. "The camp rules are posted on signs around the camp. I suggest that you read them carefully," he said sternly. "If you disobey the rules, you will be severely punished."

"Since you have not had a chance to read the full set of rules yet, let me emphasize the more important ones," he said, as he pulled a piece of paper out of his shirt pocket:

1. "You must bow to all guards and camp staff that you encounter.

2. Do not talk or otherwise try to communicate with fellow prisoners.

3. Everybody is of equal rank, although at times individuals may be chosen to lead work parties.

4. Stay ten feet away from the barbed wire fence at all times.

5. Do not try to escape."

To emphasize his point about severe punishment, he selected, for no apparent reason, a frail-looking, gray-haired Senior Chief Petty Officer standing in the third row. Comrade Disciplinarian bulled his way through the ranks, pushing men out of his way as he charged toward his victim. He grabbed the Chief and body-slammed him on the ground. We were all stunned by the suddenness of this vicious attack and concerned about the physical condition of the Chief, who was lying motionless on the ground with a small trickle of blood coming from his right ear. A stretcher was hastily called and the injured man was carried away, never to return. In thinking about this later, I am convinced that Comrade Disciplinarian overplayed his role and did not intend to injure the man as he did. However, the message was not lost on the rest of us, and only added to the stress we were already feeling.

Returning to the head of the formation and showing no remorse for what he had done, the brute served up another object lesson.

"Who is the senior man?" he shouted.

Our senior ranking officer, Lieutenant Commander Chuck Myers, stepped forward, only to receive a slap across the face that nearly knocked him off his feet.

"The camp rules say that everyone is of equal rank, therefore there is no senior man!" he bellowed, as Mr. Myers was hauled away by two guards. "Now let's try this again. Who is the senior man?" he asked.

The next senior officer stepped forward, received a resounding slap across the face, and was abruptly taken away. This same scene was replayed over and over, until my turn came to step forward as the ninth senior officer of the group. Wham! Although, I knew it was coming, it still stunned me.

As I was being dragged off by two guards toward a building, my pent-up stress boiled to the top. What was next—water-boarding, the boxes, or something worse? From what I had witnessed thus far, my pre-conceived notion that they wouldn't kill or maim me was beginning to crumble. I was fearful, just like a real POW not knowing what was coming next.

They took me inside a rather large, dimly lit room. Scattered about were a number of wooden boxes of various sizes, all painted black, with a number of half-inch holes drilled in the sides to let in air. The moment I had been dreading for months had arrived. Would I be able to control my emotions or would I panic? They selected a box and made me get into it. My knees were drawn up under me and my head was touching my knees. To close the lid, the guard had to apply pressure to force the top of my back down, thus compacting me into a smaller ball. Even as I write about this experience many years later, I can feel the same desperate feeling well up inside. Fortunately, I could barely see out of one of the small holes, which also allowed a little stream of cool air to enter the box and onto my face. This hole was a godsend because it allowed me to somehow control my panic, although I was never far from losing it.

Every ten minutes or so, a guard would bang on the box with a stick, and I had to repeat my prisoner number so he would know I was still breathing. This concession to the training environment, of course, would be absent in a real POW camp. After thirty to forty-five minutes—I lost track of time since I was merely trying to survive one minute to the next—they opened the lid and pulled me out of the box. I could not stand for several minutes, until circulation returned to my lower extremities. I was not put in the box again, like some of the others, because I tried very hard to observe the camp rules, like bowing to guards. I did not want to rock the boat. But I had conquered my worst fear and I was proud of myself.

According to the Code of Conduct, we were required to attempt an escape if possible, and one SEAL in the group did exactly that. I, on the other hand, wanted to get through the two days without bringing any more attention to myself than possible. I guess I didn't play the game like I should have—but so what? I am basically a chicken and don't like pain. My roommate, Tom Gilliam, tried several times and paid dearly for each failed attempt.

By the middle of the second day in the POW compound, we were totally exhausted from lack of food and sleep, being in a constant state of agitation and apprehension, and from the physical exertions of the past five days. To make matters worse, rumors started to swirl that we were going to be released early from the POW phase and not have to complete a full two days. I now realize the guards started the rumors on purpose, to stir up hope only to dash it. Constant mind games were all part of the plan to break us down psychologically.

At the end of the allotted time, we were called together and told that the exercise was over—we were free men! We were pretty darn happy. I can't begin to imagine what it must be like for real POWs when they are finally given their freedom.

After the successful completion of any Navy school, students are given a graduation certificate, SERE school being no different. Rumor had it, if you lost your graduation certificate, you would be forced to complete this awful training again. I still have my graduation certificate in a safe place to this very day—I am still not taking any chances!

We all piled onto the Navy bus for the ride back to Coronado and sank wearily into our seats. There was little conversation on the way back. Not only were we bone-tired, but we were not really free either—a big aluminum bird was waiting to take us to meet another demon.

Chapter 6

Combat Pay

A HOT SHOWER. HOW WONDERFUL! AFTER RETURNING TO THE NAVAL Amphibious Base, I stood under the cleansing water for nearly an hour to wash away not only dirt and grime, but also fear, apprehension, fatigue, and sleep deprivation. As I was slowly rejuvenated by the soothing flow from the shower head, my mind turned to pleasant thoughts that had been temporarily suppressed at Warner Springs. I missed Barbara very much and was seriously questioning the wisdom of volunteering for Vietnam. However, it was too late to back out. It was nearly game day—time to put on my war paint.

Two days before we left for South Vietnam, Tom Gilliam and I flew to San Francisco. It was the first time either of us had been in the Bay Area, and we made the most of it. We rode a streetcar, ate at Fisherman's Wharf, took pictures of the Golden Gate Bridge, and gazed at Alcatraz through patchy fog in San Francisco Bay. It had been a carefree interlude, one we both hoped to explore further one year later, when we returned to United States soil.

At approximately 1600 on Friday, May 26, 1967, the Captain of a Northwest Orient Airlines' Boeing 707 advanced all four throttles for takeoff from Travis Air Force Base, located fifty miles east of San Francisco. Our departure from "the world," as those serving in Vietnam fondly called the United States, had begun. On board the military contract flight headed to Saigon were 188 soldiers, sailors, airmen, and marines; and one over-the-hill movie star. Sitting in first class, ten rows in front of me, was Lana Turner, a pin-up favorite of GIs during World War II. She was embarking on a USO Tour of Vietnam. A soldier sitting nearby dryly observed, "She's two wars too late!"

In a window seat, with Tom sitting next to me, I settled in for the twenty-hour flight, which included refueling stops in Seattle and Okinawa. Other than a few catnaps, sleep would not come; I just couldn't find a comfortable position. Perhaps, it was due to heightened anticipation of finally entering combat or, maybe, it was because it never got dark as we chased the sun across the Pacific. Whatever the reason, when we arrived, I was exhausted but glad to be getting on with it.

Saigon

As the aircraft crossed the coastline of South Vietnam on its approach to Saigon's Tan San Nhut Airport, I peered into the darkness, expecting to see anti-aircraft fire, ground explosions, and other signs of violence. I saw none—only a few twinkling electric lights here and there. In fact, it looked so peaceful and calm, we could have been flying over farmland anywhere in the United States. Maybe I had watched too many war movies. We would not be arriving in a hail of gunfire after all. One other bit of good news is that I would now begin drawing an extra $65 per month in hostile fire pay. Being a soldier of fortune was going to be mighty lucrative.

Even though it was five in the morning, when I exited the plane, the heat and humidity were decidedly unkind to my air-conditioned body. It felt like any afternoon on the Florida coast in mid-August. Because it was, the beginning of the rainy season, I had better get used to it.

After clearing Customs and Immigration, we were directed to several lines leading to cashier windows, where we had to exchange all U.S. currency into Military Payment Certificates (MPC). This policy, which was implemented in Europe following the end of World War II and continued during the Korean War, was used to discourage black market currency activity and to help stabilize local monetary systems. I don't know how successful MPCs were in shoring up the Vietnamese *piastre*, but I do know that it was illegal for GIs to use "green backs" in-country.

After arrival formalities were concluded, fourteen Navy pilots from my stateside training class and I piled into a blue Air Force bus for transport to our temporary living quarters. Being a non-air-conditioned vehicle, all of the windows were wide open except for a wire mesh that covered the gap. I asked the driver why chicken wire covered the window openings. "To keep the VC from throwing grenades into the bus," he answered nonchalantly. *Well okay, but couldn't grenade fragments easily pierce the sides of this bus? Shouldn't we be traveling in an armored vehicle of some sort?* Not wanting to appear like a sissy, I kept my questions to myself, but I was beginning to wonder if $65 extra a month was worth all the excitement this place obviously had to offer.

Although it was early Sunday morning, Saigon—it will always be Saigon to me, no matter that it was renamed Ho Chi Minh City after the Communists took over in 1975—was already in full stride. Sidewalk vendors and shopkeepers were getting ready for the start of business; open-air markets were filled with fresh produce, recently slaughtered pigs and chickens, seafood of many types, and mounds and mounds of rice. The streets were jammed with every form of transportation imaginable: ox-drawn carts; bicycles; cyclos; motor scooters; military jeeps; large delivery trucks; a few very old French cars; and, of course, hundreds of people on foot, all going in different directions as fast as possible. There was absolutely no semblance of right-of-way, a left-hand or right-hand side of the street, traffic lights, stop signs, or traffic cops—nothing. It was all a big game of bluffing the other person out of your way, and the bigger you were the better your hand. It made New York City at the height of rush hour seem tame and orderly by comparison. It was like a cattle drive, except there were no cowboys to ride herd. I was thankful for being a pilot and not a bus driver.

Our bus pulled up in front of an old French hotel that had been converted into a transient officer billet, one of numerous temporary and permanent housing facilities for U.S. military personnel in the city. Other than Tan Son Nhut Air Force Base on the outskirts of the city, Saigon did not have one large military compound. Instead, the huge Military Assistance Command, Vietnam (MACV) apparatus was spread among hundreds of smaller buildings scattered throughout the city in a decentralized fashion.

Our billet, called the Annapolis, presumably because they sent Navy guys there, was a two-story, white-concrete structure with a tall barbed-wire fence surrounding the building, a sand-bagged guard post at the front entrance, and chicken wire covering all the windows. Since I was beginning to get street smart, I didn't ask any questions.

We lugged our gear up to the second floor, which consisted of two rooms: a large open area containing about twenty-five metal cots and a small bathroom at one end with a toilet and one shower. Three bare light bulbs hanging from the ceiling and two large floor fans churning noisily at each end of the room completed the décor. About the only thing missing that would have earned this place a *one-star* rating was a mint on the pillow. Truthfully, the lack of amenities did not matter at this point; we were still on California time, and it was time for "nighty-night" on the West Coast. We each claimed a rack, stripped down to our boxer shorts to get some relief from the stifling heat and humidity, and fell into the deep slumber of a mid-afternoon nap.

I don't know how long I had been asleep, but it was after nightfall when I was awakened by a couple loud booms off in the distance. Several of us went to the front window to see what was going on. An artillery battery was firing somewhere nearby, sending large pieces of lead into the darkness and seeking to destroy an unsuspecting quarry. I was thankful it was outgoing and not incoming. In another sector, several illumination flares drifted slowly to earth, suspended below small parachutes, while casting eerie shadows on the scene below—just like in the war movies. We had front-row seats but no popcorn.

With sleep taken care of, next on the list was getting some chow. Unless you want to count the miserable boxed lunches served on the airplane as food, we had not eaten since we left San Francisco. There was a military mess located four blocks away that served around the clock, so we pulled on our wrinkled khaki uniforms, and headed into the alley behind our billet. We had been warned not to travel on foot alone or in groups larger than four. Large groups invited a hand grenade and being alone might attract an assassin's bullet. So, we broke up into groups of four and wandered down the dark alley toward the messing facility. In every possible hiding place that we passed, I imagined Viet Cong sappers suddenly lunging out with knives to slit our throats, or sneaking up behind us with a garrote. If someone had tapped me on the shoulder and said boo, I probably would have needed to change my drawers. Nothing like that happened, and the food wasn't too bad either.

On the way back, with our stomachs satisfied and feeling a little more comfortable in our new surroundings, we took more notice of the milieu in the alley. There were a number of hole-in-the-wall bars that obviously catered to American service personnel judging by the number of short-haired Westerners inside and the ever-present bar girls demurely asking, "You buy me Saigon tea, GI?" Hired by the owner to drive up profits, most of these girls were not prostitutes, nevertheless, they used their considerable charm and sex appeal to get servicemen to buy them very expensive, non-alcoholic drinks, preying on the hopes of the gullible GI that the evening would somehow end up in their bedroom.

Another inescapable feature was the unbelievable stench that assailed the olfactory senses. Sanitation methods common in the Western world were absent in this city of two million. Garbage piled chest high was everywhere, and raw sewage ran in the gutters. When the Vietnamese, male and female, felt the need to relieve themselves, they squatted wherever they were and did their business. This unsettling aspect of daily life took some getting used to.

The day after our arrival was spent shuttling from one military compound to another, all part of the check-in process. At MACV headquarters, we received intelligence briefings, more lectures on Vietnamese culture and traditions, and presentations on how to avoid becoming a casualty of war. Besides using rifles, machine guns, mortars, rocket-propelled grenades, and other conventional weapons, the enemy also employed a bewildering and harrowing array of unsophisticated devices, like simple pits lined with punji sticks tipped with human excrement and booby traps cleverly constructed with grenades and artillery shells. The pressure and stress on the ground forces was relentless—one reason I was glad to be a pilot.

There were other ways to get an early ticket home that were not enemy-controlled: wild animals and poisonous reptiles. For example, good friends of my parents had a son serving in Vietnam who was abruptly awakened in the middle of the night by a tiger that had seized his left leg and was dragging him out of his tent into the bush. Hitting the tiger's face as hard as he could with his fists caused the beast to momentarily release its grip. Hollering for help, his buddies arrived just as the tiger was returning. A volley of rifle fire ended the threat, but left the unfortunate young soldier with a life-long limp as result of calf muscles that had been completely stripped from the bone.

At the Naval Forces Vietnam (NAVFORV) compound, we were each issued a large box of in-country military survival gear, which included five morphine syringes to be self-administered if wounded, a survival radio to use in the event of being shot down, four sets of lightweight jungle fatigues, two pairs of quick-drying jungle boots, a lightweight blanket, and a web belt with attached canteen and leather pistol holster. We were given a choice between a .38 caliber or a .45 caliber pistol as our personal sidearm. I chose the .45. I don't know why—maybe because it looked meaner. I commented to someone standing next to me that I wasn't a very good shot. His less-than-reassuring reply was, "We're not going to use these to kill the gooks, we are going to use it to kill ourselves." *Oh, wonderful. Maybe I should inject all five morphine doses first to bolster my courage.*

I put my pistol in the holster and strapped the gun belt containing two extra clips of ammo and a canteen around my waist. It's amazing how much false bravado a gun can provide a timid soul. With my luck, I would probably shoot myself trying to get the gun out of the holster. *Maybe I should have my gun out and at the ready the next time I walk down the alley to the mess hall.*

At one of the stops in the check-in process, we were each issued a ration card for purchasing items at the PX, items that were highly desired on the black market, such as cameras, tape recorders, radios, beer, liquor, and tobacco products. The idea was to limit the amount of these items that could be purchased by a single GI in the hopes it would discourage illegal activities.

With my new ration card in hand, I headed to the big military PX located in the Cholon District to purchase a slide camera and a movie camera. This excursion, like all trips outside the protective confines of our housing billet, was made against the backdrop that sudden death awaited the careless or the unlucky. Two days before our arrival, two GIs had been shot and killed in broad daylight in Saigon, and the same day I went on my shopping trip, a soldier was assassinated in front of the PX several hours before I arrived.

Moving about Saigon was creepy. You knew that VC were intermingled with average civilians, but you couldn't tell one from the other because everybody looked and dressed the same. I was constantly looking over my shoulder. It was unnerving. From those first few days, I developed a visceral distrust of Saigon, a feeling that gripped me each time I returned. On those rare trips to the big city, I couldn't wait to get back to the war zone, where bullets and mortars were a daily routine—at least out there, I had some idea who and where the bad guys were.

Vung Tàu

With our two-day indoctrination completed, it was time to put Saigon in our rearview mirror and head off to war. In three round-trips, a helicopter dispatched from HAL-3 managed to transport the bunch of us and our gear to squadron headquarters in Vung Tàu. Located seventy-five miles southeast of Saigon, on the South China Sea, Vung Tàu was a popular resort town before and during the war. Despite hostilities elsewhere in the country, this charming port city, noted for its beautiful sand beaches, seemed to have escaped enemy scrutiny, at least as a battleground. It was rumored that the Viet Cong came to Vung Tàu for their R & R.

Squadron administrative offices, located just off the east-west runway, were housed in a fairly small, one-story white-washed building with light-green window shutters. Inside, several strategically placed desk fans labored in vain to dislodge heavily laden air from its slow embrace of those toiling within.

Noting the commotion of our arrival in the outer office, a silver-haired Navy Commander, with a baby-face and big smile, emerged from his office in the rear of the building. "Hello. I'm Bob Spencer. Welcome to the Seawolves." He enthusiastically shook everyone's hand. Gesturing to a tall, slender man on his left, also with silver oak leaves on his collar, Spencer said, "This is Commander Conrad Jaburg, my Executive Officer." After another round of handshakes, Commander Spencer continued, "It's great to have you guys here. With your help, we are going to kick some ass. Before we go home a year from now, Charlie will definitely know who the Seawolves are." (*Seawolves* was the unofficial name given to the new squadron and it also served as our radio call sign.)

"Yeah, and we're going to show the Army what Navy gunship pilots can do," chimed in Commander Jaburg. Everyone nodded in agreement. This meet-and-greet was taking on the characteristics of a pep rally.

"All of us in the new guard only arrived about two weeks ago ourselves, so we are still trying to get things sorted out," said Jaburg. "Our biggest problem right now is lack of aircraft to fly. We only have three detachments operating, and these were inherited from HC-1 when the squadron officially commissioned on April the first. The Army has been promising to transfer more helicopters to us, but we haven't seen any yet."

"Yes, it's frustrating because we are all anxious to take the fight to the enemy," Commander Spencer agreed. "However, I'm confident that we will have our act together in short order. In the meantime, we have a plan to get some of you junior officers flying real soon, but I'll let the Ops Officer, Commander Ron Hipp, cover that."

With one last "Welcome aboard," the CO returned to his office, and we headed over to the squadron maintenance area where the Operations Office was located. My first impression of the CO and XO were positive, especially Commander Spencer. He had a friendly, approachable personality, and he seemed genuinely concerned for our welfare.

Commander Hipp also welcomed us aboard and gave us a brief rundown on the current status of operations in the three HAL-3 detachments working in the Delta. "The long-range plan is to stand up four more detachments as gunships become available from the Army," he said. "In the interim, I am going to divide the majority of you fifteen guys up among the three detachments, to get your feet wet and gain a little operational experience."

"Will we be able to do much flying?" one of the pilots asked.

"I'm not going to lie to you—probably not much," Commander Hipp responded. "Each detachment will be crawling with extra pilots, all wanting to fly. It's not the ideal situation, but it's the best I can do for now." In an attempt to raise the morale of at least part of the group, he said, "The seven of you going to Det 3 at Vinh Long might be able to weasel some flight time out of the Army up there. Their aviation company commander told me they were shorthanded and would welcome some extra bodies."

Commander Hipp then passed out the assignments: three would be going to Det One in Nha Be; two would be going to Det Two on the *USS Harnett County*, a World War II LST anchored in the middle of the Mekong River; three would stay behind to work at the *home guard*, as squadron headquarters came to be known; and seven would be going to Vinh Long. I was going to Vinh Long. Hot diggity dog! Since I had been rather successful in scrounging up extra flight time at Lakehurst, I was certain I could talk my way into some Army flights. Boy, was I ever happy! My morale was sky-high, but I did feel a bit sorry for the rest of the group, especially those having to stay behind at squadron headquarters.

We all piled into the back of a deuce and a half truck, with all of our gear for a fifteen-minute ride to a small U.S. Navy base at Cat Lo, which was home to a small flotilla of Swift Boats and U.S. Coast Guard cutters. Since the road between Vung Tàu and Cat Lo was "owned" by the VC after dark, we settled in for the evening and soon discovered what a pleasant little oasis our temporary home really was—a transient barracks which offered some degree of privacy, good chow, cold beer for sale, and movies each night.

The next day, I turned in my service and pay records and took out a five-hundred-dollar allotment which was deposited each month in a voluntary ten percent saving plan instituted for U.S. forces serving in Vietnam whereby ten percent interest was earned on money placed into the account. At that rate, I figured I could save nearly seven thousand dollars during my year-long tour of duty. Coupled with the two hundred dollars a month Barbara was saving from her bank teller job in Fairhope, we should be able to afford a nice down payment on a house when I returned to the States. (The reader will notice that I had gotten over my initial pessimism of being killed in Vietnam and was now planning for our future.)

On the third day, we were told to pack up our gear and be at the airfield at 0700 for a flight to Vinh Long. We waited all day but, for a variety of reasons, did not get off the ground. So, we again loaded our gear on a truck and headed back to Cat Lo. I was getting plenty fed up with all of the waiting, not to mention packing and unpacking and loading and unloading my gear, which amounted to a large footlocker, a heavy seabag, and a cardboard box full of survival equipment and jungle uniforms. The military saying "hurry up and wait" was alive and well, and as frustrating as ever. That night, I wrote in my diary: "I hope I see some action before my year is up." And then I wrote, tongue-in-cheek, "I have been in Vietnam for five days now and haven't killed a Communist yet."

On the fourth day, it was back to the airfield to wait around for another possible flight. The morning came and went, and the afternoon wasn't looking much better, when our luck finally changed. An Army C-7 Caribou, a twin-engine fixed-wing transport, would take us as far as Can Tho Airfield, where we would catch a helicopter for the rest of the trip to Vinh Long. I lugged my gear up the rear ramp and strapped myself into a spot on a long sling seat that ran the entire length of the aircraft on both sides. We were finally off to our appointment with the gods of war.

Not long after takeoff, we watched two U.S. Air Force F-100 fighter-bombers deliver a punishing airstrike into a tree line that paralleled our course. They dove at the target in a steep angle, dropped their bombs, and pulled abruptly into a climb, zooming several thousand feet higher than our altitude. They then repeated the same ballet under the able direction of a forward air controller (FAC), a master choreographer circling overhead in a light observation airplane. This was war up-close and personal—it was unbelievably thrilling!

After getting off the C-7 in Can Tho, and while waiting for a helicopter to take us the rest of the way, I asked three of my closest friends to gather on the tarmac so I could take a photograph of the trio: Ensign Jim Burke, Lieutenant Junior Grade Hal Guinn, and my constant companion, Lieutenant Junior Grade Tom Gilliam. It was a happy time for the four of us, with no hint of the tragedy that lay ahead for the three young men in the photograph.

A haunting photograph I took of three close friends and fellow pilots taken at the Can Tho airfield several days after our arrival in South Vietnam. Their smiles give no hint of the tragedies that would befall all three. *l to r:* Jim Burke, Hal Guinn, and Tom Gilliam. June 2, 1967

Chapter 7

The Long Green Line

As our helicopter approached Vinh Long from the southwest, I gazed out the open cabin door and saw my new delta home. The predominant feature of this large American base was the airfield located on the northwest end. It had a single, three-thousand-foot-long Perforated Steel Planking (PSP) runway, with individual parking spots that branched off both sides that contained over fifty aircraft, mostly helicopters and a few fixed-wing airplanes. On the east end of the runway, were several hangars containing aircraft maintenance facilities, and beyond those were housing, messing, and administrative buildings. Surrounding the entire base was a tight perimeter of guard towers, barbed wire, and minefields. Bathed in the warm glow of the setting sun, the base seemed orderly and peaceful. I had a good feeling.

As the rotors coasted to a stop, the six of us climbed out of the Huey, glad to be where we could finally do some flying. While we stretched our tired limbs and wondered what was next, a jeep, trailing a small dust cloud behind it, approached at a high rate of speed. It came to an abrupt halt alongside our pile of gear. The driver, a bare-chested, sandy-haired man sporting a million-dollar tan, hopped out to greet us.

"Hi, I'm Petty Officer Danforth from Det 3," he said. "Welcome to the Seawolves. Throw all your gear in the jeep," he instructed. "I'm sorry I don't have room for you all to ride, but it's only a couple blocks to your hooch, so just follow me."

Feigning indignation over the plan, a thirsty member of our tired band of brothers said, "The hell with the hooch, where can I get a cold one?"

"No sweat," Danforth said. "Let me drop you off at your living quarters first and then I'll point the way to the O club, where you will find plenty of cold brews. In Vietnam, you may at times be short of ammo, fuel for the helicopters, fresh eggs and milk, and toothpaste—but never beer!"

"It is nice to see that the bean counters have their priorities straight for a change," one of the pilots chimed in.

With seabags and footlockers piled four high in the back of the jeep, one pilot climbed in alongside the driver, and the rest of us followed the short distance on foot. All living quarters for U.S. forces in Vietnam, no matter what the construction or appearance, were called *hooches*. Most were wooden structures with metal roofs and screened-in open sides for maximum ventilation. The only war-time modification to these "Frank Lloyd Wright designs" was a double row of sandbags piled halfway to the roof line to provide a modicum of protection from shrapnel blasts of incoming mortar rounds.

Instead of a typical hooch, however, Danforth stopped in front of a significantly more solidly built structure that resembled a World War II Quonset hut, an iconic design with curved steel sides and roof blended into a continuous 180-degree arc. It was painted forest green on the outside—thank God it wasn't battleship grey—had a concrete floor and was divided into six small rooms, three on each side of a central hallway, with wooded partitions that did not reach all the way to the ceiling. Each room had a metal frame bunk bed, a small desk, and a vertical steel clothes locker.

As we had ever since Fort Benning, Tom Gilliam and I roomed together—Tom in the bottom bunk and me in the top. We did not know how long we would be in Vinh Long, but at least we were no longer in a transient status. It felt good to unpack our bags, settle into some sort of a routine, and get on with learning the business of waging war.

Shortly after returning to our hooch from the O club, where we got a bite to eat and a beer, a call came in from the Army wanting to know if any of us wanted to fly the next day. Less than two hours after my arrival at my first Mekong Delta base, and one week after my exit from the Northwest Orient Boeing 707 in Saigon, I was about to embark on my combat flying career—a period in my life marked by danger, sadness, excitement, boredom, pride, loneliness, regret, and unforgettable memories.

Lay of the Land

South Vietnam, about the size of the state of Washington, is approximately 585 miles long, one hundred miles wide, and, in 1967, had a population of sixteen million. The landmass looks like a left-curving banana with a general north-south orientation. The eastern boundary of the country, running from the tip of the Ca Mau Peninsula in the south to the Demilitarized Zone (DMZ) in the north, abuts the South China Sea; while the western border is shared with Cambodia in the south and Laos in the north. North of Saigon, the topography is composed of a coastal plain in the eastern part of the country and highlands to the west, comprised of mountains 3,000 to 4,000 feet in elevation.

The climate of the Delta is hot and humid, with average temperatures ranging between 80°F and 90°F. The average annual rainfall is eighty inches, with most of it coming during the wet season, mid-April through mid-October. Rainfall during the wet season comes in the form of two or three daily torrential downpours that last twenty to thirty minutes each. This abundant rain transforms the land into lush, dense, green vegetation along the waterways; and thousands of rice paddies under a knee-high water blanket created by raised earthen dikes that surround each paddy. In the dry season, the rice paddies look like a desert: dead brown vegetation on parched soil with large cracks. The contrast between seasons is startling.

Outside of the rain showers, the flying weather in the Delta was generally VFR; with scattered, broken clouds forming at two to three thousand feet, with good visibility underneath. Flying with the windows and doors wide-open in the Huey made for a comfortable, breezy ride no matter how stifling hot it was on the ground. The secret would have been to fly all day and sleep all night when it was cool, but waging war did not play out that way.

The Mekong Delta, which occupies about one quarter of the country, is a vast, flat, sea-level plain located to the west and southwest of Saigon. The Delta is often called "the rice bowl" of Asia because much of the rice consumed in this part of the world is grown there. One half of the total population of South Vietnam resides in this fertile and important agricultural region.

The Delta was also important to the enemy in their quest to overthrow the South Vietnamese government. Without traditional means of transport—air, rail, and road—the only way for the North Vietnamese Army (NVA) and their South Vietnamese proxies, the Viet Cong, to move and position their troops and war material to control the countryside and to mount a successful and sustained attack on the government in Saigon was by water.

The Delta is split into long fingers of land running northwest-southeast by four major tributaries of the mighty Mekong River, from south to north: the Bassac, Co Chien, Ham Luong, and My Tho rivers. Complementing these four major rivers is an extensive network of smaller, navigable streams and man-canals, four thousand miles in all. There are few places in the Delta that cannot be accessed by water and a short overland trek. This extensive water network provided a ready-made solution to the enemy's transportation needs. In large measure, winning the war depended on who controlled these waterways.

The Combatants

Politically, South Vietnam was divided into forty-three provinces and each province was subdivided into districts. The Province Chief, a career South Vietnamese military officer of the rank of colonel or lieutenant colonel, had absolute control over civilian and military affairs in his province. He was assisted by a U.S. advisory team, usually commanded by an Army colonel. Districts were commanded by South Vietnamese majors and supported by a small contingent of U.S. advisors. South Vietnam was divided into four military regions or zones: I, II, III, and IV Corps. The Mekong Delta fell entirely within IV Corps.

The enemy forces that operated in the Mekong Delta were mostly comprised of locally recruited Viet Cong (VC) and a smattering of NVA cadre and the occasional small unit of NVA infantry. The VC wore traditional peasant garb, which consisted of loose-fitting black "pajamas" and a conical white straw hat. The NVA, on the other hand, wore an olive-green military uniform and pith-type helmet. Footgear for both units consisted of flip-flops made from old tires, which the Americans immediately dubbed "Ho Chi Minh sandals." Both groups of enemy forces were tough, determined soldiers capable of putting up a fight.

Friendly forces in the Delta included regular South Vietnamese infantry divisions called ARVN (Army of the Republic of Vietnam); Vietnamese Air Force units, Vietnamese Navy units, and Regional Forces (RFs) and Popular Forces (PFs)—the latter two units were collectively referred to as *rough-puffs*—leave it to the American GI to have irreverent slang names for everyone and everything. The RFs and PFs were locally trained militias whose primary purpose was to defend their villages and surrounding countryside. They were trained and assisted by U.S. military advisors, wore typical peasant clothing, which made it hard to distinguish them from the Viet Cong, and, generally speaking, they were some of the best fighters in the Vietnamese military establishment—much better than regular ARVN troops. On the coalition side, the Delta played host to every American branch of service except the Marines.

Fortunately for me and all helicopter pilots who flew in the Delta, the anti-aircraft weaponry used by the enemy was relatively unsophisticated. Aside from the occasional appearance of the .51 caliber heavy machine, which really got your attention, especially at night when tracer burnout would occur at about 4,000 feet, enemy forces did not have radar-controlled AAA sites or Surface-to-Air missiles in IV Corp, like they had in I and II Corps. Every now and then an enterprising enemy soldier would fire a B-40 rocket-propelled grenade, usually without success, unless the helicopter was hovering in a landing zone (LZ). Really, the only weapons the enemy could direct at our aircraft were small arms: light machine guns and the ubiquitous AK-47 rifle. Although aircraft were shot down and aircrew killed and wounded by small arms fire, the odds were definitely in our favor. We knew if we flew at least 1,200 feet above the ground we were all but immune from being hit. Obviously, the mission often dictated that we fly lower, including landing in an LZ, and this is where the odds diminished. Another factor in our favor was that most enemy soldiers did not lead a helicopter enough when aiming their weapons. Consequently, if he hit the helicopter at all, it was in the tail section, aft of the cockpit and cabin, or in the main rotor blades.

The anti-air lethality of the battlefield during my time in the Mekong Delta was child's play compared with modern-day weapons and technology. A similar comparison could be drawn in the annals of military history before and after the use of gunpowder. Even with the use of chaff, flares, electronic countermeasures, and better battlefield intelligence, the military helicopter pilot of today is much more at risk than we were in 1967. Otherwise, you would probably not be reading this book.

Army Aviation Mission in the Delta

Broadly, the mission for Army aviators and aircrew in the Mekong Delta was threefold: combat assault (CA), direct combat support (DCS), and medevac. There were also some ancillary missions, like reconnaissance, forward air controllers (FAC), downed aircraft recovery, and electronic countermeasures, but in terms of overall sorties, they were small in number.

Combat assault missions involved the insertion and extraction of friendly forces on the battlefield, usually to and from an LZ in close proximity to enemy forces. During my time flying with the Army, the only forces we flew on CA missions were ARVN troops. Two types of helicopters were used: gunships and slicks—both variations of the venerable H-1 Huey. The UH-1B/C gunship, flown by two pilots and two door gunners, was a heavily armed machine, with multiple machine guns and 2.75-inch air-to-surface rockets. The "slick" UH-1D model was slightly longer, with a larger cabin than its gunship brother. It too was flown by a crew of four, but its only armament was an M-60 machine gun fired by each door gunner. Without machine guns and rocket pods carried on the side of the helicopter, it had a more streamlined appearance than the gunship, hence the nickname *slick*.

Direct combat support missions provided logistical support to American and Vietnamese forces scattered throughout the Delta and were flown in slick helicopters (and some fixed-wing airplanes). Just about anything that could fit inside a helicopter was delivered: military and civilian

Top photo: I'm pointing at two bullet holes in the tail of my aircraft. Fortunately the majority of the time, enemy gunners did not lead a helicopter enough which resulted in hits aft of the cockpit and cabin or in the main rotor blades.

Bottom photo: Occasionally, enemy gunners got lucky and put one through the cockpit, like this round that just missed my right foot.

personnel, including wounded and killed-in-action (KIA), the paymaster, and families of Vietnamese troops; ammo; food, including soft drinks and beer; mail; Px merchandise; spare parts; and building materials. If the item was too big to fit inside, it was carried in a sling load beneath the helicopter. For many of the remote government outposts, the DCS helicopter was their lifeline and only contact with the outside world.

Even though any helicopter could be pressed into service to transport the wounded, medevac flights, especially from the battlefield, were normally flown by helicopters and crews dedicated to that specific mission. Their call sign was "Dustoff" and they flew unarmed helicopters with a big red cross painted on the nose and sides of the helicopter. In my opinion, they were the real heroes of the Vietnam War. Their bravery under fire and the very demanding and risky flights they performed in all weather conditions, day and night, is legendary. Many wounded soldiers owe their lives to these selfless and unsung heroes.

First Taste of Combat

I didn't sleep very well. I wouldn't call it combat jitters because I had never been in combat before. Let's just say I was anxious and excited to be going on my first flight into harm's way—after all, this was what I had volunteered for. I set my alarm for 0500, but I was awake well before then. I shaved and showered, pulled on my two-piece jungle fatigues, laced-up my jungle boots (black leather toes and heels with canvas sides designed to dry out quickly), and headed to the chow hall. After breakfast, I grabbed my army-issued flight helmet, Nomex fire-retardant flying gloves, kneeboard, .45 caliber pistol, and headed for the flight line of the 114th Assault Helicopter Company. A typical aviation company was divided into two platoons: one flying gunships and the other flying slicks. For my first in-country mission, I would be flying copilot in a slick.

Looking at the large, flight status board in Flight Ops, I saw that I would be flying aircraft 832 with WO Whitlow. I began searching nametags of the pilots standing around, hoping to spot my aircraft commander. There he was, standing in the corner; a tall, thin fellow with a helmet bag slung over his right shoulder.

Sticking out my right hand, I said, "Hi, I'm Mike Stock, from the Seawolves. I'll be your copilot today."

"Pleasure to meet you, Mike, Jerry Whitlow. How long you been in-country?"

"One week."

"Wow, you are a newbie," he said pleasantly.

"How about you, Jerry?"

"I'm gettin' short—fourteen days to go. In fact, this is my last flight," he stated with a big smile. "I'm mighty glad to be going home, but I am going to miss the flying and my buddies. We have been through a lot together," he said, his eyes misting ever so slightly. He explained that it was his Company's unwritten policy that they wouldn't fly you during your last two weeks unless they desperately needed your services. "I guess they figure if you've made it this far, you deserve to go home. All I have to do is get through today and I've got it made."

"Well, let's hope you get through today because that means that I do too!"

"Amen," Jerry replied emphatically. "Why don't you preflight our bird and I'll join you after the mission briefing? We're scheduled for a 0700 takeoff."

"Okay, Jerry. See you in a bit."

Returning to Vinh Long well after dinnertime, Jerry shut down the helicopter. It had been a long and tiring day, but satisfying. My introduction to combat flying could not have been better. We flew DCS missions in the morning and CA missions in the afternoon, without being shot at, and logged exactly nine hours of flight time, which went into my aviator's flight logbook in green ink—green being the color used for combat flights. I felt lucky to fly my first flight with a warrant officer who had a year's worth of combat experience to share. I learned many things, including: how to finesse the Huey with a heavy load; the general procedures used during CA and DCS missions; radio communication frequencies and phraseology; elementary navigation around the Delta using key landmarks; where the bad guys hangout; ways to minimize our chances of being hit; and more subtle kernels of wisdom, such as carefully watching my personal belongings in the helicopter, like cameras, flight gear, and canned drinks, so they didn't disappear into the hands of ARVN troop thieves.

Speaking of petty theft, on my first day out, I witnessed two events that made an impression. While waiting at a staging airfield prior to commencing our first CA troop extraction flight, I watched with mild amusement as a young boy, who had stolen a case of C-rations, was being chased on foot by an ARVN MP. As the boy scrambled under a fence with his treasure, the MP reached down to his gun belt. I recoiled in horror—*he's going to shoot the boy!* But instead, he brandished a long knife and waved it menacingly at the perpetrator, who was rapidly opening the distance.

The other caper was a little closer to home. Jerry and I surprised an ARVN soldier who had liberated Jerry's survival knife from his gun belt. We gave chase, but he ran into a hooch with lots of other soldiers. Since they all looked alike in their uniforms and toothy grins, we had to admit defeat. Having now been forewarned, I was able to prevent my camera from being stolen during flight on several occasions during the days ahead.

As the two of us walked off the flight line, Jerry said, "Well, Mike, I hope I have given you a few tips to save your butt during the coming year."

"You did indeed. I am glad I was able to fly with a combat veteran like yourself, and, by the way, congratulations on finishing your flying tour. It must feel great."

"You bet it does," he beamed. "Good luck this next year and keep your head down."

Anatomy of a CA mission

For the most part, combat assault missions were boring, although the potential for all hell to break loose was always present. You went looking for trouble, actually hoping to give the enemy a bad day. An old aviation saying pretty well sums up the adrenaline meter for combat assaults: "Flying is hours and hours of sheer boredom punctuated by moments of stark terror."

The typical CA mission involved three types of helicopter assets: fifteen slicks, two to four gunships, and a single command-and-control helicopter (C&C), normally another slick. The slicks carried twelve combat-loaded ARVN troops per helicopter (if carrying American troops, which we didn't, the load was reduced to eight troopers because Americans weighed more than the typical Vietnamese soldier). The task of the gunships was to reconnoiter the landing zones before the arrival of the slicks. The C&C helicopter carried the overall mission commander, normally a Vietnamese colonel and his U.S Army counterpart-advisor, also a bird-colonel. Their job was to circle over the battlefield, out of small-arms range, to control the movement of troops on the ground, to make tactical decisions, call for medevac support to lift out the wounded, and to request reinforcements and tactical airstrikes if needed.

The mission began with the slicks departing their home airfield and proceeding to a secure staging area, normally a small airstrip, to pick up the ARVN troops. About three miles before landing, the slicks would arrange themselves in *trail formation*, one behind the other in a long straight line. Because the Hueys were painted olive-drab, this procession became famously known as *the long green line*. Unless you were flying the lead helicopter, having to follow the helicopter directly in front of you at a distance of no more than one hundred feet was extremely challenging. Not only did you have to maintain proper spacing to keep from colliding with the helicopter in front, but this delicate maneuver had to be accomplished while flying through the disturbed air and rotor-wash of the preceding helicopters—the farther back in the line, the worse it got. Rapid and large movement of the flight controls were required to maintain proper position during this hectic time. It was some of most demanding and dangerous formation flying I have ever done.

The troops were arranged in sticks of twelve men each and positioned on the left side of the runway about one hundred feet apart. After the pilot fought through the turbulence to the ground, the troops would immediately begin loading onto the choppers, some sitting on the cabin floor, while the rest sat in both doorways with their feet dangling outside. The boarding process only took a minute or two. The ARVN troops had been instructed to remove the magazines from their M-1 rifles before boarding to prevent any accidental discharges, but invariably the two door gunners would find weapons loaded and be forced to intervene. Despite the watchful eye of the gunners, some loaded weapons managed to slip by with

Top photo: The Long Green Line. D model Hueys in trail formation descending to pick up ARVN combat troops at a staging airstrip. June 1967

Bottom photo: Trail formation about to land opposite sticks of troops on left side of runway. June 1967

disastrous results. One of my Navy friends, Mike Hammergren, was shot down when an ARVN discharged his weapon and holed the fuel tank of the slick he was flying. Fortunately, no one was hurt in the forced landing.

After takeoff from the staging field, the slicks joined into flights of five helicopters each—two on each side of the flight leader and arranged into a V formation, with the lead helicopter at the apex. Each flight of five was designated with a different color: gold, white, red, green. Proceeding to the LZ, each flight flew, one behind the other, at 1,500 to 2,000 feet above the ground to remain out of small-arms range. Aside from having to dodge the occasional cumulus cloud and maintaining position in the formation, this period of the mission was relatively stress-free. The doors were open, the air was cool and smooth, the sun was low on the eastern horizon, and we were one day closer to going home—life was good.

About fifteen miles from the LZ, the radio chatter between the gunships, the C&C helicopter, and the flight leader of the slicks intensified. The discussion revolved around the safest way to get the slicks into and out of the LZ considering wind direction, obstacle clearance, size of the zone, and the location of known or suspected enemy positions. There might be several possible LZs to choose from, or maybe the mission called for a feint towards one and a landing in another. Since the gunships were responsible for escorting the slicks into and out of the zone and suppressing enemy fire if needed, the flight leader of the gunships made the call as to the final approach path and the departure route once the troops dismounted.

Helicopters in a "V" formation heading to an LZ with ARVN infantry troops onboard. June 1967

After receiving last-minute instructions, the helicopters in each flight pulled into a tighter formation, with the objective of touching down at nearly the same moment to minimize the time spent in the LZ, when helicopters were the most vulnerable to enemy fire. If the gunship leader said it was "a hot LZ," meaning that they had spotted enemy soldiers or taken fire, the heartrate increased, the adrenaline began to flow, and a sweaty presence began to form in your armpits. Game on!

If it was a hot LZ, the sounds of battle were everywhere—like sitting in a theatre with surround sound. The escorting gunships would be delivering rocket and machine gun attacks to your immediate right and left flanks as you approached the landing zone, with resounding booms and blinding flashes as the rockets exploded on impact. At the same time, both door gunners in each helicopter would open up with their M-60s, adding to the cacophony and filling the back of the helicopter with spent brass shell casings. Occasionally, Air Force F-100 fighter-bombers would drop a 500-pound bomb in an adjacent tree line that would absolutely scare the bejesus out of you because there was no warning it was coming. Through it all, you would occasionally hear a dull thud as an enemy bullet hit your helicopter. A hot LZ was like a giant sound machine—fortunately it was not set to maximum volume every mission.

After disgorging the troops, the slicks flew back to the staging field to do one of several things: pick up the next load of troops and return to the LZ, shut down and wait in case troops kept in reserve might be needed later in the fight, or wait until it was time to extract the troops from the battlefield at the end of the day.

Helicopters on takeoff from an LZ after discharging their troops.

My experience supporting ARVN troops was not positive. Besides trying to steal anything not bolted down in the helicopter, they were not aggressive fighters. Normally, we dropped them off about 0900 in the morning and picked them up around 1600 in the afternoon. Although some ARVN remained in the field overnight, I never witnessed it. Thanks to our helicopters, the ARVN we transported enjoyed banker's hours. When they did engage the enemy, they seemed to fight in a three-sided box, thus leaving a way for the VC to escape. Most of the time they did not want to press home the attack, even though they had numerical superiority. On one operation, we picked them up in the exact same spot where we dropped them off that morning—they had not moved at all! On another occasion, as the slicks were climbing out of the LZ, the American advisor in the C&C ship asked the slick leader to check for any soldiers remaining onboard. Sure enough, one helicopter reported an ARVN soldier who hadn't gotten off. The exasperated advisor yelled, "Well, for Christ's sake, take him back. He's the company commander."

The troops were more interested in plundering the small villages they encountered. More often than not, the men got back on the helicopters at the end of the day with pots and pans hanging from their belts and live chickens and pigs poking their heads out of the top of their rucksacks. So much for winning the hearts and minds.

In a way, I couldn't blame them. They didn't have one-year tours of duty like we did. They were in for the duration, and some had been fighting for many years. But, on the other hand, Americans were over there fighting for their freedom, maybe they should be doing more for themselves. Their attitude seemed to be "If the Americans are willing to do the fighting and dying, why should we?"

Down Time

In a dispatch filed by Ernie Pyle during World War II, he described the day-to-day existence of a frontline soldier as follows: "Danger comes in spurts; discomfort is perpetual." The same could be said for infantry troops in Vietnam during a mission in the field. No matter which war, the grunt on the ground has it much tougher than combat aircrew. True, death in the air is just as brutal and final, but living conditions for pilots and gunners when not flying were infinitely better. We had three hot meals a day, a real bed and mattress to sleep on, a roof over our heads, shower facilities (not always hot, but still, a means to wash away the grime), clean clothes, and a cold beer or soft drink. We had it pretty darn good compared with our infantry brethren. The worst part for everyone, grunt and flyer alike, was having to endure a year-long separation from family and friends and, perhaps, not being able to hop in your car and drive somewhere fun.

Many of our daily needs were attended to by a *mamasan*—a Vietnamese woman who worked on base during the day to do our laundry, make our bed, clean our hooch, and spit-shine our boots. Each man paid his mamasan the equivalent of four dollars per month—a huge bargain for us and enough money to help support her family. Our mamasan at Vinh Long looked to be in her mid to late thirties and had five children. Since she didn't speak any English and we couldn't speak Vietnamese, there was a lot of gesturing and smiling to get the job done. The extra price we did pay, however, was a total lack of privacy. The women didn't seem to mind and we got used to it—sort of.

I spent my nonflying days reading and working out, and whether I flew or not, I usually watched the nightly movie—a pleasurable habit I developed during my two short cruises with HC-4. Some of the pilots spent lots of their time bellied up to the O club bar. Fortunately, I did not fall prey to the alcohol master, although I will say that a cold beer now and then tasted mighty good after a long day in the cockpit. Even though my days outside of the cockpit were somewhat boring and limited in variety, I was fairly content. My only disappointment was not being able to fly every day, but that desire was neither realistic nor healthy.

When deployed to a combat zone, where rumor and hearsay are staples of everyday life, reliable news from any source was most welcome; to give us a glimpse into what was really happening in the war, on the home front, and in the world. Our best source was a daily newspaper published and distributed free to the troops called the *Stars and Stripes*. Although this paper, first published during the Civil War in 1861, was sponsored and partially funded by the Department of Defense, it retained complete editorially independence. Some of the guys preferred listening to Armed Forces radio broadcasts from Saigon, made famous by Robin Williams in the movie *Good Morning, Vietnam*. The station featured not only news of the war and around the world, but also played the pop tunes of the day. I never bought a radio, so I was content with reading the *Stars and Stripes*.

Letter writing was the only practical means of staying connected with loved ones in the States. (Remember, this was well before long-distance phone calls were the norm, and well before cell phones and the Internet.) So, I tried to write Barbara every other day, and she did the same. She saved all of my letters and I have referred to them frequently while writing the Vietnam chapters of this book. After reading and re-reading Barbara's letters, I destroyed them. I knew if I was killed, an officer would be assigned to gather all of my personal effects for shipment to Barbara. Included in that gruesome task was the requirement to read all correspondence and to destroy anything that would upset or embarrass the next of kin. The thought of one of my peers reading my personal mail was abhorrent, so I burned them.

We did have a few scares and close calls to spice up the days when we weren't earning green ink in our logbooks. One day, a couple Seawolf pilots were on top of our hooch, attempting to erect a taller radio antenna to improve communications between our airborne helicopters and Det Three operations personnel on the ground. The antenna suddenly twisted out of their hands and contacted a high-voltage power line. Mike Louy, who was my flying partner at Fort Benning, received severe burns to his hands and legs and had to be evacuated to Japan for four months of extensive medical treatment. Fortunately, no one was electrocuted.

On another day, we got word that one of the Seawolf helicopters had crashed on landing. Not knowing the fate of the four crewmembers, we rushed to the airfield, expecting the worst. We found the helicopter upside down in a shallow pond just short of the landing pad. Thankfully they all survived without major injury—the Huey was a total loss. Sadly, the downed bird was carrying the detachment mail that had been picked up at squadron headquarters in Vung Tàu. After retrieving the mail bags from the submerged aircraft, the soggy contents were dumped out on the ground. My spirits took a nosedive when I discovered three letters and a few bags of peanut crunch from Barbara and my first box of slides from the Kodak processing center. Happily, after drying out my loot, everything was in usable condition, including the slides.

One Sunday, while returning from church services, I was greeted by a flurry of activity as I entered our hooch. Instead of people sleeping in, everyone was up and had their personal weapons and ammo lying on the desk or lower bunk—some were cleaning their weapons, others loading extra magazines, and all had a serious look on their faces.

"What's going on?" I asked.

"Haven't you heard? The Viet Cong are going to try to overrun the base tonight," Larry stated matter-of-factly as he pushed another bullet into the magazine in his left hand.

"You're kidding," I said, thinking this must be some sort of a joke the heathens were pulling on us churchgoers.

"Nope!" Larry stated flatly. "We got some very good intel that they are gearing up for a big push tonight."

"Well, holy shit," I exclaimed—probably shouldn't have said that just coming back from church and all. "What's the plan?"

"The word is that everyone should sleep tonight fully clothed, with their boots on and weapons at the ready in case we have to help defend the airfield."

Being the eternal skeptic that I am, I chuckled to myself that the VC wouldn't have to actually overrun the base to achieve their objective. All they had to do was just fire a few rounds and lob in a couple of mortars and leave the rest to us. We would most likely kill each other while firing blindly at shadows and other bumps in the night. As you may have guessed, nothing happened—although, I did sleep with my boots.

A Bad Day

The day was shaping up like many of late: quiet. Tipped off by high-placed informants in the South Vietnamese Army, the Viet Cong usually slipped away from the target area well before the first helicopters arrived on the scene. This mission promised to be another milk run—drop off the troops at 0900, go to a nearby reserve staging airfield to wait, pick them back up at 1600, drop them off at their base camp, and fly back to Vinh Long in time for happy hour at the O club.

It was our third flight into the same LZ. The two previous trips that morning had been uneventful. There was no sign of Charlie, a nickname for the Viet Cong. The ARVN troops of the 21st Infantry Division that we dropped off earlier were casually milling around in the clearing, waiting for us to bring in the last lift of men before they moved out to their assigned objective.

Fifteen transport helicopters and four gunship helicopters providing overhead cover were involved in this day's operation. The slicks were arranged in three V formations of five helicopters each. I was the copilot of one slick in Gold Flight, the lead formation and the first to touch down in the LZ. It was customary to alternate flying duties—a complete roundtrip from the staging airfield to the LZ and back was flown by the same pilot, with the next roundtrip being flown by the other pilot.

Chief Warrant Officer Sean McCarthy, the aircraft commander, was flying this last trip and I was backing him up on the flight controls. Army policy dictated that within five hundred feet of the ground, the nonflying pilot must position his hands and feet close to the controls in case the flying pilot was killed or wounded during landing or takeoff. Our approach and landing in the rice paddy was uneventful, just like the first two. The twelve troopers dismounted quickly and Sean lifted the helicopter into a ten-foot hover, ready to depart straight ahead over the tree line one hundred yards away.

Suddenly, I heard the unmistakable sound of heavy machine-gun fire (.51 caliber) coming from our left side. Looking down through the plexiglass chin bubble of our helicopter, I saw a steady stream of huge, mean-looking, green tracers crisscrossing just inches below our aircraft. Glancing to the left, I saw muzzle flashes erupting up and down the tree line. The transformation from a tranquil morning to all-out combat happened so abruptly it seemed surreal, like an out-of-body experience. We were all but doomed. All the enemy gunner had to do was elevate his barrel an inch or two and he would instantly convert our flight crew into martyrs for our country.

For a merciful instant, it was like someone hit pause on the remote. Unfortunately, action quickly resumed with a "Holy shit! Do you see those tracers?" shouted by our left-door gunner. I desperately wanted to withdraw all of my extremities into the safer confines of my armored seat, but dutifully, I edged my hands and feet closer to the controls. Instinctively, Sean pulled the collective up to his armpit and the empty Huey shot straight up to a hundred feet. Simultaneously, he lowered the nose and we began to accelerate out of the maelstrom below. The gunships rolled in on the tree line, pouring rocket and M-60 machine-gun fire into the enemy positions. The tactical frequency was abuzz with shouted warnings and commands from the formation leader. Three helicopters behind us were shot down—their smoking wreckages littered the LZ. Extracting the troops on the ground, along with the dead and wounded, would take the better part of this day. There would be no happy hour.

To cap off this tumultuous day, I also experienced my first mortar attack. I was sitting at the desk in our cubicle, talking with Tom, who was lying down, when I heard a loud ka-rummpt in the distance. Someone shouted "Mortar attack!" and the race was on to get inside a large sandbagged bunker located next to our hooch—I was the first one in as other men streamed in from adjacent hooches. It was more of a grand adventure than a frightening experience because the rounds were impacting some distance away on the airfield. The targets this night, as usual, were the helicopters and fixed-wing aircraft parked alongside the runway. In rapid succession, about ten rounds fell and then it was eerily quiet. The brief tranquility was abruptly replaced by the sound of Army helicopter gunships scrambling to takeoff to find and silence the enemy mortar. It was like someone swatted a bee's nest with lots of angry fliers swarming around to locate the intruder. The Viet Cong, however, were smart and clever: a good mortar crew could fire ten to fifteen rounds before the first one hit the target. So, by the time the first gunships got airborne, the enemy had packed up its mortar tube and retreated into a hole in the earth. Later, the ground shook from airstrikes by Air Force jets called in to hit suspected enemy positions around the base.

During mortar attacks, we were told to bring our pistols with us to the bunker in case the VC tried to overrun the base. Boy, would that ever be wild—a bunch of pilots not known for superior marksmanship running around shooting at everything that moved.

After experiencing many mortar attacks in subsequent months, at other bases, including some that hit within feet of my bunker, I developed a healthy fear, unlike the cavalier attitude displayed during this first one.

Brother Bill

My mother proudly displayed two blue stars on a white background in her living room window during 1967 and 1968, signifying that she had two sons serving in the Vietnam War. The Blue Star Mothers of America was formed in January 1942 in Flint, Michigan, for the purpose of organizing the efforts of the many mothers in the United States who had sons and daughters serving in the armed forces, so they might be able to band together to contribute to the war effort. The Blue Star Mothers served as volunteers in hospitals and train stations, sending care packages to troops overseas, and augmenting homeland security forces. Part of their outreach was to pass out blue star placards to the families of service members involved in overseas combat operations. As this book goes to press, this fine tradition continues.

Fortunately for my mother, she never had to trade her blue stars for gold ones which are given to mothers who have lost loved ones in combat.

My younger brother Bill joined the Navy Seabees in 1966 and was sent to the Da Nang area of South Vietnam in April 1967, where his battalion worked on various construction projects. Around the middle of May, he was assigned to a small detachment of Seabees heading south to the Mekong Delta to build a small naval establishment at Dong Tam, a large army base situated on the banks of the My Tho River, home to the 9th Infantry Division.

I knew Bill was in the Da Nang area, but had no idea he had been transferred on a temporary assignment just down the river from my base at Vinh Long, not until I received a letter from Mom. I immediately decided I would try to visit him.

The next day I was scheduled to fly, but begged off. I hated to miss a day of flying, but I was more eager to see Bill. I managed to catch a ride on a slick going to Dong Tam and arrived there mid-morning. Then, I hitched a ride in a jeep from the airfield to the new Navy base being built from scratch by Bill and his fellow Seabees.

I wanted to look sharp for Bill and his friends, so I put on a fresh pair of fatigues, spit-shined boots, and strapped on my .45 pistol—big brother was arriving! Dong Tam didn't exist a year before, except in the form of a very large rice paddy. A one-square-mile base was created by three huge dredges running twenty-four hours a day that pumped the mud and silt from the river bottom into the former rice paddy, raising it from sea level to an elevation of eight feet. It was a gigantic engineering feat, but not without difficulties; one of which was mud.

You can imagine what river bottom silt became when mixed with torrential rain delivered three times a day. So, before even laying eyes on brother Bill, my carefully spit-shined boots were caked in thick river mud;

so much for my grand entrance. At least I still looked cool with my pistol strapped to my hip.

Not knowing where to start looking, I enlisted the help of a naval officer I bumped into. We walked up to a squad leader who was handing out work assignments to his men and asked if he knew a man by the name of Stock. "You mean this guy over there?" he said, pointing to Bill.

Bill was surprised to see me. He knew I was in Vietnam somewhere, but that was about it. In fact, Bill didn't know exactly where he was either. He knew he was in the Delta, but had not seen a map to pinpoint his exact location—the military likes to keep things simple.

Although the Seabees were working seven days a week, Bill's squad leader cut him a little slack and gave him the day off, which prompted a few of Bill's buddies to give him a good-natured ration of crap. For Bill, it was a welcome relief from the monotony of sawing boards and pounding nails.

Bill looked fit and sported a dark tan. Pointing to my lily-white skin, he said, "You can tell how long someone has been in Vietnam by the depth of their tan or lack thereof." Even though I was a new guy, I couldn't let his comment go unchallenged. Job description played a role too. He worked all day with his shirt off, while I wore a flight suit with long sleeves and sat in a cockpit partially shielded from the sun. Sibling rivalry never ceases.

He gave me a tour of the small base and showed me the various buildings and structures he and his detachment had built: a large mess hall, administrative offices, lots of hooches, maintenance and storage facilities, and a few strategically placed outhouses. In less than a month, they had accomplished an impressive amount of work. Their job was nearly finished, and they were scheduled to return to Da Nang in four days. It was fortunate I had decided to see Bill when I did.

After eating some good Navy chow and spending the better part of the day together, it was time to say goodbye. I told Bill that I would try to catch a flight to Da Nang in a few months to see him before he rotated back to the States. For both of us it had been a chance to talk of home and family—it was a brief, but wonderful interlude.

PBR Patrol

On another day off, I decided to tag along on a PBR patrol, to see what it was like on the river with the guys we Seawolves were tasked to support. Truth be known, I also wanted a break from my nonflying routine of reading, napping, and watching movies. If we got into a little firefight with Charlie, that would be an extra bonus. Oh, the ignorance of youth.

Departing from the PBR base in Vinh Long, we were on the My Tho

PBR on patrol in the Mekong Delta. These 31-foot, fiber-glass boats had a top speed of 34 mph and a crew of four. *(U.S. Navy photo)*

River at 0600 and heading downstream to our assigned patrol area. Two boats worked together as a unit for mutual protection, much like a fire team of two helicopter gunships.

The PBR was a thirty-one-foot fiberglass-hulled boat powered by twin diesel engines with jet propulsion drive and a top speed of thirty-four miles per hour. With a shallow draft of only two feet and no propeller, it was ideally suited to operate in virtually any river or waterway in the Mekong Delta. It was heavily armed for a craft its size: twin .50 caliber machine guns forward; a single .50 caliber machine gun in the rear; one or two M-60 machine guns mounted on the sides; and various handheld weapons, such as the M-79 grenade launcher, M-16 rifle, and .45 caliber pistol. A crew of four operated the boat and manned its weapons. Aside from a few ceramic armor plates around the twin .50-gun tub and the bridge control station, the PBR depended on its speed and firepower to defend against enemy attack.

Unless called on to engage an enemy target along the shoreline, the primary mission of PBRs was to stop and board waterborne traffic, such as sampans and water taxis, to check for enemy personnel, weapons, and other contraband material. While one boat was alongside a vessel being searched, the companion PBR stood off about fifty yards, weapons at the ready should its sister boat need help.

Our thirteen-hour patrol was totally uneventful. The PBR crews stopped a lot of vessels, but did not find anything amiss. The only action was shooting at floating pop cans and coconuts. It was boring and it made me appreciate again how much better pilots have it. Later in my Vietnam tour, I sadly came to realize that not all days in the life of a PBR sailor were this placid.

I was glad for the opportunity because it gave me a better appreciation of their mission and how best the Seawolves could support them when they got into trouble. I also realized just how vulnerable they were to enemy ambush from the shoreline—a point driven home several times during the coming months.

Seawolf Introduction

On June 9, 1967, I flew my first Navy flight with the Seawolf detachment based at Vinh Long. It was a *routine patrol*, meaning we were looking for something to shoot at, but without any specific mission to focus our efforts. In reality, we trolled up and down the waterways at low level, hoping someone would be foolish enough to shoot at us so we would be justified in attacking them. It was similar to another tactic called *recon by fire*, where the door gunners would light something up with their M-60s, hoping to provoke a response. As I write this, it seems preposterous that we would intentionally try to get shot at. But we were an adventuresome breed with a strong sense of immortality coursing through our veins—and young!

We finally got what we wished for. The lead gunship reported receiving fire in a designated *free fire zone*. We rolled in on two sampans in a narrow stream and sank both of them. I was flying copilot in the wing ship and, as such, my job was to aim and fire the *flex guns*, the two M-60 machines guns mounted on each side of the helicopter. I had fired them before on the gun range at Fort Benning, but this was my first time shooting at a real target. It was just like watching gun camera footage of a World War II fighter strafing a road convoy—bullets from my four machine guns impacting on the water all around the sampans and some presumably finding their mark, although I couldn't see those hits.

In the moment, it was fun and exhilarating, but disturbing when I thought about it that evening. There were human beings in those sampans. Whether we killed any of them, I don't know, but we certainly wounded some because there was blood in the water. Granted, they were in a prohibited zone and thus could be engaged without provocation or permission from the province chief. Supposedly, these people were bad guys, otherwise they wouldn't be in this area. But what if they were innocent fishermen who had wandered into a free fire zone by mistake? The government didn't post warning signs along the entrances to these zones, and, furthermore, maybe this zone was recently created before word-of-mouth could filter down to the local inhabitants who had fished this area for many years. Although I continued to attack sampans discovered in free fire zones during the remainder of my Vietnam tour, I was never completely comfortable with the concept.

Aside from the seven new guys like myself, the rest of the pilots in Det Three were former HC-1 pilots who had been absorbed into the new Seawolf squadron when it was formed on April 1, 1967. They were not overly friendly or helpful toward us new guys. Having been in combat for more than eight months, they were cocky and confident. Some, but not all, interacted with us in a condescending or aloof manner. Their resentment toward us was understandable given they had been used to doing things their way for many months, and with very little direct oversight. Now, they had a whole new set of authority figures in Vung Tàu, dictating how the war was to be fought, what reports needed to be filed, and other intrusions into their unfettered lifestyle. The relationship between the old guard and the new grew better over the next few months as we adjusted to one another, but it was never a happy marriage.

My next and last flight with the Seawolves from Vinh Long was another eye-opener. We flew two low-level recon missions, one in the morning and another in the afternoon, during which we received fire and put in a strike on the suspected enemy positions. The last attack was directed at a small village. As both gunships rolled off the target, we came upon three young boys riding water buffaloes, two on one animal and one boy on the other, in a rice paddy about a quarter mile from the village. The fight leader made the immediate assumption that they were VC and we rolled in and killed the three boys and one of the animals. Maybe they were Viet Cong, but the sudden, ruthless, and unprovoked attack on three unarmed boys stunned me. I could not believe I had just witnessed cold-blooded murder. To this day, it bothers me deeply.

That single event was a defining moment for me in Vietnam, and I am glad it happened early in my tour of duty. Yes, I had thought that I might be killed, but I hadn't come to grips with the opposite side of the war equation, namely the idea that I was being asked to take another human life. It was one thing when the enemy was directly trying to kill me—that was an easy decision. For me, it was quite another when an enemy or suspected enemy was helpless before our guns. Flying in a helicopter gunship, relatively immune from retaliation, I felt like a bully on the playground—we seemingly held all of the advantage. That evening, I prayed I would never lose my humanity during combat and I recalled what a Warrant Officer by the name of Gibson told me during my training at Fort Benning, "I would rather not fire a shot, than kill one innocent person." Months later, as a fire team leader, I would be put to the test, and would be grateful for this early exposure to the dark side of war.

Pack Up Your Gear

On June 24, I was told that five Navy pilots and myself from Vinh Long were being sent to Soc Trang to fly with the Army. We were being assigned directly into the 121st Helicopter Assault Company, just like a replacement Army aviator. Supposedly, we would fly us as much as we wanted. No more would I have to beg for flights every night. Hooray! Things were beginning to look up.

Although I was frustrated and disappointed with the lack of flying, the overbearing attitudes of the old HC-1 pilots, and the sense of abandonment by the home guard in Vung Tàu, the experience at Vinh Long was, on balance, a good introduction to combat flying and life in the Delta. I flew ten days out of twenty-one and accumulated forty-seven flight hours with the Army and five hours with the Navy. I had gained valuable experience in CA, DCS, and gunship missions; and I felt comfortable flying the Huey.

Chapter 8

Soc Trang Tigers

DURING WORLD WAR II AND THE OCCUPATION OF INDOCHINA, THE airfield at Soc Trang was constructed by the Japanese and operated as a fighter base. Several times during my stay, the ghosts of a long-ago enemy seemed close at hand. I could almost hear Zeros and Zekes thundering down the runway to engage Allied forces. Twenty-five years later, the roles were reversed. Soc Trang was now an American base that dispatched aircraft to seek out and destroy another Asian brother—the sound of fighters replaced by the *whopp, whopp* of Huey helicopters.

The hamlet of Soc Trang is located about nine miles west of the mouth of the Hau Giang River—most locals and Americans called it the Bassac River from its origin in Cambodia—and the airfield was two miles southwest of the town. Thanks to the Japanese, the airbase boasted one of the few paved runways in the Mekong Delta.

121st Assault Helicopter Company

No sooner had the main rotor of our helicopter coasted to a stop when a tall, lean chief warrant officer strode up. As we stretched our tired limbs in the mid-day sun, he said, "Welcome to Soc Trang. I'm Dave Rynearson from the Tigers." We shook hands. "Boy, am I ever glad to see you guys. We've been flying almost every day, averaging 140 to 150 hours a month and, frankly, we are worn to a frazzle. I hate to call you *fresh meat*, but with you fellas filling in on the flight schedule, we Army pilots will finally get a little bit of a break."

Pretending to be offended, Nick Press retorted, "We don't usually answer to fresh meat, but in this case, bring it on. We came here to fly."

"Amen, brother," another member of our group added.

"Well, that's great," Dave replied. "Sounds like a win-win for everybody. Here, let me show you gents where you will be bunking, it's not far.

Oh, by the way, after you get some chow, we've got an operational briefing scheduled for you guys at 1300 at Base Ops."

Our new living quarters looked more like a quaint honeymoon cabin than the average Delta hooch. With its faded-wood exterior, louvered shutters hiding screened window openings, a steep gable metal roof, and banana trees guarding the exterior, it was inviting and comfortable. I wondered if it too was a legacy of the Japanese.

The inside was a more austere, but clean and functional. There were four small rooms off a central hallway, each with the obligatory metal-framed bunk bed. I grabbed the top rack and Tom Gilliam the bottom—we each knew the drill. The location of our new abode was perfect: three doors down from dining facility/O club; two blocks from the flight line; and, for good measure, the PX was two doors in the other direction. With the promise of lots of flying, this place was shaping up to be a Delta Shangri-La.

"Good afternoon, gentlemen. I'm Major Driscoll, commander of the 121st. I would like to add my personal welcome aboard to our Seawolf comrades-in-arms." He paused a moment and then continued, "I understand from speaking with your CO, Commander Spencer, that you all will serve as the backbone of his new squadron after the Army delivers some more B-model Hueys. He outlined the minimal training you received at Fort Benning and asked if we could provide some additional OJT, to which I replied, 'Can we ever.' Perhaps, I should have given him an aye, aye, sir," the major said with a slight chuckle, obviously pleased with his attempt at some nautical humor.

"As you probably know, our pilots have been stretched pretty thin lately and they are worn out, plain and simple. You guys can provide some much-needed rest for them while learning the ropes from some very experienced, slick and gunship drivers. I hope your time with us will be positive and productive. If there is anything I can personally do for you, please stop and see me—my door is always open. At this time, I would like to turn the briefing over to my operations officer, Captain Wilson, who will lay out what's in store for you and provide the necessary tactical information to enable you folks to blend smoothly into our flight operations." With a final, "Thank you all for coming," the major strode briskly from the room.

After Captain Wilson finished his welcome remarks and the tactical briefing, we were unanimous in our initial impression that the 121st was much more squared away and organized than the 114th at Vinh Long. They seemed genuinely pleased to have us and willing to make our time at Soc Trang as educational and smooth as possible. To be fair, at Vinh Long we were officially assigned to the Seawolf detachment and not to the Army—maybe that was the difference. But the attitude at Soc Trang was much different: we felt welcome and needed. It promised to be a great relationship.

Two days later, I completed a two-hour checkride with Captain Wilson, which stressed emergency procedures. The following day, I flew nearly seven hours with the Tigers, the call sign of the slick platoon. In a letter to Barbara that night, I wrote, "Although I am pretty tired right now, after flying all day, I am very happy and in high spirits." Nothing made my morale soar more than flying. I was thankful I had chosen this line of work.

Mission Potpourri

In the ensuing fifty-one days at Soc Trang, I flew thirty-two of them. I was in heaven. Most of my missions were combat assault and direct combat support operations flown with the Tigers. During the later portion of my stay with 121st, I also flew a few gunship missions with the Vikings, the call sign of the gun platoon. Most missions were uneventful in terms of enemy contact, with a few notable exceptions that served to reinforce the notion that there really were bad guys down there trying to kill us.

DCS missions to resupply Special Forces outposts were always interesting and potentially dangerous, especially in the Seven Mountains area. In the northwestern corner of the Mekong Delta, along the Cambodian border, seven individual mountains rose to 3,000 feet, incongruously jutting up from the sea-level rice paddies that surrounded these aberrations of nature.

The enemy controlled the sides of these mountains, while units of fierce Montagnard tribesmen and their U.S. Army Green Beret advisors, held the summits. Their only means of contact with the outside world was by helicopter, so that meant twice weekly slick missions to sustain these isolated and surrounded men. It was always a rush approaching the mountaintop LZ they had marked with colored smoke, especially when they said over the radio, "Don't fly over the tree line at your nine o'clock position because we have been taking fire from there all day," or some other blunt warning of close enemy contact.

Beside these mountaintop enclaves, there were numerous outposts located at strategic canal and waterway junctions throughout the Delta that were manned by RF troops and their American advisors. Most of these fortifications were built in the shape of a triangle, with high earthen walls surrounded by ring upon ring of barbed wire and minefields. Most buildings inside the compound, such as command centers and living spaces, were fortified to protect from enemy mortar and rocket fire. To add to the complexity of life at these outposts, each RF soldier brought his wife, children, and extended family with him. That was all fine and dandy until the enemy mounted a determined attack to overrun the strong point.

One day, we landed inside an outpost and were immediately mobbed by about thirty of the most desperate looking people I had ever seen. The night before, a patrol from the outpost had been savagely attacked and nearly decimated, and these dependents of the dead soldiers wanted to get out of there in the worst way. Our helicopter was the only immediate way back to civilization. We could not take anyone with us because we still had several more missions to complete. It took our two door gunners and the senior American advisor fifteen minutes to literally pry everyone off the helicopter and restore order. It was so sad to witness such an outpouring of human emotion and not be able to help.

On takeoff, as we flew beyond the southern wall, we saw the shattered wreckage of a Huey that had suffered an engine failure months before and crash-landed in the middle of the minefield. Miraculously, the four crewmembers survived the crash and the ensuing walk back to the outpost through the minefield. Days like this one were a not too subtle reminder that we were not on a training exercise in the States.

The largest aircraft formation of my military career occurred during a CA mission involving helicopters from Soc Trang and Vinh Long. The operation involved thirty slicks, eight gunships, a C&C chopper, fixed-wing aircraft dropping tear gas, and a single smoke-dispensing helicopter. From my vantage point in the last diamond formation, I could see twenty-five helicopters in front of me as we proceeded en masse to the LZ. It was a sight to behold. I was proud to be part of such a large strike force. Yet, when compared with thousand-bomber raids over Germany, it was miniscule.

Although we had been briefed before takeoff at Soc Trang that the Air Force would be prepping the LZ with tear gas prior to our arrival, and we would have to wear gas masks while flying, it was still strange to see the ARVN troops boarding the slicks at the staging field wearing their masks. It was even weirder to look across the cockpit and see the other pilot peering out from behind a full faceplate, like an astronaut in a space capsule. Of course, the masks were ill-fitting and uncomfortable—score another one for the low bidder—which raised immediate doubts as to their reliability in keeping the gas out of our eyes and nose. Fortunately, by the time we landed in the LZ, most of the tear gas had dissipated.

As we approached on short final to the landing zone, a smoke ship was laying a thick cordon of smoke to screen our arrival from enemy positions located in a thick tree line to our right. I pitied the crew of that machine—talk about having a target painted on your back.

This operation, for all its complexity and size, was still like the others: drop 'em off at 9 and pick 'em up at 4; with a few pots, pans, chickens, and pigs to show for their effort. Hey, why should I complain? It was more green ink in my logbook, more combat pay in the bank account, and another day closer to going home.

I will never forget another particular CA mission that had my nerves on edge. The mission began with a takeoff before daybreak, which was my first experience flying formation at night. I discovered that in the darkness, it was actually safer to fly a tighter formation because we could detect relative movement, vis-à-vis other helicopters, sooner and thus were better able to correct any dangerous rates of closure.

Right out of the chute, my heartrate shot up and stayed there most of the very long day. After getting the hang of it, I admit formation flying at night produced a sense of accomplishment, and watching the sunrise over the distant horizon, amid the gaggle of helicopters, was an extra bonus.

What made this particular mission noteworthy was the amazing fact we never once shut down our helicopter during the ten-hour mission. We hot re-fueled with the rotors turning and got out of our seats only to relieve ourselves in the refueling pits. What little we ate and drank, we did while flying. Every bit of the ten-hour day was flown less than fifty feet from the helicopter in front of us. The only break we received from the constant stress of formation flying was when the other pilot took his turn.

Heaped upon the bone-weary fatigue, was the enemy fire we took on at almost every insertion and extraction that day. The constant chatter of the M-60 machine guns being fired by our door gunners added to the general haze of weariness and adrenaline. At one point, as we approached to land in an LZ, covering machine-gun fire from one of the gunships started kicking up water in the rice paddy about thirty feet in front of our helicopter. All in all, it was a hell of a day. When we finally landed at Soc Trang that evening and shut down our helicopter, I was so exhausted and spent I could barely crawl out of my seat.

Fortunately, this was not the norm for CA missions. After inserting ARVN soldiers into an LZ, we typically retired to a staging field, where soldiers being held in reserve were positioned. Until we were summoned to insert the reserve force or extract the troops from the field, the flight crews engaged in various activities to kill time—sleeping, playing cards, and reading were the usual pastimes.

Some men, however, engaged in other endeavors of questionable sanity. One favorite among door gunners was constructing and firing what they called *mini-mortars*. First, the erstwhile shooter would remove a 7.62 tracer round out of a belted clip feeding an M-60 machine gun, pry out the lead slug, dump out the powder, drop the slug into the empty shell casing, and place the powder on top of the bullet. After sticking the loaded shell casing into the dirt at the proper angle, the powder was ignited with a match or a cigarette lighter. The objective was to see who could shoot his tracer round the highest. There were, of course, misfires and other calamities, but to my knowledge no one was seriously hurt. These spirited contests took their mother's admonition "not to play with matches" to a whole new level of concern.

I engaged in some horse trading with some of the ARVN soldiers that was equally risky. Anybody who has ever watched World War II movies is familiar with the "pineapple" style hand grenade used during that conflict and the Korean War. Infantrymen carried several of them on their chests, hanging from their combat harness. In Vietnam, U.S. soldiers carried grenades that had smooth exteriors. For some reason, I thought those old pineapple grenades were so much more appealing—more manly maybe. ARVN soldiers were equipped with the old-style pineapple grenades and someone told me they would be willing to trade one for a pack of Salem cigarettes—why only Salems I don't know. Maybe they never heard of the Marlboro man. Well, I just had to have one of those old grenades, so I bought several packs of Salem in the PX for fifteen cents apiece and went scouting for war souvenirs.

You wouldn't believe the reaction of an ARVN soldier after making such a trade. He would go running toward his buddies, whooping and hollering like he had just won the lottery. After several of these transactions, the word got out, and lots of troopers came up to me, pointing to grenades on their chests.

Over the course of several operations, I managed to collect six grenades, which I intended to pass out to my brothers and friends, keeping one for myself. My source, who told me about the Salem cigarettes, also told me how to disarm the grenades by simply unscrewing the top from the base and dumping out the black powder. Since these were live grenades and he wasn't around to guide me when I tried this for the first time, I was more than a little jumpy. As I think back on this, I realize it wasn't the brightest thing I had ever done—but it worked, just as he said.

During most flights, the two door gunners on an Army slick had a boring, sedentary job. They sat opposite their machine gun, hour after hour, with little to do but watch the unchanging countryside flow past their perch—unlike the pilots who were actively engaged in piloting, navigating, and communicating on even the most routine mission. So, when the need arose to shoot their M-60 to provide suppressive fire or to shoot at an actual target, they did so with great gusto. After arriving back at home base, after a long day of flying, their job was not done. They would spend another two hours performing maintenance and cleaning the machine guns to get their helicopter ready for the next day. Pilots, on the other hand, were free to relax after engine shutdown. The life of a door gunner was not easy, yet they seldom complained. I have the utmost respect for the outstanding job they did to protect us pilots.

Speaking of door gunners, one day while waiting at a staging field to extract the ARVN troops, I noticed a gunner from an adjacent helicopter who had removed his shirt to work on his tan. He had four distinct, round scars evenly spaced across his stomach, so I asked him what happened. On a previous tour in Vietnam, he had been in the infantry and was cut down by an enemy machine gun. He turned around to show me the even larger scars from the exit wounds in his back—unbelievable! How he survived wounds of that magnitude was mind-boggling. After spending one year recovering in a military hospital in the States, he volunteered to come back as a door gunner, figuring it might be safer than being a ground-pounder. Specialist Mattheson was a young soldier who had given a lot for his country, and came back to give a little more.

On DCS missions to small hamlets and villages, we often landed on the public soccer field in the center of town. Invariably, a group of young kids, usually boys, would soon gather around the helicopter, hoping for some kind of hand-out from the generous Americans. They were particularly fond of chocolate, so we saved the mini candy bars in our C-rations for these occasions.

Their English was limited to being able to say, "Okay, GI numba one," which they delighted in saying over and over, followed by a military salute. ("Numba ten" was reserved for anything despicable.)

After receiving their candy, the kids would soon evolve into the type of play that boys of

While parked in a village soccer field waiting for our passengers to arrive, a group of village boys gathered in the shade of one of our helicopter main rotor blades in anticipation of receiving some chocolate or other goodies from our crew. July 1967

any country like to do, and that is to chase each other. But, as soon as one of our flight crew took out a camera, the boys would instantly stop what they were doing and line up for a posed photo. On one particularly hot, sunny day, after they tired of chasing each other, they all squatted down in single file in the shadow of our main rotor blade—the only shade in the soccer field. I furtively got my camera out to record this cute human adaptation before they saw me.

Now and then, I encountered VC prisoners. One day, we transported a Viet Cong who had been shot through both legs. On another occasion, while waiting at a staging field, I came upon four POWs who were being brutally treated by ARVN interrogators. I snapped a photo with my ever-present camera. As I walked away, I was accosted by an ARVN soldier who demanded I turn over my film. I had apparently stumbled on something I wasn't supposed to see. I ignored

While waiting at the reserve staging field one day, I happened upon four Viet Cong POWs being harshly interrogated by ARVN forces.

his request and kept walking, hoping he did not shoot me in the back. I had heard rumors that the South Vietnamese usually executed their prisoners after interrogation, or dropped them from helicopters if they failed to talk. I wondered if those four unfortunates ever saw the light of another day.

Interspersed with the serious business of waging war, we did manage to have a little fun. On my first DCS mission to the tip of the Cau Mau Peninsula—a *two-ship area*, meaning slicks flew in pairs because of the large concentration of Viet Cong in the thick forests and mangroves that predominated—we decided to put on an impromptu airshow on take-off from the dirt airstrip. The gunners tied one colored smoke grenade to each skid of both helicopters with a lanyard. On takeoff, we flew in close line-abreast formation at one hundred feet, as fast as the old Huey could go. When we reached the end of the runway, the gunners pulled the lanyard on the smoke grenades, as we broke sharply in opposite directions and began to climb. I am positive the troops on the ground were suitably impressed with our antics—I have no clue what the VC surrounding the airfield thought.

Another interesting sidelight of this particular mission was having to land in a tight landing zone created in the coastal mangrove by the explosion of a 500-pound bomb dropped by the Air Force. We only had about ten feet of main rotor clearance as we settled down into the crater to drop off a reconnaissance patrol. All in a day's work—more green ink in my logbook and another day to cross off on my Vietnam calendar. Life was good.

Night Missions

Aside from the night formation flight, my night flying in Vietnam, involved two specific Army missions, one flown in a slick and the other in a gunship. The *snoop mission* was flown every night in two shifts: 2200 to 2400 hours, and 2400 to 0200 hours. During these periods, a single slick flew in a lazy orbit at two thousand feet over the Soc Trang airfield to look for muzzle flashes from enemy mortar positions and to pinpoint their locations so that gunships on the ground could scramble into the air to engage the targets. Why they didn't fly these missions beyond 0200, I don't know—maybe that's when Charlie went to bed. These missions must have been fairly successful as a deterrent because I can only remember being mortared once during my time at Soc Trang.

The mission I flew was boring—no action whatsoever. I was glad I only flew one of these lonely two-hour patrols. One night, however, a bizarre thing happened to another crew. The aircraft commander told me that he felt the helicopter suddenly lurch and the door gunner in the back screamed, "He just fell out of the aircraft." Whether the other gunner accidentally fell or he committed suicide was never determined. They found his body the next day in a rice paddy.

The other night mission I flew had the potential for more action, but it too fizzled. Called a *firefly mission*, it consisted of one slick with a million-candle-power searchlight and two gunships. The light ship flew at five hundred feet above the Bassac River, hoping to illuminate enemy sampans, while the gunships trailed behind at about two hundred feet with their lights out and ready to pounce. Although the light ship seemed to be an inviting target, the VC had long ago learned that shooting at it was a bad idea. Since nobody took the bait, and we didn't turn up any sampans, it was another long, boring three-and-a-half-hour mission.

That night, I did, however, record a first of my aviation career—I fell asleep in the cockpit. I had flown a three-hour gunship mission earlier in the day; so by nightfall, I was already beat and, with nothing to shoot, it set the stage for a startling lapse of protocol. As the copilot, I had the M-60 flex gunsight in my hands. ready to fire if needed. When I fell asleep, despite my best efforts not to, the heavy gunsight and trigger mechanism contacted the cyclic stick with great force, causing the helicopter to suddenly pitch nose down, alarming the entire crew, who thought we had been hit. I was now wide awake and profoundly embarrassed. After apologizing to my crewmates, I did the very same thing twenty minutes later, except this time they were wise to my shortcomings. (As I write this fifty-one years later, it is the only time I ever nodded off unintentionally while flying—and on a combat mission no less!)

Leisure Hours

My days off from flying fell into a predictable routine: play three to four games of chess, read, take a nap, and watch the nightly movie shown in the O club. Just before turning in for the night, I crossed another day off my calendar—already counting the days until my combat tour was over. As I did so, I thought of our armed forces engaged in World War II, who were in for the duration and had no idea when they might be going home.

Soc Trang had an Olympic-sized swimming pool with a helicopter main rotor blade that served as diving board (it actually worked quite well). The only downside was the thick green algae that grew on the sides and bottom of the pool, giving the water a yellowish tint. Despite some initial misgivings of contracting a deadly tropical disease, I did do some lap swimming to keep in shape. Since no other Delta airbase had a swimming pool, I wondered if it too was a relic from the Japanese occupation. If it was, it certainly hadn't been cleaned since they left.

Seawolf Down

On July 21, in the middle of my short stint flying with the Vikings gunship platoon, Soc Trang control tower received word that a Seawolf gunship had been shot down just across the Bassac River from the base. The Seawolf fire-team had been low-leveling across a rice paddy, searching for a reported enemy bunker complex, when the wing ship took a lucky shot that severed the fuel line to the engine. With only a split second to react, the pilot yawed the aircraft to the side just before ground contact, hoping to avoid crashing head-on into a tree line just ahead. The sideward momentum at impact caused the helicopter to roll violently numerous times before coming to rest with all its appendages gone—main rotor and transmission, tail boom and tail rotor, skids, machine guns—and crushing the cockpit and cabin to nearly half its former size. When I looked at the wreckage later in the day, I could not believe that anyone could possibly have survived such a violent event.

In fact, three of the four crewmembers survived with only bruises and contusions. It was understandable why the two pilots securely strapped into their armored seats faired pretty well. The two gunners in the back faced a much more difficult situation. They were only attached to the helicopter by an eight-foot long gunner's belt wrapped around their waists. So, as the helicopter made the series of extremely rapid rolls, they were slung around at the end of their tether—one second inside the helicopter and the next on the outside, like an astronaut performing a spacewalk. Sadly, as the gunship came to rest, one of the gunners was trapped under the wreckage in a rice paddy covered in water—only his left arm was free, as if asking to be pulled to safety. The surviving gunner, Tex Swofford, held his buddy's hand until he died.

The lead helicopter jettisoned its rocket pods and ammo cans to shed weight and swooped in to rescue the three surviving crewmen before the enemy in the surrounding tree lines could send a patrol to the area.

The Vikings scrambled a two-ship fire-team to the area to provide cover for a ground party being sent in to recover the body and a heavy-lift helicopter recovery team that would hoist the wreckage out of the rice paddy and return it to Soc Trang. I flew copilot in the lead gunship.

It was easy to spot the crash site as we crossed the river. Smoke billowing up from the wreckage was being blown downwind, parallel to the large paddy, like a giant directional arrow. It took a little over an hour to extract the dead gunner and the wreckage. Apparently two fully armed gunships circling above the fray like birds of prey discouraged the enemy from trying to interfere.

I landed at Soc Trang just before *Hill Climber*, call sign of the heavy-lift Chinook helicopter, arrived at the airfield with what remained of a once lethal Navy helicopter gunship slung underneath. After gently placing the wreckage on the ground, *Hill Climber* moved off to the side to unload the body of the dead gunner. As crewmen rolled the gurney away from the helicopter, I saw his outstretched arm, frozen in rigor, bent ninety degrees. Now, instead of reaching for his buddy, he was reaching to accept the hand of his Savior. This mournful loss of a fellow Seawolf is a haunting memory I will never forget.

Near Disaster in Cambodia

Flying at normal cruising altitudes of 1,500 feet in the Seven Mountains area meant that the VC and NVA soldiers occupying the mountain sides could fire directly into the helicopter at eye level or use plunging fire from above. To minimize the chances of getting hit while resupplying sea-level outposts in the area, slicks would fly at five to ten feet above the ground at a top speed of 120 miles per hour to try to blend in with the topography. Not only was it safer, but it was a blast as well—the equal of any attraction on a carnival midway. As we zipped along, dangerously close to the ground, we had to momentarily climb over tree lines, rice paddy dikes, water buffalo, and peasants riding bicycles. Occasionally we scattered a herd of cattle, much to the dismay of the herdsman. I am sure we did not make friends among the local populace with these low-level escapades, but we were young and immature as statesmen. We had the reins of a marvelous steed in our grip, so we dug in our spurs and enjoyed the hell out of it.

In the Seven Mountains area, the border between South Vietnam and Cambodia was a fairly straight canal that was one to two hundred yards wide. Cambodia, like Laos, was officially a neutral country, but openly harbored NVA and Viet Cong forces directly across the border from Vietnam. Destruction of these sanctuaries was the objective of a series of large-scale military operations by U.S. forces into Cambodia in 1970, authorized by President Nixon. In the summer of 1967, flying into Cambodian airspace was strictly prohibited—and very dangerous.

One day, while conducting DCS missions in the Seven Mountains area, we were blithely low-leveling near the border of Cambodia. We knew from experience that the canal marking the border was fairly wide and unmistakable; so when we crossed a narrow canal, we were not concerned in the least. All of sudden, we came upon a military bivouac with neat rows of tents! It was not until we saw many uniformed soldiers carrying rifles scattering in every direction that we realized we had inadvertently strayed across the border. It was truly one of those "Oh, shit!" moments. Chief Warrant Officer Bill Raney was flying at the time; he realized our dire predicament at the same moment I did, and immediately began a hard-right climbing turn, heading back to the safety of South Vietnam.

As we turned away, the enemy soldiers quickly recovered from our surprise intrusion and began to fire with everything they had. Loud hits began to register on our fleeing machine. As we made our right turn, the left-door gunner had a perfect angle at close range to engage the confused enemy troops. I am certain if he had opened up with his M-60 machine gun, he could have taken out lots of the enemy. He did not fire one shot. After we had safely crossed the border, I turned in my seat to administer a good, old-fashioned ass chewing to the gunner for not shooting. But, when I saw him, I realized there was no point in chastising him—he was frozen to his gun, unable to move or talk. I have never seen anyone in combat so scared that he was unable to defend himself.

We were incredibly lucky that day. Later, a U.S. Green Beret Captain told us that we had stumbled into an enemy encampment numbering over three hundred NVA soldiers. Had we been shot down in their midst and survived the crash, we most likely would have been executed. It was one of my closest calls in Vietnam.

End of an Assignment

Although initially frustrating, it was a blessing in disguise that the Navy did not have enough helicopter gunships to immediately put all of us junior pilots to work on arrival in-country. Instead, the time we spent with the Army, gaining experience flying the Huey and being able to extract maximum flight performance, learning the geography of the Delta and how to navigate using a scarcity of good landmarks, and learning enemy tactics and capabilities, was priceless. It was the best thing that could have happened to us newbies. Otherwise, we would have been forced to learn the hard way: from our own mistakes—an unforgiving teacher, especially during combat.

At Soc Trang, I flew a total of 196.5 flight hours for a daily average of 6.1 hours with the 121st Helicopter Assault Company. In my remaining ten months in Vietnam, I never came close to flying this much. It was a great experience—thank you, Army!

Sadly, my time at Soc Trang also marked the death of one of my friends: Ensign Jim Burke. Earlier, I related taking a photograph (p. 87) of my three traveling companions at the Can Tho airfield (I will refer to it as *the photograph*), and I hinted that tragedy would strike them. Jim was the first to die. He was flying copilot with the Army out of Vinh Long, at night, on the first day of August. We were told it was an accident caused by bad weather and not hostile fire. Regardless of the cause, Jim died in the service of his country, fighting a war we all believed in at the time.

Chapter 9

Seawolf 62

A FTER ALMOST TWO MONTHS AT SOC TRANG, IT WAS TIME TO PACK our gear. Mother Navy was calling us back to perform the mission we were sent to Vietnam to do: protect and support the Brown Water Navy. And finally, we would be changing our call sign from Knight, Maverick, Tiger, and Vikings to the one we most wanted—*Seawolf!*

My last day at Soc Trang started early on August 17. Det 3 was sending one of their birds to pick up Tom and me to transport us to our permanent Navy assignments: Tom to Det 3 in Vinh Long and me to Det 6 at Dong Tam. After packing our gear and saying goodbye to our Army friends, we manhandled our footlockers, seabags, and cardboard boxes to the airfield in fervent hope this would be our last Vietnam move—our impedimenta had increased since our arrival in-country, with the addition of PX purchases such as cameras, tape recorders, and trinkets for family back home.

A Seawolf gunship like the one that dropped me off at Dong Tam. August 17, 1967

As the helicopter crossed the My Tho River and made its approach to the airfield at Dong Tam, two thoughts crossed my mind: one, how much larger the base was since the last time I visited; and, two, the irony that ten thousand miles from home, I would be living in a hooch that my brother had helped build.

After landing and off-loading my gear, I thanked the Det Three crew for the lift and shook hands with Tom, wishing him well at Vinh Long. Just being twenty minutes up the river, I figured I would see Tom fairly often during the remainder of our Vietnam tour. But it was still strange to be parting company after being roommates since Fort Benning. As it turned out, I would see Tom again in five days at Dong Tam, except this time he could no longer shake my hand.

Welcome to Dong Tam

Lieutenant Commander Roy Hollingsworth, Det 6 Officer-in-Charge (OIC), met me at the airfield in a beat-up, grey, Navy pickup truck that looked like it had been in continuous use since the French abandoned Vietnam in 1954. Hollingsworth was a soft-spoken, warm individual who started his naval career as an enlisted man, working his way up to chief petty officer before being commissioned. He immediately impressed me as being one of the sharpest and most genuine naval officers I had

Aerial photo of the naval base at Dong Tam. My brother Bill and his Seabee detachment built all of the buildings in the foreground. To the left is the turning basin used by the Mobile Riverine Force.

encountered thus far in Vietnam—an opinion that was reinforced in the days ahead.

Holly, as we called him (but not to his face), drove me around the Army portion of the base, pointing out key operating units that directly supported our mission, such as the Tactical Operations Center (TOC), the armory, supply depot, the hospital, and the PX. At one point, as the dirt road neared the perimeter of the base, Holly offered a reassuring assessment of the base defenses.

"You see that guard post over there," he said, pointing to a white wooden structure about thirty feet high that resembled a beach lifeguard tower on steroids. "That position is manned around the clock with two Army soldiers with a .50 cal machine gun. and those guard towers are spaced about one hundred yards apart around the entire perimeter of the base."

"That's some heavy firepower," I replied, thinking about the awesome .50 caliber demonstration I had witnessed at Camp Pendleton.

"And that's not all," Holly said in a matter-of-fact tone. "The land is stripped bare of all vegetation for three hundred yards in front of these towers, to the distant tree line you see over there. In this no-man's land, there are a series of barbed-wire fences and claymore mines for good measure."

"I wouldn't want to be a VC patrol trying to attack through those defenses," I said.

Saving the best for last, he said, "If they did manage to penetrate the perimeter, then the two artillery batteries would level their gun barrels and fire beehive rounds full of nails and other nasty stuff at point-blank range."

After this quick lesson on base defense, I never once worried about being overrun by the enemy during the remainder of my tour at Dong Tam.

We finished our tour at the small naval enclave at the southwest corner of the base. Much had changed since my short rendezvous with my brother Bill in June: all of the buildings were finished, a network of dirt roads divided and linked the Navy base with its big Army brother, and wooden boardwalks connected all of the hooches and other buildings to keep pedestrians out of the mud. And the most obvious change was the presence of a large number of small watercraft tied up to barges in the West Turning Basin that belonged to the Mobile Riverine Force. This was no longer an installation under construction, it was a fully operational naval base that was humming with activity and purpose. Det 6, on the other hand, had been formed less than a month prior; there was much to be done before we reached our full potential. I was excited to finally be in a detachment and I was eager to contribute as much as I could.

After off-loading my gear, Holly introduced me to another detachment pilot, Lieutenant Steve Beguin, who showed me to my hooch—nothing fancy, just your basic four walls with screening, a metal roof, and sandbags piled halfway up the walls around the perimeter. If I would have known I would be occupying this particular hooch, I would have asked my brother to build in some special amenities while he was at it, like an attached basketball court, Jacuzzi, and workout room. War doesn't have to be awful if you know the right people.

Just as I threw my seabag onto my rack, I heard a loud boom that caused me to jump two feet in the air. "What the hell was that?" I asked, as I looked around for suitable cover. Steve started to laugh, "Sorry about that. I should have warned you about the artillery battery over there." He pointed to eight 105 howitzers located about seventy-five yards from where we were standing—one still smoking from the fired shell that nearly caused me to load up my jockey shorts. "They fire day and night around the clock, but you'll get used it," Steve said.

"Oh really," I exclaimed still shaking a bit. "I hope you're right, otherwise sleep will be hard to come by."

Steve was right, of course. It didn't take many days before I was sleeping soundly through nightly barrages. It is amazing how the human body is able to adapt to sights and sounds that constitute a new normal. In a war zone, your senses become even more acute to danger and your body quicker to react to those signals. Case in point: about two months later, I was lying in bed just about to drop off to sleep when I heard the whistle of a shell going overhead. In an instant, my mind registered that I had not heard a boom prior to the whistle—meaning that it was incoming and not outgoing. In a flash I was on my feet, rushing toward the bunker located just outside the back door of our hooch.

Just after finishing evening chow that first day in Dong Tam, we received word that a Det 6 helicopter had ditched in the South China Sea off Vung Tàu on its way back to Dong Tam. Lieutenant Raleigh Smith was the pilot, Lieutenant Junior Grade Jeff Smith (no relation) was the copilot, and Petty Officer Second Class Bob Seaman was the crew chief. They were bringing back a new door gunner who had recently arrived in-country. When the helicopter entered the water, it sank so fast that both pilots had difficulty getting out. Bob Seaman dove underwater to assist both pilots and pulled them to the surface. He was later awarded the Navy Marine Corps Medal for his quick heroic actions. Unfortunately, the new gunner could not swim and he drowned. My first day in Det 6 ended on a somber note.

Somehow, the dead crewman's black beret was found floating near the submerged wreckage. Holly asked if anyone needed a beret, and I raised my hand. He asked if it would bother me to wear a dead man's beret. I said that I would be glad to honor his memory. Fifty-one years later, I still have his beret in my collection of Vietnam memorabilia.

Jeff Smith, who nearly drowned that day off Vung Tàu, sadly and ironically lost his life ten years later during a night ditching in the Pacific Ocean when he failed to get out of his sinking helicopter.

My New Home

Six months before my arrival, Dong Tam did not exist. In fact, it was a large open area of former rice paddies inundated with water from the My Tho River, which formed its southern boundary. MACV decided to send a statement to the Viet Cong: "By constructing and occupying Dong Tam we are announcing that we are coming in force and we are coming to stay with the ultimate goal of driving the enemy out of the Delta." To show solidarity with the South Vietnamese people, the Army chose the name Dong Tam which means *united hearts and minds.*

Two significant downsides to this reclamation project were mud and dust. Dong Tam might have been the only place in the world where you could be standing knee deep in mud and have dust blowing in your eyes, nose, and ears at the same time. It was a tough environment in which to live, work, and operate the machinery of war.

In March 1967, the 2nd Brigade of the storied 9th Infantry Division took up residence in the muddy flats of Dong Tam. They were soon followed by the U.S. Army's Third Surgical Hospital, which treated most of the combat casualties in the Delta. Dong Tam continued to evolve and grow while I was there, and long after I left. In addition to its important combat role, the base became a showplace featuring stateside amenities such as a golf course, churches, a swimming pool, athletic fields, indoor gymnasium, a large PX, and Vietnamese-operated concessions. The intention was to create a haven where GIs could relax and unwind between combat operations. Most of these improvements came after my time, not that it mattered. I was too busy learning to be an effective helicopter gunship pilot, flying missions, and keeping up with my other detachment duties to worry about R & R.

The U.S. naval base, which occupied a small portion of Dong Tam, consisted of a small Naval Support Activity that provided administrative support to the Mobile Riverine Force units operating in the area; the YRBM-17, a floating, non-propelled craft that provided repair, berthing, and messing facilities for Riverine boats and their crews; Detachment 6 of the Seawolves; and later, a contingent of hovercraft.

On the land side of the naval base were hooches, shower facilities, heads (six-holer outhouses), a chow hall, an O club and EM club that served cold beer and alcoholic drinks, a rudimentary softball and volleyball field, and various admin buildings for personnel and supply—everything a man could want! Well, most everything.

Unlike aboard ship, there was no shortage of water and no risk that the engineering department would suddenly shut off the water after getting all soaped up. There was an important shortcoming, however, as compared with a ship—the water was COLD! Not just some of the time, but all of the time, because there were no water heaters. I never learned why.

The outhouses, or *heads* as they are called in the Navy, were another matter. These weren't individual port-a-potties like you find at a state fair. No, it was a raised platform with six oval holes carved into the top. There was no privacy, no mercy flush—not even some lime to keep down the smell. (I now know why you should never let a fly land on your food.) Typically, men like to read and meditate while on the throne, but this was not the case in Dong Tam. It was hard to concentrate with the sounds from your five companions reverberating off the walls. It is also important to note that our waste did not drop into a deep cavernous pit to decay over time; no, instead the waste went into a sawed-off fifty-five-gallon drum, one under each hole. Once a day, some "lucky" guy from the Naval Support Activity would drag each container a short distance, douse it with fuel oil, and burn it. This choreographed maneuver was affectionately called *burning the shitters*. It was obvious when this daily chore occurred due to the thick, black smoke that rose into the air, like the aftermath of an air attack. Hopefully, you were anywhere but downwind of this ritual burning.

The detachment officers were quartered in two hooches separated by a forty-foot open space, which was eventually turned into a barbeque and lounge area, complete with wooden deck, a bar, banana and palm trees, and covered by a large cargo parachute. The enlisted crew of the detachment had similar housing arrangements. The senior officer hooch was divided into a conference room/lounge area in the front, a small office with two desks and filing cabinets in the center, and living quarters in the rear. Our hooch, which housed eight of the twelve officers, was devoted primarily to a sleeping area with a small lounge in the front.

Immediately behind each hooch was a totally enclosed sandbagged bunker large enough to hold about ten people. During a mortar attack, you could literally run out the back door of the hooch and right into the opening of the bunker located five feet away.

The only bedroom furnishings we had were military-issue cots. The day after I arrived, I began building a large wooden cabinet that had a place for hanging uniforms and a few civilian clothes; a place for underwear, socks, and towels; and a fold-down front that served as a desk. I painted it grey (it's the only color paint the Navy buys) and wired it for lighting for reading and writing, and also to remove the dampness so my uniforms would not mildew. It turned out to be quite nice and functional, although I took a bit of ribbing for my "big grey monster."

We did not have mamasans to do our laundry, keep our hooch clean, and to shine our boots. So, we took our laundry over to the YRBM to be washed, cleaned our hooch occasionally, and never shined our boots. Despite what anyone tells you, shined boots are the first casualty of war.

Emotional Goodbye

Tuesday, August 22, started out like the previous four days since my arrival at Dong Tam: happiness in being assigned to a detachment and a sense of eagerness and anticipation of what I might learn. However, when the day came to a close and I crawled into bed, sleep would not come because I had learned that your life can be whisked away in a fraction of a second; and aside from a battle buddy in the field and family back home, the world would not mourn your passing and the war would continue to grind on.

Since I was not scheduled to fly that day, I busied myself helping Larry Kier design a lounge area for the front of our hooch and performing other mundane tasks. About one hour before dusk, Holly called me aside to inform me that Tom Gilliam had been killed on a mission several hours earlier. His body had been brought to Dong Tam to begin the transit back to his family in Ohio. Someone needed to make a positive identification of his remains, and since I knew him the best, Holly asked me to do it. As he explained where I should go on the Army side of the base and whom to contact, I was not listening. I had stopped processing his words after hearing *killed in action*. In a dream-like state of total denial, I got into a jeep driven by one of the other pilots, to perform a task I certainly did not want to do.

Hours earlier, a fire team from Det Three in Vinh Long had stumbled on a huge gathering of over one hundred enemy sampans pulled up on a deserted beach along the coastline of the South China Sea. After receiving clearance to fire from the sector advisor, the two gunships of the fire team proceeded to make attack after attack on the empty watercraft, destroying great numbers. The Seawolf crews did not see any sign of the enemy and did not receive any hostile fire during the thirty-minute encounter. Just as they were pulling off the target, on their last run before returning to base to rearm and refuel, a lone enemy soldier jumped out of a spider hole and fired a "John Wayne hipshot" that penetrated the side window of the left cockpit door. The bullet just nicked the top of Tom's one-inch-thick ceramic chest protector and continued into his heart. According to the aircraft commander, Bill Pressey, Tom said, "I'm hit" and then slumped forward onto the cyclic stick, making it difficult for Bill to control the helicopter.

The two door gunners tripped a release lever on the bottom of Tom's armored seat and rotated it back into the cabin so they could begin first aid. Tom was unconscious and had gone into deep shock. They landed aboard a nearby LST to pick up a corpsman before heading to Dong Tam in a desperate attempt to get him to the 3rd Surgical Hospital. Unfortunately, my good friend, roommate, and constant companion for five months, died en route without regaining consciousness.

I will pick up the rest of this story by quoting from a letter I wrote to Barbara after I returned to my hooch from identifying Tom's body. That evening and the following day, I was an emotional wreck. Fortunately, I bounced back.

> This is going to be a very difficult letter for me to write. I desperately need someone to talk to, someone to whom I can vent all of the emotion tied up inside of me. Naturally, my closest 'somebody' is you, honey.
>
> You remember the fellow I roomed with at Fort Benning, Tom Gilliam—well, he was killed today while flying as copilot in a Seawolf chopper. He probably never knew what hit him because he was shot right thru the heart. I have been with Tom ever since Fort Benning. We went to California together, survival (where incidentally he escaped three times from the POW camp, the high man), we flew to Vietnam together, we went to Saigon, Vung Tau, and Ving Long. We went to Soc Trang where I was his roommate once again. Finally, last week Thursday we took off on our FINAL flight together when they dropped me off at Dong Tam on their way to Vinh Long. That was the last time I saw him. To make it worse, Tom was brought to Dong Tam shortly after being killed (all U.S. personnel in the Delta whether wounded or killed are brought here for further processing).
>
> Well, since I knew Tom the best, I had to make the positive identification of his body. That was the tough part. I was pretty well shook up by then anyhow, but to have to see your fallen comrade in death was just too much. First off we couldn't find the place where he was. It probably took the better part of 45 minutes asking directions and getting false information before we found out where he was. I fully expected to be taken to a morgue which was clean, air conditioned, and dignified—just like in the movies or on TV. Graves Registration (the name of the place that handles dead soldiers) had moved today, so they had no facilities whatsoever except for a little shack with a typewriter, etc. Three men were busy filling sandbags and building a bunker and rightfully so. It was just after dark by the time they led me to a parked truck, an ambulance I guess. A guy started up the truck so we could turn on the dome light in the back of the truck. Lying on a stretcher, exactly as he was when he was

shot, was my friend Tom. His body wasn't cleaned or anything. It wasn't a very good memory to be left with of a guy who had everything to live for and was a very carefree, happy-go-lucky guy.

I thought to myself as I walked away from the truck, 'what a terrible way for an American boy and fellow pilot to end up—in the back of some dirty old truck, lying in his own blood, in the middle of a muddy lot with everybody busily pursuing the business of war all around him.' I knew I was in a war zone. I've been shot at before and had some close calls, but not until that moment in that truck did the frightening reality of this whole situation hit me. I felt rather immune and safe while flying over known VC areas far removed from the earth beneath oneself. Undoubtedly, Tom was feeling the same way when he was called from this world. It made me realize that I could be lying there in Tom's place. Honey, I know how this letter must be affecting you, but bear with me, I just have to get it off my chest. Babe, I don't want to die over here. I love you so much and I want to come home to you and raise our family. The way I feel now, my life would be in vain if I were killed over here.

Two men in *the photograph* were now dead.

Man and Machine

By virtue of the Navy flying I had done in Lakehurst, I had more flight time than any of my contemporaries; consequently, I was designated an aircraft commander soon after my arrival in Dong Tam. The next step was to become fully qualified to fly the wing position in a light fire team (LFT), which consisted of two helicopter gunships operating as an attack unit. (A heavy fire team consisted of a third gunship, which we rarely used.) For the first few weeks, I flew missions with Steve Beguin. He did his best to impart what he had learned about the ins and outs of flying the wing position. He was a great teacher and a heck of a nice guy. On the recommendation of Steve and Holly, Commander Spencer, our squadron skipper, designated me an Attack Helicopter Aircraft Commander (AHAC) on September 12, 1967, and authorized me to fly the wing position with my own crew.

In assigning detachment call signs, we borrowed from the Army playbook, where the CO of a unit is referred to as "6," the XO was "5," operations officer was "3," and admin officer was "2." Since I was the detachment admin officer, my call sign became *Seawolf 62*: six for the detachment and two for my job position.

Larry Kier was assigned as my copilot, a decision I heartily endorsed. Larry and I went way back. We were in the same Pre-flight Class, went through flight training together, and were assigned to HC-4 for our first duty station. Not only was he a friend, but he was a good pilot and a

My crew shortly after I was a designated aircraft commander and qualified to fly the wing position in a two-ship fire team. (*l to r:*) Copilot Larry Kier, me, gunner and crew Chief Paul Andrus, and gunner Bobby Boone. September 1967

talented navigator. I depended heavily on Larry to get us to the correct target and he never failed that important task, day or night. We became a good team and flew sixty-five missions together.

Door gunners were not assigned to a permanent crew for a variety of reasons, primarily because of the influx of new gunners and the length of time it took to become fully qualified. The gunners I flew with most frequently were: Paul Andrus, Bobby Boone, Art Ibarra, Earl Kennedy, Allan Roper, Dennis Crabtree, and Dan Higgins. But I flew with every gunner at one time or another. They were a great bunch of hardworking, dedicated professionals who saved our butts time and again with their bravery and expert marksmanship. I will forever be in their debt.

In mid-October, when four pilots were assigned to another detachment, thereby leaving us with eight pilots, we implemented a 24-hour-on-24-hour-off duty cycle, which meant that the fire team on duty flew all routine patrols and emergency scrambles that came up during their 24-hour watch. With four less pilots, it also meant more flight time for all of us, which was important as we honed our skills and improved our tactics.

Our UH-1B helicopter gunships were heavily armed fighting machines and feared by the enemy. Our typical weapon and ordinance load was impressive: six M-60 machine guns with ten thousand rounds of 7.62 belted ammunition and fourteen 2.75-inch (diameter) folding-fin rockets.

This photo of a Det 6 crew shows the impressive weaponry of a helicopter gunship: six M-60 machine guns, 10,000 rounds of 7.62 ammo, and fourteen 2.75-inch rockets.

We could arm the rockets to fire two types of warheads: high explosive (HE) or white phosphorus (WP). We fired HE rounds most of the time because they were best against sampans, bunkers, and personnel. WP rounds, commonly called *willie pete*, were used for marking targets and starting fires. The rockets were aimed and fired by the aircraft commander sitting in the right pilot seat. Lacking precise guidance systems common to modern-day air-to-surface missiles, the rockets we used did not have pinpoint accuracy when fired at long ranges from the target. They were effective as an area weapon against dispersed enemy personnel. If there was a specific target, such as a bunker or sampan, the only way to achieve a modicum of success was to press home the attack to very close range before firing. In doing so, however, the helicopter and crew were exposed to increased risk from enemy small arms fire or being hit by shrapnel from their own rocket explosions.

Rockets could be fired one at a time or all seven at once, called a *salvo*, or any number in between. Not knowing any better, we started out firing a pair of rockets on each attack run. It was a lot of fun firing rockets, so why fire them all on one pass? Sort of like the difference between sucking on a popsicle or chewing it. As our experience with enemy tactics improved, we realized that after our first attack, the VC would retreat to prepared holes in the ground, where they were immune from subsequent firing passes. So,

Fire team on routine patrol looking for targets of opportunity. Photo taken from my helicopter flying the wing position. 1967

to inflict maximum casualties, we normally fired all of our rockets on the first run—not as much fun, but more effective.

Four machine guns (flex guns), two on each side of the helicopter, were remotely fired and controlled by the copilot. They were bore-sighted to converge at about three hundred yards in front of the helicopter. When all four guns were firing properly, they put out a lot of lead, however, the guns were prone to jamming. Each door gunner fired a handheld machine gun that was a free gun, unlike on Army slicks where they were installed on a fixed gun mount.

A free gun gave the door gunners a much wider firing arc which, in turn, allowed better suppressive fire during rocket attack runs. Attached to an eight-foot long gunner's belt, it was not uncommon for a gunner to stand on the skid to deliver machine-gun fire under the helicopter as it was pulling off the target.

The downside of a free gun was the possibility of target fixation by the gunner and the danger of sweeping the gun forward into the cockpit during the heat of battle and shooting the pilots. I never heard of that happening, but sometimes less critical parts like skids, rocket tubes, and wind deflectors were hit by errant gunfire. We pilots had complete faith that the gunners would not accidentally fire into the cockpit, just as the gunners trusted us not to fly into the ground on a rocket run. It was a team effort where each of the four crewmembers had a specific job to do and we had total confidence and trust in each other.

Seawolf Missions

The missions flown by our detachment, listed in order of frequency, were: targets of opportunity, PBR support, maintenance and logistics, Mobile Riverine Force support, and SEAL support. Even though our original charter and the reason the Seawolves were created was to protect and support the PBRs, that mission didn't begin to fully utilize our availability or capabilities. So, like gunslingers of the Wild West, we went looking for targets of opportunity. During most 24-hour duty periods, two routine patrols were scheduled, including some night patrols. Each patrol was typically one-and-a-half to two hours in length.

Since Seawolf detachments were not assigned rigid geographical patrol areas, we had the flexibility to range far and wide. However, due to limited locations where we could refuel and re-arm, as a practical matter, we did not usually venture too far from our base at Dong Tam. Our normal patrol area was west of Dong Tam in Go Cong and Kien Hoa Provinces and included the My Tho River and its tributaries and canals west to the South China Sea—an approximate radius of fifty miles.

The smoking wreckage of a PBR hit by enemy fire. Even though our fire team arrived fifteen minutes after the pair of PBR's called for help, we were too late to save the crew of this boat.

Top photo: The Mobile Riverine Force used a number of highly modified amphibious landing craft to support their mission of landing infantry troops of the U.S. 9th Infantry Division. Shown here is an Armored Personnel Carrier. 1967

Bottom photo: Our fire team is flying overhead cover for this Mobile Riverine Task Force as they make their way up a narrow canal to insert troops of the U.S. 9th Infantry Division. Shortly after this photo was taken, the convoy was ambushed killing five U.S. servicemen and wounding a number of others.

Standard procedure was to check in by radio with the American advisors in various sectors of our patrol area to ask if they had any targets of opportunity that we could attack. Since Army aviation assets were devoted to higher-priority missions and hard to come by, these advisors were overjoyed to have gunships at their disposal. They usually had several targets to give us, ranging from specific objects such as watercraft, buildings, and bunker complexes, to supporting RF and PF forces in the field during sweep operations.

On those rare days when the sector advisors had nothing for us, we scouted out free-fire zones for enemy sampans or other suspicious activity that we could engage without the requirement to secure permission before attacking.

More than half of the total missions we flew involved targets of opportunity that arose during these routine patrols. Not only did this activity furnish much-needed fire support to the American advisors, it also gave us a sense of accomplishment and broke up the monotony of just boring holes in the sky. We sank hundreds of sampans and destroyed or damaged numerous enemy structures. We undoubtedly killed or wounded a considerable number of enemy forces as well, but we could not obtain a reliable body count from the air. Sometimes RF and PF forces and their American advisors were able to provide accurate battlefield assessments that spoke to the effectiveness of our attacks.

Missions to support PBR operations did not occur with a predictable frequency. Most of the time, they went about their daily river patrols without the need for gunship support. Occasionally, as a precaution when they were transiting a dangerous waterway, they asked that we fly overhead cover. Most of the time when they called for help, they were already in extremis and getting the crap kicked out of them. These missions were called *scrambles* and usually involved an ambush situation. If we were lucky enough to be in the air at the time of the desperate call, we had a decent chance of arriving in time to make a difference. If we were on the ground, we could be on the scene in fifteen to twenty minutes, but most of the time we arrived too late to influence the outcome—either the PBRs were able to successfully fight their way out of the trap or their boats were a smoking wreckage with the loss of all hands.

At the detachment level, the only maintenance performed on our helicopters was of a preventive nature, so most repairs and major inspections were done at either Vinh Long or Vung Tàu. Flights devoted to fulfilling these requirements and other logistical needs provided a welcome change in the routine and allowed us to occasionally go to squadron headquarters to take care of personal business.

The Mobile Riverine Force (MRF) was a joint operation involving the

U.S. Navy and the 2nd Brigade of the 9th Infantry Division at Dong Tam. Using a variety of specially modified landing craft operated by Navy personnel and carrying Army infantry troops, the MRF conducted amphibious combat operations throughout the Mekong Delta. On several occasions, Det 6 provided overhead coverage while MRF boats and troops moved along narrow waterways en route to their objective.

The last type of mission for the detachment was quick reaction support to U.S. Navy and Vietnamese SEALS. We did not insert or extract SEALS by helicopter, as other Seawolf detachments did later in the war. Our sole purpose was to attack enemy positions if these clandestine teams ran into trouble that they could not handle themselves. The SEAL team would usually stop by Dong Tam mid-afternoon to tell us their general operating area and about how long the operation would last. The briefing never specified precisely where they would be or exactly what they would be doing, although they hinted their missions often involved assassination or capture of Viet Cong leaders. They would consume a few beers with the off-duty fire team and then, as the sun was going down, they would man their boats and slide silently into the night. While a SEAL team was on an operation, we could only expend half of our ordinance and fuel during a routine patrol in case we had to respond to a call for help. In my time with Det 6, we only had to bail them out two or three times—they were usually able to take care of business themselves.

Rescue in the Mekong

"Mayday! Mayday! Mayday, this is Army Helicopter Vanguard 6, engine failure! Going down four miles west of Dong Tam!" The frantic cry pierced the otherwise quiet emergency-radio frequency. And, those words would set into motion events that would take forty-one years to play out.

The beginning of my twenty-four-hour shift as Aircraft Commander of the wing aircraft began in a rather lazy fashion on October 15, 1967. Usually, after relieving the off-going flight crews at noon and reading the latest intelligence reports, the fire team would take off on a routine patrol of our operational area. This afternoon, however, was different. The lead helicopter had been flown the day before to squadron headquarters in Vung Tàu for some maintenance and was not due back until late in the day. Since Seawolf SOP prohibited offensive patrols by single helicopters and the afternoon patrol had been cancelled, my crew and I were in no particular hurry. At about 1400, we decided to ready our helicopter for flight by performing a thorough preflight inspection of the aircraft and ordinance systems, refueling, and re-arming. I had started the gunship in preparation to hover-taxi over to the re-arming area located about three hundred feet across the runway from its normal parking spot in an L-shaped revetment.

Since the distance was short and the move did not involve forward flight, the canvas tarps that served as make-shift gun covers for the two M-60 machine guns mounted on each side of the aircraft, were left tied in place, and the copilot and one of the door gunners had decided to walk. With only one gunner, Petty Officer (AO3) Arthur G. Ibarra, sitting on the right side, I had just lifted the helicopter into a hover when I heard the Army pilot's call for help.

During my twelve-month tour in Vietnam, I heard many Mayday calls from Air Force jets to Army helicopters to small reconnaissance airplanes. Each one commanded your immediate attention because you knew that a fellow aviator was in peril and, at that very moment, was fighting for his life and that of his crew. Each time I was riveted to the ensuing radio transmissions between the aircraft in distress, potential rescuers, and others eager to lend a hand. In the past, these events were either a long way off or help was already on the way. This time was different—it was happening close to our position and, quite possibly, I could influence a favorable outcome.

My first thought was that this poor Army pilot was going down in a very bad area that was known to be swarming with VC. I knew if he was not picked up within five to ten minutes, he would probably be captured and executed. Just two weeks prior, the pilot and observer of an Army light-observation airplane had been executed in the cockpit after being shot down five miles north of Dong Tam. Without thinking through the consequences of my actions, I made a hurried takeoff in the direction of the downed helicopter, oblivious to the fact that I had left behind my copilot and one door gunner. Even more foolish and dangerous, I had not removed the gun covers, which could easily have become unfastened in the slip-stream and flown up into the main rotor or tail rotor causing the helicopter to crash out of control.

In a matter of several minutes, we arrived in the general area and began to look for the stricken helicopter and its crew. After establishing radio communications, the downed pilot did his best to direct me to his location, but I was still having difficulty spotting him due to multiple tree lines. Then I saw a red flare shoot three hundred feet in the air at my ten o'clock position. The Army pilot had made a perfect dead-stick autorotation landing onto a small rice paddy surrounded by thick tree lines on three sides. I dumped the collective and made a steep approach to the site, putting my helicopter between the Army chopper and the closest tree line. The adrenaline rush caused my left leg to shake so badly I thought I might lose control of the rudder pedals during the landing. Almost immediately on touchdown, we began to take enemy fire from the tree line one hundred yards to our right. Fortunately, Petty Officer Ibarra was sitting on the right side and began to deliver suppressive fire from his handheld M-60 machine gun.

In the meantime, the Army pilot and his passenger, a Vietnamese Army colonel on a high-level secret mission, made their way through knee-deep muck to my helicopter. I remember wondering what was taking them so long when, in reality, it probably took less than forty-five seconds. But when you are under fire, that's an eternity. Adding to the surreal scene was the business suit and tie worn by the Colonel—not what I expected to see in a rice paddy under fire.

They had barely climbed aboard in the rear of the helicopter before I took off and headed the four miles back to the airfield at Dong Tam. The Army pilot stood in a bent-over position, with his head thrust into the cockpit between my seat and the empty copilot's seat. He was clearly elated at being rescued and, if he thanked me once, he thanked me fifteen times on the short flight back to base. I thought he was going to kiss me, he was so happy!

After thanking me once more, he and his VIP passenger got off my helicopter, and I returned to the re-arming area to face the rest of my crew, who did not have the slightest idea what had happened. I explained the situation and sheepishly apologized for not stopping for them before dashing off.

After re-arming, the tower asked me to return to the scene to provide overhead cover until an Army recovery unit arrived to extract the downed helicopter. I told the tower that I was not comfortable going back single ship, but was persuaded to go when the controller said that there was no one else available. I decided to circle the area at one thousand feet above the ground to give us a little protection from small-arms fire.

Upon reaching the scene, we noticed about seven men with weapons walking down a narrow path toward the downed helicopter. Since these soldiers were dressed in the traditional black pajamas worn by just about everybody, we couldn't tell whether they were friendly or enemy forces. Although we suspected the latter, we did not have permission to engage them, so, I instructed the gunners to fire in front of them. They got the message and retreated into some thick vegetation.

After circling for about one hour, Dong Tam tower told us that a local PF outpost was sending ten soldiers to set up a defensive perimeter around the downed aircraft and that we had been ordered to return to base.

About forty-five minutes after returning to Dong Tam, we received word that the PFs were taking fire and needed help. Once again, my crew ran to our pickup truck for the mad dash back to the airfield. Once airborne, I contacted another Seawolf fire team operating nearby and asked them to join me, thus creating a heavy fire team of three gunships. Our presence in the area caused the VC to stop firing at the PFs for the moment—because ten minutes later, we received word from the American advisor in the area that the VC were moving in a company-sized force.

About the same time, we received a radio call from the Army recovery team that they would be arriving on the scene in ten minutes. To prepare for their arrival, we dropped down on the treetops to perform a low-level recon to determine enemy locations and movement and to plan the safest approach path for the two helicopters in the recovery package: a Huey carrying the rigging crew and a CH-47 Chinook that would lift the downed helicopter from the LZ.

We escorted the rigging helicopter into the tight landing zone and they completed their work without incident. We brought in *Hill Climber* (call sign of the CH-47) and, just as the sling harness from the downed chopper was attached to the hook on the belly of the hovering heavy-lift machine, the enemy opened up with heavy automatic weapons fire. A terse transmission from *Hill Climber*—"Taking fire! Let's get the hell out of here!"—set the tone for the mad scramble that followed.

We had set up a low-level circular pattern around the LZ, with the three gunships evenly spaced so that we could deliver maximum suppressive fire if needed. As I glanced across at one of the other gunships, I saw him suddenly pop up in the air in an odd manner. Though abnormal, I thought he was just maneuvering aggressively to attack the enemy positions. Then, as mortars began to drop all over the place, I realized he had been blasted upward by an exploding mortar.

The combination of the swift retaliatory attacks by our three gunships and the late timing of the enemy onslaught, allowed both recovery helicopters and the downed aircraft to safely depart the maelstrom below. With the recovery team safely airborne, we turned our full attention to the VC. We each delivered four rocket and machine gun attacks on the enemy positions. The next day, the American advisor credited us with seven confirmed enemy KIA and two probable KIA, two structures destroyed, and one damaged. Although nip and tuck at times, the Navy and Army's joint effort resulted in two downed airmen and their helicopter being recovered with no U.S. casualties, while the enemy paid a dear price for their intervention.

In rehashing the events in the following days, I reached several conclusions about my chances of survival should I ever experience a forced landing due to mechanical issues or enemy action. With so many U.S. aircraft in the air at any given time, and all monitoring the emergency-distress radio frequency, if a pilot was able to transmit a quick mayday with approximate geographical position on the way down, help should be overhead within ten minutes. Every pilot, unless actually engaged with the enemy, would stop what he was doing and respond to the crew in peril, just as I had.

If a gunship was able to land or crash without serious injuries, the crew had considerable firepower with which to defend itself until help arrived, in the form of two M-60 machine guns and two M-16 assault rifles. Landing in the middle of a clearing or rice paddy would make it is easier for rescue aircraft to spot you, and would also afford the best opportunity to see and engage approaching enemy forces.

Lastly, this event reinforced the importance that all pilots should carry survival equipment that was readily available. I was able to quickly locate the downed pilot because he had used his survival radio and flare gun to good advantage.

Since I had been a devoted disciple of survival training from the beginning of naval flight training, I was well prepared, even before this rescue. Shortly after arriving at Dong Tam, I managed to obtain a standard-issue survival vest worn by all Air Force pilots. The vest was made of light-weight nylon mesh with a generous number of individual pockets attached. I modified it by having a holster sewn under my left armpit to accommodate my .45 caliber pistol. Among the items I carried were a battery-operated aircraft survival radio, red-flare gun, first-aid kit, two extra pistol clips, and morphine syrettes.

Mortar Attacks and High Alert

As mentioned previously, when MACV built its garrison at Dong Tam, it intended to make a statement to the enemy. The Viet Cong and their NVA masters received the message, and they clearly did not like it because they took the liberty of lobbing mortar, rocket, and recoilless rifle fire whenever the spirit moved them. At night, on occasion, the enemy also probed our large perimeter. For example, a VC frogman was killed one night in the turning basin in front of our hooches while attempting to attach a mine to one of the Riverine boats.

These hostile efforts were certainly meant to inflict as many casualties and as much damage as possible, but their real purpose was to harass the American occupiers. Due to the large number of combat troops and two artillery batteries located at Dong Tam, the enemy had no chance of overrunning the base, as they did at smaller outposts.

Dong Tam used colored flares at night to warn its residents of enemy activity—red flares for incoming rounds (usually mortars), and green flares to signal a ground attack. There was also a daily password that would be used to challenge unknown forces in the unlikely event the enemy was able to penetrate our defenses. Everyone on the base, including us Navy guys, had an assigned section of the perimeter to man in case of an all-out enemy assault. That would have been a scary prospect; fortunately, the plan never had to be executed, although we had a few occasions when intelligence indicated a major raid was imminent.

One morning just before dawn, I awoke to the staccato of machine-gun fire on the eastern berm about 150 yards from my hooch, which lasted for about thirty minutes. We learned later that a VC platoon had attempted to infiltrate past the .50 caliber machine gun towers on the perimeter.

Another night, when the base was supposed to be hit, the artillery batteries fired illumination rounds like a Fourth of July fireworks display—except this one lasted all night. It was spooky to watch these brilliant white flares descending slowly under their tiny parachutes, casting shadows that danced and swirled among the buildings, creating fleeting images of imagined enemy sappers.

On still another night alert, we watched in awe as *Puff the Magic Dragon* (an old World War II C-47 cargo plane converted into a fixed-wing gunship) hosed down large areas just outside of our perimeter. The machine-gun fire from their mini-guns, which were six-barrel Gattling guns capable of firing six thousand rounds per minute, was a solid stream of red tracers—like a firehose dispensing red water. When I realized that for every tracer round there were four invisible bullets in between, "hosing down the area" was an apt description. The roar that accompanied a burst

The hole in the foreground was where the first of a seventeen-round mortar barrage hit our small naval base. The second round landed just to the left of the photo severely wounding a sailor assigned to a roving patrol. The senior officers' bunker and hooch is in the foreground and my hooch and bunker is the next in line. October 9, 1967

from a mini-gun could be heard for a couple miles. That same night, we could hear the rumble of a B-52 strike many miles to the north. All in all, it was quite a show—sleep, however, was a fantasy.

According to my diary, January 2, 1968, marked the twelfth mortar attack since my arrival at Dong Tam—I stopped counting after that. As a result, the base suffered numerous casualties, some serious, but only two KIA.

Since the Army did not have any gunships based at Dong Tam, the Det 6 fire team on duty would scramble to get airborne in a futile attempt to find the enemy mortar crew. We never did, but at least they didn't continue to fire after their initial salvo; so in that sense, our response was helpful.

Although most of the incoming rounds landed on the Army portion of the base, the Navy was not totally spared. On several occasions, mortar rounds landed close enough to our bunker that we heard pieces of shrapnel zinging through the air or ricocheting off the metal roof of our hooch. We knew that sooner or later our luck would run out, and it did in the early morning of October 9, 1967. Shortly after midnight, seventeen rounds impacted in quick succession on our small naval base. The deadly barrage scored six direct hits on buildings: four on hooches and two on the chow hall. Twenty-six personnel were wounded, one seriously. With such a tight impact pattern, it was a miracle that no one was killed.

Every night there was a roving watch, whose job was to patrol the

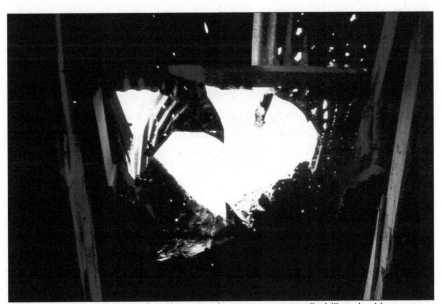

Three pilots from a sister detachment, who were temporarily billeted with us, were wounded by this mortar round which hit their hooch. October 9, 1967

naval base on foot to warn sleeping personnel of red or green flares, fires, or enemy intruders. The man on duty that night was a second-class petty officer who was known by everyone as Pappy. He was probably only in his mid to late thirties, but it seems in all wars, anyone who was ten to fifteen years older than their young comrades, was called names like *Pops*, *Gramps*, and *The Old Man*.

Pappy was on the sidewalk near our senior officer hooch when the second mortar round hit only five feet from him, causing grievous wounds. Several seconds before he was felled, I heard him screaming, "Mortar attack! Mortar attack!" His shouted warning and the sound of the first round hitting nearby allowed everyone in our hooch to scramble out of bed and into the safety of our bunker. Mingled in with the *ka-rumpt, ka-rumpt* of incoming mortars was Pappy's feeble and pleading cry for help, as he lay helpless on the ground. Braving a blizzard of shrapnel, Holly dragged Pappy into the safety of their bunker and began administering first aid. We heard several months later that Pappy was back in the States, recovering nicely having lost an eye and one leg. For his act of courage, Holly received the Bronze Star for valor.

It was amazing how fast we went from a sound sleep to a mad dash for the bunker—talk about hitting the decks a' running. As all eight of us hit the screen door at the rear of our hooch at the same moment, we must have looked like a giant centipede rearing up on its tail. Once inside the bunker, we put on our steel helmets and listened nervously as the bombardment continued all around us. I wondered if our sandbagged bunker could withstand a direct hit. I instinctively cowered into a ball to make myself a smaller target. I'll freely admit, I was fearful—much more so than during my most stressful moments in the air. I can't begin to imagine what it was like for infantry troops caught in the open with no protective cover. In E. B. Sledge's World War II classic, *With the Old Breed*, the author spoke of the nearly unbearable stress he and his fellow Marines faced on Okinawa: "From my experience, of all the hardships and hazards the troops had to suffer, prolonged shell fire was more apt to break a man psychologically than anything else." What I experienced that one night was child's play compared to the horror faced by the infantry.

Three of the wounded were Seawolf pilots from Det 5 who had been staying temporarily at Dong Tam while their LST was in the Philippines for repairs. The day after the attack, General William Westmoreland, MACV Commanding General, toured Dong Tam and, while visiting the 3rd Surgical Hospital, he awarded Purple Hearts to the soldiers who had been wounded the night before. When he met one of the Seawolf pilots, Lieutenant Junior Grade Gordy DeGraw, the General asked the commanding officer of the hospital why DeGraw wasn't getting a Purple Heart.

The commanding officer of the hospital replied that he had no authority because Gordy was in the Navy. General Westmoreland snapped, "Well, I do!" and presented the award to a surprised and grateful naval officer.

The morning following the attack, many Navy folks were seen filling sandbags and strengthening their defenses—nothing like a close call to motivate procrastinators.

The Status of Forces Agreement between the U.S. and South Vietnam stipulated that a certain number of indigenous Vietnamese civilians, male and female, had to be employed on U.S. bases to perform certain jobs, ranging from gardeners to barbers. It was well known that VC or enemy sympathizers gained access to military installations in this manner. Several days after the deadly attack, a Vietnamese worker was caught with a detailed map of Dong Tam on which all key buildings were paced off from a tall radio antenna in the center of the base. As stated before, a big problem in Vietnam, like all wars of insurrection, was the difficulty in determining friend from foe.

Scramble the Seawolves

A scramble usually began with a radio call from our controlling operations center in My Tho.

"Seawolf 66, this is Druid, over."

"Druid, this is Seawolf 66, over."

"Seawolf 66, I have two PBRs, call sign Red Arrow One and Red Arrow Two, on the Ben Tre Canal just south of the My Tho River receiving heavy automatic weapons fire. One boat has been hit by an RPG and is dead in water. Request that you scramble, over."

"Druid, this is Seawolf 66. A fire team led by Seawolf 63 should arrive on scene in approximately one five minutes."

Whoever took the radio call in the senior officer's hooch activated the scramble alarm, sending the duty crews running to climb aboard our beat-up Navy pickup truck. With three in the cab and five in the back hanging on for dear life, the truck sped the mile to the airfield, along a dusty uneven road—it really was a "cloud of dust and a hearty, 'Hi-ho, Silver!'"

When the pickup truck lurched to a stop and the crews ran to their helicopters—which had already been refueled and re-armed—each man had a specific task to perform. The left door gunner untied the main rotor blade and moved it to the nine o'clock position. The aircraft commander got into the right pilot seat, turned on the battery switch, checked to make sure the main rotor was untied, and hit the engine start button. The right door gunner removed the canvas covering from the right flex guns, climbed into his seat, and strapped in. The copilot got into the left pilot seat, fastened his shoulder harness and lap belt, and put on his flight helmet. After untying the main rotor and stowing the tie-down strap, the left door gunner pulled the cover off the left flex guns, climbed into his seat, and strapped in. By this time, the pilot had the main rotor up to flying RPM and was ready for takeoff. After the copilot received takeoff clearance from the tower, the pilot lifted the aircraft into a hover, slid sideways to the runway, and took off without being strapped in or wearing his flight helmet—less than one minute had elapsed since arriving at the helicopter. After becoming safely airborne, the pilot gave control of the helicopter to the copilot while he buckled in and put his helmet on. CWO Wade Kern at Fort Benning had been right—you didn't have time to use a damn checklist.

After clearing the base perimeter, the pilot moved the armament switch from "safe" to the "armed" position, providing electrical power to the firing circuits for the flex guns and the rockets. When clear of human habitation, usually out over the My Tho River, the pilot would give permission to test fire the guns and the copilot and each door gunner would fire a short burst from the M-60s to ensure each gun was operating normally before reaching the target area.

In the meantime, the copilot of the lead helicopter was busy navigating to the scene of the ambush and the fire team leader was on the radio with Druid or, perhaps, the endangered PBRs themselves to get an update on the tactical situation.

"62 switch 40 fox mike." With that transmission, the fire team leader instructed me to switch from Seawolf tactical frequency to that of the PBRs.

"Red Arrow One, this is Seawolf 63. We're ten minutes out. Request sitrep, over."

"Seawolf 63, Red Arrow One. Boy, am I ever glad to hear your voice. We ran into an ambush on the south side of the canal and my other boat was hit by an RPG. They're dead in the water about one hundred and fifty yards off the bank with two seriously wounded. Due to the volume of enemy fire from the bank, I can't get alongside, over."

"Roger that, Red Arrow. Hang on partner, we're almost there," replied Lieutenant Raleigh Smith, the fire team leader in the lead gunship.

Ahead, we could see a heavy volume of green tracers spitting from the bank in the direction of the two patrol boats and answering fire in the form of red tracers from the two beleaguered PBRs, mostly from Red Arrow One. This was my first night mission as aircraft commander of the wing ship and, from the looks of it, slow immersion into night ops was out of the question. I eased in a little closer to the fire team leader and waited for his attack instructions.

"Enemy fire seems to be concentrated from the bank just slightly upstream from Red Arrow Two," crackled the nervous voice of the boat captain of Red Arrow One over the radio. "If you can keep their heads down, I will try to maneuver alongside to remove the wounded and the rest of the crew."

"Roger, Red Arrow. Stand by for a little payback."

Once on the scene, and after pinpointing the location of all friendly and enemy forces, the fire team leader decided the best method and direction of attack and communicated this information to me. I then maneuvered my helicopter into the best position to cover the lead ship during the attack run and while pulling off the target.

"62, do you have the two boats in sight?"

"Affirmative."

"Okay, here's what we're going to do. A standard attack run from the water on a forty-five-degree angle to the shoreline. The first run will originate downstream of the PBRs with a left break. Out over the water, I will reverse direction to the right and commence the second pass from upstream with a right break over the water. Fire four rockets on each pass. Any questions?"

"Negative. I'm ready when you are," I replied, as I maneuvered my helicopter to provide covering rocket and machine-gun fire for Seawolf 63.

"Rolling in," the fire team leader said, as he commenced his attack.

As he called, "Breaking left!" at the end of his firing run, we opened up with four rockets and six machine guns. I had never fired rockets at night and I was not prepared for the blinding flash as the missiles swept past the cockpit and disappeared into the black void directly ahead, followed by a bright eruption as they exploded into the trees along the shore.

"62 breaking left," I radioed, as I executed an abrupt left climbing turn off the target.

The sight of a steady stream of red tracers from twelve machine guns on the two choppers coupled with the slower, but steady, .50 caliber fire from Red Arrow One was impressive and devastating; even more so, when a string of dancing red balls moved closer and closer to the front of my blacked-out helicopter. "Cease fire! Cease fire!" I yelled into the radio. Fortunately, the right door gunner of the lead gunship heard my anguished cry and letup on the trigger just before his bullets reached our cockpit.

By the end of our second attack run, enemy fire had ceased, which allowed the undamaged PBR to rescue the crew of their sister boat. Sadly, as we found out the next day, it was too late to save the two wounded sailors—two more names to be chiseled into the haunting black granite of the Vietnam Veterans Memorial in Washington, D.C.

Misdirected Firing

Before reporting to Vietnam, the last aircraft I flew in HC-4 was the UH-2B helicopter. That particular aircraft had an automatic feature that allowed the pilot to make a shallow coordinated banked turn without having to use the rudder pedals. To engage this feature, the pilot depressed a small red button on the cyclic stick with his right thumb. The stick in the Huey helicopter also had a small red button in the same location—this one, however, fired the rockets. One day shortly after I was qualified to fly the wing position, I was in my normal flight position about a hundred yards behind the lead gunship and off to the right. Without thinking, I reverted to habit and depressed the "coordinated turn button" and fired two rockets that went screaming past the leader out into space. I can't print what he said to me over the radio. He was not pleased, and rightfully so, because I could have shot him down. Where the rockets landed was anybody's guess—hopefully, not on someone's home. If that would have happened back in the States, there would have been a thorough investigation and lots of paperwork to fill out. In Vietnam, the only paperwork involved was crossing off another day on your "going home" calendar.

* *

On another flight, when I purposely fired the rockets, the rocket on the left side of the aircraft malfunctioned, which caused it to fire out of the launcher in a corkscrew motion and hit and bust out the plexiglass chin bubble at the copilot's feet. Fortunately, the rockets did not arm until they travelled a set distance in front of the aircraft, otherwise I could have shot us down. I was well on my way to becoming the first ace in U.S. military history to shoot down five friendly aircraft.

* *

Whenever the left door gunner fired his handheld M-60 machine gun in flight, the spent brass shell casings flew out of his gun into the helicopter cabin at a rapid rate. If the gunner held his gun in a certain way, he could purposely direct the steady stream of very hot casings down the back of the copilot's flight suit—this was called *brassing the copilot*. I don't remember if we had a name for the impromptu dance that resulted. It was a standard initiation rite for a newbie pilot.

* *

Artillery fire posed a deadly hazard to any aircraft that inadvertently strayed into the path of the large projectiles. Anywhere in the Delta, where U.S. Army batteries were firing, there was a specific radio frequency called

"Arty" where pilots were given the "azimuth" and "max ord" (firing direction and maximum altitude of the shell's apogee) so the danger area could be avoided. To drive home the importance of always checking with Arty, a photo of a twin-engine Army cargo plane (C-7 Caribou) upside down, five hundred feet from impact, with its tail missing was widely distributed. The caption on the photo read: "This is what happens when you fly into friendly artillery fire." It was a disturbing image because we knew that within seconds, everyone aboard that aircraft died. It delivered a vital message—one I never forgot.

Almost every sizeable Vietnamese village had a single 105 howitzer that fired in support of RF and PF troops in the field. Unfortunately, they did not have an Arty frequency, so we had no way of knowing when or in which direction they were firing. Consequently, we sometimes flew fat, dumb, and happy directly into the line of fire. Our first indication of trouble was usually a registration round that exploded in the air in front of us, leaving a puff of black smoke like World War II flack.

One day, a shell burst directly in front of my helicopter, in close proximity, scaring the bejesus out of us. In the split second I was deciding what escape maneuver to perform, Allan Roper, the left door gunner, hollered into the intercom, "Go up! Go down! Do something!" After getting out of harm's way, I chided him on his impertinence, but I definitely knew where he was coming from.

**

One night, as we were returning from a mission after the control tower had closed. I noticed what looked like a fire that had just started near the airfield. I circled the location several times to investigate, and reported my findings to the Army operations center. About thirty minutes after landing, there was an enormous explosion that sent a fireball seven hundred feet into the night sky. The location I had been circling only minutes before was a large ammo dump. My guardian angel was watching over my crew and me that night because we would have been incinerated in an instant. The dump continued to explode and cook off until early the next morning.

**

One evening in the Navy O club, one of the Seawolf pilots from Det 5 had a little too much to drink. He drew his .45 caliber pistol and fired several holes through the roof before he was restrained by his fellow revelers. Talk about the Wild West.

**

Early on New Year's Eve, well before midnight, I was startled by explosions that sounded like incoming rockets. I was just about to head for the bunker, when I realized it was some soldiers celebrating a little early. There ought to be a law against using fireworks in a war zone. At the stroke of midnight, the entire red- and green-flare system went to hell—even the gun emplacements on the perimeter opened up. Maybe the Viet Cong were celebrating too.

* *

This story of misdirected fire is personal—too personal. One morning when I awoke, my blanket felt damp. I thought maybe it had rained during the night and the wind had blown some raindrops onto my bed. No big deal. Several nights later, however, I was awakened from a deep sleep by water crashing down on my blanket. I soon realized that Lieutenant Bill Lloyd, whose cot was next to mine, was standing over me peeing on my stomach. I sprang out of bed, cursing a blue streak, and threw my blanket through the air, where it landed on the face of Lieutenant Commander Chuck Oyler across the room. By this time, everyone was wide awake and the lights came on. Bill was so drunk he must have interpreted my outrage as belligerence because he started flailing his arms trying to punch me. I felt like decking him, but instead I pinned his arms to his side. Bill, of course, had no recollection of his indiscretion in the morning. I, on the other hand, had no trouble remembering—still don't!

* *

As long as I am sharing "potty stories," I should mention one other bizarre event. Periodically, the senior officers' bunker was visited by an individual who earned the moniker of the phantom crapper. He took perverse pleasure in doing his business in the dark, cool confines of the usually empty, sandbagged enclosure. To make matters worse, his dirty work was not usually discovered until everyone had ran into the bunker during a mortar attack—a moment when its occupants were not fully awake and watching their step.

Although the phantom crapper was never caught, Holly applied a little battlefield humor to defuse the disgusting situation. On the white canvass flap that hung over the entrance to their bunker, he wrote in large letters: "He who sneaks and craps in here buys the hooch a round of beer."

Fort Apache

Even though we were able to get into the air in less than one minute after arriving at our helicopters, we lost precious time driving to the airfield in the old Navy pickup. If the on-duty fire team could be positioned at the airfield, near the parked helicopters, our overall response time would decrease by six or seven minutes.

The main challenge to this goal was constructing a structure large enough to house eight crew members and their gear in a manner that would provide reasonable security from incoming mortar and rocket attacks. Since we needed this capability as soon as possible, we did not have the time to write a formal request and submit it up the chain of command for approval, and then back down to the Seabees or a civilian contractor for construction. Instead we resorted to good, old American ingenuity and resourcefulness—we employed the time-honored beg, borrow, and steal method.

The Army at Dong Tam was receptive to our idea and said they would support us anyway they could, within limited material and manpower constraints. They agreed to grade the site and run electrical power to our new facility. The rest of the project was up to Det 6.

Somewhere along the line, I must have mentioned I had my own masonry business when I was nineteen and that I had helped my dad in his construction business for years while growing up, because at the end of November, I was given a new collateral duty: officer in charge of construction. Since I had been relieved as admin officer by Nick Press earlier in the month, I was free to devote my energies to this major project. I enjoyed working with my hands and having a sense of purpose, so I eagerly jumped into my new job.

Assigned to the Naval Support Activity at Dong Tam was a senior chief petty officer in charge of the admin office by the name of John Williams. Senior Chief Williams, in addition to his official duties, was a *master cumshaw artist*. It seems that every military outfit has a person who is adept at coming up with needed equipment and supplies outside of normal channels. There are numerous names attached to this nefarious activity, like *moonlight requisition* and *grand theft*. No matter what the name, it was sometimes as important to mission accomplishment as those forces on the point of the spear.

Leaders of the various operating components on the naval base would give Senior Chief Williams lists of items they needed or desired. He would disappear for days at a time, venturing all over South Vietnam, in search of them. He never came back empty-handed. You want a .50 caliber machine gun—no problem. You want a Boston Whaler with a 150-horsepower outboard—when do you want it delivered? Williams was simply amazing.

One day, Holly casually told Williams it would be nice to have a jeep, in addition to our pickup truck. Two days later, a jeep showed up, that had obviously once been an Army vehicle, but now sported a grey paint job and a fictitious Navy serial number on the bumper. We stopped asking Williams where and how he acquired items because his standard reply was "Got it from a friend." He either had a lot of friends or a lot of enemies, probably both! As far as I know, he never got into any serious trouble for his snatch-and-grab missions.

To complete my assigned task, my first priority was to turn to Senior Chief Williams. Within a matter of days, he had located two used twenty-foot travel trailers that the Army wasn't using. How he got them or what he traded for them remains a Dong Tam secret. He even arranged for a large mobile crane and a low-boy trailer to transport them to the airfield and to set them up back-to-back on a section of PSP on a freshly graded site at the base of the airfield control tower and about three hundred feet from our helicopters.

My design was to build a post-and-beam structure to fully enclose the two trailers and an attached briefing room that would be strong enough to support a protective layer made from discarded wood boxes. The boxes, which measured approximately ten inches wide by ten inches high and four feet long, were used as shipping containers for the rockets fired by our helicopters. When filled with dirt and stacked two wide on the sides of the enclosure, and two on top, they provided good protection from mortar fire. The design also incorporated a large conex box to store spare parts for our weapons systems and other flammable materials.

The construction team consisted of the off-duty enlisted crew; I was the only officer who worked on the project. We worked four hours in the morning and three hours in the afternoon, seven days a week. I found out many years later that the majority of the enlisted guys did not share my enthusiasm for the project. At a Seawolf reunion held in Portland, Oregon, in 2012, several of them told me they hated the project, especially filling rocket boxes with dirt.

We built the supporting structure in just two days, but it took over three weeks to fill and stack hundreds of boxes. With the electrical power, air conditioning for each trailer, an operations radio setup in the officer's trailer, bunk beds for eight, and a large wall map for our briefing room, the project was completed and ready for use before the start of the Tet Offensive at the end of January 1968. The whole project took six weeks, start to finish, without costing the Navy a dime thanks to materials provided by the Army and Senior Chief Williams—and the sweat equity of our hardworking enlisted crew and myself. Not bad for a government project—the U.S. taxpayers should be proud.

Our redoubt must have reminded an Army soldier with too much time on his hands of a popular Western on TV in the 1960s called "Fort Apache," because one morning we discovered "Fort Apache" spray-painted in large black letters on the runway side of our bunker complex. There was some talk of retaliation by painting "Go Navy Beat Army" on a suitable façade on the Army side of the base, but that threat was never carried out. The first rule of combat survival: never antagonize an enemy who outnumbers you five hundred to one.

Bob Hope Show

Entertainment tours sponsored by the USO were few and far between, at least in the Delta. When actress Martha Raye visited Dong Tam as the headliner of a musical production of *Hello, Dolly*, I was only able to catch the last few minutes of the production due to a flight, but did hear her pep talk to the troops after the curtain call in which she told us not to worry about the peaceniks demonstrating back in the U.S.

The finished bunker complex with a fighting positon on top, Dong Tam airfield. January 1968

L-shaped revetment housing one of our gunships. Just to the right of the airfield control tower is our duty bunker complex.

The one celebrity who had a long history of entertaining the troops was Bob Hope. His first show was at March Field in California in May 1941, seven months before Pearl Harbor. He continued to perform throughout the war, in every theatre of operations, often joined by his good friend Bing Crosby.

In his book *The Home Front*, Bob Hope wrote about his first show at March Field: "We didn't realize that all the rules of comedy were going to be changed. We represented everything those new recruits didn't have: home cooking, mother, and soft roommates. Their real enemies, even after the war broke out, were never just Germans or the Japanese. The enemies were boredom, mud, officers, and abstinence. Any joke that touched those nerves was a sure thing."

The Korean War, in the early 1950s, saw Bob Hope once again making troops laugh to take their minds off the horror of combat, if only for a couple hours. When taken out of context, his one-liners were corny and anything but uproarious; however, when delivered to thousands of GIs far from home, they were sheer genius. The Vietnam War presented yet another opportunity for Bob Hope to work his magic, and I wanted to be a part of it.

By the end of the Korean War, Bob Hope's annual tour for the troops during December had evolved into the Bob Hope Christmas Show. Filmed excerpts from the various performances were combined into a primetime television special that aired every year to stateside audiences during the month of February.

The only performance in the Saigon area was held on Christmas Day 1967 at Bear Cat, a large Army base twenty miles east of Saigon. To limit the size of the audience at the popular show, each military unit was given a certain number of tickets. Det 6 was given five tickets, three for enlisted and two for officers. Nick Press and I were the only pilots who cared to make the long journey to see Bob Hope, so there was no need to draw names out of a hat. We convinced one of the duty crews into flying us to Saigon, which turned out to be the easiest part of the whole day. Next, we rode in the back of a deuce and a half Army truck on hard wooden bench seats to Bear Cat. Then, we waited in the hot sun for over two hours, on more hard seats, before the two-hour show began. It was more than worth the wait. When Bob Hope strolled onto the stage, wearing a short-sleeved shirt, a red baseball cap, and carrying a golf club in his left hand, the large crowd leaped to its feet and went berserk. Thousands of soldiers screamed, clapped, and whistled, with cameras everywhere trying to capture, per-haps for many, the most joyous moment of their Vietnam tour of duty. The tumultuous welcome for the sixty-four-year-old entertainer was well-deserved; he seemed to be enjoying it as much as we did.

Hope, of course, stole the show with rapid-fire jokes he read from large, hand-printed cue cards held up by staff members in the audience. He poked fun at every military foible and snafu known to man, and then some. He was fabulous.

His supporting cast, which included a bevy of beautiful women such as Raquel Welch and the reigning Miss World, sang, pranced, and danced across the stage to the delight of love-starved GIs. But it was "old ski nose" that everyone came to see, and he did not disappoint.

Our return trip to Dong Tam was just as arduous, but more tolerable since we had just witnessed American military history.

Chapter 10

Hot Re-Arm

THE TET OFFENSIVE WAS THE MOST SIGNIFICANT BATTLE OF THE Vietnam War, by any standard or measure, including: scope, length, audacity, tenacity, ferocity, number of troops involved, and number of casualties. It was also the turning point in the war, for two reasons: Tet marked, perhaps, the first time an enemy suffered a huge military defeat on the battlefield, while achieving victory in the war of public opinion. Long before the magnitude of the enemy's losses was known, the most respected journalist in America, Walter Cronkite, stated on the *CBS Evening News*, on February 27, 1968, that the war was lost and the only honorable way out was to negotiate a settlement. Although the Vietnam War would drag on for another five years, with successes and setbacks for American military forces, the overall trajectory of the war was cast by the Tet Offensive.

The NVA and the Viet Cong had been planning a major offensive for many months, as they moved men, weapons, equipment, and supplies into position to support coordinated attacks over the width and breadth of South Vietnam. The overly ambitious enemy campaign, which became known as the Tet Offensive because the principal fighting occurred around the Tet Lunar New Year, was actually a year-long military operation. It began with the so-called border battles in the fall of 1967, which were meant to draw U.S. forces into the border regions and away from the large cities. The countrywide assault, which began on January 30, 1968, and lasted into March 1968, was Phase I. More limited actions were the focus of Phases II and III, which were launched on May 5, 1968, and August 17, 1968, respectively.

The Tet Offensive also marked a significant change in enemy tactics. Instead of fighting for two or three hours with platoon or company-sized units to inflict maximum casualties and then melting away into the countryside, during Tet, the enemy attacked in force, using battalions and regiments with the objective to seize and hold cities and towns whatever the cost.

The failure to determine enemy intentions before the battle began was the most significant intelligence breakdown of the Vietnam War.

By February 5, 1968, the gigantic enemy onslaught had stalled and they were systematically beaten back on all fronts, while suffering huge casualties. But those first six days produced some desperate times for the South Vietnamese and American defenders.

Backs to the Wall

In October 1967, Hanoi announced that its forces would observe a seven-day truce beginning January 27, 1968, to observe and celebrate the Lunar New Year. It was intended to lull the South Vietnamese and American forces into letting their guard down. The North Vietnamese and Viet Cong had no intention of observing a ceasefire.

The South Vietnamese government and MACV responded that they would also observe the proposed truce. After all, there had been other ceasefires in the past that had worked reasonably well. The South Vietnamese military granted leave to one half of its soldiers during the ceasefire so they could go home to be with their families over the holidays. The stage was set for a shocking military campaign that would engulf over one hundred cities and towns throughout South Vietnam, including thirty-six of the forty-four provincial capital cities and involve nearly 85,000 enemy assault troops.

Seawolf crews from another detachment reported seeing enemy units marching openly toward their intended target cities after the ceasefire went into effect. They said it was spooky to see enemy soldiers carrying their AK-47s and waving Viet Cong flags. Everyone, it seemed, was in a holiday mood—although not all were going home to see their families.

The enemy offensive kicked off in the Dong Tam area in the early morning hours of January 31, 1968, with largescale simultaneous attacks on the provincial capitals of Ben Tre, My Tho, and Vinh Long. In after-action reports, the naval intelligence officer stationed in My Tho estimated the size of the enemy force that attacked his city to number around two thousand.

The Det 6 fire team on duty was scrambled at 0400 to help the beleaguered garrison at Ben Tre, just across the river from Dong Tam. The fire team returned to Dong Tam long enough to hot refuel and re-arm before returning to the raging battle in the center of the city. The situation was so desperate on the ground, the fire team did not shut down their helicopters for ten hours straight—and only stopped flying then because of bullet damage to both aircraft. At one point, a U.S. advisor on the ground pleaded over the radio saying, "If you don't return, I won't survive until daylight."

The volume of hostile fire directed at our helicopters was far more intense than anything previously experienced. In the past, the VC did not fire at gunships during the run into the target, but waited until the gunships were pulling off the target, which reduced their direct exposure to our concentrated firepower. During Tet, enemy fire was continuous throughout the attack run. Additionally, the VC were employing a much greater number of .51 caliber heavy machine guns. A hit from one of these fearsome weapons nearly killed the aircraft commander of our wing ship. Fortunately, the round hit a glancing blow on the pilot's sliding armor plate and was deflected upward, blowing out the plexiglass window directly above his head. To see the deformation and damage to the three-quarter-inch armor plate made all of us realize just how powerful this weapon really was and how lucky the pilot, Bill Lloyd, was to be alive.

After helping beat back the enemy attack on Ben Tre, the fire team shifted its focus to the heavy fighting in and around the city of My Tho, located three miles downriver from Dong Tam. This battle would last over two days.

The odd part of the hellish events that occurred on the first day of Tet was the fact that Dong Tam, the largest military base in the Delta, was not probed or even mortared. That would change in the days to come, however, when the base was hit by numerous recoilless rifle, rocket, and mortar rounds. The enemy never did mount a ground assault, probably because the base was too well defended.

Purple Heart

A significant milestone for me happened to coincide with the beginning of the Tet Offensive. It was the date I was designated a fire team leader—one of the first LTJGs in the squadron to be so qualified. I was proud of my achievement and eager to prove myself on the battlefield, although I had much to learn. Because of the intensity of the fighting in the early days of Tet, the more experienced fire team leaders took those missions and I filled in where needed. I would get my chance to lead later in February.

During my first mission briefing as fire team leader, I addressed an issue I had been thinking about for some time—what would I do if my wingman was shot down? I told the other crew that I would immediately jettison my rocket pods and throw excess ammo overboard to lighten the aircraft. Then, no matter what the odds or how much enemy fire, I would come in to pick them up. It was a decision that was already made, so there would be no hesitation on my part. We would either all get out alive or we would all die trying. It was as simple as that. I didn't realize how much that pep talk meant until the senior door gunner in the other helicopter, Petty Officer Second Class Bob Seaman, got me aside and told me how much he appreciated knowing that I would be coming for them, no matter what. His candid statement, in turn, made me feel good. I said a silent prayer that this plan of action would never have to be executed.

Although I was not scheduled to fly on the first day of Tet, I decided about mid-morning to go down to our scramble trailers to see if I could be of help to our tired flight crews. I ended up spending the rest of the day and that night there because I felt an officer should be on the scene to man the radio and coordinate the hectic pace of ground operations.

One of the first tasks I tackled was to install a second layer of wood boxes filled with dirt on the roof of the complex. I had been procrastinating doing this job, but given the scope and intensity of the enemy offensive, an extra layer would give additional peace of mind during the mortar attacks that would surely come as the struggle continued. With the help of a twenty-five-man working party from the Riverine squadron, we got the job done, and none too soon.

Apparently deciding that the Dong Tam airfield needed a wakeup call, the enemy detonated about twenty mortar rounds close to our position shortly after midnight. Even though I was fairly confident that the bunker and the recently reinforced roof would withstand a direct hit, I and other personnel who had gathered to escape the bombardment, were hugging the floor to keep a very low profile. The sound of mortars impacting that close was the most terrifying sound I had ever experienced. I can't imagine what it must be like to be on the receiving end of an artillery or mortar barrage and having no protection. (Battle-hardened infantry troops reading this are probably laughing or mocking me for being such a pansy.)

The next morning, I picked up about ten mortar fins that had landed within twenty feet of our bunker—one was two feet from the northeast corner (a war souvenir I retain to this day). Other than some obvious damage to the outer layer of wooded boxes, none of the shrapnel penetrated our inner sanctum.

During one of the mortar attacks that night, someone came running into our bunker to report than an Army pilot had just crashed his light observation airplane on landing and had veered off the runway near our bunker. As the only officer on the scene, I felt it was my duty to go out and help rescue the pilot from the wreckage. But I was paralyzed with fear. As much as I wanted to go, I could not bring myself to leave the safety of the bunker. In the air, I never flinched from doing my duty, no matter the danger or personal risk. But at this particular time, I was a coward. It deeply bothered me then and it bothers me to this day. Fortunately, others were up to the task and the pilot survived with minor injuries.

I finally got into the fight on the afternoon of February 1, 1968, as copilot for Lieutenant Commander Savage in the lead ship of the fire team. The fight for My Tho was still raging in the western half of the city. Over the past twenty-four hours, our fire team had returned time after time to deliver accurate rocket and machine-gun fire to help besieged friendly forces trying to dislodge a stubborn and determined foe.

While on the ground at Dong Tam to refuel and re-arm after a mission to the city, we received information that the Viet Cong had sailed a number of large covered sampans up a canal into the city in a bold move to withdraw some of their forces. We launched immediately to see if we could thwart those plans. Since this was my first flight since the offensive began, I witnessed the tremendous amount of fire enemy ground forces had been directing at our two helicopters over the past thirty-six hours. It was an eye-opener, the likes of which, I had not experienced before or after that harrowing day. I also saw the amount of devastation that had been heaped on the once beautiful Delta city by the vicious fighting. Scores and scores of whole city blocks were nothing but piles of rubble. It was reminiscent of newsreel footage that showed bombed out cities in Germany during World War II.

As we rolled into our first attack run, I opened up with the four M-60 machine guns under my control. I could see my bullets hitting sampans and the water around them. We bored in closer to the targets in front of us. All of a sudden, I had an unshakeable premonition that I was about to be hit. At that very moment, an enemy bullet with my name on it was on its way, traveling at 3,600 feet per second. It crashed through my windshield, missing my head by five inches, before lodging in the vertical bulkhead between the two door gunners. Pieces of glass shrapnel hit me in the neck and another fragment passed cleanly through the upper part of my right forearm. Seeing the blood on my arm and feeling it run down my neck, I announced "I'm hit" over the intercom. It must have looked worse than it was because Lieutenant Commander Savage broke off the attack and returned to Dong Tam where I was transported to the Surgical Hospital for treatment.

After the medical staff removed a couple pieces of glass from my neck and bandaged the wounds, I was released back to duty. I certainly didn't think I deserved a Purple Heart, but the medical staff filled out the required paperwork and the system cranked out the obligatory medal.

When asked, I told the attending nurse that I did not want next of kin (NOK) to be notified. Somehow, that got mixed up in message transmission and the Navy sent two uniformed naval officers to locate Barbara in

Alabama. When they called the house, my mother-in-law, Mrs. Lindsey, told them that Barbara was at work, at the bank in Fairhope. She immediately thought I had been killed; fortunately, the officers told her that I had not been killed, but would not divulge any further information. After they delivered the news to Barbara, at work, that I had been wounded, but not seriously, she was finally able to phone her anxious mother.

From the first of February until the middle of March 1968, Dong Tam was singled out for special treatment almost every night with two to three mortar attacks. Occasionally, the VC would add variety by sending in some rockets or recoilless rifle rounds. These nightly intrusions didn't kill or wound many troops, but they did play havoc with sleep. One day, the harassment began at 1600 in the afternoon and continued at two-hour intervals until the next morning. As a consequence, everyone on the base, including me, was always tired and grumpy. It got so bad that a few of us began sleeping in the bunker in back of our hooch. Aside from a damp, dank smell, it sure beat having to get up several times a night to dash to the bunker. I felt like Londoners who slept every night in underground subway stations during the Blitz.

There is one other memory of mortar attacks on Dong Tam that is worthy of note. As mentioned previously, our fire team would often scramble during an attack in an attempt to find the culprit. Our helicopters were

The hole in the windshield (top center) is where a bullet entered, narrowly missing my head and spraying me with glass shrapnel during the Tet Offensive. February 1, 1968

parked about one hundred yards from our bunker complex. Since we slept in our flight suits with our boots on, all we had to do at the sound of the first mortar round was get up and make a mad dash for our birds. I was never a fast runner. My father used to say that I ran too long in the same place. However, I surprised myself by just how fast a slow person can run with mortars dropping all around.

Three Nuns to Vinh Long

On the evening of February 2, 1968, as I was getting ready to take one of our birds to Vinh Long for some minor repairs, three Catholic nuns, clothed from head to toe in white habits, suddenly approached the helicopter. They appeared out of the darkness like an apparition from the edge of my consciousness. I had no idea where they had come from.

"The airfield commander told us that you were flying to Vinh Long. Do you have room to take us?" one of the sisters asked.

I hesitated, knowing the danger involved. "Sister, we have room to take you, but it will be a risky flight. The airfield up there is still surrounded by the VC with heavy fighting."

"We understand the risk, but we really need to get back to our orphanage. Our girls need help. We have received reports that the Viet Cong are using our campus to launch attacks on the airbase." She then explained that when the ceasefire was announced, the three of them had decided to travel to My Tho by water taxi to celebrate the holidays with friends.

"Hop in, sisters. I am sorry, but I am afraid your white habits are going to get a little dirty," I said.

"Occupational hazard," she laughed. "Thank you so much for your kindness."

As we flew upriver in the pitch-blackness created by an overcast sky, the glow from our flight instruments faintly illuminated our three passengers seated in the cabin. Aside from the whop, whop, whop from our rotors, our progress was quiet and orderly, with no hint of the inferno that awaited us.

Rounding the last bend in the river, we were immediately taken aback by the ferocity of the battle being waged for control of the base. Six Army helicopter gunships were continuously circling the perimeter of the airfield, pouring rocket and machine-gun fire into enemy forces in a desperate effort to drive them back. Green tracers rising from the ground crisscrossed the night sky, hoping to shoot down their American attackers. Mortar fire was impacting on both sides of the barbed wire, causing momentary brilliant flashes of red-white light. Illumination rounds were exploding all over the sky and parachute flares drifted slowly to earth, casting long shadows on the ghastly scene below. It was like watching a mammoth Fourth of July fireworks display.

I was beginning to wonder if we could safely fly through this gauntlet of fire. Maybe I should turn around and fly back to the relative security of Dong Tam. I called the tower.

"Vinh Long tower, this is Seawolf 62, five miles east for landing."

"Roger, Seawolf 62. Cleared to land."

That was it—"cleared to land"? Just like a normal, everyday transmission? Was he not looking out the windows of his tower? Did he not realize I might be a bit apprehensive about flying into this maelstrom? What about some extra guidance concerning the safest path to take? Nothing—just "cleared to land."

I wondered what our three passengers were thinking as we flew toward the light show up ahead. They were either resigned to their fate or they were making extra circuits on their rosary beads.

Timing my approach, I slid between two gunships patrolling the perimeter and landed uneventfully on the runway, and then hover taxied to the Seawolf parking ramp. After thanking us for the ride, the nuns disappeared into the night. I never learned how they and their girls fared.

As we waited for the repairs to be completed on our helicopter, we heard tales of death, close calls, and some of comic relief. Usually, a mortar barrage preceded the Viet Cong's attempt to overrun an outpost; however, last night was different. A sizeable force penetrated the perimeter first and then they mortared the base, thus hoping to solidify their gains before the defenders could respond. The airfield commander, a U.S. Army lieutenant colonel, was shot and killed in his jeep as he patrolled just inside the perimeter during this initial thrust. Before the battle was over, seven more Americans would be killed and eleven wounded.

The invaders succeeded in overrunning half of the airfield before they were driven back. Testimony to the heavy fighting was the mound of enemy bodies stacked ten feet high at one end of the runway.

One of the Seawolf mechanics was wearing his black beret with a bullet hole clean through the crown. He explained that he was in one of the perimeter defensive bunkers, visiting an Army buddy, when the enemy silently penetrated the barbed wire. He was lucky to escape with only a bullet hole to prove just how close he had come to being sent home in a body bag.

A Seawolf pilot from Det 3, Ensign Jim Martz, had been drinking in the O club and was not feeling any pain when word was passed that the VC had penetrated the perimeter. He ran to his hooch and grabbed his M-1 carbine and proceeded to the airfield to do what he could. He saw some shadowy figures dart into a revetment containing an Army Birddog observation airplane. Jim foolishly ran up to the entrance of the revetment and shouted, "Halt! Who goes there?" He had obviously been watching too many war movies. The enemy soldiers were not intimidated or amused by his brash command, and answered with a volley of bullets that hit Jim three times. He managed to duck out of the way and escape further injury. Luckily, the rounds passed completely through both arms without hitting any bone. When he returned after spending a month in Japan recuperating from his wounds, he was able to laugh at his stupidity and tremendous good fortune in not being killed. Besides, he had a good war story to tell his grandchildren.

Hasty Med-Evac

As the next three missions illustrate, the Tet Offensive was still very much ongoing during the middle of February, although not as intense as the first several days.

In the early afternoon of February 15, our detachment received an urgent request for assistance from the senior American advisor just across the river from Dong Tam. Arriving on the scene with my fire team, we found an RF company and four U.S. advisors pinned down in the middle of a rice paddy by heavy enemy fire coming from an adjacent tree line located about one hundred and fifty yards away.

I led three attack runs on the enemy positions. Climbing out after the first run, one of the advisors warned us over the radio that the VC were now directing all of their fire at our fire team. As usual, they were not leading us enough, so their rounds passed harmlessly behind us. After the third pass, the enemy stopped firing. Thinking we had silenced the enemy position, the friendly forces began to move forward toward the tree line.

The wily Viet Cong, however, were holding their fire and waiting. The advance had no more gotten underway when a fusillade of enemy bullets seriously wounded one of the advisors and a Vietnamese soldier. Due to the severity of their wounds, they asked if we could med-evac them to the hospital at Dong Tam. Most ground troops don't realize that gunships are so heavily loaded that it is dangerous, if not impossible, to safely perform a medical pickup. They think that all helicopters are created equal in that they can land and takeoff anywhere—which is mostly true. Landing is not the problem, takeoff is the issue.

Three negatives had to be considered: the extra weight of the two men, the close proximity of bad guys possessing lots of firepower, and the squadron SOP that stated gunships were not supposed to be used in this manner. As I was weighing all of this in my mind, a radio transmission made the decision for me.

"Seawolf 62, this is Lava Prize 32 Echo. My two guys are in real bad shape. Will you be able to help us? Over."

"Lava Prize 32 Echo, this is Seawolf 62. On my way. Over."

Okay, smart guy. You just committed to this risky move; now how are you going to pull it off? This was another time when I was amazed by how fast the human brain can process information and make decisions. In a flash, a plan came to me.

"Seawolf 68, this is Seawolf lead. I want you to time a low-level attack run directly into the enemy position just as I land to pick up the wounded."

"Roger, boss," Bill Lloyd in the wing ship radioed. "Let me know when you begin your landing approach."

The execution was flawless, the timing perfect. It unfolded as if we had practiced this maneuver countless times. Just as I touched down, Bill flew directly overhead, straight into the face of the enemy force, with rockets and machine guns blazing. In describing the action later, he said most of the enemy force, about twenty-five strong, had moved out of the protective cover of the trees into the open to get a better shot at me. They were so focused on my helicopter they didn't see Bill approaching from their left at high speed and twenty feet above the paddy until it was too late.

It must have been a frightening sight to see a helicopter gunship bearing down on them in their exposed positions. In an attempt to escape, two VC soldiers tried to climb a tree at the same time and got wedged in the crotch ten feet above the ground. We all had a good laugh afterward, as Bob Seaman described their desperate antics as he blasted them out of the tree with his M-60 machine gun.

The success that Bill and his crew achieved, was, of course, unknown to me as I made my approach right on top of the trees. I remember thinking I had to do a fast pickup and get the hell out of there before the Viet Cong had a chance to riddle our very exposed and vulnerable chopper. I came in at high speed and executed an abrupt side-flare just short of the friendly forces to kill off my speed. I landed with the tail facing the enemy position to provide as much aircraft structure as possible to absorb the onslaught I knew was coming. In less than a minute, we had the two wounded soldiers on board and we hightailed it out of there for the hospital at Dong Tam.

Not only did Bill's attack kill and wound a large number of the enemy force, but it allowed me to land unscathed. We found out the next day, that the U.S. advisor would have bled to death in the field had we not picked him up. That knowledge vindicated my decision to go against SOP. The rest of the fire team felt damned good too!

Turkey Shoot

Two days later, in the early morning, my fire team landed at the capital city of Go Cong Province to be briefed on an important airstrike the province chief wanted us to make on a canal system in the northwest corner of his province. The Viet Cong were using this canal network to move large quantities of men and equipment to support ongoing operations connected with the Tet Offensive. The briefing indicated some large vessels were being employed. To underscore the significance of this operation, one of the advisors flew as a passenger in my aircraft to observe the strike and to gain valuable intelligence on enemy movements.

When we arrived in the area, we could not believe what we saw: four very large, covered junks; ten large sampans; and numerous smaller craft traveling up the canal, more or less in single file. The junks were the largest watercraft I had seen in the Delta. It was a veritable enemy fleet and was indicative of how brazenly and openly the Viet Cong operated during Tet. These fat targets were a gunship pilot's dream.

To preserve the element of surprise and to increase the accuracy of our firepower, I decided to launch a low-level attack rather than rolling in from our normal high perch of eight hundred to one thousand feet, even though we would be more vulnerable to enemy counter-fire. I also knew, from experience, that we would only have one chance to inflict maximum damage. After the first attack run, the enemy would beach their watercraft on the shoreline, abandon ship, and disperse into the trees.

With my helicopter in the lead and my wingman following in trail, we commenced the attack run at two hundred feet above the canal. With so many large targets to shoot at, it was like Christmas in July. Damn, it was exhilarating! To keep from getting a bad case of "buck fever," I bored in on each large vessel until I could hardly miss before firing my rockets. It was gratifying to see my missiles find their mark, sending pieces of debris flying high into the air. The continuous chatter of our six machine guns added dramatic punctuation to the firing run.

In less than a minute, it was over. We had raked the entire enemy column from one end to the other with deadly results—over thirty enemy killed, many more wounded, one junk and four large sampans sunk, and numerous smaller sampans sunk or damaged. It was the most successful raid of my combat tour and it caused the VC to rethink the feasibility of operating in broad daylight on that particular canal.

Hold Your Fire

"If you see any sampans between the island and the coastline, you are cleared to take them under fire." Those words from the American advisor of Go Cong Province would soon create a moral dilemma for me as the leader of my fire team.

We were on a routine afternoon patrol of the lower My Tho River when we checked in with the American advisor in the area to see if he had any targets we could attack. He said that the Go Cong Province Chief wanted us to check out an area between the mainland and Son Tan Island, located about two miles out in the South China Sea.

We proceeded to the coordinates given; sure enough, there were about fifteen sampans in the area. Rather than immediately taking them under fire, I instructed my fire team that we would go down on the deck and check them out.

We descended to about twenty feet and flew over the little fleet, looking for suspicious activity. We did not see any evidence of weapons and no one fired at us. The only passengers in the small sampans were old men and young boys. There were no *eligible males*—those of fighting age—to be seen. We already had permission to engage them, but I just couldn't bring myself to issue the order to fire. The Province Chief may well have been right; perhaps they were Viet Cong. But they were helpless before our massed firepower. It would have been a slaughter.

I slept well that night and have never had any regrets about sparing their lives—even if they were enemy combatants.

Short Timer

March 1968 was a slow month. The NVA and Viet Cong were licking their wounds and trying to regroup after their big push and disastrous defeat in the Tet Offensive. I only flew twenty-four hours, the lowest monthly total of my Vietnam tour, including January when I went to Hawaii on R and R. The reduced tempo was a welcome relief from the hectic pace and round-the-clock flying the detachment experienced in February.

The first half of April, my last month in Det 6, fell into the predictable pattern of twenty-four hours on duty and twenty-fours off. What did change was my routine on the evenings of my days off. After dinner in the mess hall, I went over to the YRBM at about 1830 and played ping-pong until 2030. Then I watched the movie in the wardroom and returned to the base for a shower before hitting the sack. I enjoyed these evenings "aboard ship" because they made me feel like I was a part of the real Navy—besides the YRBM had air conditioning. Perhaps these leisurely evenings were subconsciously preparing me for return to a normal way of life back in the States.

As my career as a Navy gunship pilot was coming to a close, I was beginning to realize that maybe I wasn't immortal after all—that it doesn't always happen to the other guy.

In a letter to Barbara dated April 8, 1968, I wrote:

"Well, I figured out today that I have only 5 more flying duty days left. As the days get shorter, I get less and less eager to go out there and mix it up. As a matter of fact, I seem to be flinching a little lately on an attack. It makes me sort of mad too because I can't seem to help it. I get mad because it makes me feel like a coward. I never felt this way before and never worried about getting hit. But that is a natural reaction for just about everybody when it comes time to go home. But as I say, I only have 5 more days and my combat flying will be over, forever I hope! It was a good experience and one I will never forget and probably will oftentimes reminisce about, but one that I will never care to go through again."

As it turned out, I actually flew eight more days. On April 17, 1968, I flew my last combat flight while leading my fire team on an attack of an enemy bunker complex in Go Cong Province. As I shut down the engine of my trusty old friend for the last time, I had mixed emotions. On one hand, I felt profound relief that I had survived; and on the other, a twinge of sadness that a defining time in my life was over. However, the overriding feeling was one of immense pride in having flown 409 combat missions without losing a member of my crew or my fire team.

Clearing Vietnamese Airspace

There was a rumor going around that our CO, Commander Spencer, was trying to send everybody back to the States a few weeks earlier than their scheduled rotation date. Since the military seemed to run on rumors, I didn't place anymore faith in this one than all of the rest I had heard in Vietnam. So, I was pleasantly surprised when I was told to pack my bags and head to Vung Tàu at the end of April to check out of the squadron, even though I had a firm flight reservation departing Saigon on May 23.

I was officially detached from HA(L)-3 on May 1, 1968, and flew to Saigon in the hope of catching an earlier flight home on a standby basis. In my last letter to Barbara, I told her I would call her when I got back to the U.S. and to expect my call any time between May 2 and May 23—so much for the precision of military operations. Luckily, I caught a flight out on my first day on the standby list.

As I stood in line on the tarmac at Ton Son Nhut Air Base, waiting to board the military charter flight to Travis AFB in California, I remembered the article I had read in *Stars and Stripes* several months back that described a rocket attack that had killed two GIs at this very spot while waiting in line to board the plane to go home. I didn't dwell on that possibility because, after all, "it always happens to the other guy."

On the takeoff run, there was dead silence on board. Everyone was lost in his own thoughts—perhaps of buddies they had lost; possibly of the sights and sounds of bloody jungle firefights they would like to forget; or maybe even the good times, when laughter and camaraderie washed away the tears and fears. But, as soon as the large aircraft lifted into the air, the entire cabin erupted in thunderous applause.

"We made it! We were going home!"

Chapter 11

Epilogue to War

PILOGUES ARE TYPICALLY PLACED AT THE END OF A BOOK, TO BRING closure to the events that were discussed in the narrative. This memoir is no different in that regard, because there is an epilogue at the end; however, there is also an epilogue here, in the middle.

My return from war left many loose ends and unanswered questions; so many, in fact, I want to address them here, while the events are still fresh in your mind. Much of what I wrote for this chapter, concerning my attitudes, beliefs, and reflections, are the result of the clarity of thought that comes after fifty years of fermentation and distillation.

End of the Vietnam Nightmare

Spanning six presidencies, the United States sought to influence the political process in Indochina with the primary objective being the containment of Communism within the borders of China and the Soviet Union. Starting with a handful of military advisors introduced by President Harry S. Truman in 1950 and ending with the final evacuation of the U.S. Embassy staff in Saigon, ordered by President Gerald R. Ford on April 29, 1975, the American effort spread over a quarter of a century and yet, failed to stop South Vietnam from falling to North Vietnamese forces or to halt the spread of Communism in southeast Asia.

The military effort cost 58,267 Americans killed in action; another 10,789 lives lost due to non-hostile causes; and 153,303 wounded—the fourth highest casualty total in U.S. military history. It was a terrible price to pay in a losing effort, perhaps, even in a winning one. The Vietnam War so divided the country that the wounds to the national psyche are still raw and slow to heal, especially for those of my generation who either fought for the war in uniform or against the war as a protester.

I want to make one thing clear, though. The military did not lose the war. The politicians and civilian leadership, through a number of misguided policies, never implemented a viable plan to win and imposed ridiculous rules of engagement that hamstrung our military capability. I am a firm believer in the LeMay Doctrine proposed by General Curtis LeMay, which, roughly translated, says: "Once you commit to war, then use whatever means necessary to win the war as quickly as possible and, in doing so, you will save lives on both sides."

Case in point, immediately following my tour in Vietnam, I was talking with a Navy jet pilot who had flown missions over North Vietnam from aircraft carriers in the Tonkin Gulf. He was bitter about the conduct of the war. "I flew day after day over the port of Haiphong and looked down at many North Korean and Soviet bloc ships carrying all sorts of military equipment, but I could not attack them. Two days later, however, I risked my neck to take out just one truck on the Ho Chi Minh Trail."

However, in fairness to the leaders in Washington, the threat of China and the Soviet Union entering an expanded conflict, which could have led to World War III, influenced decisions and strategy.

The military, when unfettered by micro-managing from the White House and the Pentagon, won all major engagements with the enemy and inflicted disproportionate casualties. For example, during the Tet Offensive—which most Americans think we lost decisively due to the shock and awe of early media reporting during the first days of the offensive—the enemy suffered about 32,000 KIA and 5,800 captured; compared to the loss of 3,895American and 4,954 Vietnamese lives. However successful U.S. forces were on the battlefield, it did not change the trajectory of the conflict. During the Paris Peace Talks of 1973, a U.S. Army officer remarked to a member of the North Vietnamese delegation, "You know, you never beat us on the battlefield." Without pausing, the Vietnamese official replied, "This may be true, but it is irrelevant."

Vietnam veterans have every right to be proud of their service and their accomplishments. At the height of the evacuation of Saigon in April 1975, Secretary of Defense James R. Schlesinger sent the following message to members of the U.S. Armed Forces that eloquently addressed the military's contribution to the war effort in Southeast Asia:

> *As the last withdrawal of Americans from Vietnam takes place, it is my special responsibility to address to you, the men and women of our Armed Forces, a few words of appreciation on behalf of the American people.*
>
> *For many of you, the tragedy of Southeast Asia is more than a distant and abstract event. You have fought there; you have lost comrades there; you may feel that your efforts and sacrifices have gone for naught.*
>
> *That is not the case. When the passions have muted and the history is written, Americans will recall that their Armed Forces served them well. Under circumstances more difficult than ever before faced by our military*

services, you accomplished the mission assigned to you by higher authority. In combat you were victorious and you left the field with honor.

Though you have done all that was asked of you, it will be stated that the war was futile. In some sense, such may be said of any national effort that ultimately fails. Yet our involvement was not purposeless. It was intended to assist a small nation to preserve its independence in the face of external attack and to provide at least a reasonable chance to survive. That Vietnam succumbed to powerful external forces vitiates neither the explicit purpose behind our involvement nor the impulse of generosity toward those under attack that has long infused American policy.

Your record of duty performed under difficult conditions remains unmatched. I salute you for it. Beyond any question, you are entitled to the nation's respect, admiration, and gratitude.

Sadly, the last day of our nation's twenty-five-year involvement in Indochina touched me personally. Captain William C. Nystal, United States Marine Corps, was one of the last two Americans to die in Southeast Asia when their helicopter had to ditch in the South China Sea while participating in the evacuation of Saigon. Bill and I both worked in the admin office of HT-8 in 1971, when we were both flight instructors in the training command. He was a soft-spoken, gentle, and kind human being—almost the antithesis of the profile most people expect of a combat-hardened Marine. I was very distressed to hear of his death and to realize that I was indirectly connected to the last casualty of the Vietnam War.

The Seawolf Legacy

In the nearly six years of its existence, Helicopter Attack (Light) Squadron Three and its predecessor detachments from HC-1, better known as *the Seawolves*, chalked up a combat record that will be remembered as being one of the most remarkable in the history of the United States Navy. Approximately 2,800 officers and enlisted personnel served during the squadron's Vietnam years, including 714 pilots and 650 door gunners.

Some highlights of the squadron's distinguished combat record are: flew over 130,000 flight hours; killed 8,696 of the enemy, destroyed or damaged 8,737 enemy sampans; destroyed or damaged 9,489 enemy structures, and performed 1,530 medical evacuation flights.

The Seawolves are one of the most highly decorated flying units in United States military history. As such, the squadron was recognized by a resolution passed by the United States House of Representatives on June 29, 2010. Individual Seawolves received many high-level decorations for their valor and heroic actions as summarized in the table below.

I was awarded the Silver Star and the Vietnamese Cross of Gallantry for actions surrounding the rescue of a U.S. Army pilot and his high-ranking

Vietnamese passenger in October 1967. The Distinguished Flying Cross, Purple Heart, and Navy Commendation Medal were awarded to me for combat missions flown during the Tet Offensive. Air Medals were awarded on a point system depending on the type and number of missions flown.

Although I am proud of the decorations I received, I didn't do anything more extraordinary than any other Seawolf pilot would have done in similar circumstances. However, the glory reflected in the many decorations and accolades bestowed on the squadron and its personnel came at a high cost—44 killed and 156 wounded. During my tour, three pilots and four door gunners were killed, including my friends Jim Burke and Tom Gilliam.

Decoration	Squadron Total	The Author
Navy Cross	5	
Silver Star	31	1
Legion of Merit	2	
Distinguished Flying Cross	219	1
Purple Heart	156	1
Bronze Star	101	
Air Medal	16,000+	32
Vietnamese Cross of Gallantry	142	1
Navy Commendation Medal	439	1

Rescue in the Mekong

Since I did not get the names of the pilot and his VIP passenger when I rescued them in October 1967, and he did not have mine, that should have been the end of an unremarkable story. There were hundreds, if not thousands, of helicopter rescues made during the Vietnam War; and my rescue was by no means the most daring—perhaps the most stupid—certainly not the most heroic or dangerous. What happened forty years later, however, transformed a mediocre war story into a serendipitous happening worthy of retelling.

One blustery winter night in March 2007, I was sitting in my Northern Michigan home by the fireplace, thankful that I did not have to be outside in the cold and blowing snow. For some reason, my thoughts drifted to my combat tour in Vietnam. I remembered that some members of my old Vietnam squadron had started a website devoted to the Seawolves of HAL-3. I had not been on the website for a number of years and the nostalgia of the moment persuaded me to turn on my computer.

On the Seawolf homepage was a menu option titled "Mail Call," so I clicked on it. What I found was a large number of letters that had been sent to the association over the years. I began scrolling rapidly down the list, looking only at the first few lines of each entry, making a mental note that I would go back someday to read each one carefully, when I had more time. Suddenly, one letter caught my eye: "Army pilot looking for Navy helicopter pilot who rescued him in 1967." I stopped to read the letter, which had been posted eight years earlier, in 1999. As I slowly read each line, it began to dawn on me that I was the pilot this individual was searching for.

I cannot adequately describe in words the feeling that swept over me. I began to tremble slightly and tears welled in my eyes. For almost forty years, whenever I reflected on that 1967 rescue, the details remained clear and vivid, but I had no memory of his face and I never did know his name. The letter was signed Rick Roll—I now had a name. All I needed was a face to go along with it.

At the end of Rick's letter was a Chattanooga, Tennessee, address. I made a copy of his original letter and wrote the following in longhand at the bottom: "Rick, I believe that I am the Navy pilot you are looking for" and wrote my phone number down and asked him to give me a call. I dropped the letter in the mailbox the next morning. What I didn't know at the time was that Rick had moved from Chattanooga to Wilmington, Delaware, three years before. The man who bought his house was kind enough to forward my letter on to Rick, otherwise it would have been sent back.

I didn't hear anything for over a week; then, one evening while I was out of town on business, my wife, Barbara, received a call from Rick. In the course of their brief conversation, Rick asked what my adult beverage of choice was. My wife said, "Kendall Jackson Chardonnay." About a week later, a case of Kendall Jackson "Reserve" arrived on our doorstep. In the meantime, I had contacted Rick via phone and email and a friendship bloomed overnight that can only occur between comrades-in-arms who have been tempered by the same defining moment.

But I still didn't have a face. Rick had sent a dated photograph of himself wearing sunglasses, but it just wasn't good enough. Finally, a year later, Barbara and I traveled to Delaware for a tearful reunion with former Army Captain Rick Roll and his lovely wife, Pat. The Rolls pulled out all of the stops. They hosted a fabulous luncheon at their beautiful home so we could meet some of their relatives and close friends. They showed us the sights around Wilmington and treated us to a sumptuous dinner at a local eatery. They were most gracious and appreciative that I had saved Rick's life so many years ago. Their oldest son, Adam, weighed in by saying, "I wouldn't be alive if it were not for the efforts of Mr. Stock." Ever the jokester, Rick replied, "Yes, you would, but your last name would be Fecklinberg." It seems that Pat was dating a guy by that name when she met Rick.

Before leaving Delaware, I gave Rick my Seawolf drinking flag, which I had purchased in Vietnam. On it I wrote, "We share a bond that few will ever know." It seemed like a fitting end to an emotional reunion. Two old warriors whose paths had intersected for a second time—forty-one years later!

Two aging warriors reunited after forty-one years. Rick Roll, on the right, is holding the Seawolf drinking flag I presented to him to mark the occasion. April 2008

As a postscript to this story, I received emails from several of Rick's friends who had served with him in Vietnam, thanking me for rescuing their good friend. One of the emails and my reply sheds light on the bond felt between "Brothers-in-Arms," regardless of the color of their uniforms.

Mike,

I got your email address from an email that Rick sent to me. I wanted to personally thank you for saving Rick in Vietnam. He and I attended flight school together and ended up flying with the same unit in Nam, D Troop, 3/5 CAV, 9TH INF DIV. He's a great guy and a dear friend.

Sonny Kayser
Crusader 11

Hi, Sonny,

Thank you for your heartfelt email. You are the second of Rick's friends that has thanked me today. I sure do appreciate the thanks and the obvious deep affection that you feel for Rick. I am very thankful that I happened to be listening to Guard that day. The great part of being in

*the military, no matter what branch, is we all salute the same flag which
makes us brothers in arms. This bond, in turn, makes us risk everything
to save a fellow warrior. Lord knows that Army pilots rescued many a
Navy or Marine pilot or SEAL in Vietnam. It was a pleasure to do my
duty. Rick and you would have done exactly the same for me.*

*In fact, at one point in the tour our top echelon commander, a Navy
0-6 non-pilot, decreed that we Seawolves could not fly farther than one
click from a major river or canal in the Delta during a rescue attempt
because it would detract from our primary mission. Right! Did he suppose
that we were going to obey such an absurd order? All of us Seawolves felt
that he may just as well court-martial us right now. . . .*

Best regards,
Mike Stock

The Photograph

The reader will recall that Jim Burke and Tom Gilliam were the first
and second of my three friends in *the photograph* to die. Hal Guinn, the
third pilot in the frame, was seriously wounded, but survived his tour of
duty.

I lost track of Hal for a number of years after Vietnam, as our naval
careers diverged in different directions. In February 1975, at a gathering
of Navy helicopter pilots in Jacksonville, Florida, I ran across Hal. It was
so good to see him again, and we instantly picked up where we had left off
seven years earlier at his bedside in the hospital at Dong Tam. We talked
about our wives and families and our duty assignments during the inter-
vening years. Our conversation inevitably drifted back to Vietnam and
some of the memories we both shared.

At one point, I said to Hal, "I hope you are not superstitious because
I have a photograph of you, Jim Burke, and Tom Gilliam taken on the
tarmac at Can Tho, those guys are gone."

Hal flashed that warm smile of his and said, "Yes, I remember the occasion. But no, I am not superstitious."

Less than six months later, Hal Guinn was dead—killed on takeoff
from a Navy frigate. His copilot was making the takeoff and allowed the
helicopter to drift into the ship's superstructure, causing the aircraft to
crash into the water alongside the ship. The copilot and crew chief were
able to get out of the submerged wreckage. Hal, for whatever reason, was
unable to escape and drowned.

I was stunned and deeply saddened by the news. I wrote a letter to his
widow, in which I closed by saying: "As sincere as I can be, Hal was probably the finest gentleman that I have ever had the privilege of knowing, a
truly super person!"

My three comrades are all dead. If you look closely, you can see my shadow (bottom left) as I took this photograph. Someday, in the not too distant future, the shadow will be gone as well.

Not only had I lost a good friend, but now everyone in *the photograph* was dead. I am the last remaining link to that image. Two serendipitous incidents further connected me to the photo and reminded me of my own mortality. When I learned more of the details of Hal's death, I was shocked to hear that his copilot on the day he was killed was Tim Stone, who had been my fuels officer two years earlier, when I was the air officer on the *USS Raleigh*.

And an even more bizarre connection occurred during my last Navy cruise aboard the *USS Aylwin* (FF-1081) in 1978. As I was checking into my stateroom, which I shared with the supply officer, I noticed that my safe had been opened with a cutting torch and re-welded. I pointed to my safe and asked my new roommate, "What happened here?"

"Oh, that was Hal Guinn's safe. They had to break into it after he was killed taking off from the ship back in 1975," he replied.

I am not a superstitious person, but with the many helicopter-capable ships in the U.S. Navy, what are the odds of my being assigned to Hal's ship and stateroom, and given his old safe? It was an eerie feeling.

A Lingering Sense of Guilt

Because my war memories have been allowed to ferment for fifty-one years, it has given me a more balanced and healthier perspective on one event that had been deeply troubling for years. It involved a decision I made as fire team leader in the waning months of my Vietnam tour.

One day, my fire team was called to assist some RF troops and their American advisors who were engaged in a heavy firefight with the Viet Cong. When we arrived on scene, the exact location of the friendly and enemy forces could not be readily determined due to heavy vegetation and palm trees. Obviously, we could not commence an attack until we pinpointed the exact location of the friendlies, so I asked them to activate a colored smoke grenade at the end of each flank. Over the radio, the American advisor said, "Popping yellow smokes" and soon, two yellow smoke columns billowed up through the trees.

Great, now we know where the friendlies are, I thought to myself. To my dismay, however, two more yellow smoke columns began to rise in close proximity to the first two. The clever enemy, known to sometimes listen in on tactical frequencies, had thwarted our attempts to pinpoint the RF troops by launching their own yellow smoke. We were right back to square one. The American advisor attempted to give us his location relative to some ground features that were indiscernible from the air. The situation was becoming more confusing by the minute. I frankly had lost situational awareness—I felt like a failure.

Rather than risk hitting friendly forces, I left the field of battle in their hour of need and took the fire team back to Dong Tam. This utter failure on my part to grasp the tactical situation on the ground and then my decision to abandon friendly forces who were calling for help, rocked me to my very core. Aside from having to identify Tom's body, it was my lowest point in Vietnam. I have lived with profound guilt all of these years.

It wasn't until January 2010, as I was reading Jon Krakauer's book about Pat Tillman, *Where Men Win Glory*, that I was finally able to find closure. In the book, Krakauer relates an incident that occurred during the battle of Nasiriyah, during the early days of the Iraq War, when two Air Force A-10 Warthogs mistakenly fired on U.S. Marines and killed ten. Krakauer wrote about the subsequent guilt felt by the pilots.

In reading about the horrific loss of life in that friendly-fire accident, I realized that it was okay that I left the scene of the battle rather than have to live with the realization that I had killed friendly forces. I was finally able to let it go—my conscience was finally free!

A Worthy Adversary

During in-country briefings for new arrivals to Vietnam, I was given a pocket-sized booklet titled: *Handbook for U.S. Forces in Vietnam*. In it was a short paragraph that summarized the enemy we would be facing:

"The VC is an elusive and determined foe. He is well organized politically and militarily, and employs both conventional and guerrilla tactics. He is an expert in the arts of camouflage, deception, and ambush. He is a hardy and ruthless fighter ..."

When I received this summary on my second day in Vietnam, it held little meaning to a newbie still suffering from jet lag and trying his best to adapt to new sights and sounds. After completing my combat tour of duty, however, I found this official military synopsis to be right on the money and reflective of my experience.

I had witnessed firsthand how the Viet Cong could quickly hide a large sampan in a narrow canal by cutting down trees along the bank. Flying during the early days of the Tet Offensive, I can personally vouch for their ferocity and determination in pressing the attack. On other occasions, I watched from overhead as the enemy launched attacks on superior American forces despite underwhelming odds of success.

The United States didn't understand the enemy: why they were fighting and what they were fighting for. We could inflict great suffering on the enemy, but not change their willingness to accept any amount of casualties or damage to infrastructure in order to achieve their ultimate objective of reunifying the North and the South. The disposition of the North Vietnamese government to pay any human cost to defeat the U.S. is borne out by their staggering losses: two million soldiers killed; six million wounded; 300,000 missing; and 150,000 civilians killed and many times that number wounded.

Even though the VC and North Vietnamese forces sustained casualty rates over twenty times higher than the United States, what they accomplished on the battlefield was worthy of grudging respect. In South Vietnam, the enemy had no airpower whatsoever—no helicopters to quickly move troops around or to med-evac wounded soldiers from the field, no transport aircraft to move cargo and equipment, no attack aircraft to support their advances, and no large bombers to lay waste to everything below. They did not have access to sophisticated, high-technology weapons, like smart bombs and cluster munitions. In fact, in the Delta area, they generally lacked conventional weapons like heavy artillery, heavy machine guns, and AAA sites. The enemy did not have a robust logistical operation backed by a large military-industrial complex. What the enemy did have in ample abundance was the will to win at any costs, an ability to endure incredible hardships, and lots of patience—none of which were strong suits in the American arsenal. The Viet Cong and NVA were relentless and formidable antagonists—I am thankful to have survived the encounter.

Reflections and Feelings

My war mementoes lie in an old cardboard box in the attic: a fin from an enemy mortar round that impacted two feet from my bunker during Tet, two smashed bullets that passed through the cockpit narrowly missing me, a captured VC flag, a leather holster used to carry my .45 caliber pistol, a rubberized escape and evasion map of South Vietnam, my olive-drab flight helmet on which I had painted "Hired Gun," a tactical map of the Delta I used on all of my combat missions—all grim reminders of an exciting period of my life when I was incredibly lucky and naïve.

As I mentioned earlier, I volunteered for Vietnam not out of patriotism but because I wanted excitement and adventure. I got plenty of both. The following two quotes aptly summarize the thrill of war.

> In the book *Ernie Pyle's War* by James Tobin, the author quotes Ernie Pyle: "… war is not romantic when you're in the midst of it. Nothing has happened to change my feelings about that. But I have to admit there is an exhilaration in its inner excitement that builds up into a buoyant tenseness which is seldom achieved in peacetime."

> In an article titled "Building Marines Hollywood Style," published in the April 2010 issue of *Naval History* magazine, the author Captain Dale Dye, USMC (Ret.) states: "It is a given that war is hell, but it's combat—where a skilled enemy is just as anxious to kill you as you are to reciprocate—that makes it such a seminal experience."

When discussing my Vietnam experiences with people who have not served in combat, I have often said: "Provided you don't come home in a body bag or are permanently maimed in some way, war is the ultimate human experience." Since I returned home with all of my parts, and didn't witness firsthand any of my buddies being blown to bits, my war was like a glorified Hollywood movie where John Wayne or Gregory Peck vanquish the enemy against insurmountable odds and return home unscathed to the arms of a beautiful woman.

Although I had plenty of hair-raising moments in Vietnam, Tom's death was the only time I came close to losing my grip on reality. How the foot soldiers who witness blood and gore and the loss of their buddies on a daily basis manage to cope I do not know. For many the nightmares surface only after they return home. Their wounds are as severe, if not worse, than those who have been seriously wounded in a physical sense. Fifty-one years after Tom's death, I speak as a father who is watching his youngest daughter struggle mightily with PTSD from her four combat tours in Iraq and Afghanistan. I was extremely fortunate to only have a twenty-four case of PTSD with no lingering after effects aside from profound sadness at Tom's untimely passing.

Despite a few low points and the year-long separation from Barbara, my Vietnam tour was satisfying, even fun at times. I believed in the war, at least in my limited sphere of influence, and I did my job to the best of my ability, which included killing as many of the enemy as possible. I was okay with that at the time because that is, after all, the underlying objective of all wars. Today, I very much regret that admission.

However, I was very thankful I did not actually see an enemy soldier fall before my guns or rockets. We received confirmation of kills from friendly ground forces from time to time; so I knew I was responsible for taking human lives, but I was spared the graphic horror of watching the moment of dispatch.

Renowned photojournalist, Kevin Sites, who has spent most of his career covering wars, had this to say about the act of killing:

> "Killing turns everything on its head. Watching people being killed, especially those you know, is a memory that can't be erased. But actually doing the killing or being complicit in it is a lifelong sentence to contemplate the nature of one's own character, endlessly asking 'Am I good, or am I evil?' And slowly going mad at the equivocation of this trick question whose answer is definitely yes."

My decision to not annihilate those defenseless old men and young boys bobbing in their sampans in the South China Sea saved not only their lives, but mine as well. If I had given the order to fire and had witnessed the bloody aftermath, I would have been condemned to live a life filled with guilt, sorrow, and the loss of my humanity; what some behavioral scientists call *moral injury*—when we perform inhumane acts that go against our moral and ethical upbringing. Perhaps that decision is another reason why I did not suffer from PTSD after returning from Southeast Asia. I was one of the lucky ones.

For years after returning from Vietnam, and certainly during the remainder of my military career, I was a conservative Republican in my politics and thinking about the justification for war. I supported President George W. Bush's decision and rationale for invading Iraq in 2003. After no weapons of mass destruction were found and the whole raison d'etre unraveled, my support for wars of liberation and war in general began to wane. My transformation from a war hawk to quasi-pacifist was hastened by watching our youngest daughter, Julie, a career Army officer, suffer through three, long deployments to Iraq and one to Afghanistan that left her with crippling PTSD and a medical discharge. I say "quasi-pacifist" because I still believe that certain military actions are justified and required. World War II is an example.

Because I did not suffer mentally and emotionally from my tour in Vietnam, initially, I thought those veterans who did were weak human beings and would have had to deal with those same issues whether they had gone to Vietnam or not. For years I was unsympathetic. How wrong I was. I now feel profound guilt for my calloused dismissal of their suffering. How could I have been so smug and disrespectful, to think that I could have weathered their combat experiences and not been similarly affected? *One day* in the life of a ground soldier on patrol in the steamy jungles—filled with enemy ambushes; incoming artillery, rocket, and mortar rounds; impenetrable vines; deadly snakes, leeches, and hordes of mosquitoes; and constant misery, exhaustion, and death—was more than I had to face in *an entire year*.

As I began to adjust my feelings on unnecessary wars, like the Iraq War, I also reflected back on Vietnam. We fought Ho Chi Minh for being a patriot and trying to unify his country that had been partitioned by colonial powers. It would be the same as a foreign country landing troops on U.S. soil during our Civil War to stop President Lincoln from keeping our Union together. How would Americans react today if an Arab nation invaded the United States for the purpose of establishing an Islamist theocracy in order to save us from "the evils of democracy"? Yet, that is exactly what we did in Vietnam. Who is to say that our form of government and the American way of life is what all other people in the world long for or should have?

I will always remember what a U.S. Army Captain and advisor told me one day when I visited his headquarters:

> "We Americans come over here and we are appalled that most public buildings have no indoor plumbing. So, we install urinals in the men's bathroom. And what do you think they do? They plant flowers in them!"

One day, when I was waiting at the Saigon heliport hoping to catch a ride back to Dong Tam, I sat in the shade of a small building, watching a slick approach and land off to the side of the pad about fifty yards away. Two waiting soldiers approached the right side of the helicopter and opened the big cargo door in the back. Assisted by the crew chief inside, the two men began tugging on a large, green sack. As they maneuvered it to the edge of the door, one got on each end and carried it twenty feet, put it down, and went back for another. As they were carrying the second sack, I realized that they were body bags—I had never seen one before, let alone with a body inside. The two soldiers off-loaded eight dead warriors from that helicopter, and eight from the next one that landed. After the second chopper took off, the two soldiers stripped down to their Army-issued T-shirts and mopped their brows with a dirty towel—it was a hot day and there was more work to be done.

I watched as three more helicopters followed the first two to disgorge their precious cargo. There were no waiting dignitaries to render a hand-salute, no band playing a funeral dirge, no Honor Guard carrying the American flag to welcome these lads from the field of battle and to thank them for their sacrifice for our nation—just two sweaty soldiers from the Graves Registration unit doing their job.

For me, it was a sobering and sad occasion. It was an opportunity to reflect on the real cost of war and the very real possibility that I could end up in one of those bags. But I did not seize the moment, because I was still clinging to the mantra that it won't happen to me. I missed the incongruity that most likely all of those dead soldiers, up to the last nanosecond of their lives, also believed it wasn't going to happen to them.

Perhaps my final realization of the futility of war and the Vietnam War in particular occurred in June 2010, as I sat alone watching a two-hour National Geographic documentary titled *Inside the Vietnam War*. The excellent production showed graphic footage of death and destruction and included many interviews of veterans who lost buddies and feared for their own lives. It recounted many battles where a piece of real estate was taken or held at great cost, only to be abandoned soon after. Places like Hill 881, Hamburger Hill, Firebase Ripcord, Khe Son, and forays into Cambodia. Ultimately, after 58,000 American, scores of Australian and South Korean, and nearly four million Vietnamese lives on both sides were taken, we abandoned the entire country.

Upon conclusion of the documentary, I sat in the darkness of my living room in stunned silence for thirty minutes. It finally dawned on me what a waste most wars are—and the Vietnam War in particular. It took me forty-five years to reach that conclusion.

Although I had always felt that Vietnam didn't leave me with any lasting scars—no flashbacks, nightmares, or personal recriminations—as I sat there, I realized I did have some baggage left over from my combat service: the glorification and over-simplification of war.

Chapter 12

Muddy Wheels

As I topped a small rise, I saw a vehicle in front of me that looked like it might be a police car. For the past several hours, the speedometer on my Chevy station wagon had settled in nicely at eighty-four. The roads in southern New Mexico were straight and the traffic was light, so I felt comfortable in pushing the seventy-mile-per-hour speed limit as we headed west toward my new duty station in San Diego.

Sure enough, it was a state trooper just poking along below the speed limit. I slowed down well before I overtook his vehicle and kept it just slightly under seventy until he was out of sight in my rearview mirror; then I bumped it back up to eighty-four.

About twenty minutes later, I noticed a car behind me, traveling at a high rate of speed. It reminded me of the epic desert chases between the Road Runner and Wile E. Coyote, when they each trailed a cloud of dust behind them. I didn't know who it was, but I figured I had better slow to the speed limit, just in case.

Much to my surprise, the same trooper I had passed earlier was now behind me with his lights flashing. I pulled over. After checking my license and registration, he solemnly informed me that he had clocked me driving eighty-four. Impossible—I was doing the speed limit when I was within his line of sight and radar range. I was flabbergasted that he had nailed my speed; so I asked, "Officer, how did you do that?"

"You looked like a speeder when you passed me, so I started my stopwatch and noted the distance on my odometer. When I caught up to you, I used simple math—speed equals distance divided by time."

I must have given him a look of grudging admiration for being an adversary who had outwitted me because he only gave me a warning to "Slow it down."

Stateside Assignment

Even before receiving my wings, I had tentatively decided that I wanted to be a commercial airline pilot after completing my obligated service to the Navy. In addition to satisfying my passion for flying, I did everything I could do in Lakehurst to build flight time to enhance my prospects with the airlines. After returning from overseas, I wanted to continue accumulating hours as fast as possible.

About halfway through my Vietnam tour, it was time for the Navy to decide where to assign me for the few remaining months of active service. I was not in a good position to be re-assigned to squadron duty because I had less than one year left and nobody wanted a short-timer. But, after several letters back and forth with my detailer (the officer responsible for new duty assignments) in Washington, D.C., and my agreement to extend on active duty for several months, I landed my dream job: a one-year tour in VRF-32, a ferry squadron based at Naval Air Station North Island in San Diego, California. As a junior officer in a ferry squadron, my job would be to fly a variety of aircraft all over the country—fat logbook, here I come!

Anatomy of a Ferry Squadron

When I reported to VRF-32 in June 1968, the Navy had two ferry squadrons: VRF-32 in San Diego and VRF-31 in Norfolk, Virginia. Whenever the custody of a Navy or Marine Corps aircraft was being transferred from one squadron or installation to another, one of the two ferry squadrons provided pilots and crew to fly the aircraft from one geographical location to the next. In certain circumstances, regular Navy and Marine crews were assigned to fly the mission, but only if the ferry squadrons decided not to do it.

Some examples of ferry missions were: squadron to squadron, squadron to overhaul facility and return, new aircraft from manufacturer to squadron, squadron to the *boneyard* (a long-term desert storage facility at Davis-Monthan Air Force Base in Tucson, Arizona), boneyard back to a squadron, naval or Marine Corps air station to another air station, etc.

The world was split in half along the meridian that passed through Dallas, Texas. Any aircraft movement originating to the east of Dallas was controlled by VRF-31 and to the west by VRF-32. Although most aircraft deliveries occurred within the lower forty-eight states, flights were made to Alaska, Hawaii, and anywhere in the free world. The ferry squadrons truly had a global reach.

Once a ferry crew flew into the jurisdiction of the other squadron, it was "owned" by that squadron and could be assigned deliveries wholly within that squadron's territory. For example, if a West Coast crew flew an aircraft to Quonset Point, Rhode Island, once the aircraft was delivered, the flight scheduler at VFR-31 in Norfolk could assign a new delivery from Miami to Minneapolis. However, the two squadrons did not abuse this "slave-labor clause" and tried their best to get you headed back to your home territory as soon as possible. The longest crews were away from their home base was about three weeks, but the norm was seven to ten days on the road.

VRF-32 was not a typical Navy squadron in terms of the number of officers and enlisted personnel assigned. It was top heavy in terms of officer rank: one captain, six commanders, fifteen lieutenant commanders, thirty-two lieutenants, and only three lieutenant junior grades. I was one of the lieutenants after I was promoted on July 1, 1968.

The commanding officer was Captain Hugh J. Tate and the executive officer was Commander Dean S. Laird. Both were decorated World War II fighter pilots, with Laird being a double ace credited with ten aerial victories: two German and eight Japanese. They were congenial gentlemen who still loved to fly.

Enlisted personnel numbered just over one hundred, which was about one quarter the number assigned to a normal squadron due to absence of an aircraft maintenance department.

Ferry duty was not considered career enhancing, so the squadron was populated by those whose naval careers had peaked or those who were close to retirement or separation from active duty, like me. But, if you enjoyed to fly unencumbered by the normal bureaucratic paperwork and politics of squadron life, this was the place to be—I couldn't wait to get started!

Introduction to Life on the Road

Because ferry squadrons moved every model of aircraft in the Navy and Marine Corps inventory, both active and reserve, the more types of aircraft an individual was qualified to fly the more valuable he was to the officer responsible for writing the daily flight schedule. So, the Training Department set about re-qualifying me in aircraft I had flown in the past and added a few I had never flown.

My first flight was to re-qualify in the T-28, which I had flown in the training command prior to receiving my wings. It turned out to also be a lesson in desert heat.

To escape the busy air traffic in the San Diego area, my instructor pilot directed me to fly across the mountains to the Naval Air Facility at El Centro, California, which is located in the Imperial Valley due east of San Diego. On this June day, the temperature on the ground at El Centro was

112°F. After completing a series of touch-and-go landings, the instructor told me to exit the runway and taxi to the ramp so we could take a break. As we always did in Pensacola, as soon as I was clear of the runway, I opened the canopy. I expected to feel the rush of cool air delivered by the big prop into the hot cockpit—instead I felt a blast of hot air as if I had just opened the door to a wood-burning stove. My instructor suggested that I close the canopy. It was cooler with the canopy closed, but cool is a relative term in the summer desert.

In the coming days, I quickly re-qualified in the H-2 and H-34 helicopters and the T-34 and C-45 fixed-wing aircraft. I was already current in the Huey, so I was off to a good start with six qualifications or quals under my belt. Before many months had passed, I added five aircraft that I had never flown before: two helicopters, the H-3 and H-53; and three multi-engine fixed-wing airplanes, the C-1 and two different models of the S-2—bringing my total quals to eleven. This was a respectable number, especially for a first-tour aviator.

I also requested a jet transition so that I could ferry jet aircraft as well. In the best tradition of military generosity, the Navy said, "Do we have a deal for you. If you agree to extend your active duty commitment an additional ten months, we will check you out in the Gruman F-9F Panther jet." I said, "No thank you." Delaying my airline career was not worth the chance to fly the legendary Korean War fighter.

In addition, I was occasionally assigned to fly copilot in an aircraft that required two pilots even though I had never set foot in the cockpit. I flew the C-130, P-3, C-118, and C-54. Essentially, I was a warm body who had been warned: "Don't touch anything—the plane commander and the flight engineer will handle all flight duties."

Throughout my flying career I have always enjoyed flying different aircraft and I think the ferry squadron was where that preference germinated. For example, during the month of September 1968, I flew the C-117, C-45, C-130, T-34, T-28, H-34, and S-2 aircraft, while accumulating 85 flight hours.

There was, however, a downside to having so many quals—and that was the vast amount of flight-related gear I had to carry on every ferry trip. When I left my home base in San Diego, the only thing I knew for certain was I would be flying a specific aircraft from point A to point B. After completing that delivery, I could be assigned to fly any aircraft in which I was qualified. Therefore, I had to carry all of the flight paraphernalia necessary to fly eleven different models of aircraft. In two large parachute bags, I carried the following items: eleven NATOPS manuals (similar to owner's manuals); eleven pocket checklists; two flight helmets; two flight suits; flight gloves; a variety of headset cords, adaptors, and microphones; a backpack parachute; low altitude IFR and VFR charts for the lower forty-eight states; and various types of survival equipment. Each parachute bag was jammed full and weighed seventy-five pounds. Additionally, I carried a travel bag containing enough personal clothing for three weeks, including a sport coat and tie used when flying on a commercial airline. I didn't need to work out in a gym. Just lugging all of that gear gave me arms like a gorilla's.

After completing my aircraft checkouts, the last step before becoming a fully qualified ferry pilot was to learn the *road procedures*, which primarily pertained to the paperwork and message traffic concurrent with the receipt of an aircraft from the transferring unit and delivery to the receiving squadron, station, or other facility. To prevent the temptation of a transferring unit to strip an aircraft of usable parts and equipment prior to arrival of the ferry pilot, we were backed up by the authority of a three-star admiral. So, if an aircraft had been stripped, or wasn't safe to fly or ready to fly when we arrived, we had the authority to send out a "nastygram" to their chain-of-command putting them on report. Consequently, everyone was fairly cooperative and eager to help us.

For my first road trip, I was assigned to fly with Lieutenant Roger Hulson, who would teach me the ropes. We picked up an H-2 helicopter at Naval Air Station Lemoore and flew it to the Kaman factory (the manufacturer of the H-2) at Windsor Locks, Connecticut. Not only was this my first road trip, but it was coast to coast—the longest cross-country flight of my naval career.

Roger was a great teacher and an easy-going, fun guy to travel with. On our second day, as we sat in the cockpit prior to starting the engine, he leaned toward me and said in a conspiratorial tone, "You do know the abbreviated engine-start checklist used by ferry pilots?"

"No, what is it?" I asked innocently.

"Testicles, spectacles, wallet, and watch," he said with a sly smile on his face as he watched for my reaction.

It sounded silly, but I had to admit that it had a nice ring to it—like a song you can't get out of your head. *Testicles, spectacles, wallet, and watch.*

Another mantra Roger passed on was: "If you can start it, you can fly it." This bit of wisdom proved more prophetic than useful. When you haven't flown an aircraft for nine months, getting it started could be a challenge. In my case, the C-1 and the S-2 were similar multi-engine aircraft made by Grumman and with almost identical cockpits, with one notable exception—the location of the magneto switches. One day, I climbed into a C-1 and spent what seemed like minutes trying to find the mag switch as a fire guard stood impatiently in front of the aircraft waiting for me to start the engines. I could imagine what was going through his mind—"He is going to fly this aircraft one thousand miles and he doesn't even know where the mag switch is."

Despite the fact that ferry pilots had numerous aircraft quals and sometimes had an alarming lack of recent flight experience in a particular aircraft, the safety record of both ferry squadrons was excellent. The primary reason for this superior record was that aircraft being ferried were only flown on relatively easy, cross-country flights and not flown on tactical missions. Although ferry pilots were authorized to fly under instrument flight rules (IFR) conditions, they were not required to push the weather, and didn't.

Across the Country at Five Hundred Feet

When the daily flight schedule was posted the night before, each pilot on the list wanted to know four things: type of aircraft, where it was located, where it was going, and what mode of transportation would be used to get him to the departure point. I was always excited to find out which aircraft I would be flying—I felt like a kid on Christmas morning.

When a ferry pilot began a road trip from San Diego, three means could be used to connect the pilot with his aircraft: fly as a passenger in another ferry aircraft, fly on a commercial airline, or the aircraft might be located right here in San Diego on the NAS North Island transient line.

All of the aircraft I was qualified to ferry required only one pilot, except for the H-3, which required two rated helicopter pilots. So, most of the time, I flew with an enlisted crew chief, which was nice because I did not have to share flight time with another pilot or have to deal with personality conflicts—I was my own boss.

Most of the enlisted crew chiefs had lots of ferry experience and functioned as copilots, in addition to handling daily inspections and other minor maintenance issues that might arise. One of the crew chiefs I often flew with in helicopters was Petty Officer second class Don Schultz. He had been in VRF-32 for over twelve years. In terms of basic helicopter flying, he was almost as good as any helicopter pilot, even though he had no formal training. I regularly let Schultz do some of the flying, including takeoff and landing.

One day while flying over the Arizona desert in the summer, in an H-34 with cockpit temperatures over 120°F, and the doors wide open, I began to nod off. Try as I might, I could not fight falling asleep. I reached the point where I could either land in the desert and take a short nap or give the controls to Schultz and take a snooze.

"Schultz, I can't stay awake any longer. Do you think you can keep this machine safely in the air while I take a short nap?"

"Yes, sir. No problem"

"Okay, you've got it."

I had complete faith that he could keep us from crashing into the desert. I awoke fifteen minutes later, refreshed and ready to tackle more of the endless cactus-covered landscape.

Another skill that Schultz had in abundance was his uncanny ability to read a sectional chart. We could be in the middle of nowhere, with nary a landmark in sight, and if I asked, "Schultz, where are we?" he would invariably pause for a second and then jab his right forefinger to our exact location. This was a handy skill flying at five hundred feet above the ground, where we were often below the altitude to receive navigational radio signals.

Since most helicopters had approximately a two-hour fuel range, coupled with the requirement to use military or contract fuel sources as much as possible, the refueling stops when flying across the country fell into a monotonous routine. Starting in San Diego heading east, the refueling stops in geographical order were: Davis Monthan AFB in Tucson; El Paso and Midland, Texas; Dyess Air Force Base near Abilene, Texas; and then on to Barksdale Air Force Base in Shreveport, Louisiana. From there, many routes were available depending on the delivery location.

I flew across the U.S., coast-to-coast, twenty-nine times during my year in VFR-32. I knew it by heart. In fact, I could fly from San Diego to Shreveport without using a chart. This was good in the sense that navigation was a no-brainer, but boring in terms of new scenery. On the other hand, though, how many helicopter pilots have ever had the chance to fly across the United States? I was grateful for the opportunity.

Because of Midland's location about halfway between Forth Worth and El Paso and the contract it had with the federal government to sell fuel to transient military aircraft, a military helicopter flying east or west, had little choice but to land in Midland for fuel. The Fixed Base Operator (FBO) was reaping a bonanza of government cash. To show their appreciation, each military flight crew was met at the aircraft with a six-pack of iced-down Coke in a Styrofoam cooler. After a hot summer flight, it was a welcome refresher, and an act of generosity we appreciated.

One day, I picked up a brand-new echo model Huey from the Bell Helicopter plant in Fort Worth to ferry to the Marines at Camp Pendleton, California. Rather than take the familiar route to Midland and then to El Paso, I wanted to fly a more southerly route to Del Rio and fly the Rio Grande River to El Paso. I had been told by another ferry pilot that flying the river at fifty feet through Big Bend National Park was spectacular, with towering cliffs on both sides.

The only problem was the lack of an airport with jet fuel between Forth Worth and Del Rio. I had read in the aircraft manual that AVGAS (aviation gasoline) could be used as an emergency fuel. I was not sure whether I should risk this since I did want to destroy a brand-new engine. Paying roughly $100,000 to replace a new engine or being court-martialed was not appealing. I decided to seek advice from the tech rep for the engine manufacturer, Lycoming, who was located at the Bell plant. He said absolutely no problem with burning AVGAS. In fact, he said, "If you could find a way to get *Crisco* into the engine, it would burn it." Hmmm, I filed that information in my ferry pilot bag of tricks!

There were two specific helicopter deliveries that were memorable. The first involved flying a H-3 from San Diego to Naval Air Facility Detroit in the dead of winter. When we picked it up, I was told that all systems were functioning properly except for the cabin heater. Understandable—not much need for a heater in Southern California. However, where we were headed, a heater would be a necessity. They asked if I would be willing to ferry without a heater. I talked it over with the other pilot and crew chief and we decided to give it try. So, we pulled on our long johns and winter flying jackets and off we went.

Well, I am here to tell you that I have never been colder in my life. Even though each leg of our flight across the U.S. was only about two hours, I don't think we could have lasted another ten minutes. It was misery. Oh, how I regretted the decision to not have the heater repaired. But, we persevered and delivered the aircraft to Detroit—then we headed for our motel and a tub full of hot water.

The other flight also involved extreme temperatures, but this time on the other end of the thermometer. I was headed east from San Diego in an H-34. Just after clearing the coastal mountain range and over the Imperial Valley near El Centro, I suddenly lost the primary hydraulic system. I immediately switched to the auxiliary system. Although the helicopter could be safely controlled using the backup system, emergency procedures dictated that an immediate precautionary landing be made because if the auxiliary system failed, the helicopter would become uncontrollable.

Just below me was a section of Interstate 10 still under construction, so I spiraled down for a landing. On the way down, I made contact with Yuma Flight Service Station to inform them of my predicament and the location of my landing. I asked them to notify Naval Air Facility El Centro and ask them to send someone to pick us up. Even though we were only twenty miles south of the airfield, it took them three and a half hours to get to us. The Navy doesn't do very well on land.

In the meantime, with only two small canteens of water to stave off summer desert temperatures, we were two very thirsty hombres by the time the Navy finally reached us. From that experience, I began carrying a five-gallon plastic jug of water on all desert flights—one more item to put into my already crammed parachute bag.

Angola Follies

One day our CO, Captain Tate, was talking informally with several of us helicopter pilots after our monthly all-officers meeting. The topic drifted to some of the unauthorized shenanigans that we helicopter pilots were doing during our ferry trips, like landing in the backyards of relatives and friends to spend the night, taking helicopters on hunting and fishing trips, and taking unauthorized passengers for a ride.

"I know what you guys are doing—just don't get caught," he said with a straight face. "If one of your escapades is brought to my official attention, I will have no choice but to hammer you." Without waiting for our reaction, he spun around and disappeared into his office.

He appreciated that ferrying helicopters was a tough job. We flew at slow speed and low altitude in noisy, vibrating machines that lacked most of the creature comforts found in most fixed-wing airplanes. We spent more time away from our families than other pilots. We worked hard and did our job. He appreciated our special talents and hard work, so he cut us a little slack because that's what good leaders do to reward those who do good work. Yes, we occasionally diverted from our assigned mission to take advantage of the "land anywhere" capability of the aircraft we were flying, but we did not abuse the privilege—and we never got caught!

I will freely admit it was intoxicating to have what amounted to my own personal helicopter and, better yet, Uncle Sam paid for the fuel. Consequently, I did not always take the shortest route to my ultimate destination. One of my favorite diversions was to the Buffalo area of western New York State, where I grew up and my family still lived. Whenever I was ferrying a helicopter in the northeast part of the U.S., I usually managed to stop for a day or two in Angola due to "bad weather." To make up for time lost during these unscheduled stops, I pushed hard during the remainder of a road trip by flying longer each day.

Several of my trips to see my family created vivid memories of exciting times that could have landed me in the U.S. military penal institution in Fort Leavenworth, Kansas. Most of these adventures included my brother David, who at the time was serving as a weekend warrior in the Army National Guard.

David and his wife, Mary, were renting a small house on the large estate of a wealthy businessman, and it was about one mile from my parents' home on Bennett Road. Directly across from David's house was a twenty-acre grass field—an ideal location to land any helicopter I was ferrying. In addition to being large and free of obstructions, the site was also well away from public roads and prying eyes.

My first trip to David's "helipad" was in an H-34 with my trusted crew chief, Schultz. We landed without difficulty and spent the night. The next morning, as we were doing the pre-flight inspection of our helicopter, Schultz called down to me from his position up on the rotor head. "We have a popped BIM indicator."

Each of the four main rotor blades was pressurized with an inert gas used to detect cracks or fractures in the blade that otherwise might go unnoticed. There was a small tube-like indicator inserted into each blade that would alert the air crew if a blade lost pressure. If a BIM indicator popped, indicating a loss of pressure, the standard procedure called for resetting the indicator. If it did not immediately pop again, then it was simply a false indication. If it did trip again, then the blade had to be removed and replaced.

Before Schultz had a chance to reset the indicator, my mind was racing. My first thought was, *Oh, hell now what?* My second thought was, *I am not going to call my squadron and tell them to send a maintenance crew to change a blade in my brother's front yard.* Captain Tate's words were, "Don't get caught." So, in a matter of seconds, I devised a plan to fly the helicopter solo to the local Angola airport three miles away, despite the possibility of a defective rotor blade. It is simply amazing how fast the mind can work when you are facing a good ass chewing or worse. Fortunately, the indicator remained normal after Schultz reset it. *Testicles, spectacles, wallet, and watch*—and off we went.

On my next visit, I was flying an H-2. Instead of landing in my brother's field, I decided to land at Buffalo International Airport because I was concerned about FOD (Foreign Object Damage—slang for any object that could be sucked into a jet engine causing significant damage).

I decided to take my father, my brother John, and David for a ride over the family homestead and around the Angola area. David, being in the National Guard, was a legal passenger. My dad and John were definitely not authorized to fly in a military aircraft. So, as not to attract too much attention to my illegal flight, I dressed Dad and John in a Navy flight suit and David wore his Guard uniform. I doubt I fooled anybody watching "my crew" as we manned our Navy aircraft—a soldier sitting in the copilot's seat and two crew chiefs in the back, one fourteen years old and the other fifty-four. But, we pulled it off and had a great flight.

Somewhere during the remainder of the ferry trip to the Kaman factory in Connecticut, the automatic blade track system malfunctioned, causing a pronounced vibration—not dangerous, just annoying. It wasn't long before my jostled bladder demanded to be emptied. Under most pilot's seats in military aircraft there is a relief tube designed for the critical situation I was facing. Hard to believe, but I had never used one before this moment.

I gave control of the helicopter to my crew chief, removed my flight gloves, removed the relief tube from its clip on the bottom of my seat, and proceeded to pee into the funnel. Soon the receptacle was filling to the top, with no sign of the urine draining out. Due to the heavy vibration of the helicopter, urine was being slung out all over the cockpit.

My crew chief was shouting at the top of his lungs, "Squeeze the trigger! Squeeze the trigger!" while trying to dodge drops of yellow liquid flying in his direction. Being a newbie at this, I didn't realize there was a trigger on the side of the funnel to allow the fluid to drain overboard. I don't think my crew chief spoke to me the rest of the day. I can't say that I blamed him. He was probably thinking to himself, *Those dumb ass officers.*

My subsequent venture into the uncharted landing fields of western New York was nearly my undoing. I had picked up a brand-spanking-new H-53 Marine helicopter from the Sikorsky factory in Connecticut. It was one of the first "D" models to be delivered to the Corps. This behemoth weighed 35,000 pounds empty, had all of the latest electronic gadgetry, and the paint was barely dry. Since I had not flown the "D" model, I received a two-hour introductory flight from a company test pilot.

I wasn't able to depart until after dark—mistake number one. Because I was anxious to get to David's house, I pressed on to Binghamton, New York, for fuel and on to Angola. When I arrived in the area, I made a low pass over David's house at three hundred feet. At that altitude, this monster created so much noise and turbulence, it could rattle dishes in the china cabinet and get the dog barking—David was expecting me, but now he definitely knew I had arrived. What the neighbors were thinking as they sat in their easy chairs watching television was anybody's guess. UFO enthusiasts were probably running outside to get a glimpse of the spaceship that had descended from the heavens.

Sure enough, on the second pass over the "helipad," I saw David standing in the middle of the big field where I always landed, waving two flashlights. I thought he was pinpointing where I should land; I never suspected he trying to warn me *not* to land there.

After landing, shutting down the two powerful engines, and braking the immense main rotor to a stop, I opened the crew door on the right side of the aircraft to greet my brother.

"Mike, you better take a look at this," he said with urgency in his voice.

"Look at what?" I replied.

"Come here and I'll show you." He pointed to the double tires on the right main landing gear with his flashlight.

As I looked at the beam of light, I could see the landing gear slowly sinking into the mud. At this point, the muck was halfway up on the wheels. I quickly realized the danger. In several more minutes, this eighteen-ton aircraft would be resting on the fragile aluminum underbelly, crushing the underside of this ten-million-dollar helicopter.

I made a mad dash for the cockpit, started the engines, engaged the rotors, and gingerly pulled it out of the mud and flew it to higher ground at the edge of the field—without bothering to fasten my seatbelt or to put my flight helmet on. I had plenty of practice with that sort of takeoff in Vietnam. After landing, I took a deep breath and sat for several minutes

Top photo: With my brother David in the copilot's seat, dressed in his National Guard uniform, I am about to land a Sikorsky H-53 in the field across from his house the day after the near disaster in the same field. March 1969

Bottom photo: To give a sense of the size of the Sikorsky H-53 that I landed in my brother's field, I am standing next to it after arriving in San Diego several days later. March 1969

trying to slow my heartbeat and to allow the adrenaline to escape from my exhausted body. I was proud of myself for reacting so quickly, but then I had plenty of motivation—nothing like facing a long prison sentence to get the old juices flowing!

In discussing the situation afterward, it was clear what had happened. There was a slight depression in the center of the field and heavy rain in previous days had collected there to create a quagmire. David, with his flashlights, tried his best to warn me away—at some personal sacrifice, I might add. One of the loafers he was wearing came off in the mud and he never did find it. As the old saying goes, "All is well that ends well." David had a story to share with his fire department buddies; I had a true tale for this book; and, best of all, I didn't get caught, although there was a suspicious mudline on the wheels that several sharp-eyed military linemen spotted on the way out to the West Coast.

Several other things happened during this ferry trip that were worthy of note. The day after landing in Angola, on March 31, 1969, our son, Brian, was born in San Diego. Barbara's parents were with her, but I would not see my new son for several days.

After departing Angola, I did not head home, even though Barbara pleaded that I do so. Instead, I headed east to Utica, New York, the head-quarters of Mohawk Airlines. My good friend Len Turrito, the owner of the Angola Airport, had contacted a captain for Mohawk who worked in the training department. Captain Dave Laxtercamp agreed to interview me, so I flew the H-53 to Utica to meet with him. The flexibility of being a ferry pilot afforded me the opportunity to accept a last-minute inter-view—even if it meant seeing my newborn son a few days late.

The last Angola tale involves another brand-new helicopter: a UH-1D going to VX-6, the Antarctic support squadron based at Naval Air Sta-tion Quonset Point, Rhode Island. After departing the Bell plant in Fort Worth, I made a beeline for western New York.

I arrived about mid-day, so I decided to suit David up in his Guard uniform for a little joy ride around the area. Flying the Huey again must have re-awakened the Vietnam "killer instinct" because I decided to show David what real low-level, nap-of-the-earth flying looked and felt like. I flew at treetop level at 120 mph and headed for Cattaraugus Creek, a long meandering waterway that looked more like a river than its name implied. In some places, steep cliffs rose on both sides as the creek made its way through desolate but stunningly beautiful terrain, on its way to Lake Erie.

I dropped down toward the fast-flowing stream, leveling at twenty feet above the water. David was having the time of his life and so was I. There is nothing quite like low-level flying—God it was fun, but dangerous and foolhardy.

At one point, David told me that we had flashed by a guy fishing along the bank. I didn't see him because I was concentrating on the business at hand. David often wondered what went through that guy's mind as we appeared out of nowhere and rocketed downstream and out of sight. We will never know what he told his family and friends that night, but I'll bet his story began, "You won't believe what I saw today."

Arriving back at the "helipad," we noticed a police car driving down the private road leading to David's house with its lights flashing. I immediately figured the cop was after us for our low-level escapades, so I decided not to land. Twenty minutes later, I landed without incident.

Later that day, when I was talking with Len Turrito, he said he had a conversation with that cop during the heat of the chase. Apparently, the policeman was complaining to Len about chasing a crazy military pilot all over the township. Whereupon, Len told him in his characteristic blunt fashion, "Why you dumb sonofabitch, you're never going to catch him." I am glad the cop didn't catch up with me because I don't think I would have enjoyed what he had to say.

When David learned I would be bringing this helicopter to Angola, he asked if I would be agreeable to doing a flyover of the village cemetery as part of its annual Memorial Day celebration. I said yes, and David spoke with the parade chairman to work out the details. The plan was for us to take off and go into a high orbit over the village as the parade made its way from downtown to the village cemetery located about a mile away. As the last unit in the parade made its way into the cemetery, that would be our signal to swoop down and perform a high-speed flyover.

This was not going to be your average ho-hum flyover. I intended to make this flyby so spectacular that my fellow Angolians would be telling their great-grandchildren about this apocalyptic event from their nursing home beds. I planned to dive out of the heavens in a screaming descent, so that when I crossed over the assembled masses, I would be going as fast as a Huey could possibly go—maybe more. I intended to pass over so low that the tuba player would have to hang on to his instrument out of fear it would be sucked out of his hands. The whop, whop, whop from my rotor blades would be so loud reverberating off the tombstones that the crowd would think they were at a rock concert. This was definitely not going to be your grandmother's flyover.

David, who was looking out the copilot's side window, said, "Mike, the last marching unit just entered the cemetery." Like an Olympic athlete tensing to deliver the performance of his life, my vision narrowed, my body coiled in anticipation, my breathing slowed, and my concentration reached a laser-like focus as I lowered the collective and pushed the nose over. Down we came—it was glorious!

Execution of the flyover, by all accounts, was breathtaking. There was, however, a problem with the timing. My first pass occurred just as the mayor began to speak. To make matters worse, nobody had bothered to inform the mayor of our participation or the timing of our arrival. In fact, nobody in the assembled crowd knew about the flyover.

But everyone *did know* who was perpetrating this obscene desecration. Angola is a small town. Most people knew that I was a Navy helicopter pilot and had served in Vietnam. I am sure that many in the crowd were upset that I was showing off and upstaging the solemnity of the occasion.

The mayor paused in mid-sentence and looked up in disbelief and growing anger at this intrusion. As the last whop, whop, whop faded, he adjusted his glasses, looked down at his notes, and began speaking again. He was just getting up a head of steam when I reversed course and did my best imitation of a Vietnam attack run in the opposite direction.

Having fulfilled the mission to the best of my ability and oblivious to the chaos below, David and I departed the scene before the firing squad of old veterans could change from blanks to live ammunition.

Other Misguided Adventures

Not all of my stupid stunts were centered in western New York. I managed to work myself into jams from Louisiana to Arizona and once even in Mexico. Through it all, I kept my ferry pilot record intact—I did not bend any metal and I didn't get caught—*testicles, spectacles, wallet, and watch.*

On one trip headed to the East Coast out of San Diego, I decided to divert a little north of my usual route. The Grand Canyon had been begging me to visit for some time now. Before dropping down into the "big ditch," I thought it prudent to get some advice from someone experienced in such matters. Calling ahead to a helicopter operator who flew tourists from the South Rim, I asked if I could land at his helipad to seek some fatherly advice. He was happy to oblige.

His helipad was located about a half mile from the edge of the abyss. All of my helicopter experience thus far had been gained at sea level, where maximum air density allowed the engine and rotor blades to perform at peak capacity. As I approached to land at his pad, situated at seven thousand feet above sea level, I ran out of engine power and hover performance at about ten feet above the ground and plopped unceremoniously to a hard landing as he watched safely out of harm's way. As I climbed down from the H-34, I was embarrassed for my less than professional military arrival.

"Hi, Mike, I'm Bill Hatfield. Welcome to the Grand Canyon," he said cheerfully.

"Hi, Bill. Sorry about the sloppy landing. I ran out of power," I said, hoping to salvage a bit of my pride.

"No sweat. You are not the first flatlander to discover that landing at these higher elevations can be tricky. But you'll get used to it. By the way, takeoffs can be just as demanding, so be careful when you depart."

"I've got a lot to learn. Eating a little humble pie now and then will serve to keep my ego in check," I said with a sigh, knowing he was letting me off easy.

"So, you want to know what it's like to fly down into the canyon. Well, at this time of the year, there is nothing to be afraid of. In the summertime, it's a much different story because you would have dangerous air currents and downdrafts to contend with. So, you won't have any problems."

"Thank you, Bill. That's a relief to know. I really appreciate you taking the time to fill me in."

"Well, I appreciate that you were courteous enough to ask before venturing into the big hole. I don't mind you military pilots flying in the Grand Canyon. I've seen all kinds of different military aircraft flying in here—even big bombers. What I do object to, though, are the jet jockeys who like to break the speed of sound below the rim of the canyon. The shockwaves cause dangerous rock slides that tumble into the Colorado River, sometimes narrowly missing hikers and rafters. The erosion to the canyon walls and other damage is something they should consider before hotdogging down there. I've been complaining about it for years, but nobody seems to care." (In 1968, there were no rules about flying in the Grand Canyon. Today there are strict rules and flight corridors. No one but the U.S. Park Service can fly below the rim of the canyon.)

"Well, I better get going, Bill. I plan to park over at the airport for the night and fly into the canyon in the morning on my way to Albuquerque," I said as I looked at my watch.

"One quick story before you go. Last year, I was giving a ride to a man and his wife from Texas. Neither had flown in a helicopter before. So, I took off from my pad and flew at treetop level to the edge of the south rim, dumped the collective, and dove into the gorge five thousand feet below—just like I always do. She yelled, "I just wet my pants!" and I thought I just lost my tip. When we got back, her husband handed me a one-hundred-dollar bill and told me that was the best damn ride his wife had ever had."

"Have fun in the canyon tomorrow, but don't pee your flight suit," Bill said with a broad smile on his weathered face.

"Thanks again, Bill. I'll try not to dislodge any rocks tomorrow," I said as I climbed up into the cockpit.

The next morning, my crew chief and I flew down into the canyon. I descended to about one thousand feet below the rim and flew around for about fifteen minutes. All the while, I was nervous and uncomfortable. All I could think was that if the engine quit there was no place to go except to ditch in the fast-flowing Colorado River. The chances of surviving that disaster would be slim. I breathed a sigh of relief as I climbed out of the deep chasm, and at least I could say that I had flown into the Grand Canyon.

The next day, heading east and not long after our departure from Albuquerque, a movement caught my eye off to the right. I turned my head to see a giant B-52 bomber flying about one hundred feet directly below me. It happened so suddenly that I had no chance to be scared or to take evasive action. It was unnerving to be that close to a mid-air collision. The bomber crew probably saw us off in the distance and said, "Hey, let's see if we can scare the bejesus out of that Navy helicopter pilot." Do you know how many square feet there are in the wing of a B-52? Lots!

The gentle curvature of the Gulf of Mexico was a familiar landmark. I followed it from Brownsville, Texas, to Pensacola, Florida, or vice versa over twelve times ferrying T-34s between the overhaul contractor in Brownsville and VT-1, the primary training squadron at Saufley Field, where I had trained in 1964.

A one-way trip took a little over five flight hours, with a fuel stop in Lake Charles, Louisiana. It was boring beyond belief. At 5,500 feet, all I had to do was follow the shoreline. There were no navigation calculations, no position reports to be made, no challenges whatsoever—nothing but mindless flying. "Boring holes in the sky" we used to call it. Since the T-34 was an acrobatic airplane, numerous times I felt like rolling it upside down or doing a snap-roll—anything to relieve the tedium. But because I had my two humongous parachute bags tied down in the backseat, I dared not try anything too radical for fear they might break loose and jam the controls.

To compound my misery, after delivering the aircraft to Brownsville and spending the night in a rundown motel, guess what? Yep, hop into another T-34 the next morning and fly it back to Pensacola. I once delivered six airplanes in as many days. I told the flight scheduler, "If you give me another T-34, I will be forced to go AWOL, defect to Canada, or engage in some other unnatural act."

Then, one day, the scheduler gave me a new assignment: fly a freshly overhauled UH-1D Huey from Corpus Christi to Pensacola. I had to fly the same route and stop at Lake Charles for fuel, just like in the T-34, but I was determined to make this delivery more fun. I decided that I would fly low-level the entire route.

Once I reached the coastline of the Gulf, I dropped to twenty feet and stayed there all the way to Pensacola except for having to pop up over an occasional tree line. As I tore through the wetlands along the coast of Louisiana, water fowl by the thousands scattered before my thunderous dash across the swamps. I am sure that any birders or Sierra Club members reading this will be appalled at this gross assault on bird sanctuaries. I wouldn't do this today, but back then, I was reckless and immature, with a hint of immortality in my swagger. I had also recently returned from Vietnam, where moral values were rearranged. Interestingly, I never hit one bird.

Sure, flying low was more tiring and dangerous than droning along at 5,500 feet, but it was not boring. Halleluiah! Amen brother. I have seen the light!

During the time I was in the ferry squadron, my brother Bill completed his commitment with the Seabees in Vietnam and was attending Louisiana Tech in Ruston. Since he was in close proximity to the Gulf Coast route, it was easy to drop in to see him from time to time. I even gave him an unauthorized ride in a Huey one day—another low-level "blast from the past."

On one of my visits to see Bill, I was ferrying a C-45 to Naval Air Station Dallas. The aircraft had been stripped of all navigational equipment, but that didn't concern me because I could follow Interstate 10 all the way.

On the morning of my departure, the sky was overcast in Ruston. It was one of those homogeneous layers that make it difficult to visually determine the height of the overcast. Since there was no official weather reporting at Ruston, I estimated the height to be five or six hundred feet—enough room to take off and fly north underneath the layer until picking up the I-10.

As I was getting ready to depart, I happened to notice the base of a small radio tower next to the FBO building; the top disappeared in the clouds. That random observation would figure dramatically in the minutes to come.

I waved goodbye to Bill and advanced both throttles for takeoff. No sooner was I airborne when—poof—I entered the clouds. Before I had time to lament my predicament, I climbed through the thin overcast layer and was now on top, looking at clear blue skies and bright sunshine. Basking in my sudden good fortune, I realized that as far as I could see in any direction, the ground was obscured by a solid layer of clouds. The hope of finding I-10 and flying to Dallas was impossible. In fact, without any navigation equipment, I couldn't go anywhere. I had about four hours of fuel, so I suppose I could have flown around with the hope that the overcast would burn off. But what if it didn't? And if it did, would I be able to locate my position on a sectional chart? Now what, coach?

As I pondered my serious situation, I noticed the top of the radio antenna that I had observed before takeoff. It was sticking up through the clouds. A plan began to form. I knew that the tower was approximately one hundred yards due west of the north-south runway. Using the tower as a guide, I figured that I could locate the cloud-covered runway.

Although exceptionally risky and stupid, I lowered the landing gear and flaps and began a slow descent into the solid mass of clouds ahead. It was a tense moment as I left the safety and security of sunshine and was enveloped in cloud and uncertainty. Down I went, hoping that when I broke out of the cloud layer there would be a runway to greet me and not a building or a large tree. The clouds parted, the runway appeared out of the gloom, exactly where expected. I reduced the throttles and landed. There is no feeling like cheating death—again!

On another longer-than-usual ferry trip, I had been gone for two weeks and I was missing Barbara something awful. I had promised Barbara the night before that I would be home the next day, and I intended to fulfill that promise. At that point, I surrendered logical decision-making to a strong force in aviation called *get-home-itis*—a dark motivation that has killed many an aviator and the passengers riding with him.

The aircraft I was flying was a T-34, which had a cruise speed of 120 knots. To fly from Abilene, Texas, to San Diego in one day meant I would have to get a very early start. So, I took off at 0400 and flew west to Midland in the darkness of the Texas prairie. Then it was on to El Paso, Tucson, and Yuma with a brief refueling stop at each. One more leg to go.

Despite the early takeoff from Abilene, and having already flown eight hours, I was eager to push on to San Diego. This T-34 was not equipped for IFR flight, but this limitation had not been an issue thus far. Up ahead, though, it would be another matter. San Diego was reporting a solid overcast at three thousand feet with visibility greater than ten miles.

Since I could not let down through the overcast, I decided to try to go underneath by following the main east-west highway through the mountains. Flying two hundred feet above the automobiles, I cautiously made my way toward San Diego. At first, the visibility was three miles, but then it began to slowly deteriorate and the clouds pressed lower and lower. It soon became apparent that I could not proceed any farther. Fortunately, I had enough room to make a 180-degree turn—many pilots have died in similar situations when box canyons proved their undoing.

After safely emerging from the mountains on the east side, I decided to climb up to seven thousand feet and fly over the mountains to San Diego to see if I could find a hole in the overcast that I could spiral down through. No such luck.

Thwarted by my second attempt, I should have given up for the day and retired to a motel. I normally would have, but this particular day I had a real bad case of get-home-itis. I had a brainstorm—I'd fly into Mexico and try to work my way along lower terrain to the Pacific Coast and then head north to San Diego under the overcast. Readers are probably scratching their head at this point and saying, "Now, let me get this straight. You decided to make an illegal and unauthorized flight into Mexican airspace, without any navigational aids or aeronautical charts, in an area you had never before flown, with less than one hour of fuel?" Yes, indeedy, that's exactly what I planned to do—and did!

It didn't take long before I was hopelessly lost in the badlands of the Sonoran Desert. One cactus looked like the next, one hill looked just like the one I just flown by. With my fuel supply dwindling, fear began to well up in the pit of my stomach. I was berating myself for being so stupid. Somehow, I managed to stumble back across the border. My guardian angel was still flying copilot.

After spending the night in a motel near Naval Air Facility El Centro, I woke up to clear skies over San Diego and flew home—thankful to be alive.

Goodbye to the Active Navy

After reading the foregoing, most people would conclude that the year I spent in the ferry squadron was one high jinks after another; perpetrated at taxpayer expense. To be sure, there were a few naughty side trips, but the preponderance of my time involved long hours, day after day, moving a variety of aircraft from one place to another in the most direct manner possible. Evidence of my hard work and dedication to my job is borne out by the monthly flight-time totals. Of the fifty-seven pilots in VFR-32, I was usually in the top five. For two of my twelve months in the squadron, I was number one in total hours, including October 1968 when I flew 102 hours. My monthly average was 65.4, which meant that I flew 850 hours during my one-year tour of duty without accident or mishap. I could finally retire my two huge parachute bags and give my arms a rest, and I was proud of what I had accomplished.

Appropriately, my last ferry flight involved a coast-to-coast trip. I picked up a Grumman S-2E, a twin-engine airplane used in carrier-based anti-submarine warfare, at Naval Air Station Quonset Point, Rhode Island, and flew it to San Diego. On June 8, 1969, the day before I was officially detached from VRF-32, I flew a NAS North Island T-28 on a farewell flight around the San Diego area. Since I was leaving active duty and thought that this was going to be my last flight in a Navy aircraft, I was sad and nostalgic as I taxied into the chocks for the final time. As I sat in the cockpit after shutting down the engine, I took a deep breath of maritime air and marveled at my good fortune of having been a naval aviator. Little did I know that I would soon re-don my uniform and serve for another fifteen years.

The next day, Barbara, our new son, Brian, and I headed east to Fairhope, Alabama, in our overloaded station wagon. And this time, I would be on the lookout for that New Mexico state trooper.

Chapter 13

On Furlough

I DID NOT USUALLY WATCH THE LATE-NIGHT NEWS, BUT FOR SOME REASON on this chilly November night, I turned on the TV. The lead story flashed across the screen: "Mohawk Airlines Flight 411 crashed on landing approach to Glens Falls, New York, early this evening. There were no survivors." This stunning announcement caused an ominous feeling of foreboding to begin churning in the pit of my stomach. This evening, one of my three airline roommates was scheduled to fly his last flight for Mohawk before beginning an indefinite furlough from the airline. Even though I did not know which flight Jack was flying that night, I had a strong premonition that I had just lost another friend in a flying accident.

Grabbing the phone, I called crew schedules at Mohawk's headquarters in Utica, New York. If I had stopped to think for a second before dialing the number, I would have realized that nobody in that office would release any information to me and certainly not over the phone. It was a desperate bid to refute what intuition had already revealed. The next day, I learned that Jack Morrow was killed, along with the rest of the crew and eleven passengers, when the Mohawk Airlines Fairchild FH-227 twin-turboprop aircraft hit the top of a mountain while flying a night instrument approach to the airport at Glens Falls in light rain and very gusty winds.

Having flown into this airport as a Mohawk first officer just three weeks prior during daylight hours, I remember thinking to myself, as I looked at the tops of nearby mountains, that this would be a tricky approach and landing at night and especially in bad weather. In a bizarre twist, the mountain they impacted was named "Pilot's Knob"—how it got its name, I don't know. Whether there was a deeper meaning or not, I will leave up to the reader's imagination. One fact that was shorn of any subtlety was that I had also flown this very aircraft on my last line flight with Mohawk, only six days before.

Two-Week Airline Career

On May 22, 1969, about seven weeks after my interview with Captain Dave Laxtercamp at the Mohawk Airlines' corporate headquarters in Utica, New York, I received a Western Union telegram: "Congratulations! You have been accepted for pilot employment letter to follow." I was thrilled beyond description. My goal, since I began Navy flight training five years earlier, was to be a commercial airline pilot. All that was left to do was finish my tour of duty in the Navy, sell our mobile home, pack the car, and head east.

Exactly one week after I was discharged from the Navy in San Diego, I had to be in Utica, New York, for the beginning of airline training. In those seven days, I drove Barbara and our two-month old son to her parents in Fairhope, Alabama, and then continued to my parents' home in Angola, New York. The last leg of my journey, from Alabama to New York, was driven straight through. I only stopped for gas and an occasional bite to eat. I was so physically spent at the end, I could barely keep my eyes open. Five miles from my parents' home, a man pulled out from a side street into my path. If I had been more alert, I could have easily swerved to avoid him. Instead, I locked up the brakes and slid into the front of his car. Fortunately, there were no injuries, just two totaled vehicles. Without an automobile to drive and needing to get to Utica the next day, I asked Dad if I could borrow the only family car—just like the old days when I asked for the keys to go on a date. My budding airline career was off to a less than auspicious beginning.

In 1969, airline passenger service in the United States was dominated by a handful of major airlines called "trunk carriers"—Pan American, Eastern, United, American, TWA, and Delta—operating from large-city hubs. Air service to smaller cities with connecting flights to the major hub airports was provided by nine regional airlines: Ozark, Piedmont, Frontier (not related to the modern-day Frontier Airlines), Hughes Air West, Southern, North Central, Allegheny, Texas International, and Mohawk.

Although I didn't have a pilot slot with a major airline, as a helicopter pilot I was lucky to have any airline job. At that time, military helicopter pilots were not considered to be strong airline candidates, unlike their fixed-wing counterparts who comprised the vast majority of airline new hires. Helicopter pilots suffered from an institutionalized bias within the military, which rationalized that they were less capable pilots because they didn't have the flying skills to fly fixed-wing aircraft and were, therefore, relegated to the "second string." The fact that Army helicopter pilots of that day did not receive the same level of instrument training required of fixed-wing aviators further contributed to the negative perception. Navy helicopter pilots, on the other hand, received the same level of instrument training as fixed-wing students and often flew in instrument conditions while operating at sea, but that didn't seem to matter. Naturally, since most of the senior executives in the airlines had cut their teeth as fixed-wing pilots during World War II and Korea, they carried the ingrained bias against helicopter pilots to their civilian jobs. Unlike today, when military helicopter pilots are no longer viewed as second-class citizens when it comes to airline hiring, in my day it was an uphill battle. So, I was very thankful to have a job with Mohawk Airlines.

World War II provided the underpinnings of the birth of passenger air travel on a wide scale. The many aeronautical innovations made to aircraft, the large number of military airfields constructed worldwide, especially in the United States, coupled with the availability of the thousands of surplus military transports and former military pilots to fly them, provided the resources to jumpstart a fledgling industry.

One of the new upstarts was Robinson Airlines, which began operations in 1945 to provide passenger service to the Mid-Atlantic States. In 1952, Robert Peach bought Robinson and changed the name to Mohawk Airlines, as the result of a public contest. Despite its status as a regional airline, Mohawk was a rising star in the airline business with several industry firsts: 1954—first airline to introduce helicopter service when it offered roundtrip flights between New York City and the Catskills Mountain resorts (discontinued after one summer); 1958—first U.S. airline to hire an African-American flight attendant (she broke one barrier only to be sidelined by another when she got pregnant and was discharged because stewardesses could not be pregnant in that day); 1961—first airline to use a centralized computer reservation system; 1965—first regional airline to use flight simulators for pilot training; 1965—first regional airline to fly jets.

When I joined Mohawk, the airline flew to forty-four cities and its route map ranged from Montreal in the north, Boston in the east, Washington, D.C. in the south, to Detroit in the west. The carrier had over forty aircraft comprised of two models: the BAC-111, an eighty-passenger turbojet manufactured by British Aircraft Corporation, and the FH-227, a forty-four-passenger high-wing twin turboprop produced by Fairchild Hiller. I was hired to fly as first officer on the latter.

Rising at 3:00 a.m. on Monday, June 16, I hurriedly loaded my suitcase into Mom and Dad's car and departed Angola for Utica, two hundred and twenty miles to the east. I didn't want to be late on my first day as an airline pilot.

As I looked around the room at my fellow classmates, it seemed like we were cut from the same mold—suit and tie, clean shaven, and short hair. The airline world did not accept hippies, protesters, or those wishing to make a style statement by wearing outlandish clothing. It was a conservative club, still is. Of the ten individuals in my class, most were former Air Force or Navy pilots with a couple of guys who had gone the civilian route to get their flying ratings and experience, including a former New York City cop, who shared some hair-raising stories of his days as a foot patrolman in Manhattan.

The first day was devoted to welcoming pep talks from senior executives, filling out endless paperwork, getting our airline ID badges (my badge number was 8519), and getting measured for our uniforms. My uniform coat, two pairs of trousers, a hat, and a black tie cost $132.10; to be paid through payroll deductions of $10 every two weeks. We also received an armload of training manuals in preparation for our formal ground school training, which would be conducted Monday through Friday over the next three weeks.

During the following days, we studied in great detail the various operating systems of the FH-227 aircraft, including the electrical, hydraulic, pneumatic, air conditioning and pressurization, flight controls, landing gear, engines, cockpit instrumentation, navigation, and avionics systems. We performed numerous weight and balance calculations to ensure the aircraft would be properly loaded for safe flight. We learned how to calculate takeoff, climb, and cruise and landing performance under varying climatic, wind, and runway conditions. We drilled on the emergency checklists that delineated step-by-step procedures to handle various aircraft emergencies, such as engine, cabin, and electrical fires; loss of an engine on takeoff or during cruise flight; loss of pressurization; and a runaway propeller. We studied company manuals to learn the Mohawk way to handle anything and everything that pertained to our job. We poured over government and company manuals to learn how to safely and efficiently fly the FH-227 in instrument flight conditions. It was intense, it was demanding, and it was draining. After eating a late dinner and doing my homework each night in my hotel room, I had no trouble falling asleep.

With two weeks down and one more week of ground school to complete before beginning flight-simulator training, we were given a week off, which included the Fourth of July holiday. I eagerly hopped in the car and drove back to Angola to enjoy a brief respite from the rigors of becoming an airline pilot.

Several days into the hiatus, I heard the mailman beep his horn as he drove into my parents' driveway. This was the signal that he had an important delivery or package and needed someone to meet his car. I walked over to his vehicle and greeted Sam, who had been our mailman for as long as I could remember. He handed me a certified letter and had me sign the delivery receipt. It was addressed to me. This was odd and I wondered who in the world knew I was temporarily staying with my folks. It was from Mohawk Airlines.

Dear Mr. Stock:

Several months ago, we embarked on a pilot hiring and training program designed to produce the crews necessary to implement Boeing 727 service at year's end.

The currently abnormal prime interest rate, nation-wide failure of passenger traffic to meet 1969 forecasts and inflationary pressures caused by both labor and material increases have forced Mohawk Airlines to delay acquisition of the B-727 which, in turn, reduces our training requirements and pilot employment.

I regret to inform you that, due to the above circumstances, you will be temporarily removed from the payroll effective July 18, 1969.

The letter went on to say that I needed to turn in my company manuals, ID badge, and other Mohawk property by July 18; that I should keep the company informed of address or telephone changes; and to say they "sincerely regret the concern and hardship it will cause you."

My airline career had lasted exactly two weeks; it was over before it started. Now what? As usual, I did not have a Plan B.

Flying Tourists over Niagara Falls

Before I left the Navy, my father mentioned to me one day over the phone that Jerry Clark was back in the local area and was the Chief Pilot for Heussler Helicopters out of Buffalo. Although Jerry was several years older than me, he and I had been good friends ever since our scouting days in Troop 28. In fact, he and I became Eagle Scouts at the same ceremony in March 1955.

After a hitch in the Army as a helicopter mechanic, Jerry got a job "wrenching" for some helicopter operators in the South and gradually worked his way into a pilot position flying pipeline inspection work all over the country. He had been with Heussler Helicopters for about a year, when I decided to give him a call to see if he needed any helo drivers. It just so happened that he did, and he invited me to interview with Don Heussler, the owner. As one of my Navy colleagues was fond of saying, "What's a friend for if you can't use him?" After a short discussion, Don offered me a part-time job flying the Bell 47, a piston-engine helicopter that looked very much like the helicopter that was used in the long-running TV series *MASH*. It also happened to be the first helicopter that I flew in the Navy.

Heussler was engaged in three main revenue-producing operations: flying tourists over Niagara Falls, flying a traffic-copter over the city of

Buffalo during the morning and evening commute, and gas pipeline patrols in western New York and northern Pennsylvania. I was soon checked-out for all three missions.

Majestic Niagara Falls is one of the more enduring natural wonders of the world. Located seventeen miles northwest of Buffalo, New York, on the Niagara River between Canada and the United States, Niagara Falls has been a major tourist attraction for over one hundred years, drawing visitors from all over the world. It has a long history as a destination for honeymooners and thrill seekers who have gone over the Falls in barrels or crossed above on a tight-wire.

The water that flows over Niagara Falls comes from the wide and swift Niagara River, which empties the eastern end of Lake Erie into Lake Ontario. Niagara Falls is actually comprised of two main sections: *Horseshoe Falls* on the Canadian side and *American Falls* on the U.S. side of the border. The two falls are separated by Goat Island, a small body of land in the middle of the Niagara River. Horseshoe Falls, curved in the shape of a horseshoe, is 2,600 feet long, 167 feet high, and is the most powerful waterfall in North America in terms of height and flow rate. American Falls is more or less straight across and at 1,060 feet long and only 70 to 100 feet high, is not nearly as spectacular as Horseshoe Falls. Combined, Niagara Falls has the highest flow rate of any falls in the world, with nearly two million gallons of water per second flowing over the edge in peak season, which occurs in late spring. To stand overlooking the edge of

Bell 47 over the Niagara River, approaching the American Falls, with the Horseshoe Falls at the top of the photo.

Horseshoe Falls and hearing its mighty roar is a sight and sound spectacle that is both breathtaking and unforgettable.

Flights over Niagara Falls in rotary-wing aircraft date back to May 1931, when an autogyro flew over both falls. Don Heussler began offering tourist flights over the falls in 1958, and by the time I started flying for Heussler Helicopters in 1969, there were two other competitors offering helicopter rides: Prior Aviation, which operated from a heliport on Goat Island and a Canadian operator.

The Heussler helipad, an elevated structure twenty feet above the ground, was built in the parking lot of the Howard Johnson's Restaurant. It was perched just north of the American end of the Rainbow Bridge going to Canada and about three hundred hundred yards from the edge of the Niagara Gorge, downstream of the falls. Beneath the helipad was a small ticket office and an above-ground aviation fuel tank. The helipad could accommodate two helicopters during busy times, but normally only one machine was used, while the other Bell 47 owned by Heussler was used for traffic copter and operations elsewhere.

A ride cost $7.50 per person and the helicopter could carry two passengers sitting on a bench seat alongside and to the right of the pilot, who sat on the left side of the helicopter. The routine was simple: the ticket agent would load the passengers into the helicopter and strap them in; the pilot would lift into a hover and depart directly across the gorge toward the Canadian shoreline while climbing to five hundred feet; he would then proceed to a point just above Horseshoe Falls, reverse course following the same route and land back on the helipad—six minutes exactly from take-off to landing, just like clockwork.

From a pilot's perspective, multiple flights back-to-back was mind-numbing and boring—most of the time! Occasionally, a passenger sitting next to the pilot, usually the female member of the party, would get spooked when they suddenly found themselves staring two hundred feet straight down into the Niagara Gorge containing the churning, swirling, frothy waters of the Whirlpool Rapids at the base of the falls. One lady abruptly grabbed my right bicep in a death grip so fierce that she left fingernail marks. She was seriously impeding my ability to control the helicopter, but I was able to muscle my way through until she became more relaxed and released her grip. I didn't say anything. A few minutes later, when I swung out over the Niagara River to reverse course, she grabbed my arm again, this time with such force that it caused the helicopter to suddenly pitch up. I had had enough. I said to her, "Lady, this is the arm that is controlling this helicopter." She instantly realized the gravity of her actions and let go of me. Other passengers got so excited by the spectacular sights that they tried to hand their camera to me and wanted a photo of them with the falls in the background. They didn't realize that I needed all of my extremities to fly the helicopter. It seemed, at times, that control of the machine was being jeopardized by the frightened and the giddy—but these emotional outbursts did serve to break up the monotony!

Late in the afternoon on August 5, I had just returned from a flight and had shut down the helicopter since there were no passengers waiting for a ride. Jerry, a Buffalo cop who worked part-time as a ticket agent, came running up the stairs to the helipad. "Mike, there's been a helicopter crash in the river just upstream of Horseshoe Falls," he said out of breath. "I think it's Prior."

Survivors of boating accidents in the past had managed to grab on to some large rocks just above the edge of the falls until they were rescued. If the occupants were able to get out of the sinking helicopter, perhaps they might be clinging to those rocks.

"Hop in," I said. "Let's go check for possible survivors."

As we took off and climbed toward Goat Island, we received a radio report that the helicopter had crashed just upstream of the water intake for the large hydroelectric power plant on the Canadian shoreline. A weir with huge hydraulic doors jutted into the Niagara River to divert about ten percent of the flow through the power turbines. We found out later that workers on the weir closed the massive doors when they saw the crash in the hopes that action would keep the wreckage from being swept over the falls.

From a hundred feet in the air, over the brink of the falls, we scanned the rocks for any people. Seeing none, we shifted our focus toward the gates of the intake. Although the workers had managed to close the gates, it wasn't in time to stop the wreckage from passing through. Their quick action did succeed in drastically slowing the flow of water immediately downstream of the gates, which caused the helicopter to sink in about twenty feet of water about three hundred yards from the brink of the falls. We could clearly see the wreckage but could not see well enough to locate the occupants. Realizing we could not be of any help, we flew back to our helipad. Frankly, I was glad to get out of there. It was unnerving being so close to the edge of the monstrous waterfall and its thunderous roar, knowing if the engine suddenly quit, there would be absolutely no chance for survival.

Sadly, I found out the next day, the pilot was a thirty-year-old former Navy helicopter pilot, who I had met a couple weeks prior to the accident. Two passengers from New Jersey also perished. Much later, we learned the helicopter had run out of gas and was not able to glide to the Canadian shoreline. Since we never carried full fuel on passenger flights due to weight limitations, our standard policy at Heussler was to fly three six-minute flights and then refuel. Prior Aviation, the operator of the crashed helicopter, probably had a similar policy, but human error will always be inextricably linked to the human endeavor.

Performing a traffic copter or pipeline-patrol flight every now and then was always a welcome break from the tourist flights. When I joined the Heussler staff, the company was in its eleventh year of providing a helicopter to WEBR radio for an hour and a half each morning and afternoon, Monday through Friday, to provide live traffic reports in the Buffalo metro area. It was the second-longest running traffic copter operation in the country. Jack Sharpe was the well-known voice of the WEBR traffic reports for many years. A small kit that rested on the floor of the chopper behind his feet contained a radio and a headset with an attached microphone. After picking him up in the parking lot of the radio station, or at some remote location if he happened to be covering a local news story, he would tune his radio and call the control room at the station to be sure that the communication link was satisfactory. He would then listen to the live radio broadcast and wait for his cue to begin broadcasting. While he was on the air, he would point in the direction of the next location he wanted to scout. I was content with his pointing finger because I didn't have the foggiest idea where I was most of the time.

Flying pipeline patrol was another case of not knowing where I was or where I was going, but at least I had an observer from the utility company with me and a right-of-way to follow. Looking for the telltale signs of natural gas leaks amongst the grass and vegetation was not the most exciting mission either, but, overall the three months I flew for Heussler were enjoyable, and it did bring a little money into the family coffers during some lean times.

Weekend Warrior

Even before leaving active duty, I had been considering joining the Navy Reserves. I didn't leave because I disliked the Navy, I left to achieve my number one goal of becoming an airline pilot. The unexpected furlough from Mohawk and the ensuing scramble to find part-time work, simply caused me to join the Reserves sooner than I had planned.

On Friday evening, July 12, 1969, I waited at Buffalo International Airport with a group of other naval reservists from western New York for the arrival of a C-118 Navy transport aircraft that would fly us to Naval Air Station Willow Grove, located just to the west of Philadelphia. It felt good to be back in uniform and I looked forward to being able to fly Navy helicopters once again.

Moreover, the Reserves provided a much-needed source of income during the long furlough from Mohawk Airlines. During my nine months as a reservist, I applied for every school and training activity I could—anything that would allow temporary recall to active duty and the paycheck that went with it. I attended SH-3A helicopter familiarization training at Naval Air Station Key West, Basic and advanced anti-submarine warfare courses and more helicopter training at Willow Grove. Counting the two weeks of training that all Reservists must perform annually, I served a total of two months on active duty.

I was assigned to HS-1W3, a Navy Reserve anti-submarine warfare (ASW) squadron flying the SH-3A Sea King helicopter. Although I had flown this helicopter as aircraft commander in the ferry squadron in San Diego, I did not have any ASW background, so my time in the squadron was spent in the copilot's seat learning the basics about hunting enemy submarines.

Beginning with Operation Desert Shield in 1990 and Operation Desert Storm in 1991, the Navy Reserve force transitioned from being simply a mobilization force waiting to be called up in time of national crisis to serving as an integral component of the total naval structure, with virtually no appreciable difference in combat readiness as compared with the active duty Navy. That was not the case when I joined the Navy Reserves in 1969. The anti-submarine warfare helicopter squadron I was assigned to was no more combat ready than the local Boy Scout troop. Our general lack of tactical mission skills and expertise was laughable. It was more like a good ole boys club that allowed grown men to put on their uniforms and play Navy one weekend a month. I remember one pilot who would hold court at the bar in the officer's club on Friday and Saturday night, but was conspicuously absent the remainder of the drill weekend.

To further illustrate the prevailing mindset of the typical reservist, one Saturday morning I was assigned to fly as copilot for a senior commander who had been a fighter pilot in World War II. In addition to receiving two day's pay for a drill weekend, a pilot could receive an extra day's pay for flying four hours in one day. So, if a pilot flew four hours on Saturday and four on Sunday, he would receive four day's pay for that drill weekend—good, easy money. Well, we took off to fly four hours—or at least that was my impression. Instead, we flew thirty minutes west, turned around and flew back to the naval air station and landed. But, instead of logging one hour of flight time, this crusty old commander logged four hours to ensure that we would receive the extra day's pay.

Apparently, this was common practice throughout the Reserve force and it was time for a crackdown. Each aircraft squadron in the Navy Reserves received a formal message from the Chief of Naval Operations, the top admiral in the Navy, which began with a rhetorical question: "Why do helicopters flown by the Reserves burn so much less fuel per flight hour as compared to the active duty forces?" The admiral knew what was going on and he said to "Knock it off. In the future, if you want to receive an extra day's pay, you better, in fact, fly four hours."

On my very next drill weekend, I was paired with this same commander. This time, I thought we would be flying the full four hours. Wrong! We took off and flew thirty minutes west and thirty minutes east. Just before landing at the air station, he reached up and hit the fuel dump switch and dumped three hours' worth of fuel. He then landed and logged four flight hours. Welcome to the combat-ready world of the Naval Air Reserve forces. The general lack of professionalism that I encountered during my short stint in the Reserves was troubling and greatly contributed to my eventual decision to return to active duty.

Of the thirty-two flights that I flew with the Reserves, two were memorable. The first occurred during a winter flight from Willow Grove to Naval Air Station Norfolk in Virginia. Due to low cloud ceilings and visibilities along the route, we were forced to fly in the clouds on instruments with the real possibility of encountering icing conditions. Helicopter manufacturers have tried various anti-ice and de-ice systems over the years, but none have proved to be very effective. Consequently, the main defense against potentially dangerous ice accumulation on the rotor blades is one of avoidance altogether or exiting icing conditions immediately at the first sign of ice buildup.

For most of the trip south, we did not encounter any icing, even though we were in the clouds most of the way. About twenty miles northeast of our destination, we noticed ice starting to build up on the upper part of the front windshield just below the air intakes for the two jet engines. While debating the best course of action, we heard and felt two extremely loud bangs as the ice broke loose and was ingested into both engines. We quickly glanced at the engine instruments. All temperatures and pressures were completely normal. Thinking that the ice must have harmlessly passed through the engines, we continued on to Norfolk. Only after landing did we realize just how close we came to suffering a dual-engine flameout and having to autorotate into the frigid waters of the Chesapeake Bay. A mechanic motioned for us to climb up to take a look into the engine intakes. The damage we saw was truly unbelievable: the first three rows of turbine blades in each engine were twisted and distorted almost beyond recognition. Why or how both engines continued to operate normally is a mystery to this day. We were two very lucky and grateful hombres. The Navy, on the other hand, was not as happy. Both engines had to be scrapped, to the tune of several million dollars.

The second noteworthy flight occurred at Key West during a night ASW training exercise. The principal system aboard the SH-3A helicopter used to detect enemy submarines was a dipping sonar, which consisted of a large cylindrical transducer that was lowered on a long cable from the belly of the helicopter. Once lowered into the water, the transducer would send out a series of pulses of sound energy in all directions. If one of those pulses hit a submarine, it was reflected back to the transducer and the range and direction to the submarine was displayed on the operator's console in the back of the helicopter.

Before the transducer could be lowered into the water, the helicopter had to be established in a steady hover at forty feet above the sea. Because this vital mission had to be conducted day or night and in weather conditions that did not provide sufficient visual references to the pilot for maintaining a manual hover, an automatic, hands-off approach and hover capability was installed in the helicopter. The pilot would simply position the helicopter at a specified altitude and airspeed, depress a switch on the instrument panel, and the autopilot would take over control of the aircraft and bring it into a stable forty-foot hover.

Hovering above the ocean at forty feet, even on a clear day with calm seas, was enough to elevate the old heartbeat. Try it at night, enveloped in fog, and it becomes downright frightening. And, by the way, the pilot is supposed to sit on his hands and place total trust in the autopilot to keep his machine from crashing into the water only a split second below. As the old saying goes, "This was not for the faint of heart."

For a twenty-four-hour period, our squadron had the services of a training submarine, USS Mackerel, to hone our skills by locating and tracking a live submarine. At 131 feet long, with a crew of two officers and twelve enlisted, the diesel-powered Mackerel was one of the smallest subs ever built for the U.S. Navy. Being small, slow, and quiet, it was a difficult target to locate, but the Reservists from Willow Grove piled out of the Officer's Club eager to show the active duty Navy what we were made of.

The extent of my experience with this "dipping" operation was one day flight. I think we got a few pings off the Mackerel, but I can't remember for sure, it was all blur of brand-new sights, sounds, and activity. What I do remember distinctly about this daylight flight was looking down from our forty-foot hover and seeing several large hammerhead sharks circling—perhaps they realized that Reservists were not good at this and might fall into their laps.

So, that night, with one dipping sonar flight under my belt, we took off into the blackness to find the USS Mackerel. After arriving in the "operational box" in which the submarine was supposed to be, the aircraft commander manually flew our helicopter through the approach gate, punched the automatic coupler and relinquished control to the autopilot. I watched the flight instruments in tense anticipation as the airspeed

Sikorsky SH-3 Sea King helicopter similar to the one I flew in the Naval Reserves. Shown here lowering its sonar transducer into the ocean. *(U.S. Navy photo)*

slowed and the radar altimeter began to slowly unwind as we descended toward the ocean somewhere below. Egad, it was a nerve-wracking and helpless feeling. I wanted to scream, "We're all gonna die!" As I wondered if those same sharks were still patiently waiting.

Finally, after a minute or two, we were firmly established in a steady hover and the ASW operator in the back lowered the transducer into the water. I knew we were in a forty-foot hover only because it said so on the radar altimeter—I couldn't see the water or anything else outside the aircraft. It was like being on the inside of an ink bottle. Only the soft glow of the red instrument lights provided a subtle hint that the situation was normal. The operator in the back reported that he was receiving a strong return echo from the sub—I was glad that someone was getting positive feedback from this unnatural situation. Twenty minutes later, we broke the hover and flew back to NAS Key West, mission accomplished. I was never so relieved to set foot on dry land. That was my last flight in the Navy Reserves, and a memorable one it was!

Flying the Line

Two months after being placed on furlough from Mohawk, I was recalled and told to report to the airline training center in Utica on September 22. The dream of being an airline pilot wasn't dead after all. My classmates and I spent the next seven days reviewing aircraft systems and company manuals and preparing for the twenty hours of flight-simulator training that each new hire must complete before moving to the aircraft itself for inflight training.

Although I already had over five hundred multiengine flight hours in my Navy logbook, the simulator training provided by Mohawk was the first formal multiengine training I had received. It was disturbing to realize just how little I knew about handling emergencies, especially engine-out procedures.

Like flight-simulator training the world over, two students are paired together, one flying in the left seat doing the actual flying and the other acting as copilot to assist the flying pilot. Midway through the training session, the two students switched positions, all the while being directed and coached by a third person in the device, an experienced simulator instructor.

In 1969, the use of full-motion flight simulators was relatively new in the airline industry and it was well before they found their way into military flight training. "The box," as everybody affectionately or derisively called the control module, was perched atop huge hydraulic arms rising from the floor that caused the box to gyrate in pitch, roll, and yaw to mimic an aircraft in flight. The control module consisted of an actual FH-227 cockpit and an instructor console behind the pilots' seats.

Fairchild FH-227, a twin-turboprop airplane I flew for Mohawk Airlines. 1969

These early simulators did not fly like the real aircraft, as they do today, but they were useful in teaching basic instrument-flying skills and cockpit procedures, such as executing normal and emergency checklists. Also, unlike modern flight simulators, there was no outside visual presentation that would simulate the airport environment necessary for takeoff and landing practice because computers of the day were not sufficiently advanced to present visual images with the requisite fidelity.

My flying partner was Mike DiPirro, a former Navy S-2 (a twin-engine carrier-based ASW airplane) pilot and a cheerful, fun-loving individual. I guess Mohawk sought to contain the fallout by pairing both Navy pilots named Mike to the same crew so they could keep a close watch on us. Over a one-week period, we each flew twenty hours, passed our sim check, and moved on to flying the real McCoy.

Mohawk did not have enough FH-227s in their fleet to be able to dedicate an aircraft solely to training. So, we used line aircraft after they finished the daily schedule. That meant that we usually started flight training at two o'clock in the morning—this was before I had ever heard the term "flying the red eye." After flight simulators became sophisticated enough in later years to precisely replicate the flying qualities and performance of the real aircraft and were able to produce high-quality outside visual presentations, the airlines eliminated the need to fly actual aircraft during pilot training. The first flight in a real airplane for most copilots today is a revenue-producing line flight. After four early-morning flights with seven hours spent in the copilot's seat, we each passed our check flight and were duly pronounced qualified to fly the line as first officers.

Most of my classmates were assigned to be reserve first officers flying out of LaGuardia Airport in New York City. Four of us, Jack Morrow and another former Air Force Officer whose name I can no longer remember, Mike DiPirro, and I, rented an apartment "crash pad" within walking distance of the airport. With our brand-new Mohawk uniforms and black-leather flight cases, we slowly settled into the rhythm of being airline pilots. On October 26, I flew my first line flight, which involved seven short legs—the longest being one hour and nineteen minutes from LaGuardia to Watertown, New York—with a final landing at Plattsburg, New York, where we spent the night in a rundown crew hotel. Ah, living the dream!

Eleven days later, it was all over. That was the day that I, along with everyone else in my class, received another certified letter from Mohawk headquarters stating that we were being placed on indefinite furlough, effective November 21, due to unexpected tough economic conditions.

Years later, I learned that Mohawk was on financial life support due to declining passenger loads, high debt related to jet aircraft purchases, and labor strife with the pilots. In retrospect, it was a wonder that I was recalled in the first place. Robert Peach, the embattled CEO of Mohawk and highly decorated World War II Navy pilot, was forced to the sidelines by the board of directors and creditors after guiding the airline to prominence during the 1950s and early 1960s. In 1971, shortly after it was announced that Allegheny Airlines was buying out Mohawk, Robert Peach committed suicide at the age of fifty-one.

I flew my last line flight on November 13 and, once more, was forced to ponder the course of my aviation career without an airline job.

Although my commercial airline career lasted less than two months and contained two furloughs, it was punctuated by several events that, for better or for worse, defined this short period in my aviation history.

While making a visual approach and landing at Albany, New York, the captain overshot the base-to-final turn so badly and so close to the end of the runway that I feared for the safety of the airplane. I briefly considered taking control of the aircraft from him before he managed to make a hairy landing aimed toward the side of the runway. Back in that day, crew resource management, a modern concept where every crewmember has an obligation to act decisively if the safety of the aircraft is in jeopardy, was not yet invented. In those years, the captain was God and no one dared to challenge his authority. If I had taken control of the airplane that day, I am not sure what would have happened immediately or after we taxied to the gate. It would have been ugly, I'm quite certain.

In the late 1960s and early 1970s, the equivalent of modern-day terrorism was the frequent airline hijackings to Cuba perpetrated by young idealists wanting to join the Fidel Castro's social revolution or others just wanting to escape their problems in the United States. This craze reached a frenzy between 1968 and 1972. In 1968, fourteen American aircraft were hijacked to Cuba from the United States; and in 1969, there were thirty-two.

Nearly all of these hijackings were bloodless, so the prevailing thought among law enforcement agencies was to let the hijack continue to Cuba rather than risk the safety of passengers and crew and let the Cuban authorities arrest and imprison the perpetrators. In later years, the U.S. and Cuba reached an agreement whereby hijackers were extradited back to the United States to stand trial, which pretty much put an end to that fad. Of course, after 9/11, a more lethal approach was taken regarding aircraft hijacking, including the potential use of deadly force by military jet fighters. During our training with Mohawk, we were briefed to cooperate with a hijacker and fly him to Cuba if necessary. To be prepared for that possible event, the Mohawk secreted instrument-approach procedures for Havana International Airport behind a plastic placard located on the rear bulkhead of the cockpits. I was never hijacked to Cuba, but did indirectly participate in a major hijacking event.

Late one afternoon, we were on final approach to Kennedy International Airport and cleared number one to land when we were suddenly commanded by the tower controller to go around and proceed to a holding pattern off the coast of New Jersey. There was no explanation, we were just told to do it. We heard other aircraft following us being given the same instructions. Pretty soon, air traffic control had airliners parked in holding patterns all over the northeast. No aircraft were being allowed to take off or land. We wondered what was going on and asked the controllers several times, but we were curtly told "to be quiet" and to continue to hold. And, hold we did—for the next two hours. We finally called Mohawk operations on the radio and were told that an aircraft hijacking was in progress at the airport.

We were number one to land once things got straightened out, and we heard new arrivals being told that they were number eighty-seven for the approach. Soon, airplanes were calling in with low-fuel reports and being told that they would have to divert to other airports because Kennedy was locked down tight. At one point, we were cleared out of holding and started inbound to the airport only to be told to return to the holding pattern. Fortunately, we had plenty of fuel and we were finally cleared to land.

The cause of all of this high drama was a disgruntled Marine and Vietnam combat veteran who hijacked a TWA Boeing 727 in the air over Fresno, California, at gunpoint and demanded to be flown to Rome. The hijacked aircraft and crew, however, were not capable or qualified to fly internationally, so they landed at Kennedy where the hijacker was put on a different airplane, which then took off for Rome. After landing in the Italian capital, the hijacker, who was Italian born, supposedly asked to see the Pope, but instead was shown the inside of a dreary prison cell.

My exceptionally brief career at Mohawk involved equal doses of tragedy and irony. At the beginning of this chapter, I described a Mohawk Airlines' crash that killed everyone on board, including my Mohawk classmate and roommate. My association with Jack Morrow was brief, less than two months, but we had instantly formed a bond, which was commonplace among aviators who shared the same mission, whether in the military, an airline, or elsewhere within the aviation community. Further, we had each been military pilots and each had served a combat tour in Vietnam. We were born and raised in the same neck of the woods in western New York, he from Orchard Park and me from Angola, only eighteen miles apart. He had one child, a son, and so did I. But perhaps our most intimate connection occurred during a five-hour roundtrip flight we flew together, shoulder-to-shoulder, in Len Turrito's Cessna 150 from Angola to Utica to turn in our books and manuals after the first Mohawk furlough.

Maybe for the above reasons, or perhaps because Jack was just a few hours away from being on furlough like me, I took his death hard. After all, it could just have easily been me—I had flown the same identical airplane on my last flight with Mohawk several days before. To be sure, I was deeply affected by the loss of Jim Burke and Tom Gilliam in Vietnam. But those deaths occurred in a war zone where death was not unexpected. Jack's sudden demise was the first fatality of a friend in the civilian world of aviation. It would not be the last—and it never got any easier.

During my ten days flying the line, I flew four with Captain Robert McAdam. Three years later, he perished in another Mohawk crash when he heroically fought to save his passengers and crew following loss of an engine on final landing approach to Albany, New York. Thirty-one of forty-five passengers survived thanks to his skill and daring. I had flown this same airplane when I was with Mohawk—two aircraft, two fatal crashes, and I had flown them both. It simply wasn't my time to go, but it does make you stop and reflect, nonetheless.

Those in my class who chose to ride out the furlough waited over three years before being called back. Although my short time with Mohawk was new and exciting, I don't know if an airline career would have provided enough challenge and variety to satisfy my aviation wanderlust, money notwithstanding. Most airline careers are unremarkable and could best be described as mundane. Aside from a few pilots, like Captain Al Haynes (Sioux City, Iowa) and Captain Sully Sullenberger (miracle on the Hudson) who survived spectacular crashes and went on to international aviation fame, the vast majority of commercial airline pilots plod along in the shadows—just the way they like it. So, if I had chosen a commercial airline career, you wouldn't be reading a book about my aviation exploits.

Almost a Spy

Most people today have heard of Air America, the clandestine aviation arm of the CIA that was used primarily to support top-secret combat operations in Laos during the Vietnam War, but also employed to make forays into North and South Vietnam, Cambodia, Burma, and China. Much has been written about this shadowy air service and it was cemented into pop culture by the 1990 Mel Gibson movie *Air America*, a comedy that highlighted the antics of a band of Air America pilots. During the fall and hasty evacuation of Saigon on April 30, 1975, one of the iconic and enduring photographs of the Vietnam War was taken of an Air America Huey helicopter lifting desperate Vietnamese from the rooftop of the Pittman Apartment building (not the U.S. embassy as widely reported at the time). But in 1969, most Americans had not heard of this secretive organization.

Air America was created in 1950 to support CIA intelligence operations in China. Although the airline remained under the umbrella of the CIA during its lifespan, the agency farmed out its services to other branches of the U.S. government that needed "plausible deniability," including the Army and Air Force, which were prevented from using military aircraft because of various treaty limitations. During the later stages of the Indochina War, Air America flew in support of the French forces at Dien Bien Phu.

Air America's slogan was "Anything, Anywhere, Anytime, Professionally." You name it and the airline flew it: soldiers, commando teams, saboteurs, mercenaries, search-and-rescue missions for downed military pilots, civilians, diplomats, drug enforcement officers, doctors, war casualties, VIPs, food, medicine, weapons, ammunition, domestic animals and, as some have alleged, illicit drugs. Operating from bases in South Vietnam, Thailand, and Laos, Air America's fleet numbered over eighty fixed and rotary-wing aircraft of every description from World War II bombers to specialized short-field airplanes like the Pilatus Porter and the Helio Courier. On the helicopter side, the fleet included every type of military helicopter used since the Korean War.

Flying this motley collection of aircraft were hundreds of hand-picked aviators plucked from the ranks of former military pilots or civilian pilots who wanted to inject a little spice into their ho-hum flying careers. Christopher Robbins described these hired guns best in his 1979 book titled *Air America*: "This group of tin jockeys has been dubbed flying legionnaires, aerial cowboys, airborne buccaneers, and the CIA high flyers, but by any name they formed the finest bunch of airplane drivers that has ever been gotten together anywhere."

At one of my drill weekends with the Navy Reserves, I was talking with one of the pilots in my squadron when he casually mentioned that he had flown for Air America. My antenna immediately went up since I had recently received my second furlough notice from Mohawk Airlines. He invited me to stop by his BOQ room later that evening so we could talk about flying for Air America.

Air America helicopter evacuating desperate Vietnamese from a makeshift helicopter pad on top of the Pittman Apartment building in downtown Saigon. April 30, 1975

John Tarn was a short, balding, soft-spoken Lieutenant Commander who looked nothing like someone who had flown in the jungles of Southeast Asia for the CIA. He told me he had flown Sikorsky H-34 helicopters out of Udorn, Thailand, for three years. Most of his missions were into Laos, in support of nationalist troops fighting Communist insurgents, the Pathet Lao, with occasional flights into North Vietnam and Cambodia. I was somewhat familiar with Air America operations in South Vietnam, from which I concluded that my missions with the Navy Seawolves were much riskier and dangerous. John confirmed that on the vast majority of the Air America flights, he felt safe and secure because they had good intelligence about where the bad guys were. Occasionally, they came under small arms fire, but he said their flight profiles and tactics minimized the risk of being shot down. He went on to say that maintenance of the choppers was top-notch. If a part was defective, it was often replaced with a new one rather than being repaired. The only negative was the flying weather, but he said the good news was there were only three types to worry about—foggy, windy, and rainy!

John said that life was good on the Thai Air Force Base at Udorn. Within the Air America compound, there were dining, commissary, and good athletic facilities. There was nice housing and schools for married pilots and their families. He said that the social scene and comradery reminded him of being on a military base in the States. Best of all, the pay was outstanding and after being out of the country for eighteen months, it was tax free. John told me that his financial goal was to make enough to buy a farm in Pennsylvania, and that's what he did. He thoroughly enjoyed his time with Air America and had no regrets. He encouraged me to look into it and told me to contact a Mr. Harry Dawson in the Washington, D.C. headquarters. As I walked out of his room, he told me that they were looking for qualified H-34 pilots and that my chances were probably good to get a job.

Boy, was I ever pumped-up when I got home! Surprisingly, Barbara was all for the idea of moving to Thailand. She had not adjusted well to living among the Yankees of western New York and she was more than ready to get out of town. An overseas assignment sounded rather glamorous and exciting.

So, the next day, I fired off a letter to Harry Dawson. Six days later, I received a letter asking me to fill out an enclosed pilot application, which I did. Within a week, I received a Western Union telegram offering me a job—starting pay: $35,000 per year (equivalent to $230,000 today). There was one catch: I had to resign my seniority number at Mohawk.

At that point in time, I still wanted a career as a commercial airline pilot and I wasn't willing to resign, even for the glamour and pay of Air

America. (As it turned out, that's exactly what I did five months later, when I re-entered the Navy.) Even though I turned down the job offer, every three months, over the next year, just like clockwork, I received another telegram from Harry Dawson asking me to call him collect if I wanted a job. I never did and there went my chance to fly with a legendary outfit that is still spoken of with awe and reverence. Air America was disbanded in 1976.

Return to Pensacola

In late January 1970, during one of my active-duty stints with the Navy Reserve, I was eating lunch in the snack bar at NAS Willow Grove when one of my fellow reservists stopped by my table.

"Hi, Mike."

"Hello there, Tom," I replied.

"Say, I just got off the phone with the detailer and the Navy is offering to take guys like you and me back on active duty," he enthused.

"What did he have to say?"

"Well, apparently they are in need of flight instructors in Pensacola and are offering two and three-year active duty contracts to Reserve officers to fill that need. Besides limiting duty station choices to training squadrons, the other stipulation is you will not be eligible for promotion during the period of the contract."

"I won't be up for Lieutenant Commander for another three years, so that's no problem. Do you plan to apply?" I asked.

"Yes, I think I will. What about you?"

"Well, I could use some steady employment and being a flight instructor in Pensacola sounds pretty damn good. I'm going to call the detailer right after lunch. Thanks for the tip, Tom."

That was great news and I was excited about this new possibility. I wolfed down my cheeseburger and fries and called my detailer in Washington, D.C. Less than a month later, I loaded Barbara, our eleven-month-old son Brian, and our meager personal belongings into the station wagon and headed south to begin a three-year contract—which would morph into a fabulous twenty-year naval career.

Chapter 14

A Cut Above

I T WAS A BEAUTIFUL, CLEAR DAY IN MILITARY RESTRICTED AREA R-4005, ten miles southeast of Naval Air Station Patuxent River, Maryland. From my perch in the backseat of a T-38A jet flying at thirty-three thousand feet over the Chesapeake Bay, I could clearly see the Atlantic Ocean, the Potomac River, and Washington, D.C. We pilots often took for granted the magnificent views we were afforded by our profession, but not this day. For some reason, the sensory images outside the cockpit were never more vibrant and alive. Perhaps it was because of my eager anticipation to do what few helicopter pilots ever had the opportunity to do—fly faster than the speed of sound!

My reverie was cut short by a "You've got it" command from my flight instructor in the front seat. He then contacted range control and we received clearance into the high-speed corridor reserved for supersonic flight. Every time a naval aircraft exceeds the speed of sound over the continental United States, the geographic coordinates, date, time, altitude, and duration are documented in the event some civilian homeowner decides to file a damage report against the Navy claiming a wall in his house was cracked or an irreplaceable chandelier was smashed by a sonic boom. If the date and time matches a supersonic event in the official records, the U.S. government will usually pay damages to the homeowner. Otherwise, c'est la vie. The clever ones, of course, who know how to play the system, wait until an actual sonic boom occurs before submitting their carefully documented claim.

"Okay, Mike, here's what I want you to do," the instructor said. "Maintain straight and level flight and slowly advance both throttles to the firewall."

"Sounds easy enough," I replied.

"It's a piece of cake. Once the afterburners are lit, it won't take any time at all to reach Mach one."

As the aircraft began to accelerate, I wondered what the sensation would be like as we passed through the sound barrier. Would there be a sudden change in aircraft attitude? Would I be able to feel it in the stick? Would there be a change in airframe vibration or noise level? I watched the Mach meter rise—.85, .90, .95, .99—almost there. Then, with a slight shudder in the aircraft, we shot through the barrier and continued to accelerate.

"Gosh, is that all there is too it?" I exclaimed over the intercom. "If I wasn't watching the Mach meter, I would have missed it all together."

"Yep, that's it," he replied. "As you know, when Chuck Yeager did it for the first time, some of the brightest minds in aerodynamics predicted that his aircraft would break up."

"Yes, I do remember reading that."

"Mike, go ahead and pull the throttles back to disengage the afterburners. Otherwise, we won't have enough fuel to get back to the airfield."

With that, I headed back to the air station and aviation immortality. Well, not exactly, but I did have a big grin on my face.

Pax River

Sixty miles south of Washington, D.C., a point of land encompassing some six thousand acres juts out from the western shoreline of the Chesapeake Bay. Surrounded by the gently rolling farmland of St. Mary's County, this remote location in southern Maryland, close to the seat of government, made an ideal place for the Navy to consolidate secret testing of new aircraft, new weapons systems, and captured enemy aircraft during World War II. One year after the start of construction, Naval Air Station Patuxent River was established on April 1, 1943. Pax River, as it is affectionately called, has continuously served the aeronautical testing needs of the Navy with great distinction, even up to the present day.

Initially, the flight testing of new aircraft was performed by Navy and Marine fleet pilots, who were selected because of their superior flying skills and engineering backgrounds. In the waning days of World War II, the Navy decided that test pilots should receive formal training and standardization in the test techniques and procedures that would bring a high degree of safety and sound analysis to the oftentimes dangerous world of flight testing. Founded in March 1945, the U.S. Naval Test Pilot School (USNTPS) has evolved from a three-hour-per-day, ten-week course of instruction to an eleven-month intensive academic and flight program.

The exact reasoning for my application to Test Pilot School has long been forgotten. Perhaps I was attracted to the glamour and aura surrounding Pax River pilots as being the best of the best. Four of the original seven Mercury astronauts (Glenn, Carpenter, Schirra, and Sheppard) and many astronauts to follow, were graduates of this illustrious school. Maybe it was the challenge of applying and hopefully being selected to a highly competitive and prestigious program. No matter the specific rationale, I fired off an official application letter to the Selection Board in September 1973. With a selection rate of only twenty percent, I did not expect to be chosen. A brochure describing the application process was not encouraging:

> Selection to USNTPS is highly competitive. Military aviators are evaluated by a selection board which takes into account flight qualification, professional performance, academic background, and the needs of the service....

> Attendees normally have a BS degree in engineering, physical science, or math but this is not absolutely required. Those without requisite math or engineering courses can make themselves more competitive by completing correspondence courses or attending a local college/university. Don't second-guess what the board is looking for--if you don't apply you can't get picked. Over 1000 hours of flight time is desired at the time class convenes but, again, this is not a firm requirement.

Not only did I not have an engineering, physical science, or math degree, I had less than stellar grades at the University of Buffalo and Penn State in those types of courses (official transcripts were included in the application packet). The one thing in my favor was having 3,055 flight hours, in eighteen different models of military aircraft, in my logbook—well above the flight experience for most any fleet aviator who might be applying. Additionally, I had accumulated over six hundred pilot hours in civilian aircraft off-duty. Later, I learned that one of the hallmarks of a test pilot was the ability to quickly transition and master a totally unfamiliar aircraft. Apparently, the Selection Board minimized my poor academic credentials in favor of my strong flight background.

On January 10, 1974, I entered U.S. Naval Test Pilot School, one of only four test pilot schools in the free world and the second oldest. The other three were the U.S. Air Force Test Pilot School at Edwards Air Force Base; the Empire Test Pilot School at Boscombe Down, England; and the French Test Pilot School at Istres le Tube Airbase, France. If I managed to handle the rigorous eleven-month curriculum, I would be joining a select fraternity of international pilots.

Class 66

My classmates in Class 66 at the United States Naval Test Pilot School at NAS Patuxent River were a diverse group of pilots, flight officers, and engineers from six countries and representing nearly every branch of military service. The class roster included twelve U.S. Navy pilots, three U.S.

Marine pilots, one Navy and one Marine flight officer, one pilot from the U.S. Air Force, six pilots from the U.S. Army, one pilot and one engineer from the Canadian Forces, one pilot from the British Royal Navy, one engineer from the Italian Air Force, one pilot from the Australian Royal Air Force, and a civilian German engineer—twenty-nine in total. There were fighter and attack-jet pilots, carrier-based ASW pilots, long-range patrol pilots, and helicopter pilots with a wide range of operating experience. Many in the class were combat veterans of the Vietnam War. For all of our varied backgrounds, we shared a common passion for aviation and a strong desire to capitalize on our good fortune to have been selected for this very special training.

Spending long hours each day for eleven months with a bunch of guys in pursuit of a common goal lends itself to a deeper understanding of your fellow classmates. Some I got to know better than others, but all were true gentlemen and professional in their interactions with me. A few of my classmates stand out for a variety of reasons and, thus warrant mention.

Strictly by rank, I was selected to be the group leader of three other students also going through the helicopter curriculum: Captain Jim Arnold, U.S. Army pilot; Lieutenant John Burks, U.S. Navy pilot; and Flight Lieutenant Bob Redmond, Royal Australian Air Force pilot. During normal work hours, Monday through Friday, if we were not in class or flying, the four of us were crammed into a small office with four standard-issue military wooden desks that seemed to date from the War of 1812, five slightly more modern swiveling office chairs, and a small window with a venetian blind that was last dusted the day before Pearl Harbor. The walls were barren with the exception of a blackboard. I assumed that the spartan trappings of our work space were meant to send a signal to us TPUIs (Test Pilots Under Instruction)—the military has an acronym for everything—that creature comforts were simply a distraction to the serious work at hand.

Although smelly flight suits were unwelcome guests at times, the close contact of our small office afforded numerous opportunities to help one another. If one of us was struggling to master a particular academic concept or flight technique, it was a sure bet one of the other three had the answer and could provide a little on-the-spot tutoring.

John Burks, for example, who had a master's degree in aeronautical engineering from Princeton University, spent many an hour trying to explain difficult aerodynamic theory to his office mates. Even though I was without question the most academically challenged of the group, John always seemed to have an infinite amount of patience trying to hammer things into my thick skull. I am sure that many times he must have wondered how in heaven's name I was ever accepted to TPS. After the Navy,

John went on to a sterling career with NASA, rising to become Director of Aeronautics for NASA Ames, the premiere aeronautical research center in the United States, perhaps in the world.

Since military test pilots must evaluate new aircraft on their ability to perform a variety of flight missions that differ depending on the branch of service, the U.S. Army sends their future test pilots to Pax River, which has the only rotary-wing curriculum of the two U.S. test pilot schools. Our groupmate, Jim Arnold was a soft-spoken southerner with a dry sense of humor that belied a keen intellect. After serving his time in the Army, Jim enjoyed a long career as a test pilot for the FAA flight certification branch.

Rounding out our study group was Bob Redmond, a happy-go-lucky Aussie who kept up our morale with his constant upbeat assessment and minimization of the trials and tribulations of TPS. His greeting each morning of "G'day mate" and unfailing good humor pulled us through some tough stretches when course workload threatened to bury us.

Bob was my flying partner on the majority of the required syllabus flights, so I got to know him better than any other classmate. Not only was Bob a good pilot and well prepared for each flight, he also was a man of great determination and force of will because he got airsick to the point of vomiting at least once, sometimes twice, on every flight. By all rights, he should not have made it through military pilot training, where students who are plagued by chronic airsickness are washed out. Not that the military is heartless, but it is entirely understandable they can't have pilots upchucking during a dogfight or during a carrier landing, not to mention the resultant mess and smell in the cockpit. I have heard of pilots who had an occasional sudden bout of nausea and resorting to barfing into one of their flight gloves. Bob, on the other hand, had the unusual talent of being able to swallow his own vomit. Time and again, I would look across the cockpit to watch him contort his face as he struggled to force a mouthful back down his throat. Not a drop ever came out of his mouth. (Think back to the last time you imbibed a little too much and were forced to "hug the porcelain god." Now, think about trying to keep your mouth closed while swallowing all of those bits of lunch and dinner floating in a delicate cream sauce of beer and stomach acid. Do you see now why Bob had a very, very special talent?) Watching him in action was the most amazing display of bodily self-control I have ever witnessed. I'll have to admit, it did make for great theatre during our many flights together.

Several of my other classmates also achieved notable recognition after their days as a Pax River test pilot ended. Captain Tim Dineen, USMC, became a pilot with the Blue Angels, flying the number 2 positon during the 1981 and 1982 show seasons. Captain Ken Fugate, USMC, flew President Jimmy Carter in Marine One, the presidential helicopter. Ken was also an all-Marine tennis champion and frequent doubles partner of President Carter at Camp David. Lieutenant Mark Gemmill went on to command a fighter squadron and the USS Eisenhower, a nuclear-powered aircraft carrier. He retired from the Navy as a rear admiral.

Two classmates became NASA shuttle astronauts: Lieutenant Mike Coats and Lieutenant Mike Smith. Over the years, I have often told people about my claim to fame: "There were three guys in my TPS class named Mike. The other two became astronauts."

Mike Coats blasted into space three times aboard the shuttle, serving as the commander on his last two missions. After retiring from the Navy and being employed as a senior executive in the aerospace industry, he was tapped to be the Director of the Johnson Space Center in 2005 and retired from that position in 2012.

One year before he retired, Barbara and I stopped for a thirty-minute visit with Mike in his spacious fourth-floor corner office in the headquarters building at the Space Center in Houston, Texas. As we were about to leave, I asked Mike about a persistent and unique habit that he had when I knew him at Pax River, which involved a one-handed twirling and flipping of his pen. He would perform this amazing bit of manual dexterity while carrying on a serious conversation and oblivious to what the pen was doing—as if his hand had a mind of its own.

"Mike, do you still have that habit of flipping your pen?" I asked.

He started to laugh. "In fact, I do. On my last shuttle mission, we had to orbit the earth an extra time due to a last-minute hold from Mission Control. Since we had already completed our re-entry checklist, there was nothing to do but wait while we circled the earth one more time. Out of boredom and not thinking about the effect of zero gravity on my earthbound routine, I absentmindedly flipped my pen. I watched helplessly as it floated away and ricocheted around the cockpit for quite some time. Fortunately, it didn't delay our return to earth."

As for the other Mike, after completing our tour of duty at Pax River, Mike Smith and I were assigned to different squadrons in the Norfolk, Virginia, area. Though separated professionally, our two families continued to socialize occasionally on the weekends. One weekend, I borrowed his old lime-green pickup truck to transport a load of bricks I was using in the construction of a patio deck on the back of my house.

In 1980, our Navy careers diverged: Mike was selected to be an astronaut and I was sent to the Navy ROTC unit at Purdue University. After I retired from the Navy in 1984, I accepted a job teaching at Purdue University in their aviation department. On January 28, 1986, I was walking across the Purdue aviation maintenance hangar when I heard the stunning news over the PA system that was tuned to a local radio station: the space shuttle Challenger had blown up seventy-three seconds after lift-off from Cape Canaveral, killing all of the astronauts, including my friend Mike Smith. He had worked so long and so hard to achieve his dream of flying in space, and I am sure that his characteristic big grin was on full display right up until the end.

Death also stalked our days as students at USNTPS. One month before graduation, on October 23, 1974, the only U.S. Air Force officer in our class, Major Pete Vermaire, was killed when the jet he was flying crashed into the Chesapeake Bay. While still trying to make sense of Pete's death, the very next day, a student in Class 67 was killed when his jet also crashed. These two deaths in close proximity were reminders that the test pilot profession, even during training, was a dangerous business and not to be taken lightly.

The First Two Weeks

"Attention on deck." Sixteen Navy and Marine officers sprang to their feet, while the remaining thirteen members of Class 66 looked around, wondering what was going on, but soon followed suit. A tall, thin Navy Captain in a dress-blue uniform bedecked with multiple rows of military decorations, entered the room and strode briskly to the podium. Captain Carl "Tex" Birdwell, Jr., the Director of the U.S. Naval Test Pilot School, looked like a movie matinee idol of a bygone era with his pencil-thin mustache, dark eyes, jet-black hair, and rugged-looking face. The first day of TPS was about to begin.

"Seats, gentlemen," he said, as he scanned the room of eager, but anxious, faces. "I am happy to be the first to officially welcome you to Test Pilot School. I also want to congratulate everyone on your selection to this program. The old saying, 'Many are called, but few are chosen' certainly applies here, so you can be justifiably proud to be sitting in this classroom today.

"Now, the hard part begins. In the next eleven months until you graduate, the TPS staff will do their best to transform you from an above-average fleet pilot to one of the best test pilots in the world. We will expose you to the academic knowledge and test piloting skills and techniques to make you successful, but most of the heavy lifting will be done by each of you. Spending twenty hours per week in the classroom and the rest of your days, nights, and weekends preparing test plans, flying test flights, and writing technical reports, will severely test your mental abilities and physical stamina. Admittedly, the workload is very high, and it will seem there aren't enough hours in the day to get it all done. Time management is the key to success at TPS because no one subject or test project taken individually is beyond your capability, but everything taken collectively can be overwhelming."

As I sat there, listening to Captain Birdwell walk a fine line between scaring the hell out of us and encouraging us that we were equal to the task, I thought to myself, I have seen this man before. Although he bore some resemblance to Clark Gable, the 1930's and 1940's movie star, I knew our paths had crossed, but where? Then, it came to me. When I was a ferry pilot in VRF-32, I flew as copilot on a C-130 transport aircraft in August 1968 that flew then Commander Birdwell from California to Pax River. Before takeoff from Naval Air Station North Island in San Diego, the crew chief lowered the rear ramp and Birdwell drove his fancy sports car into the cavernous cargo bay where it was latched down for the trip to the East Coast. I knew that rank had its privileges, but this was a whole new world.

"Gentlemen, before I turn the podium over to my staff," he said with obvious feeling, "I would like to encourage each of you to try to devote one day a week to your family; and if you are single, a day just for you. The workload at TPS has been known to wreck marriages and cause other personal problems. So, I implore you to have a little fun along the way. Again, congratulations and welcome aboard."

After a couple more glad-you're-here type speeches, delivered perfunctorily by staff members way above my pay grade, the rest of that first day was devoted to important briefings critical to our success at TPS: flight operations, maintenance, safety, and use of the technical library. The last briefing for the day was titled "Physical Fitness Program." My mind went AWOL for a second—on top of everything else heaped on our plates, we had mandatory calisthenics and six-mile runs at 0500 every morning aka boot camp? No, we were simply encouraged to build some physical exercise into our daily routine. It sounded like a good thing to do on the first day, but in the months to come, it would be wishful thinking.

On day two, like every Monday through Friday for the next eleven months, we spent the morning hours in the classroom cramming in the academic knowledge that would, hopefully, make us better test pilots—we had "to talk the walk" first. The first two weeks were devoted to a quick review of algebra, trigonometry, geometry, complex numbers, and the beginning of a thorough review of calculus. Since I had done reasonably well in math in high school and college, I was able to hang in there with the rest of my classmates. But, in the weeks to come, it didn't take long for that to change.

On the flying side, the afternoons during the first two weeks were dedicated to flight physiology training, learning how to perform a proper preflight inspection of different models of aircraft, and familiarization flights with TPS instructors. Several of the physiology exercises were a repeat of training that I had encountered during my student training days: low-pressure chamber, parachute hang, parachute drag, and swim test.

One was a brand-new experience—the ejection-seat ride. Since I would be flying some jet airplanes during training, in addition to the primary focus of helicopters, I would need to know the steps to safely eject from a stricken aircraft. After receiving classroom instruction on the various types of ejection seats, how to prepare for and activate the ejection seat, and the post-ejection sequence of events, it was time for each student to perform a simulated ejection by pulling the face curtain handle above your head and shooting rapidly to the top of a thirty-foot vertical rail. Even though the explosive charge in the trainer was one-quarter of that used in a real jet, it was still quite a kick in the pants.

By Monday of the second week, in our "free time," we had to read five thick aircraft manuals and take a comprehensive open-book exam on each of the different aircraft we would be flying as pilot-in-command during the eleven-month curriculum. In my case, it was three helicopters (OH-58, UH-1, and CH-46) and the two fixed-wing airplanes (T-28 and OV-1). We also were encouraged to log as much cockpit time as possible sitting in the pilot seat and going over operating checklists and procedures—making "motor noises" was optional.

In keeping with the basic premise that a test pilot must be able to rapidly transition to a brand-new aircraft and that flying the machine must be subordinate and second nature to the primary task of flying test routines and collecting data, TPS policy for checking out in a new aircraft consisted of two flights with an instructor—the first being a general familiarization flight and the second being a checkride. So, after three hours in an aircraft you have never laid eyes on before, you were designated "safe for solo" and entrusted with a multi-million-dollar piece of military equipment. Talk about on-the-job training—this was almost like my ferry pilot days back in San Diego where the motto was "If you can start it, you can fly it."

As a test pilot, you might be the first person to fly a newly designed aircraft or to venture into an unexplored corner of the flight envelope. There was no instructor pilot to take you there or any published data that you could consult before takeoff. The onus was squarely on the test pilot to prepare himself as best he could before braving flight into the unknown. So, it was completely understandable that TPS would want to kick us out of the nest when we could barely fly. Actually, this methodology wasn't much different from World War II fighter pilots checking out in a new single-seat airplane: read the manual, hop in, and give it a go. Having said all of this, I still felt a bit like Linus without his blanket during the second week at TPS when I checked out, after only two flights in the OH-58, a light turbine-powered observation helicopter used by the Army and similar to the civilian Jet Ranger.

During the first two weeks, the TPS staff did an excellent job of preparing us for the days and weeks to come when we would be spending eighteen to twenty hours per day pursuing the goal of becoming a Navy test pilot. As one instructor told us half in jest, "Between flying, classes, and study, you have four or five hours a day of wasted time that's taken up sleeping." How right he was!

Academics

At Test Pilot School, the curriculum was divided into three parts in which to excel—or fail—Academics, Flight, and Report Writing. Unsatisfactory performance in any of these three areas would result in dismissal, and just about every facet was graded by staff instructors. I knew going in that my academic preparation was less than desirable. Although I had been able to keep up during the first two weeks of math review, I knew after reading the list of future courses that I would be in over my head down the road. Courses like mechanics, aerodynamics, thermodynamics, stability and control theory were scary sounding to a fellow like me with a bachelor's degree in management.

One bright spot was the invention of personal handheld, battery-powered, scientific calculators and permission from the staff to use them. Those of my vintage, who cut their teeth on a slide rule, can attest to the constant struggle to accurately place the decimal point when performing mathematical and engineering computations. I bought one of the first HP-45 calculators on the market, and it was not cheap—I paid nearly five hundred dollars, a lot of money in that day—but it was worth every penny not having to worry where the decimal point belonged.

The Head of Academics was world known in the field of flight-test methodology and an intimidating presence in the classroom. Mr. Tom Moore, a highly decorated World War II and Korean War Marine fighter pilot, was a large bald-headed man who seldom smiled. It was obvious from the onset that he favored those students who had the solid academic background to stay with him as he wrote one obscure mathematical equation after another on the blackboard. He had little patience for those students who could not quickly grasp the advanced concepts he was presenting. He called on me twice to answer a question he had posed to the class, and found me wanting both times. Mercifully, he never called on me again. Early in the term, I went to his office for some extra help, but left deflated and demoralized—I never went back. Fortunately, the other three academic instructors—Bob Miller, JJ McCue and Bob Bowes—were able to teach less gifted students like me and were approachable. If it were not for their patience, understanding, and encouragement, I would likely not have made it through the academic portion of TPS.

At the end of normal working hours, most of my classmates dashed home to grab dinner and say hello to their wife and kids before returning to TPS and their officemates to study and prepare for the challenges facing them the following day. I have never been one who liked group study or group projects. I have always worked best alone. Consequently, I converted an extra bedroom in the basement into my study, where I toiled until midnight most days. Unlike my counterparts who saw very little of their families, at least I was in the house and available for snippets of conversation now and then.

After the first month of working day and night seven days a week to keep up with the academic, flight, and report-writing requirements, I came to the realization that there just was not enough hours in the day—at least for me—to get everything done to my satisfaction. Something had to give. Then I had an epiphany—this is a test pilot school, with emphasis on "pilot"! I reasoned that the quickest way to get kicked out was to perform in a sub-standard manner in the flight or report-writing sections of the curriculum. So, I decided to concentrate my efforts there and devote what time I had left to my academic studies. I had, unknowingly, broken the code. As I was to find out later, when I returned to TPS as an instructor, students were given a fair amount of leeway when it came to sub-par academic performance, but next to none in the other two areas. As the old question goes, "How do you eat a five-hundred-pound marshmallow?"—you eat the flight and report-writing parts first. At least now I had a survival strategy that would hopefully lead to graduation day.

Flight

After spending each morning in the classroom trying my best to discern complex flight theory, it was a relief to spend the afternoons in a realm in which I felt more the master. It was a tremendous morale booster to spend the latter part of each day preparing test plans, discussing the procedures to be used and the sequence of events with my flying partner, and finally walking out to the flight line and taking off.

To most people, the mere mention of being a test pilot conjures up an image of an extremely dangerous occupation populated by daredevils and risk-takers who put their lives on the line each and every time they take to the air. Nothing could be further from the truth. To be sure, many test pilots have lost their lives, but not because they were careless or reckless—if they were properly trained. So, one of the primary missions of TPS was to create a test-pilot culture that promoted safety, careful test-plan preparation before takeoff, and rigid in-flight discipline.

"Plan the flight and fly the plan" was a recurring motto that was drummed into us from day one. In other words, meticulously plan the flight on the ground, and prepare test cards that will be used during flight to control the precise sequence of events and methods used to achieve each data point. Once airborne, the test pilot should religiously adhere to the test plan laid out in the test cards and refrain from any temptation to explore an uncharted area of the flight envelope or to investigate a new phenomenon that was accidentally uncovered during the flight. In other words, don't deviate from the script—no ad-libbing in the air.

Perhaps it would aid you, the reader, if the various types of test pilots who work within the aviation industry were defined in regard to their specific job descriptions. At the top of the profession, at least in terms of glamour and notoriety, is the *experimental* test pilot. These are the pilots who make the first flight of a new prototype design and, through subsequent flights, expand the so-called flight envelope in terms of takeoff and landing distances, airspeed, altitude, range, weight, and configuration of landing gear, flaps, and other aerodynamic devices. You might say that they establish the outer limits for a particular aircraft. They fly into the unknown, where no pilot has ever been. Most experimental test pilots are employed by aircraft manufacturers and flight-research institutions, such as NASA. A good example of the latter would be Chuck Yeager, who broke the sound barrier for the first time in 1947. Private individuals who fly their own designs or set aviation records could also be classified as experimental test pilots. Charles Lindbergh, who was the first to fly across the Atlantic Ocean in 1927, and Dick Rutan and Jeana Lee Yeager, who were the first to circumnavigate the world unrefueled in 1986, are well known for their record-setting feats.

Engineering test pilots are the unsung heroes of the profession. They are the ones who do the grunt work of gathering the flight data necessary to compile and document the aircraft's performance and handling information that goes into the detailed flight manual that is published by the manufacturer or military service to be used by pilots flying a specific model of aircraft. One might say that experimental test pilots define the extreme outer edges while the engineering test pilots fill in the gaps between the limits. Pilots who graduate from military test pilot schools are classified as engineering test pilots. Not that they couldn't perform experimental work—in fact, many experimental test pilots are former military test pilots—it is the unwritten rule that military test pilots do not venture into any part of the flight envelope not previously cleared by the manufacturer's test pilots. However, military test pilots do perform experimental flights that are not the charter of the manufacturer, like ordnance and weapon separation testing, aircraft carrier suitability testing, the development of operational and tactical flight procedures, and the research and development of airborne electronic and navigation systems.

As new aircraft, both military and civilian, roll off the assembly floor, each must be flown to ensure that it is safe to fly and that it conforms to the specifications contained in the design and manufacturing contract. A *production* test pilot performs this tedious, but important work before a new aircraft is turned over to the buyer, whether that be the military, the airlines, a corporation, or a private owner.

After major repairs have been performed on an aircraft, it usually must be flown by a pilot with experience in that particular model to ensure that the repairs corrected the original discrepancy and that the aircraft is safe to fly by any line pilot. The military and other organizations with large flight departments usually designate one or more pilots to perform this important work and they are called *maintenance* test pilots. Normally, this is a collateral duty and not their primary job description. For example, during my tour of duty at the test center, I was designated as a maintenance test pilot for the OH-58, AH-1, and SH-2F helicopters and the X-26 glider.

The flight curriculum at TPS was anchored by the two main areas used by the test community to describe the behavior of any aircraft—Flying Qualities and Performance, or as it is commonly called "FQ & P."

Let's discuss the easy one first, the one that even a layman can identify with. Wow, does that aircraft go fast! Wow, does that aircraft fly high! Wow, does that aircraft take off and land in a short distance! Years later, when I was teaching private-pilot ground school at Northwestern Michigan College, I introduced the subject of aircraft *Performance* with those exclamations. I called them the "wow factors." Way back in the infancy of a new aircraft's design, a test pilot determines just how fast it can go, how fast it can climb, how far it can go without refueling, and the takeoff and landing distances. Consequently, at TPS, we had to learn how to accurately measure aircraft performance.

Flying qualities is a little more difficult to comprehend, especially for non-pilots. First, this general area is sub-divided into two major parts: *longitudinal* and *lateral-directional* flying qualities, which corresponds to the three principal axes of rotation that allow the pilot to control an aircraft in pitch, roll, and yaw using the stick/yoke and rudder pedals.

Embodied within a test pilot's quest to correctly document the flying qualities of an aircraft, he must delve into specific areas that most pilots have never heard of, like static and dynamic stability, aerodynamic coupling, control damping, and control harmony, to name just a few. Some flying qualities can be precisely measured, others are more subjective—much like art is in the eye of the beholder. These subtleties are of little concern to the average pilot because test pilots have identified problems and deficiencies in these areas and they have been largely corrected before the first new aircraft rolls off the production line.

So, the job of TPS flight instructors was to teach and demonstrate the proper techniques used to collect inflight data and to assist the student test pilot in developing the subjective skills used to assess and document the FQ & P of a new aircraft.

The flight syllabus consisted of eleven one-on-one demonstration flights by instructors, forty data-acquisition flights flown by students with another student flying as copilot, and three progress checks or check-flights administered by staff instructors. In my case, I flew four helicopters (OH-58, UH-1, CH-46, and AH-1G) and six fixed-wing airplanes (T-28, OV-1, T-2, T-38, B-26, and X-26), and accumulated 156 total flight hours during my eleven months as a student at TPS. Even though it was a lot of hard work, it was still a fantasy world for someone like me who loved to fly. Nowhere else in the world could a pilot fly so many diverse aircraft in the span of less than a year.

Rehashing details of the majority of my data-acquisition flights as a student would be boring in the extreme for the average reader, but there was one notable exception and several demo flights that are worthy of being included in this book.

One of our flight syllabus exercises had the innocuous sounding name of *Asymmetric Power*. It was a dangerous test—only I didn't realize how dangerous it was until I began teaching multi-engine flight students after I had retired from the Navy. The test aircraft for this exercise was the Grumman twin turbo-prop OV-1 Mohawk, used by the U.S. Army as a reconnaissance and surveillance aircraft. The assignment itself called for students to investigate and document the FQ & P of the OV-1 flying on one engine, including determination of the airspeed at which directional control is lost, which all multi-engine pilots know as Vmc.

On top of the dangerous nature of the test was the minimal checkout given to all students, by design, in any aircraft they flew at TPS—one instructional flight and a checkride, less than three total hours. I was fortunate to have over seven hundred hours of multi-engine time, while most of my TPS classmates had none. Such is the nature of being a test pilot: being able to step into any aircraft and do the job, no matter how unfamiliar the machine.

My first flight in the Mohawk was an eye-opener. My flight instructor, Lieutenant Willie Williamson, was at the controls flying at two thousand feet, when he said, "Watch this"—two words, when paired together in an aircraft cockpit, usually spell trouble. He then proceeded to yank the yoke

Four of the ten aircraft I flew as a student at TPS. *From top to bottom:* Bell OH-58, Grumman OV-1, Boeing-Vertol CH-46, and Schweizer X-26

back into a 4-G pull-up. I had never started a loop so low, but over we went, nice as you please. He was trying to demonstrate just how agile the airplane was, and he succeeded! I was thankful that he didn't offer me a chance to replicate his stunt.

I passed my checkride, flew one familiarization flight as pilot-in-command, and then proceeded to make two data-acquisition flights with my officemate Captain Jim Arnold. Ignorance really is bliss, because Jim and I merrily yanked an engine to idle thrust in straight and level; performed climbs at higher and higher nose attitudes, in steep turns—you name it, all without knowing just how close we probably came to losing total control of the airplane. The Mohawk was equipped with ejection seats, so maybe we could have saved our skins, but maybe not.

The half-day of glider flying built into the flight curriculum was another example of the steep learning curve expected from all TPS students. I had flown gliders briefly when I was stationed in San Diego, so I wasn't a total neophyte, but I was the only one in the class with any glider experience. The reader will begin to appreciate just how quick things are thrown at you when I describe the flight profile on the very first flight in X-26A, a tandem two-seat glider manufactured by Schweizer (the civilian designation is the SGS 2-32). Incidentally, the X-26As operated by TPS were the only gliders in the Navy inventory.

The only concession to sanity was that the instructor pilot flew the first flight from takeoff to landing. The profile went like this: aero-tow behind a U-6 Beaver to three thousand feet, release from the tow plane, 360-degree descending steep turn, stall and recovery, loop, enter three-turn upright spin, recover, and land. Then, it was the student's turn. Although it was stressful to cram all of those maneuvers into a six- or seven-minute flight, it was a blast. And the best part: there was no report to write!

I mentioned the supersonic demo at the beginning of this chapter, which was a thrill, but the most interesting demo flights we flew were those in specialized aircraft whose stability characteristics could be changed during flight. The Cal-Span Corporation of Buffalo, New York (formerly Cornell Aeronautical Lab), was contracted by TPS to bring a "vari-stab" B-26 and a T-33 to Pax River two times per year. These vintage aircraft were modified with a fly-by-wire control system which allowed the instructor pilot from Cal-Span to change the electronic signals to the flight controls during flight to make the aircraft fly like any number of other aircraft. For example, during my first flight in the B-26, a World War II era bomber, the instructor made it fly like a B-747 and then, by manipulating a few dials, he made it fly and behave like an F-16 fighter.

On the helicopter side, TPS had its own vari-stab aircraft, a modified CH-46 tandem-rotor helicopter that could be set up to fly like a variety of different helicopters. These variable stability aircraft were invaluable tools to teach fledgling test pilots how to evaluate the flying qualities of different aircraft without actually having to fly all of them separately.

Technical Reports

The third and final area that students had to master at TPS was learning how to translate inflight data and impressions to a form that could be understood and used by decision-makers up the chain of command. If a test pilot could not successfully bridge the gap between flight observations and the world of engineers and bureaucrats, then he could not possibly hope to influence the process by which deficiencies and problems uncovered during test flights were corrected. The end result of that failure could be the delivery of new aircraft to the fleet that were dangerous and incapable of mission success. Although this phase of training was not nearly as much fun as flying, and was the dread of most students, it was arguably the most important.

Mirroring the need in the real world, there were two types of reports: written and oral. Written reports could vary from a couple pages to ten to twelve typewritten pages, depending on the assignment. There were thirteen written reports and nine oral reports, which in some ways were more difficult and time consuming to prepare than the written ones.

The first step in the preparation of a technical report was called "data reduction"—taking the raw data captured by special onboard test equipment and physical measurements made by the test pilot himself and displaying this information in a usable manner, usually in the form of a graph.

The special flight-test instrumentation devices and associated electrical wiring were colored orange to distinguish them from standard aircraft components. TPS aircraft were not equipped with state-of-the-art flight-test equipment—such as computers, digital recording devices, strain gauges, accelerometers, and air-to-ground telemetry—for two reasons: cost and to mimic situations when a test pilot may be called to perform a quick evaluation of a standard production aircraft. So, TPS aircraft were generally only equipped with a sensitive airspeed boom and a photo-panel. The latter piece of equipment was so low-tech that it could have been used by the Wright brothers. It was simply a device that took a photograph of the standard aircraft flight instruments, like airspeed, altimeter, vertical speed, and needle and ball, whenever the pilot pushed a button on the control stick. The tedious part of using the photo-panel was the necessity to look frame-by-frame after a flight to manually record the readings—it required many boring hours.

Much of the equipment used by the students was definitely old-school, such as stop watches, handheld force gauges and control jigs, and pocket tape recorders.

Once the data reduction was completed and the numerous graphs were constructed, then the student had to combine hard data and subjective impressions into a succinct technical report. Good test pilots were known for their ability to concisely describe an inflight event in as few words as possible, yet convey to the reader precisely the point they were trying to make. Famed test pilot and air racer, Jimmy Doolittle, once came back from a flight and wrote: "Wings broke off. Thrown out." I must say that he set the brevity bar pretty high for us new technical writers.

Fortunately for me, I have always enjoyed some success as a writer, so the written reports, although time consuming, were not too difficult. Mercifully, the school hired women in the local community to type student reports. My typist, Joyce Grabelchic, was a dear lady, who was almost old enough to be my mother. Her husband was a wealthy businessman, so she certainly did not need the small amount of money that this job paid—she did it because she loved working with student test pilots and helping them to succeed. She had been doing it so long that she probably could have written these reports herself. Consequently, she caught many of my mistakes. Small ones, she just corrected without even telling me. If she came across something that didn't sound just right, she would call me to discuss it—and she was usually right!

Once the reports were typed into the proper format and handed in to the grading instructor, he would carefully and thoroughly correct and critique our efforts and give us a grade. By the eleventh month, we student test pilots had been molded into Hemingways of technical discourse—at least that's what we liked to think!

NPE and Graduation

The final exercise and culmination of months of hard work was the NPE, which stood for Navy Preliminary Evaluation. It involved a complete FQ & P evaluation of an aircraft we had never flown before—we were allowed a maximum of six flight hours spread over four individual flights. During those six flight hours, we had to utilize all of the skills and techniques that we had learned. Completion of this task in the time allotted required a monumental amount of ground preparation making test cards and choreographing the precise sequence of events.

My assigned aircraft was the AH-1G Cobra attack helicopter manufactured by Bell Helicopter. Being a former gunship pilot from Vietnam and marveling at the Army Cobras that I saw when they were first introduced into the Mekong Delta, I was thrilled to be able to finally fly this sleek machine. Some of my classmates were sent to manufacturer's facilities and

Bell AH-1G Cobra attack helicopter like the one I flew as a student and flight instructor at TPS.

warbird museums around the country to be able to fly an aircraft totally new to them if a suitable aircraft could not be found locally at Pax River. In my case, TPS had Cobras in its inventory, so I didn't have far to go—which turned out to be a fortuitous happenstance for me.

After completion of the flying and data reduction, a voluminous technical report—mine was eighty-three pages—had to be written. It really was the equivalent of a master's degree thesis. In fact, within a short number of years after I graduated from TPS, first, the University of Maryland and then the U.S. Naval Postgraduate School at Monterrey, California, began awarding master's degrees in aeronautical engineering to TPS graduates who completed an additional six academic courses. Such was the academic rigor accorded to the Test Pilot School curriculum.

My NPE exercise took an unexpected detour the last week in October 1974, shortly after I was informed that I would be flying the Cobra. I awoke one morning with acute stomach pain on my right side. I told Barbara that I had appendicitis. She immediately threw cold water on that idea and said that I was jumping to conclusions. Ever since my two younger brothers, David and Bill, experienced a ruptured appendix as young boys, I was primed and ready. I just knew that I would be next and, therefore, every pain on the right side of my body was immediately put through my "appendicitis filter." I put on my uniform and convinced my wife to take me to the naval hospital on base. At 2200 hours I was on the operating table having my appendix removed. Needless to say, I was medically grounded during the time the rest of my classmates were completing their NPE. I was told that I would be allowed to graduate with my class and be able to complete the NPE during the Christmas holidays—which I did.

Graduation exercises for Class 66 from the United States Naval Test Pilot School were held on November 26, 1974, at the Cedar Point Officer's Club. It was a formal black-tie affair, befitting the significant milestone in the education and training of the next group of test pilots to proudly represent their respective military services. Members of Class 66 and the military staff were in their mess dress uniforms, civilian staff and male visitors and fathers were in their tuxedoes, and the ladies were dressed in splendid evening gowns. My mother and father were there—it would be the first and only graduation of mine they attended since high school.

After a social hour and dinner, and short speeches by various military dignitaries, the graduation certificates were handed out, each encased in a fine-leather binder—mine had a blank certificate inside. It was hard for me to get excited like my fellow classmates—they were completely finished, while I had the NPE hanging over me. It was definitely a bittersweet moment.

Class Field Trip

As a reward for completion of a grueling course of instruction, Class 66 was given a "victory lap" around the country to visit various aircraft manufacturers. In the days before the ethics police of the federal government got involved to stamp out what they perceived to be subtle bribes on the part of contractors wishing to do business with the military, the contractors we visited rolled out the red carpet and wined and dined us royally. Over a twelve-day period, we visited Raytheon, Pratt and Whitney, Sikorsky, Grumman, McDonnell Douglas, Beech, Bell, and Vought. Many of these famous aviation brands have since merged into other companies with different names or disappeared completely.

We were briefed by chief test pilots on their company's latest and greatest technological achievements—famous men who had made the first flight on many of the aircraft in the military inventory. We were taken on walking tours of their production facilities and laboratories where cutting-edge research was being performed. Best of all, we were treated with respect and as professional equals. It was certainly an eye-opening and humbling experience for all of us.

During our visit to Vought Systems in Dallas, a division of LTV Aerospace, we each received two very nice gifts, apparently in keeping with a longstanding tradition of TPS visits. In our hotel room was a bottle of Chivas Regal, and at dinner that night, each of us was presented with an expensive cowboy hat with our name embossed in gold lettering on the headband—the students were given a white hat and the instructors were given a black hat, I guess to symbolize the "good guys" and the "bad guys."

That evening after dinner, many of us retired to a lounge in the hotel for a few drinks and to listen to live music. One of our classmates—who shall remain anonymous to protect the guilty— apparently got along well enough with one of the ladies to be invited to her apartment. All well and good, except our Navy transport aircraft was departing Naval Air Station Dallas promptly at 0800 the next morning. All of us were standing around the airplane as the time for departure drew near. The only hitch: we were missing one guy. Commander Pete Gorham, the executive officer of TPS, was pacing back and forth, looking at his watch and then to the parking lot, wondering what to do. Should we leave on time or wait a few more minutes to see if he would show up? Finally, a few minutes after our scheduled departure, Gorham was given a message that our playboy was en route and should be there within five minutes.

Someone had the bright idea that we should form two lines, one on each side of the path leading to the airplane boarding stairs, wearing our cowboy hats—much the way that sideboys line up when a dignitary is welcomed aboard a Navy ship. Pretty soon, we heard a taxi screech to a halt in the parking lot and saw a bedraggled naval officer with his tie askew leap out of the car and run toward the waiting reception committee. With a sheepish grin, our wayward sailor made his way down the gauntlet. As he passed down the line the "sideboys" removed their hats in a sweeping hand motion and bowed. It was the highlight of the trip!

When we returned to Pax River, I completed my NPE and traded my blank certificate for one with my name on it. I had accomplished a significant goal. When I graduated in 1974, less than one thousand Navy and Marine pilots had graduated from TPS before me, so I was in some select company.

Would I do it again? The short answer is no. As one student put it, "It's like taking eleven months of final exams." That being said, I am glad I did it!

Chapter 15

The Ragged Edge

T HIRTY MILES NORTHWEST OF SAN CLEMENTE ISLAND, OFF THE coast of Southern California, the *USS Chicago*, a guided missile cruiser measuring 673 feet long, plowed through the placid waters of the Pacific Ocean at twenty knots. Overcast skies prevented any moonlight from intruding into the blackness that enveloped the ship two hours before midnight. The ship's mission was to provide flight-deck services for the repeated launch and recovery of a helicopter involved in a flight-test project conducted by the Naval Air Test Center.

Being an old ship, the *Chicago* was not equipped with the latest lighting and visual equipment that allowed helicopter pilots to operate more safely at night. After a couple landings, during which I had some difficulty picking up the outline of the ship and judging closure rate, the ship's crew, with my concurrence, started to experiment with various combinations of standard exterior shipboard lighting trying to improve the situation. After several landings, it was determined that the red floodlights used to illuminate the main deck during night replenishment operations greatly improved my visual cues.

On the fourth starboard-to-port approach to the flight deck using this ad hoc lighting arrangement, I was feeling comfortable and relaxed—a dangerous mindset for any type of night landing, especially on a small platform fifty feet off the water with a missile launcher and towering superstructure just forward of the touchdown point. At a quarter mile and three hundred feet above the dark swells, I noticed that one of the red floodlights was reflecting off the water. It appeared to provide a good visual cue to my height above the ocean. As I continued to descend, I shifted my instrument cross-check to this newfound discovery, marveling at the improvement it made. Everything seemed normal—almost like a day landing with good visual altitude references. Suddenly, it didn't feel so normal. I quickly glanced at my radar altimeter. To my horror, it read fifty feet and descending! A second or two from crashing into the Pacific Ocean, I abruptly pulled up collective and started an emergency climb to a safe altitude.

Shaken at how close we had come to flying into the water, I turned the flight controls over to the copilot. As was the case so many times during my aviation career—it wasn't my time to buy the farm.

Flight Test

When I graduated from Test Pilot School in 1974, the Naval Air Test Center at Patuxent River was divided into three major divisions: *Flight Test*, *Service Test*, and *Weapons Test*. Flight Test was responsible for the more traditional aspects of flight testing, such as documenting flying qualities and gathering performance data on new aircraft entering the fleet, spin testing, carrier suitability and shipboard flight operations, and conducting preliminary evaluations of new aircraft designs that manufacturers were trying to sell to the Navy and Marine Corps.

Service Test carried out accelerated flight operations of existing aircraft in the naval inventory in an attempt to uncover mechanical and mainte-nance issues before the fleet encountered them—a "beat the fleet" concept. The idea was to discover problems early and correct any deficiencies before they impacted operational readiness at sea.

As mentioned in the previous chapter, airframe manufacturers did not perform flight testing on the various weapons that could be dropped or fired from naval aircraft. The job of *Weapons Test* was to operate the dif-ferent weapons systems inflight to ensure missiles, bombs, rockets and bullets separated cleanly from the wing or fuselage without endangering the aircraft or crew. Of parallel importance was to determine and refine the accuracy and efficiency in destroying the intended target.

Over half of my TPS classmates selected Flight Test as their first choice, which was rumored to be the more glamourous and plumb assignment; apparently only the "best sticks" were picked. As a result of the deliberate division of labor I made during my first month at TPS, I finished number three from the bottom of my class in academics, but near the top in flight and report writing. So, I suppose I should have applied for Flight Test. But I thought blowing things up with rockets and torpedoes sounded more fun, so I put Weapons Test as my first choice. "Needs of the Navy," which translates into "We'll assign you wherever we damn well please," trumped my desires and I was assigned to Flight Test.

Since I was the new guy in the rotary-wing section of Flight Test and had to learn the ropes in the real world of test pilots, I was assigned to be copilot for some of the seasoned veterans on their projects, but without any real responsibility. For the first three months, it was pretty slow, without much to do—quite a turnaround from the hectic, seven-day-a-week pace as a TPS student. I did a little routine proficiency flying and requalified in the H-1 and SH-2F helicopters as aircraft commander and transitioned to the dual-engine Cobra, the Bell AH-1J attack helicopter.

Three months after reporting, the Test Center underwent a major reorganization and Flight Test, which had existed for thirty years, was abolished. The old test divisions were carved into new entities organized according to aircraft mission: *Strike Directorate* was for fighter and attack jets, *ASW Directorate* for fixed-wing anti-submarine aircraft, both carrier-based and land-based, and *Rotary Wing Directorate* for all helicopters. Naturally, I was reassigned to the latter. Other than our official name and the gathering of all helicopter test pilots under one roof, nothing else changed for me personally.

Landing on a Pitching and Rolling Deck

All classes of ships in the U.S. Navy that are capable of landing helicopters on their decks have a wind-operating envelope designed for that specific class so that fleet helicopter pilots can safely land and take off within specified wind direction and velocity parameters. These wind envelopes are developed empirically by Navy test pilots performing repeated landings and takeoffs in varying wind conditions and sea states (wave heights), both day and night. These oftentimes dangerous test projects—one for each class of ship—were called Dynamic Interface testing (DI).

A month before Flight Test closed its doors, my section head assigned me to take over the DI projects involving the SH-2F helicopter aboard *non-aviation ships*, the term given to all non-carrier type ships that had a helicopter landing area. To hasten my education and transition to this new job, I was assigned to be the understudy for the test pilot currently doing that job: Lieutenant Mike Coumatos. Even better, I would be his copilot for the upcoming DI tests aboard the *USS Detroit* (AOE-4), a Fast Combat Support ship capable of providing fuel, ammunition, food, and other supplies to U.S. Navy ships at sea.

I was indeed fortunate to be paired with Mike Coumatos. Not only was he an experienced and

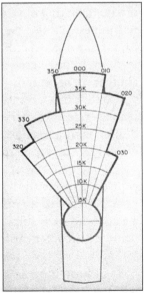

Example of a wind operating envelope published after completion of DI testing.

gifted test pilot, he was also an excellent mentor and teacher. With an easygoing manner and ever-present smile, he was extremely well-liked and respected by his seniors, peers and coworkers. Just above a bushy mustache that bordered on being non-regulation length were eyes that had the slight twinkle of a man who played as hard as he worked. As evidence of his reputation as a consummate test pilot, Mike was assigned as a member of the NATC test team that would evaluate two competing helicopter models, one from Boeing-Vertol and one from Sikorsky, that were vying to replace the venerable Huey helicopter in the military inventory. (Several years later, Sikorsky won the competition, which resulted in the production of the Blackhawk, a helicopter that has become almost as famous as the one it replaced.)

About a week before the start of testing aboard the *Detroit*, Mike cornered me in the passageway leading to our office spaces.

"Say, what are you doing this afternoon?" he asked.

"Nothing much really," I responded.

"Good, let's meet right after lunch so you and I can discuss the fundamentals of DI testing. It would be helpful if you had a basic understanding before we head to the ship next week."

"That would be great, Mike," I replied. "I would appreciate that very much. I'll stop by your cubicle about 1300."

During a three-hour stretch that afternoon, Mike patiently explained the process used to gather the necessary test data to allow construction of safe operating envelopes for fleet aviators. "Mike, before we get down to business, I'd like to get a feel for your previous shipboard experience. About how many landings do you have on small decks?" he asked.

"Oh, I don't know. Probably around seventy in my first squadron and another six or seven in Vietnam," I stated.

"Well, that's a respectable number and way more than the H-3 drivers that operated off carriers," he smiled, seemingly relieved that he wasn't dealing with a total greenhorn. "I also heard that you were the air officer on an LPD before coming to TPS."

"Wow, bad news travels fast," I laughed. "No, actually I very much enjoyed my tour on the *Raleigh*."

Mike screwed up his face in mock surprise. "You're a strange duck—an aviator who likes ships," he chuckled. (Ironically, Mike went on to command a helicopter carrier later in his naval career).

"Yeah, I suppose I am."

"I'm beginning to see why the powers-that-be selected you to replace me. You have experienced flight ops on non-aviation ships from the pilot perspective as well the ship's point of view. You'll do well, I'm sure." Turning serious, Mike began to provide a broad overview of DI testing. "In the early days, before the early 1970s, there was no official guidance, so it was up to the pilot and the ship's captain to decide if it was safe to operate. Oftentimes the ship's CO thought it was safe and browbeat or forced a takeoff against the better judgment of the pilot flying the helicopter. So, NAVAIR—Naval Air Systems Command—decided that the twin goals of mission accomplishment and safety would be best achieved by some sort of official guidance. And so, Dynamic Interface testing was born.

"The idea," he continued, "was to provide a wind-operating envelope that determined the maximum limits for day, night, and degraded flight control modes, like ASE off or hydraulics off. Furthermore, these operating envelopes should allow takeoffs and landings up to a wave height of thirteen feet or sea state five."

"Man, that's some big waves," I said, somewhat surprised.

"Yeah, it can get pretty sporty out there, trying to land in those big rollers," Mike said matter-of-factly.

He went on to explain that every ship, depending on its design and loading, has "a null period"—a five- to ten-second timeframe when the deck smooths out and stabilizes—that occurs in a random fashion no matter how badly the deck is pitching and rolling. So, if the pilot is in position, a relatively safe landing can be made during this null. However, staying put on the deck and not sliding off when violent deck motion resumes, is dependent on the ship's deck crew quickly placing chocks on the wheels and chaining down the aircraft to the flight deck—not an easy task.

"Obviously, these tests involve some dangerous operating conditions," Mike said seriously. "As you learned at TPS, the most important factor when engaged in critical flight testing is a gradual build up to the end points. In other words, we are going to start out making takeoffs and landings with light winds over the deck, right down the lineup stripe, in fairly calm seas. Then we increase the relative wind over the deck in gradual increments up to the maximum limit. Then we'll shift the relative wind ten degrees either side of the lineup marking, and do it all over again. Naturally, we will begin with day operations before proceeding to night and degraded mode flights."

"How do we know when we have reached the maximum limits for a given wind direction?" I asked.

With a mischievous twinkle in his eye, he let me in on a trade secret. "When the landing scares the living shit out of you."

Hmmm, not a very scientific or test-pilot-like conclusion, I thought, but then his explanation left little room for argument.

"The only time when we might alter the gradual buildup process is in the matter of wave height. The only variable we really can't control is the sea. Since we usually only have four days of dedicated ship time, sometimes we are forced to fly in less than ideal water conditions."

"I can understand that, I said. "That's why they pay us the big bucks."

"Yeah, right," replied my mentor.

After spending the rest of the afternoon discussing in greater detail the procedures used by test pilots during DI tests, he ended with a not-so-subtle reminder that we pilots are not the sole center of the testing universe. Flight-test engineers, instrumentation technicians, aircraft maintenance, and administrative personnel all play a vital role in every final report produced by the test center. It was a good lesson to remember that our work was a team effort. Closer to home, a flight-test engineer was aboard ship during every DI test project.

Other than the fact that my flight logbook shows that I made eighteen day landings and eleven night landings, I have long since forgotten the specific details of the five days Mike and I spent aboard the *USS Detroit*.

Three months after my initiation aboard the *Detroit*, I was running my own project on the West Coast aboard the *USS Chicago* (CG-11), along with flight-test engineer Dave DuFresne. Rather than take the time and bear the additional expense of flying a test center SH-2F to California,

NAVAIR tasked HSL-35, a squadron based at Naval Air Station Imperial Beach just south of San Diego, to provide an aircraft, copilot, and crew chief for the DI tests. As it turned out, a former squadron mate at HC-4 in Lakehurst, Commander Chuck Craft, was the CO of the host squadron, which certainly helped to grease the skids.

The *Chicago* was the third World War II-era heavy cruiser to be converted to a guided-missile cruiser, replacing her main

Flight deck of the *USS Chicago* (CG-11). *(U.S. Navy photo)*

battery of nine, 8-inch naval guns with Talos and Tartar missile launchers. She was re-commissioned in 1964. Aside from four wartime deployments to the waters off the coast of North Vietnam, she served much of her remaining sixteen years of service as the flagship of the Third Fleet on the West Coast. As a flagship, she routinely operated helicopters carrying senior officers and dignitaries, but like all non-aviation ships before the advent of DI testing in the early 1970s, the ship's crew simply painted a line-up line on her flight deck that provided a takeoff and landing path clear of the ship's superstructure and did their best to provide a relative wind straight down the line-up stripe for landing and departing helicopters. My job was to create an officially sanctioned operating envelope for the SH-2F helicopter.

Although not a test pilot, my copilot contributed greatly to the success of the project. In addition to normal copilot duties and providing an extra set of eyes and ears, he helped me navigate and operate in the complex civilian and military airspace lying off the coast of Southern California.

The tests were conducted over a period of five days, including one night test in benign sea conditions with winds less than ten knots. One day, the winds picked up to twenty-six knots with twenty-foot waves, but the large ship barely noticed—the flight deck remained relatively stable and usable at seven degrees in roll and four degrees in pitch. A surprising result of the tests was the significant decrease in turbulence over the flight deck caused by the ship's superstructure as the relative winds were shifted toward the bow. This discovery was unlike most ships and was just the sort of counterintuitive finding that justified DI testing.

Aside from nearly flying into the water on a night approach—described at the beginning of this chapter—the only other time the pucker factor went off the scale was during a routine takeoff with a following sea and a relative wind of only five knots directly astern. We were sitting on the deck with all chocks and tie-down chains removed from the helicopter as we awaited takeoff clearance, when, all of a sudden, the ship lurched violently into a fifteen-degree roll to port. The unrestrained aircraft began to slide to the left, slowly at first, but picked up speed as the roll intensified. It happened so fast, we almost rolled off the side of the ship into the water before I managed to jerk the helicopter into the air. Fortunately, the deck crew had removed the chains from the left and right landing gear at the same time. If the roll would have happened with the left wheel still fastened to the deck, we would not have been able to lift off and we would have pivoted about that wheel into the Pacific Ocean.

Upon conclusion of the at-sea portion and the return of the borrowed helicopter to our host squadron, Dave and I headed back to Pax River to construct the various operating envelopes and to write the technical report that would be given wide dissemination within the naval community. I now knew why, as a student, I had to write so many reports at TPS. It was well and good to gather all of the inflight data, but until that information was analyzed and condensed into a readable technical report for the chain of command, it had little value to effect needed change.

Four months after returning from California, I was off to Pascagoula, Mississippi, in charge of a much larger test team that consisted of two additional test pilots, a crew chief, and five maintenance personnel to conduct DI testing on a brand-new class of ship, the DD-963 Spruance class destroyer.

USS Spruance (DD-963). *(U.S. Navy photo)*

The *USS Spruance*, the first of a thirty-ship procurement contract, was the first U.S. warship to use gas turbine engines for propulsion. In fact, the four engines were a modified version of the jet engines used in the C-5 and DC-10 transport aircraft. With the simple movement of a throttle on the bridge, much like the throttle in a jet airplane, the *Spruance* could go from dead in the water to over thirty knots in a remarkably short period of time. At 563 feet long, with a beam of fifty-six feet and a displacement of 7,800 tons, it was almost twice the size of older destroyers. Through liberal use of technology and automation, the total size of the crew was 280 men, an eighty percent reduction from other ships of comparable size.

The test team and I arrived on the Gulf Coast on Saturday, September 20, 1975, the same day that the *USS Spruance* was commissioned at the Ingalls shipyard in Pascagoula. Although we missed the official ceremony, it felt like we were members of the commissioning crew as we checked aboard later that afternoon to find our assigned berthing areas. Two days later, shortly after the ship had reached open water at the beginning of her transit to her new homeport of Norfolk, Virginia, I guided a SH-2F helicopter to a smooth landing on her flight deck, a first for the U.S. Navy.

The ship was on a tight timeline to reach Norfolk—only four days were allotted to make the trip around the tip of Florida and up the Atlantic

Coast—so, unlike most DI testing where a ship was dedicated solely to the project, we were unable to chase varying wind and sea conditions and had to accept the data we got, which was winds less than ten knots and relatively calm seas. Consequently, we were only able to publish preliminary operating envelopes with a recommendation that further testing be conducted at a later date.

We did manage to accumulate thirty-eight day landings and twenty-seven night landings during our beeline for Norfolk—all routine and uneventful.

By any description, the *Spruance* represented a remarkable new breed of warships and I had the privilege of being the first Navy pilot to land aboard her type—you might say that I earned a very tiny place in the history of the United States Navy.

A Change of Pace

Not all of the flight test projects I was involved in at Rotary Wing were particularly dangerous. One was routine to the point of being boring and another existed only on paper.

A Test Center UH-1N—a Huey equipped with twin engines—was outfitted with Bell Helicopter's first prototype automatic flight control

The first helicopter landing aboard the *USS Spruance* (DD-963). September 22, 1975 *(U.S. Navy photos)*

system (AFCS). The goal was to put as many flight hours as possible on the new system to uncover bugs and problems, which would allow Bell's design engineers to refine the product. Most of the test pilots assigned to Rotary Wing were given plenty of opportunity to "bore holes in the sky" performing routine training, instrument flying, and going on cross-country flights—anything to accumulate flight hours. There was little preparation required before flight and a minimum amount of post-flight paperwork, so it was a cushy assignment and a chance to get out of the office.

Other than DI testing, the only other project-officer assignment—meaning I was in charge—that came my way was the Recovery Assist, Secure and Traverse (RAST) program. This was a shipboard system designed by a Canadian company to safely recover helicopters on pitching and rolling flight decks beyond the current limits for a hand-flown landing. Essentially, it involved establishing a stable hover over a wildly gyrating flight deck and being quickly winched down and secured to the deck. Other than flying as copilot with a Canadian test pilot on a very early prototype flight, and several trips to Montreal to attend design review meetings, the project was mainly one of observation due to the immaturity of the design. I am sure that test pilots after me, who flew and certified the final design, probably had a few hair-raising stories to tell.

Like a squadron in which every officer had a primary duty assignment in addition to his flying duties, Rotary Wing was no different. I was the test directorate's safety officer responsible for maintaining a safe flight and workplace environment. Fortunately, during my tenure, we did not suffer any aircraft accidents or major injury on the ground, although I take little credit for that achievement.

My last flight test assignment before leaving the Rotary Wing Test Directorate was serving as the second pilot on a Navy Preliminary Evaluation

Bell Helicopter Model 214ST, like the one Lieutenant Dennis Rowley and I tested at the Bell factory in Ft. Worth. March 1976

(NPE) of the Model 214ST helicopter produced by Bell Helicopter. The project officer and lead test pilot was Lieutenant Denny Rowley, a six-foot-four mountain of a man, who played as hard as he worked. Denny was smart, organized, hard-working and good humored—a great guy to work with.

Because Model 214ST was a skid-mounted helicopter, the Navy had decided it was not suitable for shipboard operations. Then politics got involved and Bell cried foul, claiming that Sikorsky and Boeing-Vertol were being given preferential treatment in the search to find a new aircraft to replace the aging Sikorsky H-3 and the Kaman H-2 helicopters in the fleet. To assuage ruffled feathers, the Navy agreed to send a test team, including a senior flight test engineer, to the Bell plant in Fort Worth, Texas, to conduct an NPE on one of their fully-instrumented Model 214s.

Denny and I spent the first few days at the Bell flight-test facility flying a couple familiarization/checkout flights in the 214 with a company test pilot, meeting the players we would be interfacing with during the course of the NPE, and preparing the test cards we would be using during each flight to gather the necessary data. It was exciting for me to actually put to use the training I had received performing a traditional FQ & P evaluation of an aircraft we had never flown before. By March 19, 1976, Denny and I had flown nineteen flights and were nearly finished with the flying portion of the evaluation when my world turned upside down.

Shortly after landing, I was handed a handwritten note asking me to call my wife as soon as possible. I was puzzled by the telephone number because I didn't recognize the area code. Where was she? What was so urgent that she needed to talk with me during the middle of the workday? I asked if I could use one of the phones in the pilot office and hesitantly dialed the strange number.

"Bethesda Naval Hospital, Pediatric Ward, Corpsman Johnson speaking, sir," the voice said. My heart sank.

"This is Lieutenant Commander Stock. I was given this number to call my wife, Barbara Stock," I stated, my voice trailing off.

"Hold on, sir. I'll get her."

After several minutes, I heard Barbara's quivering voice, "Babe, Ashley has spinal meningitis."

I was stunned. My mind was desperately trying to process what she had just told me. I only knew one thing about meningitis—it was fatal! Our five-month old baby daughter was going to die. Big tears welled up in my eyes and cascaded down my cheeks. Seven hours later, I landed at Dulles International Airport outside of Washington, D.C. fearing the worst, but hoping for a miracle. Fortunately, Ashley beat the odds and pulled through after a two-week stay at the nation's premier naval hospital.

Off-Duty Flying

During the sixteen months I was assigned to Flight Test and the Rotary Wing Test Directorate, I was also active after work hours and on the weekends as a civilian pilot with the base flying club. Although most of the 150 hours I accumulated in my civilian logbook during this timeframe were devoted to cross-country flying to visit relatives—Angola, New York, to visit my family and down south to visit Barbara's family—I did do some flight instructing. I also flew to Winter Haven, Florida, to obtain a single-engine seaplane rating and to Elmira, New York, to acquire a glider flight instructor rating. Along the way, I served as president of the Patuxent River Navy Flying Club and taught a private pilot ground school course for St. Mary's County adult education. I will freely admit that I had an addiction to flying—a day without flying was a downer. As I write this, after a professional aviation career spanning fifty-three years, flying still invokes memories of great satisfaction, but it is no longer the air that I breathe.

Two events that occurred as result of my off-duty aviation activities serve as an exclamation point to the notion that flying can prove to be dangerous to the unprepared and the complacent. The first incident involved hand-propping an airplane with a dead battery. In my role as a flight instructor at the flying club, I was checking out a TPS classmate in a Cessna 182. As he turned the ignition key to the "start" position, there was a whimper of life, but it soon became obvious that the battery did not have enough juice to start the engine. Not to worry, I had hand-propped airplanes before, so I hopped out of the cockpit and took a position in front of the propeller. Since my friend had never been involved in this arcane process, I carefully explained the steps I would take and exactly what I wanted him to do and when. So far, so good. We started the time-honored ritual:

"Mags off, mixture off, and battery master off," I challenged.

He replied, "Mags off, mixture off, and battery master off."

I then turned the prop through several revolutions and placed it at the 10 o'clock position, ready for the downward swing of my arms that would, hopefully, start the engine. "Mags on, mixture rich, and battery master on," I commanded. He repeated the words as he took the appropriate action. As I was about to extend my arms and place both hands on the leading edge of the prop, a sixth sense made me hesitate. Suddenly, the engine started and I was staring into a five-foot propeller whirling at 1,000 RPM only eighteen inches in front of my face.

He had mistakenly moved the ignition switch to the start position and this time the battery provided enough power to crank the engine. I jumped back and immediately got the shakes as I realized how close I had come to being pulled into and consumed by the spinning mass of aluminum blades. My friend didn't know what had happened—but he soon found out, although my choice of words could have been chosen more delicately.

The other near disaster was clearly my own making. A unique aspect of the Navy flying club at Pax River was that it operated two gliders, in addition to eight fixed-wing airplanes. In terms of glider experience, I was definitely a new guy with lots to learn. All of my meager glider hours were logged in gliding flight, i.e., being towed to three thousand feet above the ground, releasing from the tow plane, performing a few basic flight maneuvers, and gliding straight back to the same airport for a landing.

I knew from studying glider-training manuals that there were three types of soaring flight: thermal, ridge, and wave. *Ridge* and *wave* soaring required specific terrain and wind conditions that were unique to certain geographic locations; whereas, *thermal* soaring, with varying degrees of success, can be done almost anywhere the heat of the sun is absorbed by the earth and then re-directed into the surrounding atmosphere as a rising current of air. One only has to observe a hawk circling lazily in the afternoon sun without flapping its wings to appreciate what a glider does during thermal Soaring. There are certain locations that spawn good thermals almost any day the sun is shining. Cumberland, Maryland, is one of those locations.

On this particular day, with a grand total of nine glider hours in my logbook, I took off from Pax River in a Schweizer 1-26 single-seat glider being towed by a flying club Cessna 172. The objective was to be towed on a two-hour flight north to Cumberland, so that I could experience some good thermals. My only experience being towed in a glider up to now was twenty-nine flights to a release altitude near the airport. I did, however, have a lot of formation flying experience in the Navy, which helped bridge the gap in my experience being towed.

About twenty-five miles north of Pax River, at 2,200 feet above the ground, I was settling nicely into the *high tow* position and getting comfortable for the long tow flight. The high tow was more comfortable than the *low tow* position because the glider was above the downwash and turbulent vortices coming off the tow plane. The downside was that the glider naturally wanted to climb well above the tow plane to an unsafe position. So, I had to pay close attention to maintain the tow aircraft in the proper sight picture. Something distracted my concentration—all of a sudden, the tow plane was nowhere in sight beneath me. About the same time, the tow rope became taut with a violent jerk that simultaneously pitched the nose of the glider down and pulled the tail of the tow plane sharply upward. Nothing like looking at a forty-five-degree angle at the tow plane below while tethered to a two-hundred-foot-long tow rope to get your undivided attention. I reached for the red handle of the tow rope release and gave a mighty tug to release me from the Cessna 172. The tow pilot was as surprised as I was, and he too reached for the tow release handle. I can still remember vividly the tow rope being suddenly released from both ends and falling horizontally to earth.

I was now a glider in free flight, unencumbered by a tow rope or a tow plane. However, before I could pat myself on the back for my safe extraction, a new problem emerged: where was I going to land? It was a new situation for me as a glider pilot. The base was too far away. My mind raced. Would I have to attempt a landing in a farmer's field or a cleared area? Then, I remembered we had flown directly over St. Mary's County Airport only a few minutes earlier. So, from a position ten miles north, I headed for the airport, hoping I would have enough altitude to make it. I didn't have a lot to spare. Much to my relief, and the tow pilot's, I was able to land on the runway. Another lesson learned: never take your eyes off the tow plane. Aviation experience might be defined as a series of lessons learned without killing yourself, your passengers, or destroying the air-craft. Thus far, in my eleven-year flying career, I had learned many lessons and only destroyed two helicopters.

Chapter 16

Aviation Legends

THE ALTIMETER UNWOUND AT A DIZZYING RATE AS THE JET AIRCRAFT I was flying plummeted to earth, out of control despite my best efforts to level off. A minute before, at twenty-seven thousand feet, my student in the front seat, a Lieutenant Commander in the British Royal Navy, deliberately put the jet we were flying, a North American T-2C Buckeye, into an upright spin maneuver—with my concurrence.

The British pilot was a flight instructor at the Empire Test School in England and was accompanying a group of test pilot students from his country. A highlight for any flight instructor when visiting another test pilot school was the opportunity to fly aircraft not previously flown. So, by luck of the draw, Andrew and I were paired together to "ring out" the T-2C, a basic jet-training airplane used by the Navy.

Toward the end of our flight, after Andrew had performed a variety of test-flight maneuvers designed to gauge the performance and flying qualities of this "new" aircraft, I decided to have him enter a spin to lose altitude before returning to the airfield for some touch-and-go landings.

"Okay, Andrew, let's do a clearing turn to make sure there's nobody below us," I commanded from the rear seat. "We'll plan to recover from the spin at seventeen thousand feet, so we'll need about ten thousand feet of clear airspace."

"Roger," he intoned over the intercom, as he rolled the airplane into a tight 360-degree turn to the left while scanning the area below.

"It looks clear, so whenever you are ready, enter an upright spin using the entry procedures we briefed on the ground," I said as I tugged on my oxygen mask, trying to relieve some of the constant pressure on my cheekbones.

"Okay, here we go," he replied eagerly.

Throttles to idle, nose above the horizon, let the airspeed bleed off, at the first indication of stall, stick full back and right full rudder—classic spin entry. As we spun to the right, losing about seven hundred feet per turn, Andrew played test pilot as he varied the control inputs: pro-spin and anti-spin ailerons and longitudinal fore and aft stick position, all the while producing a running commentary over the intercom describing the resulting aircraft reaction using standard test-pilot terminology.

At seventeen thousand feet, Andrew applied standard spin recovery controls: full rudder opposite the direction of spin, ailerons neutral, and stick forward. Nothing—the jet continued to spin! At this moment, a flight that had been unremarkable and enjoyable suddenly turned desperate. Apparently, the various flight-control inputs Andrew had made to investigate the spin characteristics during our descent from flight level 270, had shifted the aircraft into a spin mode that was resistant to normal spin-recovery techniques.

I let Andrew try his luck for an additional two turns.

"I have the controls!" I shouted, trying to hide a growing sense of urgency. I tried every trick I could think of. Nothing I did seemed to make a difference. We were fast approaching ten thousand feet—the altitude at which Navy flight procedures mandated a bailout if an aircraft was still out of control. Suddenly, just as I was contemplating pulling the face curtain on my ejection seat which would have catapulted both of us clear of the stricken aircraft, the jet came out of the spin and I was able to level off—at nine thousand three hundred feet! As the old adage goes: "Only the person doing my laundry will ever know how scared I really was."

Back to the School House

One day as I was crossing the hangar deck, the chief pilot of Rotary Wing, Commander Orville Wright, asked if I would be interested in returning to TPS as a flight instructor. I had heard the school was looking for volunteers, so his question did not catch me totally off guard. I asked if I could think it over and let him know in the morning; he said that would be okay.

That night, I performed a ritual I used whenever I had an important decision to make: I sat down with a pad of paper and listed the pros and cons. It was an easy decision. There weren't any major test projects in the wings and DI testing was slow; whereas TPS offered a lot more flight time and a chance to get checked out in jets. The only downside was having to grade lots of technical reports written by the students. I reported for my new duties on April 27, 1976.

The first order of business was to re-qualify in the OH-58 and AH-1G, which were the main instructional helicopters. By the end of my first month back at the school, I was also fully checked out in the T-2C—the first jet of my naval career. Even though I never regretted selecting helicopters over jets when I was a flight student in Pensacola, it was an ego boost to be able to fly both types of aircraft.

Although on paper, I was qualified to solo a jet, I was far from being a "jet jock." This disparity was aptly demonstrated during my checkout syllabus while flying my second instructional flight with Major Walt Costello, USMC, the Chief Flight Instructor and my TPS

North American T-2C like the one I flew as a flight instructor at TPS. *(U.S. Navy photo)*

classmate. He was, sitting in the instructor seat behind me and we were in the training area at 17,000 feet when we were "jumped" by another T-2C flown by another TPS instructor, Lieutenant Ed Schneider. Like me, Ed was a Navy helicopter pilot by trade, but he desperately wanted to fly jets when he left the test center and returned to the fleet. He seized every opportunity to build jet time and to improve his skills, including mock dogfighting. This day, with the "fight on," my instructor mercifully took the controls as Ed's aircraft flashed by on a simulated gun run. For the next eight minutes, I gamely tried to hang on to my seat and keep my oxygen mask attached to my face as Walt and Ed alternatively pulled six positive and two negative Gs as they turned, climbed, and dove in an effort to gain a good firing position

DeHavilland U-6 Beaver towing a X-26 glider at TPS. *(U.S. Navy photo)*

on the other. I didn't have a clue as to what was going on. Occasionally, I got a glimpse of Ed's jet, but most of the time I felt like I was in a different world of sights, sounds, and feelings—almost like I was having an out-of-body experience. The only good thing to come out of the brief experience was that I didn't puke. I also knew that I would never make a real jet pilot. By all accounts, Ed held his own that day, and he did go on to fly jets, eventually becoming a NASA research pilot flying the SR-71.

By the end of my first month back at TPS, I was earning my keep as a contributing member of the instructional staff performing flight demos, checkout flights, and progress checks in helicopters and occasionally in the T-2C, as well as grading technical reports—my least favorite part of the job. Two months later, I took over the glider program because I had the most glider experience of any staff member by virtue of my off-duty civilian glider activities. As the lead glider instructor, I also got checked out in the U-6A De Havilland Beaver, a tailwheel airplane used for glider towing.

A Cornfield Never Looked So Good

It was a beautiful sunny afternoon with just a hint of fall in the air. We were flying an OH-58 single-engine, turbine-powered helicopter over the gently rolling terrain of beautiful St. Mary's County, just to the east of Leonardtown, Maryland. My student, Captain Rudolf Fredericy of the Royal Netherlands Air Force, and I were in the middle of a Performance Demo flight in which the student learns and practices the various flight-test techniques required to gather valid helicopter performance data for level flight, climb, and autorotation. We had finished the level flight portion and were engaged in completing the last two areas of investigation, which consisted of climbing several thousand feet at varying climb airspeeds while doing the same to measure autorotative descents. To make the best use of allotted training time, a climb was initiated at a specific climb airspeed and immediately followed by an autorotation at a predetermined speed. My student had completed one climb-descent profile and the climb portion of the next profile.

The autorotation tests were started at four thousand feet above the ground by lowering the collective to full down and rotating the throttle to the idle detent, which decoupled the engine from the main rotor. Even though the engine was still running, it was no longer powering the main rotor and the helicopter behaved exactly as it would if the engine had suddenly quit. The plan called for initiating a power recovery from the autorotation at two thousand feet by re-engaging the engine.

Everything was normal on the second descent profile until the recovery was initiated at two thousand feet. "The engine is not responding," my student stated, with a hint of alarm in his voice.

"What do you mean?" I asked, as I grabbed the throttle to make sure he had rolled it full on.

"The engine is not accelerating!" he shouted.

I could see from the engine instruments that he had correctly diagnosed the problem, which meant that we were still in autorotative flight and descending toward the ground at over one thousand feet per minute. We were rapidly running out of altitude, time, and ideas.

"I have the flight controls," I stated in my best command voice.

Perhaps the most important pre-condition before entering a practice autorotation—one that I constantly emphasized to my students—was to have a suitable landing area within gliding distance in the event the engine fails to respond. I had violated my cardinal rule. As I looked around for a place to land, all I saw were trees. And more trees.

Directly in front of the helicopter, at a distance of one-half mile, was a small cornfield carved out of the surrounding forest. It seemed too far to reach, but it was our only hope if we wanted to avoid going into the trees. I lowered the nose of the helicopter to increase our ground speed and miraculously made it over the field with one hundred feet to spare—just enough altitude to pitch the nose up and land the chopper vertically into the cornstalks, which were as high as the top of the helicopter. After congratulating ourselves on our good fortune to have landed without damage, we trudged three hundred yards to the farmer's house to call the base, after first telling the farmer that the Navy would pay for damages to his crop.

That night, as I re-played the narrow escape over and over, several thoughts came to mind: I was thankful that we instructors were proficient in executing full autorotation landings due to constant practice back at the base, which allowed me to react instinctively in the short time that we had; this was my first engine failure in a single-engine aircraft in my twelve-year flying career; and, lastly, I would never enter autorotation again without a safe landing area nearby.

Rubbing Shoulders with Aviation Legends

The main ballroom of the Beverly Hills Hilton Hotel was dressed in its finest and ready for some very important guests. Round tables with starched white-linen tablecloths were adorned with the best china, crystal, and silver the iconic establishment could produce; enough for the expected three hundred guests. The only missing formality was a red carpet from the curb to the entrance, perhaps because there would be no Hollywood celebrities attending this dinner. The night, however, would not be without royalty because this was the formal black-tie banquet that marked the end of the three-day annual gathering of the Society of Experimental Test Pilots. Luminaries from the world of aviation—famous test pilots, astronauts, movie stunt pilots, record-setters, titans of industry, acrobatic champions, and military leaders—would be rubbing shoulders with lessor known test pilots and engineers from the aerospace community, including members of Class 70 from the U.S. Naval Test Pilot School on their end-of-course national field trip, and a few of us instructors along to coordinate the various planned activities.

At the cocktail hour that preceded dinner, small groups formed into circles, drink glasses in hand, to renew old friendships and to engage in lively banter. At one point, I glanced over my right shoulder at a small group nearby. There was a short, older, bald man who looked familiar. Without being too obvious, I shifted my feet slightly to get a better view. *Oh my, it's Jimmy Doolittle!* The noted air racer, aviation pioneer, and leader of the famous bombing raid on Tokyo during World War II, was standing three feet from me. I couldn't have been more excited if it had been Orville Wright. I wanted so much to lean over and shake the hand of the great man. But, I did not; although I will admit I cocked one ear to see if I could pick up any scraps of his conversation.

The ten-day field trip for TPS Class 70 and us instructors began at Edwards Air Force Base in Southern California on September 21, 1976. This famous flight-test facility, which includes Rogers Dry Lake, was home to numerous aviation accomplishments, including Chuck Yeager's sound-breaking flight in the X-1, flights of the North American X-15, first landings of the space shuttle, and the around-the-world flight of the Rutan Voyager.

Our first stop was the U.S. Air Force Test Pilot School, where our host accorded us the traditional opportunity to fly an aircraft that was new to most of us—the legendary C-130 Hercules. It was not new to me since I had logged over twenty-five hours in the "Herc" while I was assigned to VRF-32, the ferry squadron in San Diego, but I dutifully crawled into the copilot's seat when my turn came and wriggled the controls for a few minutes. After touring the U.S. Army flight-test facility, our last stop at Edwards was the NASA Dryden Flight Research Center and a visit with its director, David Scott, the seventh man to walk on the moon.

The next day, we went to Palmdale, California, where we toured North American Rockwell's space shuttle facility and had the rare opportunity to see the first space shuttle, *Enterprise*, which had officially rolled out just five days earlier. Another highlight at Palmdale was having a ringside seat for a flight demonstration by Bob Hoover, that he performed just for our group. We were standing on the flight line, ten feet from his twin-engine Shrike Commander, as Hoover casually walked up in a three-piece beige suit, yellow tie, and his trademark wide-brimmed straw hat perched on top of his bald head. After shaking hands and talking with us briefly, he removed his suit coat and hat, strapped himself into the left front seat, started the engines, and took off.

During the twenty-minute show, he looped and rolled the Shrike with both engines, on one engine, and finally with no engines. Hoover's grand finale started at about two thousand feet, when he shut down and feathered both engines and dove for the runway to build up speed. Upon reaching the end of the runway, he abruptly pulled up into a full loop. At the bottom of the loop, he dropped the landing gear, landed, and then proceeded to coast to the flight line where we were all standing, and pulled into the parking spot from which he had departed, just as he ran out of momentum. He opened the door, put on his suit jacket and straw hat to the applause of a bunch of incredulous onlookers. It was a tour de force in the art of energy management—and he hadn't even broken a sweat.

The last stop on the West Coast portion of our field trip was the symposium and awards banquet at the Beverly Hills Hilton Hotel. Each day was crammed full of presentations by world-famous test pilots from industry and the military concerning the latest, cutting-edge flight-test research and development projects. For us novice test pilots, it was a backstage glimpse into the rarified atmosphere belonging to experimental test pilots and their exotic machines. The most amazing thing was that they treated us like equals and valued members of the fraternity. It was a heady experience indeed.

Everywhere I turned, I bumped into a famous aviator. Sitting in a booth next to me at breakfast was Alan Shepard, a naval aviator, test pilot, and the first American into space and the fifth man to walk on the moon. I saw astronaut Vance D. Brand getting off the elevator; Mercury astronaut Gordon Cooper perusing items in the gift shop; Frank Tallman III, the famous stunt pilot (*Flight of the Phoenix*, *The Great Waldo Pepper*, etc.) walking across the lobby; and Sir Frank Whittle, the inventor of the jet engine, was a luncheon speaker. One night, in one of the hospitality suites, I spotted one of my squadron mates from my Naval Reserve days at Naval Air Station Joint Reserve Base at Willow Grove. Warren Hall was a test pilot for the Calspan Corporation, a science and technology company headquartered in Buffalo, New York. As he and I were talking about our Reserve days, an older man approached and shook hands with Warren.

Warren turned to me and said, "Have you met Tony LeVier?"

"No, I haven't," I said as I extended my hand to one of the most famous test pilots in the world, and the first American to fly a jet airplane, the Lockheed XP-80 Shooting Star, in January 1944.

On our return trip to Pax River, Class 70 stopped at Fort Worth, Texas, to tour Bell Helicopter and General Dynamics. Unlike during my class field trip when Vought gave each of us a bottle of whiskey and a one-hundred-and-fifty-dollar Stetson cowboy hat, this time, due to new Pentagon regulations which sought to sever any potential conflict of interest in the procurement of military weapon systems, we received nothing but a handshake. It was so ridiculous, we couldn't even accept a ride to the airport from a contractor doing business with the federal government.

Chief Flight Instructor

In the military officer community, your date of rank determines many things, including your job assignment within a squadron, ship, or organization. The military is so hidebound when it comes to seniority that most often, the officer with the most senior date of rank is selected for an important position rather than the one who is best qualified. So, when Major Walt Costello, the incumbent chief flight instructor, was transferred back to a Marine squadron, I became his replacement on December 16, 1976, because I was the next senior test pilot at the school. Despite the hierarchical selection process, I like to think that I was also a good fit for the position, and that I made some improvements that had a lasting impact.

As the Chief Flight Instructor, I was responsible for the content and delivery of two of the three main components of a student test pilot's education: flight training and technical report writing. Assisting me in this difficult and demanding job of overseeing the progress of sixty student test pilots were seventeen military flight instructors, all who reported directly to me. To say this job kept me busy would be an understatement. But the rewards and job satisfaction more than made up for the long hours.

One of those rewards was being able to check out in the Northrop T-38 Talon, a supersonic jet trainer capable of 858 mph. It was an ego trip for a rotor-head like me. It certainly did not further the capabilities of the instructional staff because I didn't have enough experience in jets to be able to instruct students in this high-performance airplane, as evidenced by the fact that I flamed out one of the two engines at the top of a loop on a solo flight, caused by applying too much right rudder—a habit from flying propeller-driven airplanes.

One event involving the T-38 is fondly remembered. It involved a cross-country flight to visit my brothers in western New York. Since military flights had to land at a military base, I landed at Niagara Falls International Airport, which had an Air National Guard facility. After a brief visit over lunch, I said goodbye to my brothers, who stayed behind to watch the takeoff. I decided to put on a little show to demonstrate the power of the

Northrop T-38 Talon like the one I flew as a flight instructor at TPS. *(U.S. Navy photo)*

nimble jet. After lining up on the runway, I requested a "high performance climb to 10,000 feet," which was approved. Even though I had never done one before, I had watched many jet-jocks do them—so why not me? I lit both afterburners and streaked down the runway, deliberately keeping it on the ground well above normal lift-off speed. I then abruptly rotated to a seventy-degree nose-up attitude and blasted into the heavens. My brothers told me later that it was definitely impressive—even I was amazed at just how fast I reached 10,000 feet. The T-38 is well known for having "short legs," meaning it doesn't carry a lot of fuel, and I managed to squander a fair amount with my full afterburner climb. So much so, that I almost had to declare a low-fuel emergency on my return to Pax River. (The next section in this chapter might convey the notion that my track record for running on fumes in a jet was a growing phenomenon—and not a particularly healthy one!)

Running on Empty

One of the major projects I completed as the Chief Flight Instructor was a comprehensive staff study to determine the ideal mix of training aircraft assigned to TPS in terms of model types and quantity of each type. One of the replacement helicopters I was considering was a French helicopter manufactured by Aerospatiale. Since I had never flown this particular helicopter, I decided to visit their North American distributor located near Dallas, Texas, for a test flight.

My plan was to fly to Texas in a T-2C in the morning, fly the new helicopter, and return to Pax River the same day. During the weather briefing I received from the duty meteorologist at base ops, he told me that the jet stream winds forecasted at my cruising altitudes were not too bad at seventy knots, but a direct headwind. So, based on the forecast winds and my projected ground speed, I decided that I could make the trip comfortably with one fuel stop in Fort Campbell, Kentucky.

In the days before GPS and other fancy onboard navigation equipment, I could not compute an accurate ground speed until I reached my cruising altitude of 34,000 feet and determined the elapsed time between two known checkpoints on the jet airway I was flying. Consequently, nearly one hour had elapsed since takeoff before I realized the actual jet stream headwinds were about one hundred knots greater than forecasted—those dang "weather-guessers" led me astray once again! (To be fair, the meteorologists in 1977 did not have the sophisticated weather satellites and the spot-on computer models in use today.)

I wondered if I could reach Fort Campbell with the remaining fuel. The T-2C did not have an autopilot and I didn't have a copilot to fly the aircraft while I made some hasty navigational computations. So, I trimmed the jet up as best I could to fly hands-off and pulled out my nav charts, plotter, and E6B manual flight computer (a circular slide-rule modified for aviation use), and got to work. After five minutes, with an occasional pause to right the aircraft, I determined that I could not make it to Fort Campbell.

Okay, now what? Although I could divert to a civilian airport with longer runways in an emergency, my preference would be a military air-field—for a number of reasons. A quick scan of my nav chart, showed that Fort Knox would shave about one hundred miles off my route.

About this time, as the old saying goes, "When it rains, it pours." My sole onboard navigation equipment (TACAN) decided to quit working. No worries—at least not yet. I contacted ATC:

"Memphis Center, this is Navy 328."

"Navy 328, this is Memphis Center, go ahead."

"Memphis Navy 328, I am running a little short on fuel, change my destination to Fort Knox. I also lost my only navigation capability, so I will need a radar vector, over."

"Navy 328 Memphis, roger. Fly heading 320 for Fort Knox. Are you declaring a low-fuel emergency?" the controller asked.

"Memphis Navy 328. Negative, not at this time. Fly 320 for Fort Knox," I replied.

For the time being, things were under control—although that was about to change.

In addition to only having one nav, the jet only had one communication radio. As long as this radio worked, ATC would be able to vector me to Fort Knox for an uneventful landing. But, if the radio quit, I would suddenly be in a world of hurt. No sooner had those negative thoughts entered my mind, when the radio quit working—my only link to the out-side world and salvation was suddenly severed.

My mind shifted into an agitated state of high gear. I began to quickly assess my predicament and possible courses of action. Sitting on top of a solid layer of clouds as far as the eye could see in any direction, meant that visual navigation using surface features was out of the question. Other than the 320-degree heading given by ATC, I had no idea where Fort Knox was and I was low on fuel. I decided that it was pointless to stay at thirty-four thousand feet until I ran out of fuel, so I pulled both throt-tles to idle to conserve as much fuel as possible and began descending toward the solid overcast layer below me. On the outside chance that only the radio receiver had failed and that my transmitter was still working, I declared an emergency over the universal distress frequency: "Mayday, Mayday, Mayday, this is Navy jet 328 in the vicinity of London, Kentucky, on a heading of 320 descending out of Flight Level 340." As I found out later, ATC did hear me and were able to clear lower aircraft out of my way.

I entered the top of the overcast at thirty-one thousand feet. As I descended lower and lower, still tightly enveloped in gray clouds, a new worry began to take shape—what if the clouds went all the way to the surface? Luckily, I broke into clear air at nineteen thousand feet. As I descended below ten thousand feet without a clue as to my location, I began to look for airports, but saw none. I did, however, continue to cling to the last lifeline thrown to me by ATC. I steadfastly maintained a compass heading of 320 degrees.

As I leveled at three thousand feet, the low-fuel warning lights illuminated. I had twenty minutes of fuel remaining. It was getting down to crunch time. Although my heart was racing and the adrenaline was surging, my head was clear. I had two options: bailout or land on a highway. Even though ejections from jet aircraft usually resulted in a positive outcome, there were plenty of malfunctions too. I did not want to eject. I did not want to take a ride on the "nylon elevator"! I didn't want to trust my life to a mechanical sequence of events, regardless how successful they'd been in the past.

Glancing to my left, I spotted a four-lane divided highway and quickly abandoned any notion of ejecting. I eased over toward the highway and began to formulate a landing plan. The traffic was fairly light, so I figured that I could time my approach such that I could plop down just in front of a car with enough room to brake before hitting the car ahead. If it looked like I was going to hit the car ahead, I could always veer into the median. It was a risky decision, even if I managed to pull it off without injuring any innocent people on the ground or myself and somehow managed to save the airplane. Navy policy dictated that I should eject over a rural area in this situation. So, there was no way I was going to be labeled a hero, no matter the outcome. Not to mention that a safe landing was far from being guaranteed.

Then, I spotted it! I had blundered right on top of the Fort Knox airfield. Maybe the tower was half expecting me from my earlier Mayday call, I didn't know, but the traffic pattern was strangely empty. I quickly turned downwind, lowered the landing gear and flaps, and landed—with five minutes of fuel remaining!

As Dr. Richard A. Pellerin, a civilian FAA Designated Medical Examiner, is fond of saying, "If you are not living on the edge, you are taking up too much space." I do believe I lived up to his challenge that day. But then, I have often wondered how a landing on the highway might have turned out versus an ejection. Either way, I'll bet I would have made the ten o'clock local news.

Return to the Fleet

A month after assuming the mantle of Chief Flight Instructor, it was already time to begin planning for my next set of orders, which would take me back to sea duty. I knew I wanted to fly the SH-2F helicopter in a Light Airborne Multi-Purpose System (LAMPS) squadron——but on which coast? Barbara and I had enjoyed our one-year tour in San Diego right after Vietnam, so my first inclination was to put in for a West Coast squadron. The big downside to living in San Diego though was the cost of housing. Rumor had it that a West Coast house would cost twice as much as an East Coast home of similar size and amenities. So, I decided to fly to San Diego to find out for myself.

It was easy to convince another pilot on the staff to take a cross-country to sunny California. Lieutenant Bernie Kneeland was qualified in the TA-4J Skyhawk, a two-seat, advanced-training jet that was faster and had longer legs than the T-2C. While Bernie took in the sights, I spent a whole day with a real estate agent looking at homes for sale. I quickly confirmed the rumor: prices for small homes on postage-stamp lots, ten feet from your neighbor, were outrageous. Sunny weather and comfortable year-round temperatures were simply not worth it. So, I came back to Pax River and requested to be assigned to a squadron in Norfolk, Virginia.

Although July 5, 1977, was officially my last day at TPS, I decided to go for all the gusto on my last flying day, five days earlier. At 1000, I flew the T-38; at 1215, I took off in the AH-1G; and I finished with a mid-afternoon flight in the OH-58. Two helicopters and a jet—a fitting end to one of the best flying gigs I ever had.

Chapter 17

Torpedo Away

I T SEEMED LIKE AN EASY NIGHT MISSION. TAKE OFF FROM OUR SHIP AND head south about fifty miles, locate the "enemy" carrier task force, and return to the ship. With high clouds, ten-mile visibility, and calm seas, weather would not be a factor. With any luck, I should be back in my stateroom sound asleep by 2200. But then, no flight mission in the military, even in peacetime, is a guaranteed slam dunk, especially at night.

My ship, the USS Aylwin (FF-1081), and several other U.S. Navy warships had departed the naval base at Charlestown, South Carolina, the day before. Another task group of ships, centered on the aircraft carrier USS Forrestal, had set sail at the same time from Mayport, Florida, bound for the Mediterranean. The two task groups were scheduled to rendezvous two days out and make the Atlantic transit together as one large task force. In the meantime, the Charleston task group, acting as an aggressor force, would attempt to sniff out the Forrestal group for a simulated attack.

The one complication for the planned mission was that both task groups would be in total EMCON, as would be the situation during wartime. EMCON meant that all electronic emissions—sonar, radio, radar, and navigation signals—would be shut down to prevent an enemy ship or aircraft from locating and targeting surface vessels using passive detection methods. So, my crew would be on its own in terms of navigation. We could not rely on the Aylwin to provide any navigational assistance. Even though EMCON would make it more difficult to find our ship when we returned from our search mission, I minimized the risk because of the relatively close proximity of the Forrestal group.

We launched in our SH-2F helicopter and climbed to two thousand feet on a pre-determined southerly heading. With good visibility, sporadic use of our onboard radar, and a fairly accurate prediction of their location, I figured that we would be able to easily spot the "enemy" task group. Along with me on this dark night was my copilot, Lieutenant Junior Grade Steve

Park, and AW3 Ken Bradt, the radar and sonar operator. Both of these guys were on their first deployment and inexperienced, but eager to learn.

I told Petty Officer Bradt to make an occasional single sweep of his radar before shutting it down again, hoping to spot a telltale group of blips signifying the task group. Meanwhile, the two of us up front peered into the dark void ahead, hoping to catch the silhouette of a ship's superstructure highlighted against the dark grey ocean. When we reached the projected location of the task group, based on pre-takeoff calculations, the ships were nowhere to be seen and no blips turned up on our radar.

"Okay, here is what we are going to do," I said. "We'll fly this heading for another ten minutes. If we still have not made contact, we will turn around and head back to the ship." Both concurred with my plan— although they didn't have much of a choice but to go along given their inexperience and the fact that I was the aircraft commander.

Ten minutes later, with no success, we turned around and headed back to our ship. At this point everything still seemed normal.

But then things began to get complicated. Since the Aylwin was not radiating its TACAN navigation aid, we had no way of using our onboard equipment to home in on the ship. And, of course, we could not request a radar vector because the ship was not transmitting on their radio or operating their radar. Steve used his plotting board to project where the ship should be and we altered our course accordingly.

I did not begin to worry until we arrived in the area where our task group should have been and there was nothing but vast ocean staring back at us. In addition to electronic silence, all of the ships in the task force were sailing in a "darken ship" condition, which meant that not even a hint of light was allowed to escape from the interior or exterior of the ship.

My pucker factor began to build. Not only could we not find our ship, but we were beginning to run low on fuel. If we did not find our ship within the next fifteen minutes, we would be faced with having to make a night ditching in the ocean—a thought I dared not contemplate.

At this point, I thought to myself, *To hell with EMCON*. I turned the flight controls over to Steve, so I could devote full attention to the rapidly deteriorating situation. Broadcasting in the clear, on the international distress frequency, I transmitted, "*USS Aylwin*, this is Navy helicopter 190 in your general vicinity, with fifteen minutes of fuel remaining, over."

Nothing! I repeated the same desperate plea. Nothing!

"Mayday, mayday, mayday. This is Navy helicopter 190 requesting radar vector from any U.S. Navy ship. I will be forced to ditch in the next fifteen minutes if I do not receive help."

Nothing but dead silence.

"This is bullshit," I said to my crew. "I know those bastards are listening on the radio." My anger was about to overtake sound judgment. Then, I noticed a large commercial container ship, all lit up and heading toward Europe. "Okay, guys, this is what we are going to do. We are not leaving sight of that ship down there. If we have to ditch, I will fly close aboard the port side at bridge level with all of our lights on full bright and raise and lower the landing gear several times to get their attention. Then I will fly about two miles ahead on their port bow and establish a hover. I want the two of you to jump into the water on my command. I will then move a safe distance off and ditch the helicopter. Hopefully, this ship will stop to pick us up. Any questions?"

"No, sir," they replied weakly, in unison.

I desperately hoped it wouldn't come to that, but at least we had a survival plan that might work if we were lucky.

I was about to broadcast another Mayday when the *Aylwin* came on the radio to give us a radar vector. With seven minutes of fuel remaining, we landed. Although I was relieved to be standing on a dry deck and not floating in my life vest, I was still angry at what my ship had put us through in the name of a war game. An officer on the bridge confided to me later that the ship had been listening to our desperate radio calls and wanted to break radio silence, but they were overruled by the captain until the situation was about to spiral out of control. I was in bed by 2200 as planned, but sleep came much later as I replayed the near disaster over and over in my mind. My crew and I were lucky to be alive!

Fleet Replacement Squadron

Keeping my record intact of always receiving my first choice for my next assignment, I received orders to one of the two LAMPS fleet squadrons homeported at Naval Station Norfolk, Virginia. Before reporting for duty at HSL-32, I took a four-month detour for schooling and training in the LAMPS mission.

Before any naval aviator, regardless of experience, reports to a fleet squadron, he must first attend transition training to learn how to fly the specific model aircraft. Once that is mastered, he must learn the tactics used to successfully accomplish the mission assigned to that aircraft. When the concept of having a squadron dedicated solely to training fleet aviators was started in the late 1950s, these specialized squadrons were called a Replacement Air Group, or RAG. By the mid-1970s, the name had changed to Fleet Replacement Squadron, or FRS—most aviators still referred to them as RAGs—but the mission remained the same.

In July of 1977, I reported to HSL-30 at Naval Station Norfolk, the East Coast FRS for the SH-2F helicopter. Although I had been qualified as aircraft commander in this specific helicopter at Pax River, I knew next to nothing about anti-submarine warfare or some of the other missions assigned to LAMPS.

Since I was reasonably current in the SH-2F, I was able to complete the basic aircraft transition syllabus, including re-qualifying for day and night shipboard landings, in less time than a pilot without previous experience. Learning the LAMPS mission was a whole different story. I needed all of the time allotted, just like any newly minted naval aviator.

The primary mission assigned to LAMPS was anti-submarine warfare, or ASW for short. In 1977, the United States and the Soviet Union were still locked in the potentially deadly embrace of the Cold War. One of the principal weapon systems used by both countries was the submarine. Although the Soviets enjoyed a nearly four-to-one advantage over the U.S. in the total number of submarines, their force was mostly comprised of old, outdated diesel boats. The number of nuclear-powered attack and missile submarines operated by both sides was more evenly matched. The one significant advantage of U.S. nuclear submarines over their Soviet counterparts was in the level of noise they made. Russian subs were noisier than U.S. boats, a fact that made Soviet models easier to detect—and destroy, if the cold war ever turned hot. The lofty goal of the U.S. Navy and its allies was to locate and track every Soviet submarine operating on the high seas. Of course, this objective was impossible to totally achieve, but considerable ASW resources were deployed around the world by the U.S. and its allies to do as much as possible. LAMPS was one such resource.

There were two main types of ASW sensors used by the SH-2F helicopter to locate and track submarines: sonobuoy and MAD. A sonobuoy was an expendable, cylindrical device about five inches in diameter and three feet long that was dropped from an aircraft into the water. Once in the water, a floatation collar inflates to keep its radio antenna above the water and to allow hydrophones to descend into the ocean to a preset depth. There were two types of sonobuoys: *passive* and *active*. The passive type simply listened for any sound in the water that might come from a submarine in the area. An active sonobuoy actually transmitted a burst of sound energy called a "ping," which traveled outward, hit a submerged sub, and was reflected back to the hydrophone of the sonobuoy. The passive and active signals were then transmitted back to an aircraft or ship to be processed and analyzed. Passive means of detection were best because the enemy submarine would not know there was a hostile force in the area. Once a sub knew there were ASW forces looking for it, the sub would initiate defensive measures like stopping engines to reduce noise, deploying false sounds, or fleeing. In theory sonobuoy technology sounded like a foolproof method of detection. In practice, however, this method often fell short of actually detecting a lurking submarine. Factors like salinity and temperature of the water that affected sound propagation and reception, hydrophone depth, and defensive counter-measures used by submarines, all greatly impacted detection rates. The SH-2F was equipped with a sideward firing launcher that carried fifteen sonobuoys.

The other main onboard sensor, MAD, stood for Magnetic Anomaly Detection. The MAD equipment used by the SH-2F consisted of a cylindrical device seven inches in diameter and five feet long, called a "madbird," attached to a two-hundred-foot cable wound on an electric winch mounted on the right side of the helicopter. When deployed, the madbird "flew" behind and one hundred feet below the helicopter. The scientific principle behind MAD was that a large steel shape like a submarine would disrupt the normal magnetic lines of flux surrounding the earth, which could then be detected by the madbird. Unlike sonobuoys, which could search a relatively large area, MAD was used primarily to confirm and pinpoint a suspected target prior to launching a torpedo attack.

To a far lesser degree, the surface- search radar of the LAMPS helicopter could be used to spot a submarine on the surface. Similarly, the aircrew, using the good, old, human eyeball, might get lucky and spot the hull outline of a sub operating near the surface in clear water or a periscope—as my crew did once during an exercise with a U.S. fast attack submarine in the Mediterranean Sea.

The only weapons carried on board the helicopter when actively hunting enemy submarines were two MK 46 homing torpedoes. With a range of six miles and a speed of forty knots with a ninety-six-pound warhead, it was a respectable sub-killer if dropped on a good "datum" (possible submarine position).

Another LAMPS mission, which was taking on greater importance in 1977, was the detection and targeting of enemy surface vessels. This mission, like all things military, was tagged with an acronym—ASST, which stood for Anti-Surface Surveillance and Targeting. The primary reason why this mission was steadily growing was the introduction of the deadly surface-to-surface Harpoon missile system on U.S. Navy combatant ships in early 1977. The Harpoon missile had a maximum range of twenty-four miles, a distance that put the target beyond the horizon and therefore beyond radar or visual detection from the firing ship. The helicopter was used to provide geographical coordinates of the enemy ship, which were then fed into the missile-guidance system. Once fired, the active homing system on board the missile took over and guided it to its intended target.

Secondary missions flown by LAMPS were general utility—transport of personnel and equipment from ship-to-ship or from ship-to-shore installations—and Search and Rescue.

Previous tours of duty had given me enough exposure to the utility and

SAR missions to be reasonably proficient; ASW and ASST were a different story. Although I had some exposure to anti-submarine warfare during my short time in the Naval Reserves, I was basically starting from scratch with ASW, and I was totally ignorant about ASST.

The primary tool used by the FRS to train students in the execution of ASW and ASST missions was a Weapons Systems Trainer. The WST was a Star Wars-looking curved box mounted on top of three long hydraulic arms that caused the device to gyrate and swoosh as if possessed by evil forces from a faraway galaxy. This was my first exposure to state-of-the-art flight simulators that made a pilot feel just like he was actually flying the real aircraft. The WST flew so much like the SH-2F, you couldn't tell the difference. Not only did it fly just like the real helicopter, but the computer-generated visual system projected onto the cockpit windows was just like looking at the real world—good enough to simulate takeoff and landings aboard Navy ships, like a frigate or a destroyer. Because of the near-perfect replication of the actual helicopter by the WST, all ASW and ASST mission-training in the FRS was flown in the simulator and none in a real aircraft.

Through a combination of classroom lectures, flights in the WST, and self-study, I slowly mastered the fundamentals and tactics necessary to fulfill the LAMPS mission—at least at an entry level. Accordingly, I graduated from the FRS on November 18, 1977, and checked into HSL-32. Hopefully, on-the-job training during deployment aboard ship would complete my transformation from a neophyte to master tactician. Cold War, here I come!

The Home Guard

After reporting to HSL-32, I was nominally assigned to the Maintenance Department, but my primary duties revolved around getting Detachment Four ready for deployment in April 1978. As the officer in charge (OIC) of the thirteen-man detachment—three pilots, two airborne sensor operators, and eight aircraft mechanics—it was my job to ensure that each individual was able to perform his duties in a professional manner and in accordance with accepted norms and Navy regulations. It would be a challenging task because only three of the thirteen men had ever made a long deployment on a small ship. None of the pilots, myself included, or the two sensor operators in the back of the helicopter, had any real-world experience with LAMPS. As I told the men during our first all-hands meeting, my principal obligation as OIC was to ensure the safety of everything we did during the deployment. To put it more succinctly, I promised that I would bring everybody back alive. Our growth and development as an effective warfighting unit would be secondary.

So, we all rolled up our sleeves and got to work in our individual areas—the aircrew to gain more familiarity with flying the SH-2F and the maintenance personnel to ensure that our assigned aircraft was in the best mechanical shape possible. The aircrew studied and rehearsed tactics in the WST, the first time we had flown together as a crew on simulated LAMPS missions. The maintenance gang completed a torpedo-loading course and made sure that our pack-up kit (spare parts we would carry with us to the ship) was completed and certified for flight. Slowly, over the next four months, we came together as a team. We no longer associated ourselves with the parent squadron. We belonged to Det 4 and were proud of it.

During one night-training flight, I was flying straight and level at two thousand feet when suddenly my heartrate shot up to stratospheric heights. The SH-2F had a very large, sliding cargo door on the right side of the aircraft that served as a combination cockpit door and entrance into the rear of the helicopter. It was approximately five feet high and eight feet long. As we were flying along, with the cargo door closed, I felt a slight vibration and noticed that the cargo door had opened about one inch. In the time it took me to transfer my left hand to the stick and my right hand to the door handle to close it, the whole door was suddenly ripped from its tracks and flew off into the night. I was stunned and speechless as I contemplated just how close we had come to disaster.

Many fatal accidents have occurred in helicopters when a door or access panel comes off in flight and flies into the main or tail rotor. One year before, a friend had been killed at Pax River when one of the lower engine doors on the same type of helicopter came off and flew into the main rotor. Then I began to think about where our door had landed. Did it hit someone's house or an automobile, injuring the occupants? The rest of the flight back to Norfolk was breezy and cold—a time to reflect on how fragile life is for airmen who tempt the laws of gravity in pursuit of their passion.

Set Flight Quarters

As April rolled around, Det 4 was as prepared as we could be. It was time to put our game faces on and say goodbye to spouses, children, friends, and sweethearts. It was time to move to the USS Aylwin, our floating home for the next six months.

Homeported in Charleston, South Carolina, the USS Aylwin (FF-1081), was a Knox Class frigate, 438 feet long with a crew of eighteen officers and 267 enlisted. She was armed with missiles, torpedoes, and a single five-inch gun.

Lieutenant Greg Matthes, the second pilot and detachment maintenance officer, flew down to Charleston from Norfolk on the first of April aboard a military airlift, along with eight mechanics and the pack-up kit. Two days later, Lieutenant Junior Grade Steve Park, the third pilot and detachment operations officer; the two airborne sensor operators; and I flew directly to the *Aylwin*, which was tied up at a pier in the Charleston Naval Base. Our last day in port was spent stowing and lashing down all of our gear so we would be ready to face whatever sea conditions the Atlantic might throw at us during the ten-day transit to the Mediterranean.

There was one last order of personal business before we departed—buy a ping-pong table. On a visit to the Aylwin several weeks earlier, I was shown the two-man stateroom I would occupy during the cruise and met my roommate, Lieutenant Steve Putnam, the ship's Supply Officer. Somewhere in our conversation, it came out that both of us enjoyed playing ping-pong, which spawned an idea that probably wasn't exactly in line with Navy regulations. Why not buy a ping-pong table and stow it somewhere, out of the way, in the helicopter hangar, located just forward of the flight deck?

We may well have had the first and only ping-pong table on a frigate of the United States Navy. It was a godsend. Whenever the ship was anchored or in port and the helicopter was "sunbathing" on the flight deck, the two of us spent many hours testing each other's skills. We were pretty evenly matched, with a slight edge held by Steve. And almost every night after dinner, we played chess in our stateroom. Here again, Steve was a slightly better player. So, between the two activities, I remained a frustrated but happy competitor throughout much of our deployment.

The stateroom was also the scene of a recurring nightmare I had, played out in dramatic and dangerous fashion. This horrible dream, where I was trapped and slowly being crushed between the overhead and my bunk,

When our helicopter was on the flight deck "sunning itself," my roommate and I were often inside the helicopter hangar playing ping-pong. *USS Aylwin* (FF-1081) 1978 *(U.S. Navy photo)*

began on the *Raleigh* and continued occasionally at home after I was transferred from that ship. In every dream, I leaped out of bed to escape my impending doom. Naturally, when I hit the deck, I immediately woke up feeling foolish—but relieved. On the *Raleigh*, my bunk was three feet high, so my desperate leap did not break any body parts. On the *Aylwin*, I slept in the top rack, six feet off the floor. The first time this happened, I landed with a sprawled thud on the steel deck, just missing the sharp corner of a desk. My surprised roommate flicked on the reading lamp above his head and stared into the darkness. Not knowing what had just happened or what to say, he managed a weak, "Are you all right?" He got used to this occasional middle-of-the-night spectacle and I, luckily, never seriously hurt myself.

On the morning of April 4, 1978, the *Aylwin* departed Charleston Harbor, bound for the Mediterranean and a six-month deployment. Our ship and the rest of the task force "in-chopped" to 6th Fleet operational control on April 14 after a ten-day transit of the Atlantic, devoid of rough seas. Our first port of call immediately after in-chop was Malaga, Spain, located just inside the Med on the famed Costa del Sol. Founded in 770 BC by the Phoenicians, it is one of the oldest cities in the world and the sixth largest city in Spain. I don't remember much about Malaga, but I do recall flying past the Rock of Gibraltar several times on our way to and from the large naval base at Rota, Spain, located on the Atlantic side of the Strait of Gibraltar. At 1,398 feet, the Rock was not that tall, but its iconic image and long history as an impregnable fortress made for a thrilling fly-by nonetheless.

Scratch One Submarine

Each month of the deployment featured one major training exercise that lasted four to six days. Four of the six exercises only involved U.S. Navy forces, one was a NATO exercise, and the other involved the Italian and U.S. navies. Each exercise had an ASW component to it, some larger than others; but due to a variety of reasons, Det 4 only flew seventy-one flight hours on ASW exercises during the entire six-month cruise. That being said, we did have some notable success.

During the first exercise of the deployment, which was held in the western Med, a surface ship in our task force generated a submerged contact using its active sonar. We launched from the *Aylwin* and placed a passive sonobuoy pattern around the submarine's estimated position. Using the sonobuoys to narrow the search area, we were able to use our trailing MAD gear to obtain six consecutive hits." Had this been wartime, we likely would have scored a "kill" with one of our torpedoes. The success we achieved in our first real-world submarine prosecution injected a lot of confidence into a beginner LAMPS detachment.

To maintain certification, each LAMPS detachment must annually drop a live torpedo with a dummy warhead. Det 4 was scheduled to drop one during the exercise described above, but other fixed-wing airplanes "hogged" the show, contrary to the operations order, and the allotted time with the exercise sub expired. We did get our chance two months later in an ASW exercise with the *USS Sturgeon* (SSN-637), the lead ship in a class of nuclear-powered fast-attack submarines.

As mentioned earlier, U.S. submarines were very quiet and hard to detect. The "Silent Service" is justifiably proud of its ability to operate undetected and relished the opportunity to humiliate and frustrate ASW forces, friendly or otherwise, trying to hunt them down. Basically, if they did not want to be found, they wouldn't be found. So, when my copilot Greg Matthes and sensor operator Ken Bradt and I took off from the *Aylwin* fifteen minutes before the start of the exercise with a live MK-46 torpedo hanging from the right pylon, we had little hope of actually gaining contact with the sub. But we planned to drop our torpedo anyway to satisfy the annual requirement.

Not having a clue as to where the *Sturgeon* might be lurking within the relatively small chunk of ocean designated for the exercise, we flew to the northern boundary on a whim. What we found when we got there was a total surprise. Greg spotted it first.

"There's the sub!" he shouted. "It's on the surface!"

Sure enough, about four miles away, was a sight you don't often see—a U.S. nuclear submarine on the surface in the open ocean.

"I don't believe it!" I exclaimed. "This is unbelievable!"

"I wonder if she sees us?" asked Ken from the back.

U.S. fast attack submarine on the surface. *(U.S. Navy photo)*

"Oh, I'm sure she does," I responded. "I'm sure she has radar and four or five lookouts posted in the sail looking for aircraft and surface contacts."

We continued straight for her, expecting she would pull the plug and submerge even though the exercise would not begin for another five minutes. But, she didn't.

"Well, this may be considered cheating, but we're gonna hang around until the exercise commences and then we're gonna drop this torpedo right on their head," I said, barely containing my excitement.

"This is too good to be true," Greg said. "Maybe they don't know we're carrying a torpedo."

"Yeah, maybe not, but won't they be surprised?" I replied.

Sure enough, as soon as the exercise officially started, the sub dove into the dark-blue depths of the Mediterranean Sea.

We could have dropped the torpedo directly on her submerging wake, as we would have during wartime, but I felt we should play the ASW game—at least for a little while. Since the sub obviously knew we were there, and there was no need to hide behind passive detection methods, I told Ken to drop an active sonobuoy pattern.

Almost immediately, Ken said, "I've got contact on two buoys."

"Fantastic!" I cried. "Greg, deploy the madbird and let's see if we can convert to attack criteria."

MK-46 torpedo with inert warhead attached to the right side of our helicopter, just before takeoff and successful "kill" of the *USS Sturgeon*. Note the "madbird" mounted just outboard of the torpedo. 1978

"Yes, sir," my copilot replied, as he activated the winch that would stream the madbird behind and below the helicopter. I then commenced flying a crisscross pattern at four hundred feet above the water.

"Madman, madman," Ken said over the intercom, indicating positive contact with the sub. "It looks like she is heading one hundred and forty degrees at fifteen knots."

That's all we needed. We had achieved attack criteria within five minutes of the sub submerging.

"Drop the torpedo," I commanded.

"Torpedo away," Greg replied, after pulling the release handle.

The sudden shift in the helicopter's lateral center of gravity with the release of the 508-pound weapon, which caused the aircraft to sharply tilt to the left, told us that we had achieved a clean drop. If the torpedo guidance and propulsion systems performed properly after water entry, we stood a decent chance of scoring a direct hit on the "enemy" submarine. It would take several days to find out if we had been successful.

In the meantime, we needed to find the expended torpedo, which was designed to bob to the surface and float. These exercise torpedoes cost thousands of dollars and were reusable if they could be recovered. Once on the surface, the torpedo emitted a lime-green dye that aided visual detection. After ten minutes, we spotted the torpedo and gave the Aylwin the approximate geographical coordinates. We also told the ship we would mark it with a smoke flare.

In my haste to accurately drop the flare near the torpedo, I descended without reeling in the madbird—neither Greg nor I remembered that not-so-small detail. We all heard a loud thunk and, before anyone could say "What was that?", we instantly knew we had lost the madbird and cable when it hit the water behind us. At a price of $37,000 ($225,000 in 2017 dollars), it was a costly lesson and tempered our short-lived taste of victory.

Five days later, at the post-exercise debrief aboard the submarine tender *USS Puget Sound*, I was told by those in attendance that the commanding officer of the *USS Sturgeon* was hopping mad. Apparently our torpedo chased him down and hit the side of his submarine with a resounding bang.

"It's not fair!" he shouted, as he hit his fist on the table. "The helicopter knew exactly where we were when the exercise started," he fumed. "Otherwise, he never would have found us, much less kill us."

When I heard about his rant, I couldn't help but smile. He was right—if he hadn't been on the surface, we never would have found him. "All's fair in love and war" as they say—and maybe exercises too!

If it Floats, Sink it

Even though locating and tracking a submarine was exciting and heady stuff, I was okay with the fact that we spent about twenty-five percent more time looking for and targeting "enemy" surface combatants during major exercises. Granted, the Med is a gigantic area to search and there were plenty of islands and coves to mask a surface raider lying in ambush, but at least when one was finally spotted, there was no ambiguity as to her exact location, like there was with a submarine. Of course, an enemy surface vessel adds a dangerous dimension to this "big-boy" game of hide-and-seek that submarines do not—the ability to shoot down intruding aircraft. But, since we were not at war and nobody was shooting at us, it was just plain fun to sneak up on an "orange" vessel long enough to obtain targeting information (during an exercise, friendly forces were labeled "blue" and the bad guys were dubbed "orange" units).

The only time it wasn't so much fun was at night. To avoid radar detection, we usually flew at one hundred feet above the water. On moonless nights, we could not see the surface, so it was like flying inside the proverbial "ink bottle" (a term that would be unfamiliar to the younger generation who have never had to fill a fountain pen with ink from a bottle). At that altitude, an inattentive helicopter pilot could fly into the water in a matter of seconds. On these flights, both pilots would focus their attention on the flight instruments, especially the radar altimeter. And you also had to contend with the real possibility of literally running into a darkened ship, especially one at anchor. I vividly remember one night, flying in and around an "orange" anchorage containing the aircraft carrier *Forrestal* and her escorts. We could just barely make out their ghostly shapes with our naked eye.

But all of those black nights were soon forgotten when flying a search mission in the daytime, with sunny skies and unlimited visibilities; like the mission we were given during Dawn Patrol, a NATO exercise in the Greek islands in the Aegean Sea. Two fast Greek patrol boats, acting as "orange" forces, were reported to be waiting in ambush in a small bay on the northern coast of Crete, about thirty miles from the *Aylwin*. Since our ship was headed west, I figured that the "enemy" boats would most likely be lurking along the eastern shoreline of the bay, waiting for the *Aylwin* to sail past the mouth before launching a simulated missile or torpedo attack. So, I decided to hug the western shoreline of the bay and follow it around to hopefully surprise them from behind. And that's what we did. Flying at fifty feet and a hundred and twenty knots, and using the hills surrounding the bay as cover, we were suddenly on top of them before they knew we were there. We caught them with their pants down—well almost.

They did have their laundry strung out on the fantail. For a moment, I thought I was back in Vietnam on a gun run against Viet Cong sampans along a muddy riverbank. Unlike later-day Navy helicopter squadrons, which were armed with machine guns and air-to-surface missiles, LAMPS squadrons were not armed for surface engagements. Our sudden appearance made for a few laughs, however, as the Greek sailors scrambled to man their battle stations while dodging clotheslines filled with underwear, socks, and uniforms.

We had two direct contacts with the Soviet Navy during this deployment and one indirect exposure. The first occurred at a large Soviet anchorage off the Greek island of Kythira, located at the southwestern exit from the Aegean Sea. This spot had been a traditional crossroads for maritime travel for centuries, which is, perhaps, why the Soviets chose that location to site a large part of their Mediterranean fleet. Our mission on this particular day was to photograph a Soviet Tango-class diesel submarine reported to be in the anchorage. Among other duties assigned to the sensor operator in a LAMPS helicopter was that of taking photographs of Soviet Navy vessels with a handheld camera equipped with a telephoto lens whenever the opportunity presented itself. To be assigned a specific task of photographing a Soviet vessel was rare indeed, but off we went.

I will admit that my first experience flying close to a potentially hostile surface force was a bit unnerving, especially because we could see Soviet sailors train a few gun mounts on our helicopter as we flew by. We didn't see any submarines, but our guy in the back got some good photographs of a Krivak-class frigate, a Kara-class destroyer, a submarine tender, and a surveillance vessel used to shadow U.S. aircraft carriers. All the time we were flying around the anchorage, I was thinking, *What if the Soviets decide to provoke an international incident by shooting us down?* I was mighty glad to put those Ruskies in our rearview mirror as we flew back to the *Aylwin*.

The second encounter with the Soviet Navy, which also occurred in the Aegean, did not involve Det 4. The *Aylwin* was steaming independently when she stumbled upon a Soviet Navy vessel dead in the water, conducting a Nuclear, Biological, and Chemical (NBC) drill, with all of its topside sailors dressed in protective suits from head-to-toe, running to and fro—just like the drills conducted on U.S. Navy ships. The Aylwin slowed to five knots and gave the Soviet ship a wide berth while each captain saluted the other.

On August 12, the ship, along with other naval assets, was dispatched on a secret mission through the Strait of Gibraltar to a position off the Atlantic Coast of Spain. Intelligence reports indicated that a Soviet submarine would soon be entering the Med and our mission was to assist in locating the sub as it approached the narrow confines of the Strait. As mentioned before, the U.S. and allied navies did their best to keep track of all Soviet submarines, so that if hostilities were to break out, they could be neutralized.

In the early 1960s, the United States laid on the floors of the oceans a series of sophisticated hydrophone arrays that were connected to shore stations by underwater cables. These systems were called SOSUS, which stood for Sound Surveillance System, and were so highly classified that even the name SOSUS was confidential. I first learned about this technology in 1969, when I attended an ASW training course in the Navy Reserves. At the end of the Cold War, in 1991, SOSUS came out of the shadows when it was declassified.

These extremely sensitive arrays could detect acoustic power of less than a watt at ranges approaching two hundred miles. The system was so sensitive that it could detect low-flying Soviet bombers, although it was not used for that purpose. Using triangulation methods, SOSUS had the ability to pinpoint and track submarines, both unfriendly and friendly, as was the case when it enabled the U.S. to locate the wreckage of the *USS Thresher* in 1963 and the *USS Scorpion* in 1968, two nuclear-powered submarines that sank with the loss of all hands.

The intelligence received by 6th Fleet and passed to the *Aylwin* had been generated from SOSUS contacts, probably after the sub had departed her homeport. Unfortunately, Det 4 missed a golden, real-world opportunity to hunt for a Soviet Sub when our helicopter was not called on to assist the other ASW forces. I guess they had the situation well in hand and did not need our superior talent to deliver the coup de grace.

Although we missed our chance to find the Soviet sub, we did participate in a humanitarian mission during this period that was gratifying in a couple ways. One afternoon, the *Aylwin* received a distress call from a Spanish commercial fishing boat saying that one their deckhands had sustained a serious leg injury and needed immediate medical attention. We launched our helicopter, located the boat about ten miles away, and directed our ship alongside the Spanish vessel, which turned out to be fishing for swordfish. Large pointed hooks are used to move these large fish on the main deck and the injured man had caught a gaff in the upper thigh. After our corpsman patched him up and returned him to his boat, their captain presented our ship with three freshly caught swordfish to express his gratitude. One fish went to the officer's wardroom for the evening meal and two went to the mess decks for the crew. I am not a big seafood fan, but those swordfish were out of this world.

Cavorting in Saint-Tropez

One month later, the *Aylwin* anchored off the French Riviera city of Saint-Tropez for a six-day visit. The seaside resort, made famous in the latter part of the twentieth century as a destination for American and European jet-setters, was better known in my youth as the home of the curvy and seductive actress Brigitte Bardot.

Going back to my two-year tour on the *USS Raleigh*, I was not a big liberty hound who had to go ashore at every opportunity to sightsee or grab a beer at a local dive on the waterfront. If there was something really worthwhile seeing, I would go ashore, but otherwise, I was content to stay on the ship to read, play chess, or catch up on my sleep. As my wife and children have told me many times, "Dad, you're so boring."

I figured that Saint-Tropez would be no different, until the XO of the ship said something about checking out some nude beaches reportedly in the area. Now, that fit the category of "something really worthwhile seeing!" So, off we went to perform a recon mission—"we" being the CO, XO, Weapons Officer, and myself—crammed into a French rental car built for two. I noticed that the other three had each brought along a small, folding, aluminum beach chair. I didn't have one, and I didn't think much about it until a few hours later.

We finally found the right section of beach; so, we grabbed our towels, a cooler filled with cold drinks, a football, and, yes, three beach chairs. We headed to the water's edge and were told that there were really three beaches all in a row. First, was a family beach where everybody had on proper swim attire. The next was a topless beach, and the third was a completely nude beach. Why waste any time? We headed straight for beach number three. By a nude beach, the French meant that swim tops and bottoms were optional; we did see a few cautious individuals—like the four most senior officers from the mighty *USS Aylwin*—who were modestly attired.

Talk about whiplash! There was so much to look at it was difficult to take it all in. Our morale was inching up by the second. After taking in all of the sights for about an hour, the four of us decided to play some catch in the gentle surf with the football. The XO looked at the CO who looked at the Weapons Officer who looked at me—in unison we shouted "What the hell!" dropped our swim trunks and dashed into the water.

After playing catch and running pass plays that would be the envy of the Green Bay Packers, we returned to our encampment on the beach, sans swim trunks, to rest up and take in more of the local sights. And then, it happened.

A couple in their late twenties or early thirties approached and identified themselves as Canadian tourists. They had figured we were Americans when they saw us playing with the football. She was topless, but both wore suits on the bottom. The trouble with this encounter was that they happened to stop right in front of me, and I was getting more embarrassed by the minute. I suppose they took my very red features to be sunburn. My mind was desperately looking for an escape from this French tragedy. I looked to my right, at my three compatriots, for help. They were smugly sitting proudly on their beach chairs with their towels swirled in an impressive cone conveniently covering their private parts. Since I did not have a chair, I was sitting on my towel with nothing to hide behind. Now, I knew why they had brought those chairs—they were pros at this nude beach stuff.

Luckily, the two Canadians did not ask what we were doing in Saint-Tropez because I could picture the front-page headline the next day: "Commanding officer of U.S. Navy warship caught cavorting in the nude with three of his most senior officers."

Homeward Bound

Although there had been several operational successes, and Det 4 would be returning home as an experienced LAMPS detachment, it had been a frustrating deployment due to lack of spare parts, which resulted in lots of aircraft downtime. For example, the helicopter was *hard down*, meaning unable to fly at all, for almost the entire month of September. Pilots and sensor operators like to fly, and mechanics like to work on aircraft and fix problems. But that was all behind us when the *Aylwin* departed the Med for Charleston on October 15, 1978.

Aside from several utility missions and two brief radar exercises, the ten-day transit to the States was low-key, which gave the mechanics time to prepare the helicopter for the all-important post-deployment corrosion inspection conducted by Helicopter Sea Control Wing One. While the maintainers were doing their thing, Greg, Steve, and I were busy gathering data and compiling reports that would be included in the extensive end-of-cruise report that I would be writing after our return to Norfolk.

One day, for the heck of it, during the transit home, I joined the rest of the *Aylwin's* OODs (officer of the deck) in conning the ship during man-overboard drills. Handling a smaller single-screw ship was somewhat different than the *Raleigh*, but after several tries, I got the hang of it. Little did I know that the CO and XO were observing me and hatching a plan to put me on the bridge watch bill in the coming days.

On the day before the ship entered port, the captain wanted to hold an all-officer meeting in the wardroom. He couldn't have one hundred percent attendance because one officer would have to be the OOD on the bridge. So, the XO asked me if I would be willing to assume the watch for an hour or so. This request was highly unorthodox and contrary to naval regulations—but, of course, those minor details never stopped this hard-charging captain. I agreed and reported to the bridge to get a turn-over briefing from the OOD on watch. The ship was steaming independently, so I didn't have to worry about maintaining station in a formation of other ships and the weather was good and there were only two merchant shipping contacts that would pose no problem. So, even though I was not qualified as officer-of-the-deck on the Aylwin, I put the binoculars around my neck, saluted the off-going OOD, and announced in a loud, clear voice, "This is Mr. Stock, I have the deck and the conn"—just like the old days on the USS Raleigh. I thoroughly enjoyed my brief return to the bridge. Thankfully I didn't have to deal with any sudden emergencies or other calamities.

After my short watch on the bridge, I sent a message to the home guard, HSL-32, at Naval Station Norfolk, alerting them that Det 4's helicopter would be arriving at the squadron hangar tomorrow at 1230. I began the message titled "Arrival of Fantastic Four" as follows:

> At the end of one message from the home guard that Det 4 received during a particularly trying aircraft crisis was the advice, 'Remember it's not just a job, it's an adventure." Looking back over the events of this deployment from a vantage point where time has dulled a few painful memories, it has indeed been an adventure. But six months of LAMPS daring-do is about all we can hack—so we are coming back tomorrow.

On October 26, at 0800, on a clear morning fifty miles off the coast of Charleston, Det 4 helicopter 190 was granted takeoff clearance from the Aylwin tower one last time. Before heading north, there were two pieces of unfinished business we needed to take care of.

Three miles off our port beam sailed the USS Blakely, with a LAMPS Detachment from our sister squadron in Norfolk, HSL-34. Off and on during the cruise we had worked with Det 7 and enjoyed a spirited and friendly rivalry. But we owed them. So, armed with three water balloons, we flew over their helo deck and scored three direct hits on their helicopter about to takeoff. The moral of the story is to never let your guard down, even on the last day of deployment.

The other bit of unfinished business was a personal goodbye to the XO of the Aylwin, Lieutenant Commander Terry Clark. He and I had gotten along fabulously during the cruise. He was unfailingly good-natured with a great sense of humor. Almost every day, he would end a conversation with the cute phrase: "If I don't see you again, so what!" I don't know that it had any particular meaning, but he always threw it out there.

One day during the transit home, I discovered a large, flat piece of solid brass, one-quarter inch thick, in a storage area at the back of the helicopter hangar. I had a sudden inspiration for a fitting farewell and enlisted the help of the machine shop on the ship. I also enlisted the help of the captain and asked him to call the XO to the bow of the ship after we returned from water bombing the *Blakely*.

I entered a hover over the bow and Ken Bradt lowered a nicely engraved brass plaque on the rescue hoist to the XO who was waiting below. The inscription, in the format of a proper naval memo, read:

From: Officer-in-Charge, Helicopter Detachment Four
To: Executive Officer, USS Aylwin FF-1081
Subj: Farewell

1. If I don't see you again, so what!

Very Respectfully,
M. J. Stock

And, you know—I *never* did see him again!

Two months before the end of the deployment, I had ordered hand-carved plaques from the Philippines for each member of Det 4. In a letter to Barbara, I told her that I wanted to have a detachment party at our house on October 31. In the letter, I wrote:

I realize it's Halloween. The reason I want to have a party on this day is because that is the day our aircraft will be inspected by the Wing for corrosion and it will mark essentially the end of Det 4 as we know it. I will be leaving, "Junebug" is leaving HSL-32 the same day, Graves is going to Rota, etc., etc. I owe a lot to these men. They have worked hard for six months and have made my aircraft safe to fly. In essence, they are responsible for my coming back alive. So, I want to have a party to mark the end of the cruise and Det 4. I have told them it will be a masquerade party, so it should be fun. Babe, I will make the party a little later in the evening so that I can take Brian and Ashley trick-or-treating.

Thank you to Barbara's forbearance in agreeing to host a party only five days after her husband returned from a six-month deployment. The gathering was a great success. I don't remember everything that I said to the men before handing out the plaques, but I do remember one: "I promised you before the cruise began that I would bring you all back home alive. I have fulfilled that promise and as an extra bonus, we brought the aircraft back in better condition than when we left."

The occasion was a fitting end to a time when thirteen men came together for the common good of our country, the U.S. Navy, and each other. I was very proud to have been their leader.

Chapter 18

The XO

I PARKED THE CAR A BLOCK DOWN THE STREET FROM HER HOUSE. THE chaplain pulled in behind me. I gripped the steering wheel tightly and looked at Barbara sitting in the passenger seat—I did not want to get out. Desperately, I wished I could flee and leave my body to the terrible task at hand.

Four hours earlier, on this overcast Sunday morning, the phone rang on the nightstand. Blinking my eyes, I tried to focus on the clock. Whoever was calling at 0630 can't be the bearer of good news.

"Hello, Mike Stock," I said, trying to sound awake.

"XO, this is the SDO (squadron duty officer). Sorry to call so early, but we just received a call from the Massachusetts State Police saying that one of our helicopters crashed into a field during bad weather late last night. Apparently, it took them this long to trace the aircraft back to us."

"Any survivors?" I asked, hoping against hope.

"No, sir," he replied with obvious emotion.

"Have you already called the skipper?"

"Yes, sir, I called him first"

"Okay, do not tell anyone else about this. I'll be there in twenty minutes."

Not bothering to shave, I hurriedly threw on my khaki work uniform and hopped in the car. As I drove north on I-64 toward NAS Norfolk, I remembered that one of our helicopters had departed Friday afternoon for a weekend cross-country flight to New England with six on board: three pilots and three enlisted aircrew. In my fifteen years in the Navy, I had been down this road before—squadron mates killed in the prime of their lives. But this time, I wouldn't be able to grieve privately. As the second-in-command, I would be dealing with next-of-kin notification, memorial services, the accident investigation, and a host of issues I knew nothing about. Grieving would have wait until later.

By the time I arrived, the CO, Commander Ron Jesberg, and the operations officer, Lieutenant Commander Jerry Baker, were congregated in the skipper's spacious office on the second deck. The mood was solemn, but business-like. They quickly brought me up to speed.

"Morning XO," the ops officer said. "All we know at this point is that the State Police have confirmed what appears to be five deceased crew-members in and around the crash site. There was a post-impact fire, so the bodies and the wreckage itself are in pretty bad shape."

"I thought there were six guys onboard," I stated.

"That's right. Six were on board when they left here on Friday," the CO interjected. "We know their plan was to drop off one of the enlisted guys at a small airport short of their final destination, which was NAS Brunswick, Maine. We just don't know if he was dropped off before the crash or not."

"Well, that shouldn't be that hard to confirm," I allowed.

Baker weighed in, "The problem is we don't know exactly where they were planning to drop him off. The SDO is trying to run that down right now."

As I was trying to process everything, the CO got right to the heart of our dilemma. "All six of these guys were married and have wives and families living in the area. We need to personally notify the spouses as soon as possible, before they find out through the news media."

For the next several hours, while we desperately tried to determine if we were dealing with five deaths or six, we began to assemble notification teams, which would fan out shortly to deliver news that no spouse ever wants to hear. Each team was comprised of a Navy chaplain and an officer from the squadron. I was assigned to notify Allison Mellott, wife of Lieu-tenant Paul Mellott.

The skipper thought it would be a good idea if each of our wives went along, to provide additional support and comfort to the grieving widows. I immediately called Barbara and asked her to get ready. I told her I'd be home within the hour to change into my dress-blue uniform.

As the minutes ticked away, it was becoming more and more obvious that reaching a quick determination as to the precise number of deaths was not going to happen. And it was only a matter of time before the local media got wind of the fatal crash. We just couldn't bear the thought of these unfortunate women finding out about their husband's death in this manner—we had to act!

As if to accentuate the need for quick action, the SDO popped his head into the office to tell us he had just received a call from one of the wives asking if he knew when the helicopter was scheduled to return. Appar-ently, her husband was bringing back Maine lobsters for a cookout with some friends later that day.

"We can't wait any longer," the CO stated emphatically. "The only unanswered question is whether the sixth man was dropped off or not. So, let's notify the five we are sure of and deal with the sixth individual later." (Later in the day, we were able to confirm that the sixth sailor had been dropped off before the crash.)

It was the chaplain's recommendation that we park down the street, so that Allison would not see us pull up front—anything to prolong the dreaded moment of reckoning was okay with me.

It was late morning, on a gloomy spring day, when we walked up the short driveway to the Mellott residence. The front door was open, and through the screen door we could hear Allison vacuuming somewhere out of sight. The chaplain was slightly in the lead, so he rang the doorbell. I wanted very much to hide behind him—but I didn't.

Military families are all conditioned to and understand the meaning of several uniformed personnel standing unannounced on their doorstep. No words have to be said. The family instantly realizes that their loved one will never be coming home again.

Allison turned off the vacuum and rounded the corner. As soon as she saw us, she stopped and began to slowly walk backward, saying in a loud voice, "No, no, no!"

Finding the screen door unlocked, the chaplain did not wait for an invitation to enter. He just opened the door and walked in with Barbara and me on his heels. Notification of NOK is part of the job description for chaplains, so he knew the ropes.

We followed Allison to the living room and sat down. She was quiet and did not ask any questions. She just sat there, looking around the room as if she was trying to process this sudden turn of events. I gently explained that the squadron did not know many details at this early stage, but I told her what little we knew. She seemed appreciative. Barbara remarked later that everything that was done or said seemed to be unfolding in slow motion.

Allison was obviously in shock. She did not cry or break down the entire forty-five minutes we were sitting in her living room. She was teaching a psychology course at a local college at the time and at one point said, "I will have to practice what I have been teaching my students about handling grief."

The chaplain asked Allison if she wanted to call anyone while we were there. She said, "No. I especially do not want to call Paul's parents because the news will forever change their lives."

Another touching statement Allison made that fateful day was: "I will never be able to smell Paul again."

Over the next month, Barbara and I saw Allison two more times in our official capacities: a memorial service held on base for all five of the deceased and a private memorial service held at the U.S. Naval Academy—each time she was the model of strength and composure.

Notifying Allison, that Sunday so long ago, remains one of the most difficult things I have ever had to do.

Surprise Orders

Before I left on deployment to the Mediterranean, HSL-32 had programmed me to be the maintenance officer on my return. Due to my unconventional career path, I had never had a squadron department head assignment and I really needed that box checked to be viable for squadron command.

One month prior to the end of the cruise, I received a message from the parent squadron asking if I wanted to be XO of HSL-30—a large squadron of forty-six officers and over four hundred enlisted. At first glance, this seemed to be a dream assignment, even though it meant giving up my chance to be a department head. I assumed, wrongly as it turned out, that having more responsibility as the second-in-command outweighed the career benefits of being a department head. So, lured by the bright lights of the "front office," I accepted their offer.

Settling into the Number Two Slot

In the Navy, the CO sets policy and interfaces with the naval establishment external to the command and, of course, is the final authority and ultimate decision-maker within his or her command, whether that be a ship, a squadron or a shore activity. The traditional job of the XO is to run the day-to-day internal affairs, subject to the oversight of the CO. In the business world, the XO is like a chief operating officer, while the CO is akin to being the CEO.

Fortunately, I worked for a splendid CO, who let me do my job with minimal guidance and direction. Commander Jesberg could have been an intimidating presence had he wanted; at six-foot-five he was a hulk of a man. But instead, he chose to lead with a big smile, a word of encouragement, and a slap on the back. HSL-30 was Commander Jesberg's second squadron command, his first being a fleet HS squadron. He went on to command two deep-draft ships and all U.S. naval forces in the Persian Gulf. He retired as a rear admiral.

In many ways the XO's job is more difficult and broader in scope than that of the CO. During fifteen months on the job, I worked harder than in any other position I had in the Navy, but it was also one of the most satisfying and rewarding assignments. Within the broad policy dictates set by the CO, I was free to tackle and implement most any improvement program I thought would benefit the command in the short or long term. I am most proud of my efforts on many fronts to promote a people-oriented approach to everything the squadron did. Partly due to my efforts, HSL-30 won the coveted Golden Anchor Award given annually to the command that posted the highest rate of re-enlistments for the entire Atlantic fleet.

Moving On

On October 5, 1979, I reached a milestone in my career when I donned a cover (hat) with scrambled eggs on the bill signifying the rank of commander or captain in the United States Navy. Unlike the Army, Air

Force, and Marine Corps, which divided its officer corps into company grade, field grade, and general grade officers, the Navy divided its ranks into junior officers, senior officers, and flag officers (admirals). Now, as a commander, I was officially a senior officer.

Although I didn't fly as much as I would have liked, due to my administrative responsibilities, my tour of duty as the XO of HSL-30 remains one of the highlights of my naval career and certainly the most satisfying in terms of personal accomplishment.

But it was time to move on to my next assignment. When I called my detailer in Washington, D.C. to see what jobs were available, the first one he put on

Newly promoted to commander. September 1979 *(U.S. Navy photo)*

the table was XO of the naval air station on Guam. Although an overseas tour on an island, living in a nice house on the base, overlooking the Pacific Ocean, had a certain amount of appeal, it would have been a "killer job" and I had already decided that I was not going to bust my hump anymore for the Navy, not after I was passed over for squadron command. I would do my job to the best of my ability, but nothing extra.

"Okay, how about being the XO of a Navy ROTC unit?" my detailer asked.

"Well, that sounds like it could be fun and not too stressful," I replied. "What openings do you have?"

"Do you have a master's degree?" he asked.

"No, not yet, but I am only six credit hours short of obtaining one," I answered, thinking my chances of an ROTC assignment were slipping away.

"Well, Mike, most schools require a master's or higher, but a few will accept some level of graduate credit," he said. "Let's see, what I might have available in the latter category." There was a pause and I could hear papers being shuffled. "Looks like Purdue and Cornell will accept less than a master's," he said.

"Those are certainly two good schools," I answered.

"But let me caution you ahead of time," he said. "I can't just issue you orders to one of these schools. A faculty committee at each school must approve my nomination. So, even though they may advertise that they will accept less academic qualifications, the faculty members will decide who is acceptable based on their review of your application and overall record."

"Let me talk it over with my wife, and I will call you tomorrow."

"Sounds good."

That night, Barbara and I discussed the pros and cons of each university. I knew that Purdue was known for the excellence of its engineering programs and I also thought I may be able to do a little flying since Purdue owned its own airport. For her part, Barbara figured that the winters in Ithaca, New York, would be more severe than those in West Lafayette, Indiana. So, Purdue was our choice, if they would have me. After going through a rather lengthy vetting process, the Military Affairs Committee of Purdue University approved my application in early January 1980, and I received my official transfer orders shortly thereafter. After receiving my orders, Barbara and I and our two kids piled into our motorhome and drove to Indiana to house-hunt. Ironically, after rejecting Cornell as being too cold, we encountered one of the coldest months of January in recent memory in northwest Indiana. It was so cold, the water pipes in our RV froze solid.

Since the officer who was replacing me as XO at HSL-30, arrived earlier than expected, I turned over the job to him in mid-February and really didn't have a job to do. In the meantime, I got wind of a ferry crew in need of a copilot to fly a SH-3 helicopter from the East Coast to the West Coast. With my good friend Commander Woody Knight in the pilot's seat, we departed Norfolk Naval Station and arrived five days later at Naval Air Station North Island in San Diego. There I hopped into the copilot's seat of a Huey helicopter with another ferry pilot and headed back east for a delivery to Naval Air Station Corpus Christi, Texas. In eight days, I flew thirty-two hours—and managed to relive my carefree days as a ferry pilot back in VRF-32 in the late 1960s.

On March 26, 1980, I officially detached from HSL-30 and headed west. My first Navy squadron, back in 1965, had been HC-4, which was re-designated HSL-30 in 1972 and moved from NAS Lakehurst to NAS Norfolk. So, I started and ended my fleet aviation career in the same squadron—a bit of trivia not many naval aviators can claim!

Chapter 19

Navy Farewell

NEAR THE END OF A THREE-HOUR FLIGHT THAT HAD ORIGINATED earlier that morning from NAS Patuxent River, Maryland, I was looking forward to lunch and a cold Pepsi. The Cessna 182 I was flying had recently undergone an engine change and the primary purpose of the flight was to put time on the new engine before it was released to be flown by other members of the Patuxent Navy Flying Club. Since I had to fly a few hours anyway, why not fly to Angola, New York, to visit my mom and dad and brothers, as opposed to making lazy circles around southern Maryland?

The IFR flight, at a cruising altitude of nine thousand feet, had been uneventful and smooth in the clear on top of a solid overcast below. Forty miles southeast of my destination, Buffalo Approach Control broke my reverie, "Cessna 52581, Buffalo Approach, descend and maintain 4,000, Buffalo altimeter 30.12."

"581, descend and maintain 4,000; altimeter 30.12, leaving 9,000," I replied as pulled the carb heat on and reduced the throttle to begin the descent.

At 4,500 feet, I entered the top of the solid overcast layer of clouds and a few seconds later, as I was leveling off at my assigned altitude of 4,000, the engine emitted a loud *whoooosh* sound, like the prop lever had suddenly been reduced to low pitch. At first, I didn't know what had happened. Then I knew full well—the engine had quit!

What could have caused the engine failure? I had applied full carb heat, so it wasn't likely carb ice. I quickly stopped trying to comprehend why it had quit. I had more pressing concerns.

The latest weather report from Buffalo International Airport was ceiling 500 overcast and one-mile visibility. Being familiar with the local topography, I knew I was flying over some foothills and higher ridges that surround the Buffalo area. My first thought was, *Given the low clouds, I will never see the terrain before crashing into it.* So, instead of initiating a flaps-up, best glide nose attitude, which is recommended, I immediately lowered full flaps and slowed to fifty-five knots. My reasoning was that I would be going as slowly as possible when I hit the higher terrain. My next thought was to let approach control know what was going on. "Buffalo approach, Cessna 581, my engine just quit."

"Your what?" replied the controller, either not hearing or not believing what he had just heard.

"My engine just quit," I responded more emphatically.

"581, there is a grass airport three miles off your left wingtip," the controller replied coolly and instantly, like he had been rehearsing this emergency for years.

"Give me vectors to it," I stated.

"Turn left heading 280 and the airport should be at your twelve o'clock."

"Roger, 581. I'm still in the clouds."

"Understand, report the airport in sight."

That was the last radio transmission with the controller because I had descended below radio reception altitude.

Sometime during my brief communications with Buffalo approach, I remembered way back, "in the gray matter," that someone had told me that pumping the throttle (thereby using the accelerator pump in the carburetor) might restore some power. I decided to try it. Sure enough, the engine roared back to life providing about one-half power. So, as long as I kept pumping the throttle, I had some power. On this particular flight, for some reason, I forgot to bring my radio headset and had to resort to the cabin speakers and a handheld mic. Consequently, each time I had to use "my right-throttle pumping hand" to grab the transmitter handset to communicate with Buffalo approach, the engine quit again. This scene would have been comical to watch if the stakes weren't so high.

Still tightly enveloped in white clouds, I tightened my seat belt and watched the altimeter unwind to an uncertain fate. I split my attention between "flying the gauges"—heading 280 degrees and airspeed fifty-five knots—and peering over the top of the instrument panel hoping to catch a glimpse of the ground in time to quickly maneuver to a softer impact.

Suddenly, there it was! Just clearing a tree-lined ridge, I broke clear of the clouds at four hundred feet above the ground and found that I was perfectly lined up with the grass airstrip. It was like I had just flown a precision instrument approach to minimums. The landing was anticlimactic, but oh, so sweet!

What can I say? I was lucky—again! All the pieces came together perfectly: altitude, proximity to an airport, groundspeed and rate of descent, a controller who gave me a perfect heading to fly, and a few bursts of power from a sick engine. The chances of being able to replicate that successful outcome to the same airport would be nearly impossible.

A humorous postscript to this near-accident involved my interaction with a FAA operations inspector from the Rochester, New York FSDO. As is customary whenever an emergency landing is made, the FAA conducts a routine investigation, usually over the phone, to see if any regulations were broken. He was going down his checklist of questions when, at some point, I mentioned that I had removed the carburetor to check for possible contamination and, finding none, reinstalled it on the aircraft. There was a long pause before he said, "Do you have an A&P (airframe and powerplant) license?" He probably thought he had me since a non-mechanic pilot cannot perform a carburetor removal.

"Yes, sir, I do," I replied jauntily.

"Just checking," he said.

I never did find out what caused the engine to quit. My best guess is that some water had become trapped in the wrinkles at the bottom of the rubber fuel bladder, a well-known problem in that model Cessna.

My Last Set of Orders

When it came time to leave Purdue ROTC, I had exactly seventeen months left in the Navy to reach retirement eligibility. I was fairly certain I would opt to retire after twenty years of active duty, even though I could remain on active service until the twenty-eight-year mark. The best option was to return to Pax River. We still owned a house there, and after I retired, there was a good possibility of landing a job with a civilian defense contractor in the area. My detailer in D.C. offered me a job at BIS, which stands for Board of Inspection and Survey. The BIS unit at Pax River, more commonly referred to as the "Aviation Board," was the aviation arm of the main board headquartered at the Navy Yard in Washington, in D.C. It was responsible for the acceptance of all new aircraft designs into the naval inventory. As an added bonus, I would be back on flight status and able to fly a variety of airplanes and helicopters.

My job at the Aviation Board was to serve as project officer on four helicopters and two fixed-wing aircraft. Being a project officer at BIS, unlike my previous test-pilot tour at the Naval Air Test Center, did not involve any test flying in the project aircraft that I managed, nor did it encompass any direct oversight and direction of flight-test operations. My job was to be the eyes and ears for the Secretary of the Navy at various program meetings, design reviews, yellow sheet reviews (maintenance issues), and other conferences held by the Naval Air Systems Command in Washington, D.C. or chaired by the manufacturer at their facilities. I was directly responsible for preparation of a monthly written report on the current status of each aircraft program that I monitored, which was sent up the BIS chain of command and ultimately to the Secretary of the Navy. I was a paper-pusher extraordinaire, but then, I could handle anything for the seventeen months I had left in the Navy. I could have been assigned to a worse job, like a staff assignment in the Pentagon.

Since there were only three project officers on our small staff, the OIC, Captain Pete Gorham, divided up the aircraft requiring oversight in such a way as to balance the workload and to play to our fleet and previous test-pilot expertise. The four helicopters I managed were the Sikorsky SH-60B Seahawk, Sikorsky MH-53E Sea Dragon, Bell AH-1T Super Cobra, and the Kaman SH-2F Seasprite. On the fixed-wing side I had the Lockheed S-3B Viking and Grumman E-2C Hawkeye, both carrier-based airplanes, which would have stretched my meager carrier-landing experience in a T-28 back in 1964 to its limit. But fortunately, both aircraft were being upgraded in the avionics and weapon systems areas and not in the basic airframe, which might have impacted carrier suitability.

Additionally, I was the project officer for the brand-new JVX air-craft under development by a team composed of Bell Helicopter and Boeing-Vertol. JVX stood for Joint-Service Vertical Takeoff and Landing Experimental Aircraft—the reader can now fully appreciate why everyone simply referred to as "JVX."

JVX arose from the 1980 Iran hostage-rescue operation that failed to rescue the fifty-two members of the American Embassy in Tehran. Because existing helicopters did not have the range or payload capacity to perform the roundtrip mission from Navy ships at sea to Tehran, a complex joint mission involving MH-53s flown by Marine pilots, Air Force C-130s carrying fuel for the helicopters, and the Army's Delta Force was mounted. Tragically, the mission was scrubbed at the Desert One landing zone in the middle of the Iranian desert due to insufficient helicopters after three of the original eight had to abort. As the U.S. forces were withdrawing from Desert One, one of the remaining helicopters collided with a C-130 on the ground, resulting in the death of eight U.S. servicemen.

After the dramatic and embarrassing failure of the rescue operation, military planners decided build a new vertical-takeoff and landing air-craft similar to a helicopter, but with the increased range and payload of a fixed-wing airplane. In April 1983, a joint Bell-Boeing team was awarded a preliminary-design contract to build an aircraft patterned after the success-ful XV-15 tilt-rotor demonstrator aircraft designed, built, and successfully flown by Bell Helicopter in April 1977.

The tilt-rotor concept involves a fixed-wing fuselage with a large wing mounted on top. On the end of each wingtip is a pylon that contains a jet engine and a fairly large rotor called a "prop-rotor" because it serves as both a lifting rotor during vertical takeoff and landing and as a conventional propeller in cruise flight. The conversion from vertical flight to cruise flight is accomplished by rotating each pylon at a safe altitude from the vertical position ninety degrees forward to the horizontal position.

During my tenure at the Aviation Board, I was privileged to have a front row seat and insider's perspective on the design and development of this military aircraft and to witness the birth of a totally new aviation concept, the tilt-rotor. It was certainly one of the highlights of my professional test-pilot career. Forty-five days after I retired from the Navy, the Pentagon announced the name for the JVX aircraft: the V-22 Osprey. Its first flight occurred four years later, in March 1989. After years of development and flight testing, the V-22 Osprey delivered some impressive performance figures: top speed of three hundred and sixteen miles per hour; a range of one thousand and eleven miles; and an internal load capacity of twenty thousand pounds, which equates to thirty-two combat troops. The debacle at Desert One would not happen again!

Jets, Helicopters, and King Airs

While at BIS, I did manage to get one flight in the huge Sikorsky MH-53 Sea Dragon at Pax River and a flight in XV-15 tiltrotor simulator at the Bell Helicopter plant in Fort Worth, but that was the extent of my "project" flying. Fortunately, the four aviators assigned to the Aviation Board, were designated as part-time instructor pilots at Test Pilot School, just across the base. We didn't have the aircraft currency or the intimate familiarity with the test-pilot curriculum to engage in the more critical aspects of test-pilot training, so we were used as instructors on familiarization and orientation flights. I suppose we did help out some, but I believe we old geezers were allowed to fly as more of a courtesy to us than a necessity.

Courtesy or not, I was thankful for the opportunity and tried to get out of the office as often as I could to go flying. I was re-checked out in the Bell OH-58 helicopter and the North American T-2C Buckeye, twin-jet trainer, logging ninety-one hours in the OH-58 and forty-seven hours in the T-2C during the seventeen months I was assigned to BIS. Although I was not qualified as plane commander in the Beech C-12 (the military equivalent of the civilian King Air 200), I logged sixty-five hours as a copilot.

I was able to fly the T-2C home to Indiana to see my family on a couple occasions. One of the biggest perks for military aviators during my time of active service was the ability to fly "cross-country training flights" on the weekends to almost anywhere in the U.S. where there was a military base or a civilian field with military landing rights and contract fuel. I can't begin to count how many such "training" flights I took during my military career to visit family and friends, house-hunt, checkout a new duty station, or just for the fun of it.

On August 29, 1984, I flew a TPS student in the T-2C who needed some night-flying time to satisfy his annual minimums. We flew for 1.6 hours in the local area, doing night landings and instrument approaches, without a hint of aircraft trouble; he was in the front seat and I was in the instructor's seat in the rear cockpit. On the very next flight the following morning, that same airplane exploded inflight and erupted into a huge fireball, killing the student who was flying in the backseat and severely burning the instructor pilot in the front seat before he was able to eject. Had the jet exploded the night before, I would have been consumed in the fireball. This was one of many exceedingly close calls I had during my long professional flying career. No question, I have lived an exceptionally charmed life.

After Normal Working Hours

Free of the day-to-day family responsibilities and home maintenance issues when I left my family behind in Indiana, I threw myself into a frenzy of leisure-time pursuits to ease the loneliness and boredom of being a geographical bachelor. My first order of business was to finish two graduate courses from Embry-Riddle Aeronautical University, in which I had received incompletes back in the spring of 1980. Usually outstanding coursework has to be turned in no later than the following semester; so, I contacted my professor, who had taught both courses, to see if he would be willing to waive the time requirement. He must have had a soft spot in his heart for the military because he agreed to accept my late term papers. After receiving a grade for the two delinquent courses, I received my master's degree *with distinction* from Embry-Riddle Aeronautical University in April 1984. With a graduate degree in hand, I was ready to pursue a teaching job at Purdue University upon my retirement from the Navy.

Having received the FAA Powerplant Mechanic's rating while I was at the Navy ROTC unit at Purdue, I was eager to complete the requirements for the Airframe Mechanic's rating so that I would be able to claim a full A&P certificate on my aviation résumé. I obtained the Powerplant rating by attending classes at an approved school (Purdue), but there was no such school available in the Pax River area. The other option was to apprentice under another A&P mechanic and then take the practical test from a Designated Mechanic Examiner (DME). Well, it just so happened the mechanic for the Patuxent Navy Flying Club, Ed Childers, was also a DME.

Ed was a retired Navy Chief Petty Officer, who had worked on reciprocating engines during his Navy career. Since I was the Maintenance Officer for the club, Ed technically worked for me, but our friendship flourished on the basis of mutual respect.

Ed agreed to take me on as his apprentice, and then, when I had logged the required experience, he administered the practical test after I had taken and passed the FAA written exam. I was now a Certificated A&P Mechanic, at least on paper. I had a heck of a lot to learn about being a mechanic! As I have always told people, I am was a pilot with a mechanic's license, not a mechanic with a pilot's license.

At this point in my aviation career, I set about to obtain as many certificates and ratings as I could, figuring it would look good on my résumé and possibly lead to the next job. (I believe my success in the job market over the years supports that logic.)

During the seventeen months I spent at Pax River, I learned a lot about maintenance techniques under the able supervision and mentoring from Ed. He and I totally overhauled the engine of the club's T-34, refurbished the airframe, and returned to service an airplane that had not flown in over three years. I also assisted in maintaining six other airplanes owned and operated by the flying club, eventually being able to perform certain maintenance actions and repairs myself and sign them off.

Embry-Riddle Aeronautical University had a satellite campus at NAS Pax River, so I approached its director, a retired Marine colonel, to see if he had any openings for faculty, and he did. So, I taught an aviation law course and an aviation marketing course in the evenings as an adjunct professor. I also taught an instrument-pilot ground school in the evenings for St. Mary's County adult-education program. And then, flipping my hat around from teacher to student, I took a welding class in the adult-education program.

As if the above activities did not keep me busy enough, I also flew a fair amount in the flying club, I instructed two primary flight students and one pilot working on his instrument rating; flew two trips on official business as part of my Navy job; flew four times to Lafayette, Indiana, to visit my wife and three children and three times to Angola, New York, to visit my parents and brothers; flew to the Ridge Soaring Gliderport in central Pennsylvania to do some ridge soaring, something I had not done before in a glider; and flew to Florida on two different occasions to acquire more pilot ratings: a Multi-Engine Sea rating and a multi-engine ATP certificate. In total, I flew ninety-one hours in 1983 and two hundred and twenty hours in 1984 during off-duty hours.

My Last Day in the United States Navy

In April 1984, with some regret, I officially started the countdown to my retirement from the Navy, when I sent a letter to the Secretary of the Navy, via the chain of command, to formally request I be transferred to the retired list effective December 1, 1984. Even though I had more or less decided four years earlier, after not being selected for squadron command, to retire at the twenty-year point, it was still a difficult step to sever my ties from an organization that had been my life for so long and formed so much of who I was. The Navy had been like a patient parent, mentoring and guiding me, as I matured from an adolescent to a young man with purpose and direction. I'll freely admit that it was a sad moment when I signed my retirement letter.

In addition to starting the retirement process, I also had to begin planning for my second act. Toward that end, I sent out feelers to the Aviation Technology Department at Purdue University, to see if they might have any faculty openings for spring semester 1985. Because I had taken a number of courses at AvTech when working on my FAA mechanic's license, I knew a fair number of the faculty members in the department, including the department head, Bill Duncan. On two different occasions, when I was home visiting Barbara and the kids, I met with Bill to discuss job prospects. He told me he did not have any immediate openings,

Receiving my U.S. Navy retirement flag from Captain Pete Gorham, USN on my last day in the United States Navy just before taking off to fly to West Lafayette, Indiana to visit my family. November 30, 1984 *(U.S. Navy photo)*

but that he would certainly give my application a favorable endorsement should one arise.

Several days before my actual retirement date, I started thinking about how I wanted to spend my last day on active duty. At first, I thought it would be cool to fly a helicopter, a jet, and a multi-engine airplane—three flights that would encompass the different types of Navy aircraft I had flown over the past seventeen months. Go out with a bang! But then, I thought it would be selfish of me to not share my last day with my family in Indiana, who had taken a backseat to my naval career all of these years.

So, I decided to fly a T-2C jet to Lafayette, spend a few hours, and fly back. The plan seemed simple enough, but the execution nearly turned into a disaster.

My preflight planning indicated that I should have sufficient fuel to fly nonstop from Pax River to Lafayette. It would be a little tighter than I preferred but I figured I would be able to land with just over thirty minutes of reserve. However, once airborne and leveled off at my cruise altitude of 24,000 feet, the jet stream struck again, with much higher headwinds than forecasted—just like it had a number of years earlier when the radios and navigation equipment failed on the T-2C I was flying. As Yogi Berra once said, "It was déjà vu all over again"—except this time, I didn't have to contend with any mechanical failures.

My dwindling fuel supply was causing a great deal of anxiety, so I decided to take a bold step. "Cleveland center, this is Navy 58178 declaring a low fuel emergency."

"Roger Navy 58178, Wright-Patterson AFB in Dayton is at your eleven o'clock 56 miles. Fly heading 250, descend and maintain 8000."

"Navy 178 heading 250 descend and maintain 8000, leaving flight level 240," I replied, reading back my clearance verbatim, as required.

"Navy 178, Cleveland center, state souls on board and fuel state."

It is always disconcerting after declaring an emergency that the first thing ATC always asks for is "the number of souls on board." Hey, wait a minute! I'm not a soul yet. That's why I called you in the first place and declared an emergency—in the hope that we could prevent that from happening!

"Cleveland center, Navy 178, one soul and thirty minutes of fuel."

The landing at Wright-Pat was uneventful although the tower rolled all of the crash and rescue vehicles just in case; nothing like a little excitement and an adrenaline cocktail on my last flight in the Navy.

Back in Lafayette, Barbara didn't know what had happened to me. She had arranged a surprise retirement party, complete with cake and punch, to be held in one of the AvTech classrooms at the airport. She had invited a number of our friends and neighbors to attend, but as the minutes and

Top photo: Just after shutting down my engines at Lafayette, Indiana, somebody boosted my youngest daughter, Julie (4 years old), into the cockpit for an arrival kiss.

Bottom photo: Family photo shortly after landing at the Purdue Airport on my last day in the Navy. *Back row (l to r):* Barbara, me, Brian. *Front row (l to r):* Julie and Ashley. November 30, 1984 hours dragged on with "no Mike in sight," most of them had to leave. Finally, I was able to get word to Barbara to explain what had happened, and that I would be arriving as soon as I could.

When I finally arrived at Lafayette Airport, I decided to make it a memorable arrival, albeit two and a half hours late. "Lafayette Tower, this is Navy jet 58178, fifteen miles east, request high speed low pass with an overhead break, over."

"Navy jet 58178 approved as requested, report five miles east."

"Navy 178," I replied, barely able to contain my excitement.

I shoved both throttles to the forward stop, lowered the nose to descend to three hundred feet above the ground while building airspeed. I roared down runway 28 at just a little over 450 knots, rolled into an abrupt ninety-degree angle of bank turn to the left, popped the speed brakes, lowered the landing gear and flaps, and greased it on. All in a day's work—after almost running out of fuel, that is!

After posing for a few pictures with family and friends and eating some cake, I strapped on my G-suit and torso harness and climbed back into the cockpit of the Navy jet one last time. It was a sad moment when I pushed the throttles up for takeoff, but at least I knew I would be reunited with my family in several days, when I unpacked my seabag for good.

When I arrived at Pax River later that same day, with the jet stream at my back, it was after dark. Upon clearing the runway, I released one side of my oxygen mask, raised the canopy, and allowed cool air to brush gently across my face. It was a bittersweet moment to be sure. I was three hours from retiring from the greatest career a man could possibly have. I was in an expansive mood as I taxied to the TPS line.

"Pax tower, 178, that was my last landing in the United States Navy. I am retiring at midnight."

"Congratulations! Good luck in your retirement. Continue taxiing to the TPS line and good night, sir."

After arriving at my motorhome in the Goose Creek campground on base later that evening, I crawled into bed a tired, but happy hombre and promptly drifted off to sleep. An hour or so later, something woke me up. I looked at my watch and it was precisely midnight. I was now a civilian!! What are the chances of waking up exactly at the stroke of midnight? I guess I didn't want to miss a second of the next chapter in my life!

Chapter 20

Flying Professor

ALL FLIGHT STUDENTS PLAY A MACABRE GAME CALLED "KILL THE Flight Instructor." Not that they ever deliberately set out to cause grave bodily harm to their flight instructor, and, by extension, to themselves, but the suddenness of their incorrect actions and mistakes can catch an instructor off-guard. I was usually wise to their little tricks and, therefore, operated in the "spring-loaded position" ready to jump on the flight controls to stave off impending disaster. But, not this day.

Jay Reed was one of my instrument students in the Purdue University flight program. This particular day, we were practicing ADF instrument approaches to Frankfort, Indiana, a small non-towered airport located twenty-six miles southeast of the Purdue Airport. It was a beautiful fall day without a cloud in the sky; we were the only aircraft for miles. To add to the illusion that flying doesn't get much better than this was the fact that Jay was the best pilot I had ever flown with, period! Military or civilian, it didn't matter. Jay was a gifted, natural aviator. He didn't need a flight instructor to critique his performance or to suggest ways to improve his technique. The very first time he tried something new, he did it perfectly—and he did it flawlessly from then on.

We were nearing the end of the flight lesson and Jay was flying one last practice instrument approach before returning to Purdue. As usual, he was flying another perfect maneuver, and, for anyone who has never attempted an ADF approach using a bearing needle, it is the most difficult and demanding of all instrument-approach procedures. As Jay approached the "missed approach point"—the position where a pilot must decide whether to land or to execute a missed approach and go around—I told him to make a touch-and-go landing.

Like every maneuver, Jay's landings were a thing to behold. He greased them on every time. Because Jay was so good, I had let down my normal instructor guard. In fact, my mind wasn't even in the airplane. I was sitting with my arms folded, lost in thought, miles away.

Jay crossed the end of the runway and allowed the main wheels on our Cessna 172RG to touch ever so lightly on the pavement, like a feather floating to earth. And then, while holding the nosewheel off the runway, he suddenly reverted to a normal human prone to error. I saw his right hand move from the throttle to the landing gear lever, but it happened too quickly for a daydreaming instructor to prevent. He slapped the gear handle to the up-position and the landing gear immediately began to retract.

To prevent accidental retraction of the landing gear while an airplane is on the ground, manufacturers install a safety device called a "squat switch" on an oleo landing gear strut that senses when the airplane is on the ground and deactivates the retraction mechanism. On low-wing airplanes, the squat switch is normally installed on one of the main landing gear struts. On high-wing airplanes, like the C-172RG, the squat switch is installed on the nose gear, because it is the only oleo strut on the airplane. Since Jay was holding the nosewheel off the runway and the oleo strut was fully extended, the squat switch was not activated. This allowed the landing gear to begin the retraction sequence.

There is nothing like looking out the front windshield of an airplane on the ground as the landing gear is retracting to stimulate action. I grabbed the flight controls, pitched the nose up to the takeoff attitude, and simultaneously applied full throttle as the airplane continued to sink. I had done everything possible, but I just didn't see us escaping the inevitable. I fully expected the propeller to begin making ugly sounds as each blade contacted the runway as we slid to a grinding stop.

Somehow, though, we narrowly escaped and the airplane climbed away from the close encounter. After we were safely at altitude and my heart had slowed below two hundred beats per minute, I looked over at Jay and said, "What the hell did you do that for?"

"I have no idea why I did that," he said sheepishly. "But thanks for saving my bacon."

Lesson learned: even the best flight students occasionally try to kill their flight instructor.

Cockpit and Classroom

My primary duties as a faculty member in the Aviation Technology Department (AvTech) at Purdue University were evenly split between flight instructing and classroom teaching. On the flight side, I conducted FAA Part 141 phase checks for private and commercial students in the PA-28 Piper Warrior; I flew the Cessna 172RG teaching instrument flight students; and I taught students working on their multi-engine land rating in the PA-44 Piper Seminole and later in the BE-76 Beech Dutchess.

Typically, I did two or three phase checkrides per week and I had two or three instrument and two multi-engine flight students at any given time.

In the classroom, I taught one course per semester. Since I was a licensed A&P mechanic, I often taught entry-level classes to students enrolled in Aviation Maintenance Technology, such as Airframe Mechanic Responsibilities and Helicopter Aerodynamics and Systems. For students working on their flight ratings, I taught Piston Engines for Pilots, Aviation Law, and Emergency Survival Skills. The latter course, which I developed based on my Navy survival training, was a first for Purdue and was offered to the university at-large as well as to AvTech students. The novel course, which included an optional three-day survival experience in the Hoosier National Forest, became a very popular three-credit elective on campus. The first time it was offered in the fall of 1987, eighty-one students enrolled.

Weekend Ground Warrior

Every instructor must renew his or her flight instructor certificate every two years. There are several ways to accomplish this, including attending a weekend seminar that did not involve any actual flying. At first, only the FAA offered these renewal ground classes, but eventually a couple of nongovernmental organizations received approval to conduct them. One of the first to do so was the Aircraft Owners and Pilots Association (AOPA), a 300,000-member organization founded in 1934.

During my time on active duty with the Navy, I had attended several Flight Instructor Renewal Courses (FIRC) put on by the AOPA Air Safety Foundation. I thoroughly enjoyed them, learned a lot, and thought they were professionally presented. Because I was always scouting for new aviation opportunities, coupled with my enjoyment of classroom teaching, I decided that I would apply to AOPA to see if they had any openings for part-time staff positions teaching FIRCs. On my next to the last day in the Navy, I flew the flying club's T-34 to AOPA headquarters in Frederick, Maryland, to interview with Russ Lawton, the head of the flight instructor department. He told me that he liked my résumé and wanted to hire me but he did not have any openings. Six weeks later, Russ called with a possible job offer. He asked if I would drive down to Indianapolis in two weeks to present several lectures, so I could be evaluated by some of the staff instructors. That was the beginning of a satisfying five-year relationship as an AOPA staff instructor; primarily teaching FIRCs, but also an occasional safety seminar for general aviation pilots.

A weekend FIRC was a fairly intense, somewhat grueling experience for flight instructors who wished to renew their license. It consisted of twenty-four classroom hours presented over a three-day weekend: four hours on Friday night and ten hours each on Saturday and Sunday.

(The number of hours was later reduced by the FAA to sixteen hours, but that did not happen until after I had left the AOPA team). On any given weekend, AOPA might be teaching at three or four different locations around the country. The AOPA team for each location consisted of three instructors, each presenting eight hours of instruction during the course of the weekend. As I recall, sixteen of the twenty-four hours were on topics required by the FAA and the rest were subjects chosen by AOPA as electives. Each of the individual instructors had their favorite topics split between required and elective classes. The classes I taught on a regular basis included: Practical Test Standards, New Trends and Developments, Introduction to Helicopter Operations, Emergency Landings, Medical Aspects of Flight, and Basic Survival Techniques.

The usual FIRC had approximately one hundred attendees, most of whom were not full-time flight instructors and many of those were not actively instructing but were attending solely to keep their certificates from expiring. It was rare to see a young flight instructor less than thirty years old, most were fifty and older. I would usually try to determine the oldest flight instructor in attendance and invariably that person would be in his or her late eighties or early nineties. Some of the attendees were airline pilots and other professional aviators, but most did something else for a living and came from all walks of life: judges, corporate executives,

AOPA Air Safety Foundation staff instructors. *Front row (l to r):* Annabelle Fera, me, Chuck Berry, Tom Emanuel. *Middle row (l to r):* Chas Harral, Andy Serrell, Russ Lawton, Jerry Fairbairn. *Top Row (l to r):* Bob Carter, Catherine Fish, Pete Campbell, John Hammons, Ken Medley (missing Rod Machado). 1986 *(AOPA Photo)*

college professors and teachers, engineers, attorneys, farmers, scientists, government employees, active and retired military, you name it. It was always fascinating and a great honor to meet and talk with such a talented, smart, and accomplished group of individuals.

Before beginning my first class with a new group, I would conduct what I called my "Rich and Famous Survey." I would start out by asking, "Is there anyone in the room who is filthy rich?" That would usually bring a great deal of laughter because it is common knowledge that no one gets rich as a flight instructor. A common retort was, "Filthy yes, rich no." I would follow up with a series of questions in an attempt to identify individuals in the class who were worthy of special recognition. Questions like: "Are there any holders of the Medal of Honor, any astronauts, any aces (three, including Bud Anderson, with seventeen and a half victories in World War II flying his famous P-51 "Old Crow"), any Olympic athletes (one guy who won a gold medal in fencing in the '36 Olympics in Berlin), any POWs, anyone shot down in combat, any admirals or generals, any world or national recordholders in any endeavor, any all-Americans, anybody who made national or world-news headlines, any members of the "Caterpillar Club," any major professional athletes, any aviation authors, and any holders of a patent? Over the years, I received positive responses to every one of those questions. Not only did we, as a group, get to applaud these great accomplishments, but it was a great ice-breaker and an excellent way to start an arduous weekend.

Early in my AOPA career, a flight instructor who was attending a FIRC I was teaching, approached me during a break and asked, "Have you ever seen one of these?" He pulled a piece of worn paper from his wallet. It was a pilot certificate signed by Orville Wright. The Aero Club of the United States, following the lead of the Aero Club of France, began issuing pilot licenses in 1911 and continued until the first U.S. government pilot certificate was granted in 1927. Until the federal government took over, Orville Wright personally signed every license. I was looking at a piece of aviation history. Over the years, several other fellows were eager to show me their certificates signed by the famous aviation pioneer.

As equally accomplished and colorful as the course attendees were my fellow instructors on the FIRC staff. They were not only extremely good aviation presenters, subject-matter experts, and highly experienced aviators, they were also fun to work with and hang out with after the classroom lights were turned off for the day. We became close friends on and off the lecture circuit. As I write this in 2018, a few of my instructor colleagues have "gone west" as they say in aviation circles, to denote those who have passed on. A few are still at it—teaching weekend FIRCs some twenty-eight years after I left AOPA. One of my co-instructors, Rod Machado, went on to become very famous within the aviation community as a writer and author and as a keynote speaker at high profile events.

A typical FIRC assignment for me began with a commuter airline flight on Friday from Purdue Airport in Lafayette to Chicago O'Hare, where I would connect to a major carrier to fly to the city where the seminar was being held. Sometimes, on shorter distances, I would drive or rent a C-182 and fly myself, often taking my wife and kids along for a weekend get-away. Since I did not finish my teaching duties until late Sunday afternoon, I usually returned home to Lafayette on Monday. Because I averaged two FIRCs per month, this schedule meant that I was away from home eight days a month. When I retired from the Navy, I thought I would be spending more time in my own bed—but at least I was racking up a lot of frequent-flyer miles.

One weekend, when I was scheduled to do a FIRC in Dallas, I woke up very early on Friday morning with an overpowering and unshakable feeling that I was going to die sometime this weekend. I didn't know how or on what day, just that I was going to die that weekend. It was the strangest feeling I had ever had—and it was downright scary. So, before I left the house that morning, I sat down at my desk and wrote a letter to my wife and family telling them how much I loved them and how much I would miss them. I sealed the letter in an envelope marked "To Be Opened in the Event of My Death" and stuck it in the top drawer of my desk.

Now, all I had to do was wait for it to happen. As the commuter airline flight I was on approached the Chicago area, we ran into a thunderstorm cell and the worst prolonged turbulence I had ever encountered. My immediate thought was, *This is it. The airplane is going to break apart any second now.* Well, somehow, I survived. Later, as I stood on the curb outside baggage claim at Dallas-Fort Worth Airport, waiting to cross a busy street, the thought occurred that maybe I was about to be hit by a car. And so, it went all weekend: trapped by a fire on the seventh floor, plunging to my death in a freakish elevator accident, shot and killed during a botched hold-up while walking to a restaurant. By the time I arrived home on Monday, I was totally exhausted and a nervous wreck. Fortunately, I have never had a premonition of my death since—thank goodness!

In January 1989, I was promoted to team leader, which meant I had to introduce my two colleagues prior to their first lecture, handle all of the course paperwork, make sure the coffee and doughnuts were ready each morning, coordinate with the hotel to make sure the sound system and slide projectors were working properly, prepare and hand out the course graduation certificates on Sunday evening, and complete a report and send it back to AOPA headquarters. The upside was I earned an additional $150 for the weekend.

Teaching my last Flight Instructor Refresher Course for AOPA. January 14, 1990 in Rochester, New York.

Like a longtime TV news anchor who announces at the end of the broadcast that this was his or her last show, I similarly announced, just before handling out the graduation certificates at the completion of a FIRC in Rochester, New York, on Sunday evening, January 14, 1990, that this would be my last Flight Instructor Refresher Course for AOPA. It had been a great five-year run. I had taught one hundred and twenty-four FIRCs in thirty-three states and one foreign country (West Germany). This position was one of the highlights of my career—I hated to turn the lights out!

Kalamazoo Air Zoo

At first, I didn't take particular notice of the tall, slender guy in the Nomex flight suit walking toward the flight line snack bar on this sunny mid-November day. But as he got closer to me, his hawkish, angular face; pencil-thin mustache; and jet-black hair combed straight back looked vaguely familiar. By golly, he looked a lot like my first Navy flight instructor at Whiting Field in T-28s. Could it be? It had been nineteen years since I last saw John Ellis. At that moment, our eyes locked and a small smile of recognition swept over his face.

"John Ellis, is that you?" I asked.

"Yes," he replied, desperately trying to place a name with the familiar face standing in front of him.

"Mike Stock," I said as I shook his hand. "You were my T-28 flight instructor at Whiting, back in 1965."

"Good to see you again, Mike," he stated. "Yes, I do remember. Gosh, it's been a long time."

"What brings you to Pax River, John?" I asked.

"Well, I brought an SNJ to TPS for a student NPE," he responded. And then, anticipating my next question, he explained: "The SNJ (the navy version of the ubiquitous AT-6 Texan World War II trainer) is owned and operated by the Kalamazoo Air Zoo based in Kalamazoo, Michigan. My younger brother, Bob, is the executive director of the Air Zoo, a world-class museum dedicated to preserving World War II aircraft in flying condition."

Over the next five minutes, we quickly shared our individual experiences since we had last seen each other. I mentioned that I would be retiring from the Navy in another month and re-joining my family in Lafayette, Indiana.

"Mike, after you get settled in Indiana, give me a call. We are sometimes in need of an experienced pilot to join the museum staff. It is strictly a volunteer position, but you get to fly some of our amazing collection of warbirds."

"It sure was great to see you, John. I will definitely give you a call in a few months."

The Kalamazoo Aviation History Museum was founded in 1977 by Sue and Pete Parrish, a wealthy couple living in Kalamazoo, Michigan. Both were pilots during World War II: Sue was a Women Air Force Service Pilot (WASP) and Pete was a Marine pilot. The museum, better known as the Kalamazoo Air Zoo because of its flying collection of Grumman "cats"— Wildcat, Hellcat, Tigercat, and Bearcat—is dedicated to "Preserving the military aviation heritage of this nation for present and future generations. It is also devoted to educating the public about the contribution of air power to the Allied victory in World War II."

The Air Zoo was unique from most air museums because almost all of its aircraft were in pristine condition and regularly flown. Weather permitting, museum pilots flew one of these aircraft in a daily exhibition called "The Flight of the Day." Museum aircraft also participated in airshows around the U.S. and Canada. The Air Zoo quickly became one of the largest nongovernmental aviation museums in the United States.

Ever since I joined the Navy, I have been enthralled by World War II aircraft, especially fighters. I would have given anything to have flown during the war, but I was born eighteen years too late. I have long fancied being able to fly some of the classic war planes, the P-51 being my all-time favorite. This chance encounter with my old flight instructor might just turn a dream into reality.

In March 1985, I wrote a letter to John expressing my interest in becoming a museum pilot and provided a list of my qualifications and background, which, I felt, could make me a useful addition to the staff. I ended my list of qualifications by saying, "Lastly, I am an 'Ellis trained man' and that should count for a whole lot." This letter started the clock on a three-year quest.

Two weeks later, I rented a C-182 and flew to Kalamazoo to meet with John at the headquarters of Kal-Aero, a large FBO and aircraft refurbishment center, of which, he was the president and CEO. He showed me around the museum, but his brother was not available. A month later, I did receive a letter from Bob Ellis, stating that I appeared to be well qualified and that the board of directors of the museum would be meeting in a month to discuss "the guidelines for future museum pilots" and that I should be hearing from John or him soon thereafter.

Over two years later, I was invited to a meeting over lunch with Bob Ellis and Sue Parrish, one of the founders. Apparently, Sue had to sign off on any new pilot and she wanted to do a "preflight inspection" on me. She was a charming and engaging person, who immediately put me at ease. Bob, who I also was meeting for the first time, was equally nice and offered subtle encouragement that I may be offered a pilot slot.

Six more months passed before I was invited to begin training in the North American SNJ, the Navy version of the famous AT-6 Texan. Since most of the museum aircraft were tailwheel airplanes, all new pilots were checked out in the SNJ, a tail-dragger, prior to being assigned to fly other aircraft.

John would once again be my flight instructor, a mixed blessing as far as I was concerned. On one hand, John was a good pilot and friend, but on the other hand, I remembered John was a "screamer" when he was my Navy flight instructor back at Whiting Field. This time around, John was totally different. He was calm, relaxed, and never raised his voice. I figured

North American SNJ, like the one I flew for the Kalamazoo Air Zoo in 1988.

that his demeanor back in Pensacola was part of an act that he thought produced the best Navy pilots. In total, I received five dual flights in the SNJ and was pronounced safe-for-solo on June 16, 1988. I immediately flew a solo flight in the touch-and-go pattern at Kalamazoo that same day. Little did I know that my career as an Air Zoo pilot would be short-lived.

After finishing my fam flights in the SNJ, John said that in the spring I would be checking out in the Douglas A-1 Skyraider, and then gradually, over time, the museum would check me out in other aircraft in the collection. Before I left to drive back to Lafayette, just for grins, I sat in the tight cockpit of the F8F Bearcat, wondering what it would be like flying this sleek machine built around a huge radial engine up front. I almost had to pinch myself. I just couldn't believe my good fortune in being able to fly these incredible airplanes from the "big rebellion," as a Marine fighter pilot friend of mine who flew in World War II was fond of saying.

Six months later, on December 26, 1988, I received a letter from Bob Ellis, with a lump of coal in it. He told me that due to a projected budget shortfall in the coming year, I was being suspended from the museum pilot staff. They couldn't justify spending any funds on my training if future airshow bookings dropped off as anticipated. While I understood the business logic, it was a crushing blow. Bob ended with, "Please be assured, when the demand for Warbirds increases, or if my predictions are totally inaccurate, the Air Zoo staff will look for your help to fulfill its mission." They never called.

Fast-forward seven years. After moving to Northern Michigan, I decided to contact Bob Ellis to see if anything had changed in regard to pilot staffing at the museum. He told me it had gotten worse. They were no longer doing the "Flight of the Day" and air show bookings had indeed diminished. As a result, they were no longer maintaining all their collection in flying condition.

He did ask if I was interested in flying as copilot on the Ford Tri-motor. As a money-maker for the museum, they offered visitors a chance for a short flight around the Kalamazoo area in the vintage airplane. It sounded intriguing. True, it wasn't a powerful and sleek fighter, but getting to fly the famous "Tin Goose," with its corrugated wings and fuselage, had an appeal all of its own. Bob told me that after passing my second-in-command checkride, they would schedule me to fly several days a month.

On June 21, 1995, I drove south to Kalamazoo. After 1.2 hours and four landings in the old girl, I was pronounced second-in-command qualified. I assumed that with so little training, my sole job would be to take

Ford Tri-motor like the one in which I qualified as second-in-command with the Kalamazoo Air Zoo in 1995.

over the controls if the captain suddenly slumped over the wood steering wheel—yes, it had a steering wheel instead of a yoke. And, instead of being fun to fly, it was a lot of work. The flight controls were exceptionally heavy and ponderous, and only moved with great effort. The only trim control was for pitch. When the check pilot simulated a right engine failure, I literally had to use both feet on the left rudder to keep the airplane from turning right since there was no rudder trim. No wonder my check flight wasn't any longer—I was pooped.

On the drive back to Traverse City, I decided it wasn't worth it. The airplane wasn't fun to fly and I had to drive three and a half hours each way, at my expense. That was the end of my casual acquaintance with the Kalamazoo Air Zoo. But then, how many pilots can say they have flown a Ford Tri-motor?

Helicopter Fantasy

When I was initially hired by Purdue as a temporary instructor in its Aviation and Technology Department (AvTech), my salary was paid from the Purdue president's discretionary fund. The reason for this unusual funding source was Dr. Stephen Beering's personal interest in starting a helicopter-training program at AvTech. I was being hired to get the job done. Coming from the military, with a what-the-admiral-wants-the-admiral-gets mentality, I naturally assumed I would be given the necessary resources and backing from the department because the president was behind the initiative. Being new to the world of academia, I had much to learn.

For spring semester 1985, officially a quarter of my workload was allotted to working on a helicopter program. Unofficially, I spent a lot more than that, because I really wanted to establish Purdue as the industry leader in providing helicopter training. Bill Duncan, the AvTech Department head, had a connection inside Bell Helicopter that spoke of a real possibility that Bell might be interested in loaning a Jet Ranger to help us get started.

In the meantime, I flew up to the University of North Dakota to tour their helicopter-training operation, the largest college-based program in the country, to see how they managed to profitably operate five helicopters. (It turned out that they were almost totally funded by an Army contract to provide initial helicopter training to Army ROTC cadets.) I began searching for the ideal training helicopter and took a demo ride in the Robinson R-22. I was also involved in finding classroom and office space for the new venture.

But, after a semester's worth of work, I didn't have much to show for my efforts. Bell Helicopter was all talk and there was no line item in the AvTech budget set aside for starting a helicopter program, much less to purchase a rotorcraft. So, reluctantly, I put it aside and concentrated on flight instructing and classroom duties in the coming semesters. Every now and then, when I would bump into President Beering waiting to board one of our airplanes for a business trip, he would ask, "Mike, how's the helicopter program coming?" I would dare say that at a university with 36,000 students and a 2,500-member faculty that not many junior assistant professors would be on a first-name basis with the president—for all the wrong reasons. He wasn't mean or demanding when asking that question, but it was always uncomfortable for me to have to give the "reserve salute" and say, "We're still working on it" or some other lame platitude. Maybe I should have jumped the chain of command and gone directly to him and asked for funding, but I didn't—I wasn't totally naïve!

The idea lay dormant until the fall of 1988, when I convinced Bill Duncan, the AvTech department head, to eliminate my flight-instructor duties in favor of working half-time on the helicopter program. I wanted to give it one more college try.

Out of the blue, the stars aligned when a former graduate of our flight-training program, who worked as a self-employed aviation consultant, approached Bill Duncan about a high-placed Japanese contact she had at Nihon University in Japan. She claimed that Nihon might be interested in partnering with Purdue to provide helicopter training for its students and they wanted to come to the West Lafayette campus to look at our facilities and flight-training operation. Our former graduate hinted that Nihon was willing to spend a considerable amount of money at Purdue to build infrastructure and buy helicopters as needed.

A four-member contingent from Nihon University arrived in mid-November, and we pulled out all the stops. We picked them up in the King Air at Indianapolis Airport, gave them the grand tour of main campus, and AvTech trotted out our best dog and pony shows. I presented scale drawings for a new hangar, ramp, and a classroom/office building, and we wined and dined them in lavish style, with Purdue University vice presidents and deans in attendance.

When staring at the potential for substantial investment from our Japanese visitors, we all sat around with our tails wagging and drool coming from the corners of our mouths. Whenever costs for new structures and helicopters were brought up, our friends from across the sea would bow and smile politely, but never once did they say they would be willing to invest hard-earned yen at Purdue. But, our graduate turned consultant kept assuring us that they were serious about making a major commitment—and we believed her.

I never did figure out what the Japanese were after. Maybe they never had any intention of partnering with Purdue or investing any money, and only wanted to gain some insight into how one of the best college aviation programs in the country operated. At the very least, there was a huge disconnect between what the consultant was telling us and what the Japanese were actually thinking.

But I didn't want to admit defeat just yet, so I started to pursue possibilities that did not require any upfront capital commitment from Purdue.

The Naval Avionics Center, located in Indianapolis, was a naval shore installation whose mission was to conduct research, engineering, and limited manufacture of airborne electronics pertaining to aircraft missiles, guidance systems, and related avionics equipment for naval aircraft. During World War II, it was the top-secret facility that developed and built the Norden bombsight. Captain Russ Henry, USN, was the commanding officer of the facility and happened to be one of my old flight instructors at Test Pilot School. In talking with Russ, I discovered that his facility had a Bell UH-1D helicopter that they used as a test platform for some of their research and development work. I also found out they didn't use the helicopter much and they had no pilots assigned specifically to fly it.

I had a sudden inspiration, which I pitched to Captain Henry: base the helicopter at Purdue, where we would maintain it and whenever they needed to use it, I would fly the mission. In return, we would be able to use the aircraft in our burgeoning helicopter flight program. He didn't have to think long about my proposal. I was a former Navy test pilot and well qualified in the Huey, and Purdue would maintain the aircraft, saving him money. It was a win-win for both sides. He said yes and we had our first helicopter.

Next, I got wind of a military surplus, multi-million-dollar, full-motion UH-1D helicopter simulator available at Fort Campbell, Kentucky. After explaining my purpose and need, the Army agreed to a no-cost transfer of the simulator to Purdue. In a matter of two weeks, I went from no equipment to having a flyable Huey helicopter and simulator to match. Boy, was I ever pumped up! Then, my world came crashing down.

"Bill, can I speak with you for a minute?" I asked as I stuck my head into the large, cheery office of the AvTech department head.

Bill looked up from the paperwork lying on his desk. "Sure, Mike. Come in," he said pleasantly.

"Well, I just got off the phone with Fort Campbell," I said excitedly. "You remember the simulator I told you about the other day? Well, they have agreed to transfer it to Purdue."

"That's great news," he said, pausing for a moment. "I think it's time that we call a faculty meeting to see if this is the direction that we want to go as a department."

I was speechless. "Do you mean to tell me that after all of this effort over a four-year period, and now that we are on the brink of making it happen, you want to call a faculty meeting?" I asked plaintively. "I thought we had made that decision when President Beering essentially hired me to start a helicopter program." My disbelief was turning into anger, so I stopped talking. He asked if I would chair the meeting, and I said that I would.

About a week later, I received a typewritten memo from Bill concerning my contract renewal for the upcoming academic year. The first two paragraphs stated:

> On the recommendation of the faculty peer review committee, your employment contract is being renewed for one year (the norm was two years). The one-year renewal period should not be interpreted as a negative endorsement. The committee felt that it would be in your best interest that a review of your progress towards promotion and tenure be made again in another year.
>
> You are recognized as being a very good classroom teacher. Concern was expressed, however, that because of your unique staff assignments, past and present, that you don't "fit the mold" of the traditional assistant professor methodically working towards promotion and tenure.

I could not believe what I had just read. So, I read it again. After busting my tail for four years on a program I was hired to do, the committee and Bill had the audacity to say that I was not earning sufficient points toward promotion and tenure. I was beyond flabbergasted. I was pissed! As I drove home that evening, replaying the contents of the memo in my head, I got madder and madder. By the time I got home, I had reached the decision to resign. I typed my letter of resignation as soon as I stepped inside the house and couldn't wait to deliver it to Bill the next morning. May 10, 1989, was my last day at Purdue University.

Job Hunt

Because I had my Navy pension and AOPA income to fall back on, I was able to make the sudden and unplanned decision to resign from Purdue without immediately affecting my family. But, I still had to find full-time employment, not only because of financial obligations but because I enjoyed working.

I began using my bully pulpit at AOPA to solicit a new job. At the very next FIRC I taught, I met Jim Stamps, a captain for Northwest Airlines, who was helping to train and staff a new startup airline in his free time. Systems International Airline (SIA) was a very small airline based in Barstow, Florida, which initially planned to offer flights between various Florida cities and the Bahamas. SIA planned to use Martin 404s, a twin, radial-engine, pressurized airplane that held forty passengers. Eastern and TWA used the airplane in passenger service from 1951 until 1962. Although displaced from the flight lines of major air carriers by jet aircraft, the airplane saw continued use up through the 1980s by smaller airlines.

Jim invited me to join SIA's first pilot class, which began in early June 1989, as chief pilot and captain trainee. As I recall, there were three captains, three first officers, and six flight attendants. Because of the small number of trainees and the austere operating budget, combined classes were taught where feasible (pilots and flight attendants together) and separate classes where necessary.

Upon completion of two weeks of ground training, the company ran out of money to pay us when a potential financial backer withdrew his support. Captain Stamps flew one training flight on a weekend I was off teaching for AOPA, so the closest I got to flying the Martin 404 was a ground taxi from the left seat. We were recalled back to Barstow the end of September to try again; and after four days, the till was once again empty. And that was the end of SIA as far as I know—at least it was the end for me. Fortunately, the company did not survive long enough to offer me a job because, as it turned out, I had much better prospects in the offing.

During the first two weeks in October 1989, I had two interviews with substantial companies: TWA and the Saudi Arabian Oil Company (Aramco). Even though I bought the first tailor-made suit I ever had for the interview, TWA rejected me for some medical reason they would not divulge. All they would say was the condition was not life threatening. Easy for them to say—hadn't they heard that starving from lack of a job was usually fatal? Maybe I didn't look *that good* in my tailor-made suit.

The Aramco interview came about indirectly from a contact made at a FIRC I taught in Indianapolis. One of the attendees approached me during a break and introduced himself.

"Hi, my name is Dave McNeil. I heard you mention that you were looking for a flying job."

"Yes, I am," I replied.

"Well, I work in Saudi Arabia for a company called Aramco, a very large, state-owned oil company. I am not a pilot for them, but I know they are hiring pilots. I would be most happy to hand-carry a résumé to the chief pilot when I go back in a couple of weeks."

"Gee, that's very kind of you," I said. "Can you tell me about their flight department? What kind of aircraft do they fly? Where do they fly, and so on?"

Dave replied, "I don't have a lot of time right now, but I'm traveling up to Lafayette tomorrow to see my ex-wife and three children for a couple days. I would be more than happy to meet you somewhere for lunch and tell you all about the flight department and, perhaps, more importantly, what it's like to live in Saudi Arabia."

"That would be fantastic. Thank you so much."

Two days later, we met at a Burger King and Dave graciously spent over three hours giving me the lowdown on Aramco and living and working in the Middle East. It sounded too good to be true, starting with the money I could make. Dave ended with a critical piece of advice, "Since you are qualified to fly fixed-wing and rotary-wing aircraft, my advice would be to apply for a fixed-wing position. You will start two pay grades higher and you will be flying, for the most part, in air-conditioned cockpits. You will greatly appreciate that last fact because the temperature routinely reaches 125 degrees in the summer."

After talking it over with Barbara, I mailed a résumé to Dave at his Saudi address. I thought it was a longshot because it sounded like a dream job that would attract many well qualified applicants. As it turned out, I had some pull in the upper echelons of the Aranco flight department I didn't know about. The chief pilot, an American by the name of Cal Mills, remembered me from a FIRC I had taught in Richmond, Virginia, a year before. The flight department manager was Marland Townsend, a retired

Navy captain and a fellow graduate of Navy Test Pilot School. This stroke of good luck got my foot in the door and a personal interview on October 6, 1989, with Mr. Townsend in Houston, Texas, the headquarters for the Aramco operation in the United States.

Aramco only hired American male expatriates who were willing to move their families to Saudi Arabia. Their reasoning was sound: men would be happier and stay longer with the company if their families were with them. Therefore, the company interviewed not only the man, but also his wife—at the same time, in the same room, so everything was out in the open and upfront.

The day-long process for Barbara and I began with a one-hour interview with Marland Townsend. He seemed to be more focused on Barbara than me. I suspect he was already more or less satisfied with my qualifications, but wanted to make sure that she was on board with this drastic move to an all-Muslim country. And, he was right to be a little wary. Barbara was in a state of shock and denial even before I had a job offer to consider.

He brought up some of the stark differences between life in the States and life on the Aramco compound near the Persian Gulf: women can't drive off camp; all TV and press was censored and controlled by the government; women must be conservatively dressed at all times, which meant no halter tops or Bermuda shorts; and there were no movie theatres and no alcohol. But he saved the biggie for last. "Barbara, you do know that the Aramco school system on camp only goes through the ninth grade," he intoned, leaving the proclamation hanging in midair somewhere between a statement and a question. "After the ninth grade, all children must go off to boarding schools with tuition paid by the company."

Barbara looked like she had been pole-axed, even though Dave McNeil had told me about this company policy over our lunch at Burger King.

"Yes, I know," she said, as large tears began to well up in her eyes. "Maybe I should stay behind with the girls and come over later."

In Marland's mind, that option was a non-starter, although he didn't put it that way. "I wouldn't advise that," he said. "Most mothers initially balk at the idea of sending their kids off to boarding school at such a young age. But Aramco does such a great job of preparing students and parents for this eventuality that, when the time comes, it is much easier to say goodbye than you think. And, the company pays all expenses for your child to fly back to Saudi three times during the school year. In fact, most students and their parents agree that boarding school is the biggest highlight of the whole Aramco experience."

Barbara gave a weak smile and mumbled something unintelligible. She was physically sitting next to me, but her mind and spirit were in a state of abject despair.

Twenty minutes later, Barbara and I were standing in the lunch line at the company cafeteria, two people behind Marland Townsend, who was engaged in a lively conversation with a friend. All of a sudden, I thought Barbara was going to collapse on the floor. She turned ghostly white, started to hyperventilate, and looked like she wanted to run for the nearest exit. I don't think she even recognized me. She was definitely on the verge of a nervous breakdown—it was downright frightening. All I could think, rather selfishly, was that if Barbara made a big scene right there, in the dining room, in front of the Aviation Department manager, I could kiss any chance of employment goodbye.

I grabbed her by the shoulders and said sternly, "Babe, get a grip on yourself. Marland is standing right there." Fortunately, she did, and I eventually got the job after a long, torturous application process.

Chapter 21

Mr. Sullivan

A LL IN ALL, IT WAS QUITE A DAY: MY ONE AND ONLY FAA VIOLATION and passenger hanky-panky all on the same flight. When the dispatcher handed me a trip ticket to pick up two passengers at Block Island, I figured it would be another milk run like I had made dozens of times.

It was a clear, sunny day as I lifted off Griswold Airport near Madison, Connecticut, in a four-seat Piper Warrior PA-28 and headed almost due east up Long Island Sound. Thirty minutes later, as I approached Block Island Airport, I noticed a fog bank rolling in from the south that precluded making a normal left downwind entry to the traffic pattern of the non-towered airport. So, in the interest of safety and being able to pick up my two passengers on schedule, I entered a right downwind, forgetting that the Federal Aviation Regulations require fixed-wing aircraft to only make left turns when entering and while in the traffic pattern.

I called entering right downwind and turning right base and landed without further incident just as the fog rolled over the field. At no time did I see or hear another aircraft in the traffic pattern or on the ground. I clearly had my mission-completion hat on.

After waiting an hour or so for the fog to lift, I loaded my two passengers, a male and female couple in their mid-twenties, in the backseat and took off for the short flight back to Griswold Airport. Shortly after reaching my cruise altitude of 4,500 feet, I felt the airplane bucking up and down and soon realized the unnatural motion was coming from the back. My first thought was, *This couple is trying to join the Mile High Club.* I was afraid to look around until I felt a tap on my right shoulder. "Captain, have you ever seen one of these?" he asked.

I hesitantly looked into the rear seat to discover that he had pulled down the right side of her tank top to reveal her breast. I softly said that I had, and immediately turned around and started fiddling with the radios.

I didn't have the heart to inform my couple in heat that we weren't quite a mile high.

A month later, after returning home to Lafayette, Indiana, I received a certified letter from the FAA—always a bad sign—that I was being investigated for a violation of the regulations. Even then, I failed to realize I had committed a violation. Luckily, the FAA chose to give me a Letter of Warning, vice formal enforcement action.

Kid in a Candy Store

One of the great benefits of being a college professor was having the summers off to pursue my passion. Along about January each year, I would begin searching for a summer flying job. The extra money earned was always secondary to my constant quest to fly new models of aircraft and to experience and develop different types of piloting skills. Up until the time I retired from professional flying, I never tired of the "chase" for a new and interesting flying challenge.

True to form, during the winter of 1985, I was scouting for the next grand adventure when I came across an ad in the employment section of *Trade-a-Plane* for a charter pilot in the New England area. I applied in early March and received a letter from the chief pilot of Shoreline Aviation, Inc. offering me a summer flying position. The letter, signed by Thomas L. Hine, also a retired commander and Navy pilot, went on to state: "Your major area of responsibility will be our multi-engine charter operations. Other duties may include single-engine land and sea charters and instruction, helicopter instruction (if required), and glider or tow flying." The potential diversity of flying duties was intoxicating. I couldn't wait for my first semester at Purdue to end and my New England sabbatical to begin.

Shoreline Aviation was founded in 1980 at Griswold Airport, Madison, Connecticut, by John Kelly, an ebullient Irishman and aggressive aviation promoter. If there was a way to make a buck flying, John would try it, which accounted for the impressive array of different models of aircraft in the Shoreline fleet: single-engine and multiengine land airplanes, a single-engine float plane, a helicopter, a biplane, and a glider. And even better, I was qualified to fly them all!

Within three weeks of my arrival, I had checked out in ten different models of aircraft: C-152, C-172, C-182RG, C-210, C-303, PA-18, PA-32, UPF-7 (Waco biplane), Enstrom F-28 (helicopter), and a Schweizer 2-33 (two-place glider). The only aircraft type in the Shoreline inventory I did not fly was the floatplane because there wasn't enough business to warrant another pilot. I was in hog heaven. There were times when I flew two or more different models in the same day. On one particular day, I

Four of the ten different models of aircraft I flew for Shoreline Aviation during the summer of 1985. *From the upper left clockwise:* Cessna 303, Waco UPF-7, Enstrom F-28, and Schweizer 2-33.

flew the Waco, the Cessna 303 multiengine Crusader, the Cessna 210, and gave three glider rides for a total of 8.5 hours of flight time. Admittedly it was challenging keeping up with ten different flying machines with different flying characteristics and emergency procedures, but it was the thrill of a lifetime. At no time before or since, did I ever get a chance to fly such a wide variety of aircraft on a daily basis. Even when I was a young naval aviator in the ferry squadron in San Diego, and similarly qualified to fly ten different models of aircraft, I never flew more than one model in any given day.

The French Riviera, in particular Monaco, might have been the inspiration for the pop-culture phrase: "The playground for the rich and famous," but some of the high-brow tourist destinations in New England were certainly on par. Cape Cod, Nantucket, Block Island, Montauk, Newport, Martha's Vineyard, and East Hampton were daily destinations for Shoreline Aviation and its diverse fleet of aircraft, carrying well-heeled charter customers.

In addition to the charters, I flew a wide variety of flights that came my way because I was qualified in so many types of aircraft. Some notable flight assignments included flying a CBS News crew to film the return of the world's first nuclear-powered submarine, the *USS Nautilis* to Groton, Connecticut, where it would become a floating museum after an extensive overhaul; flying a traffic reporter for a local TV station; flying local sightseeing flights in an open-cockpit biplane, complete with leather flying helmet and goggles; towing the Schweizer 2-33 glider with the PA-18, or the Waco and numerous glider flights themselves; dropping skydivers wearing cutoffs and flip-flops from a Cherokee Six (PA-32) on downtown

Hartford; and taking a local police chief for a demo ride with the purpose to using Shoreline's helicopter for patrol duty. It was a fun summer and one of the best flying experiences of my career.

Partners in Crime

The night before, as I was leaving work, the dispatcher told me that my first assignment for the following day would be to fly two businessmen to the Wall Street heliport. I arrived around six a.m. so that I could pull the helicopter out of the hangar, complete the preflight inspection, check the weather, and file a flight plan in plenty of time for the seven o'clock departure. The helicopter apparently did not like being aroused so early because I soon discovered a grounding discrepancy. Flying directly to Wall Street was not going to possible.

We were used to flying wealthy clients from their Connecticut homes to New York City, so when these two "businessmen" in their mid-twenties showed up dressed in jeans, T-shirts, and running shoes instead of the usual three-piece suit and black wingtip shoes, it seemed strange. I put my suspicions aside and told them about the helicopter's problems. "The best I can do," I explained, "is to fly you in one of our fixed-wing airplanes to Teterboro Airport, just across the Hudson River from downtown Manhattan. From there, it is only a fifteen-minute cab ride to Wall Street."

They were not happy with the change in plans and one of them expressed his dissatisfaction by snarling, "Well, make it quick."

Fifteen minutes later I had a Cessna 182RG on the ramp, ready to board—but my two "Wall Streeters" were nowhere in sight. I searched for five minutes before seeing just the tops of their heads in the parking lot between two parked cars. As I rounded the rear bumper of one of the cars, I noticed that the two of them were squatting down, with the contents of an aluminum metal briefcase spread out on the ground. I sensed something was not right about this picture and stopped, not wanting to see what was going on.

On the thirty-minute flight to Teterboro, my suspicions were confirmed that these two characters were, in fact, drug dealers. They were sitting in the backseat, talking loudly about various drug deals. In place of a specific drug deal, they couched it in the terms of a real-estate transaction. But it would have been obvious to a third-grader what they were really talking about. And I am certain the metal briefcase contained illicit drugs. I dropped them off and one of them gave me a crisp one-hundred-dollar bill.

The tip took some of the edge off my outrage by the time I arrived back at Griswold. It is contrary to FAA regulations for a pilot to carry known drug dealers, but the operative word is known and I didn't know for sure.

Still, I was pretty steamed about the whole affair when I walked into John Kelly's office.

"Good morning, John. Say, I think those two guys that I flew down to Teterboro this morning are drug dealers."

"Oh, I knew that," he responded matter-of-factly.

I was dumbfounded. Welcome to the world of "What's the color of your money?" Come to think of it, the hundred-dollar tip was green as could be.

My next trip to the dark side came with a warning before takeoff. This particular afternoon, the regular dispatcher had the afternoon off and John Kelly was filling that slot. He told me to take the Cherokee Six up to Hartford to pick up a man, his wife, and two young daughters and fly them to Nantucket. *Simple enough*, I thought. But as I walked out of the office, John said, "Oh, by the way. This guy is the mafia boss of Hartford." I guessed John realized I didn't like surprises, so he was going to give me a heads-up this time. In hindsight, I discovered that knowing ahead of time was worse than finding out after the fact.

The short flight to Hartford was uneventful and, after parking the airplane, I proceeded into the FBO waiting room to collect my four passengers. I didn't need to call out names, because there he was—just like he had stepped off the set of *The Godfather*. Central casting could not have done a better job. But the man was cordial and introduced me to his young family.

After strapping them into the four rear seats, giving them the required safety briefing, and loading the luggage, I hopped into the front left seat and began going through the engine-starting checklist. Now, any pilot who has ever flown a fixed-wing airplane with a fuel-injected engine will tell you that these engines have a mind of their own when they are hot. Each engine seems to have its own personality and requires a specific starting sequence, a lot of stroking, and prayerful intervention when hot. Cold no problem, hot is enough to make a pilot cry. It was ninety degrees on the ramp, in a searing summer sun, and I had landed just fifteen minutes before. So, the engine was plenty warm.

I went through all of the steps that had worked in the past, to no avail. The engine simply refused to start after several attempts. This was not good for a couple of reasons. One, I was a professional pilot and not being able to start the engine does not engender a lot of confidence in your passengers concerning your ability to safely fly the aircraft. Secondly, I was carrying the head of the Hartford La Cosa Nostra, who probably had a low tolerance for incompetence. I actually thought, *If I don't get this thing started pretty quick, he is going to pull out his pistol, press it against the back of my head, and tell me to get this airplane started now or else.* I finally did get it started, and we had a smooth flight to Nantucket. And, if I remember correctly, the color of his $100 tip was also green.

Don't Say That Again

Every Friday morning at nine o'clock, Shoreline's Cessna 303 Crusader was parked on the ramp at Teterboro, New Jersey, ready to fly Mr. Sullivan (not his real name) and his wife to their weekend getaway-home at Montauk, Long Island. I was never told much about Mr. Sullivan: what he did for a living or how he made his money, but he obviously had a lot of it. I did notice that his black stretch-limo was the only private vehicle allowed to drive onto the ramp and right up to the airplane. I didn't even know if he had a first name—everybody called him Mr. Sullivan, even though he looked to be in his mid-thirties. Given my previous experience with a couple of John Kelly's customers ... nah, don't even go there.

On this particular Friday, I arrived early so that I would be ready when Mr. Sullivan's limo pulled up. A customary plate of specially-ordered finger sandwiches was on the table between the fore and aft facing seats in the cabin, and their favorite beverages were in the cooler within easy reach.

The flight to Montauk was smooth and uneventful until I entered the traffic pattern at the non-towered airport located on the very northeastern tip of Long Island. Mid-field downwind, I lowered the landing gear handle and noticed that the left main landing gear indicated unsafe, meaning that instead of a normal green light, which indicated that the gear was down and locked, it was an amber light, which meant there was something wrong with the left landing gear itself or there was an electrical malfunction with the indicator light.

I called the FBO operator on the radio, explained my problem, and asked him to look at my left main landing gear as I made a low pass down the runway. He radioed back that the gear looked like it was in the normal down position. I knew that a safe report from an observer in a tower or on the ground did not automatically mean that everything was, in fact, okay. And I didn't want to take a chance on the landing gear collapsing on the very narrow and short runway at Montauk Airport.

Looking over my right shoulder, I hollered back to Mr. Sullivan to explain the problem and that I was going to fly to Suffolk County Airport instead, where they had crash and rescue equipment. He shook his head, wagged his finger, and said, "No, we are going to land at Montauk." He was obviously used to getting his way and, by golly, we were going to land at Montauk.

I explained the risk if the gear was to collapse on landing and reiterated that Suffolk County had crash and rescue equipment in case the worst should happen. He fixed me with a withering glare and pointed at my chest and said firmly, "Don't you dare use that word again."

"What word?" I asked, dumfounded.

"Do not use the word *crash* again," he commanded for the second time.

"Okay, we are going to land at Suffolk County where they have fire trucks."

When he realized he was not going to win the battle over the landing destination, he sat back and pouted. I called Suffolk tower and declared an emergency. By the time we arrived ten minutes later, they had all of their "fire trucks" standing by, with all of their lights flashing.

The landing was uneventful and I taxied to the ramp. Mr. Sullivan and his wife stormed off the plane and into the FBO. In the meantime, I inspected the left landing gear closely, but found nothing that looked suspicious or out of the ordinary. I assumed that the unsafe cockpit indication was an electrical problem and that I could safely continue the flight.

I gathered the Sullivans and flew back to Montauk, but I left the landing gear down as a precaution. After dropping off my passengers, I flew back to Griswold Airport. After takeoff, I decided to raise the landing gear, but on landing, the left main gear still indicated unsafe. I've seen this movie before, no biggie, and I landed and taxied the airplane up to the maintenance hangar and told the mechanics what had happened.

Thirty minutes later, the Director of Maintenance came and found me.

"Mike, I want to show you something," he said as he led me back to his shop. He proceeded to point out a small crack in the over-center drag brace for the left main landing gear. "You were lucky this gear didn't fold on landing. Because of the crack, the drag brace wasn't extending far enough to engage the electrical micro-switch, and that's why you had the unsafe indication."

"Wow, I was lucky. In fact, I was lucky three times," I replied, a little shaky.

In retrospect, Mr. Sullivan was right. Because I stopped using that word, we didn't crash.

Chapter 22

Sixty Seconds of Terror

WITHIN THE MILLIONS OF ACRES DESIGNATED AS U.S. NATIONAL Forests are thousands and thousands of huge, old-growth trees begging to be harvested. The downside of conventional logging operations was the serious environmental impact left in its wake: construction of logging roads and equipment staging areas; damage to surrounding timber as big trees were felled; serious erosion problems, which can lead to flash flooding and mudslides; and destruction of wildlife habitat to name just a few villains. Perhaps the most egregious example of environmental damage is the common practice of *clear-cutting* which leaves the forest looking like a military bombing range.

Aside from helicopter logging, which has limited lift capacity and is very expensive, the logging industry does not have a good sustainable method to harvest large individual trees without concurrent environmental damage. If only there was an aircraft that could hover with sufficient vertical-lift capacity to be able to cut a big tree at its base, lift it straight up, and transport it a short distance to a central staging area for further processing. Enter Frank Piasecki, the world's foremost helicopter and vertical-flight designer.

Most people in aviation circles have heard the name Sikorsky. Igor Sikorsky designed, built, and flew the first true helicopter, the VS-300, in 1939; and the company that bears his name has been building military and civilian helicopters since then. Contrasted with his more famous colleague, Frank Piasecki was hardly a household name—in fact, few outside of the helicopter world had heard of him. Yet, he has contributed much more to the advancement of rotary-wing flight than Igor Sikorsky.

A list of Frank Piasecki's accomplishments is both long and impressive, and includes many aviation firsts. Perhaps his greatest contribution was the invention of the tandem-rotor helicopter in 1945, which led to a series of twin-rotor aircraft, including the CH-46, used by the Navy and Marine

Corps for many years; and the world-famous CH-47 Chinook helicopter, used by the U.S. Army and sixteen other nations for over fifty years. Other noteworthy achievements include: the world record for altitude in a helicopter at 22,110 feet, in 1952; the world's largest helicopter, in 1953; the first twin-turbine helicopter, in 1955; the first nonstop transcontinental helicopter flight, in 1956; and a compound helicopter that exceeded 225 mph, in 1965. During his lifetime, he was awarded twenty-one patents and numerous professional honors, including the prestigious National Medal of Technology, presented by President Ronald Reagan.

Frank Piasecki, a noted helicopter and vertical lift pioneer, standing in front of a scale model of one of his many designs. circa 1986 *(Photo courtesy of Piasecki Aircraft Corporation)*

Since Frank Piasecki was the first to demonstrate the lifting of logs with a helicopter in 1945, it was not surprising that, years later, he would apply his considerable genius to the design of a vertical-lift aircraft that would meet the needs of the U.S. Forest Service. The result was the creation of an entirely new type of aircraft called *quad-rotor hybrid heavy lift*, which combined the static lift of an aerostat with the dynamic lift and control provided by attached helicopters.

The Aircraft

In 1980, the U.S. Navy awarded Piasecki Aircraft Corporation a contract to design, build, and fly a prototype heavy-lift air vehicle with U.S. Forest Service funding. The Naval Air Development Center at Warminster, Pennsylvania, served as the technical and contracting agent for the Forest Service, which had no experience or charter in designing and building aircraft. Although this project was being undertaken for civilian purposes, it clearly had important military applications in the areas of cargo handling and logistical support, especially ship-to-shore operations, if it was successful.

The initial budget for this technologically sophisticated undertaking was less than seven million dollars—a bargain by any measure—at a time when multi-billion-dollar new-aircraft programs were the norm. With limited funding, Frank Piasecki and his team had to be resourceful, so they scoured military surplus sites for ready-to-use parts, components, and assemblies to use in the construction of a prototype aircraft. From the military's desert storage facility at Davis-Monthan Air Force Base in Tucson, Arizona, better known as the *aircraft boneyard*, they obtained four Navy H-34 helicopters, landing gear and tail rotors from Navy H-3 helicopters, and landing gear assemblies from the B-52 bomber, among other miscellaneous parts.

Acting on a tip from an old, retired chief petty officer, who was present when the last Navy blimp squadron was decommissioned in 1961 at NAS Lakehurst, New Jersey, the Piasecki team found a complete airship envelope from a Navy ZPG-2W blimp that had been folded and hidden away in one of the huge former blimp hangars at the air station. The story goes that the Navy decreed that all of the airship envelopes were to be destroyed after the decision was made to get out of the blimp business. But he and several of his fellow chiefs, who had labored most of their careers in lighter-than-air vehicles, could not bring themselves to destroy the last vestiges of the blimp Navy. So, they carefully folded three envelopes and stacked them one on top of each other in a secret hiding place.

Piasecki's foraging for off-the-shelf low-cost materials also carried over into the civilian world, where they obtained aluminum pipes of various lengths and diameters used in farm irrigation systems. A flatbed trailer, more accustomed to hauling oversized construction equipment, was pressed into service to mount a seventy-five-foot pole to serve as a mobile mast to which the inflated prototype air vehicle would be tethered.

With a hangar full of assorted aircraft, assemblies, and parts that resembled a military surplus auction, the engineering and fabrication team at Piasecki Aircraft Corporation set about building a one-of-a-kind experimental prototype—the PA-97 Heli-Stat.

Of the three old blimp aerostats discovered at Lakehurst, the one stacked in the middle appeared to be in the best condition. After the application of several small patches, it held pressure and was deemed airworthy.

The catenary cables inside the air envelope, which served as the attachment points for the gondola when it was a blimp, were used to support and attach a large structure of welded aluminum irrigation piping called the ICS (Inter-Connecting Structure). The four H-34 helicopters were then attached to the ICS, two on each side of the aerostat. To allow for ground handling and taxi, four full-swiveling, fixed-landing gear wheels were attached to the bottom of the ICS. To provide better yaw control of this large aircraft, each H-34 helicopter was highly modified by replacing the original tail boom and tail rotor with a pusher rotor constructed using the tail rotor assembly from the H-3 helicopter.

The four helicopters attached to the ICS were employed using a master-slave arrangement. Flight control of the entire aircraft, in terms of pitch, roll, yaw, and collective was accomplished by the command pilot seated in the aft left helicopter or *master helicopter*. The remaining three helicopters were slaved to the master helicopter in terms of basic flight control. The command pilot or *master pilot*, however, could not start the engine,

Top photo: The Heli-Stat, constructed primarily of surplus military components, was the largest aircraft in the world at that time. It was 343 feet long, 187 feet wide, and 112 feet high. April 1986 *(Photo courtesy of Piasecki Aircraft Corporation)*

Bottom photo: Close-up of the tail modification made to each H-34 helicopter on the Heli-Stat, which converted the tail rotor from a Navy H-3 helicopter into a pusher propeller for yaw control. 1986

engage or disengage the rotor, or maintain main rotor RPM in the slave helicopters, which then necessitated that a qualified helicopter pilot fly in each one.

When fully assembled, the Heli-Stat was enormous—the largest aircraft ever built aside from the huge, rigid airships made by the U.S. and Germany during the 1920s and 1930s. The length was 343 feet and the height was 112 feet—both modern-day records. Only its width of 187 feet was surpassed by the wingspans of some large fixed-wing airplanes, such as the Spruce Goose and the Lockheed C-5. The dimensions by themselves do not immediately convey the immense size of this behemoth. Imagine a large college or NFL football stadium—the Heli-Stat would barely fit on the level surface between the spectator stands. The aerostat held one million cubic feet of helium gas, five times the amount of the Goodyear blimp. The first time I met this monster face-to-face was at night when I walked into the dimly lit, former blimp hangar where it was housed at NAS Lakehurst. When I looked up and saw this gargantuan shape, it took my breath away—like an evil Star Wars creation just waiting to devour the entire planet. I had trouble believing my eyes.

The Flight Crew

The members of the flight crew on the day of the accident were as colorful and motley as the odd assortment of components that made up the aircraft. The Heli-Stat required a crew of five: a master pilot, a pilot in each slave helicopter, and a pilot with blimp experience to control the pressure, shape, and trim of the aerostat, who flew as copilot in the master helicopter. All five crewmen were former military pilots: two Navy, two Marine Corps, and one Army. Three of the five were at or past retirement age and the other two were middle-aged. After leaving the aircraft boneyard in Tucson, it seemed as if Piasecki had stumbled across a tar pit that contained some ancient aviators who wanted another opportunity to *slip the surly bonds* in their old greasy flight suits.

The master pilot was Barney Stutesman, a fifty-seven-year-old former U.S. Army pilot who had over twenty thousand hours of helicopter time. After his military service, Barney started a successful helicopter flight service in Detroit, where he had the distinction of launching the first helicopter air ambulance service in the country. He also became the first combination pilot/traffic reporter in the nation.

Sitting next to Barney was retired-Navy blimp pilot Louis Prost, sixty-five years old, from Stanton, Delaware. Commander Prost was a World War II veteran who flew anti-submarine patrols and convoy-escort missions in blimps out of Naval Air Station South Weymouth, Massachusetts.

At one point during his naval career, he was copilot of an airship that set a world record for time aloft—170 hours—breaking a Russian record of 123 hours. Lou had over nine thousand hours of lighter-than-air pilot time and was the first blimp pilot to be inducted into the Delaware Aviation Hall of Fame.

Piloting the left-front slave helicopter was Gary Olshfski, the youngest member of the crew at thirty-nine. Gary served in Vietnam as a Marine helicopter pilot and later joined the Tennessee National Guard, flying helicopters, where he was awarded the Soldier's Medal for heroism on a noncombat mission. Gary was the only member of the crew who was a full-time employee of Piasecki Aircraft Corporation, not as a pilot, but as an engineer.

A whole book could be written about the pilot who occupied the aft-right helicopter, such was his fame in the Marine Corps—only I didn't know any of it until I began my research for this chapter. Kenneth L. Ruesser, at sixty-six, was the oldest member of the crew and retired as a colonel after twenty-seven years in the Corps. His service years included combat flying in three wars: World War II, Korea, and Vietnam. He was shot down five times, one of very few military pilots to have been shot down in each of those wars. He was awarded two Navy Crosses, two Distinguished Flying Crosses, five Purple Hearts, and a Bronze Star. He retired as the most highly decorated Marine aviator in the history of our nation.

Since I joined the project only eight days before the accident, I was a *Johnny come lately*. During my second tour as a test pilot at the Naval Air Test Center at NAS Pax River, Maryland, I had met Frank Piasecki after a keynote speech he gave to a group of test pilots and engineers. Nearly ten years later, and after I had retired from the Navy, I bumped into him at a helicopter conference. He told me briefly about the Heli-Stat project and said, "Why don't you join me this summer? I could use a helicopter test pilot." Since he didn't know much about me except that I was a graduate of the U.S. Naval Test Pilot School and was now teaching at Purdue University, I thought his job offer was more talk than substance. But always up for a new flying adventure, I responded that I would be interested in hearing more about the project.

Over a year later, in June 1986, Frank and I finally sat down for a thorough discussion of this unique aircraft development. Frank alluded to the fact that he was getting a lot of heat from the Navy and the Forest Service for being over budget and several years behind schedule. Although Barney Stutesman was a superior helicopter pilot, he did not have any formal training as a test pilot and Frank thought by bringing me on to the test team, the project would gain some needed credibility in the eyes of the U.S. government overseers.

In the meantime, I asked a friend at the Naval Air Test Center who had a PhD in structures what he thought about the Heli-Stat project. His answer was short and blunt: "I wouldn't touch it with a ten-foot pole." So, what did I do? I packed up my wife and two young daughters and headed to Naval Air Engineering Station Lakehurst, New Jersey, for the summer—the length of time Frank figured it would take to finish the limited-flight-test program. Why did I want to risk my life on such a dangerous venture? Because military test pilots never get the opportunity to fly the first flight of a new aircraft—a heady experience that only experimental test pilots employed by the manufacturer get to do. Since the Heli-Stat had only flown in a hover, the all-important first step into forward flight was waiting out there, sucking me in like a moth to a bright light. To a test pilot, making a first flight is the pinnacle of one's career—that quest nearly cost me my life!

The flight crewmembers were not the only seasoned personnel on the Piasecki team. On my first day on the job, I was met by Frank—as ebullient as ever in his trademark red suspenders—and given a tour of the *erection works*, as he called his fabrication and assembly operation in Hangar 6 at NAS Lakehurst. As he introduced me to the various members of his development team, it slowly dawned on me that I, at age forty-four, was one of the youngest guys. Like me, most were retired Navy or Marine Corps veterans—it was like touring an old soldier's home. Since the predominant component of the Heli-Stat was an old Navy blimp, the project would obviously require individuals who possessed airship experience and expertise: riggers, ground handlers, airship mechanics, pilots and the like. Since the Navy had abandoned airships twenty-five years earlier, there were no young recruits to be found. But age didn't seem to dampen the enthusiasm displayed by these older, but hardworking people. It was easy to see the gleam in their eyes as they reveled in one last golden opportunity to recapture some of their lost youth and relive the glory days of lighter-than-air.

The Crash

By the time I arrived at Naval Air Engineering Station Lakehurst on June 23, 1986, the Piasecki team and the federal government had been working on the project for over six years. Expectations and frustrations were running high. After countless delays, all stakeholders were anxious to prove or disprove the feasibility of quad-rotor hybrid heavy lift.

The first hover flight was made two months earlier, on April 26, but progress had been slower than anticipated due to nagging flight-control issues and problems with the installation and calibration of the onboard flight data package. On the second hover flight, the two left landing gear assemblies were damaged by a hard landing. During the last week in May and the first week of June, the winds were too high for flight testing. It seemed as if the flight gods were conspiring to keep this experimental prototype permanently grounded. Despite these setbacks, the Piasecki team kept prodding forward. By the time I arrived on the scene, there was a palpable sense of excitement among everyone involved—engineers, mechanics, pilots, ground crew—that the Heli-Sat was on the verge of its first venture into forward flight. It was unbelievably thrilling for me to be caught up in the intoxicating feeling that we were about to make aviation history.

Since it was imperative that I get up to speed as quickly as possible, so I could share the master-pilot duties with Barney, my education took on aspects of drinking from the proverbial *fire hose*. To assist and guide me, one of the other pilots, Gary Olshfski, took me under his wing and devoted countless hours trying to impart what he had learned over the last two years. He did this knowing full well that he was training me to take the job that he so coveted. As an engineer and pilot, he had faithfully devoted many long hours over the past months to ensure the success of this venture. Among other things, he was the principal author of the *Pilot's Flight Manual* and *Exploratory Flight Test Plan*. He had secretly hoped that

First hovering flight of the Heli-Sta on April 26, 1986. *(Photo courtesy of Piasecki Aircraft Corporation)*

Frank Piasecki would reward him by promoting him to the master-pilot position. I will be forever grateful and humbled by Gary's unselfish actions to educate a consummate outsider and thereby dash his dreams in the process.

After the ground training so generously provided by Gary, it was time for several flights as an observer in one of the slave helicopters. But first, I had to master the art of repelling—that's right, repelling! The distance from the ground to the bottom of each helicopter was thirty-five feet. Before flight, a hydraulic scissor-lift was used by the flight crew to gain access to their cockpits. But what if a crewmember had to exit the helicopter quickly during an emergency on the ground? A device called a *Sky Genie* was employed for just such a purpose. It involved each pilot wearing a repelling harness fastened to the aircraft. After several rather humorous and awkward attempts to repel while suspended from the arm of a crane, I was pronounced good to go. This harness would later seriously compromise my escape from the wreckage of my helicopter.

After flying three hovering flights as an observer in the aft-right helicopter, I was ready to fly as an official member of the crew. The plan was to fly several flights in one of the slave helicopters to learn the duties and responsibilities there, and then transition to the master-pilot position.

On the night before my first official flight, I casually mentioned to my wife that the company carried a five-hundred-thousand-dollar life insurance policy on each pilot. I didn't have a premonition of the next day's disaster—just one of life's curious moments.

As I knew from my days as a Navy test pilot, test flying is done early in the morning or late in the day to obtain more reliable data when winds are usually calm and the atmosphere is more stable. So, well before sunrise, on July 1, 1986, I reported to the dark confines of Hangar 6 to keep an appointment with a horrendous chain of events that would unfold later in the day.

The place was humming with activity as people darted about, making last-minute checks and adjustments, completing preflight inspections of each helicopter and the aerostat, and generally attending to the myriad of details necessary before a test flight. Soon the large hangar doors rumbled open to let the first rays of the approaching day enter and embrace the monster within. The nose cone of the aerostat was firmly attached to the top of the seventy-five-foot-high mobile mast mounted on top of a flatbed trailer pulled by a large semi. Each side of the tail of the aerostat was connected to a large aircraft tug which ensured the tail would not swing as it was being moved from the hangar to the launching pad.

After refueling each helicopter and a final briefing for flight-test engineers, ground crew, and flight crew, it was finally time to put on our

A hydraulic scissor-lift was used by mechanics, ground crew, and pilots to access individual helicopters on the Heli-Stat. The distance from the ground to the bottom of the helicopter was 35 feet. 1986

repelling harnesses and mount the hydraulic lift to be transported to our aircraft—like astronauts riding the gantry elevator to the spacecraft. I settled into the cockpit of the forward-right helicopter, fastened my lap belt and shoulder harness, made a communications check with the master pilot, completed my checklist, and waited for the signal to start the engine and engage the rotor of my helicopter. Wow! What a view from my perch forty feet above the ground. The forward and left side windows were almost completely filled with the gigantic aerostat—the only other visible parts were sections of the ICS and Gary's helicopter directly opposite me on the left side. I was poised on the threshold of the biggest day of my aviation career—it was thrilling beyond description!

Finally, Barney's voice came over the intercom, telling us to start our engines; followed by a second command to engage rotors. We were about to disengage from the mobile mast when one of the outside observers noticed a significant oil leak coming from Ken Ruesser's helicopter directly behind me. Disappointed, we all shut down our engines to await repairs. Rather than use the scissors lift, I decided to repel down for some extra practice.

By the time the oil leak was corrected, the winds had picked up to an unsafe velocity, so it was decided to wait until evening to try again. In the meantime, over our lunch break, like we did most every day, Gary and I ran two miles or so to a small lake to go for a long swim. Gary,

The Heli-Stat in hovering flight just moments before the in-flight breakup and crash on July 1, 1986. *(Photo courtesy of Piasecki Aircraft Corporation)*

ever the Marine, was in fantastic physical condition and whipped my butt every day, this day included. He was easily four hundred yards ahead of me crossing the lake. Because of his easygoing and warm personality and unstinting efforts to help me assimilate into the test team, we became good friends—as good as you can be in the space of eight days.

As the afternoon wore on, it didn't look like the winds were going to cooperate. We were about ready to call it a day and try again in the morning when the winds abruptly died down around 6:00 p.m. Suddenly, the word was passed that we were going to launch, but we had to hurry so we could complete the hover flight while we still had good daylight.

Engines were started and rotors engaged. After disengaging from the mobile mast, Barney lifted the huge aircraft into a twenty-foot hover. Over small distances less than fifty feet, he maneuvered the Heli-Stat carefully left and right, forward and backward. Due to rolling and pitching movement of the aerostat, independent and out of sync with the ICS and attached helicopters, it demanded constant flight control inputs just to maintain a semblance of controllability. It was much more difficult than hovering a conventional helicopter. As a consequence, it was extremely fatiguing to fly. After about ten minutes, Barney decided to land to rest his weary arms and legs.

A second or two after landing, Gary said over the intercom, "Barney, that was a great birthday present. Let's do it again." None of us had known it was Gary's birthday until that moment. Sixty seconds after uttering those joyous words, Gary was dead!

Shortly thereafter, my helicopter began losing rotor RPM for some unknown reason and I immediately rolled on full throttle to no avail. The RPM eventually stabilized about sixteen percent lower than required for normal flight. I notified Barney of my problem and he confirmed the loss of RPM on his gauges. He immediately terminated the test and notified ground personnel he wanted to dock as soon as possible. The mobile mast was located in our ten o'clock position, three hundred yards away.

Barney applied left rudder and the aerostat swung slowly to the left and began taxiing toward the mast. The taxi speed did not seem excessive, but almost immediately a strong vibration began to shake the entire structure with ever increasing intensity. So much so, that the cockpit was a blur and I was being thrown violently against my lap belt and shoulder harness. I tried to hang on as best I could. The next day, ugly black-and-blue marks on my shoulders and abdomen bore silent witness to the severity of the fight between man and machine. Instinctively, I knew that the vehicle could not withstand this punishment much longer. It was only a matter of time before it would simply break apart. All five of us were lost in our own internal struggles and thoughts—not a word was uttered over the intercom or radio as the huge aircraft careened inexorably toward self-destruction.

Like any experienced helicopter pilot would have thought, myself included, Barney decided that the aircraft had entered ground resonance, a destructive vibratory mode that can affect certain types of helicopters while on the ground. If left unchecked, the vibration will very rapidly increase to the point of structural failure. Helicopter pilots are trained to immediately lift into hover, which will quickly dampen out this danger-ous vibration and save the aircraft. So, Barney pulled collective and flew the Heli-Stat off the ground. Because of its thirteen-knot forward motion while taxiing and the amount of collective applied, the aircraft did not enter a hover, but a forward flight climb. Unfortunately, the aircraft did not react like a normal helicopter and the vibration continued to increase.

Passing fifty feet above the ground, the aft-right helicopter, flown by Ken Ruesser, broke loose from the ICS and fell tail-first to the ground severing its main rotor blades. One of those blades caught my attention as it rocketed past the right side of my cockpit before coming to rest on a perimeter road an eighth of a mile away. It confirmed my worst fear—the breakup and destruction of the once proud aircraft had begun!

Over the next three seconds, in ripple-fire fashion, each of the remain-ing three helicopters broke free and fell to earth—first the aft-left one containing Barney and Lou, then the forward-right ship with Gary, and finally my helicopter. At the time I did not know this sequence of events, they were revealed only during a review of the videotapes. Aside from the rotor blade flying past my cockpit, the horrifying sounds of aluminum

Top photo: Taken minutes after the in-flight breakup and crash of the Heli-Stat at NAS Lakehurst, this photo shows two of the four severed helicopters engulfed in flames and the punctured aerostat. July 1, 1986

Bottom photo: A fire truck is spraying foam on one of the two helicopters that caught fire on impact. My helicopter is in the foreground. July 1, 1986

pipes snapping and breaking apart, and the violent shaking of the whole structure, I was ignorant of the fate of my fellow crewmembers.

Due to the climbing flight path and the steadily decreasing weight of the vehicle as each helicopter broke loose, by the time my aircraft finally severed from the ICS, the height above the ground was over one hundred feet. Once free of the mother ship, the nose of my helicopter pitched straight down, almost inverted, while rolling ninety degrees to the left. I thought to myself, *Well, this is it. I am going to die.* My life did not flash before my eyes. I didn't see a bright light beckoning me forward.

As I regained consciousness shortly after impact and realized that I was still very much alive, the peaceful and serene feeling I had on the way down gave way to one of intense desperation. The aircraft might catch on fire and I needed to get out. I released my lap belt and shoulder harness, hoisted myself up and over the right cockpit door frame, narrowly missing the spinning rotor head with three-foot sections of jagged blades still attached. I did not know until the next day that my engine continued to run after impact. As I ran from the wreckage, I only traveled a short distance when I was jerked off my feet by the repelling harness strapped to my body. I was lying in 115/145-grade aviation gasoline four inches deep. My survival instincts shifted from determined and thoughtful action to unbridled panic. I got to my feet and struggled to find the quick release on the harness, to no avail. Finally, I was able to push down and wiggle out of it.

Running well clear, I turned around to survey the devastation all around: two of the four helicopters were being consumed by fire; the aerostat was partially deflated with each end pointing skyward in a final act of defiance; parts of rotor blades, aluminum piping and other debris were scattered over a large area; huge, yellow crash trucks were on the scene, spraying fire-retardant foam on the burning and smoking wreckage—it was a vista from hell.

Not seeing any of my fellow pilots, I wondered if I was the only survivor. My right hand was bleeding from a laceration, but otherwise I seemed okay. Then I did something rather uncharacteristic and bizarre for someone who had just survived a catastrophic event—I took out a small camera from my flight suit and began taking photos of the nightmarish scene. (All of the crash photos in this chapter were taken by me).

The Aftermath

Ken, the first to crash, suffered serious injuries, but was able to get out of the wreckage before his helicopter caught on fire. Barney and Lew, likewise, were able to extricate themselves from their aircraft with serious injuries. Sadly, Gary was killed on impact, but mercifully before his helicopter caught fire. Four of us survived this horrible disaster because our helicopters hit on their sides which caused each main rotor blade to break off independently, thus dissipating much of the impact force. Gary's aircraft landed upside down and crushed him. When looking at the horrific crash videos posted on the internet (Google "Heli-Stat crash"), you might naturally assume that nobody survived. We were indeed lucky.

Top photo: Taken the day after the crash, this photo shows my repelling harness hanging just to the left of the rotor head with four severed blades. I missed the spinning rotor head by three feet when I jumped out of the cockpit. July 2, 1986

Bottom photo: Stark witness to the violence of the Heli-Stat crash is a severed main rotor blade impaled in the tarmac. Photo taken the day after the crash. July 2, 1986

My survival was even more astounding. I could have been killed in many different ways on that tragic day: hit by flying pieces of rotor blade, crushed in the initial impact, dismembered by the spinning main rotor head, or consumed by fire if the gasoline surrounding my helicopter had ignited while I was struggling with the repelling harness. Another discomforting thought: what if the aerostat had not been punctured and my helicopter did not break off? The Heli-Stat was normally about five thousand pounds heavier-than-air. With three helicopters gone, the remaining structure would have suddenly become lighter-than-air and would have ascended to great heights. I did not have a parachute. Achieving my goal of a *first flight* almost turned into my *last flight*!

Fortunately, nobody on the ground was injured by the rain of lethal debris that covered a large area. Frank Piasecki, however, narrowly missed being killed. He was standing next to his white station wagon, parked on the edge of the ramp near the mobile mast. After the mid-air disintegration, the aerostat came to rest on one side of his car and a very large section of ICS and wheel assembly landed on the other side. Those pieces missed him by less than seventy-five feet. Strangely, he stood transfixed in that spot for nearly an hour after the crash, no doubt horrified by the sudden ending to a dream he had been nurturing for many years.

That evening and all of the next day, the Heli-Stat and Lakehurst, New Jersey, became headline news in the U.S. and around the world. The crash appeared on the front page of the *New York Times* and in many newspapers, large and small. It was a lead story on NBC, ABC and CBS television broadcasts. A week later, it appeared in *Time* magazine. The attraction for the press was not that some experimental aircraft had crashed, but that an airship had crashed at Lakehurst, not far from where the Hindenburg had crashed forty-nine years earlier. We had become media darlings by happenstance.

At the funeral mass and graveside service for Gary Olshfski, there was no shortage of sadness as his family, friends, and fellow crewmembers laid to rest a cheerful and upbeat young man who died in the prime of life chasing an aviation dream. Because of Gary's extreme kindness to me, I had trouble coming to grips with the finality of that day.

At the gravesite, standing in front and off to the side, was a man who seemed out of place—he was dressed casually, almost to the point of irreverence, and he had a large boombox at his feet. As soon as the priest finished the service, this strange man announced in a loud voice, "Gary and I were Marine pilots in Vietnam. We had a pact that whoever died first, the other would come to his funeral and play the bagpipe version of *Amazing Grace*. I lost." With that, he reached down and turned on the boombox. Everyone under the protective awning burst into tears. It was a perfect exclamation point to a short life well lived.

The direct cause of the accident can be readily determined by watching the crash videos. Almost immediately, as the taxi maneuver was initiated, all four wheels of the landing gear can be seen wobbling back and forth and getting more violent as the taxi speed increased. The best way to demonstrate what happened is to take a typical grocery store shopping cart with two full-swiveling front wheels and propel the cart down an aisle as fast as you can run. Most people will guess that the two front wheels will begin to shimmy back and forth—just like the four wheels did on the Heli-Stat. The resulting vibration created by the wheels fed up into the ICS and created a destructive sequence of events. The final NTSB report blamed the accident on ground resonance.

The Heli-Stat program was not without its critics, even before the crash. In 1982, the Government Accounting Office termed it a *white elephant* and said that the U.S. government would never recover its investment. Senator William Proxmire from Wisconsin awarded it one his infamous *Golden Fleece Awards* which he handed out annually to federal programs that he deemed to be a colossal waste of taxpayer money. At the time of the accident, the project was four years behind schedule and over twenty million dollars over budget. In fact, a previously scheduled meeting was to be held at Lakehurst the day following the accident when it was rumored the Navy and the Forest Service were going to announce the cancellation of the program.

In this photo taken before the crash, the four, full-swiveling main wheels that started the destructive vibration that led to the in-flight breakup of the Heli-Stat can be seen at the bottom of the structure. 1986

Over the years, many people have asked if I ever regretted getting involved with the Heli-Stat project—and my answer has always been the same—an emphatic *no*. Of course, it is easy for me to say that since I was not killed and I did not suffer serious injury. In a perverse and tragic way, I got to make a *first flight* as a test pilot. I met and worked with some talented and dedicated people, but most of all, I was accorded the distinct honor of working with Frank Piasecki. After the accident, we reconnected twice a year or so, usually over the phone. The first two sentences out of his mouth were always the same, delivered in his familiar booming voice: "Mike, how the hell are ya?" and "Where the hell are ya?"

Frank Piasecki died February 11, 2008, at the age of eighty-eight. I sent his oldest son, Fred, a condolence letter which stated in part:

> *I am not ordinarily a hero-worshipper, nor am I in awe of celebrities, but your dad was different. As a helicopter test pilot, knowing and working with him on the Heli-Stat project was the highlight of my professional flying career, bar none. To have personally known the most important helicopter designer in the history of aviation is something I will forever treasure. It would be akin to any fixed-wing pilot being able to say that he had worked with the Wright brothers.*

The Heli-Stat was my third crash in a helicopter. My second one occurred at Lakehurst twenty years earlier. As a result, I have firmly resolved to never again fly a helicopter at Lakehurst—unless, of course, it involves a first flight!

Note: I am the last surviving crew member of the Heli-Stat crash.

Chapter 23

Flying for Oil

THE VIEW FROM THE COCKPIT WINDOW WAS AS BREATHTAKING AS IT was ominous, like the final scene of a science fiction movie depicting a cataclysmic end to the earth. Straight ahead was a towering, vertical wall of swirling brown matter that began on the ground and rose to well over twenty thousand feet. During my time flying over Saudi Arabian deserts, I had experienced a number of sandstorms—what the locals called *shamals*—but nothing compared to the monster storm I was staring at. Even though I wasn't exactly certain about what it was, I knew instinctively that I shouldn't fly into it.

Five minutes earlier, I had taken off in a Twin Otter from Pump Station Six with the superintendent of the east-west pipeline and several of his top aides on our way to Pump Station Seven, located fifty-eight miles west. As we approached the massive wall of brown, I searched for a safe route through the maelstrom. Finding none, I turned left and flew south along the leading edge in the chance we could circumnavigate around the tempest. But after five minutes, the dark line still stretched to the distant horizon.

At this point, I abandoned any hope of getting to Pump Station Seven and hightailed it back to Pump Station Six in a desperate bid to outrun the rapidly advancing storm as it approached from the west. I beckoned the Saudi superintendent to the cockpit to describe the situation and to tell him I was returning to land. I apologized for the inconvenience, but he assured me that he was fine with my decision. Since he was older than I, and had spent his entire life in the desert, this phenomenon certainly was not new to him.

Now the race was on to land and get the airplane inside the hangar before being inundated by blowing sand and debris. After taxiing up to the hangar and discharging my passengers, I collared the Saudi crew chief and shouted, "I don't know exactly what's heading our way, but we need to get this airplane in the hangar immediately!"

Five minutes after landing, I made my way to my room in the transient barracks, and had just barely closed the door, when day turned to night. There was a small palm tree outside my window, barely five feet away, that marked the lateral extent of horizontal visibility. I thought the tree was going to be uprooted and blown away. Fine particles of sand and dust infiltrated through the window and door seals, leaving a gritty deposit on the bed and dresser and causing a peculiar smell to permeate the small confines of my room.

I couldn't begin to imagine what might have happened had I decided to penetrate the storm. Perhaps the two turboprop engines on the Twin Otter would have flamed-out after ingesting the suffocating mixture. Fortunately, I never encountered a similar disturbance during the remainder of my flying days in Arabia.

Overseas Movement

Eight months passed between the official start to my quest for a flying job in Saudi Arabia, when I completed the application in July 1989, and when my family and I stepped off the KLM Boeing 747 in Dhahran, Saudi Arabia, on February 18, 1990. There were many hoops for my wife, our children, and me to jump through—background checks, medical and dental exams, permission from the U.S. Navy to work for a foreign government as a retired military officer, and visas to enter the country—and lots of paperwork flowing back and forth, each affixed with an official stamp of some sort, even a document from the U.S. Department of State. Being admitted to the astronaut corps might have been easier.

Early in the process, I received a phone call from the Aramco Aviation Division Manager, Marland Townsend, questioning my commitment to a long-term employment relationship, undoubtedly prompted by Barbara's reaction during our initial interview in Houston when we learned we would have to send our children to boarding school at the end of their ninth grades. I sent a Western Union telegram to Marland the same day:

> *Dear Marland, regarding our phone conversation of December 7, my wife and I have reached an accommodation that hopefully will satisfy ARAMCO and family requirements. My wife has agreed to come to Saudi Arabia and give it a good try for one and a half years. If at that point, she decides to return to the U.S., I agree to remain for at least an additional year.*

Apparently, this informal agreement satisfied Marland because I received a job offer several weeks later. Barbara, on the other hand, was not so easily swayed. She treated it like a contract and even made me sign it! I tried to convince her that since we did not have an overseas assignment during my Navy years, this job would put a check in that box. She probably would have agreed with that logic had we been heading to Italy or Spain. Going to a desert kingdom where tourists weren't allowed and women had to be covered from head to toe just didn't seem to be a fair trade in her mind.

Our three kids, on the other hand, were more than ready for a new adventure. But first, I had to show them exactly where Saudi Arabia was located. On one of the walls in Brian's bedroom was a large world map. First, we found Egypt on the continent of Africa and then due east was the Kingdom of Saudi Arabia, bound on the west by the Red Sea and on the east by the Persian Gulf. At that point, the whole family became excited, even Barbara. I think we all agreed this was going to be an experience of a lifetime.

With a firm offer of employment in hand, the real fun began. Since we didn't know how long we would be living overseas, we held the mother of all garage sales to sell much of what we owned except our furniture, personal items, and family mementoes. Then the packers arrived, and took up residence for three full days as they carefully packed everything into two wooden shipping crates: a smaller one containing essential items, which would be sent air cargo, and a much larger container that would travel by ship.

Leaving behind an empty house with a For Sale sign in the yard, Barbara, our two daughters, Ashley and Julie, and I flew to Houston, Texas, where we attended three full days of company orientation with seven other new families. (Our son, Brian, a junior at Purdue University, remained behind.)

The company treated us like visiting royalty. They put us up on the 22nd floor of a beautiful hotel, in a luxury suite comprised of two bedrooms, each with two double beds, two baths, a kitchen, and a large living room. I felt like the condemned being given anything they wanted for their last dinner.

After completing orientation, we boarded a KLM 747 for the long flight to Saudi Arabia, with a five-hour layover in Amsterdam. After flying through eight time zones and looking weary and in need of a shower, we finally arrived in Saudi Arabia—or as most expats call it: "The Kingdom." The first step was to pass through immigration to have our passports and entry visas checked and stamped; and then on to a line where our personal luggage was searched for contraband.

During orientation in Houston, we had been thoroughly briefed about the items that were not permitted into the country and about how we could be arrested and immediately deported for attempting to bring in any illegal or prohibited items. We were totally traumatized and stressed.

When the entry cards for Saudi Customs were passed out to us by our flight attendants before landing, we couldn't help but notice the following warning in bold-red ink: "DEATH FOR DRUG TRAFFICKERS." We certainly weren't carrying any drugs, but the message was clear that we were entering a country with a radically different system of laws and justice.

For example, any doll, statue, figurine, photograph, or painting depicting the human body would be confiscated. Our nine-year-old daughter, Julie, was adamant that they were not going to take her favorite doll, so she clutched it in her arms like a fullback plunging into the end-zone. Fortunately, the Customs men were charmed by this little girl and paid no attention to her doll. Much to our relief, the Customs procedure went smoothly and quickly.

After clearing the arrival formalities, we were met by Steve Davis, my company sponsor, and a couple company drivers in a van to pick up our thirteen pieces of luggage. As a training captain for the Fokker F-27, I would fly a number of flights with Steve over the coming weeks to qualify as a first officer.

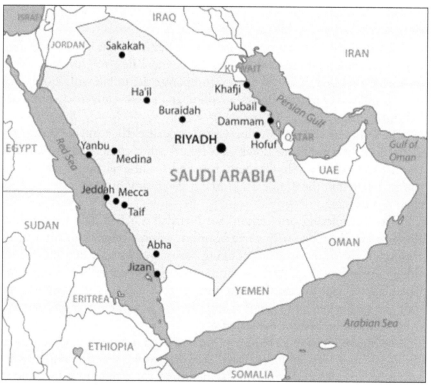

Map of Saudi Arabia and surrounding countries.

We had been warned in Houston that, due to a big influx of new employees, we might be assigned to a mobile home instead of a townhouse. So, we were expecting the worse. Much to our good fortune, we moved into a beautiful, two-story, four-bedroom, two-and-a-half bath, 2,500-square foot townhouse that had been totally refurbished, including new carpet throughout. When we walked inside like four zombies, we found it fully furnished with furniture, bed linens, blankets, towels, china, silverware, pots and pans, and a couple days' supply of food. Thankfully, the beds were made because we could have slept vertically like weightless astronauts.

And with that, a new Aramco pilot and his family completed their first day in Saudi Arabia.

The Desert Kingdom

Many books on the culture and customs of Saudi Arabia have been published, so anything written here won't even begin to scratch the surface. My purpose is to provide the broadest overview to serve as a backdrop and provide some perspective on the four years we spent living and working in Saudi Arabia. The information presented in this section is nothing more than a snapshot of conditions as they existed in the 1990 to 1994 timeframe.

Saudi Arabia was founded in 1932 when a strong, intelligent, and charismatic leader by the name of Abdul Aziz banded together various nomadic tribes and warring factions to form a unified desert kingdom. The House of Saud has ruled as an absolute monarchy ever since.

In terms of landmass, Saudi Arabia is a large country: one-third the size of the lower forty-eight United States, or about the size of Western Europe. The country occupies most of the Arabian Peninsula and lies at the crossroads of three continents: Africa, Europe, and Asia; and sits astride the major waterways that link much of the civilized world. The country is bordered on the north by Jordan, Iraq, and Kuwait; on the south by Yemen and Oman; on the west by the Red Sea; and on the east by the Persian Gulf, Bahrain, Qatar, and the United Arab Emirates. Aside from a 7,000 to 9,000-foot mountain range in the southwest, Saudi Arabia is a relatively flat country interspersed with occasional hills, called *jebels*, that jut up from the monotonous landscape of sand, rock, and scrub vegetation.

Because annual rainfall is so meager, the country is basically a vast desert, with temperatures ranging above 120°F in the summer and to below freezing in the winter.

In terms of population, in 1990, the country had sixteen million people, less than the state of New York. Of the total population, about ten percent were nomadic Bedouins. An additional three million foreign workers, mostly male, and mainly from India, Bangladesh, Philippines, Pakistan, and Egypt, performed manual labor and other nonprofessional work.

All Saudi citizens were Muslim, as were most of the foreign workers. Two of the three holiest sites in Islam—Mecca and Medina—lie within Saudi Arabia and were off limits to non-Muslims. (The third holiest site is located in Jerusalem),

There was no such thing as a tourist visa in Saudi Arabia. (In 2018. there was some speculation that this policy might change, to make the Saudi economy less dependent on oil production.) Outsiders were not permitted to enter the country unless they were diplomats, foreign military exchange personnel, or those on government-sanctioned business. The only exceptions were Muslims making the annual Hajj pilgrimage to Mecca.

Although oil and natural gas are the foundation of Saudi Arabia's economy, manufacturing, agriculture, and service industries are playing increasing roles in the country's efforts to become less dependent on oil.

Although Arabic was the official language, most Saudi professionals and businessmen spoke English; many had earned degrees from universities in the United States or Europe.

Gleaming five-star hotels and Bedouin tents. A desert country that exports wheat, even though expensive irrigation systems are necessary to do so. Luxury automobiles on eight-lane boulevards share space with free-range camels apt to show up anywhere. Heterosexual men talking, laughing, holding hands, and kissing one another on the cheeks while their wives and daughters, dressed in black, without any skin showing, trudge along in total silence. These are but a few of the contradictions that travelers to Saudi Arabia will notice.

Sharia is the law of Islam and regulates not only public behavior, but also private behavior and beliefs. It is more than just a set of rules and laws; it is a way of life derived from the teachings of the Prophet Mohammed and the holy book of Islam, the Quran. Other Muslim countries also follow Sharia dictates, but Saudi Arabia is the strictest in its observance because the Saudis feel obligated to safeguard Islam from the encroachment and evil influence of Western society.

To most others, Saudi law is overly intrusive in the private lives of its citizens. In Saudi Arabia, there is no such thing as freedom of religion or freedom of speech. Religions other than Islam are prohibited from openly expressing their faith or maintaining houses of worship. Foreign newspapers and magazines were either banned entirely or heavily censored by the government. The publications that were allowed had complete pages torn out or were heavily redacted with black magic marker, mainly to cover up any exposed skin on a woman. We found it amusing to think that someone's job was to color the arms and legs of fashion models, for example, in a catalog featuring women's clothing. Only government-owned and operated radio and TV stations were permitted. Listening to the outside world on a shortwave radio was illegal. Public demonstrations of protest were out of the question.

Punishments for violation of Sharia law were harsh, brutal, and uncompromising. Minor offenses might result in a public flogging with a whip, or prison sentences. Thieves, even those guilty of shoplifting, could have their right hands cut off. It was shocking to occasionally pass a man on the city street who had a stump on the end of his right arm. Individuals convicted of armed robbery, rape, murder, drug trafficking, major corruption, or blaspheming the Prophet or the Quran were executed, usually by public beheading. Women guilty of adultery could be stoned to death.

All civil and criminal court proceedings were bench trials, meaning no juries; and since Sharia law is uncodified, with no legal precedent, interpretation of the law was left up to individual judges. However, the general absence of crime, is noteworthy. I never hesitated to walk down any city street in Saudi Arabia in the darkest of night, fearing that I might be victimized. The biggest risk was possibly stumbling into a construction hole not properly barricaded—OSHA-type regulations were apparently not incorporated into Sharia law.

Because of immense oil wealth, the King and his ministers have passed some of the bounty down to their subjects, including free health care; free schooling through university; interest-free loans to homeowners and businessmen; very low utility rates; a monthly stipend to help less fortunate families; and, just for good measure, no personal income tax or sales tax. Oil revenues have also allowed the Kingdom to build modern cities and infrastructure to improve the life of its citizens.

Saudi Arabia is a man's world and women are treated as second-class citizens—or worse. The old adage "A man's home is his castle" certainly applies in Saudi Arabia, where men act as the supreme ruler of their families. A man can have up to four wives at a time, although he must treat all of them equally. If he buys one a new dress, he must buy all a new dress. Additionally, a man can divorce his wife by simply stating "I divorce you" three times in front of the prescribed number of witnesses; no member of his family can travel without his written permission; in the summer heat, he can wear a white, loose-fitting, one-piece garment called a *thobe*; whereas women must be covered from head to foot in a heat-absorbing black *abaya* in public.

Most Saudi men that I dealt with were college-educated, spoke excellent

In public Saudi women must be covered head-to-toe in a black garment called an *abaya*.

English, and only had one wife. They were cordial and friendly to outsiders. I never witnessed Saudi men arguing or showing displays of temper or impatience. Certainly, Saudi men have character flaws like all of us, but in public, they were charming, polite, hospitable, and, frankly, likeable.

Since the left hand was used to attend to toilet matters, touching anyone with the left hand was a serious sign of disrespect. When shaking hands, Saudi men used a loose grip, which most Westerners would consider unmanly. Also, Saudi men tended to stand very close when conversing, which other cultures might feel as encroaching on their personal space.

In the Saudi culture, women and men did not mix or mingle in public; conversation between the sexes outside the home, even within the same family, was not permitted. New Aramco employees were instructed during orientation in Houston to never speak to or even look directly at a Saudi woman in public.

If a married couple was invited to a Saudi home for dinner, the man of the house would greet them at the door and direct the wife to enter the women's living room, while the man would be hosted in the men's living room. At no time would everybody gather together, not even for dinner. Sadly, Barbara and I never got to experience being invited into a Saudi home. But other expatriate women told us that it could be an awkward and uncomfortable evening, especially if the woman of the house didn't speak any English and her female guest spoke no Arabic. One can only smile just so long.

Inside the country, Saudi women towed the mark, but outside the country it was a different story. On one occasion, Barbara and I flew Saudia, the Saudi national airline, to and from New York City. On the outbound

At a stateside costume party, I'm wearing a white *thobe* and a red and white checkered *ghutrah* held in place by an *iqal*. My wife, Barbara, is wearing an *abaya* and a head scarf that might be worn by non-Saudi women.

flight from Jeddah, as soon as the airplane was outside Saudi airspace, the Saudi women emerged from the bathroom having shed their black attire. They were stunningly beautiful in their colorful Western clothes, tight-fitting jeans, and carefully applied makeup. Alcoholic beverages were sipped with delight. On the flight back, the reverse happened; they were properly encased in black before crossing into Saudi territory. We often wondered which world they would have chosen given the opportunity.

From time to time, Barbara and our two daughters experienced cultural meltdowns; an issue I addressed in a letter to family and friends:

> *During moments of frustration, both Julie and Ashley have been heard to say that they were going to take the next airplane out of here. Actually, I have heard Barbara express similar sentiments. Fortunately, the three of them have not reached crisis proportions at the same time. I was wondering why they mentioned in Houston during our orientation that Aramco has a full staff of mental health counselors over here.*

Western expats privately joked that we lived in "the magic kingdom" and that the frequently used Arabic expression *enshallah* (God willing), tacked onto the end of a sentence, really meant "It ain't gonna happen." In the end, my family and I had a good experience living and working in Saudi Arabia. As soon as an outsider realized that he or she couldn't change things to their way of thinking, they began to adapt to cultural differences and, by doing so, started to appreciate and value the benefits of living in another country—even one as foreign and strange as Saudi Arabia!

Saudi Aramco

In 1933, shortly after the Kingdom of Saudi Arabia was founded, the King signed a concession agreement with Standard Oil of California (known today as Chevron), allowing the company to explore for oil. In 1936, another American company, Texaco, acquired half-interest in the enterprise; and in 1944, the company formally became known as the Arabian American Oil Company (Aramco). In 1948, the wholly owned American company took on two more partners, Exxon and Mobil, and moved its company headquarters from San Francisco to New York City.

Although geologists were quite certain that oil in large quantities existed below the surface of the Arabian Peninsula, initial drilling efforts were disappointing. In March 1938, a deep well known as Dammam #7 began producing large quantities of oil, just as Standard Oil of California and Texaco were beginning to doubt the wisdom of their sizable investment. And as the old saying goes, "The rest is history." Incidentally, Dammam #7 is still producing today.

In 1973, the Saudi government acquired a twenty-five percent stake in Aramco; and by 1980, it owned all the assets. In 1988, reflecting the change in ownership, the name of the oil conglomerate was changed to the Saudi Arabian Oil Company (Saudi Aramco).

When describing the totality and reach of Saudi Aramco, superlatives abound: the world's largest oil producer and exporter; second largest oil reserves in the world (slightly behind Venezuela); operator of the largest offshore oilfield in the world; and the richest company in the world, with assets estimated as high as ten trillion dollars. Since 1938, the region has produced fifty-seven billion barrels of oil and at peak capacity, it produced over nine million barrels per day. The company owns and controls its entire supply chain, from exploration, drilling, and refining, to distribution to world markets using a large fleet of ocean-going Very Large Crude Carriers, down to the gas pump in certain markets.

Saudi Aramco has 43,000 employees from over fifty countries; with Saudis comprising seventy-five percent of the workforce and nearly all management positions.

The Aviation Department

It comes as no surprise that the largest oil company in the world also has the largest corporate flight department. In terms of total number of aircraft and financial valuation of the entire operation, the Saudi Aramco flight department has no equal. Not only do they own aircraft and maintenance facilities like most corporate operations, they also own and operate a large number of their own airfields and all that goes with supporting a large ground-based infrastructure.

Like all great business ventures, the Aramco flight department started out small, with one aircraft under contract. In 1934, shortly after Standard Oil of California signed an agreement with Saudi Arabia to explore for oil, the company contracted with American Dick Kerr to photo-map the entire Kingdom as the first step to determine where drilling operations should begin.

Dick Kerr was uniquely qualified for the job. Not only was he an experienced ex-Navy pilot who owned his own aerial surveying company, he was also a university-trained geologist, an aircraft mechanic, and a skilled photographer who developed his own film—fortunately for me, new pilot hires in 1990 did not have to be this versatile!

Kerr contracted with the Fairchild Aviation Corporation in Hagerstown, Maryland, to build a new Model 71, a high-wing monoplane with an enclosed cockpit and cabin, and powered by a single 420-horsepower radial engine. By the time Kerr placed his order, the Model 71 had an established history of being a rugged and reliable bush plane preferred by U.S. and Canadian operators. With wide, low-cut windows in the aft cabin and vertical camera ports in the bottom of the airplane, it had also been used for aerial photography. So, with the addition of large, low-pressure tires and an extra gas tank in the cabin, it made the perfect platform for carrying out this ambitious project in a vast desert environment. In addition to transporting the new airplane to Saudi Arabia, Kerr also arranged to ship five thousand gallons of aviation gasoline in five-gallon tin containers.

Before leaving for Saudi Arabia, and knowing that he would not have access to cold water in the desert necessary to develop photographic film, Dick Kerr worked with Eastman Kodak in Rochester, New York, to find a new process using water temperatures as high as 120 degrees.

Although the Aramco Aviation Department continued to use a small number of aircraft during the late 1930s and early 1940s, it wasn't until after World War II that the department began to grow into the large operation it is today. In 1947, with limited options for commercial airline service to and from the Middle East, Aramco decided to form its own international airline to facilitate the transportation of employees and their dependents, visitors on company business, and cargo to and from the United States.

Starting with DC-4s and then DC-6s, the company operated three aircraft in trans-Atlantic service between New York City and Dhahran, Saudi Arabia, offering two roundtrip flights per week, with an overnight stop in Amsterdam or Rome. The names given to these three aircraft reflected their desert mission: The Flying Camel, The Flying Gazelle, and The Flying Oryx (a desert antelope). Common to international flights of that era, the crew of six consisted of a captain, first officer, flight engineer, navigator, purser, and a stewardess. When Aramco got out of the international airline business in January 1961, the operation had flown 87,600 passengers; 7,300,000 pounds of cargo; and made 2,400 Atlantic crossings without a single fatality or injury—a remarkable record of achievement.

After the World War II, in addition to international flights, the Aviation Department continued to build up its domestic fleet to support the increasing expansion of in-country oil exploration and production. By 1951, the department counted thirteen aircraft, including eight DC-3s and five single-engine Navions. By 1984, that number had grown to eighteen aircraft, and by 1990, when I joined the pilot staff, there were eighteen fixed-wing airplanes and nineteen helicopters—many airlines in the world didn't have that many aircraft, let alone a corporate flight department.

On the human side of the equation, in 1966, there sixteen pilots and 108 total personnel in the department; and in 1992, there were sixty-two fixed-wing pilots and a similar number on the helicopter side of the house, with just over 450 total personnel. And there were the thirty-two airfields constructed, owned, and operated by the department. Aramco Aviation was a huge enterprise no matter how you sliced it.

The Flying Camel, a DC-4 operated by Aramco in the early 1950's to provide international air service between the U.S. and Saudi Arabia. *(Photo courtesy of Saudi Arabian Oil Company)*

The annual production figures for the Aviation Department during the four years I flew for Aramco were stellar: 700,000 passengers; 8,000,000 pounds of cargo; and 17,000 flights. The department's safety record matched its production: from 1979 to 1990 the company flew 184,000 accident-free hours.

Planes, Pilots, and Missions

From a pilot and aircraft standpoint, the Aviation Division was divided into two sections: the fixed-wing branch and the rotary-wing branch. The chief pilot of each branch reported to the division manager. To give the reader a broad sense of the types of flights flown by fixed-wing pilots, I will briefly discuss each type of airplane and the missions assigned to that model.

The most unique airplane in the inventory was a DC-8, which flew the Oil Minister and Foreign Minister of Saudi Arabia. The airplane was based in Houston and flew deadhead from the States to Saudi Arabia to pick up one of the principals whenever he had a trip abroad. Because foreign trips for these two ministers often originated from either Riyadh or Jeddah, the airplane was seldom on our ramp in Dhahran. One day, when it was, one of the pilots invited me to come aboard for a quick tour. All I could say was "Wow!" The interior cost more than the airplane itself. The fixtures in the lavatories were gold-plated. The bedrooms and lounges were appointed with the most luxurious leathers, fabrics, and carpeting money could buy. He also showed me the liquor cabinet and bar area, fully stocked with a vast assortment of top-shelf liquors and the world's best wines. Apparently, the Islamic ban on alcohol did not apply to the country's elite.

Next in the pecking order were three Gulfstream G-IV top-of-the-line corporate jets. These airplanes, based in Dhahran, flew all over the world, carrying members of the Saudi Royal family and high-ranking executives of Aramco, for both business and pleasure.

There were five Boeing 737s used within the country to conduct daily passenger and cargo flights. Although these aircraft were equipped with special engines capable of operating from hard-packed desert runways, they were generally flown to and from paved airports. The department also had four Fokker F27s that operated from both paved and unpaved strips within the Kingdom.

Also flying company missions within Saudi Arabia were three de Havilland DHC-6 Twin Otters that were used primarily for desert operations from unimproved landing strips. These were the only airplanes in the fleet that were typically flown with just one pilot on board.

Rounding out the stable of airplanes was a Cessna CE550, a small twin-jet modified for photo mapping. So, nearly sixty years after Dick Kerr arrived with his Model 71 photo plane, Aramco still had a bird devoted to photo reconnaissance.

Of the sixty-two pilots on the fixed-wing roster in January 1992 (two years after I started), only fifteen were Saudi nationals, and most of them had joined the pilot ranks within the last year. The remaining pilots were Americans, many were former military aviators, a few were former commercial airline pilots. However, the pilot staff was in transition. Since the company was no longer an American-owned corporation, the goal was to hire qualified Saudi pilots to replace the expatriate staff as soon as feasible. The goal of the Americans was to ride the gravy train as long as possible.

Any Saudi employee of Aramco could live anywhere in the Kingdom and the company would provide free roundtrip air transportation once a week from his home to his place of work as long he was able to get to one of the Aramco-owned-and-operated airports scattered around the country. So, on Saturday mornings ("Monday" in the Muslim world), B737s and F27s would fan out to the four corners of the Kingdom to pick up workers; and Wednesday afternoon the ballet would be repeated in the opposite direction. The Saturday and Wednesday shuttles were essentially a company airline operating on a fixed schedule. The remaining five days were devoted to scheduled and unscheduled flights, carrying the passengers and cargo necessary to support the far-flung Aramco operation. Within the scheduled category, two routes were flown almost daily: the *east-west pipeline* and the *northern area*.

Starting at the east coast on the Persian Gulf, a fifty-six-inch diameter pipeline capable of moving four and a half million barrels of oil per day stretched 746 miles to the west coast on the Red Sea. Running parallel to the oil conduit was another pipeline carrying liquid natural gas. The motive force used to move these large quantities of oil and gas was a series of gas-turbine-driven pumps located at eleven pump stations along the pipelines. Each Pump Station (PS) has an associated airstrip with four of the eleven having a paved runway long enough to accommodate a B737. So, almost daily, a B737 flew the pipeline with stops at PS-3, PS-6, and PS-10.

The northern area route connected major oil production facilities and refining plants along the western shore of the Persian Gulf at Tanajib, Ras Tanura, Abqaiq, and Al Ahsa. This route was also flown almost daily.

Unscheduled flights, for the most part, fell into three categories: *support flights*, which transported cargo and employees to wherever needed, including flights to support exploration and drilling; *equipment malfunction flights*, where technicians and parts were rushed to the scene to make speedy repairs; and *medical evacuation flights*.

My First Ten Weeks

Most new pilots that arrived between 1990 and 1994 were assigned to fly the Fokker F27 as their first airplane. One week after my arrival, I advanced the throttles for takeoff in the high-wing twin-turboprop to begin checking out as a first officer. Before that first takeoff, however, I spent several days in ground training, learning aircraft systems and flight profiles of the F27, as well as company standard operating procedures and how to conduct flight operations within Saudi airspace. And, like so many times throughout my aviation career, I curled up at night with the flight manual, trying to ingest all of the numbers and facts of a new aircraft— and as before, I promptly fell asleep!

Before I started to fly, I had to look the part of an Aramco pilot. My sponsor, Steve Davis, took me to an old warehouse on main camp, where I was issued two pairs of tan-colored trousers; two brown belts; eight white uniform shirts; a nice pair of brown-leather, ankle-high dress boots; a pair of first officer stripes; a set of gold-colored wings; and a spiffy-looking brown-leather jacket for chilly winter mornings. I felt like I was back at *Clothing Issue* at the Supply Department in Pensacola when I joined the Navy.

The next stop was the Aviation Department front office, located in a beautiful, modern high-rise, appropriately called "The Tower Building," which housed senior management of Aramco. As we entered the Aviation Department suite, Steve pointed to a middle-aged lady sitting at a desk in an office adjoining the reception area. "Mike, this is the person who will exercise dictatorial control over your daily life," he laughed. "Please meet Sue Lawford, the aircrew scheduler."

"Nice to meet you, Sue," I said, extending my hand.

"A pleasure to meet you as well," she replied in a pleasant British accent. "Welcome to Saudi Arabia."

"Well, thank you. I appreciate that," I said.

"Are you ready to go to work?" she asked with a big grin, knowing full well that I had several days of ground training to complete before stepping into an airplane.

"I am so jet-lagged right now, I'm not sure I'll ever be ready," I pleaded. "How long does it take to get over this hangover?"

Steve and Sue laughed. "Oh, in about a week or so, you'll feel good as new," Steve replied.

"Oh, wonderful," I groaned.

Returning to business, Sue said, "Well, here's how this process works from my end. Requests for unscheduled air transportation flow into this office from all over the company to Ed Flynn, the aircraft scheduler," Sue said, as she pointed to an empty desk.

"On Wednesday," she continued, "Ed takes all of the recurring scheduled flights, like the pump station and northern area runs, and unscheduled requests, and, after coordinating with the maintenance section to determine which aircraft will be available, he assigns aircraft to cover those tasks. My job is to then assign a flight crew to each airplane, taking into account pilots who are on repat or in the States for training or are otherwise indisposed," she explained.

"What is repat?" I asked. "That's a new one for me."

"Oh, I'm sorry. Repat stands for Repatriation Leave, a fancy term for annual vacation, or as we Brits say, 'annual holiday.' After I'm finished assigning the flight crews, I print up a weekly schedule that runs from Saturday through Friday," she stated, as she held up the flight schedule for that week. "And then one of the flight crew drivers will deliver a copy of the flight schedule for the coming week to the front door of your house on Thursday morning."

"That sounds like a very efficient system, Sue," I said.

"Well, I try to make it as painless as possible for you pilots," she nodded. "Please, let me know of any medical or dental appointments, important school functions, or any other scheduled commitments that come up, and I will try my best to ensure that you have those times off."

"Sue is very accommodating and easy to work with," Steve interjected.

With that, we excused ourselves and stuck our head in the office of the Aviation Manager, Marland Townsend.

"Hi, Mike. Welcome aboard," said the retired U.S. Navy captain and former aircraft carrier skipper. "After your interview in Houston, I wasn't sure your wife was going to buy into this program."

I shook his hand and laughed, "I am almost as surprised as you are, but I'm glad she decided to give it a try."

"Well, so am I. You'll make a great addition to our department."

"Thank you, sir," I replied as Steve and I exited his office.

Since all company aircraft were registered in the United States, U.S. Federal Aviation Regulations governed Aramco flight operations in Saudi Arabia. This was a good thing, not only because the U.S. regulations imposed a high standard on day-to-day flight operations, but also because expatriate American pilots were already well-versed and familiar with these rules.

Since there was no recreational flying and because of the general paranoia of the Saudi government to intrusion by outsiders, all flights within Saudi airspace were carefully monitored and controlled by Air Traffic Control (ATC). When talking to Saudi radar controllers, the American pilots felt right at home because the majority of the controllers were ex-PATCO (Professional Air Traffic Controller Organization) employees fired by President Reagan when the union instigated an illegal strike in 1981.

Basically, the only aircraft that were allowed to fly VFR (Visual Flight Rules) were Aramco aircraft flying below six thousand feet. All other aircraft, including company airplanes flying at higher altitudes, were on IFR flight plans and in constant contact with ATC. Whether flying VFR or IFR, all Aramco aircraft were in constant communication with company flight controllers, call-sign Y3, who performed flight tracking and coordination functions for all flights. Upon departure from each airport, all Aramco aircraft were required to contact Y3 with a departure report that contained takeoff time, ETA at next destination, passengers deplaning at next destination, total passengers on board, cargo on board, and any weather observations or other remarks. This contact was especially important for low-level flights, which were often below line-of-sight radio communication with ground-based ATC. Using long-range HF radio frequencies, Y3 could talk with any company aircraft and vice versa no matter where in the Kingdom or at what altitude. In a desolate country, it was comforting to know that search-and-rescue forces would be alerted if an aircraft was overdue.

My first training flight in the F27 occurred on February 26, 1990. An hour and a half before scheduled takeoff time, a crew van driven by a Philippino man pulled up in front of our townhouse to pick me up for the fifteen-minute ride to the Aramco flight line located off-camp at Dhahran International Airport. At the end of the flight, the crew van would bring me home. Talk about being spoiled.

Since I had flown its larger sister, the FH227, for Mohawk Airlines back in 1969, the cockpit had the feel of an old pair of shoes. The training captain was Claude O. "Bud" McBroom, a senior pilot who joined the company in 1983. After going over a preflight inspection of the airplane, I went through the usual drill for checking out in a multi-engine airplane: four takeoffs and landings, two instrument approaches, steep turns, approaches to stalls, shutdown, feather, and re-start of an engine. All went well apparently, because Bud wrote on my training sheet: "Mike's performance today was more than satisfactory in all areas. Recommend F27 F/O checkride."

Later, I learned that Bud was a retired U.S. Army Special Forces operator and pilot. Like all special warfare types, he was tightlipped about his activities in the Army. However, one day, he did tell me that he had helped pioneer HALO (High Altitude Low Opening), the parachute jumps Special Forces used to penetrate an enemy's battlespace undetected.

Imagine my surprise many years after I left Aramco, when I came across

Bud's name in the book *Guests of the Ayatollah* by Mark Bowden, having to do with the 1979-1980 Iran hostage crisis. After retirement from the Army, Bud joined the CIA and was assigned to the Air Branch. On March 31, 1980, twenty-eight days before the failed rescue operation, under the cover of darkness, he flew as copilot on a CIA Twin Otter to reconnoiter suitable landing sites for the C-130s, which would take part in the rescue mission. After selecting a site that was later named *Desert One*, Bud got out of the aircraft to help set up a lighting system that would be used to guide the C-130 and helicopter rescue package to a safe landing. For this mission, Bud was awarded the Distinguished Intelligence Cross, the highest award given by the CIA.

Two days after my training flight with Bud, I flew my second-in-command check with Steve Davis, and was pronounced qualified to fly the line. On March 3, I flew my first flight as first officer, also with Steve. In my logbook, in the remarks section for the flight, I wrote: "Many mistakes, a lot to learn." I have always been hard on myself, so maybe it wasn't that bad because they let me keep flying and collecting a paycheck.

On the next three days, I flew a succession of firsts, as duly noted in my logbook: first landing on a hard-packed desert airstrip that was outlined with oil in the sand; first landing at King Khalid Airport in Riyadh, the capital of Saudi Arabia; and my first time flying the east-west pipeline. The flying was fun, challenging—and different!

Flying for Aramco was similar to flying with any other airline—uniformed flight crew, passenger terminals with security lines, checked luggage, boarding passes, and PA announcements about fastening seatbelts—albeit with a few notable exceptions: instead of female flight attendants, we had male stewards from the Philippines; instead of being able to purchase a cold beer or a glass of wine, water and apple juice was served; instead of a

Aramco Fokker F-27 being unloaded at a desert airstrip. March 1990

cabin full of people, you might be sharing a flight with a critically needed repair part or a set of huge desert tires for an exploration vehicle.

Perhaps the biggest difference was the total desolation of the landscape we flew over. As one of the first Aramco pilots, Moe Morris, said, "You'll fly for hours without seeing a living thing: man, bird, beast, or vegetation. No roads or railways, no lakes or streams, no woods, no villages—just great stretches of sand or gravel between the rolling dunes, or occasional limestone hills and escarpments. The changing light makes some striking shadow patterns, though."

Just as I was beginning to find my rhythm, I was reassigned to fly the B737 to help fill a shortage of first officers on that airplane. So, on May 9, 1990, I flew my last flight in the F27 having logged a total of 110 flight hours.

Flying the Boeing

The chief pilot must have been anxious to get me trained in the Boeing because I departed Saudi Arabia later that evening after my last flight in the Fokker. All B737 initial and recurrent training for Aramco pilots was contracted with Southwest Airlines. So, on May 14, I found myself sitting in a classroom at the Southwest Training Center in Dallas, Texas. My initial course consisted of eight days of ground training followed by five days flying the B737 flight simulator. Upon completion of training, I flew to London where I spent the night before proceeding the next day back to Dhahran.

Three days after returning to Saudi Arabia, I flew my second-in-command checkride with Jim Wooley, the B737 Training Captain. Management must have wanted to recoup some of its training investment because I flew thirty-eight flights in the next fifty days, accumulating 106 flight hours.

Things were moving fast for this new jet pilot—and then I went on a forced Repat due to the invasion of Kuwait. I didn't fly again until September 9 (see following chapter).

My return to the cockpit was less than auspicious. We were flying a northern area route, and I was landing at Tanajib in a strong ninety-degree crosswind. The crosswind was much stronger than any I had encountered before in the Boeing. During my training with Southwest, and subsequent flying with a number of Aramco captains, I was never warned that when switching from a crab-type crosswind correction to the slip method just before touchdown a sizeable increase in thrust was required to arrest the resulting sink rate. All of a sudden, the bottom dropped out and I landed hard—very hard—the hardest landing of my flying career! It was

One of five Boeing 737-200 Advanced model aircraft operated by Aramco Aviation. *(Photo courtesy of Saudi Arabian Oil Company)*

bone-jarring. As we taxied to the ramp, I thought the only harm was to my pride. But as soon as we came to a stop, the lead flight attendant ran to the cockpit and exclaimed, "Captain, all of the oxygen masks are down in the cabin!" We both swiveled around in our seats and looked over our shoulder. Sure enough, there were 119 masks hanging in the faces of the startled passengers. I found out later that this stunt is called "Getting the rubber jungle." I'll bet those passengers are still talking about that landing.

The five airplanes flown by Aramco were B737-200 Advanced models powered by two Pratt and Whitney JT8D-17 turbofan engines that produced 16,000 pounds of thrust each. Each airplane had a total capacity of 119 passengers with a maximum takeoff gross weight of 125,000 pounds. Three of five airplanes were "combi" versions, meaning they had a large cargo door on the forward left side of the aircraft through which palletized cargo could be loaded. Although the entire airplane could be filled with pallets, the more normal configuration was cargo in the forward part of the airplane with a passenger section in the rear.

The Boeing 737 was a dream to fly—very responsive to flight control inputs and easy to maintain a desired heading, altitude, and airspeed. And, oh my, what power! In short, it was a nimble performer. Of the more than one hundred different aircraft I have flown, I would rank the B737 as my number three favorite aircraft, behind the Huey helicopter and the de Havilland Beaver. Since my aviation background had been in smaller aircraft, it was thrilling and satisfying to be in control of a large airplane. For me, knowing that I was the master of a large aircraft was special. Maybe I am a hopeless romantic.

I'm standing in front of a de Havilland DH6-300 on a desert airstrip in Saudi Arabia

Twin Otter Captain

After mastering the Boeing, it was time to become dual qualified in the DHC-6 Twin Otter. Many of the permanent landing strips serviced by the Aviation Department were too short for the B737 or the F27, not to mention the temporary strips created on a flat piece of desert to support exploration crews operating far from established support facilities. Hence the need for a reliable aircraft with short takeoff-and-landing performance coupled with the ability to operate in a harsh desert environment, with limited maintenance and crew infrastructure. And, perhaps, no aircraft does it better than the Twin Otter.

Built by legendary aircraft manufacturer, de Havilland of Canada, known the world over for producing some of the best bush flying airplanes ever made, the Twin Otter first flew in 1965 and immediately became popular with companies operating far from civilization. Fitted with large low-pressure tires, skis, or floats this versatile aircraft could operate from just about any landing surface. Equipped with two Pratt and Whitney PT6 engines—arguably the most successful small-turbine engine ever built—the Twin Otter offered impressive performance with turboprop reliability and reduced maintenance intervention, all important factors in remote operations.

The three Twin Otters operated by Aramco were DHC6-300 models with PT6A-27 engines producing 680-shaft horsepower each. One airplane was configured to carry eighteen passengers, while the other two carried thirteen passengers each. All three planes could quickly be converted to all-cargo aircraft by simply folding the web passenger seats and securing them to the side of the aircraft. With a maximum takeoff gross weight of 12,500 pounds, and a useful load capacity of 4,700 pounds, this nimble performer had a cruise speed of 150 knots, a stall speed of 58 knots, and amazingly short takeoff and landing distances.

Next on the agenda were five training flights with the DHC6 Fleet Captain, Art LeBlanc, a Louisiana-born pilot whose early career was spent flying float planes in support of oil operations along the Gulf Coast of the United States. Remaining in the oil business, Art traded his pontoon floats and saltwater for big tires and desert sand when he moved to Saudi Arabia. He was outgoing and friendly, and fun to fly with. Then it was on to IOE (Initial Operating Experience), where I flew an additional twenty-seven hours with Art flying the line on regular Twin Otter missions. Finally, with four brand-new stripes on my uniform, I flew my first line flight as captain on November 11, 1990.

Aside from landing on true desert landing strips carved out of the trackless wasteland and flying in cockpits that were not air conditioned, Twin Otter missions were similar to B737 and F27 flights—repetitive, routine, and sometimes boring flights between Points A and B, carrying people and cargo. A notable difference, however, with the two other types of aircraft, was the lack of a supporting cast. Since most Twin Otter flights were flown without a copilot and never with a flight attendant, the captain was it. He did all of the flying, navigating, and communicating, but he also made all passenger-safety briefings and supervised the loading, securing, and off-loading of cargo. An exception to the single-pilot norm began in 1993, with an influx of new Saudi pilots. During the last eight months with the company, I often flew with young Saudi copilots, who were fresh from initial pilot-training programs in the States and elsewhere.

Although most Twin Otter flights were monotonous and unremarkable, a few stood out. The closest I came to disaster was a routine northern area flight operation with three intermediate stops. The sudden appearance of widespread fog, combined with major errors on the part of a Saudi radar controller, nearly resulted in a fuel exhaustion accident. Luckily, I had just enough fuel to make it to an inland desert airfield that had clear weather. I landed with fifteen minutes of fuel remaining!

If you've been keeping score, this latest low-fuel emergency made number four! And you might be wondering if I ever learned. Unfortunately, this situation goes with the territory. If you fly long enough, running low on fuel, despite your best intentions, will happen sooner or later. Luck also plays a part in pilot longevity, and I will freely admit, I had more than my fair share.

In late spring of 1991, the decision was made to base a Twin Otter at Pump Station Six on a more or less permanent basis to accommodate an increasing number of flight requests to support upgrades being implemented to increase the efficiency of the east-west pipeline. I was assigned the first seven-day rotation, with the additional task of writing the SOP to govern this new basing concept.

One of the recommendations I made was: "Due to the debilitating heat and the presence of only one pilot, a maximum of five (5) flight hours per day should be scheduled in the interest of flight safety. Naturally, emergencies and other critical flight requirements will be handled on a case-by-case basis." Two years after my recommendation was approved by the Chief Pilot, I exceeded that limit nearly twofold—why I don't recall—when I flew from Dhahran to PS-6 to PS-11 to PS-10 to PS-8 to PS-6 to PS-1 and back to PS-6, racking up 9.8 flight hours, my longest day of flight in Saudi Arabia. Talk about being tired! I could barely drag myself out of the cockpit to my room. That day was reminiscent of even longer days flying in Vietnam, but there I shared a cockpit with another pilot.

On one of my seven-day stints, while waiting for my passengers to return at Pump Station Eight, I was sitting in the cabin of my Twin Otter, looking at the shimmering desert panorama that stretched as far as the eye could see. While enjoying the only shade available for miles, punctuated by a slight zephyr blowing in through the open door, I spotted a goat herder approaching the airstrip with his flock in tow. I was excited. Finally, after three years in Saudi Arabia, I would finally get to meet a Bedouin. As he approached closer, I got out of the airplane and waved. He acknowledged my greeting, so I walked over and greeted him with the standard Arabic salutation, "*As salaam-alaikum.*" He responded with the standard reply, "*Wa aliikum salaam.*"

Great, now what? I had just about exhausted my limited Arabic vocabulary. I was about to launch the big-smile-hand-gesture routine, when he asked in perfect, but heavily-accented English, "Are you waiting on your passengers?"

"Well, yes I am," I exclaimed, surprised by the sudden turn of events. Still thinking he was a native Bedouin, I commented on his good English.

"Many Pakistanis speak English," he said matter-of-factly.

"You mean to tell me you're from Pakistan?" I asked, incredulous.

"Yes, sir," he offered. "I'm here on a two-year contract.

"Do you have a family back home?" I queried.

"Yes, I have a wife and four children."

"It must be hard to be separated from your family for two years," I offered.

"Yes, it is, but I can make a better life for them with the money I make as a herder," he stated proudly.

Well, so much for meeting a Bedouin. The quest continued.

On another landing at one of the smaller pump stations, I was introduced to a hazard that most pilots in the rest of the world don't have to contend with—a dead camel lying in the middle of the runway! This was a situation where the short landing and takeoff capability of the Twin Otter came in handy.

Over the course of my four years with Aramco, I averaged a Twin Otter stint about every fourteen to twenty-one days, sometimes lasting only one day, but more often involving an extended assignment of five to seven days. In fact, I served fifteen seven-day stretches at PS-6 and two seven-day stretches at PS-3. All in all, being dual-qualified was a welcome change to the airline-type predictability and ho-hum routine of flying the B737.

More Boeing Stories

The east-west pipeline was flown daily during the workweek, Saturday through Wednesday, by a B737 and occasionally by a F27. The daily milk run began at Dhahran and made stops at PS-3, PS-6, and PS-10; and again at PS-6 and PS-3 on the return to Dhahran. Normally, the Boeing was refueled at PS-6 on the outbound trip, with enough fuel to fly the remaining route back to Dhahran.

On this particular day, Saudi Captain Basam Barghouti had left the cockpit while the aircraft was taking on fuel at PS-6. It was my job, as the first officer, to watch the fuel gauges in the cockpit to determine when the proper fuel load had been reached and to signal the ground crew to cut off refueling. However, I was distracted by an animated conversation I was having with a company engineer who was getting off at PS-10. When I finally looked back to the fuel totalizer, I realized, to my horror, that I had inadvertently allowed too much fuel to be pumped into the aircraft. A quick calculation revealed that we would be approximately three thousand pounds over our maximum landing weight when we arrived at PS-10, our next stop.

About this time the captain returned to the cockpit and I confessed what I had done. Basam was an easy-going guy, and he didn't chew me out for my unprofessional conduct, but he was clearly flummoxed by this new development and unsure of what to do.

"Mike, we can't land at Pump 10 this much overweight, and there is no easy way to defuel the airplane here," he stated as he wrestled with the dilemma I had created. I didn't know what to do either, but then, a brainstorm came to me:

"We can fly to Pump 10 with the gear down, which will burn a helluva lot of fuel," I stated confidently. He seemed a little confused at my suggestion, so I explained, "After takeoff, instead of retracting the landing gear, we'll leave them down and advance the thrust levers to achieve the maximum gear down airspeed of 270 knots. By the time we fly the 218 miles to Pump 10, we'll be below our max landing weight."

He seemed a bit skeptical, so I added, "Trust me, it'll work." As soon as those words were out of my mouth, I thought to myself, *Why in the hell would he trust me when I had just pulled such a bonehead mistake in the first place?*

"Okay, let's try it," he said, smiling ever so slightly.

So, for the thirty-minute flight to PS-10, there was a rumble like you never heard before as the turbulent airflow around the extended landing gear rattled the entire airplane from stem to stern. I can't imagine what the regular passengers were thinking because we did not make a PA announcement to relieve their anxiety.

And, it worked!

In September 1992, a little over two years after I started flying the B737, the company paid Southwest Airlines to run me through their type-rating course on the airplane. Aramco routinely substituted the annual recurrent training course for the more stringent type-rating course for most company pilots at their two-year anniversary to enable a quick upgrade to captain should that become necessary due to a thinning of the pilot ranks. Note: For all airplanes that weigh over 12,500 pounds, the captain has to have a special FAA rating for that specific model of aircraft, which is called a *type rating*.

So, it was back to the classroom for a thorough review of all aircraft systems and flight-operating procedures. I had to pass an oral examination given by a FAA Operations Inspector. Although I passed, I can't say that I excelled on it. Next, the inspector gave me a checkride in the flight simulator to ensure my emergency procedures were up to snuff. That exam went much better than the oral, and then it was on to a real airplane. (Today, the entire check flight is flown in a flight simulator, but in 1992, the simulators did not have sufficient fidelity, so a flight in the airplane itself was required.)

At two o'clock in the morning, I boarded an empty Southwest Airlines jet parked at a vacant gate at the terminal, along with a Southwest training captain, who sat in the right seat, and the ever-present FAA inspector, who sat in the jump seat between the two of us. This was my first time using the nose wheel steering mechanism, so it was a bit of a learning curve as I jerked and over-corrected my way along the taxiway to the active runway. Being at night made my task somewhat more difficult; however, by the time I finished the test, I had gotten the hang of it.

Two instrument approaches, three night landings, and 1.5 flight hours later, I taxied to the gate and shut down the engines. The FAA inspector reached for my hand and said, "Congratulations, you passed." By FAA regulations, a candidate for a pilot rating or certificate is the pilot-in-command during a check flight; thus, I was a *Captain for a Day*, and it felt good.

The other grand adventure I had while flying the B737 was the first, and only, trans-oceanic flight of my flying career. Transport category aircraft like the B737 must undergo periodic detailed maintenance inspections after so many cycles, flight hours, or months of being in service. These inspections, called "checks," are labeled A, B, C, and D, with "A Checks" being the least intrusive and time-consuming to "D Checks," which essentially dismantle the entire airplane and take two to three months to complete. Aramco's Aviation Maintenance Division performed A, B, and C Checks in-house, but farmed out D Checks to an outside contractor. So, when N719A came due for a D Check, Steve Davis and I were assigned to fly it to Dallas, Texas, where the maintenance contractor was based.

Steve had previously flown the Gulfstream G-IV business jets for Aramco and he had delivered a F27 to Malaysia for a D Check, so he had plenty of international flying experience. Since I had none, Steve did all of the flight and trip planning and coordination necessary to pull off this long cross-country flight.

We left Dhahran on December 6, 1992, refueled in Athens, Greece, and spent the night in Shannon, Ireland. On day two, we refueled in Keflavic, Iceland, and Gander, Newfoundland, and spend the night in Boston, Massachusetts. On day three, we flew nonstop from Boston to Dallas. Total flight time for the trip was 22.4 hours.

Besides speaking to ATC controllers with a variety of English accents—the French controllers were the hardest to understand—and learning about great circle Atlantic flight tracks and oceanic position reporting, some personal highlights of this trip included: flying over the Alps at 31,000 feet on a cloudless day and watching the sunlight glisten off snow-covered peaks; singing drinking songs in an Irish pub in Shannon; making a tricky crosswind landing at Gander; and visiting with my son, Brian, who had taken his first job out of college in Boston.

Chapter 24

Scud Attack

N OMINOUS VOICE OVER THE INTERNATIONAL DISTRESS FREQUENCY
crackled in my headset. "Unidentified aircraft at eighteen thousand
feet, heading zero nine zero this is a U.S. Navy warship. Identify
yourself and state your intentions, over."

We had just taken off from Dhahran International Airport five minutes earlier, heading for Dubai in an Aramco Boeing 737 and under the
direction of Bahrain Approach Control. The military authorities had just
reopened the airspace to limited use by civilian commercial aircraft; and
this was the first flight the company had flown since the Gulf War started
on January 17, 1991.

All company pilots had received a terse one-page summary from Saudi
government officials warning us of the ongoing air war over the gulf and
adjacent land, and the extreme danger of being shot down of any aircraft
that appeared to pose a threat to coalition forces. It specifically advised aircraft to adhere to the following procedures to minimize the risk: respond
immediately to radio communications from military units; fly at or above
twenty-five thousand feet; avoid off-airways routing; and avoid unusual
changes in heading and/or altitude which may be construed as inconsis-
tent with normal civil aircraft flight patterns.

The "unidentified aircraft" was us. Iran Air Flight 655, which was shot
down by the *USS Vincennes* on July 3, 1988, during the so-called "Tanker
War" in the Persian Gulf popped, into my mind. The thought of a sailor
on a guided missile cruiser at this very minute with a finger poised on the
button that would shoot us down was chilling.

"U.S. Navy warship, this is Aramco 716, a Boeing 737 bound for
Dubai, over," I replied in a clear, but strained voice.

"Aramco 716, you are cleared on course," stated the air controller on
the unidentified warship somewhere in the Gulf below us.

Within the space of fifteen minutes, this same scenario repeated itself three more times, as a different U.S. naval vessel challenged our progress. The fifth was different—radically different! This ship, for whatever reason, could not hear my responses. An insistent voice repeated his challenge four times, each time I could sense growing alarm in his voice.

I shouted to the captain, "If we don't establish contact with this guy quickly, he's going to shoot us down, I know it!"

Chuck Alexander, who was flying the airplane, was a retired Marine F-4 fighter pilot and was as unflappable as they come. I suspect, in his mind, this was a pretty low "pucker factor" situation compared with most of his missions in Vietnam. "Try him, again," he muttered.

Since we were being controlled by Bahrain Approach Control, I decided to inform them of our plight.

"Bahrain Approach, this is Aramco 716. I've got a U.S. Navy warship who has challenged us four times on 243.0 and he isn't reading me. Is there any way you can get a message to them?"

"Aramco 716, stand by. I'll see what I can do."

Apparently, approach control was able to contact somebody in the military chain of command because we did not hear from that ship again. But I will tell you, it was a tense and frightening few minutes for me!

Have You Heard the News?

The date was August 2, 1990. Our family had been invited to another Aramco pilot's home for dinner. Charlie and Sally Yancey met us at the door and welcomed us into their living room.

After shaking hands, Charlie said to me, "Have you heard the news?"

"No. What news?" I responded.

"Saddam Hussein invaded and occupied Kuwait this morning, and his armies are poised on the Saudi border."

"Oh, my God," I blurted.

"Yeah, it could get bad down here. He is only two hundred and fifty-two miles north of us. He could be in town by tomorrow morning," Charlie said evenly.

"How did you find out?" I asked.

"I heard a BBC news bulletin on my shortwave radio."

"Boy, now what?" I asked rhetorically.

"Well, I've got my Chevy Blazer packed with sleeping bags, food, and water. I plan to join up with some other Aramcons (informal name for Aramco employees and their families) with four-wheel drive vehicles. We intend to head south, into the remote desert."

"Got room for five more?" I asked with a laugh, knowing full well that he didn't.

"Sorry, bud. My friendship with you only extends to a dinner invite."

Charlie was a retired Green Beret and U.S. Army officer, so it was no surprise that he was not going to give up without a fight. I immediately thought of several other American expats, including one pilot, who had escaped with only the shirts on their backs during a government upheaval in Libya several years back.

I'm sure that Sally had set a beautiful table and prepared a delicious meal that night, but the ominous events unfolding four hours north of us overshadowed the festivities and monopolized the conversation.

By the next day, the rumors floating around the camp indicated that Saddam's forces were still holding on the border and that the international community, led by the United States, was mobilizing to thwart any further territorial ambitions the Iraqi leader may have envisioned.

Being the eternal optimist, I thought the heading-into-the-desert mentality was a little over the top and that the mild panic sweeping the camp was a bit overhyped. So, without a shortwave radio or a four-wheel drive vehicle, the Stock family played Ostrich by sticking their heads in the abundant sand of Saudi Arabia and hoped for the best. Incidentally, our son, Brian, who had arrived for his first visit to Saudi Arabia only five days earlier, was getting a lesson in geopolitics up close and personal.

We did have an ace up our sleeve, though—if only Saddam cooperated for a few days. We were already scheduled to depart the country three days later for a week's vacation in Germany. So, on August 5 we boarded a U.S. Air Force C-130 Space-A flight from Dhahran to Frankfurt, and then boarded a train that took us to the U.S. Armed Forces Recreation Center in Berchtesgaden. Once we got to Germany and had access to a free and uncensored press, the gravity of the situation in Saudi Arabia began to sink in. Despite this downer looming large over our immediate future, we did our best to make the most of our family vacation. We toured Hitler's Eagle's Nest and other World War II sites, a salt mine and local attractions, drank some good German beer, and had our fill of wiener schnitzel and sauerkraut.

The week passed quickly, and now it was decision time—do we return to Saudi Arabia or do I quit the company and return to the U.S.? From talking with friends at the camp, we learned that Aramco was arranging and paying for charter flights to take dependents out of Saudi Arabia on a volunteer basis. The media portrayed a massive buildup of U.S. forces and coalition troops in Saudi Arabia and the Gulf region. War seemed to hang in the air. One thing was certain: there was no way I was going to take my family back to Saudi Arabia.

I called the chief pilot, Cal Mills, to discuss my options. He suggested that I take my annual Repat leave. I jumped at the opportunity, figuring that in a month's time, the tense standoff might have blown over and we could safely return to Dhahran. So, we took the train back to Frankfort, bought airline tickets, and flew to the States, settling in at our lake property in North Carolina.

As the month of August wore on, it became increasingly apparent that the brouhaha in Kuwait was not going to be solved anytime soon, and all the indicators seemed to point in the direction of armed conflict. We had a huge decision to make—do we return to Dhahran as a family, or do I go back and leave Barbara and our two girls in North Carolina? Aramco painted my own personal decision in black and white—either return when my vacation was up or lose my job.

In talking with several of our good friends who remained on camp, and who had school-aged children, we got the impression that life had slowly adjusted to the new reality. Schools were reopening and life was getting back to normal. They didn't feel threatened in any way, and they encouraged us to return.

We had a family meeting. The girls wanted to get back to their friends and they thought living at the lake was *boring*. How do kids learn that word at such a young age Remaining in the U.S. would mean the girls would have to assimilate into a new school, their second in six months. Barbara and I certainly didn't want to be separated again. We had endured enough of that during my naval career. So, we decided to go back, even though there was a certain amount of risk involved. I did have the utmost confidence that our military forces would keep us safe from harm. We returned to Saudi Arabia on August 8 and I flew the next day in the B737. It was good to be home!

Operation Desert Shield

When 140,000 Iraqi troops, supported by 850 tanks, occupied Kuwait on August 2, 1990, declaring the conquered nation would henceforth be known as Iraq's 19th Province, few Americans could have found Kuwait on a world map. That geographical ignorance would quickly change as the Western world mobilized to counter Saddam's brazen move.

Saudi Arabia would not be able to prevent Iraq, which had the fourth largest land army in the world at the time, from quickly seizing the oil-rich facilities of its Eastern Province. On August 6, the Saudi government officially requested the assistance of the United States. The very next day, President George H.W. Bush launched Operation Desert Shield by sending forty-eight F-15 fighter jets from Langley Air Force Base to Saudi Arabia, where they immediately began to patrol the northern Saudi border. On August 8, sizeable contingents from the 82nd and 101st airborne divisions arrived in-country and the *USS Independence* and *USS Eisenhower* battle groups were ordered to the region. On August 12 a naval blockade of Iraq was imposed, and on August 22 President Bush called up the National Guard and reserve forces, marking the largest mobilization of U.S. military forces since the Korean War. Saddam Hussein had kicked a hornet's nest.

The sleepy desert kingdom was transformed by the sudden and massive influx of coalition military forces, mostly American. Military vehicles hauling troops and supplies, towing artillery pieces, and transporting tanks and armored vehicles were a familiar sight on the roadways around the Aramco compound. Uncommon was the presence of female military drivers in a country where women were not allowed to drive. Female troops wearing fatigue uniforms with trousers also caused quite a stir. To enter the Saudi Air Force Base adjacent to the Aramco camp, all vehicles had to weave through a maze of barriers and heavily armed troops before arriving at the guard post where military IDs were closely checked and the underside of each vehicle was checked for hidden explosives. Before Desert Shield, a single lax Saudi guard would wave you through with a cursory glance at your ID.

On a personal level, the military presence brought a couple welcome changes to our restricted lifestyle. We could now receive news and other programing carried by U.S. Armed Forces Radio and TV stations, like CNN and the other major American news networks. Going from a controlled news environment to unfettered access was like the euphoria surrounding the invention of the electric light bulb. For retired military, like myself, we were now able to shop at the nearby U.S. Air Force PX that had recently been expanded to accommodate the dramatic increase in American military personnel on the airbase, thus providing access to consumer goods unavailable in Saudi stores off-camp.

In the Aviation Department, it was business as usual during Desert Shield. The only noticeable difference was the increased presence of U.S. and coalition military aircraft in the air and on the ground at various airstrips around Saudi Arabia. One day, I landed at an airstrip near the Iraq border in northwestern Saudi Arabia, that had been transformed into a military encampment complete with a military control tower, where no tower had previously existed. I asked one the U.S. Army soldiers walking by, "What's going on here?" His clipped answer, "Special Forces," as he walked off, told me he didn't want to answer any more questions.

Most of the time, military pilots used tactical radio frequencies instead of the usual ATC channels, so they would often appear out of nowhere with no advance warning. The potential for midair collisions was definitely elevated during the Gulf Crisis, especially with military helicopters flying around airports at low level in poor visibility conditions.

Sometimes these aerial conflicts were exacerbated by hotdog military pilots showing off. One day, I was on short final, five hundred feet above the ground in a Twin Otter, landing at Al Ahsa, when two French Mirage fighter jets suddenly streaked across my flight path in front and slightly below my altitude. It scared the crap out of me. They had heard my radio communications with the control tower, saw me coming, and decided to have a little fun at my expense. Well, I was not amused. I complained loudly to the French tower controller and asked to speak to the commanding officer of the French squadron that had recently taken up residence at the airfield. I taxied over to the ramp and shut down my engines as two French officers approached. After threatening to write an incident report when I got back to Dhahran, they apologized for the actions of their junior pilots and said that it wouldn't happen again.

Overzealous military pilots were also causing consternation among employees living on the Aramco compound immediately west and adjacent to the Saudi airbase. After enduring the noise and dangerous low-altitude flying over our camp for three months since the beginning of Desert Shield, I decided to write a letter to the man in charge, General H. Norman Schwarzkopf—not really expecting any change in flight profiles, much less an answer to my letter. Surprisingly, I got both!

November 24, 1990

Dear General:

Those of us living on the Saudi Aramco compound in Dhahran have a serious complaint involving low-flying military jet aircraft.

The Aramco compound, as you probably know, is located about one-half mile to the west of the departure end of Dhahran runway 34 Left. The problem is this: the vast majority of aircraft are beginning a left turn shortly after takeoff which takes them directly over Aramco housing areas at low altitudes—100 to 500 feet. These jet aircraft are usually still in afterburner, so the result is highly predictable ear-splitting noise occurring around the clock that is literally terrorizing some of the inhabitants of Aramco housing. From observing jet aircraft departures for over three months, it appears that a few pilots deliberately see how low they can fly over the housing area.

I am a retired Navy pilot and currently a pilot for Saudi Aramco, so the sound of jet noise is normally music to my ears. I clearly remember the bumper sticker making the rounds near military bases in the early seventies that proclaimed: "Jet noise—the sound of freedom." So, I am not normally one to complain about aircraft noise, but this situation is much worse than normal. Several weeks ago, from a sound sleep, I literally (no exaggeration) leaped out of bed and flattened myself on the floor because I feared that the deafening roar I heard was a jet about to impact my house. I have heard other families expressing similar fears and frustration. Inability to get uninterrupted sleep is a common complaint. One woman supposedly is leaving because she simply is unable to cope any longer with her fear that a jet aircraft may hit her house. So, I am not alone in my complaint.

Noise, although the principal focus of complaints, is not a threat to life. The following possibilities, however, could result in a tragedy of grave proportions:

- *Aircraft slamming into densely packed housing after the pilot had to eject.*
- *At high airspeeds and low altitudes, a slight miscue by the pilot, especially at night, could result in flying the aircraft into the ground.*
- *Mid-air collision over the housing area.*
- *Items falling from the aircraft into the housing area, e.g. inspection panels, armaments, etc.*

The good news is that these dangers and the noise problem can be nearly eliminated without any reduction in tactical efficiency through the following actions:

- *After takeoff, climb on runway heading using a noise avoidance profile.*
- *On takeoff on runway 34L, do not turn left until reaching 1,500-2,000 feet and then do not overfly the Aramco compound.*
- *De-select afterburner after reaching a safe climb airspeed and altitude.*

General, I am sure you are aware of the tremendous outpouring of generosity exhibited by hundreds of American Aramco families through the nightly hosting of soldiers for dinner in our homes and the weekly 4-wheel drive vehicle caravans bringing ice, cold drinks, cookies, etc. to soldiers in the desert on the front lines. We deeply appreciate the sacrifice being made by all of our brave service men and women. Our efforts on their behalf are a small token of thanks for safeguarding our way of life here in Saudi Arabia. So, we don't want the jets to go away, in fact, we take great comfort in the protection they provide to us. All we ask is that they fly in a more neighborly manner.

I know there are jet aircraft of many nationalities flying out of the airbase at Dhahran and that you only directly control U.S. aircraft, but, perhaps, you could appeal to our friends from other nations for cooperation.

Lastly, General, I would like to invite you and some of your staff for dinner. I assume that generals, as well as privates and sergeants, would like a good home-cooked meal. (phone: 878-7518)

Thank you for your time and consideration of this request.

Sincerely,

Michael J. Stock
Commander, U.S. Navy (Ret.)

General Schwarzkopf's reply, written on his personal four-star stationery, dated December 20, 1990, follows:

Dear Mr. Stock,

Thank you for your letter of 24 November calling to our attention the problem of low/afterburner overflight of the Aramco compound area. We appreciate your genuine concern for the safety as well as the comfort of the Aramco community.

Lt. Gen. Horner, my Air Force Commander, is giving the problem his personal attention. Copies of your letter were provided to the appropriate air commanders of units (Saudi, American, and British) conducting regular tactical air operations from Dhahran Air Base. Squadron operations supervisors have been contacted directly and we have reviewed published departure guidance. Existing procedures, if followed, should not present the deafening noise problem you describe. Frankly, this appears to be the case of overly aggressive, premature turnouts from the airfield by some pilots. With the supervisory emphasis requested, this problem will be significantly curtailed. I cannot promise you that objectionable noise will not occasionally occur in the future. Intensive, round the clock tactical operations must continue under the present military situation. However, rest assured that we will carefully monitor the situation to reduce the risk and noise levels to the adjacent population to the minimum practical levels.

I am keenly aware of the generosity of the Aramco community to our Desert Shield troops, and I thank you for that. I regret that I am unable to accept your invitation to dinner at this time. Thank you for your concern and support.

Sincerely,

H. Norman Schwarzkopf
General, U.S. Army
Commander in Chief

Even before the General's letter arrived, the problem of jets overflying our camp ceased. It was extremely gratifying for me that in the middle of the biggest military crisis in the Middle East since World War II, the commanding general had taken time to correct the problem and to write to me. It was a measure of the great leader that he was.

Aside from a reduced resident population reflecting those dependents that temporarily departed Saudi Arabia when the crisis began, work, school, and camp activities continued as before. A week after we returned from North Carolina, Barbara wrote a letter to her family in Alabama:

It is very quiet here on camp. Many of the families are still out of Kingdom, especially the Americans. I am a rare species now! You see very few white-skinned women on camp. There are only about 1/5th of the students in school. Many have enrolled in schools back in the States.

Several of Ashley's good friends are attending boarding school and will not be returning. The school officials are expecting more students to trickle in during the next couple of weeks. After that period of time they predict that most of the remaining students will wait until Christmas or until things have stabilized in the Middle East.

On September 30, 1990, all employees of Aramco received a letter from the president and CEO of the company acknowledging the impact of the current crisis on employee morale, their safety concerns, and the demands being placed on the workforce to meet production goals. As a reward for continued diligence, all employees would receive a temporary extra fifteen percent in their base salary effective October 1 and until the crisis was resolved. It was a welcome gesture on the part of company management, which up to this point had been strangely silent about the brewing crisis.

Supporting Our Troops

A profound grassroots movement, unique in the annals of American military involvement on foreign shores, sprang up on the Aramco compound shortly after Operation Desert Shield kicked off. Wars in the past did not have thousands of American civilians in close proximity to U.S. frontline troops—but the Aramco compound in Dhahran did, and these employees and their dependents wanted to help. This desire to assist resulted in three volunteer ad hoc organizations: *Host-a-Soldier, Desert Dogs* and *Hospital Support.*

Host-a-Soldier involved individual families opening up their homes to two or three soldiers at a time to provide a brief five-hour respite from the monotonous heat and sand of their desert foxholes and outposts. The participating host families were each assigned a day of the week to welcome their assigned group into their houses for a home-cooked meal, a hot shower, do their laundry, call home, watch TV, listen to music, or just relax and enjoy good conversation with someone not wearing a desert camouflage uniform.

After returning from our "vacation" in North Carolina, we immediately volunteered to host every Wednesday. So, on September 18, I drove to the parking lot of the Hills Elementary School to await the Army buses bringing in the troops. After collecting three soldiers with their duffel bags of dirty clothes, I drove them to our house to begin a routine that we honed to precision in the coming weeks.

To put their needs in perspective, these three men had been in the desert nearly six weeks since their sudden arrival in Saudi Arabia, without a hot meal, a shower, air conditioning, a place to wash their dirty clothes, or contact with the outside world. The first priority was to clean 'em up!

We gave each of them a pair of loose-fitting shorts and a T-shirt to put on so we could begin doing multiple loads of wash while allowing them the luxury of taking a long, hot shower. Next, we let each of them call the States to talk with their loved ones. At some point during their stay, Barbara put a delicious home-cooked meal on the table, along with as much cold milk, iced tea, soda, and water they wanted. This was followed up with a tasty dessert and coffee. Perhaps what they wanted most was a chance to be in a real home again, to unwind and talk about their lives and their families—anything except what might lie ahead if peace negotiations broke down. Making conversation and lending a sympathetic ear was a job our two daughters, Ashley and Julie, performed well. The soldiers were appreciative of our kindness, but do you know who benefited the most? We did!

Before this program wrapped up, as the last of the troops and their equipment departed the area after the war ended, over four hundred participating families hosted over twenty-five thousand men and women in their homes.

Desert Dogs involved civilian convoys of four-wheel drive vehicles that drove into the desert on Thursdays and Fridays to bring cold drinks, hot food, ice cream, desserts, books, and stationery to thousands of combat and support troops that could not take advantage of the Host-a-Soldier program. In coordination with the Army and Marine Corps, these convoys would fan out across the desert and set up barbecue grilles in the forward operating areas. Ice cream, as you can imagine, was a particularly welcome treat, so the Aramcons would buy as many five-gallon containers

Two of the many soldiers *(on the left)* hosted by our family in our home during the Gulf War crisis. Fall 1990

of ice cream at the commissary as they could cram into their coolers and ice chests.

The Desert Dogs program, which grew to thirty convoy leaders and four hundred four-wheel drive vehicles, traveled six hundred thousand miles and serviced one hundred and eighty thousand forward-deployed military forces.

Hospital Support allowed volunteers to take newspapers, magazines, brownies and cookies, audiotapes, and warm conversation to our men and women who were being treated in the U.S. Army Evacuation Hospital on the Dhahran Air Base. Several other Aramco pilots, who were also retired military, and I offered to drive the civilian volunteers to the hospital and return since they could not get on base without a military ID.

As the Gulf War wound down and our victorious military forces redeployed from the Middle East, accolades, certificates, and letters of commendation came pouring in to the Aramco volunteers from President George H.W. Bush, Secretary of Defense Dick Cheney, Chairman of the Joint Chiefs of Staff General Colin Powell, Commander-in-Chief of Central Command General H. Norman Schwarzkopf, and others in the military chain of command, expressing their profound gratitude and support rendered by the "volunteer corps" of Aramco.

ABC News

In August 1990, a Joint Information Bureau was set up by the Saudi government in the Dhahran International Hotel to handle and coordinate the tremendous influx of foreign print and TV journalists, mostly American, who arrived shortly after the start of Operation Desert Shield. Fortunately for us Aramcons, who were starved for the latest news on the fluid and dangerous situation occurring just 250 miles north of us, the foreign press corps filled a desperate need for current information on the developing crisis. As mentioned earlier in this chapter, we were now able to receive live TV broadcasts on camp via the Armed Forces Radio and TV Network.

Barbara played a small part in the news-gathering effort of ABC News during Desert Shield and Desert Storm. In a letter written to her family on September 17, 1990, she told how she got the job:

> *Speaking of news, I will be working for ABC two nights a week at the Dhahran International Hotel. My friend, Micki Harmon, who is also a pilot's wife, and I went out to lunch at the hotel on Saturday. Micki suggested that we go up to ABC's headquarters and offer our assistance, even though I had no real desire to work. I was shocked when Mr. Rex Granum, the Bureau Chief, said that he could use some extra help in*

the evenings. I told him I would have to consult my husband first. To my surprise, Mike was supportive! So, I start working this Thursday night from 6pm to 2am. I will also work on Fridays. Micki will cover Monday thru Wednesday evenings. I am apprehensive, but also excited about this new role. Hopefully, it will be interesting and rewarding working around reporters. Mr. Granum said he hired us because "he liked our spirit."

Barbara's job included general office duties, like greeting visitors, copying, faxing, filing, answering the phone, making travel arrangements for correspondents, and making coffee. Nothing challenging, but the general tempo of activities having to do with gathering and reporting the latest breaking news from the military front and the Middle East in general, which was most often the lead story on *ABC World News*, was a heady experience nonetheless.

Working with some of the biggest names at ABC, like Peter Jennings, Ted Koppel, Sam Donaldson, and Forrest Sawyer was also an experience of a lifetime for a small-town girl, although Sam Donaldson could be prickly and gruff at times. The biggest downside was getting off work at two in the morning and then having to get up on Saturday morning to get the girls off to school. But having Godwin, an Indian driver hired by ABC, drive Barbara to and from work, made commuting a snap.

The night the war started in January, Barbara happened to be working and had an unpleasant experience when the air raid sirens went off and all staff from the various news agencies rushed to the basement of the hotel and tried to put their gas masks on while jammed into a crowded space. Barbara said the overwhelming feeling of claustrophobia brought on by

My wife, Barbara, who worked for the ABC News bureau in Dhahran, Saudi Arabia, during Operation Desert Shield, is shown with Peter Jennings. November 1990

the gas mask almost did her in. She was apparently not alone in her feelings because none of the ABC staff went to the basement during future air-raid alerts. They decided to take their chances with Saddam's scuds and the Patriot missiles.

Preparations for War

On November 29, 1990, the UN Security Council passed Resolution 678, which gave Iraq a deadline of January 15, 1991, to withdraw all forces from Kuwait and it also gave the coalition forces led by General Schwarzkopf the authorization "to use all necessary means" to evict Saddam's forces if he didn't leave. By the first week in January, the U.S.-led military forces were ready for war—Saudi Aramco and the Mike Stock family not so much.

In true Arab fashion, Aramco had been downplaying the odds that the confrontation with Iraq would lead to war ever since Desert Shield began. "There will be no war, enshallah." If there is such a person as a true, eternal optimist, then an Arab would be the poster child. As a culture, their natural predilection is to always be positive, while minimizing negative and unpleasant consequences. So, it was a natural extension of these core beliefs that very little contingency planning had been done by Aramco in the event war were to break out—at least from the perspective of the rank and file. Maybe they had plans and just didn't share them with the worker bees.

Take gas masks, as an example. Everyone knew that Saddam had used poisonous gas during the Iran-Iraq War and against the Kurds in northern Iraq. We also knew that he had scud missiles capable of reaching Dhahran. So, putting two and two together, it was logical to assume that he might launch a gas attack on or near the Aramco compound. Did the company pass out the gas masks that were rumored to be stored in a warehouse on camp, or publish instructions on what to do in the event of such an attack? No—not until four days before the war actually started. Then employees were given a specific time to go to a warehouse to draw enough gas masks for themselves and their dependents living on camp.

Standing in that long line, waiting to receive four brand-new gas masks was a sobering experience. All sorts of thoughts swirled through my head. Chief among them was the nagging feeling that I may have screwed up big time by bringing my family back to Saudi Arabia instead of leaving them in North Carolina. To reinforce my self-recrimination, of the thirty-two American pilots living in Dhahran, only nine had their wives still with them, and only one other pilot, Tom Harmon, had children at home. They were either much wiser than me or a bunch of pantywaists.

Along with the gas masks, we each received some Chemical Agent Detection strips with a few instructions including: "If pink or red spots appear on the chemical detection paper, take necessary protective action."

Even though the company passed out the gas masks and detection strips—which I feel they did only because of mounting pressure—they still didn't publish any official guidance on what to do in case of an attack. I suppose, like so many lost opportunities in life, I must have missed the class in grammar school on how to properly don a gas mask. So, a Good Samaritan member of the Aramco underground, with a sense of humor, passed out a one-sheet summary that included the following tips:

A. If you are outside:
  - You will die. Do nothing

B. If you are inside:
  - Seal all air leaks: dryer vent, bathroom ceiling vent, pet door
  - Turn off AC
  - Look outside for birds dropping from trees, cars crashing and general chaos—these are signs of poison gas
  - Gas will disperse in one or two hours
  - Your best bet is to stay inside and level headed

After discussing the three main types of gas: mustard, cyanide, and nerve, he ends his homemade cheat sheet with some reassuring words: **GOOD LUCK**!

The Aramco schools, on the other hand—probably because they were headed by Americans—were much more proactive. In a memo to parents dated October 6, 1990, Jess Arceneaux, the principal of Dhahran Junior High, laid out the steps the school would take in the event of hostilities.

As the January deadline approached, with no signs that Saddam had any intention of removing his forces from Kuwait, the company did encourage each family to designate a safe room, like a bathroom, in their home and stock it with extra water, food, medicine and medical supplies, blankets, duct tape to seal off vents and around the door, and a radio. Residents were also told to place large masking tape X's on all windows to lessen the dangers from flying glass.

What did Mike Stock do to prepare for Armageddon? Nothing! I guess I had gone native—*enshallah*. Although I didn't know for certain that Saddam wouldn't launch a gas attack, I felt comfortable that the U.S. military was well prepared to deal with any offensive actions the Iraqis might initiate. And furthermore, *procrastination* is my middle name. And it made it easier to give directions to our house: look for the only house on the block without X's on the windows.

The War Begins

At approximately 2:30 a.m. on January 17, 1991, my wife and I were awakened by the sound of one military jet after another taking off from the air base just southeast of us. The sheer number of aircraft could only mean one thing. I said to Barbara, "The war has started." Thirty minutes later, the phone rang.

"Mike, just wanted to let you know that the war has started," my brother David said. He had been watching live CNN coverage being broadcast from the Dhahran International Hotel. Like many around the world, he would follow the Gulf War as it unfolded via live broadcasts from the field—the first U.S. war to be delivered to your living room in near real time.

"Thanks for the heads-up, David, but we already know," I said, relating the large number of military aircraft continuing to take off.

The next night, a siren sounded at 3:45 a.m., which we assumed was an air-raid alert. As it turned out, what we heard were the air-raid sirens from the nearby air base. Aramco, in its infinite wisdom, did not get the air-raid system on camp working until two weeks after the war commenced. The air base had detected an incoming threat and fired a Patriot missile—later, the threat was determined to be a computer glitch, but we didn't know that at the time. All we heard was a tremendous explosion-like sound about ten minutes after the sirens went off. I thought we were under missile or air attack—only later did we find out the explosion we heard was a Patriot missile being launched from the air base. Very shortly after launch, the missile achieves supersonic speed, so the loud noise we heard was the sonic boom created when it broke the sound barrier.

Nothing like a perceived air attack to make one wish he had a safe room ready. We all crowded into the hall bathroom and slammed the door. Oh, hell, no duct tape! I rushed downstairs and into the garage, looking for some tape, glancing out the window to look for dropping birds—the memo didn't say what to look for at night. Five minutes later, I have the door and the ceiling vent taped shut. One of our girls says, "Daddy, aren't we supposed to put our gas masks on?" Good point. If we had them in our safe room, we would surely put them on. It was not my finest hour.

About ninety minutes later, we heard a different siren and assumed it was the all-clear signal. We emerged from our safe room cold and subdued, but unbroken. However, I did have a renewed sense of purpose and motivation to get my act together.

Even though the limited company guidance recommended a safe room on the second floor because poison gas is heavier than air, I reasoned that a room enclosed with more wood structure would better protect against a Scud with a conventional warhead. A fairly large closet under the stairs leading to the second floor was chosen to be our safe room. So, I got busy stocking it with the necessary items we would need during future attacks—duct tape and gas masks headed the list. As an added benefit, we could turn on the TV in the adjacent living room for local updates and, more importantly, to know when the all-clear was given. The TV reporters often beat the air base sirens by thirty minutes or more.

Two days after the hostilities began, the U.S. State Department and Department of Defense offered to fly American Aramco employees and their dependents who were having second thoughts out of the Kingdom for a nominal charge. The company, however, reaffirmed its policy of terminating any employee who left; their families could leave, but not the employee. In a letter to family back in the States, Barbara wrote:

> *Overall, we have been dealing well with the stress associated with living in a war zone. However, this is minor compared to what the civilians in Bagdad are experiencing. I hit a low point yesterday when I heard that several of my good friends were leaving. I felt abandoned and wondered if we were doing the right thing in staying. But the mood passed and I feel okay today.*

On January 20, we experienced our first real Scud attack at 9:45 p.m. and the next day, we had five Scuds enter our airspace—all were successfully intercepted and destroyed by Patriot missiles. Thus far, no gas attacks and every Scud missile aimed at Dhahran had been taken out. Five days into the war, we were feeling confident that the Patriots would protect us and that Saddam had abandoned any idea of using gas. We became almost blasé about these daily intrusions, to the point of walking, not running, to our safe room; no longer sealing the doors with duct tape. We even stood in our front yard sometimes to get a better view of the aerial fireworks. Our next-door neighbor and block warden, Ken Burnell, would often climb onto his roof with his camera when the air-raid siren went off. His wife, Marjorie, said with a laugh, "Ken, if it's a gas attack, please bang on the roof so I can get my gas mask on."

Our bubble of perceived invulnerability was burst several days later, by two earth-shattering explosions.

Our family had decided to make one of our rare visits to the dining hall on camp. Because so many dependents had evacuated, the place was nearly deserted. We selected a table next to a wide expanse of glass, with a good view of an adjacent park accented by beautiful palm trees and exotic desert plants. Halfway through our meal, a deafening explosion rocked the camp, causing the windows to rattle and the dining room floor to tremble. We figured it must be another Patriot launch, but decided to move away from the windows as a precaution. The next day, we heard that a Scud warhead had exploded only a half mile from us, just over the camp boundary on the air base side. Fortunately, it exploded harmlessly in the desert. Julie and Ashley, along with some of their friends, descended on the impact site the next day to collect small pieces of the missile, which they made into trendy Scud bracelets and necklaces.

The second incident turned deadly. It was 8:35 p.m. on Monday, January 25, when the air-raid siren sounded. Barbara and I were sitting at our respective desks that faced each other in our den. We had always proceeded to our safe room whenever the siren went off, yet this night, she looked at me, and I looked at her and said, "Nah, let's just stay here. I don't feel like wasting time in the safe room." She agreed and we both went back to what we were doing. Then we heard and felt a tremendous explosion. It seemed different than previous Patriot launches or the Scud that hit near our camp. Next, we heard sirens and saw the lights of first responders and military helicopters as they converged on a site off-camp. We decided to turn on CNN to see what had just happened. Over the next hour, live reports filtered into the newsroom and into our living room to deliver devastating news—a Scud missile had hit and destroyed a warehouse being used as a billet to house U.S. troops.

Years later, it was revealed that a computer error in the Patriot tracking software had allowed the incoming Iraqi missile to slip through unchallenged. Since the Scud was not a smart missile with terminal guidance, the hit on the billet was totally random and not the result of a deliberate attack on that specific target. Sadly, the final death toll was twenty-eight, with many more wounded.

Three miles from our house, the war had suddenly taken on new meaning. The one night we had decided not to take refuge in our safe room, tragedy struck close to home. Fortunately, only two more Scuds came into our area before the war ended—and we were in our safe room both times.

After closing for two weeks after the war started, Aramco officials and school administrators felt it best to reopen the schools on camp, even though hostilities were ongoing. Our girls and their friends were overjoyed at the news. The boredom of just sitting around the house, day after day, with nothing to do except watch CNN, was not pleasant for them or their parents. So, each school day, Barbara packed a lunch for Ashley and Julie and made sure their homework assignments and *gas masks* were in their backpacks.

Limited Flight Operations

When the Gulf War started, airspace was closed to all but military flights and Aramco Aviation did not fly for the first nine days of the conflict. It took two months after the war ended for flight operations to return to their pre-war level.

Not knowing when commercial airlines would be allowed to resume service out of Dhahran, the company sought work-arounds that would allow employees traveling on official business to be able to connect with international airlines that were being allowed to operate from Jeddah, far away from the military action ongoing in the Eastern Province. On January 23, the Aviation Department announced that it had dispersed five airplanes to Jeddah and one to Riyadh, along with flight crews. Employees would be bussed from Dhahran to Riyadh and then flown to Jeddah. This plan barely got started before it was abandoned after the military authorized Aramco to fly two flights per day, one to the United Arab Emirates and one to Jeddah from Dhahran. Over the course of the next month, I flew four roundtrip flights to Jeddah in the B737, which took twice as long to fly as normal because we had to fly well to the south of a direct route to avoid military airspace. During the same period, I also flew twice to Dubai and once to Sharja in the U.A.E.

On January 25, Iraqi forces in Kuwait opened valves at the Sea Island oil terminal and released approximately five million barrels of oil into the Persian Gulf causing the worst oil spill in history. The strategic objective of the massive release was to inhibit any amphibious landing by the U.S. Marines. The next day, three U.S. F-117 fighter-bombers destroyed the pipeline leading to the sea terminal to prevent further discharge into the Gulf, but the damage had already been done. The oil slick, which eventually covered an area approximately one hundred miles long and sixty miles wide to a depth of five inches in places, blanketed most of the Saudi Arabian coastline. It threatened to shut down the huge industrial water plants that provided electrical power and drinking water to much of the Eastern Province, not to mention the unfolding environmental disaster. Since loss of electrical power would essentially shut down oil operations, Aramco took the lead in the mitigation efforts, which included flights by two company F27s specially modified to spray oil dispersant chemicals.

It wasn't until March 26, nine weeks after the war started, before I flew the Twin Otter again. One of the Twin Otter flights was memorable. I flew several of the company's management team responsible for oil recovery and cleanup efforts to survey the entire coastline up to the Kuwaiti border. It was one thing to read reports of the massive oil spill, but it was quite another to see it with my own eyes. Flying at five hundred feet along the shoreline, the oil slick extended out into the Gulf as far as I could see. It completely covered the beaches and, in some locations, had spread inland via tidal marshes and lowland areas. We saw many water fowl, either dead or struggling, in the oily morass. The scope of the environmental disaster was hard to comprehend. As we flew past the northernmost Saudi city of Khafji, we saw the widespread destruction caused when Iraqi forces invaded and briefly occupied the city on January 29 before being ejected by Saudi ground forces supported by coalition air strikes and artillery.

During the ten-week slowdown, I only flew sixty-six hours, so it was good to get back in the groove again after the war ended—there are only so many books you can read in the comfort and security of your safe room.

Ceasefire and Beyond

Before and after the start of the ground war, which began on February 24, Iraq ignited over 650 Kuwaiti oil wells causing dense black smoke to envelope the country. The reasons for doing so were manifold: inhibiting coalition air strikes by foiling precision guided weapons, thwarting spy satellites, screening Iraqi troop movements, and punishing Kuwait with a scorched-earth withdrawal. Dense black clouds drifted as far south as the Aramco camp at Dhahran. Although the company downplayed any health risks associated with air quality, I had to wonder about that self-serving pronouncement after the day my white uniform shirt became covered in small black dots walking from the airplane to the flight operations building. Extinguishing the oil fires involved a huge international effort that lingered well after the cessation of hostilities; the last wells were finally put out in November 1991.

The ground war, which everyone thought would last weeks, was over in one hundred hours. A formal ceasefire negotiated on March 1, ended the most successful military campaign in U.S. history. Of the 500,000 U.S. forces involved only 148 were killed in action and 467 wounded with an estimated 20,000 to 30,000 Iraqi dead.

Toward the end of our involvement in the Host-a-Soldier program and before the war started, I jotted down some general observations concerning the brave men and women that passed briefly through our home. I titled my thoughts *America, You Can Be Proud*:

- They serve as Goodwill Ambassadors
- Women serving in active combat roles
- They serve in a country with a radically different culture from their own, but they are trying to understand
- The deprivations they endure in the field are staggering: extreme heat, no air conditioning, no showers, no clean laundry, MRE's to eat and warm water to drink
- They are polite, respectful, uncomplaining, physically fit, and very appreciative of the least bit of kindness
- They signal the rebirth of the U.S. Armed Forces after the Vietnam experience

- They hope for a peaceful resolution of the present conflict, but they are ready to do their job if necessary

As it turned out—no ground invasion by the Iraqi army, no poison gas attacks, and no widespread injuries or death from Scud missiles—our family decision to remain in Saudi Arabia during Desert Shield and Desert Storm was totally vindicated by a stroke of good fortune. In fact, we were accorded a front row seat during the unfolding of a major historical event. It was an exciting and memorable period in our lives.

Chapter 25

Northern Exposure

U NABLE TO CLIMB AFTER TAKEOFF DUE TO LACK OF ENGINE POWER, the airplane paralleled descending terrain in ground effect toward the valley below. Suddenly a powerline loomed large in front of us. Would we pass underneath, go over, or hit the high-voltage wires and become a gigantic fireball? Time stood still as our fate played out in slow motion.

Forty-five minutes earlier, my two flight students and I had landed at Leadville, Colorado, the highest-elevation public airport in North America at 9,927 feet above sea level. On our way from Cortez, Colorado, to Colorado Springs, we decided to divert north out of our way just so we could say we had landed at the very top of the continent. (This flight was part of an extracurricular mountain-flying course offered by Northwestern Michigan College in Traverse City.)

The weather in the eastern Rockies was superb on this June day: smooth air with a few, small cumulous clouds scattered about. Since we descended into Leadville from our cruising altitude of 12,500 feet, the effects of density altitude on available engine power were not evident at reduced-throttle settings. The landing at ten thirty in the morning and the taxi to the ramp seemed normal in all respects.

We were hungry, so we decided to head into town to grab a bite to eat while the line crew refueled our Cessna 172RG. But the temperature, which was already 81°F and unusually warm for this altitude, caused me to rethink our plan. The temperature would be even higher after lunch, thus making the density altitude higher and further degrading engine and aerodynamic performance. A quick calculation showed the density altitude was currently at 14,500 feet, which meant the airplane would perform as if it were taking off from an airport of the same height above sea level. A check of the Pilot's Operating Handbook (POH) for takeoff distance and climb performance revealed no data—it was off the top of the chart! We had two choices: spend the night and depart very early the next morning, when the temperature would be much lower, or leave immediately. I should have chosen option number one.

I filled out a FAA flight plan form for our VFR flight to Colorado Springs, and was about to pick up the phone to call it into the FAA Flight Service Station, when the FBO manager stopped me.

"Let me file that for you, after you take off," she said.

Thinking this was a strange offer, but appreciative of her willingness to help, I asked, "Why do you do that?"

"Oh, because so many aircraft crash shortly after takeoff, I wait until they are safely on their way before calling the FAA. If they crash right after takeoff, I know exactly where they are and there is no sense involving the FAA in the search-and-rescue effort," she said matter-of-factly.

Chuckling at the wisdom of this procedure, instead of calling a hotel to make a reservation for the night, I handed her our flight plan. The only logical thought process I had was to observe that the runway sat on top of a mesa and the immediate surrounding terrain sloped downward on all sides. Had it not been for that fact, I would not have attempted the take-off. I also reasoned that a 6,400-foot long, paved runway would be plenty for a C-172RG, regardless of the density altitude.

My second mistake was letting one of the students make the takeoff.

So, Steve taxied to the departure end of Runway 16, announced his intentions on the Common Traffic Advisory Frequency (CTAF)—there being no tower at Lake County Airport—and commenced the takeoff roll. About halfway down the runway, he apparently became concerned that the takeoff was taking much longer than normal and pulled back on the control wheel, forcing the airplane into the air before it was ready to fly. Compounding the problem was a ninety-degree crosswind from the right at eight knots. The airplane settled back down on the runway, and I quickly discarded my instructor hat and said, "I have the flight controls."

I should have aborted the takeoff—but I did not.

We literally rolled off the end of the runway, barely airborne, and started to follow the downward-sloping terrain. Okay, so far we were staying in the air, but barely. *Oh, no! Powerlines!* There was nothing I could do but hold on. We passed over the top so close I thought the bottom of the aircraft might impact the wires. *Whew, that was close!* But we still weren't gaining any altitude. We were holding steady about twenty feet off the ground. I was convinced we were going to crash. At least the lady at the FBO would notice the black smoke and alert the first responders.

As I told my flight students many times, the human brain has a capacity to process information and make decisions during an extreme emergency that is astounding—even an emergency of your own making.

We were headed south-southeast down a relatively flat valley tucked between mountains that rose to nearly 15,000 feet on either side. My experience with ridge soaring in a glider suddenly popped into sharp focus. Perhaps if I could ease over to the left, we could pick up some lift created by the wind flowing up-slope. Sure enough, we began to climb ever so slightly. A full six minutes after takeoff, I finally realized that we were not going to crash. The two students never uttered a single word during the whole episode—they didn't need to—their eyes told the whole story. Notch another narrow escape in Mike's flight logbook!

Return to the U.S. in Need of a Job

After resigning from Aramco and returning to our lakefront property in North Carolina in April 1994, we initially got our hopes up of landing another overseas assignment. Singapore Airlines was advertising for flight instructors to fly Lear jets in their in-house training department, where all new hires received flight training before advancing to a line position. I was told that I was on "the short list" for a job. We started to get excited about the possibility of living and working in Singapore. We had some Aramco friends who had lived there and they absolutely loved it. But it was not to be.

My next résumé went to American Trans Air (ATA), a scheduled and charter airline founded in 1973 and based in Indianapolis. ATA was heavily involved in providing charter flights to transport U.S. military forces worldwide. I remembered seeing their aircraft taking off and landing at Dhahran during Desert Shield and Desert Storm. The pilot recruiter I spoke with at ATA told me the upgrade time to captain was only two to three years due to anticipated expansion. However, this was not to be either because I accepted a different job the day before ATA called to invite me in for an interview.

Reading a listing of available pilot jobs in *Trade-a-Plane*, a popular classified newspaper catering to the aviation industry, I saw an ad for a chief flight instructor position at Northwestern Michigan College in Traverse City. Since I had enjoyed my time teaching at Purdue, I was intrigued by the possibility of returning to academia. But first, I had to find out where, exactly, Traverse City was located. I remembered hearing the name, but that was it. Getting out the atlas, I soon discovered the city of fifteen thousand was located in the northern part of the Lower Peninsula on the eastern shore of Lake Michigan, three hundred miles north of the Indiana border. The winters were probably longer and colder, but the low-humidity summers should more than make up for it. I fired off a résumé, flew up for an interview, and accepted the job. The Stock family was once again on the move—our twelfth in twenty-eight years of marriage.

Northwestern Michigan College

Northwestern Michigan College (NMC) was founded in 1951. Although NMC was a two-year community college, it had the feel and swagger of a much larger institution, primarily because some of its academic programs were not typically found at a junior college, like the Great Lakes Merchant Marine Academy, the Great Lakes Culinary Institute, a nursing program, and an observatory. It also had second-largest aviation flight program in the state of Michigan.

When I arrived in Traverse City, late in the afternoon on August 25, 1994, I was not aware of the sterling credentials of my new employer. All I knew was classes would start four days later and I would be filling the shoes of two full-time aviation faculty members who had departed in May. To say that I had to hit the deck running would be a gross understatement—but then, I have always enjoyed a challenge.

NMC Aviation

The aviation program was started in 1967, with two airplanes operating from privately owned T-hangars at Cherry Capital Airport and a handful of flight students. By the time I arrived, the Aviation Division had its own hangar, classroom and office complex; a hundred and twenty students, and eighteen airplanes—fifteen single-engine Cessnas and three multi-engine aircraft (one Piper PA-23 Aztec and two Beech BE-65 Queen Airs).

As the chief flight instructor, I didn't do much flight instructing except for the occasional multi-engine student. My primary focus was conducting Part 141 Private Pilot checkrides and training and certifying new staff flight instructors.

The most satisfying aspect from a flying perspective was piloting the twin-engine BE-65 Beech Queen Airs operated by the college. Both aircraft were "straight-tail" Queen Airs built in the early 1960s that had been former U.S. Army model U-8s obtained through government surplus. Each airplane had the Excalibur Conversion, which increased engine horsepower to four hundred by installing ten-cylinder Lycoming IO-720 engines, which increased gross takeoff weight to eight thousand pounds. These seven-passenger, non-pressurized aircraft, with a range of thirteen hundred miles were the forerunners of the extremely successful Beech King Air models.

These two aircraft were used in a variety of ways: transport college administrators and members of the NMC Board of Trustees to meetings and conferences, provide limited air transportation at a reduced cost to local Grand Traverse County departments, and transport aviation students on a wide variety of field trips, primarily to points of interest east of the

NMC's Queen Airs in formation for a photo-op. I'm flying wing *(top aircraft in photo)* on Bob Buttleman, the Aviation Director. September 19, 1996 *(Photo courtesy NMC Aviation. Photo by Don Rodriguez)*

Mississippi River. In addition to facilitating college-business operations, the Queen Airs provided a unique opportunity for advanced students to fly as copilot, thus gaining valuable experience flying in all types of weather, while logging additional multiengine hours which was important to further their aviation careers.

As a perk, the other two captains and I could rent the Queen Airs for personal use, only having to pay direct operating expenses. So, between college business and personal use, I accumulated just over a thousand enjoyable flight hours in the venerable aircraft.

Sabbatical Tease

One of the important perks of being on a college faculty is the opportunity to periodically take a leave of absence to pursue scholarly work that improves the professional competence and experience of the individual faculty member while benefiting the institution as a whole. The application process and the funds provided to each faculty member during a sabbatical vary from college to college. At NMC, there were two types of sabbaticals: a six-month at full pay and allowances and a one-year at half pay.

At the start of the spring semester 2003, I decided to apply for a one-year sabbatical and began looking for opportunities that would meet

NMC's stated goals to *Improve Teaching and the Learning Process* and to keep *Learning at the Center*. After reading a glowing magazine article about the International Aviation Academy of New Zealand located at Christchurch International Airport on the South Island, I decided to give them a call. After speaking with the operations manager of the Academy several times, it seemed like his school would be a good fit, and he said he could definitely use me on his instructional staff. So, based on his encouragement, I submitted a letter up the college chain of command, which approved my request.

The next step was to visit New Zealand to firm up the details of my employment and to look for a house to rent for the upcoming year. Over spring break, Barbara and I made the long flight to Auckland, on the North Island, and then boarded a local flight to Christchurch. The beauty of the country, especially the South Island, was incredible; and people were very friendly and welcoming.

My first stop was to confer with the operations manager of the flight academy. His enthusiasm and encouragement over the phone, back in January, did not carry over to our face-to-face meetings in April. He now seemed lukewarm to the idea and refused to give me a firm commitment, instead holding out the possibility of future employment. Needless to say, I was extremely disappointed.

Driving toward the airport exit, I noticed a hangar on the left emblazoned with a large sign: "Christchurch Helicopters." *Gee, I wonder if they might have any openings?* I introduced myself to the receptionist and briefly told her my purpose in stopping. After a brief wait, I was ushered into the office of the CEO. Also in attendance were the Chief Pilot, a business partner, and an Air New Zealand B767 captain. After listening to my story and reading over my résumé, the CEO said that my timing couldn't be better because they were in the process of starting a fixed-wing charter business using a Cessna Citation jet and needed a pilot to spearhead that project. He also liked the idea that I could also help with helicopter-flight instruction as well as some ground training. He ended my impromptu job interview by saying that he could probably use my services as early as June.

So, in an hour's time, I went from being discouraged to optimistic. I was excited about this new opportunity I had stumbled on quite by accident. As I left his office, he said to email him as soon as I arrived back in the States, so we could get the ball rolling. Barbara and I were so excited about the prospect of living overseas again and recapturing the expatriate lifestyle we so enjoyed in Saudi Arabia—and we were enchanted with New Zealand! We couldn't wait to get started.

Then, the air slowly escaped from my balloon. In response to my email, the CEO stated that the Citation project had been delayed, so he wouldn't need me until September. He also asked what my salary requirements would be.

Since I would be receiving half of my college pay each month, along with my Navy pension, I figured that all we needed was enough to cover our living expenses in New Zealand, or about $25,000 U.S. As I had told him, this opportunity was not about money, but about the experience of living and flying in a different country. However, I was not prepared to go into debt to do it.

Despite several phone calls and emails, sadly, I never heard from him again. My assumption was that he expected me to work for much less because NMC was paying my salary. I can understand that maybe he wasn't prepared to pay even a modest stipend, but I was disappointed that he didn't have the common courtesy to let me know the plan had changed.

During my twelve years at NMC, I never did go on a sabbatical but Barbara and I did get to make a quick visit to a beautiful country, albeit at our expense.

Extra-Curricular Flight Activities

A recurring theme during my career has been an insatiable quest to fly different types of aircraft. Often new opportunities arose outside of my day job. The Traverse City years were no different.

In the summer of 1995, I read in the local newspaper that a new tour company, Biplane Adventures, was offering rides in a 1941 Waco UPF-7 biplane from Cherry Capital Airport. Since I had given tours in a Waco during the summer of 1985, I decided to pay a visit to find out if they needed a part-time pilot.

I'm about to pilot a local sightseeing flight in a Waco UPF-7 owned by Biplane Adventures at Traverse City, Michigan. August 1995

I approached a tall, fit-looking man wearing a brown flight suit standing in the main lobby of Cherry Capital Aviation, one of two FBOs at the airport. "Excuse me, sir. Are you the owner of Biplane Adventures?" I inquired.

"That would be me," he answered.

"Hi, I'm Mike Stock," I said, extending my right hand.

"Pleased to meet you, Mike," he said. "I'm Jim Muennich. Would you like to go for a ride?" he asked as he pointed to a red-and-yellow bi-plane parked on the ramp.

"No, sir," I replied. "I was wondering if you needed any pilots."

"Well, I'm just getting this thing going and I haven't thought that far ahead," he stated honestly. "Have you got any Waco time?"

"Not a lot. Sixteen hours back in 1985," I answered.

"What were you doing with the Waco?"

"I flew aerial tours out of Madison, Connecticut, and also towed a glider," I responded.

"Tell me a little about the rest of your flying background."

"Well, I'm a retired Navy pilot, taught at Purdue University for five years, and flew B737s and Twin Otters in Saudi Arabia. Currently I teach in the aviation program at NMC."

"That's impressive. How many total hours do you have?" Jim asked.

"About nine thousand three hundred," I said.

"Mike, I'll be honest with you. Business has been rather slow since I started two weeks ago, but then, I haven't had a day off either. I guess having a second pilot would be good, especially if business picks up," he said, pausing for a moment. "Let's get you checked out."

In two months, I only flew a total of nine rides and four of them were with family and friends. Jim apparently didn't fly a whole lot more because he closed his business shortly after Labor Day and did not return the following year.

My next after-hours venture involved a local physician, Dr. Sean Rivard, who bought a beautiful, used Cessna 182RG. He and I had met when he was a student in the Private and Instrument Ground School courses that I taught at NMC. So, he approached me to see if I would be interested in working with him to meet the insurance requirements to fly his new airplane and then be his flight instructor to get an instrument rating. We worked out a deal whereby I would instruct him for free if I could use his airplane for personal use without charge, only paying for fuel. Over a period of two years, I got the better end of the bargain because I flew thirty-one hours with him and flew almost double that on trips with my immediate and extended family.

Rather liking a deal where I could trade my instructor services for free personal access to an aircraft, I launched into another similar arrangement, but this time in a helicopter; an arrangement that turned into a long and enduring personal friendship beyond the cockpit.

One day after class, one of my Private Ground School students happened to mention that he was thinking seriously of buying a helicopter. Dale Nielson was a successful businessman in town and certainly had the financial wherewithal to purchase a rotorcraft, although I did not know that at the time. I didn't know if Dale was simply seeking affirmation for his plan, feeling me out on being his flight instructor, or just making conversation. But the chance to fly a helicopter again—it had been fourteen years since I left the Navy and last flown one—was tantalizing. I took the bait. "I'll tell you what. If you buy a helicopter, I will teach you for free," not really expecting anything to come of it.

Two years went by. Then, in October 1998, out of the blue, I received a call from Dale. "I just bought a brand-new helicopter. Can you go pick it up?"

"What did you buy?" I asked, reeling from the surprise announcement.

"I bought a Schweizer 300CB," he replied enthusiastically. "It's at the factory in Elmira, New York."

Over the next seven years, I taught Dale, his wife, Barb, his son, Keith, his son-in-law Jon Crosby, and his pastor Carey Waldie to fly the helicopter; in addition to giving countless rides to Dale's family, friends, business associates, and townspeople—all for free. In return, I was able to fly my family and friends for free—Dale even paid for the fuel. Being able to

I am conducting an instructional flight for Dale Nielson, the owner of the Schweizer 300CB helicopter. Circa 1999 *(Photo courtesy of the Nielson family)*

pursue my first love of flying helicopters, more than compensated for my time. So, it was with a tinge of sadness, when Dale decided to sell his helicopter in 2009, after he and I ferried it to Florida. It was a great relationship and I will be forever grateful to Dale for the opportunity to log two hundred and eighty-six hours in his great, little whirlybird.

Before leaving this helicopter saga, two occurrences that would have added more grey hair if my head had not already turned all white, are worthy of mention.

One day, Dale and I were practicing autorotations at the Cherry Capital Airport in Traverse City. Dale had performed a half dozen autos using various types of entry—straight-in, ninety-degree, and 180-degree—to a power recovery at five feet above ground level versus a full touchdown on the runway. To enter autorotative descent, the pilot lowered the collective full down and simultaneously rolled the throttle off to disengage the engine from turning the main rotor. Immediately thereafter, the pilot must look at the instrument panel to determine three things and take corrective action as needed: airspeed at sixty knots, main rotor RPM in the green arc, and engine RPM slightly lower than the main rotor to indicate the helicopter was indeed in autorotation and the engine was still running.

To give Dale a chance to relax, I took the controls and entered a straight-in auto to Runway 28. After initiating the maneuver and checking the instruments, I immediately noted that engine RPM was reading zero, which meant the engine had quit running. From five hundred feet above the ground, there would be no time to restart the engine. This would be the real thing—a landing without power! Fortunately, I had practiced full-touchdown autos in the past in Dale's helicopter and we had a nice, flat, smooth runway directly in front of us. We skidded to a stop on the pavement and the only sound was a whooshing noise as the main rotor coasted to a stop.

There was no damage to the helicopter, but we were sitting directly on top of the numbers, blocking the runway. We called the control tower to tell them what happened and used the ground handling wheels to push the machine off onto the adjacent taxiway. After fifteen minutes, we were able to restart the engine, and I slowly and cautiously air taxied to the maintenance hangar. The mechanic could find nothing wrong, so we both concluded that the repeated autorotations had somehow caused carburetor ice to choke off the fuel-air mixture to the engine.

The second incident involved both Dale and his helicopter. A former aviation student of mine, turned film producer and cinematographer, approached me to ask if Dale might lend his helicopter to film a car chase scene in downtown Traverse City for a movie he was making. In the scene, the bad guys in their getaway car were being pursued by several cars containing local good guys. That description may be an oversimplification, but you get the idea. Dale enthusiastically embraced the plan and even volunteered to drive his Dodge Viper as one of the locals chasing the bad guys.

Hollywood would have meticulously planned and thoroughly rehearsed this chase scene before rolling film; our production shoot would be a one-take deal with little planning and no rehearsal. As a result, it nearly ended in disaster.

James, acting as producer, director, and cameraman on this low-budget film, told me the day before what he wanted to achieve and the route he wanted to take through the downtown area. I called the Traverse City Police Department to alert them, and they seemed okay with our plan; actually *indifferent* might be a better word. Since helicopters are not bound by the same FAA rules as fixed-wing aircraft regarding minimum flight altitudes, I knew that I would be legal as long as I could land the helicopter in the event of an emergency without endangering people or property.

Just before the director's call for *Action!*, I took off with James in the right seat and flew lazy circles near the starting point as we waited for the chase to begin. The doors of the helicopter had been removed to allow James an unobstructed view with his large professional-grade video camera.

In the meantime, the three chase cars, including Dale in his green Viper with the top removed, were waiting in the parking lot of a nearby bank, ready to sally forth in pursuit of the bad guys in the getaway car. Dale was sitting on top of a rocket with a ten-cylinder, 450-horsepower engine, six-speed manual transmission, capable of 0 to60 mph in four seconds flat. Like a thoroughbred in the starting gate, Dale was revving the engine and waiting to pop the clutch that would release the awesome power of his four-wheeled road monster. When the moment of glory finally arrived, in a burst of adrenaline, Dale, blew out three of his four tires in a cloud of black smoke and screeching rubber, and destroyed one rim—before he got out of the parking lot. Dale's chance at movie stardom vanished in an instant, but the thought of replacing three tires and one rim to the tune of $1,597 lingered a bit longer.

"There they go!" shouted James, as he pointed to the getaway car zooming east on Grand Traverse Parkway, which follows the shoreline of West Bay, being pursued by the local posse, now reduced to two cars. Basically flying a loose formation on the bad-guy car, I flew over the water at one hundred feet, positioning James so he could capture the cars weaving in and around unsuspecting "extras" in their private vehicles. I think the Traverse City Police Department got more than they bargained for.

Things got hairy when the chase suddenly turned right onto Park Street, and then another right heading west on Front Street, the main drag through a quiet downtown. First, I didn't know their exact route; and secondly, I had to contend with buildings obscuring my view of the target vehicle from time to time. But I hung in there as best I could. Suddenly, I glanced up to see a chimney on a tall building directly in our path. I sucked the cyclic back into my lap just barely clearing the brick-and-mortar intruder. James, who was looking through the viewfinder on his camera, was blissfully ignorant of our close call. The movie never was released and I declined to join the Screen Actors Guild.

Watching the brightly colored hot air balloon drifting over the base of Old Mission Peninsula, just before sunset in April 2003, brought back memories of two previous balloon rides. My first ascension, which occurred south of Lafayette, Indiana, in the mid-1980s, left me with two indelible impressions. The first was how incredibly quiet the flight was (when the burner was not being fired); and the second was the notion of being in the cast of the movie *Around the World in Eighty Days*. My second balloon flight occurred over the Maasai Mara National Reserve in southern Kenya. During Christmas 1993, my wife, three kids, and I embarked on a ten-day African safari—a trip of a lifetime. Drifting above lions, elephants, gazelles, wildebeest, giraffe, buffalo on the grasslands, and hippos wallowing in the rivers was simply indescribable.

Deciding it would be fun to get my FAA Lighter-than-Air Balloon rating, to add to the list of aircraft I was authorized to fly, I contacted Jeff Geiger, the owner of Grand Traverse Balloons and an absolute master at piloting hot air balloons. He told me he could always use extra ground crew to assist in launch and recovery operations, and in return, he would train me as time permitted. Well, after crewing on two flights, I came to the swift conclusion that my sixty-year-old body was not in shape for the arduous work of lugging the heavy envelope, burner assembly, and basket around launch and recovery sites in the middle of large fields. So, after one instructional flight with Jeff, I threw in the towel.

A New Direction

By early spring 2006, I had become disillusioned with my job at NMC for a variety of reasons, and not the least of which was the fact that I had been at the college for twelve years—the longest stretch at any job other than the Navy. I was used to changing the wallpaper every two or three years, so I was long overdue for new flying job, a new aircraft, a new mission, new colleagues, and a new attitude.

For me, the search for a new position is exhilarating; like a scavenger hunt: you never know what might turn up. So, I updated my résumé and fired off a bunch of cover letters to prospective employers far and wide. In the span of two months, I had four interviews and four job offers. Then came the hard part: choosing which one to accept.

The first interview was with a company in Louisiana that used aircraft tankers to spray dispersant chemicals on oil spills, primarily in the Gulf of Mexico. They had an aging fleet consisting of a DC-4 and two DC-3s. Since I had a type rating for the DC-3, which I got while I was in the Navy, I thought it would be fun to fly the old Gooney Bird again. But after seeing the deplorable cosmetic condition of the fleet, inside and out; and the aircraft maintenance hangar with parts, tools, and greasy rags strewn about, I wondered about the mechanical condition of the airplanes I would be flying. I decided to pass on this one.

Next, I traveled to Wenatchee, Washington for a formal interview with Executive Flight, a provider of air-ambulance service in the Pacific Northwest. Arriving at Executive Flight's headquarters building and their adjacent hangar and maintenance complex, I was immediately impressed with sparkling quality of their facilities and the extreme friendliness of their employees. It was the antithesis of the sloppy spray operation in Louisiana. I immediately felt at home.

Having communicated with the head of the HR department on several occasions via phone and email, I knew they were looking for a captain to fly one of their air ambulances, a Lear jet permanently based in Ketchikan, Alaska. Since I had never flown a Lear, I was fairly certain I was called for an interview mainly because of my experience flying in southeast Alaska for three summers. For one, I was familiar with the lifestyle of living in Ketchikan, albeit during the summer months, and I was aware of the weather challenges of flying in the area.

After meeting individually with the chief pilot and the director of operations, we were joined by the HR director. The four of us proceeded to the conference room for a formal interview that lasted about an hour. When they were finished asking their questions and answering a few of mine, we began discussing pay and benefits and other details of the job. They told me that most of my flying would consist of transporting patients in need of advanced medical care from Ketchikan to Seattle, with the occasional flight elsewhere in southeast Alaska or the northwest United States. I would be on a fixed schedule of six days on and three days off. Other than for annual training, there would be no overnights required, and I would be on standby at home during my duty days as opposed to being on call at the airport. They also liked that I had an FAA Airframe and Powerplant mechanic's license. I would also have the opportunity, if I wanted it, to earn extra pay for performing simple aircraft inspections and routine maintenance, a prospect that appealed to me because I had always enjoyed the little bit of "wrenching" I had done in the past. They also alluded that I could most likely transfer to one of their crew bases in the Northwest after spending two or three years in Ketchikan. The director of operations said he was impressed with my background, and I should be hearing from one of them within a week. I thanked them for the opportunity to interview, shook hands, and drove back to Seattle to catch my flight back to Michigan.

With two down and two to go, I rented a NMC Queen Air and flew to Fort Wayne, Indiana, for an interview with Omni Flight, for a pilot position flying one of their EMS helicopters for a local hospital. I wasn't keen about flying this type of mission because it was dangerous. It was very demanding flying with a high accident rate industry-wide because of the necessity of landing and taking off from the scene of highway accidents or other disaster sites at night and during poor weather conditions. Even during the daytime in good weather, light poles, power lines, and other obstructions in the landing area posed a high level of risk. Adding to the danger is the self-imposed pressure on pilots to fly when they shouldn't because they know someone might die if these victims are not quickly transported to a hospital.

Right now the average person who knows anything about my aviation career to this point is probably saying, "What? Mike Stock worried about dangerous flying. You've got to be kidding me." I agree. I have done far more dangerous things in an aircraft without a second thought. This time was different for some reason; maybe because I was excited about my prospects of flying a Lear jet for Executive Flight. Even though I was offered a job, I declined to accept, despite the fact it meant turning down a chance to fly helicopters full time.

Before I had contacted any of the three companies mentioned above, I had heard through the grapevine that Air Services, Inc. (ASI), a Part 135 charter operator based in Traverse City, was looking to hire a King Air captain. I contacted John Stewart, ASI's chief pilot and a former student of mine, to find out more details. He confirmed that they would be hiring a King Air captain in the near future, but didn't know exactly when. I told John that I would be interested in applying when the time came.

When I didn't hear anything from ASI, I decided to accept the job offer from Executive Flight. I was excited about flying the Lear and moving to Ketchikan, although, Barbara was not. We had moved into a lovely, new construction home a year earlier and she didn't relish the idea of having to move again, especially to Ketchikan with its perpetually rainy and dreary climate. But, like so many times in the past, she had no choice because that's where my next job was. So, reluctantly, we started the initial planning for a move to Alaska, which, for all its complexity, could just as well have been to the other side of the world. Because the move would be so expensive, Executive Flight even upped their moving allowance by $1,500.

Two weeks later, I interviewed with Roy Nichols, the owner of ASI and was offered a job, which would keep us in Traverse City. I now had a critical decision to make. Like any time in my life when faced with a major decision, I carefully drew up a table listing the pros and cons for each job. Surprisingly, the tally sheet was pretty evenly balanced. My dilemma, however, was magnified by several facts: I had already accepted the job with Executive Flight, they had reimbursed me for all travel expenses connected with the interview, and they had increased the moving allowance. The company had, in good faith, invested a lot of time and resources on my behalf. Those legitimate concerns were counterbalanced by Barbara's valid and persuasive arguments to accept the ASI offer.

Barbara prevailed and I regrettably called Executive Flight to inform them I was declining their job offer. It was not the honorable thing to do and it bothered me greatly.

Chapter 26

Misty Fiords

A S I ROUNDED THE TIGHT BEND AT THE HEAD OF RUDYERD BAY AT four hundred feet, I reduced the throttle slightly on the de Havilland Beaver floatplane and began a slow descent for landing on the smooth, grey water below. Each flying tour to the Misty Fiords included a landing to allow passengers to climb out onto the floats for ten minutes to bear closer witness to the stunning beauty of the National Monument and to snap a few photos to capture the moment.

Since I started flying Misty tours a month ago, I had landed many times in this same location without incident. It was my spot. Anything that could bring some semblance of familiarity and routine to an otherwise stressful job with a steep learning curve was welcome.

On final now, I leveled my wings, lowered landing flaps, and checked my airspeed at 70 knots, right where it should be. The three-thousand-foot walls of the fiord reflected off the surface, indicating glassy water, which is one of the tougher landings that seaplane pilots make due to lack of depth perception. I was not unduly alarmed or tense because I had landed under these same conditions at the exact same location many times.

I remember shooting a quick glance out the side window and thinking that we were approximately two hundred feet in the air. Wham! We hit the water so hard that a male passenger in the middle seat directly behind me bit completely through his lower lip. The violence of the impact might have destroyed a less rugged seaplane. For me the shock and suddenness of hitting the water ten seconds before anticipated was worse than the extreme G-force that caused the aircraft to bounce fifty feet back into the air.

My disbelief gave way to panic. Directly ahead was a shear wall of solid granite. Adding power and going around was not an option. The distance to the rock face was rapidly diminishing. I added a short burst of power that thankfully "caught" the airplane and cushioned our second touchdown. Extremely embarrassed but relieved to be upright on the water, I shut down the engine and coasted to a stop.

As I turned around in my seat to apologize for the hard landing, I was confronted with the passenger bleeding profusely from his mouth. To describe my passengers as being speechless would understate the silence that engulfed the cabin. They were stunned and, I suppose, thankful to still be alive. I'm not even sure they heard my profuse apology or that it mattered. The time spent on the floats and the trip back to Ketchikan was unusually subdued—for them and for me.

How It All Began

Most pilots, whether they fly for a living or for fun, have fantasized about flying in Alaska. The allure of the *Last Frontier* is undeniable, not only for pilots, but for explorers, gold miners, fishermen, hunters, home-steaders, mountain climbers, outdoor enthusiasts, and tourists. It is on most everyone's bucket list. And I was no different. It had been a dream of mine to fly in Alaska as long as I can remember, but the timing never seemed right, until a chance encounter.

In December of 2000, I bumped into Josh Ruttkofsky, a 1995 NMC aviation graduate and former flight instructor who had worked for me, as he was walking down the hallway in the Aviation building.

"Well, hello, Josh," I smiled. "Are you home for the holidays?"

"Yes, I am, so I thought I would stop by to see if anyone was around, but apparently not," he replied.

"No, as you remember, it gets pretty quiet over Christmas break," I said.

"Yeah, I know," he sighed, "thought I might get lucky."

"It's great to see you again. Where are you flying these days?" I asked.

"I'm flying Twin Otters and Beavers on floats out of Ketchikan, Alaska," he responded with a big grin.

"Really! I've always wanted to fly in Alaska," I rejoined enthusiastically.

"Why don't you apply? We need some pilots for this coming summer."

"I only have twelve hours of float time," I said emphatically. "They wouldn't give me the time of day. And besides, I don't have any Alaska time." (Potential employers place a great deal of emphasis on hiring pilots that have previously flown in Alaska. But it's a catch-2, how are you going to get any Alaska time if no one will hire you?)

"You never know," he answered. "Why don't you send a résumé to Mark Easterly, the Director of Operations at Promech Air? I'll put in a good word for you when I return next week."

And, that's what I did. Two weeks later, I received a call from Mark. We had a pleasant conversation about Promech's operation and discussing my background and experience. He said he normally would not consider anyone with only twelve hours of float time, but he followed up with, "Given your experience, you probably won't hit anything"—meaning a mountain. He said, "Why don't you come up and I'll give you an evaluation ride to see if you can handle the Beaver?"

Arrival in Ketchikan

Based on this less-than-firm job offer, Barbara and I packed four huge roller bags and headed for the far north. Since our flight itinerary routed us through Seattle, I decided to stop by Kenmore Air Harbour to purchase an hour of dual flight instruction in a Beaver on straight-floats (as opposed to amphibious floats with wheels), just like the model I would be flying in Ketchikan—if I passed my evaluation flight, that is. Although it was a bit pricey at $425 per hour, it was a smart decision, as I will relate later in the chapter.

We stepped off the Alaska Airlines B737 in Ketchikan on May 15, 2001. We had been warned that it rained a lot and our advance intel was spot on. We were greeted by a steady rain and low ceilings and visibilities as we tried our best to roll four heavy bags down a steep incline to the ferry landing without being run over by them. The airport is located on Gravina Island, while the city itself is a short distance away on the adjacent island of Revillagigedo. The two islands are separated by the Tongass Narrows, a thin ribbon of water a quarter-mile wide. Other than the airport and a handful of cabins, Gravina is largely uninhabited.

Some may recall the "Bridge to Nowhere" controversy that erupted four years later, when Alaska Governor Sarah Palin and U.S. Senator Ted Stevens proposed building a bridge across the Narrows to spur economic development of Gravina Island by eliminating the cost and time spent waiting for the ferry.

As we crossed the Narrows on a city-owned passenger and car ferry that runs every thirty minutes, and gazed at the quaint frontier town built on the mountainside with cruise ships lining the harbor and floatplanes taking off and landing in random fashion, I said to Barbara, "This is going to be fun! And a great adventure!" As it turned out, it was an adventure, but it wasn't always fun.

Southeast Alaska

The Alaska Panhandle or *Southeast*, as the natives call it, is a narrow strip of mainland and islands five hundred and forty miles long and a hundred and twenty miles wide, stretching from Icy Bay in the north to Dixon Entrance in the south and bounded on the east by British Columbia and

Ferry landing on the airport side of the Tongass Narrows, Ketchikan, Alaska. May 15, 2001

the Pacific Ocean on the west. Much of the area is comprised of the Alexander Archipelago, which contains over two thousand islands, large and small.

Lonely Planet Alaska describes Southeast Alaska as being "so un-Alaska." While the majority of the state is a vast treeless expanse of permafrost, the southeast part of the state is an area of breath-taking beauty comprised of large, old growth forests, snow covered mountains, glaciers, salt water bays, abundant wildlife, and numerous fresh water lakes, rivers, and streams.

Besides the Inside Passage, the other dominant natural feature that pervades most of Southeast Alaska is the Tongass National Forest. At seventeen million acres, it is the largest national forest in the United States by far; the next largest being only seven million acres in Nevada. The forest is a major part of the largest continuous temperate rain forest in the world, with annual rainfall totals exceeding two hundred inches.

Other than local city roads and a few rugged, unpaved logging roads, there was no interconnecting road network in Southeast Alaska. Only three cities on the border with Canada—Haines, Skagway, and Hyder—have a road connection with the outside world. This means that communities large and small can only be accessed by boat or aircraft. For many small villages, a commercial floatplane is their only practical link with civilization, and the means by which they receive food, consumer goods, mail, construction materials, and new outboard motors for their boats.

Ketchikan

Located at the southern entrance to the Inside Passage, Ketchikan is Alaska's fourth largest city with a year-round population of fourteen thousand. However, on any given day in the summer, the population can easily double, depending on the number of tourists that disembark from the large cruise ships docked in the harbor. Founded in 1900, and populated by an influx of fishermen, loggers, and miners, Ketchikan grew rapidly, and was Alaska's largest city by 1930. To "support" all of the men arriving from the lower forty-eight states and elsewhere, a large number of brothels sprung up in the red-light district on Creek Street until prostitution was banned in 1953. In 1920, Ketchikan had the distinction of having the first paved street in Alaska.

Today, due to a number of environmental and market factors, mining and logging have all but disappeared. Once the self-proclaimed "Salmon Capital of the World," commercial fishing has diminished from its peak, but it is still a major player in the local economy, and sport fishing continues to draw a large number of anglers from around the world. Fortunately, tourism and cruise ships have taken up the slack, otherwise Ketchikan would be experiencing significant decline.

One of the main reasons Ketchikan is a popular tourist spot is because the city retains its frontier flavor and the looks of an early-twentieth-century fishing village. Rustic-looking homes and business establishments are built close together along both sides of Tongass Avenue, the main drag that curves along the waterfront. Most structures have a run-down appearance and are badly in need of paint. But instead of being repulsive, they have a certain pastoral charm and aura that simply grabs and captivates.

Content to drive rusted-out cars and pickup trucks, the folks who call Ketchikan home are unpretentious, friendly, and honest. There isn't a lot of crime, but then, that could have something to do with living on an island with limited getaway options. Although residents can purchase just about any consumer product they might want in the stores, trading posts, and supply houses located within the city limits, they will pay at least one third more than they would *down south*, the term the locals use when referring to Washington and Oregon.

The Weather

Ketchikan weather can be summed up in four words: rain and more rain. With an average annual rainfall of one hundred and fifty inches, Ketchikan is one of the wettest spots in the United States; it receives four times the amount of rain that Seattle does. The record, set in 1949, was two hundred and two inches—nearly seventeen feet of *liquid sunshine*, as

Typical weather in the Ketchikan area. Photo taken through the front windshield of my aircraft.

some jokingly refer to the lack of sunny days. A quote from the movie *Forrest Gump* seems to perfectly describe the constant rain: "We been through every kind of rain there is. Little bitty stingin' rain, and big ol' fat rain, rain that flew in sideways, and sometimes rain even seemed to come straight up from underneath." Because of the gloomy days and constant rain, and the fact that Ketchikan is on an island, some locals refer to their hometown as *Ketchitraz*.

The constant drumbeat of miserable weather certainly affects the mood and morale of residents to be sure, but it is not life-threatening. For pilots having to make a living in this environment it's another matter altogether. The typical flying weather involves low clouds and visibilities and a special type of fog called *rain fog*, which consists of very fine mist. In all my years of flying, I never experienced weather that could change so quickly. In less than fifteen minutes, a mountain pass could go from clear to completely socked-in. In most other parts of the world, where low ceilings, visibilities, and fog prevail, the winds are fairly light with little turbulence. Not in the Ketchikan area. Strong winds and huge waves occur frequently on foggy days. Winds of twenty to thirty knots were not uncommon in Ketchikan Harbor. In fact, Promech Air did not suspend flight operations until the wind was blowing steady at forty knots. If the above weather conditions weren't bad enough, we had to contend with turbulence, the likes of which I had never experienced. Being slammed sideways for the first time was a real eye opener. Sudden and violent downdrafts impacting on the water can actually pick up moisture from the surface in swirling air currents, much like a dust devil. The locals call these *williwaws*, and floatplane pilots try their best to avoid them during takeoff and landing.

To say that flying day in and day out in these horrible weather conditions was stressful and dangerous is to understate the obvious. There were many times during my three years flying in the Ketchikan area when I prayed to God to guide me and my passengers to a safe landing. I came close to quitting several times during my first season after surviving particularly harrowing weather encounters. My morale varied from day to day, from extreme highs to extreme lows; mostly depending on the weather. Unfortunately, the weather my first year was exceptionally bad, even by Ketchikan standards, so I didn't experience many high-morale days.

The operating minimums, set by FAA Part 135 regulations that govern VFR air-taxi and charter operators like Promech Air, were five hundred and two, meaning we couldn't fly less than five hundred feet above the surface or when the visibility was less than two statute miles. Recognizing the less-than-ideal prevailing weather conditions in the Ketchikan area, the FAA granted a specific written exemption to floatplane operators there to operate as low as two hundred feet provided the visibility was three miles or greater. At no time could we fly with less than two miles visibility. The truth was, if we abided by these minimums, we would never fly and most of the small communities in Southeast Alaska would wither and die—and the FAA knew it! So, the feds turned a blind eye to our daily transgressions, as did company management.

To avoid incriminating yourself when flying lower than legally allowed, pilots were creative when giving weather reports to other pilots over the radio. Cloud bases reported as "ragged" were actually less than the numerical value given. "Murky" meant that the visibility was less than two miles. One of our competitors used a code whereby the existing weather was obtained by subtracting five hundred and two from that given. One day, when I was brand-new on the line, I reported over the radio that I was flying at three hundred feet. Another company pilot replied, "Mike, don't you mean five hundred feet?" In other words, "Don't put yourself on report," as we used to say in the Navy.

The owner, DO, chief pilot, and dispatchers at Promech Air didn't put any overt pressure on us to fly, but there were various forms of subtle pressure, much of it self-imposed by individual pilots. Some examples: senior, more experienced pilots leading a group of airplanes on a tour saying things like: "Keep coming. It clears up as soon as you round the bend" or "Just hug the left side of the mountain and you'll be okay;" knowing that your company makes most of its money during the summer months; and lastly, pilots, by nature, are mission-oriented and want to get the job done. In his excellent book about flying in Alaska, *Flying North South East and West*, Captain Terry Reece states, "Push the weather to complete your mission and you will be a hero for an hour. Bend an airplane and you will be remembered forever."

In air-taxi operations, where the pilot interfaces directly with the passengers, it is harder to say no or to cancel a flight due to weather. Commercial airline pilots, on the other hand, are insulated from passengers by rigid company procedures, FAA oversight, ramp agents and flight attendants, and a locked, reinforced cockpit door. It is easier to make an objective and dispassionate weather decision within this safe refuge. In every Part 135 job that I have worked, I felt the same pressure to fulfill the "mission." Admittedly, it was self-imposed pressure, but it was real and carried potentially dangerous consequences.

Promech Air

When I joined Promech Air in 2001, it was the largest floatplane operator on the Ketchikan waterfront, with fourteen aircraft and twenty-two full-time and seasonal pilots. The fleet consisted of: three Cessna 185s, five DHC-2 Beavers, three DHC-3 Turbine Otters, and Three DHC-6 Twin Otters. All were mounted on straight floats, except for one Twin Otter that had wheels. Counting pilots, dispatchers, mechanics, dockhands, outlying station agents, tour staff, and office people, the company numbered over one hundred employees. Everyone at Promech was congenial, friendly, and eager to help a greenhorn like me. The seasoned pilots, some who had over twenty thousand flight hours in floatplanes flying in Alaska, were

Promech Air dock in Ketchikan Harbor with three of the four types of floatplanes operated by the company: (l to r) DHC-6 Twin Otter, DHC-3 Turbine Otter, and DHC-2 Beaver (missing is the Cessna 185). Summer 2001

especially helpful in protecting and mentoring new pilots. Other than the weather, it was a great place to work.

The types of flights flown by Promech generally fit into four categories: scheduled air service, tours, fishing-lodge support, and charter. Aside from the occasional long-range charter, all flights remained within a hundred-mile radius of Ketchikan.

Under the air-taxi banner, the company flew regularly scheduled flights to small villages on Prince of Wales Island, with "household names," like Whale Pass, Port Protection, Coffman Cove, Point Baker, Thorne Bay, and Meyers Chuck; carrying passengers, freight, and mail. We also flew to larger settlements, like Craig, Metlakatla, and Hollis on a daily basis.

Two tours generated most of the flights during the summer months and, therefore, most of the company's revenue. The mainstay was a one-hour-and-fifteen-minute tour to the Misty Fiords National Monument that operated during the cruise ship season from May through October. With no roads or trails, and being larger than Yellowstone National Park, Misty Fiords is one of America's great wilderness areas. The tour included, when possible, a landing in a fiord or lake to allow the tourists to get out onto the floats to take pictures and soak in the stunning beauty of mist clinging to the sides of shear rock faces and abundant waterfalls plunging from the tops of three-thousand-foot mountains to the sea below.

The other tour was a bear-viewing excursion to Neat's Bay during the salmon run, which takes place mid-July until the end of August. After a short walk from the floatplane dock, tourists could almost be guaranteed to see numerous black bears catching salmon as the fish swam upstream to spawn. Sometimes the lack of any barrier between bears and people made for an unforgettable Alaskan story, like when tourists got trapped in the restrooms by a bruin that had decided to take a nap in front of the door. Fortunately, the bears had a full stomach and were habituated to humans, so there were never any serious confrontations.

To support the sport-fishing business, a number of all-inclusive lodges that catered to the well-heeled were located in the Ketchikan area. Promech Air had exclusive contracts with two lodges to provide air transportation from the Ketchikan Airport to the resort and back. The larger of the two was Waterfall Resort, located sixty miles west of the airport, near Craig, Alaska. Situated forty miles north of the airport, off the Behm Canal, Yes Bay Lodge was owned and operated by the same family that owned Promech. Servicing these two lodges put additional pressure on the company and its pilots to fly in questionable weather. Incoming guests landing at the airport wanted to get to the lodge as quickly as possible, to perhaps get some fishing in before dinner. They were paying big money and certainly didn't want to spend any of their time waiting in Ketchikan.

Loading a Promech Air Beaver with fish boxes and luggage at Yes Bay Lodge. *(Photo courtesy of Promech Air)*

On the day of their departure, a weather delay could cause them to miss their airline flight out of Ketchikan. So, on bad-weather days, which were most of the time, there was a palpable sense of urgency to fly these guests. Complicating this process was the sheer size of the Waterfall contingent, which sometimes required most of the Promech fleet. It reminded me of a military operation involving multiple aircraft all converging on an enemy target at that same time.

The charter-flight business was both sporadic and varied. Some of the more-common charters included flights to support: fishing and hunting, the timber industry, real estate development, mining, photography, and personal transportation to private homes and National Forest Service cabins. Charter flights were a welcome relief to the monotony of the tours and scheduled service flights.

The duty day for pilots began at 6:00 a.m. and ended at 8:00 p.m. I averaged thirteen hours on duty for the three years I flew for Promech. By FAA regulations, we were limited to eight hours of flying time per day; I averaged five flight hours per day. When the stress of constantly flying in bad weather was factored in, on top of long duty days and the occasional eight hours in the cockpit, I was wiped out by the end of the day. I now understood where the term bush pilots came from; I was plenty bushed by the time I crawled into bed each night. (Actually, the generally accepted definition of bush was anywhere you could not drive out of Alaska using a car or truck.) Mercifully, we worked five days on and two days off. Considering that I was fifty-nine years old my first year in Ketchikan, I don't know how I lasted two more seasons.

For the privilege of living out my fantasy of flying in Alaska, Promech paid me $4,000 per month my first year and $5,000 a month for the next two summers. Getting rich flying in Alaska is a myth perpetuated by pilots who have never flown there, but want to; a modern-day version of gold-rush fever, I suppose

Flying the Mighty Beaver

Most bush pilots consider the DHC-2 Beaver to be the ultimate bush plane: rugged, dependable, able to carry a heavy load, and capable of taking off and landing in a short distance. The first Beaver rolled off the assembly line in 1947, and the last one twenty years later; after 1,692 airplanes had been produced. In between World War II and the Korean War, and before the use of helicopters, the U.S. Army purchased a total of 973 Beavers, which gave de Havilland a needed boost in sales. After Korea, the helicopter was introduced in large numbers and the Army no longer needed the Beaver; consequently, many former military DHC-2s made their way into the civilian market. Most of the Beavers in Promech's fleet were former military aircraft.

The Beaver is an all-metal airplane with a high-lift wing and is powered by a Pratt and Whitney R-985 radial engine producing 450 horsepower. Another reason this airplane was in such high demand for bush operations in Alaska and Canada was because it operated equally well on wheels, floats, and skis.

Over one thousand Beavers are still being flown today, which is remarkable considering the last one was produced over fifty years ago. Many are working bush planes, flying every day in demanding conditions.

Although I had flown the Beaver on wheels towing gliders at the U.S. Naval Test Pilot School fifteen years earlier, it didn't lessen the learning curve much—unless you count the fact that I could spell the name of the manufacturer! With twelve hours of floatplane time and an FAA seaplane rating that I had obtained many years ago, the task for Pat Magie, my flight instructor at Promech, was daunting. Fortunately, he was up to the job and I was highly motivated not to blow my only chance to achieve immortality as an Alaskan bush pilot.

As I was quick to discover, flying a floatplane once it was off the water was just like any other airplane. True, it had more drag, which decreased climb and cruise performance, but in terms of the stick and rudder skills needed to control the aircraft, they were the same. On the water, it was, however, a different story. Nothing in a pilot's previous training or experience can prepare him or her for water operations. In fact, operating a fishing vessel or driving a pontoon boat would be better preparation for handling a floatplane on the water. Being able to safely and efficiently dock and beach a floatplane in varying wind, current, and tide conditions, while avoiding a never-ending variety of obstructions was the hallmark of a good seaplane pilot. I had much to learn and many mistakes to make!

The day after my arrival in Ketchikan, I reported for my first day of work, not knowing what to expect. Since I was provisionally hired over the phone, I had yet to meet anyone from the company. Finding my new employer was not difficult because it was straight down the hill from the B&B where Barbara and I were staying until our small rental house became available. It was a rare sunny day as I crossed Tongass Avenue to a nondescript boxy building on the waterside with a sign that proclaimed "Promech Air" in large green letters. I opened the glass front door and entered a fairly large room that I took to be a waiting area of some sort because it had a number of plastic chairs lining the walls and a few people sitting around with small handbags and luggage at their feet. On the opposite side of the room, just before double glass doors leading to the waterfront, a lady stood behind a curved counter intently scrutinizing some papers lying before her. Figuring this was a good place to start; I approached her and said, "Good morning. My name is Mike Stock, one of the new pilots. I'm looking for Mark Easterly."

About this same time, a short, middle-aged man with close-cropped hair and wearing trousers held up by wide dark-brown suspenders hurried past the counter. "Mark, this is one of your new pilots, Mike Stock," she said.

The Director of Operations spun around in his tracks to face me and broke into a broad smile. "Welcome to Ketchikan, Mike," he responded. "When did you get in?"

"Yesterday afternoon," I replied as I shook his hand.

"Where are you staying?"

"We're staying at the B&B you recommended, at Sherry's place up the hill," I answered.

"Isn't she a real sweetie?" he stated rhetorically.

"Yes, she sure is."

Gesturing toward the counter, Mark said, "Mike, this is Becky, the front-counter supervisor."

"Hi, Becky," I said as I shook her hand.

"She checks in all passengers flying with us on scheduled runs to the outlying villages. So, when you are scheduled to fly one of these trips, you will check in with her or one of the other counter girls to get your manifest. The passengers will be waiting here, in the lobby; so call out the destination and then lead them to your aircraft down on the dock."

Mark led me around, introducing me to other key people in the Promech operation: Kevin Hack, the owner and son of a retired naval aviator;

Darrell and Carrie, aircraft dispatchers; Brian, head of the freight office; and a few pilots who happened to be waiting around the dispatch office for their next assignment.

Back in his office, Mark continued with the informal overview of the company. "One of the key components of any flying outfit, as you well know, is the maintenance department, and we have a good one. It is located in our hangar at Peninsula Point, which is located four miles northwest of here, up the Narrows. We've got seven experienced mechanics working up there doing a fantastic job keeping our airplanes in tip-top shape."

"How do you get the airplanes out of the water and into the hangar to work on them?" I asked.

"The guys back a large trailer down a concrete ramp into the water and you drive the plane up onto the trailer, much like hauling your boat out of the water at a marina. We'll get you checked out on launching and retrieving at Pin Point before we turn you loose to fly the line. It's really a piece of cake," Mark allowed. (As it turned out, it wasn't always a piece of cake, especially in a strong crosswind.)

"Mike, we have a flight going to Waterfall Resort in a few minutes, carrying some freight. I thought you might tag along in the right seat to get a feel for how we do things and to see a little of the countryside at the same time."

"Sounds great, except I didn't bring my headset with me, thinking this would be a paperwork and ground school day," I replied.

"No problem," Mark said. "You can use one of the passenger headsets in the aircraft."

He led me down a very steep ramp to a floating dock and over to a Beaver that was being loaded with food and other essentials by two men. "Steve, I'd like you to meet Mike Stock, one of our new summer pilots," Mark said, as he stopped in front of a tall, lean blonde-haired fellow wearing a green shirt with a Promech logo on the front and a pair of brown Carhartt pants—which I soon found out was the unofficial uniform trouser worn by all pilots working on the Ketchikan waterfront, no matter what company.

"Hi, Steve. Pleasure to meet you," I said.

Acting like this was a chance encounter, when it had actually been prearranged unbeknownst to me, Mark said, "Steve, I'd like Mike to tag along, if it's okay with you. He may not get many sunny days like this to witness our spectacular scenery." Mark laughed as he gestured to the blue sky. Oh, how right he was!

"No problem, boss," Steve replied. "In fact, Mike, why don't you grab a headset from the cabin and crawl up into the right seat? We're just about ready to shove off."

Talk about new sights and sounds. My goodness! There was a lot to take in: being turned out and held by the dock-boy until the engine was started; then taxiing in the busy harbor, trying to avoid other floatplanes and a variety of water traffic; calling the FAA Flight Service Station (FSS) located at the airport and requesting a "west departure from the harbor"; finding a clear takeoff path on the water; and then, turning to the northwest after liftoff while adhering to prescribed routes and altitudes until clear of the Tongass Narrows. It seemed hectic and thrilling.

Leaving the hustle and bustle of Ketchikan behind, we flew across Clarence Straight toward Prince of Wales Island. Steve Kahm, an easygoing and upbeat individual in his late thirties, proved to be an excellent tour guide. His running commentary proved to be a perfect exclamation point to the gorgeous vistas that paraded by our windows. Blue skies blended harmoniously with tree-covered mountains flowing down to various bodies of saltwater with romantic-sounding names like Twelve Mile Arm, Trocadero Bay, and Port Estrella. Finally, a bunch of white buildings came into view. It looked like a factory of some sort. Steve identified the cluster of structures as being the Waterfall Resort, and stated that it was a fish cannery at one time. After unloading our freight, we headed back to Ketchikan, empty.

About halfway back, Steve landed in the middle of a lake, lowered the water rudders, and shut the engine off. He turned to me and said, "Would you like to fly?"

"You bet I would," I answered.

Steve unstrapped and slid into the middle seat in the cabin and motioned for me to get into the left seat. This particular Beaver did not have a dual-yoke, so all flying was done from the left seat. As I fastened my lap belt and shoulder harness, Steve got into the copilot's seat. I then proceeded to make three takeoffs and landings in the same lake, and did some step taxiing. After my third landing, we swapped seats and Steve flew back to Ketchikan.

About a half hour after landing, Mark caught up with me and said with a big smile on his face, "Well, you passed your evaluation flight with Steve. He said that you handled the airplane real well."

Pleased, but a little surprised nonetheless, I responded, "That's great."

"Sneaky, huh?" Mark said with a chuckle. "With that little matter out of the way, the next step will be to hook you up with Pat Magie, one of our senior pilots, to get some ground and flight training under your belt. Then you can take a Part 141 standardization ride. Following that, I'll fly with you for some IOE (Initial Operating Experience) and, when I think you're ready, we'll let you start earning your paycheck as a line pilot."

"Sounds great, Mark. When do I start?"

"I'll check with Pat and one of us will get back to you. In the meantime, let's go over to the business office to start the paperwork process. On our way, we'll get you a couple of uniform shirts and a Promech ball cap."

The next two days were spent in ground school with a couple other new pilots, studying aircraft systems, computing weight and balance, and learning Promech standard operating procedures; all familiar topics in every ground school I'd ever taken in the past. There was one subject, however, that was brand-new to me: handling hazardous materials or HazMat; items like gasoline and other flammable liquids, batteries, aerosol cans, acid, propane tanks, and paint. A separate part of the Federal Aviation Regulations pertains to the transportation of HazMat by air carriers, and since Promech was an air carrier that transported HazMat, all pilots had to be well versed in the proper procedures and paperwork involved. Not only could there be substantial risk to safety of the aircraft and occupants if the dangerous materials were improperly handled, but there were significant legal consequences and stiff fines if the regulations were not followed to the letter.

After completing ground training, I spent the better part of one day with Magie, learning the subtle nuances of flying the Beaver. Appropriately, we spent most of the time making takeoffs and landings in a variety of wind and water conditions in different nearby bodies of water. More importantly, he coached me in useful techniques to use when docking crosswind or downwind. He also stressed the importance of knowing whether the tide was coming in or going out when beaching. "Mike, with an average difference of twenty-four feet between high and low tide, you can readily see what will happen if you are beached somewhere and you leave your airplane or don't pay attention. If the tide is coming in, it will float your airplane away. Even worse, if the tide is going out, it will leave your airplane high and dry until the next high tide, approximately twelve hours later. In either case, the boss is not going to be happy."

"Gosh, I never thought about the tide. That could get really ugly in a hurry," I groaned. "Thanks for the heads up."

He added, "You don't have to worry much about tides when tied up to a dock because most docks are floating structures."

Pat also passed along a useful tidbit regarding fuel management in the Beaver that made me distinctly uncomfortable when he first showed me. We were using fuel from the center tank, which was reading five gallons; so I asked, "How accurate are the fuel gauges in the Beaver?"

"Very, let me show you. When the needle drops to zero, wait until it stops bouncing, then switch tanks," he stated authoritatively. We proceeded to do exactly that, but I was skeptical because fuel gauges in aircraft are notorious for being inaccurate. Sure enough, after the needle dropped to zero and stopped bouncing, I switched to the forward tank and the engine never missed a beat. And that, is why I always believed experience trumps the flight manual. Pat shared many other tricks and bits of wisdom he had gained from thousands of hours flying the mighty Beaver. I couldn't have asked for a better teacher.

At one point during a break in our training, Pat happened to mention that he was a contract instructor for the Cessna Caravan on floats and that he had been all over the world teaching new owners how to fly their airplane. On one particular contract he was in Madagascar, a large island nation off the southeast coast of Africa. It was a very hot humid day and he and his client were taking a break sitting on the left float of the airplane with their legs and feet dangling in the water. All of a sudden a huge crocodile erupted out of the water just to the left of where Pat was sitting. With its jaws wide open, the monster lunged forward just missing the two men. Shaken, they decided to take the rest of the day off.

Thankfully, I didn't have to worry about crocodiles in Alaska, but then there were bears that could be equally determined. Another senior Promech pilot, Dale Clark, told me a frightening story of the day he was ahead of schedule and needed to kill a little time. So, he decided to land in the lake below him, shut down the engine, and take a short nap. As he was setting up to land, he happened to notice a black bear swimming across the lake. After landing, Dale decided to check the bear out, so he taxied slowly in front of the bruin on a course perpendicular to the bear's. Well, the bear apparently was not amused because the beast suddenly attacked the rear of the left float ripping out a chunk of aluminum and damaging the water rudder. Moral of the story: give bears a wide berth no matter where they might be.

After a rest break, Pat put on his check-airman hat and put me through the paces of an FAA Part 141 standardization checkride. Passing that, it was on to a series of IOE flights, with Mark Easterly sitting in the right seat, observing while I went about flying actual line flights. After four days of IOE and nearly twelve hours of flight time going to places that were all new to me, like Metlakatla, Hollis, Kasan, Craig, the Pullout, and a few Misty Fiords tours, Mark pronounced I was good to go and turned me loose on my own. My sometimes funny, oftentimes brutal, education of learning to be an Alaskan bush pilot was about to begin.

Initial Impressions and Near Mishaps

There were a number of things about flying floatplanes in general, and out of Ketchikan in particular, that my previous aviation experience did not prepare me for. Reporting for work the day after my surprise evaluation flight, I noticed three Beavers tied up at the dock, nose-to-tail, with their engines running at idle. Upon closer inspection, I was shocked to realize there was no one sitting in the cockpit. Leaving an engine running without a pilot or authorized mechanic inside the cockpit was unheard of where I came from. I soon learned that here, on cold mornings, it was the norm before the first flight of the day to warm up the engine, so that takeoff could commence shortly after leaving the dock.

For the first several days, from force of habit, I kept trying to apply "brakes" while taxiing, especially in tight quarters. Once the engine was started and a seaplane was cut loose from the dock, it will move forward even at idle power unless heading into a strong headwind. Approaching a crowded dock without brakes, it was easy to get yourself in a jam. Sometimes the only option was to shut down the engine and let the wind push you back (called "sailing") or grab the paddle strapped to the float and use it to fend off obstructions you were about to hit. Seaplane pilots had to think much farther ahead of the airplane than their landplane brethren. I was learning—slowly and sometimes the hard way!

"Blipping" the mags was another technique that landplane pilots didn't have—or need—in their bag of tricks because they had brakes. If a Beaver was approaching a crowded dock situation too fast, even with the engine at idle, a pilot could switch the mags off, killing the engine for several seconds, and then back on before the engine died completely. By doing this repeatedly, the speed of the airplane could be slowed appreciably. For any would-be seaplane pilots reading this, please understand this method only works for a radial engine with a large propeller acting as a giant flywheel. Do this with a horizontally opposed engine and you will kill the engine completely. True, you will slow down, but maybe too much and not have enough momentum to reach the dock.

Unlike the pilot in a land-airplane, who fastens his or her seatbelt before ever setting the aircraft in motion, seaplane pilots usually buckle-up once they are well clear of all obstructions and just before takeoff. This allows the pilot to hop out quickly if necessary, to fend off or keep from contacting a piling, a dock, a boat, or another airplane. After landing and before heading into a congested area, a seaplane pilot, likewise, unstraps to be ready to deal with the unexpected.

Docking a floatplane by yourself, without anyone on land to "catch you," can be a tricky maneuver, ranging from simple embarrassment to downright danger. The idea was to nimbly jump from the left float of your airplane to the dock with a float-rope in your hands and then to quickly tie off to a cleat, bringing the airplane to a stop before hitting a piling or the airplane in front of you. Because it was usually necessary to make last-minute steering adjustments using the water rudders, a pilot must, at the last possible moment, shut down the engine and then quickly jump out of the cockpit onto the float, grab a rope, and hop onto the dock from a moving airplane. The timing of this delicate ballet was critical: if the engine was shut down too early, the aircraft could weathercock into the wind; if too late, the aircraft might hit something or sail past the end of the dock, requiring the pilot to hurriedly restart the engine and try again. During IOE, I couldn't figure out why I had significant bruising on my left leg. I eventually realized it was from the constant sliding out of the cockpit. To avoid that pain, I learned how to jump out of the cockpit onto the float instead of sliding out.

During my first few weeks, I made some major docking blunders. Fortunately, I didn't damage or lose an airplane, or injure myself or any passengers. One time, I hopped out of the cockpit onto the float and up on the dock without first grabbing the rope attached to the float. I hurriedly jumped back on the float crawled back into the cockpit and started the engine to try again.

Another time, at the Ketchikan Airport dock, a passenger alerted me to the fact that my airplane had become untied and was drifting away. I was just about to jump in and swim after it when a dockhand managed to grab a handling rope attached near the wingtip. Later, when recounting this event to Mark, he warned me to never attempt to swim after an airplane that was drifting away. He said that hypothermia would overtake me in a matter of minutes. Pilots have drowned doing that. He told me to let the airplane go. It would eventually drift to a stop somewhere and could then be retrieved.

One day, as I was approaching the Promech dock in Ketchikan Harbor, I didn't notice a steel cable hanging down to the water from a large commercial fishing boat tied up to the fish cannery next door. My airplane contacted the cable about three feet from the end of the left wingtip, which suddenly pivoted the plane ninety degrees to the left, headed straight into the side of the fishing vessel. I immediately turned off the mags to shut down the engine as the hard-rudder bumper on the front of the left float contacted the side of the hull. Some seamen working down by the waterline managed to untangle me from the cable and gave me a shove. Then, the wind took over and the airplane slowing drifted into some pilings a quarter mile away, where it came to a stop. Luckily, there was no damage to the airplane and I was soon towed back to the Promech dock.

Taking off and landing in Ketchikan Harbor was always challenging. At times, it was the busiest seaplane harbor in the world in terms of the number and variety of watercraft all jockeying for position. During peak tourist season, it was common to have ten to fifteen floatplanes trying to take off and land at the same time; with no control tower and only

Standing on the left float of a de Havilland Beaver on the Promech dock in Ketchikan Harbor, I'm all checked out and ready to fly the line. May 2001

individual pilot awareness and courtesy to maintain separation and to keep aircraft from colliding. Since there were no designated water lanes for seaplane use only, pilots also had to contend with large cruise ships; marine ferries, especially the airport ferry that crossed the Narrows, oblivious to any seaplane landing or taking off; commercial fishing boats; pleasure craft, including jet skis, sailboats, and kayaks; and floating logs dislodged from the shore by high tides. And if that wasn't enough chaos, pilots also had to dodge hundreds of seagulls and bald eagles circling a small area in the harbor where fish heads and entrails from a large fish cannery floated to the surface from an underwater discharge pipe. The only bird strikes I ever had occurred in Ketchikan Harbor—two seagulls and one bald eagle.

Added to this mix were four-foot high waves, ocean swells, riptides, swift water currents, wakes caused boats and seaplane, and wake turbulence from departing floatplanes. Also, moderate to severe turbulence and extremely strong downdrafts were caused by winds blowing down from the mountain tops and ridges that surrounded the harbor, oftentimes gusting well over thirty knots.

Because of all these hazards and the narrow confines of the harbor, we were seldom able to land directly into the wind, which necessitated crosswind landings in high winds and less than ideal sea conditions. Some of the old pilots who had flown seaplanes around the world said, "If you can fly seaplanes out of Ketchikan Harbor, you can fly them anywhere."

In reading this chapter and the next devoted to flying in Alaska, you will come across numerous references to *glassy water* landings along with the implication that these operations were stressful and potentially dangerous. So, perhaps, I ought to explain why.

In any landing on land or water, a pilot relies on depth perception to judge the height above the landing surface, which in turn dictates the flight control and throttle inputs necessary to effect a smooth and safe touchdown. Smooth or "glassy" water negates the normal visual cues that a pilot uses to determine height above touchdown. In other words, normal depth perception is severely compromised even to the extent of providing a false sense that the aircraft is higher than it actually is. Consequently, a seaplane pilot may delay raising the nose of the aircraft to the proper landing attitude, which could result in a very hard landing or cause the aircraft to flip over on its back. This is what happened to me in the story related at the beginning of this chapter.

Since commercial seaplane pilots are confronted by glassy water conditions on a daily basis, how do they manage the risk? First, they recognize the inherent danger and plan accordingly. Second, they take advantage of any nearby land features, like a shoreline, that provide a substitute height reference. And finally, they set the landing attitude early during the approach to land and then use engine power to establish and maintain approximately a 150 feet-per-minute rate of descent all the way to water touchdown; in essence flying the seaplane onto the water without any flare just before touchdown, as would normally be the case when landing on a runway.

First Month on the Line

My first month on the job was a learning experience of epic proportions and one that I do not care to repeat. With a grand total of twenty-three hours of seaplane time before I flew my first solo line flight, I also needed to learn how to fly a floatplane without killing my passengers or myself. As I stated at the beginning of this chapter: the experience was an adventure, but it wasn't always fun.

Having lots of grey hair in my business usually equates to having lots of pilot experience, justified or not. Such was the case on the occasion of my very first trip to the Misty Fiords as pilot in command. After collecting my seven passengers and leading them down the gangway to the dock, I overhead an older lady in my group say to her traveling companion, "At least we've got an experienced pilot." I assumed that her point of reference was just having passed baby-faced, blonde-haired Ryan McCue, our youngest pilot at age twenty-six, who looked more like eighteen. If only she knew that Ryan had two years' experience and lots of floatplane time while I had virtually none.

My goal when I started flying the line was to finish the summer without *bending any metal*. The horrible weather, flying in mountainous terrain, not knowing exactly where I was most of the time, and being new to floatplanes and the Beaver in particular, made that goal seem unattainable at times. And it did not help my confidence or mental state during IOE when Mark would say things like, "I can't count how many funerals I've been to in Ketchikan over the years," or "So and so killed himself when he hit that peak right over there," or "So and so bought the farm down there when he aborted the landing too late."

Since I left Promech after the 2004 season, there have been three Ketchikan-based floatplanes involved in fatal accidents, two of which occurred during Misty Fiord tours that killed everyone onboard. Reading both accident reports sent shivers up my spine because I knew exactly where they crashed. I could easily relate to their predicament as they flew into low clouds because the same thing had happened to me except I survived and they didn't. The accident rate for pilots flying in Alaska is very high compared with statistics for the rest of the United States. I admit that knowing the risks took some of the luster away from my Alaskan fantasy.

Let's shift gears, away from doom and destruction, and talk about a topic that is equally dear to the hearts of bush pilots who fly paying customers—TIPS! We certainly don't require a tip for flying you from Point A to Point B, any more than an airline pilot would expect to be tipped for flying you from Phoenix to Miami. However, when we fly you on an aerial tour and go out of our way to show you interesting things and provide stimulating and interesting narration, a tip is much appreciated. To be fair, tipping never crosses the minds of some tourists. If it did, many would be happy to give their pilot a tip. On the other hand, some people are just cheap and give you the dreaded "naked handshake" as they climb out of the aircraft. While others seem to go out of their way to advance their warped agenda by giving pilots a single dollar bill.

Many of the pilots at Promech were creative in their subtle and not-so-subtle approaches to generating tips. Some pilots went out of their way to point out wildlife, real or imagined. One of our pilots, with a great sense of humor, would say over the radio for all to hear, "And if you look closely at the bend in the creek, you'll see a herd of armadillos." Others tried to be chatty and witty. Some pilots took a direct approach: holding up a sign that read: "Please don't feed the bears, but you may tip the pilot; "If you have any suggestions on ways to improve this tour, write them down on the back of a twenty-dollar bill and give them to me when you leave." And one pilot asked his passengers just before they deplaned, "Did you see any bears?" If they said "no," he would poke his head out of the cockpit wearing a stuffed bear hat.

I didn't feel comfortable using these direct approaches. It felt like I was prostituting myself. And besides, it seemed to me that no matter what I did or said, it didn't produce any more tips. So, I gave up trying.

After one particularly stressful bad-weather day, I was standing in Dispatch when another pilot asked me if I had gotten any tips that day. I responded, "Hell no! I'm just trying to get back alive." It cracked the whole place up. I was dead serious.

At the end of my first month, I was so stressed and frazzled with the experience, especially having to deal with lousy weather day in and day out, I wasn't sure I would stay the full three months. Gradually, I became more comfortable in the Beaver and flying a floatplane and I began to recognize land references, so I didn't feel lost all of the time.

And, every now and then, the skies would clear to reveal some of the most amazing and compelling vistas on the planet. With brilliant sunshine

A not so subtle sign used by one of the Promech Air pilots to encourage tipping.

streaming into the cockpit and cool mountain air flowing into my lungs, my spirit soared and the bad days faded long enough to repair my fragile psyche and to stiffen my determination to finish what I had started.

Snippets from Ketchikan

When combining the three volumes of *The Reluctant Aviator* into this single book, *Chasing the Four Winds*, I had to trim a lot of the original manuscript; one of the casualties were many of the diary entries pertaining to Ketchikan and Anchorage. I have, however, kept a few pertinent diary entries titled *Snippets* in this book.

I have carefully chosen diary entries from all three years at each location that not only describe the job itself, but also those that capture a range of emotions that infused and guided my behavior and actions as a pilot. Where necessary for clarity, I have included background information in italics.

Ketchikan—May to August 2001

May 25—First day on the line. Mistakes: 1. Attempted takeoff without flaps on a Misty. 2. Very long takeoff at Metlakatla, probably over gross weight. 3. Took off from airport dock and landed in harbor with water rudders down; cost me a case of beer. 4. Dropped sunglasses in water. 5. Headed to wrong dock at Metlakatla on second trip.

In professional floatplane circles, it is standard practice if you are caught taking off or landing with your water rudders down, it will cost you a case of beer. For example, in Anchorage all the pilots from the different operators at Lake Hood got together one day after work each season for a "Water Rudder Party" paid for by those who got caught. In the six seasons I flew in Alaska, I bought a case of beer each season, sometimes more than one, much to my dismay. You knew you had been caught when another pilot would say over the radio for all the world to hear, "Are they dry yet?"

May 27—Due to a last-minute change by Dispatch, instead of going direct Craig, I had to stop at Thorne Bay first. A male passenger became very irate because he had been told this was going to be a direct flight to Craig and in a faster Turbine Otter. To pacify him, I let him sit in the copilot's seat, but he kept loudly complaining. I told him if he didn't calm down, I would have him removed from the aircraft. The entire time we were flying to Thorne Bay (*twenty-minute flight*) he was looking at his watch and shaking his head. Then on takeoff, heading for Craig, the only way I knew (via Harris River), he said I was going the wrong way. (Actually, there was a shortcut, but I didn't know about it.) I was so distracted by the time I arrived for a crosswind landing in Craig Harbor that I didn't notice I was drifting right at touchdown and nearly buried the right float causing the aircraft to violently pitch forward and bank right. Not a good day.

It was one of two times I came close to flipping an airplane during my six seasons flying in Alaska. Had the right tip contacted the water the airplane most likely would have cartwheeled.

June 8—Busiest day yet, 7.0 hrs flight time, but it's not fun flying— very stressful. I can't relax for a minute, so many dangers lurking. My landings were OK, bounced a couple. But the most stress are the Misty Fiord tour flights. In was very turbulent in there in the PM with white-caps in Rudyerd Bay. My first Misty, I landed downwind accidentally and the bottom dropped out during the flare. Only a sudden burst of power kept us from hitting very hard. The takeoff was a tight turn at 100 feet off the water, not fun and actually rather dangerous. On the third tour, I decided to land in Punch Bowl Cove, but the downdrafts getting there were very severe. At one point I thought we might be forced into the water with max power applied. The landing was okay, but the wind was so strong that I had rush the passengers back into the airplane and restart the engine twice to keep from drifting to shore. Consequently, I was late getting back to town. On a trip to Met (*Metlakatla*), when I tried to switch to the front fuel tank, the water rud-ders were in the way. In trying to reposition them they slipped out of my hand and a cable jumped off a pulley such that I couldn't raise my water rudders before landing. I couldn't steer very well once I was on the harbor. Both my wife and I are counting the days until this Alaska adventure is over. Hope the fun will start soon!

In addition to the stress of horrible weather, very strong turbulence, and glassy water, the Misty Fiords' tours were tightly scheduled. Each pilot was allotted one hour and fifteen minutes to fly to Rudyerd Bay, land, and allow passengers a few minutes on the floats to take pictures, and fly back to Ketchikan. In the fifteen minutes between docking and the next flight, the line boys had to refuel each airplane and clean the airplane's windows of salt spray. It was not uncommon to have six Misty tours scheduled each day, with five or six aircraft on each timeslot. Because cruise ships usually departed between five and seven p.m., passengers had to be on board or they would be left behind. So, there was enormous pressure on the whole Promech operation to maintain this insanely tight schedule because this was how the company made most of its revenue for the entire year.

July 8—Another rainy day with very strong gusty winds. I experienced my first aborted flight. I flew to Met and winds were 18 gusting to 25. The waves would have been OK, but there were big swells too, so I came back to town. A flight to Waterfall was fairly nasty as well. Very turbulent on the way, but extreme gusty conditions in the bay. The landing wasn't too bad, but the takeoff was my most hairy to date because of the swells and gusts. I touched back down on the water two times before being launched by a big wave and I was finally able to stay in the air. A passenger said to me as he was getting off the airplane back in KTN, "How do you fly in this stuff? It must be very stressful." I said that it was. He thanked me very sincerely for getting them back safely and promptly reached into his pocket and gave me a $20 tip.

July 12—Another horrible weather day. I really don't know how these full-time pilots do it day in and day out year round. I simply couldn't do it. I would work at Burger King instead. I am very thankful that I have a safe comfortable job to go back to at the end of the summer (NMC).

August 3—Foggy in AM, but cleared up, partly cloudy and sunny. The a/c I was supposed to fly was fogged in at Craig, so I flew in another airplane to Hollis and then took a Promech van overland to Craig. Interesting to see some of Prince of Wales Island from a different perspective. I took off from Craig going to Waterfall to pick up some fish boxes.

If a guest wanted to ship the fish that he/she caught to their home, the lodge would pack the fish in ice in a special cardboard box. Promech would then fly these boxes to Ketchikan Airport. Each box weighed close to eighty pounds, so loading and unloading a Beaver with a full load of fish boxes was not a pilot's favorite task.

When I arrived at Waterfall, the whole bay was completely fogged in except for a very narrow strip of open water on the far side of the bay. I was a little hesitant about descending through the narrow opening because there could have been a fishing boat or a floating log that I wouldn't be able to see until I got below the clouds. After landing, I turned in the general direction of the lodge, but immediately ran in to very thick fog. I could only see about 50 feet ahead. I thought I may have been going the wrong direction, so I turned on my GPS about the same time that Gail on the dock called me on the radio to say they could hear me and that I needed to turn more to the north. After ten minutes or so, I finally groped my way to the dock. Overall a good day. Hit a seagull landing in the harbor at KTN.

August 18—Great day. A few scattered showers, but mostly sunny. Even saw the first towering cumulous clouds I've seen all summer. Saw a humpback whale breeching in Clarence Straight. What a sight! *(Jim Cagle had a terrifying experience taking off one day from Waterfall Resort. Immediately after he broke water, a humpback whale breeched right in front of his aircraft, nearly hitting him.)*

August 19—Last day of work! A real easy day, although I was hoping for a busy one. I started at 0800 and finished by 1600. Only flew two Mets and a Waterfall. All of my landings were good including my last one in the harbor with a strong crosswind and some wave and swell action; I had to work for it. I didn't know when I returned from Met that it would be my last flight. It was appropriate and ironic that my first trip as a line pilot and my last would be to Metlakatla. The past three months are sort of like life itself: all of a sudden, it's over.

Two pilots each had a cake made for me. One from Jim Cagle said, "Congratulations, Mike." Being a nostalgic person, it was a sad day because I probably won't come back next year, although it is always an option. And, who knows, I may never fly a Beaver on floats again. Promech has a tradition of throwing people in the harbor on their last day of work. I was ready for it—wallet and watch in my backpack. But they didn't throw me in. Maybe they had pity on the old man or maybe they figured they would have to jump in to save me. Anyway, I'm glad they didn't.

After arriving back home in Traverse City, I wrote the following letter to my colleagues in Ketchikan, dated September 2, 2001:

To the Pilots and Staff of Promech,

It has been nearly two weeks since I left Ketchikan. I have been back to work at the college now for a week and classes begin this coming Tuesday. Besides teaching Private and Instrument Ground School courses, I am also teaching a new course (for me) called Advanced Systems. So, life is busy at the moment, but that's the way I like it.

It has been a dream of mine for many years to fly in Alaska and I want to thank all of you for providing an experience of a lifetime. To Kevin and Mark, for taking a chance on a guy who only had 12 total hours of float time. To all of the pilots for always being so willing to give me some needed advice or drawing a sketch of a new location. To the schedulers and dispatchers, for lengthening my tether gradually by matching my ability and experience to the mission. To the front counter folks, for keeping my passengers straight and reminding me to go to the airport for a pick-up. To the freight guys and gals, for getting my freight to the dock on time and showing me ways to load my aircraft better. To the dock hands who refueled and "mystified" my aircraft, pumped my floats, and helped me load freight all without complaint. To the tour gals for patiently awaiting my return on those Misty flights early in the season as I was refining my timing. To the maintenance crew for keeping the aircraft in tiptop condition and launching and retrieving me at the pullout. And lastly, to the gals in the office, that took care of my paperwork, especially my paycheck. I can honestly say that everyone was very friendly and helpful. It was indeed a pleasure to work with all of you.

As far as my plans for next summer, time will tell. If you would have asked me at the end of June if I would be coming back next summer, I would have said, "Not only no, but hell no!" But after I began to learn the area, gain experience on the water and in the Beaver, and the weather improved thus raising my level of comfort, I am at least willing to consider returning next summer. It will depend on my situation at that time.

Whatever happens next year, I want all of you to know that I consider you to be my good friends. If you are ever passing through Michigan, I would be honored if you would give me a call or stop by for a visit. I am in the phonebook. Thank you again for a most enjoyable summer experience.

Warm regards,
Mike Stock

Ketchikan – May to August 2002

It is amazing how much I forgot in a year's time. All of those horrible weather days in Ketchikan, when I struggled to remain clear of the clouds and fog; surrounded by mountainous terrain, were distant memories. All of the takeoffs and landings on glassy water or in huge waves and ocean swells, when I feared for the safety of my passengers and my airplane were no longer cause for concern. So, when a possible job flying helicopters out of Homer, Alaska, failed to materialize, I decided to return to Promech and try it again.

May 24—First day back on the line. Started off with a Misty and a Boat-fly. Then went to the airport dock to pick up two pax for Met. I decided to land west, which was about 8 kt downwind for convenience, and attempted to tie up on the outside face by myself—no dockhand. As soon as I got out, I grabbed ahold of the front strut rope and jumped onto the dock, the wind and current started to pivot the airplane to the left. I jumped back onto the float trying to salvage the docking and then thought about jumping back to the dock, but slipped and fell into the water. It wasn't as cold as I thought, but then I wasn't in long either. I grabbed onto the rear float strut and pulled myself back onto the float skinning my right forefinger in the process. So bleeding and soaking wet, I hopped into the cockpit to start the a/c which was drifting into the shipping channel. I got it started and turned the airplane around and tied up to the inside of the dock facing into the wind. Nobody saw me fall in, thank goodness. So, soaking wet, I loaded my passengers and flew to Met. I wonder what they were thinking. Maybe they thought I jumped in to cool off—but then, Alaskans didn't get too excited about anything. I loaded some passengers at Met and flew to town. I had about ten minutes before my next flight, so I ran across the street and up the stairs to the B&B and changed clothes. Word of my dunking spread quickly and everyone got a big laugh out of it. I flew all last year without falling in (came close twice) and here on my first day back, I do it. I went on to fly 6.7 hours today. It was gorgeous and sunny.

May 29—Rain. Slow day at work, one Misty (the long way around Alva). Jim Hall *(Jim was one of Promech's senior pilots and a heck of a nice guy)* rode along *(brave man without flight controls)* into Meyers Chuck for my first time in there. It is one of the smallest places we go into and it was a minus tide today *(meaning below normal low tide)*. It will be a real challenge, but I think I can handle it. Mark let one of the new pilots go today. I guess he wasn't cutting the mustard. I really felt bad for him because his wife had quit a good job and was driving to Alaska.

Meyers Chuck deserves a little digression; not only because a pilot has to be on his game to fly into its narrow confines, but also because of its character and charm.

Located twenty-six miles north of Ketchikan on the eastern coastline of Clarence Straight, Meyers Chuck is representative of many of the tiny communities that cling to existence throughout Southeast Alaska. The 2000 census listed twenty-one residents, but that's only in the summer. In the winter, the number drops to as low as five. In the 1930s, Meyers Chuck was a booming fishing village of one hundred, with a general store, barbershop, bakery, a bar, a school, and a post office. Today, only the post office is left and the town is slowly withering as its older inhabitants die or move away.

Since the post office is the lone remaining public building, it serves a dual purpose of also being a social-gathering place, especially when the weekly mail plane in the form of a Promech Beaver arrives. The postmistress signals that the mail is ready for pick up by hoisting the American flag on a pole outside the post office. In addition to mail, Promech also provides the inhabitants of Meyers Chuck a reliable connection with Ketchikan and other small villages on Prince of Wales Island.

Landing and taking off in Meyers Chuck is always a thrill and sure to get the adrenaline pumping. Due to its banana shape and tree-studded, rocky shoreline, the seawater basin only has about 1,250 feet of usable landing distance with a slightly longer distance available for takeoff—and that's at high tide. Because of the steep sides to the basin, at low tide there is even less water available. It is like landing in a large bathtub. Due to its layout and obstructions, landings are usually made to the south and takeoffs are made to the north regardless of wind direction. To put it simply, operating to and from Meyers Chuck in a floatplane is a sporting proposition.

May 30—Rain. Busy day. Flew 6.6 hrs of steady work loading and offloading cargo. It is nice to be a returning pilot. Gives you some credibility with the locals as well as self-confidence. It is surprising how much better I feel this year. I guess I made so many mistakes last year that I don't have to repeat them again. When I got home tonight, I felt as if the house was rocking; I'd been in a rocking and rolling seaplane all day.

June 1—Rain half day. Started off this morning with vis about 2 and low ceilings. I was dispatched to Thorne Bay and Hollis with one gal from town who started out complaining to the ticket counter that one of our pilots scared her real bad the other day because she thought he was "hot dogging." On the way to our a/c she kept saying she was scared and wasn't sure if she should go or not. She kept this up in the airplane until I told her that I have been flying for 39 years and that I didn't want to die either. She calmed down and later thanked me for a great flight. Some people are so scared to fly that they become ill.

I got my first charter this year. I took a young fellow to Pond Bay (south of Met) to pick up some camping gear that had been helicoptered in. Well, we found the location OK and I landed and beached the a/c on a rather steep gravel beach. The tide was coming in so I had to keep tightening a rope tied to the front cleat on the left float to keep it from floating away. Then he and I humped all this camping equipment: huge tents, tables, a generator, etc, and loaded it into the a/c. It took about an hour and fifteen minutes of hard work. I was beat. We then took off and flew to town and offloaded it. Then I had to clean all of the sand and gravel out of the airplane. It was a long day 12½ hrs. *Being a bush pilot isn't all glamourous folks!*

June 15—Overcast, but no rain. Good day. Went to some new places. Steady flying 6.3 hrs. Flew to Port Protection on the northern tip of Prince of Wales Island to pick up 4 pax. I had never been there before, so I asked one of the pilots to draw me a little diagram. It is a small place to land, but I landed in the mouth of a small cove, which sits right on the ocean, so it gets a lot of ocean swell. I landed OK and started taxiing in the cove wondering which dock to go to. Finally, I saw 5 people standing on a very small dock, so I figured that must be the one. It was such a small dock that I had to nose the a/c in on the right front float. I taxied out to the mouth again because I thought I couldn't just blast out of the cove and disturb all of the fishermen, etc. *(As it turns out, pilots do exactly that.)* Well on takeoff I encountered those swells again and the airplane took a beating as it was continually being launched into the air before it had flying speed and then slammed back on the water. I was beginning to wonder if I could do this. It was scary! I learned as I went and figured I should lower the nose a little each time I was launched to gain a little more airspeed. Finally, to my relief I got airborne. Probably to my passengers' relief as well, although they didn't say anything.

Later in the day I flew to Meyers Chuck for the first time alone. My pulse quickened a lot. There was a Canadian sailboat anchored right in the middle of the basin. The landing wasn't much of a problem, but the takeoff was very tight. But a confidence builder. Good day. Felt like I was a real working Beaver pilot who can accomplish some hard jobs.

June 30—Rain. Steady day of flying. Went to Meyers Chuck again, getting comfortable in that small place. On first trip to Craig, I took the wrong valley west of Holis by mistake thinking it was the Harris River. It was raining very hard so I couldn't see that well, but it didn't look right. Well, I got to the end of a box canyon and had to turn around. I doubt I will make that mistake again. *(Many pilots have died trying to turn around in a box canyon that was too small.)* Then on takeoff from Craig, I decided to take off downwind with a 12-15 knot tailwind. Boy, it's a good thing I had plenty of water because it took forever to get off. I won't do that again either.

July 11—Sunny. Landing at Beaver Falls fish cannery I tried to dock downwind, which is tough. I got lined up, jumped out quickly and tried to grab the center float strut rope, but in my haste to jump to the dock, I missed the rope. With the plane rapidly pulling away, luckily I was able to jump back on the float and restart the engine. On another flight to Whale Pass I almost ran aground at low tide. Every day is an adventure on the water.

My morale was much better this year than last year. There were several factors for this turnaround: better flying weather in 2002 than in 2001; I knew my way around the area better, so I didn't have to rely on my map or GPS as much; I was more comfortable flying the Beaver; and I had more experience on the water, which after all, is the hallmark of a good seaplane pilot.

Ketchikan—May to August 2004

As recounted in chapter 25, in January 2003, I decided to pursue a sabbatical from my job at Northwestern Michigan College. After traveling to New Zealand, it looked promising that I would have a job flying a Cessna Citation and doing some helicopter-flight instruction for an operator in Christchurch starting in late summer. So I informed Promech I would not be returning for the 2003 summer season.

May 27—Clouds, some rain and some sunshine. On one of my Misty flights, as I was entering the narrow entrance to Nooya Lake, I nearly had a mid-air collision with a Tacquan Beaver coming out. It was too close, he was no more than 100 feet above me. Later Rick Seale, one of the older pilots, sat down on the couch next to me and said, "What do you know?" I said, "Not much." He retorted, "Probably shouldn't be saying that, you being a professor and all."

May 28—In negotiating some weather yesterday and today, I feel so much more comfortable now that I know the area. Gosh, when I think back on that first year, I don't know how I managed to survive or why I ever came back.

July 2—Gloomy, overcast and rain fog early. We didn't fly at all until 1000 when we launched five Promech planes on a Misty. Getting to the Behm Canal was OK, but then rain reduced visibility to ¼ to ½ mile. I crossed to the east side and proceeded north to entrance of Rudyerd Bay. I was number three in the gaggle judging from radio calls, but I couldn't see any of the rest. It was frightening. How we avoided a mid-air collision I'll never know.

July 21—Overcast AM, sunny PM. Busy day, flew 8.0 hrs. I slipped off the float at the Promech dock and fell so hard on my left shoulder that

Promech Air Beaver approaching the floatplane trailer at the Peninsula Point pullout.

I had a slight headache. I must have just missed hitting my head on the dock. I put my a/c into the hangar for the 7th straight time. Maybe I've got it down finally.

Promech had a small hangar large enough for a Cessna 185 and one Beaver located right on the waterfront next to the docks downtown. Because of the significant risk of damage due to strong winds or the possibility of a leak developing in one or both of the floats and sinking the plane, Promech aircraft were not left tied up to the downtown dock overnight. So, at the end of the flying day, each pilot either delivered his aircraft to Peninsula Point where it was hauled out of the water onto a large trailer, or he delivered it to the small hangar in town.

Ramping a plane at the entrance to the hangar in town was a demanding maneuver, especially in a crosswind because the channel leading from open water to the hangar entrance was only about forty feet wide. As the pilot approached the aluminum ramp that had been lowered into the water, he had to perfectly time when to take out any crosswind correction, straighten out the aircraft, and run the keels of the floats up onto hard-rubber tracks. The trick was to hit the ramp at just the right speed; too slow and the airplane would begin to weathercock into the wind; too fast and the bow wave would float you off the ramp. In either case, it was a mad scramble to keep from hitting anything with the wingtips. If you were straight on the ramp and got a thumbs-up from a mechanic, you then pushed the control yoke full forward and moved the throttle to almost full power to hold you on the ramp until the mechanics could raise the ramp to a level position. It was an unnatural feeling because it seemed like you were going to shoot straight forward with great force into the mouth of the hangar. It took several misfires before I got the hang of it.

July 26—It was the worst weather I had seen all summer. All flights were grounded. My company was losing lots of money because our two main revenue-producing tours to the Misty Fiords National Monument and a bear-watching tour to Neat's Bay had been cancelled. At 1315 a pilot was launched in a Cessna 185 to check the weather. He radioed back to Dispatch that it was possible to get up the Behm Canal as far as Smeaton Bay, but he wasn't certain if anyone could get to Rudyerd Bay, the normal entrance to the Misty Fiords. Based on the hope that a Misty tour could be completed and antsy to clean out the overcrowded waiting room, Dispatch set in motion a maximum effort involving eight Promech floatplanes. Tourists were hurriedly formed into groups and led by their pilot to the waiting aircraft on the dock.

After strapping everyone in and giving them a quick passenger safety briefing, each plane was cast off from the dock and its engine started. In a big free-for-all each aircraft jockeyed for takeoff position. The turbine-powered Otters, whose engines didn't need a warm-up period, took off first. As soon as the Beavers' oil temperature reached the minimum, they started taking off. Since there was no proscribed water-lane in Ketchikan harbor, aircraft were taking off in a multitude of easterly directions, some close to the waterfront and others further out in the harbor all at approximately the same time. Unlike a runway, where aircraft take off in sequence, one at a time, here it was every man for himself.

Finally, I decided to go for it. Shortly after I lifted off the harbor, about 100 feet in the air, my left wing suddenly and violently dropped and aircraft began a rapid roll to the left. I countered with full right aileron, full right rudder, and full power. The airplane continued to roll to nearly seventy degrees left wing down. I thought we were going to crash for sure. Instinctively, my muscles started to tighten and I braced for impact. Then slowly the aircraft righted itself as my control inputs took effect. I finally got the wings level about twenty feet off the water. I doubt if any of the passengers knew just how close we had come to crashing—probably only a pilot would have recognized the imminent danger. Later that day in analyzing what had happened, I came to the conclusion that my aircraft most likely got caught in the wingtip vortices of a single turbine Otter which had taken off shortly before me. It was one of the closest calls I had during my three years flying for Promech.

July 31—Sunny, boring day, only flew three times. I flew to the Quartz Hill mine again with the owner of the company that maintains the mine in caretaker status. After landing and tying up at the dock, Dan said, "You make it look easy." To which I gave my usual response, "Sometimes, I get lucky."

August 5—Partly sunny. Busy day: flew 5 Misty's and 2 Bear tours—7.4 flt hrs. The two bear tours broke up the Misty's enough to keep my morale up. Got into a predicament in Nooya Lake on one of the Misty's. After landing, I was talking to the passengers out on the left float and didn't realize that a strong wind was blowing our plane onto the shore on the west end of the lake. By the time I realized what was happening it was too late to get all the pax back on board and start the engine. The wind blew the a/c and right float into a fallen tree at the water's edge. Fortunately, there was no damage to the airplane. However, because of the curved shape of the tree, I couldn't power up and move straight ahead. So, I loaded all the pax and passed the oar through the cabin while I crawled across the forward spreader bar beneath the engine to the right float. I was able to push the a/c away from the tree, but the wind blew it right back onto the tree again. So, I enlisted the help of a male passenger sitting in the copilot's seat to get out on the right float to hold off the a/c long enough for me to start the engine and taxi clear. I then shut down the aircraft and retrieved my helper and the oar. Another first in the life of this Alaskan bush pilot.

While chatting with my passengers standing on the left float, the wind blew the aircraft into a fallen tree on the shoreline of Nooya Lake

August 8—Sunny. Last day of work and, perhaps, the last day I will ever fly a Beaver in Alaska. So, it was a sentimental nostalgic sort of day where I was thinking to myself, "Well, this is the last time I will ever see this," or "This is the last time I will ever see that." Kind of a bittersweet day; on one hand I was glad that I was all done and had survived another year, and sad that I might never return. I flew one charter, two Misty's and one Bear tour for a total of 5.9 flt hrs. At the end of my work day, I flew Barbara, my brother Bill and his wife, Nancy, on a private bear tour to Neat's Bay at company expense—a nice gesture that the owner, Kevin Hack, occasionally awarded his pilots.

As it turned out, 2004 was my last year flying in Ketchikan. When the next summer rolled around, all of the bad memories of pressing on in spite of horrible weather and hoping not to hit the side of a mountain greatly outweighed the joyous sunny days when I was on top of my game and handling the daily challenges of new locations and strong, gusty winds.

During the 2004 summer season, Mark Easterly, the DO of Promech, was having a few health issues that would sideline him for a day or two here and there. In the fall, Mark was diagnosed with an aggressive form of cancer that took him down rather quickly. I spoke to him on the phone two times during the fall and each time he was upbeat, positive, and his old cheerful self. Never once did he let on to me that his time was getting short, not until our last phone call in December 2004.

Not only did he give me a chance when he hired me back in 2001, Mark also became a trusted friend who I admired greatly. And it was in that spirit that I wrote the following email to him on January 14, 2005.

Dear Mark,

I am very sad to hear that your illness has taken a downward turn. This past fall when we talked, it seemed that you were feeling good and your life was back on an even keel. So, I was surprised and deeply troubled when you told me that things were not going well.

Mark, I will be forever grateful to you for taking a chance on a guy like me who had a total of 12 hours of float time before you hired me for summer 2001. I remember my first telephone conversation when you said that with my experience and total flight time that "You probably won't hit anything" (meaning a mountain). Well, I didn't hit any mountains during my three summers, but I did hit the dock in Meyers Chuck hard enough to dent the front of the left float. Sorry Boss.

Much of what I know about flying floatplanes, which is admittedly very little, I learned from you, Mark. You patiently sat on your hands while I struggled through my IOE. You taught me how to load a Beaver to take advantage of every bit of space. You hopped in with me to show me how to dock with a strong tailwind just after I had made a complete fool of myself. If I was going to a new location, you always took the time to draw me a diagram of the landing area and the rocks to watch out for. You let me tackle new assignments as you felt I was ready. You always called me on the radio if the weather was bad to see how I was doing...... "Mikey, are you okay?" Never once did you raise your voice or chew me out for being a dumbass, when you had every right to do so. Mark, I am in awe of your talent as a pilot. I was fortunate indeed to learn from a master and consummate professional.

Just as you have led us for many years by setting a good example and high standards, you continue to show us the way in your final months on this earth. Instead of us having to buoy your spirits, you are inspiring us by standing there, head up, shoulders erect, and charging straight ahead, just like you have been doing all of your life. I hope that if the Lord gives me a "clearance" like yours that I can be as courageous and accepting as you. Mark, you are a remarkable human being and I consider myself extremely fortunate that our paths crossed.

Mark, until we meet again, take care old friend. Thanks for the memories.

Mike Stock

Mark died on January 22, 2005, eight days after I sent this email to him. I hope he got a chance to read it.

My good friend and Director of Operations at Promech Air, Mark Easterly, shown here on the "Boatfly" dock wearing his trademark brown suspenders. Summer 2004

Chapter 27

Glaciers and Wildlife

AUGUST 4, 2009, STARTED OUT SUNNY, BUT WAS RAINY BY EARLY afternoon. Like the abrupt change in the weather, my mood toward float flying in Alaska varied dramatically from the beginning of this day to the end.

On this particular morning, I flew a Beaver to the River Song sandbar on the Yentna River, sixty miles northwest of Anchorage, to drop off some day fishermen. I then loaded two rafting guides and their equipment from nearby Wilderness Place Lodge and flew them to a small lagoon on the south end of Chelatna Lake near Mount McKinley. I then returned to the sandbar to pick up their five clients—four men and a woman from the UK—and flew them to join up with their guides, who in the meantime had the rafts all inflated and the gear stowed.

I had twice successfully negotiated the tricky approach and landing in the lagoon, which almost always had dangerous glassy water to contend with, in addition to being very small. I was feeling good; on top of my game! So much so, that I flirted with the possibility of coming back next season provided I could only fly the Beaver. For some reason, I had been having difficulty with my landings in the Cessna 206 all season and it was really getting me down.

That afternoon, I had one of the most dangerous and challenging experiences in six seasons of flying floatplanes in Alaska—my morale plummeted along with the frightening encounter.

The Great Alaska Fish Camp, located on the Kenai River south of Anchorage near Soldotna, was one of the more difficult and demanding places we flew to on a regular basis. The approach and landing were made upriver regardless of wind, and the takeoff was made downriver, retracing the inbound flight path. Not only was the river swift and narrow, but the flight path for the final mile during landing and initial takeoff was below tall trees that lined the river on both sides. Additionally, there was little option for aborting the landing and going around due to a large bridge just to the north of the lodge. If the foregoing didn't provide enough drama, it was often very gusty and turbulent while flying the winding river with its several sharp bends. However, when everything worked out as planned, it provided an exhilarating high to any pilot and an affirmation of his or her skill.

This day, the Great Alaska Fish Camp was living up to its reputation with a little extra—it was exceptionally turbulent and light rain was falling to further compromise vision and depth perception. After takeoff from Lake Hood, I swung the Beaver to the right and headed southeast across Turn Again Arm. My mission was to pick up five passengers and their luggage from the lodge and fly them back to Anchorage. Had it been a sunny day, I might have looked forward to pitting my skill against the mighty Kenai River, but the steady rain, reduced visibility, and heavy turbulence I experienced crossing the Arm foreshadowed anything but a pleasant encounter. Even though I was technically VFR, I had to stay on the gauges to keep my wings level over the water, where the sky and sea blended together in a white, opaque medium.

The approach and landing was tense, as it always was, but not too bad considering the turbulence and light rain on the river. After beaching in front of the lodge, I proceeded to load five happy fishermen from South Africa and three hundred pounds of luggage into my aircraft.

As I powered off the beach, ready for departure, I knew this takeoff would be difficult. The fact that I was heavily loaded and the takeoff would be made downriver with a fairly strong tailwind meant that the airplane would gobble up a lot of water before becoming airborne. But once off the beach, the die was cast—there was no turning back. I increased the throttle to 36.5 inches of manifold pressure, got on the step, and accelerated slowly down the river. In the past, I had always gotten airborne before the second bend, a ninety degree turn to the right, but just barely. I had often wondered what would happen if I didn't. Well, I was about to find out.

At this point, midway through my third season flying for Rust's Flying Service, I was pretty comfortable with a step-turn at full power and lifting off while still in the turn. But the narrow confines of the river and the looming bend up ahead were daunting nonetheless. Sure enough, I was not airborne before the bend. I briefly considered aborting the takeoff, but quickly abandoned that idea because I wasn't sure if the river was wide enough to takeoff further downstream after another ninety-degree bend, this one to the left.

I continued the takeoff and slid across the river to the outside of the sharp turn due to centrifugal force. At one point, I thought the aircraft might crash into the opposite bank. Once into the short straightaway

454 | Chasing the Four Winds

before the next bend, I managed to struggle into the air and followed the riverbed until I gained enough altitude to escape its deadly embrace.

The South Africans and I breathed a collective sigh of relief, although I don't think they realized just how close we had come to a disaster. Fifteen minutes later, in the middle of Turn Again Arm, there was no doubt in their minds that they might die.

As we headed back to Anchorage, at 1,500 feet the intensity of the rain had increased to the point I could barely make out the Chugach Mountains just north of the city. As we left dry land and headed out over the fifteen-mile expanse of Turn Again Arm south of Anchorage, I was flying on instruments because of the lousy weather conditions. I couldn't tell if I had flown into the clouds or not. Since I could still see whitecaps if I looked straight down, I assumed that I hadn't. I was tempted to turn around several times, but pressed on. Unsure of my exact position and stressed about accidentally flying into the clouds, I decided to contact Anchorage Approach Control to request assistance. Even though they assured me I was heading direct for Campbell Lake and the VFR entry point to the Lake Hood traffic pattern, I still felt disoriented, like I was somehow heading down Cook Inlet to the ocean. Maybe my frightening experience in Ketchikan, when I got lost in Clarence Straight, was intruding on my innermost thoughts. Eventually, the steady voice of the controller saying, "The shoreline is coming up in two miles" calmed me down.

Then, we hit the turbulence!

Before takeoff, I had alerted my passengers about the heavy turbulence I had encountered on the way down, but I don't think the warning registered because they were definitely in a party mood. Now, the turbulence was worse than what I encountered earlier. Without the presence of a visible horizon, I was desperately trying to keep the aircraft under control using the attitude indicator on my instrument panel. I was literally fighting with all I had to keep the aircraft from being turned upside down. It was unbelievably frightening. Then, suddenly, the bottom fell out and the airplane plummeted straight down, like an elevator, six or seven hundred feet. Simultaneously, the engine quit!

Unlike most piston-engine aircraft, the Beaver is equipped with a downdraft carburetor. So, the onset of negative G force caused by the sudden loss of altitude interrupted fuel flow to the carburetor, which, in turn, caused the engine to stop. Old time Beaver pilots spoke of "engine poppers" in extreme turbulence, but I had never experienced one before. The engine was only silent for a second or two until positive G forces returned at the bottom of the dive, restoring fuel flow. But it was long enough to scare the crap out of all of us. In my peripheral vision, I could see my passengers hanging on for dear life. Deadly silence permeated the cabin. It was far and away the worst turbulence of my forty-five-year flying career.

I reported "extreme turbulence" to the air traffic controller. Shortly thereafter, we exited the turbulent zone and the air smoothed out considerably. Then I sighted landfall and lots of visual references. All I had to do now was calm my badly frayed nerves and land the airplane. Shortly before landing, after the flight had smoothed out and the passengers realized that their lives would be spared after all, I could hear them beginning to talk quietly and laugh nervously amongst themselves.

When we got to the dock, I noticed the float handling ropes draped high up on the boarding ladders leading to the cockpit and cabin, which I had never seen before. I thought That's strange, until I remembered the negative G forces.

As each passenger exited the cabin, he said, "Thank you, captain." They didn't say, "For saving my life," but I silently added that phrase for them—of course, I also saved my own skin as well.

I was a little wobbly getting out of the cockpit—my nerves were shot. I went straight to Willis in the dispatch office and said, "If you really don't need me, I would like to go home." I was physically and mentally spent. If there was any lingering question in my mind about whether to come back next year or not, this flight settled it. Hell no!

King Air Captain

In the interest of accounting for all significant flying positions I've had, I want to briefly discuss May 2006 to May 2007, when I flew King Airs for Aircraft Services, Inc. (ASI) before tackling a return to bush flying in Alaska.

Roy Nichols, a Traverse City businessman and former U.S. Marine jet pilot, founded ASI in 1994, to provide aircraft charter and aircraft management services to clients in Northern Michigan. The company, based at Cherry Capital Airport in Traverse City, had the following aircraft on its operating certificate during the period I flew for them: a Hawker jet, a Lear jet, two King Air 90s, a King Air 100, two King Air 200s, and two Beech Barons. ASI owned two of these aircraft and the rest were owned by other individuals or entities, but all aircraft were available for charter operations when the owner wasn't using the equipment. Including full-time and part-time employees, there were twenty-one pilots, three office/dispatchers, and two maintenance/line workers.

The King Air was a blast to fly—impressive turboprop performance, great instrument platform, roomy and comfortable cockpit, pressurized and air conditioned. It was a pilot's airplane and fit easily into the top five favorite aircraft I have ever flown. I was checked out in all three King Air models and logged 362 flight hours during my year of employment. Nearly sixty percent of my flights were Part 135 charter, with the rest being Part 91 trips for aircraft owners, their families, and friends.

Although I only spent five nights away from home on company business, the most disagreeable aspect of the job was being on call seven days a week. Not that we got many pop-up flights, but we still couldn't make any long-range plans like, buying concert tickets, traveling to see our family in Chicago, or planning a night out with friends. So, in January 2007, I began casting about for another flying job that allowed more personal freedom. After much soul searching and carefully weighing my options, I decided to retire from full-time flying in favor of part-time summer employment. I will freely admit that my recent eligibility for full Social Security compensation played a large factor in my decision. Consequently, I submitted a letter of resignation to ASI on March 16, 2007, and left the company on May 8.

Return to Alaska

Although I was happy to give up full-time employment, I was not ready to walk away from commercial flying altogether. About this time, I began to entertain the idea of going back to Alaska. Memories of the many hours I spent groping my way through fog and rain while praying that I would live to see another sunrise were still too fresh and raw to consider going back to Ketchikan. What about Anchorage? I remembered the good vibes I had received as I drove around Lake Hood, the big seaplane-base adjacent to Anchorage International Airport, back in 1989, when I was in town teaching a Flight Instructor Refresher Course for AOPA.

After a number of phone calls and emails back and forth, and checking my references with Promech Air in Ketchikan, I received a firm job offer mid-March from Rust's Flying Service to fly floatplanes for the 2007 summer season. Rust's is the oldest, largest, and most respected floatplane operator in the Anchorage area.

In 1963, a recently retired U.S. Air Force pilot by the name Henry B. "Hank" Rust founded Rust's Flying Service with a two-seat Piper Super Cub to fly fishermen and hunters to remote areas of Alaska. Over the years, the company had grown to include nine floatplanes flying out of Lake Hood Seaplane Base and eight wheel and ski-equipped landplanes based in Talkeetna flying under the banner of K2 Aviation, a company Rust's bought in 1996. When I arrived in May 2007, the seaplane fleet included one Cessna 208 Caravan, a de Havilland DH-3 Turbine Otter, three de Havilland DH-2 piston Beavers, and four Cessna 206—all on straight floats. There were seventeen full-time and seasonal pilots and

Headquarters for Rust's Flying Service at Lake Hood Seaplane Base in Anchorage, Alaska. 2007

thirty-five total employees at Rust's. I was hired to fly the Beaver and the Cessna 206 as a seasonal pilot.

During one of my phone calls with Todd Rust, the owner and President of Rust's Flying Service and Hank's son, I asked him if there was much pressure to fly in poor-weather conditions. His reply was both welcome and encouraging: "I'm paying you to turn around whenever you feel that the safety of the flight is being compromised. We have an excellent safety record and I intend to keep it that way." His response led to my next question, "What is your safety record?" Todd replied, "We've had one fatal accident since we started forty-four years ago, and that occurred in 1998." I thought to myself, *Wow, one fatal accident in nearly a half century of Alaska bush flying is unheard of.* This was my kind of company, and I was looking forward to getting started.

My first week was devoted to recurrent ground training for all company pilots and taught by the chief pilot, Dan Baldwin. Unfortunately for me and a couple other new pilots, these classroom sessions were aimed more at returning pilots, so we newbies had more questions than answers. Dan suggested that new pilots ride along on revenue flights whenever there was an open seat and that's what we did for the next week or so. These ride-alongs proved to be beneficial, especially when we were able to occupy the copilot's seat instead of being stuffed back in the cabin. I took copious notes and asked lots of questions—it was a steep learning curve!

I had two training flights in the Cessna 206, followed by a formal checkout ride with Dan, who also administered my Part 135 checkride in the Beaver the following day. By June 1, at least on paper, I was ready to begin earning my keep. Two days later, I flew my first revenue flights as pilot-in-command: two thirty-minute Chugach Explorer tours in the local Anchorage area. I felt good to be on my own, but nervous at the same time—like every new piloting job I've ever had when you hope that the mistakes that are sure to come down the road are subtle and survivable.

No Two Days the Same

Anchorage, with a population approaching 300,000, is like most U.S. cities, with tall buildings, malls, trendy places to eat and shop, traffic congestion, and crime—but with a few exceptions, like moose running down the sidewalk or the occasional bear attack in a city park. It was the largest city in the state by a factor of four and is the economic, cultural, and transportation hub of South Central Alaska, which includes Denali National Park, Prince William Sound, Cook Inlet, the Chugach Mountains, and much of the Alaska Mountain Range.

Because South Central Alaska contains a wide variety of natural terrain features of stunning beauty, such as rugged snow-covered mountains, huge glaciers, pristine lakes, and fast-flowing rivers; and is home to a sizable number of large animals and game fish, it was the ideal location to head-quarter a flight operation that catered to tourists, hunters, fishermen, and people who value the outdoors. When Hank Rust started Rust's Flying Service, he couldn't have chosen a better place to spread his wings.

Of course, by the time I arrived in May 2007, Rust's was well established and offered a variety of different flights to its local customers and out-of-town guests. Flights fell within four broad categories: Glacier and Wildlife Tours; Bear Viewing Tours; Fishing, Rafting, and Hunting Trips; and Charter Flights. The only type of flight missing from this impressive lineup was scheduled air service like Promech Air provided in Ketchikan. The vast majority of these flights operated within a 250-nautical mile radius of Anchorage, with the occasional tour or charter flight out to four hundred miles.

Glacier and Wildlife Tours included Mount McKinley (3 hours), Prince William Sound (2½ to 3 hours), Knick Glacier (1½ to 2 hours), Triumvirate Glacier (1½ to 2 hours), and Chugach Explorer (30 minutes). Alaska has over sixty thousand glaciers, large and small, so we didn't have to fly far to find one in the mountains surrounding Anchorage. Wildlife, on the other hand, did not read the daily flight schedule and therefore did not always show up at the appropriate time and place. Usually, however, we were able to show our passengers one or two types of wildlife on every tour, such as moose, black and brown bears, Dall sheep, mountain goats, sea otters, harbor seals, or beluga whales. If all else failed, there was a mounted head of a mountain goat in the passenger waiting room we could point out as a last, desperate measure on our return.

Top photo: Alaska has plenty of glaciers within 150 miles of Anchorage.

Bottom photo: If all else failed, we could always show our passengers some wildlife on our return to Anchorage.

All of the Glacier and Wildlife tours, with the exception of the Chugach Explorer, included a landing on a nearby lake—weather and water conditions permitting—to allow passengers to get out on dry land to stretch their legs, take some photos, and soak up the cool mountain air. If the weather or turbulence wasn't conducive for the normal Chugach Explorer tour through a mountain pass to the north of Anchorage, we flew an alternate route the pilots unofficially called *The Moose and Spruce Tour*, which proceeded to flat marshy lands located between the mouth of the Big Susitna and Little Susitna Rivers southwest of Anchorage, which were populated by lots of spruce trees and usually a moose or two.

Nearly everybody who travels to Alaska wants to see a bear, so it was no surprise that *Bear Viewing Tours* were popular. There were three options: Katmai/Brooks Falls, Redoubt Mountain Lodge, and Redoubt Bay Lodge. The last two were half-day tours and included a guided tour in a boat and a sit-down lunch at the lodge, with a one-way flight time of 1.4 hours to Redoubt Mountain Lodge and forty-five minutes to Redoubt Bay Lodge. The trip to the famous Brooks Falls in Katmai National Park was an all-day event due to its distance from Anchorage—over three hours flight time each way. It included only a box lunch and a self-guided tour, which seemed like a step down from the two other bear tours. But the huge upside was the almost guaranteed sighting of a large number of brown bears. (Brown bears and Grizzlies are the same species. Brown bears live within one hundred miles of salt water and are larger than their interior cousins due to a diet rich in fish).

Fishing, Rafting, and Hunting excursions varied depending on the calendar. The number and location of fishing trips depended largely on when the salmon were running. Rafting trips depended on water levels in the

Katmai/Brooks Falls bear viewing tour.

rivers and creeks, and hunting depended on the official opening of hunting season.

The most popular fishing trips were day outings to numerous wilderness lodges located on the Yentna River. After a forty-minute flight from Lake Hood, we landed on the Yentna River and beached the aircraft on a sandbar, where the passengers were picked up by their fishing guides and transported to the lodge where they were properly outfitted and fed in

Top photo: Day fishermen were dropped off on a sand bar in the Yentna River where they were met by their guides.

Bottom photo: Two rafters getting ready to depart the lagoon on Chelatna Lake for a four-day trip downriver.

preparation for a day of fishing for salmon and other game fish. Rust's also owned several primitive cabins on lakes and streams that could be rented by fishing parties; the fee included roundtrip air service.

The majority of the rafting trips started on the rivers and creeks in the shadow of Mount McKinley, on the south side. We would fly in the rafting party, their rafts, equipment, and provisions; and pick them up four or five days later downstream on the Yentna River.

Like rafting trips, Rust's flew hunting parties and their gear to a prime hunting location and then returned in a specified number of days to pick them up and, hopefully, their trophies. Hunting season for caribou ran from August 1 to September 30, while moose season was generally from September 5 to September 20. Black bears could be taken anytime of the year in most areas. During the three years I flew for Rust's, hunting trips had decreased in numbers, primarily because the large caribou herds had been depleted or had moved out of the feasible economic range of Anchorage-based aircraft.

Charter flights were always the least predictable revenue producers for any flying-service company because the demand was random and sporadic. Theoretically, with refueling stops, Rust's could fly just about anywhere for any purpose as long as the client had the money to pay for the trip. Practically speaking, the majority of the charter customers that Rust's flew were closer to home and fell within the following broad categories: private home or cabin owners; fishing lodges; hunting and fishing camps; federal and state government entities, such as Fish and Game, Department of Natural Resources, and the National Weather Service; commercial enterprises, such as oil and construction companies; and aerial photography.

I flew an Alaska state biologist into a small cove in Prince William Sound to collect Mussel specimens. 2009

A New Ballgame

There were so many differences between flying out of Ketchikan and flying out of Anchorage it is hard to know where to begin describing them. Other than flying the Beaver again and a few other similar, but small details, it was like starting a whole different job. As you will discern after reading this section, on balance, my three years flying in Anchorage were more pleasant and satisfying and less stressful than my days in Ketchikan.

Let's begin with the most obvious and important difference—the weather! Since flying in the low clouds, poor visibilities, and rain fog of southeast Alaska, my flying-weather yardstick is forevermore: how does it compare with Ketchikan? Happily, I can report that we did not have many *Ketchikan Days* in the Anchorage area, and when we did, the weather usually improved dramatically within twenty-four hours. We had little fog in general and no rain fog. To be sure, we had *some* Ketchikan Days, but usually by mid-day the ceilings and visibilities had lifted to permit safe and comfortable VFR flight.

And, when the weather was bad, there was absolutely no pressure from management to fly—it was totally the pilot's call. If a pilot had to turn around and return to Lake Hood, the customers' money was refunded, no questions asked and the pilot often got an "attaboy" from the chief pilot, as I did one day. And since there was no management pressure, it lessened the number of "macho" pilots begging to display their skill by pushing the weather.

Additionally, there was a greater number of official and unofficial weather-reporting stations and weather cameras in South Central Alaska from which a more complete weather picture could be obtained before takeoff.

Another significant difference was the veritable smorgasbord of different flights, missions, and locations that we flew at Rust's. For example, there were seven specific glacier and wildlife tours, and the pilot had great latitude within each tour to alter the route and the sights because the tours flown by Rust's were much longer than Ketchikan and not as tightly scheduled. Consequently, few tours were ever exactly the same. Throw in hauling fishermen to fifteen or so different lodges; a rafting trip here and there; flying regular customers, provisions, and construction materials to their remote homes and cabins; and the occasional half-day charter for the DNR; on top of tour flights; and it is easy to see why I was never bored flying for Rust's. Every day was a new adventure, with a few challenges tossed in along the way.

Since we had a larger radius of operations and significantly longer flights than Ketchikan, there was less pilot fatigue. On the flip side, there was more time spent waiting onsite for passengers to return from their activities—what we pilots called "hang time." These waits were good for taking a nap or reading a good book, or both in my case. Although we were paid by the flight hour, our monthly pay included a minimum guarantee of eight-five hours, so we didn't mind these forced waits.

Another significant change was the greater variety of terrain features: taller mountains, wider valleys, abundant glaciers, and more lakes and rivers.

There were also some mundane differences, which pale in comparison with the factors previously mentioned, but nevertheless added spice and variety to our day. Pilots, for the most part, loaded their own freight with a hand from dock boys if needed. We also back-hauled garbage from a few lodges to Anchorage. Several bags could be carried in the float compartments, and when we were not carrying passengers, we often carried a cabin full of malodorous content—those were the times when you wished you had an oxygen mask!

From the standpoint of technical difficulty, the piloting and water-handling skills required in Ketchikan and Anchorage were similar, but with a few differences. Unlike Promech, at Rust's we had few saltwater operations, which meant less concern about tidal fluctuations, less concern about high waves and ocean swells, but without the advantage of unlimited takeoff distances that saltwater bodies of water generally provide. More lakes and rivers in Southcentral Alaska meant the use of more beaches and fewer docks to offload passengers and cargo. Docking generally required more skill and experience, especially in crosswind or downwind situations.

The biggest technical difference for me was river operations. In Southeast Alaska, there are limited river opportunities; in fact, I had no river experience whatsoever when I arrived in Anchorage, where river operations were a major factor. Not that landing and taking off from a river is much more difficult than taking off from a lake or a bay, it's just a different skillset and level of awareness that must be learned and honed.

In chapter 26, I described the chaotic situation that awaited the seaplane pilot taking off and landing in Ketchikan Harbor; at Lake Hood Seaplane Base in Anchorage, home to Rust's Flying Service, there was a control tower and designated water "runways." There weren't any commercial fishing vessels, private pleasure boats, kayakers, canoers, sailboats, scuba divers, and twelve seaplanes trying to take off at the same time, or hundreds of seagulls and eagles circling in the takeoff and landing path—although there was the occasional moose swimming in the water lane "without clearance" from the tower. Operating from Lake Hood was sane, orderly, and without drama—just the way we liked it! Boy, it was great.

The personality and mentality of the tourists we flew out of Anchorage were markedly better from those I encountered in Ketchikan. It wasn't so

Lake Hood Seaplane Base looking east. Lake Hood is in the foreground and Lake Spenard is at the top of the photo. Gull Island separates the east-west waterway on the right from the slow taxi canal on the left. *(Photo by Don Hartman)*

much that the people were higher-class folks, just that their circumstances were different, which caused them to be in a better frame of mind. They were more friendly, engaging, and courteous. First, they did not have the typical "cruise ship mentality," where hordes of people were crammed into a relatively small space to eat, sleep, and recreate while following a rigid time schedule. The typical tourist visiting Anchorage was on a freer schedule and usually had more discretionary income to spend on sightseeing trips. They were able to spread themselves out and relax.

On Rust's airplanes, unlike those in Ketchikan, each passenger had a good headset with a microphone that he or she could use to ask questions of the pilot or to engage with fellow passengers. Since our flights were much longer, pilots and passengers had time to get to know one another and to form a bond that was impossible to attain in Ketchikan. On longer flights, in addition to my usual narration, I would usually go around the cabin and ask each person to introduce themselves and tell us something about them. Everybody enjoys feeling important and talking about their lives a little. It was a great icebreaker. As a consequence, most passengers were in a good mood, laughing, and carrying on while taking in the spectacular scenery. And the tips were far better too. Average tips per year in Anchorage was $1,787 versus $701 in Ketchikan—a two hundred and fifty-five percent difference!

At both Promech and Rust's the aircraft maintenance departments did a superb job of keeping the aircraft fleet in tiptop condition. I had very few mechanical problems and those I did experience were of a minor nature. Aircraft-wise, the big difference between the two jobs was I flew two airplanes at Rust's: the Beaver and the Cessna 206. The latter was faster and more quiet, but not as much fun to fly as the de Havilland.

The pace at Rust's was definitely more relaxed with less emphasis, within reason, on the timing of departures and returns. In keeping with a slower pace, I averaged only 2.8 flight hours per day at Rust's, compared to 5.0 hours at Promech. Because I didn't have to get back for the start of fall classes at NMC, my season in Anchorage was twice as long as in Ketchikan.

Lastly, I had fewer injuries in Anchorage, which was good medicine for a sixty-seven-year-old body—maybe it was the result of luck and experience!

A Flight to the Big Mountain

To give the reader a sense of what it was like to fly floatplanes for Rust's Flying Service during the three summer seasons (2007, 2008, and 2009) I flew for them and to provide a glimpse into the specific details of my job, I have decided to take you along on two of our most popular tours: Mount McKinley and Katmai National Park. Each account is a replay of an actual tour as recorded in my diary and was chosen because of some unique aspect that set it apart from the everyday routine. Interspersed within the chronicle of each tour I have inserted in italics the typical narration I would be giving to my passengers along the way.

The alarm went off at 5:15 a.m. I shave, shower, grab a bowl of cereal, pack my lunch, and I'm out the door by six. Traffic on the Glenn Highway, heading to Anchorage from Eagle River, is already building as the morning rush hour picks up momentum. Thirty minutes later, I arrive in the parking lot of Rust's Flying Service at the Lake Hood Seaplane Base. Getting out of my car, I grab my backpack and hip boots, and head to the dispatch office/passenger waiting room. I wonder what my first trip will be.

Standing behind the counter is a large bear of a man with a neatly trimmed beard and ever-present smile. Willis Thayer is the Operations Manager and Chief Dispatcher.

"Morning, Willis," I said, as I walk into the office.

"Well, hello there, Mike," he replied with a slight chuckle. "I've got you on a McKinley at eight in 083," he said as he handed me the *dingus*—a rectangular metal box that contained trip information, names of passengers, any freight with weights, and aircraft information such as time remaining until the next 100-hour inspection for each aircraft. (How it got the name dingus or what it means, I have forgotten.)

"Thank you, sir," I answered. "I'll get 'er ready." I picked up my hip boots, threw my backpack over one shoulder, and headed out the door to the dock area where the nine floatplanes in Rust's fleet were tied up. The place was already humming with activity as the dock guys went about cleaning windshields, refueling airplanes, and pushing carts loaded with freight to the appropriate aircraft.

As I walked out on the wooden dock on the right, that housed the three Beavers in the fleet, I passed one of the dock hands pushing a cart of freight. "Good morning Austin," I said to the eighteen-year-old lad in his second season working on the dock and the hardest worker we had.

"Morning, Mike," he replied cheerfully. "You've got 083, right?"

I nodded.

"How much fuel you need?"

"Top her off, if you would, please. I'm going to McKinley at eight."

"Will do," Austin answered as he continued to push the cart to the Beaver in front of mine.

Following a well-practiced routine, I stepped from the dock onto the left float and climbed into the cockpit, placing my headset bag and dingus on the copilot's seat. Next, I adjusted my seat, hooked up my headset, and stowed the headset bag. Then, starting at the left of the cockpit, I checked the instrument panel, radio settings, flight controls and flaps, recorded the

Dock boys loading freight and getting ready for the first departures of the morning from the Rust's Flying Service dock at the Lake Hood Seaplane Base.

engine tach reading in the dingus, and noted the time remaining to the next 100-hour inspection. Exiting the airplane, I stowed my backpack in the rear baggage compartment and performed a complete exterior inspection of the airplane, which included pumping any accumulated water out of the float compartments and checking for proper fuel load and oil. Since this tour included a lake landing, I pulled on my hip boots and put my leather work boots in the baggage compartment. With that, I was ready to greet my passengers when they arrived, usually delivered from a local hotel by a Rust's shuttle van.

About twenty minutes before scheduled departure time, I walked out of the office onto a wide, open-air deck where groups of passengers were waiting to link up with their pilot. I started calling off names from the passenger manifest: "Cooper, Fenwick, Mattingly, and Kirtland." Three couples and a man raised their hands. "Please, follow me," I commanded as I led them to the dock in front of our airplane.

"All right, the first thing we're going to do is load the aircraft in such a way that preserves the proper weight and balance." I usually put the heaviest person in the copilot's seat, if there was a passenger who was indeed a lot heavier than the rest. Otherwise, I put a person traveling alone up front. Since I didn't have any real heavyweights, I pointed at the man traveling alone and told him to crawl up into the copilot's seat through the main cabin. I then distributed the remaining six people—one in the far back sling seat, two in the middle row, and three in the first row in the cabin.

After instructing them to fasten their seat belts, I climbed to the top step leading to the cabin and perched myself there for the passenger-safety briefing.

"Good morning. My name is Mike Stock and I will be your pilot today. We will be flying in a de Havilland Beaver. It looks like everyone has gotten their seat belt fastened. If you will give me your undivided attention, I'll go over the safety briefing." Unlike in an airliner where they have heard the same spiel countless times, I found that the folks going on tours in Alaska were all ears and paid close attention, which made my job easier.

Continuing, I said, "Please ensure your seat belts are nice and tight. I'm not expecting any turbulence this morning, but you can never be sure when flying in or near mountains. If I turn the seat belt sign off, feel free to move about the cabin." After looking around to see how jammed in they were, a few smiles and chuckles ensued at the incongruity of my statement.

"There are four exits, two back here and two up front. All four doors open the same way, by turning the little silver knob either way. To those of you sitting in the first row in the cabin, remember that the release is behind you when the door is closed," I said as I pointed to the doorknob.

"Under your seat is an airline-type life preserver. The main thing to remember in the unlikely event we have to use the vests is do not inflate them inside the aircraft. Wait until you are well clear of the airplane before doing so, otherwise you may get trapped inside the aircraft.

"There is a fire extinguisher under my seat and there is a large orange bag containing survival equipment located in the rear baggage compartment. In the tail cone of the airplane is an emergency locater beacon which can be turned on manually by using the red switch on my instrument panel." I paused and said, "This is all beginning to sound rather grim. Do you folks still want to go?" They all nodded their heads and smiled.

I continued, "In the seat pocket in front of you is a passenger safety card and an airsickness bag. If you have to use a sick-sac, treat it as an Alaska souvenir and take it with you—we don't want those back." This statement always got the most laughs. "If you start to feel queasy, please let me know and I will do what I can to lessen your discomfort.

"There are headsets located near your seat. Please put them on once I get the engine started. They will block out some of the engine noise and allow me to clearly narrate during the flight. If you want to speak to me, make sure the microphone is nearly touching your lips so the voice acti-vation feature is engaged. I encourage questions and comments, except during takeoff and landing or any time I raise my hand for quiet. Are there any questions?" There were none, so I continued. "One last thing: no smoking, drinking, or wild parties during the flight. Let's go have some fun." With that, I closed the main cabin door, applied three strokes to the fuel primer before climbing into my seat in the cockpit—ready to rock and roll.

Noting that Austin had already untied the airplane and was holding it by the tail pointed slightly away from the dock, waiting for me to start the engine, I initiated a cockpit routine I could have performed in my sleep: check the cove for other traffic, check wingtip clearance, extend the water rudders, mixture rich, throttle cracked, master switch on, call "Clear," hit the starter and crank through three blades, mags to both. The Pratt and Whitney engine belched once and roared to life, and settled into a reas-suring rhythm that only a big radial can provide. As the Beaver slowing moved away from the dock, I continued with the cockpit flow: oil pressure checked, radio master on, fasten my seat belt, close the door, put on my headset, and listen to the current ATIS broadcast—Lake Hood Informa-tion Bravo informed me that the winds were six knots out of the west and that the west water lane was in use.

"Lake Hood tower, Rust 68083, Fish and Wildlife, taxi for a west with Bravo," I stated on tower frequency.

"68083, Lake Hood tower, taxi for a west, altimeter 29.88," the air traffic controller replied.

With clearance to taxi, I crossed the east-west water lane and turned into the slow taxi channel on the north side of Gull Island and proceeded east toward Lake Spenard at idle taxi speed. "Can everyone hear me? If you can hear me okay, give me a thumbs-up." I saw seven thumbs, so I began my customary narration as we proceeded slowly to the other end of the seaplane base.

We'll begin our tour right here at Lake Hood Seaplane Base. The seaplane base is actually made up of two natural lakes, Lake Hood, which we just left, and Lake Spenard, which we will enter momentarily. In 1938, a canal was dug to connect the two lakes to give us more distance for takeoff. Seaplanes are just the opposite of landplanes in terms of takeoff and landing distances. Due to water friction, a seaplane requires more distance to takeoff than a landplane, but less distance required to land. In fact, a seaplane pilot could land in a small lake that is too short for takeoff. The boss wouldn't be happy with me if I did that, so we won't be doing that today.

There are some facts about this seaplane base that you might find interesting. It is the world's largest and busiest seaplane base. Over 800 airplanes are permanently based here and during a four-month period in the summer, eighty thousand takeoffs and landings are made.

You heard me request permission to taxi from the control tower. It is one of the very few remaining tower-controlled seaplane bases in the world, and the east-west waterway is lighted. We don't need lights in the summer with the long days we have, but in the winter, when we only have six hours of daylight, lights are essential. Back in the 1930s, during the heyday of the Pan American Clippers and the big flying boats, tower-controlled seaplane bases with lighted waterways were the norm, but not anymore.

The narrow island to our right is Gull Island and it got its name from all of the sea gulls that once nested there. Well, as you can probably imagine, lots of birds and airplanes create a dangerous combination. The local authorities tried several different methods to deter the sea gulls from nesting on the island, but nothing worked until one summer when they placed three domestic pigs on the island that eagerly ate all of the eggs. That cured the bird problem, but pilots did have to contend with a pig swimming in the water lane occasionally. The sea gulls never returned; problem solved.

Most of the seaplanes you see are privately owned. Alaska has the highest per-capita number of pilots in the world, with one person in seventy-six being a pilot. The reason is obvious: with few roads, the airplane is the only practical means of access to many areas of the state. In the winter, many of these seaplanes will trade their floats for skis and continue to *operate. The rest of the airplanes are hauled out of the water onto the shoreline. If you wanted a private slip for your float plane, you would pay approximately $125 per month year-round, which isn't terribly expensive. The bad news is you would go on a ten-year waiting list with close to three hundred names ahead of you.*

The first passenger-carrying commercial flight between Seattle and Anchorage landed here, in Lake Spenard, in 1934. It was obviously not a nonstop flight, but a journey of three days and sixteen flight hours.

After exiting the slow-taxi canal, I performed the Engine Run-up Checklist: oil pressure minimum of forty and cylinder head temperature at least one hundred, area clear ahead, yoke full back, advance throttle to 1,750 RPM, cycle propeller, check mags, throttle back to idle. Next, I completed the preliminary items on the Before Takeoff Checklist: flaps set, flight controls free, check mixture rich and prop full forward, fuel selector on forward tank and fuel quantity checked.

"Lake Hood tower, 083 ready for takeoff west, northbound."

"Rust 083, Lake Hood tower, cleared for takeoff west."

After reading back my takeoff clearance, I finished the Takeoff Checklist: pulse and landing lights on, transponder on, waterway clear, and water rudders up. The aircraft was ready, I was ready, and the passengers were eager. Let's go to the Big Mountain.

Heading more or less into the wind, I pulled the yoke full back and slowly added takeoff power of 36.5 inches of manifold pressure. The nose of the aircraft rapidly assumed a nose-high attitude as the floats plowed through the water as the airplane fought to gain speed. Momentarily, the nose displayed a second rise, indicating the airplane was ready to come up on the step. I relaxed some of the back pressure on the yoke and the nose lowered to the step or planning attitude. Free of most of the water drag from the two floats, the Beaver accelerated quickly down the west water lane. Reaching a takeoff speed of approximately fifty-five knots—I actually wasn't watching the airspeed indicator; it was more of feel-thing—I pulled aft on the yoke ever so slightly and the aircraft lifted gently off the water. Reducing the throttle to thirty inches and the prop to 2,000 RPM, slowly raising the flaps, and establishing a climb airspeed of eighty-five knots completed the after-takeoff cockpit duties.

Upon reaching the western shoreline of Lake Hood, I started a gentle right turn, heading toward Point MacKenzie on the north shore of Knick Arm, while climbing to nine hundred feet.

"083, Lake Hood tower, frequency change approved."

After acknowledging the tower, I switched the radio to 120.65, the company frequency, and called dispatch with my off report. "61A, 083 off at 8:40 to McKinley with seven passengers, four hours on the fuel, back at 11:40."

"083, 61A, got it. Have a good one."

Folks, let me give you a little geographical orientation. Under the left wingtip is Cook Inlet, which comes up from the Gulf of Alaska and Pacific Ocean. When it reaches Anchorage International Airport, it splits into two arms: Knick Arm which we just crossed on the west, and Turn-again Arm to the east of Anchorage, which we will not see on this tour.

Ahead of the aircraft is a broad, expansive valley, the Matanuska-Susitna Valley or Mat-Su Valley as the locals call it. It is fifty to sixty miles wide and stretches from the Talkeetna Mountains on the east under the right wingtip to Mt. Susitna on the left, which you can see under the left wingtip; and from Cook Inlet on the south to the foothills of Mount McKinley to the north, a distance of eighty-five miles. McKinley, itself is visible today; it is that small, white object just to the right of the nose of the aircraft. We can only see Mount McKinley from here about twenty percent of the time due to cloud cover. So, you folks are some of the lucky ones.

The Mat-Su Valley is largely uninhabited, especially when you get away from the eastern corridor running from Palmer and Wasilla in the southeast corner to Denali National Park. In fact, we are at the western terminus of the road network in Alaska—meaning that from here, we can fly fifteen hundred miles to the west and no longer be able to drive out of Alaska. In other words, we are in the "Alaska Bush," which means

Just after takeoff from the west water lane at the Lake Hood Seaplane Base. Gull Island is on the right. *(Photo by Mike Everist)*

an area that is not accessible by road; the only way in or out is by air or by boat.

Under the right wingtip, off in the distance, is the city of Palmer and the Knick River Valley, where some of the world's largest vegetables are grown. You may have heard of them. It seems rather odd that a growing season of only a hundred and five days, as compared with California's three hundred days, can produce larger vegetables. The secret is in the amount of sunshine per day. Nineteen hours of daylight in the summer allows the process of photosynthesis to go into overdrive. At the Alaska State Fair, which occurs the last two weeks of August, there is a contest to determine the largest vegetables. Some recent examples are a nineteen-pound carrot, thirty-five-pound broccoli, sixty-five-pound cantaloupe, a hundred-and-twenty-seven-pound cabbage, and a seventeen-hundred-and eighty-pound pumpkin.

So much for the geography lesson; let's talk about what we will be doing this morning. The plan for our tour will be to start a climb momentarily, to ninety-five hundred feet on a general heading of north so that we can fly up the Kahiltna Glacier toward Mount McKinley at a safe altitude. Because the Beaver only climbs about two hundred and twenty-five feet per minute, if I waited until reaching the toe or foot of the glacier to begin my climb, the rise in terrain would outpace our climb performance.

On the return flight, I will descend to about five hundred feet above the glacier. This way, you will have both a high and low altitude perspective of the ice pack, which I think you will find interesting. On the way back, I'll land on a nice lake and pull up to a sandy beach where you can get out, stretch your legs, and take some pictures.

After taking off from the lake, we'll head south back to Anchorage at five hundred feet above the ground and look for wildlife. Since we'll be climbing during the first part of our flight and therefore too high to spot any animals, I'll do most of my narration on our way to McKinley.

After crossing Point MacKenzie, I reset climb power, raised the nose slightly to achieve climb airspeed of eighty-five knots, and began a slow climb. This morning, in the clear air and unlimited visibility, navigation was simple—just point the nose of the Beaver toward Mount McKinley. Aside from keeping a watch for other aircraft, my cockpit duties were minimal, which allowed me to interact with my passengers and to give them more information and amazing facts about Alaska.

Well, folks, since this is billed as a Mount McKinley tour, I suppose I should tell you a little about the grand mountain we are going to visit. McKinley, as you know, is the highest mountain in North America at 20,310 feet. It is located in the Alaska Range, which forms a

Mount McKinley is the peak to the right of center. Mount Foraker to the left appears larger because it is closer to the camera.

five-hundred-mile-long, east-west arc around Anchorage, approximately one hundred miles inland. Two of the ten highest mountains on the continent are located in the Alaska Range: McKinley, of course, and Mount Foraker at 17,400 feet; both of which we will see today.

Even though the Alaskan natives call the mountain Denali and the Park is named Denali National Park, the official name is Mount McKinley. (In 2015, the United States government officially changed the name from McKinley to Denali.) In the Athabascan language, Denali means the "big one" or "great one." Some natives also refer to the mountain as the "home of the sun." On the longest day of the year, June 21, if there are no clouds, the sun will appear to rise on the east side of Mount McKinley and set on the west side, hence the name "home of the sun."

McKinley is not a technically difficult climb using the most popular West Buttress route. In fact, the adjoining peaks of Mount Foraker and Mount Hunter are so difficult and dangerous that not many climbers attempt them. McKinley is more of an endurance contest, like running a marathon. But due to extreme cold and severe storms, it can be a very dangerous and unforgiving experience.

McKinley is unique among the great mountains of the world. The locals are fond of saying that the mountain makes its own weather. It is buffeted by storms from two large bodies of water known for their inhospitable weather: the Gulf of Alaska and the Bering Sea. The weather can change very precipitously and dramatically in a short period of time. A balmy day of glacier travel can rapidly deteriorate into a day of having to dig snow caves to survive blizzard conditions, with winds in excess of one hundred miles per hour and temperatures minus thirty to forty below zero—and we are talking in the middle of summer.

Climbing Mount McKinley is in some ways more dangerous than climbing Mount Everest. At the same elevation, it is fifteen to twenty degrees colder and the barometric pressure is lower on McKinley, which means less oxygen available to the climbers. On average, two climbers die on McKinley each year during the climbing season: four were lost in 2007, two in 2008, and four so far this year.

The climbing season is relatively short: approximately May 1 to July 15. Before May 1, it is too cold, with too many winter storms; and after July 15, the ice bridges crossing the many crevasses are too thin to support the weight of the climbers. The ice bridge needs to be approximately four feet thick for a safe crossing.

The National Park issues twelve to thirteen hundred climbing permits each year, and about one half of these climbers are successful in reaching the summit. It costs two hundred for each permit and application must be made two months in advance.

One hundred feet prior to reaching cruise altitude, I set cruise power: retard the throttle to twenty-seven inches MAP, retard the prop lever to 1,850 RPM, then reset the MAP to twenty-eight inches, and lean the mixture.

"Well, folks, we have reached our cruising altitude of 9,500 feet. If you look straight ahead," I said, pointing with my right hand, "you can see the toe of the Kahiltna Glacier."

Everyone strained to get a glimpse of the large, white mass that was looming larger by the minute. I heard several say that they could see it. A palpable feeling of excitement was building in the cabin.

"Since we will soon be flying up this ribbon of ice, this is a good time to tell you a little about glaciers."

Alaska has a lot of glaciers—approximately 330,000 square miles, or about five percent of the total land area of the state. People always associate Alaska with glaciers, but may not realize that some of our lower forty-eight states also have some small valley glaciers. Oregon, Washington, Idaho, Montana, Colorado, and Utah have glaciers, but all of them combined could fit into the glacier we are about to fly up.

A glacier is a perennial accumulation of snow, ice, water, rock, and debris. Glacial ice is formed over a period of about twelve months by subjecting fresh snow to increasing pressures ultimately reaching seven hundred and fifty psi. If you were to take a shoebox full of freshly fallen snow and compact it by reducing the volume nine times over a period of twelve months, you would create glacial ice. The very high density of glacial ice is the reason why it is blue in color. All other colors of the spectrum are absorbed; blue is the only color to be transmitted. If you took an ice cube out of your refrigerator and placed it under seven hundred and fifty psi pressure, assuming that it would not fracture into a million pieces, it also would be blue in color. As we fly along the glacier, you will be able to see the blue color, especially in the crevasses and in the pools of melting ice on top of the glacier, which will be a brilliant turquoise color.

A glacier is called a "River of Ice" because it is always moving downhill due to gravity. The rate of movement varies depending on location and other geological factors, but the glaciers in this part of Alaska move at the rate of about one to two feet per month. Some glaciers carry an additional classification called surging. A surging glacier, for reasons not fully understood by scientists, will begin to move at a very fast rate for a short period of time. The fastest surging glacier ever recorded was moving at the phenomenal rate of eleven hundred and fifty feet per day.

One other tidbit worth knowing about glaciers—one that will make our trip this morning more enjoyable—is that our flight should be relatively turbulence free. Normally when flying in and around mountainous terrain, a pilot can expect moderate to severe turbulence almost anywhere. The glaciers, however, keep the air above much cooler than normal and thus diminish and dampen rising air currents, which are the root cause of most turbulence.

"Folks, you'll be happy to know that concludes most of my standard narration for this tour. I know I've probably given you more than you ever wanted to know about Mount McKinley and glaciers. For the rest of our trip, I'll be sure to point out prominent landmarks and features and answer any questions you may have, but I'm mainly going to let you all ponder and absorb the breathtaking beauty that surrounds us. Owing to the cloudless sky and unlimited visibility we have today, we'll be able to get a good look at McKinley as we fly farther up the glacier."

Just before starting up the glacier, I switched the fuel selector from the rear tank to the center tank—not good form to burn a tank dry over such inhospitable terrain with few good landing sites. From here to the top of the glacier, my cockpit duties were minimal: monitor the engine instruments and fuel quantity, look out for the occasional passing aircraft, and follow the glacier uphill. I could even take in some of the sights myself.

A lady in the rear of the cabin spoke up. "How big is this glacier?"

"The Kahiltna Glacier is forty-four miles long and four miles across at its widest point, making it the longest glacier in Denali National Park and, for that matter, in the Alaska Range. So, it's a big one for sure." I continued, "And we are only able to see a small part of it from here because

Toe of the Kahiltna Glacier looking towards the "Big Bend."

fourteen miles straight ahead, the glacier turns about sixty degrees to the right."

As we approached the "Big Bend" in the glacier, I pointed to a cluster of rugged peaks, five thousand feet high, just off to our right and said, "That group of peaks is called "Little Switzerland" because many tourists say it reminds them of the Swiss Alps."

Several minutes later, as we continued our trek up the glacier, another passenger asked, "Is that McKinley we're seeing up ahead, to the right?"

"No, that's Mount Hunter. At fourteen-thousand-five-hundred-and-seventy-three-feet tall, it is obscuring McKinley, which is behind it," I said. "We'll be able to see McKinley in a few more minutes."

Just then the radio crackled to life. "Kahiltna traffic, Otter 9KT, West Ridge of Hunter, heading downslope."

I replied, "Beaver 083, Ice Falls, upslope. I'll keep to the right." Pretty soon, I spotted the red-turbine Otter of our sister company K2 highlighted against the white, snow-covered mountains as it passed on our left.

"Up ahead and off to our left, that big mountain you see, is Mount Foraker. As I stated earlier, at seventeen thousand, four hundred feet, it is the second tallest peak in the Alaska Range and the sixth highest mountain in North America. It is sometimes referred to as "Denali's Mistress," but she is no easy lady. In fact, she is much more technically difficult and dangerous to climb than McKinley. A number of climbers have perished on the mountain and their bodies were never recovered."

Several miles past Mount Foraker, I banked the aircraft to the right and circled a collection of brightly colored tents on the glacier below. "Folks, this is base camp, the place where most climbers begin their assault on McKinley. The climbers and their gear fly in from Talkeetna on ski-equipped airplanes. In fact, you can see one getting ready to take off down glacier. Base camp, at an elevation of seven thousand, two hundred feet, is the first of several camps along the way to the summit where the climbers gradually acclimate to higher altitudes."

"How long does it take to reach the summit?" someone asked.

"The average is seventeen days from base camp to the top and back to base camp," I stated. "Obviously, some parties do it in a shorter period of time, but only if the weather is favorable, which is not often the case."

After making two circles to allow everyone to take pictures, I turned and flew farther up the glacier, where we spotted a number of climbers trudging uphill single-file, carrying their heavy packs and pulling sleds

At 7,200 feet, Base Camp is the departure point from which most climbers begin their quest to climb Mt. McKinley. *(Photo by Mark Stadsklev)*

"The Tall One"–Mt. McKinley

with additional equipment. Pointing off to the right, I said, "And there she is, Mount McKinley, in all of her majesty and splendor. In terms of flightseeing, it doesn't get any better than this. The air is exceptionally clear today and makes the mountain just sparkle!" Everyone nodded in agreement, as they pointed their cameras toward the massive presence. It was a special moment.

On the distant skyline, like a steep ramp to the heavens, was the West Buttress Route, the path that over ninety percent of the climbers use to ascend the great mountain because it is the least-technical route to the summit. But, as noted before, even though it may require the least amount of technical skill, it was nevertheless challenging and demanding, primarily due to the ferocious winter-type weather and cold winds that could unfold at a moment's notice.

Having reached the nine-thousand-foot level on the glacier, which put our airplane five hundred feet above the terrain below, I made a 180-degree turn to the left and headed down glacier, reducing the throttle as we went to maintain the same distance above the descending river of ice and snow.

"Okay, folks, as you've noticed, we have turned around and are heading back down the glacier. Shortly, after passing the 'Big Bend' up ahead, I will jump off the glacier and head down the narrow valley of Coffee Creek, which will lead us to Chelatna Lake, where I will land and beach the airplane so you can get out for fifteen minutes or so to stretch yours legs."

Heading down the Kahiltna Glacier toward the "Big Bend." *(Photo by Mike Everist)*

Ten minutes later and five thousand feet lower, I turned ninety degrees to the right and flew through a notch in the mountains, followed almost immediately by a ninety-degree turn to the left that put us in a sharply descending, narrow valley with steeply rising terrain on both sides of the airplane. Being closely surrounded by mountains was a sudden turnabout from the spacious and remote vistas thus far on our tour. My passengers seemed to enjoy the juxtaposition.

As I exited Coffee Creek into Chelatna Lake, I turned to the right and flew toward the north end, where I customarily landed to take advantage of a nice sandy beach with a steep water gradient that allowed a floatplane to get to the beach without running aground. Mother Nature was not following the script, however, because there was a rain shower that blanketed the beach and landing area. *Now what, coach?* I had always landed there and did not have an alternate site. I turned and flew toward the south end of the lake, looking for a suitable beach. Because of the color of the water and the ambient lighting conditions, I couldn't readily determine if the water was deep enough along the shoreline. So, I picked an area that looked reasonable and went for it.

Judging from the ripples on the water, the wind was about five knots out of the south, so I landed parallel to the western shoreline of the lake into the wind. After landing, I dropped the water rudders and taxied to a somewhat rocky beach. Unfortunately, I ran aground about ten feet from the shore. Since I have learned to always wear hip boots when I know in advance that I will have to beach the floatplane, I hopped out into fifteen

Heeled up on the west shoreline of Chelatna Lake. *(Photo by Mike Everist)*

inches of water, spun the aircraft around and dragged the heels of the floats as far as I could toward the shoreline. Despite my best efforts, the tail-ends of the floats were still in water eight inches deep. So, using my superior bush-pilot skills, I found a few large stepping stones that would allow my passengers wearing suitable footgear to pick their way to the beach without getting their feet too wet. One lady, however had flats on, so I offered to carry her on my back to the shore, which she accepted. Anything for a good tip, I always say!

As everybody was huddled together on shore, pondering their next move, I said, "The ladies' restroom is to the right and men's to the left." One of the female passengers turned and looked at me as if to say, "Really, there are

Anything for a good tip! *(Photo by Mike Everist)*

Looking for wildlife on the flight back to Anchorage. *(Photo by Mike Everist)*

restrooms out here?" But she caught herself and then smiled with the rest of her fellow passengers at my feeble attempt at some Alaskan humor.

After fifteen minutes, we loaded up and took off for the thirty-minute flight back to Lake Hood. "Okay, folks, as I stated at the beginning of our tour, I will be flying at five hundred feet above the ground on our way back to Anchorage, and this will be our best opportunity to see some wildlife. If you see something that looks like an animal, even if you don't know what it is, tell me which side of the aircraft it is on. I will then immediately turn in that direction to try to locate what you have seen. Don't be bashful about speaking up, even if it turns out to be a uniquely shaped brown rock. I will be looking out as well.

"What animals might we see?" one passenger asked.

"It is unlikely you will spot any of the smaller animals, but in the larger category, we might see black bears, brown bears, and moose or maybe a bald eagle soaring above the muskeg looking for one of the small critters we can't see," I replied.

About ten minutes later, I spotted a brown bear on the edge of a small clearing to our left, so I banked the aircraft sharply in that direction. Although we caught another glimpse of the bear as we circled around, the airplane apparently spooked the creature because it quickly disappeared into the woods. The contact did serve to whet everybody's thirst for another sighting, so all eyes were glued to the landscape passing beneath our aircraft.

Turning final for the west water lane at Lake Hood Seaplane Base. *(Photo by Mike Everist)*

Shortly thereafter, a lady in the cabin shouted, "I've got something on the right; I think it might be a moose." Sure enough, out in the middle of a large clearing was a female moose and her calf. I circled a couple times in each direction to give everyone a chance to see the animals and then resumed our flight toward Anchorage.

As it turned out, the moose were the last wildlife we spotted, but the tour had been a total success—we got a good look at the Kahiltna Glacier, saw Mount McKinley, landed on a lake in the shadow of the great mountain, and saw some wildlife on our return to civilization. My passengers clapped as we coasted to Rust's dock and thanked me for a great tour and a fantastic experience. It made me feel good to know that they really enjoyed themselves.

Bears—Up Close and Personal

I was in high spirits as I negotiated the morning rush hour on the Glenn Highway. There wasn't a cloud in the sky and McKinley was visible off to my right. July 16, 2007, would prove to be more than just a beautiful day. It would be my second trip to Katmai National Park during my inaugural season flying for Rust's, and it would be the most memorable flight I ever had to the fabled national landmark.

The logistics involved in getting ready for a Katmai trip were different from any other flight we flew on a regular basis. Since it was an all-day tour, with no opportunity to obtain food, I packed coolers containing box lunches, snacks, sodas, and, most importantly, bottled water. Because Katmai was two hundred and ninety miles from Anchorage and had no gas pumps, aircraft fuel had to be managed carefully. Also, due to the distances involved, assessing the weather that might be encountered during the trip out and back was crucial, and took some time to accomplish.

The coolers were loaded in the aircraft, all tanks were topped off with fuel, the windows inside and out were spotless, and the preflight inspection of the airplane was complete. It was time to meet and greet my passengers. With manifest in hand, I walked onto the open deck outside the dispatch office. "Good morning. Who's going to Katmai?" I asked. Four individuals raised their hands. "Please, follow me," I replied as I led them back into the dispatch office and over to a large wall map.

"My name is Mike Stock," I stated, as I shook hands with a middle-aged couple from Australia, an eighty-year-old woman traveling alone, and a single gal in her mid-twenties from Canada. "Let's start out by showing you the route we intend to take today, on our flight to Katmai and return. Tracing the flight path with my right index finger, I explained, "I plan to fly the so-called outside route going down, which will take us along the western shoreline of Cook Inlet to Bruin Bay, right here; and then on to Brooks Camp on Naknek Lake. We'll take a different route coming back, which will take us over Iliamna Lake and Port Alsworth on Lake Clark, right here, where I'll refuel the aircraft before heading back to Anchorage. Any questions so far?"

There being none, I continued. "Aside from a few passing rain showers, I'm expecting reasonably nice weather. Hopefully, you brought a light-weight jacket or sweater because it can get cool if the sun disappears behind the clouds and the wind picks up.

"One last, very important item: the flight to Katmai will take about two and a half hours and there is no restroom aboard the airplane. So, I would strongly advise getting rid of that morning coffee before boarding. The restrooms are right over there. When you're done, I'll meet you at the Cessna 206 at the end of the center dock."

Soon, we were on our way. After clearing Anchorage controlled airspace, I turned to the west toward the mouth of the Big Susitna River and leveled off about one thousand feet above the grey waters of Cook Inlet below.

"Folks, just behind the right wingtip, on the distant horizon, is Mount McKinley, which is only visible from here about twenty percent of the time due to cloud cover." There were a few appreciative nods and one passenger pointed a camera to capture the moment. Continuing I launched into my standard narration for this trip:

The expansive, relatively flat area to our right is the Matanuska-Susitna Valley, which stretches from the Talkeetna Mountains in the east to Mount Susitna on the west, a distance of about eighty miles. Among other interesting facts about the Mat-Sue Valley, is it is the starting point of the famous thousand-mile Iditarod Sled Dog Race from Anchorage to Nome held every year in March. A ceremonial start is held in Anchorage, but the actual race begins in Willow, at the southeastern corner of the valley. The first three race checkpoints are within this valley, and the dog teams and mushers typically cover this hundred-and-twelve-mile distance in about fourteen hours.

Just then I caught sight of a few white objects in the mouth of the Little Susitna River. "Folks, if you look down at the river we are about to cross, you will see a pod of beluga whales fishing for breakfast."

"Wow, look at that!" the young woman from Canada shouted as she pointed excitedly at the white shapes as they randomly breeched to breathe, thus creating a stark contrast with the light-grey glacial waters of the river.

As we continued our journey the older female passenger asked, "Is it still possible to homestead in Alaska?"

"No," I replied. "The federal government discontinued homesteading in 1986, although the state occasionally puts small parcels up for sale; they are fairly reasonable in price, but not free."

Just forward of the right wingtip, at the one o'clock position, is Mount Susitna, or as the mountain is better known, The Sleeping Lady. If you use your imagination a bit, perhaps you can see the body of a woman lying on her back. Her head is to the left and the rest of her body is spread out to the right. The legend is that her warrior fiancé went off to the north with his tribe to fight an enemy nation and never returned. She is asleep, waiting to be reunited with her lover.

That tall mountain coming up on the right is Mount Spurr, the first of four active volcanoes we will pass in the next hour. Active doesn't mean that it is erupting, just that there are signs of volcanic unrest as measured by instrumentation on site. These four mountains—Spurr, Redoubt, Iliamna, and Augustine—are part of the Aleutian Chain and the so-called Pacific Rim of Fire, which is a series of active volcanoes that encircle the Pacific Ocean. Mount Spurr last erupted in 1992.

Mount Redoubt, which you can see in the distance on the right, last erupted in 1989, and nearly caused a major disaster. A KLM B-747. on its way to Japan. flew into the ash plume from the eruption, causing all four engines to flameout. After descending fourteen thousand feet without power, the crew was able to restart the engines and the airplane landed safely at Anchorage. As result of this incident, coming on the heels of another four-engine flameout on a British Airways 747 over Indonesia in 1982, in which the engines were also restarted, volcanic ash clouds are now tracked as they circle the globe and all aircraft are diverted from their paths.

And, while we are talking about eruptions, let me tell you about a gigantic one that occurred in Katmai National Park itself. In 1912, Novarupta exploded with ten times the force of Mount St. Helens, spewing volcanic material that filled in V-shaped valleys and eventually covered an area forty square miles. In terms of volcanic material displaced, some experts think it was the second-largest in recorded history; the largest occurred in Greece in 1500 B.C. The flat plain that was created was named The Valley of Ten Thousand Smokes by a 1916 National Geographic Society expedition because of the thousands of steam vents that dotted the landscape. The huge eruption was heard in Juneau, seven hundred and fifty miles away, yet no one was killed because of the extremely low-population density. Had that same eruption occurred on Manhattan Island, it likely would have killed most everybody.

Almost two hours into our trip, as we approached St. Augustine Island on our left, I turned to the right and flew up Bruin Bay to intercept the normal Lake Clark route into the park. When I got in the vicinity of Naknek Lake and Brooks Camp, it was raining fairly hard, which lowered visibility to less than two miles. Since I had never landed on Naknek Lake before, coupled with the chatter on the radio that indicated several other aircraft were converging to land at the same time, I decided the situation was not to my liking. Since we planned to eat our lunch as soon as we arrived anyway, I decided to land on a small lake just to the north of Brooks Camp. I picked a small island about one hundred yards off the shoreline to beach the airplane, figuring there would be less chance of encountering any bears. Because of the shallow bottom gradient leading up to the island, I wasn't able to beach on the shoreline; so, I had to build a bridge of rocks so that my passengers could get to the beach without getting their feet wet.

After finishing our box lunches and getting ready to load up the airplane, someone said, "What's that?" It was a brown bear and her cub swimming from the mainland to our island. They came ashore about twenty-five yards from us. The mother bear and her youngster looked at us for several seconds before turning the other way and strolling out of sight around a bend. Fortunately, the bears in the Katmai area were used to seeing humans at close range, and didn't feel threatened. Otherwise, our chance encounter could have resulted in tragic consequences.

When trying to land on Naknek Lake by the main ranger station, I saw that bears were all over the beach. The rule was that no airplane could approach the shore if a bear was on the beach; so I circled for about five minutes until a ranger waved me in. My passengers went to "bear school," where they learned about bear etiquette and then walked on their own to the bear-viewing platforms located 1.2 miles away. In the meantime, I hung out reading a book and taking a short nap in the airplane.

Two hours later, when my passengers had not returned for departure, I found out that they were held up by two brown bears that decided to take a nap at our end of a footbridge that crossed the Brooks River, trapping them on the other side. The number one rule in the national park was to not interfere with the bears' routine to the maximum extent possible. So, all parties involved waited patiently for an hour, hoping the bears would move on their own accord. When they did not, a ranger about two hundred feet away from the sleeping bears started beating the water along the shore with a stick, simulating a fish flopping in the shallow water. This did the trick, because both bears came running to investigate, which in turn allowed my passengers and the others to cross the bridge where they were led by another ranger along an alternate path to the ranger station to meet up with their pilots.

My four passengers and other visitors were following the ranger, single file through shoulder-high grass, when all of a sudden someone shouted, "Bear!" My male Australian passenger told me later what happened next: "I was bringing up the rear of the column and when the warning was shouted, I turned around just in time to see a big brown bear charging up the trail towards me. He was on me before I could move. He put on the brakes and slid to a stop within arm's reach of me. He studied me closely

After finishing our lunch and just before boarding the aircraft, we saw a brown bear sow and her cub swimming toward our position.

These two brown bears were keeping my passengers from crossing the foot bridge to where I was waiting to fly them back to Anchorage.

for a second or two before abruptly turning ninety degrees and tearing off into the high grass. I was scared shitless, believe me." He certainly had quite a story to tell his friends back in Australia.

After departing from Katmai, I flew across Iliamna Lake—the largest lake in Alaska and eighth largest in the U.S., and one of only two lakes in the world that has freshwater seals—into Lake Clark and landed at Port Alsworth to refuel. Because of the delay caused by the sleeping bears, by the time I arrived in the lagoon and taxied up to the beach, the door to the fuel shack was closed. My first thought was, *If I can't get any fuel, we are stuck here until tomorrow morning, when the fuel concession reopened.* With that horrible thought weighing on my mind, I ran the left float up on the beach and hopped quickly out of the airplane and ran the hundred yards or so to the fuel shack to see if there were any after-hours instructions.

I heard someone call my name. I turned around to see my airplane about thirty yards offshore and drifting farther out into the lagoon. I ran as fast as I could in hip boats to the shoreline and into the water. Even though the bottom gradient was fairly shallow, the water level soon reached the top of my boots. I briefly contemplated removing them and swimming for the plane, but quickly abandoned that idea as foolhardy. *Now what, all-wise bush pilot?* A young man who worked for Lake Clark Air Service saw my plight and rowed me out to the errant aircraft in a small inflatable. I restarted the engine, beached it properly, and managed to find someone to turn on the fuel pump. My passengers were amused by the turn of events, apparently thinking this was all part of the Alaskan experience.

I learned a valuable lesson that day which became my rule #1 for seaplane flying: NEVER EVER leave your plane unattended on a beach or at a dock unless it is securely fastened or tied down.

Snippets from Anchorage
Anchorage—May to September 2007

July 3—Light rain, overcast. Even though we are having some low cloud days and light rain, we don't have the rain fog like Ketchikan, therefore the visibility is much better below the overcast, which makes for less stressful flying. On first flight to Redoubt Bay Lodge nearly collided on the water with another Rust pilot at the lodge. I was just about to touch down heading west as he began his takeoff run heading southeast. I called him on the radio, "Bob, I'm at your 10 o'clock, thinking he would abort his takeoff, but he kept on coming. I tried to come off the step ASAP, then had to gun it when a collision appeared inevitable. I yelled, "Listen to the radio." Boy, was I ever mad—and scared! I spoke with him back in ANC and he apologized.

July 10—Finally, got my baptism on the Katmai run. I was a little apprehensive as I always am when going to a new place for the first time and also because this was such a long trip. I had a great group of two couples who were very good friends. They kept us all in stitches with their humorous commentary. The trip down was uneventful. I had my map out the whole way, which didn't seem to bother my passengers and the GPS was helpful and the weather was great. Chris, one of the female passengers, had to go to the bathroom so bad by the time we landed, she was ill. I offered to land short of our destination, but she declined. Once I beached our aircraft, she didn't waste any time hopping off the float and dashing into the woods.

I attended "bear school" with my passengers and we received our Graduation Pins, which must be prominently displayed on our outer clothing. Since my job was not to guide them in the Park, I left them proceed by themselves to the bear viewing area while I ate my lunch and reviewed my map and fuel stop for the return trip. I then walked by myself to the viewing platforms located about a mile away. I was very nervous because there were numerous bear signs along the narrow trail weaving through the woods: scat, trees clawed, numerous intersecting bear trails, and fresh diggings in the ground. I scuffed my feet and clapped my hands trying to make as much noise as possible. I passed a sign that said, "Travel in groups of four." A visitor in a group going the opposite direction said to me, "You are brave." I could have added, "Or stupid." I got to the boardwalk leading to the viewing

Top photo: Narrow path leading to an elevated wooden viewing platform. Walking alone on this path with bears all around is a bit unnerving.

Bottom photo: World-famous Brooks Falls where visitors can view upwards of fifteen brown bears fishing for salmon at the same time.

platforms and breathed a sigh of relief. I watched about nine brown bears fishing at the base of Brooks Falls. One very large, old male bear had the prime spot on top at the lip of the falls.

August 5—Definitely a Ketchikan day. The worst day so far. Ceilings and visibilities were down everywhere except right in ANC. We sat around most of the day waiting for the weather to lift. Four of us pilots went out to breakfast and we started telling "tourist" stories. Scott told of the day he was doing a Prince William Sound tour on a day the waters were quite rough. A lady asked, "What are all of those fish jumping for?" Scott replied, "Oh, those are just whitecaps." She asked, "Are they good to eat?" I told the story of the lady off a cruise ship that entered the art gallery where my wife worked in Ketchikan and asked, "Do you take American money?" Tourists—you've got to love 'em!

August 12—Patches of light rain and low clouds, but cleared up nicely in PM. First flight took two rafters and their gear to Chelatna Lake located near Mt. McKinley. The lagoon was challenging as usual: glassy light blue water and a relatively short landing area. After arriving back in ANC, I realized I had forgotten to unload their oar locks, which were in the left float compartment.

To alert a pilot or dock crew that cargo was being carried in a float compartment, a red streamer was hung on the outside of the float compartment to provide a visual reminder. I had forgotten to deploy the red streamer.

I felt terrible and walked into the office and said to Chris, the dispatcher, "Do you want to spank me now or later?" Fortunately, it was a light-flight schedule day, so he sent me right back in a 206 with the oar locks. Chris suggested tying the locks to a couple of life preservers and air dropping them. I didn't think much of that idea because they could hit the horizontal stabilizer or drop in a thicket somewhere beyond their grasp.

Fortunately, the rafters were still in the lagoon when I returned. They had overcome the missing oar locks by lashing the oars to the side of the raft somehow and were within ten minutes of departing downriver. They were glad to see me and I was glad to see them. They still had their sense of humor. They said, "It is nice of you to come back." And I said, "Well, Rust's has good customer service." To which one responded, "That's not what we were saying one hour ago." He went on to say, "At first you want to blame someone—the pilot, Rust's, ourselves, my friend. In fact, I was beginning to develop a hatred for him." I noted that they had a .44 Magnum pistol on top of their stuff. He said, "Yeah, I thought about shooting my friend or maybe myself."

August 14—Started out with a drop of 3 passengers at McDougal Lodge on the Yentna River near Lake Creek then empty to K-2 Lake to pick up two and take them to Winter Lake Lodge. Halfway to Winter Lake, I got a call on the radio from Justin, one of our pilots, saying the weather was too bad to land at the lodge and that I should proceed to Shell Lake to join two other Rust pilots, Eric and Russ, who were also waiting there for the weather to improve. Well, the first problem was where in the hell is Shell Lake? My front seat passenger was a former pilot, so I solicited his help to locate it on the map, which he did. I landed on the narrow, long lake and taxied over to where the other two airplanes were tied up to the Shell Lake Lodge dock.

We went inside and met Zoe, the owner of the Lodge. The other two pilots told me Zoe wasn't too happy with Rust's pilots, who often stopped to wait out the weather, drank her coffee, but did not buy anything to eat. So, the three us ordered a sumptuous breakfast while my two passengers bought lunch. Zoe was happy. It turned out from talking to her that she was a true Alaskan pioneer. After getting divorced, she came to Alaska 33 years ago with her three children ages 12, 8, and 6. They built the log cabins comprising the lodge themselves. Simply amazing. She was a real character.

After waiting several hours, we heard that another one of pilots got into Finger Lake, so two of us launched with Eric in the lead (Russ was on a different mission). We were flying up the Swentna River Valley at 100 feet just below the clouds. I saw Eric suddenly make a 90 deg turn up over the river bank and promptly lost sight of him. As I tried my best to follow him, I was literally flying right on the tree tops going in and out of clouds. I didn't know where I was, but I knew we were heading in the direction of higher terrain. All of a sudden I was directly on top of skinny Finger Lake heading perpendicular to the long axis with no flaps deployed and going way too fast to land. I didn't have the option of going around. I had to land. So, I jerked the throttle to idle, dropped full flaps and dove into the lake with the stall horn blaring. It was real scary and frightening. I thought for sure that the aircraft was going to stall and drop right wing into the lake. After splashing down hard, my pilot passenger said, "Well, that was about a 9½ on the pucker scale." He was cool about it, not mad—just relieved to be safe.

After disembarking my two passengers, the co-owner of the lodge said that he was going to send down my passengers who were going to ANC. I told him in no uncertain terms that I wasn't leaving. I was still visibly shaken. The other co-owner approached me a little later and asked if I was going to leave. Eric had departed right away which made me look like a weak pilot. I told her not until the weather improved. She seemed putout with the prospect of extra overnight guests. I said that I would sleep in my airplane and she replied rather snotty, "What about the guests?" Not my problem. I threw up my hands and started to respond when she spun on a dime and huffed off. I did sleep in my aircraft. It was not all that comfortable, and I kept waking up fearing that one of the ever-present brown bears in the area was going to stroll down the dock to investigate my airplane.

September 15—Last day of the season for me. Yeah! The weather was fairly nice all day, partly sunny, but cool—only 60 deg for a high. When

I arrived for work everyone in the office was talking about "the termination dust" we had received last night, which refers to the first light dusting of snow in the mountains surrounding ANC. It signifies the *termination* of summer and the beginning of winter.

I started out by flying some chainsaw oil and gas to a small lake east of the big bend in the Yentna River called Gem Lake. I put the coordinates in the GPS and it took me right to it. How did the early pilots do this job before GPS, because the lake was so small it didn't even show up on my sectional chart and there were many small lakes in the vicinity?

Anyways, the wind was strong out of the west, so set up my approach heading west, chopped the power and dove into the lake over some high trees that ringed the small body of water. So far so good, then the fun began. As I approached the south shore with a crosswind from the right, I noticed a tall pine tree on the water's edge just to the left of a small group of men waiting for me. Because of the tree I decided to head straight in to the beach. I didn't have my boots pulled all the way up—big mistake! As I got out of the cockpit, the wind started to turn the airplane to the right which put the left wing in jeopardy of hitting the pine tree. So, I hopped quickly into the water while trying to pull my hip boots up. I was not successful and the deep water overflowed into my boots—the water was damned cold too! But I was able to prevent the left wing from contacting the tree. I loaded one of the workers and his gear and flew to ANC. Fortunately I had the foresight at the beginning of the season to put a change of clothes in my car based on my dunking experiences in Ketchikan.

After changing clothes and putting on my regular work boots, I was off on a McKinley tour. It was fairly nice on the mountain and I made my usual landing in north end of Chelatna Lake on the way back. I did my normal beaching angled 45 degrees to the right heading north, but the wind, being fairly strong out of the south, caused the nose of the aircraft to turn further to the right and beaching the plane broadside to the beach. The floats grounded out about 4 feet offshore with me in my work boots. I thought to myself, "Great, I'm going to get my feet wet for the second straight time today." Which I did, but I managed to wrestle the aircraft around and heeled it up on the beach so my passengers could exit off the rear of the float without getting their feet wet.

My next flight was a Tauck tour to the Knick Glacier at a lower altitude than normal due to low clouds, but my passengers seemed to enjoy themselves. I got back to Lake Hood with 6 hours of flight time already and figured I was done for the day. Wrong! I flew one last flight to McDougal Lodge in a 206 and landed back in ANC with 7.0 flight hours and $52 in tips for my last day of work. I picked up my paperwork from the admin office and my hip boots which were nearly dry, shook hands with Willis and some of the pilots, who wished me luck and hoped to see me again next year. I have decided that I will return next year—unless I get another offer too good to pass up.

Anchorage – May to September 2008

June 10—Overcast, cooler. Started out with a Triumvirate Glacier tour in a 206. Had 3 male passengers, one a, 87-year-old WWII Navy pilot. Everything went fine until the landing on Beluga Lake.

Beluga was typical of bodies of water, be they rivers or lakes that are fed by runoff from glaciers. The water was a blueish-gray color which interferes with a pilot's depth perception making it harder to judge height above the water on landing. Add glassy water and a pilot really has his hands full.

It was glassy, so I planned my landing approach along the northern shoreline to give me a reference to aid depth perception. Although I had landed there numerous times in the past, this time I extended my touchdown point so I would be closer to where I intended to beach the aircraft. Well, I ran out of room. I still wasn't on the water and with the shoreline and a ridge full of trees looming ahead, I pulled the throttle off and smacked the water hard and bounced back into the air several times before settling down. But I was going too fast to stop before hitting the shoreline and possibly running the aircraft up on the beach high and dry. In desperation, I stuffed in full left rudder and turned 90 deg to parallel the shoreline. I felt the bottom of the floats begin to drag on the bottom, and despite adding full power, I ran aground. So, after apologizing to my passengers, I put my boots on and hopped into the water to assess the situation. I determined if I could turn the a/c about 45 deg further left, I would be headed toward deeper water.

I remembered listening to the older pilots talking about flying duck hunters into very shallow lakes and how you can pulse the nose of the aircraft up and down with the elevators while applying full power to move the nose of the aircraft left or right if you ran aground. I decided to try it. I asked the two younger men to climb into the back of the aircraft to lighten the nose and was able to slowly move the nose to the left at full power and refloated the aircraft. I had dodged another bullet and added to my bag of floatplane tricks. My three pax seemed cool about it and even gave me a $20 tip on return to ANC, grateful they weren't still marooned in the Alaskan wilderness.

Next I flew pax and freight to King Point Lodge on McDougal Slough. After making a nice landing and docking, my front seat passenger asked, "Do you always make it look so easy?" With the morning fiasco still fresh in my mind I replied, "Not always."

June 14—Flew five people and gear to their cabin on Red Shirt Lake located fifty miles northwest of Lake Hood. The lake was white-capping and I estimated the wind about 15-20 knots out of the south, which meant this would be a downwind docking. I knew this would be difficult, but didn't realize just how challenging it would be. On the first attempt, I cut the engine and hopped out to grab the float rope, but the aircraft started to weathervane immediately and ended up straddling the corner of the dock. On the second approach, I was too far out to jump onto the dock. The third try worked, but I had to tug with all of my might to wrestle the airplane into the dock and tie it up. At one point, when I thought I might lose it again, I considered asking one of the passengers to help me. You would think that one of them would offer to help, but no, they just sat in the airplane and watched me struggle. Oh yes! The life of a bush pilot.

June 15—Lots of sitting around today telling "war stories." I hope the season picks up soon or it will be a long summer. I flew 4 young people in their early 20's who were born and raised in Hawaii on a McKinley tour with a drop at K-2 Lake. I gave them a good tour, but could only climb to 4,000 feet due to the ceiling. Consequently, I could only get to the "Big Bend" in the Kahiltna glacier. But they were very polite and asked some questions and seemed to be enjoying themselves. At K-2, as I was about to get into the aircraft to leave, one of the male passengers shook hands with me as did the other man. The two girls each gave me a hug and one even gave me a kiss on the cheek. When I got back to ANC, I was telling Bruce Adams, one of our pilots, that I didn't get any tips, but I got two hugs and a kiss. He said, "That may be OK in the short term, but I prefer cash." I flew a Chugach Explorer to finish out the day.

June 24—Flew the 206 all day. I'm beginning to feel more comfortable in the aircraft. The 206 has a few advantages over the Beaver: rudder trim, quieter, and faster, but I still prefer the "Mighty Beav." Flew to Winter Lake Lodge and picked up 2 and flew them to Redoubt Bay Lodge at 6500 feet along the front edge of the Alaska Range. It was sunny and very beautiful. Strandline Lake had recently emptied leaving icebergs on the lake bottom—very interesting sight.

Strandline Lake is the site of a unique natural phenomenon that usually occurs once every summer. The oval-shaped lake, with steep sides three-hundred-feet high, fills with water and icebergs from the Triumvirate Glacier. When the lake is full, the water pressure builds to a point that it breaks through the ice dam at the southern end of the lake, releasing a torrent of water that rushes down a narrow canyon and empties into Beluga Lake. The draining takes place over a period of approximately forty hours and raises the level of Beluga Lake thirty feet for a period of several days, until the normal level is restored as excess water flows to Cook Inlet. Since the lake drains so fast, icebergs two hundred feet tall are left high and dry on the bottom of the lake. It is a very interesting and rare sight to show tourists on the Triumvirate Glacier tour. Rust's pilots had a betting pool going each summer to see who could come the closest to predicting when the lake would empty.

June 28—One of my flights today was a drop at the Bulchitna Lake cabin and then over to Alexander Lake to pick up two fishermen. After landing to the south as normal, I taxied through the narrow neck of the lake just above the beach where we positioned our fishing boats. As I moved through the narrows there was a fisherman standing up in his anchored boat angrily gesturing at me like I was interfering with his fishing, tranquility, or something. He was acting very rude and he really ticked me off. All of a sudden, he lost his balance and fell backwards into the water. Talk about poetic justice—it was a sight to behold.

July 7— Landed at the infamous "Cable Crossing" for the first time solo after having done a ride-along with Bruce Adams earlier this year.

There were two river-landing sites that we went to frequently that were sure to get my adrenaline pumping because the rivers were swift, the landing approach and takeoff had to follow the river below the treetops lining each side, there was only one way in and the same way out, no matter what the wind was doing, and once committed there was no safe go-around path to abort the landing.

The first was to the Great Alaska Fish Camp on the Kenai River. The second was to a place commonly referred to as the "Cable Crossing" on the Skwentna River located approximately seventy miles northwest of Anchorage. Unlike the Great Alaska Fish Camp, the beach where passengers and cargo was loaded and unloaded at the Cable Crossing was narrow, rocky, and located just below a narrow gorge, which caused the river to flow very swiftly. So much so that you had to fall off the step landing upriver fairly close to the beach or the current would sweep you downriver tail first. The approach to the beach was so fast it almost felt like you were going to overshoot and smash into the steep terrain directly behind the rocky sandbar. The takeoff wasn't quite as scary as long you were able to lift off before the ninety degree bend a quarter-mile downstream. Both of these locations kept me on my toes.

July 21—Took a water-studies professor from the University of Alaska to a small lake a little south of Soldotna on the Kenai Peninsula. Since I was the lead pilot in a flight of two Beavers, I had to decide whether the lake was big enough to takeoff—*landing distance for a seaplane is always shorter than the takeoff distance due to water friction.* After circling a couple of times, I decided it was long enough, landed, and taxied up to a spot on the shoreline I had picked out in the air. As it turned out, the "beach" I had selected was actually floating muskeg. When you walked on it, the surface bobbed up and down like you were walking on a large water bed. It was definitely weird and another first for this Alaskan bush pilot.

August 10—A good day and a bad day! On the good side, I flew to a place I had never been to: Crazyman Lake, located near the foothills of Mt. McKinley. I took a Beaver load of 2 x 6s to Seth Bates. I received a short briefing from Scott Rocky, one of the full-time pilots, on what to expect: small lake and a good dock. I approached through a cut in the trees just a little wider than the wings—and made a good landing.

After offloading the lumber, I asked Seth if he would give me a quick tour of his place. He is a retired Army Special Forces soldier with 28 years active duty service and then worked 8 years on the North Slope as director of security for an oil company. He bought his place in 1981

Walking on top of floating muskeg was like walking on a waterbed.

for $83 and pays no taxes. He has two log buildings: his original cabin and the one he currently lives in. He turned the old cabin into a nice sauna. He received 35 feet of snow last winter, so I imagine keeping the snow plowed to his sauna, a distance of 150 feet, must be a full-time job. I thought I had it bad in Michigan.

He has a nice workshop, storage sheds, sawmill, etc. His main cabin has a 6 ft x 6 ft root cellar below the kitchen and it keeps food from freezing even when it is 30-40 below zero outside. He has a generator for power, satellite TV—all of the comforts of home except running water. He plans to drill a well next year. The drilling rig will have to arrive in the winter on a sled towed by a snow machine. *In Alaska they call snowmobiles snow machines.* He was awarded two Silver Stars and lots of other decorations in Vietnam; a real nice guy with a great place.

When he retired, he wanted to be out here and his wife didn't, and since the kids were grown, they split. He comes into town, meaning Anchorage, two times a year to buy provisions. He said that he normally leaves for the entire month of February, often going back to Vietnam. A real character.

And now, for the bad part of my day. After taking off from Crazyman Lake, I proceeded to Lake Creek to pick some fishermen on the sandbar and transport them back to ANC. I landed upstream, which was normal, but with a good tail wind, which wasn't usually the case. *At Lake Creek there was a lack of good wind indicators and rivers seldom provide any clues as to wind direction and velocity.* I came over the trees, landing to the north and chopped the throttle because I didn't want to overshoot the lower sandbar and apparently had some right drift coupled with the normal "sucking of the nose" when you are light and landing downwind. I touched down and must have buried the right float because the aircraft suddenly veered to the right almost 90 deg. Lord only knows how close the right wingtip came to hitting the water. I don't know exactly what I did, but I probably instinctively added left aileron and left rudder. This caused the left float to touch, which caused the a/c to swerve to the left. For a moment I thought this dance was increasing in amplitude and that I was going to lose control of the airplane. The guide in the fishing boat carrying my passengers saw this all happen and suddenly swerved to the right, probably thinking I was going to hit him. It scared me plenty. I came very close to being upside down in the river. I taxied very slowly to the sandbar, visibly shaken. I was going to say something to the guide and passengers, but thought better of it and just passed it off as an everyday event. I don't know what my passengers were thinking when they got into my aircraft. I

Repairing the floor of the outhouse at a wilderness cabin owned by my company is all part of being a bush pilot.

knew one thing: I had to grease it on back at Lake Hood to salvage any pride I had left—and I did. So even though it scared me bad, it served as a reminder not to get too complacent and cocky. I will be a safer pilot for the experience. It certainly was humbling.

August 12—Chris sent me out to Wilderness Lake to make a repair to the outhouse floor at the Rust-owned cabin—apparently the last tenants had complained that they felt like they were going to fall in. So, I loaded into a Beaver a piece of ¾-inch plywood, a skill saw, a portable generator, hammer and nails, and one of the dock boys to help me—and off we went. The repair went as planned and since I enjoy working with my hands, it was a welcome change from the normal routine. Before Chris assigned this job to me, he didn't ask if I knew how to use this equipment or knew anything about basic carpentry. I guess he assumed that all bush pilots must have this skillset.

August 31—Everybody is tired: pilots, office staff, dock workers, and maintenance—all counting the days until the season ends. Today was a slow day with only 2.5 flight hours, but I worked my butt off because the first two flights were to the "duck flats" to transport duck hunters and their gear to their hunting shacks.

The "duck flats" are located in the river delta area where the Big Sue and Little Sue rivers dump into Cook Inlet. Within the duck flats are three small, very shallow bodies of water that have hunting shacks used by duck hunters in September of each year: Red Duck, Green Duck, and Lewis River Slough. Every landing in these three locations results in the pilot running aground either in the bottom muck or on sunken logs lying on the bottom. The trick is to keep the aircraft on the step as long as possible after touchdown while attempting to get as close as possible to the destination hunting shack. Once the airplane falls off the step, it is usually aground. Then it is a matter of tugging and pulling on the floats, or pulsing the nose up and down at full power in a laborious attempt to get the airplane as close to the shack as possible. When that fails, then the pilot and hunters get out into the muck with their waders on to unload the equipment and cargo. The experience of the pilot plays a big role in the amount of work required to unload and load. My first year at Rust's I wasn't assigned to fly any of these flights and only three or four pilots had enough experience to be sent to Red Duck, a pond so small and shallow that the floatplane had to be maneuvered on the mud flats themselves, which is an amazing feat of skill and prowess.

My first flight to Green Duck worked out okay, but my trip to the "school house" on the Lewis River Slough was ugly. The wind was out of the north which meant a downwind landing with the aircraft going too fast after landing to make a step turn into the dock. I kept

Just dropped off these two duck hunters and their gear at their hunting shack on Green Duck Lake.

it on the step and tried to make another step turn, but the a/c started to porpoise and I ended up short of the dock. So we all got out and managed to pull and push the airplane to the dock after a good deal of effort. I was frustrated and said, "This is the worst place we fly to." I probably offended the customers because they didn't say thank you or goodbye—nothing!

September 13—Last day of work! My first flight of the day was to take three rafters and their gear to Chelatna Lake. The flight up was uneventful in light rain. The fall colors were absolutely gorgeous—the golden aspens, cottonwoods, and willows against a green backdrop of spruce trees were stunning. Even the muskeg had turned a golden hue of many colors. The landing in the lagoon was challenging as usual— short, glassy with light rain—but I chopped the power over the last stand of trees and managed a fairly decent touchdown.

My next flight was the last Tauck tour of the season, but only involved three aircraft: Justin in the Otter, John Seaman in a 206, and me in a Beaver. Sarah Palin, the GOP vice-presidential nominee, left her home on Lake Lucille earlier that morning, so the Coast Guard inflatable boat and the Secret Service detail that had been guarding her home had left. After loading up our passengers, we taxied by her home and pointed it out to our clients, which they seemed to enjoy. We flew an abbreviated Triumvirate Glacier tour. Due to low clouds, we couldn't climb above 2,000 feet, so the only wildlife we spotted were some moose in the flats on our return.

My last flight was back to Chelatna to drop the raft to the group I dropped off in the morning. Then I flew to Bulchitna Lake to pick up four guys and their gear. It was my third difficult landing of the day. Only one more step-turn takeoff and a landing back at Lake Hood stood between me and my 2008 safety bonus. I managed to grease it on evoking a comment from one of my passengers, "You've done that before." I retrieved my headset and backpack from the a/c, filled out the office paperwork, picked up my hip boots, said goodbye to Willis, and drove home to Eagle River. Another successful Alaska flying season was behind me and with no KTN weather days to boot!

Anchorage—May to September 2009

Just like the soul searching I did during the three summers I flew in Ketchikan, I went through the same agony flying out of Anchorage. To be fair, my first two seasons, although not without some drama and hairy encounters, were relatively pleasant experiences. My third summer—which you are about to read about—was an emotional roller coaster primarily because of my continuing difficulties landing the Cessna 206.

June 1—Flew a NOAA marine biologist named Mandy in a C-206 to Prince William Sound to gather mussel samples, seaweed specimens, and to count whales. The first landing in Valdez Arm was very smooth in light chop on the water. The shoreline was exceptionally rocky, but I managed to beach it OK. That's the nice part of having fiberglass versus aluminum floats in that there is less chance of puncturing a float on sharp rocks and corral. The tide was going out and the wind was picking up, so I had to hold onto the float ropes on the right side—one in each hand—to keep the wind and waves from turning the a/c broadside to the shoreline. I had to really strain for about 30 min while she collected her samples.

Next, we flew to Siwash Bay. The water was glassier than I anticipated and I rushed the landing, which resulted in a good bounce which progressively got worse. For some reason I did not add a touch of power or go around. Finally, it settled down on the water. It was a little scary and more than a little embarrassing. The beach at this location was a little better than the first, but still a bit rocky. At least the wind and water were calmer and I was able to tie the a/c off to a snag on the beach.

Next, we flew to Herring Bay, where she collected seaweed specimens. There was a little swell and again I bounced the landing, but not as bad.

After leaving there, we spent the next two plus hours looking for whales. I did not see any on my side, but then I was concentrating more on flying, so all sightings were on her side; ten in all, including two female humpbacks with calves and what she thought might be a grey whale, which I gathered from her commentary to be more of a rare sighting.

Boy, did she ever know her way around Prince William Sound. Good thing too because most of the time I didn't have a clue. I wanted to nail my landing back at Lake Hood, more for my own confidence, but also to show her I could do it—and I did! 6½ total hours with 4.1 flight hours. Good first day back on the job.

June 9—Flew to Redoubt Bay Lodge in the morning and hung there until 1330 return flight. My next flight was to drop off some German fishermen at Kings Point Lodge at Lake Creek. They come every summer; I even recognized one of the men from last year. As another pilot and I were waiting around to load our passengers, an older woman approached me and said, "Sprechen sie Deutsch?" I replied, "Nein." She then said, "Parlez-vous francais?" I gave my standard reply, "Un peu." (A little.) She smiled, I think because she finally made some sort of connection. Then I thought she said something that sounded like, "Quelle heure est-il?" (What time is it?) but I think she was asking what time do we leave. I pointed to my watch and she seemed satisfied. I felt good that I was able to communicate just a little and reinforced my desire to someday learn to speak a foreign language fluently. When she got off the aircraft, she said, "Merci."

I then flew over to Alexander Lake to pick up some fishermen who caught over 60 Pike. I made a nice glassy water landing and beached it perfectly. Made me feel good about my skills—I was back in the saddle.

July 4—Another scorcher—75 deg and downright hot. I think the reason why 75 in Anchorage feels like 95 in the lower 48 is because the sun's rays are more direct at this latitude during the summer months. I got ready for my first flight to Redoubt Bay Lodge early as is my custom, but forgot to check the weather at the lodge. So, I blasted off and soon discovered there was fog at the lodge. The overcast was quite extensive, but I continued on top of the clouds in the hopes there would be a hole I could spiral down through when I arrived at the lodge.

Fortunately, there was a very small hole at the "backdoor" of Big River Lake near the lodge. I circled the hole twice questioning whether I should do this. I had never done it before, but some of the more senior pilots talked about the technique. I slowed the Beaver and lowered landing flaps and rapidly descended into the hole while circling to avoid the mountainous terrain on all sides. I passed through the hole and slid under the overcast clouds only to find fog rolling in from the east. By the time I taxied the short distance to the dock it was socked in—zero-zero. Boy that was close! Obviously had I known it was that bad underneath, I wouldn't have tried it, but it still felt good that I pulled it off.

July 18—Flew 083 (a Beaver) all day. Kind of like having your own airplane and I like that. Flew two roundtrips to River Song sandbar and one trip to Mt. McKinley that was aborted due to weather.

On my last return flight of the day to Lake Hood, I had a teenager who promptly fell asleep in the front seat right after takeoff. I've been trying for six years flying in Alaska to land without waking up the "copilot." Well, I finally did it! I congratulated him much to the applause and amusement of his family.

I had just landed at Redoubt Bay Lodge after spiraling down through a small hole in the overcast, when fog rolled in.

July 19—Rainy, cool. Very slow day due to weather. Flew the 0800 flight to Redoubt Bay Lodge and had one of the worst landings of my floatplane career. I hit a little hard and bounced up and each bounce got progressively worse. I actually thought we might nose over. It was scary! I had three female passengers on board and I know they were scared. It totally destroyed my self-confidence. I've been having trouble off and on all season landing the 206. I can't figure it out. I think my depth perception is off because I seem to be leveling off too high and maybe stalling it in; although I don't have much problem with the Beaver. Maybe it is a mental hang-up. Yesterday, since I was flying the Beaver all day, I was feeling good and had almost decided to come back for another year. But after today's hard landing, there is no way in hell I am coming back to fly floats. Helicopters might be a different story and I intend to explore that possibility. On the other hand, maybe it is time to hang up professional flying. My morale is very low right now. I hope tomorrow is better.

July 20—Guess what? I flew the same 206 as I did yesterday. As the old saying goes, "When you get thrown from the horse, the best thing is to get right back on," or something like that. What a difference a day makes because all of my landings today were decent.

July 26—Cool, rainy. Boy! What a day. I've decided there is no way in hell I am coming back next year to fly floatplanes; helos maybe. All of my landings today were made under very difficult conditions—talk about stress. But the real nightmare happened at the Tuka Bay Lodge, which is located in Kachemak Bay south of Homer. The landing was OK, actually the best of the day. I recalled other pilots advising me that it's best to beach a Beaver instead of using the lodge's dock. When I got to the beach it turned out to be very rocky and the tide was going out. A rocky beach is always a concern that an aluminum float might be punctured.

Anyway, I proceeded to load a father and his five sons and 300 pounds of luggage. Normally, this load would not be a problem for a Beaver except all of these guys were huge—over 6 foot 3, with one being 6 foot 11. I probably should have refused to take such a large load, but they said they had a flight to catch in Anchorage and I didn't want to rain on their parade. I had plenty of water for a long takeoff and I knew from experience that the Beaver could haul a tremendous load, so I decided to go for it.

First, I had trouble getting off the beach because of the receding tide and the heavy load—it took almost full power. The takeoff run was very long as expected. But then I got launched 20 feet into the air below flying speed by a large swell. I reacted instinctively by jamming in full throttle and over-boosting the engine by 3½ inches of manifold pressure for five seconds. But fortunately we stayed in the air and flew away. I'm convinced that had we smacked down again the force might have damaged the floats. It was one of my most scary takeoffs, if not the worst one ever.

My last landing of the day was to the River Song sandbar where I landed in fog ten-feet thick right on top of the water. By the time I got to the sandbar, the fog had thickened to twenty feet. Egads, what a day! I have lost my confidence and my edge. It's about time to hang up Alaska float flying.

August 2—I am still paranoid about landings, especially in the 206. It is ironic that this is the first time in my flying career that I am not trying to "grease it on," but just trying to land safely without too much embarrassment. It just seems like I'm having more problems "finding the bottom."

On an upbeat note, one of our pilots, John Seaman, told a funny story about a flight he had a number of years ago to drop the ashes of a man and his wife. When he dropped the woman's remains, he said over the radio, "Bombs away" and everybody in the dispatch office heard him. When he got back from his flight, he was gently chided for his insensitive remark to which he said, "I meant to say 'Mom's away.'"

August 10—Sunny, nice day, but I'm back in the pits again regarding flying the 206. I flew down to Wilderness Lake to pick up a fisherman from NC—nice guy—and the flight went OK.

My next flight to Winter Lake Lodge was awful! First it was very, very turbulent and gusty on the landing approach to the southwest. At one point I had to add full power to keep from being slammed into the ground. In the Beaver, I can wrestle it to the water in these conditions, but in the 206 it's another matter. I probably tried to force the landing rather than landing long. I settled too hard onto the water and then went through three hard heart-pounding bounces one harder and higher than the previous. To make matters worse, a film crew was filming a documentary on Alaska and captured the whole embarrassing incident. Boy, did they ever get some good footage of how not to do it. After finally settling down on the water, I was at first scared, then embarrassed, and then mad.

I don't know what's happened to me. In the last two years flying the 206, although I never liked landing it as compared with the Beaver, I did OK and felt comfortable. This year, I approach every landing in the 206 with dread and stress. So what do I do? I feel I have three options: quit now, quit early, or quit flying the 206. Maybe this is the beginning of the end of my flying career because I seem to have lost my edge and skill. If so, then it's time to hang it up. I'm anxious to see when I return to Traverse City if I have the same trouble with a runway. If I do, it's time to quit flying altogether. I am leaning toward quitting the 206. I think I will talk to Dan Baldwin (chief pilot) tomorrow morning. I will sleep on it and see how I feel in the morning.

August 31—My job today was to take some passengers to Redoubt Mountain Lodge for a day of bear viewing and then bring them back to Anchorage at the end of the day. Chris and I debated whether to go or not based on phone calls and vague emails from the lodge that reported winds 30-40 mph and 2-foot waves coming directly onto the beach in front of the lodge. After flying in KTN for three years, I wasn't too concerned about the wave and wind conditions in a Beaver, so I decided to give it a try.

Sure enough, when I arrived the wind and waves definitely precluded landing and beaching where we normally did. So, I elected to land at the narrow end of the lake, located about an eighth of a mile from the lodge, I landed directly into the wind which was blowing like crazy. But once on the water I couldn't turn more than 60 degrees out of the wind line, which meant I couldn't go directly to the beach. So, I shutdown the engine and sailed back far enough that I could sail power-on to the beach while keeping my nose pointed into the wind. However, after grounding out approximately ten feet from dry ground I was parallel to the beach which meant the passengers would have to wade in knee-deep water to high ground. Finally, I hit upon the idea of the guide and me working the Beaver around a narrow point into a very small cove that was completely protected from the wind. After ten minutes of both us pulling, pushing and tugging on the floats, we managed to get the aircraft around the point and heeled the rear of the floats up onto the beach. I felt pretty darn good about my bush-pilot resourcefulness and ingenuity.

The next day back at the office most of the pilots, including the seasoned veterans, crowded around the computer in the pilot's lounge with a Google Earth map of the area. They were impressed with what I had done and several commented that it was good info for the future in similar wind conditions. This was the first time in six flying seasons

After landing at Redoubt Mountain Lodge in very strong winds and large waves, one of the guides and I managed to wrestle the Beaver into a small protected cove so we could unload my passengers.

in Alaska that I was able to offer some advice to the old timers—it had always been the other way around.

September 4—Beautiful day, clear skies and about 70 deg. I started the day with the expectation that I had five more work days and I was mentally prepared for that. Well, as I was getting ready for a 1030 departure on my first flight, Dan (chief pilot) approached me and said, "If you want, you can cut your season short; no pressure, it's up to you." My initial reaction, which I kept to myself, was no I wouldn't leave early—I was geared up to work five more days.

I took off on my first flight to Winter Lake Lodge and then to River Song sandbar back to Lake Hood and a Chugach Explorer all in a 206. I was thinking about what to do on each of these trips and I reached a decision: I would work another 3 days versus 5. My landings were not great, a little bounce each time. This continued poor landing performance, however, caused me to revise my decision—today would be my last day and I told Dan of my decision.

My last two flights in Alaska were to the "duck flats" in a Beaver. The first to Green Duck went smoothly and I didn't even have to get in the water. My very last flight was to the Lewis River Slough. The two duck hunters—a man and wife—wanted me to drop in two places: the eastern most hunting shack and the rest of the gear at a larger building nicknamed "the school house" on the western end of the slough. I made a nice short-field landing abeam the first shack and kept it on the step and made a wide sweeping left turn on top of submerged logs that vibrated the airplane much like running over rumble strips on the highway and stopped four feet from their rickety dock. Not bad, even they said so and they were not prone to offering compliments. We off-loaded their hunting equipment, hopped back in and I tried to step-taxi as best I could to the school house on the other end. This time I was only able to get within 8 feet of the dock, so we all had to get into the water and muck to move the remaining supplies from aircraft to the dock.

Information Mike

After unloading the two duck hunters, their Labrador retriever, rifles, ammunition, sleeping bags, food, beer, and water (in case the beer ran out) onto the dilapidated dock in front of their equally ramshackle one-room hunting cabin, I got back into the floatplane and fastened the seat belt for my very last flight in Alaska, and the last flight, as it turned out, I would ever fly as a commercial pilot. Using a quick cockpit flow, honed

On the next to last flight of my bush pilot career in Alaska, I dropped three duck hunters at their hunting shack on Green Duck Lake. September 4, 2009

by six seasons flying the legendary de Havilland Beaver—mixture rich, mags to both, master switch on, hit the starter—the big nine- cylinder Pratt and Whitney engine roared to life and settled into a familiar deep-throated purr at idle power. I announced my impending departure from Lewis River Slough on 122.7, pulled the yoke back into my lap, and laid the whip to her. The empty aircraft leaped onto the step and was airborne in less than five hundred feet.

As I climbed to 1,200 feet and crossed the mouth of the Big Susitna River heading toward Anchorage, I gazed one last time on Mount McKinley just forward of the left wingtip, Mount Susitna, the Sleeping Lady, just behind the wing on the left, Cook Inlet on the right, and the Chugach Mountains to my front. These picturesque and dramatic sights had been my constant companions over the last three summers—old friends now slipping from view and on their way to becoming distant memories.

As I approached the congested airspace of Anchorage, I tuned into the Lake Hood ATIS to get the recorded airport information:

"Lake Hood Information Mike, 1950 zulu. Wind 250 at 8, sky clear, visibility greater than 20, temperature 18, dewpoint 13, altimeter 29.85, west routes in use, landing and departing runway 31 and the west water lane. Read

back all hold short instructions. On initial contact, report you have informa-tion, Mike."

Did I hear that correct? Information Mike? What are the odds of the current ATIS being "Mike" on my last flight? The flying gods must be speaking directly to me—"It's okay to retire. You are making the right decision. You've had a great ride."

I flew parallel to the powerlines and made the right turn at "powerline bend" heading to Point MacKenzie and called the tower:

"Lake Hood Tower, Rust Beaver 083, two north of MacKenzie, for the water, with Mike."
"Roger, Rust Beaver 083, report the ballpark."
"083."

Mixture rich, fuel selector on the proper tank, water rudders up—I went through the pre-landing checks over Point MacKenzie as I had done hundreds of times before. I especially didn't want to land with my water rudders down on my last flight—not a cool way to exit the stage. I crossed over Knik Arm and headed toward the ballpark on the south shoreline.

"Tower, 083, ballpark."
"Rust 083, cleared to land west."
"083, cleared to land west."

On right base, I reduced the throttle to twenty-one inches manifold pressure, selected landing flaps, moved the prop lever full forward, and lowered the nose to maintain an approach airspeed of seventy knots. I flew around the Millennium Hotel and lined up on final for the west water lane. I reduced power, raised the nose to the landing attitude, smoothly slid the floats onto the water, turned left into Fish and Wildlife Cove, and taxied to the Rust dock.

At some larger airports, it is tradition on an airline captain's last flight before retirement to align the airport firetrucks on both sides of the taxi-way to create a large water arch as the captain taxis to the gate for the last time. There was no such fanfare or ceremony awaiting me—just as it should be. I rather liked the idea of just slipping away. I cut the mixture and the big radial engine became silent. The only sound was water lapping against the floats as the Beaver coasted to the dock.

Just like that, it was over! My forty-five-year professional-flying career ended the way it had begun—full of wonder and awe!

Epilogue

I BEGAN WRITING MY AVIATION MEMOIR IN 2004. THIS ODYSSEY HAS been a multi-faceted journey; at times stressful, at times joyful, and always illuminating. There were moments, as I remembered particularly dangerous times and narrow escapes, when my pulse quickened and my throat became dry. Over the course of my writing, I have developed classic symptoms of PTSD, which I attribute to reliving those days in the cockpit when my life hung in the balance. Maybe I felt guilty for having survived to fly another day, when so many of my pilot friends did not. On the flip side, I smiled and laughed out loud at some of the lighter moments that crisscrossed my flying career. And the best part of this careful introspection has been rediscovering names, places, and events that had long been forgotten.

Since beginning this project fourteen years ago, there were many times when I despaired of ever reaching the point of writing the epilogue. What started out as a single book to document my career became a three-volume labor of love. But like all human endeavors where love is a central theme, there were rocky patches that tested my commitment. True, I took breaks to go on family vacations, to complete projects around the home, and to re-charge my batteries, but I always felt somewhat guilty that I was not in my study banging away on the keyboard. In short, my quest has been all-consuming and at times very draining. So, I am very glad to be at the point of wrapping it up!

At the conclusion of the last chapter, I wrote that my forty-five-year professional-flying career came to an end in 2009 when I cut the engine to my floatplane and coasted to the dock at Lake Hood. That statement was only partially correct. It is true that I never again flew passengers for hire, but I did do some part-time flight instruction for eight years afterwards. So, in that sense, my professional flying career did not end until July 2017. Let's finish the rest of the story, shall we?

Seaplane Flight Instructor

It had been over a year since I had last flown a seaplane for Rust's Flying Service and I was missing it. So, I renewed my employment relationship with Northwestern Michigan College and signed on to be a part-time flight instructor, flying their pristine Super Cub on amphib floats. I instructed for the last five weeks of the floatplane season in 2010, before the water temperatures forced the winter layup of N644DR just before Thanksgiving.

Over the next four summers, I racked up two hundred and fifty-one instructional flight hours and a greater number of ground-training hours teaching aspiring pilots the finer points of seaplane flying. With over 2,000 hours flying floatplanes in Alaska, I felt that I had a lot to offer my students, and I had a blast doing it. What is there not to like about flying a beautiful Super Cub with an oversized 180-horsepower engine around one of the most beautiful areas in Michigan, with an abundance of pristine lakes in which to wet your floats?

I have always said that I wanted to hang up flying on my terms and not wait until someone tapped me on the shoulder and said, "Mike, I think it's about time you stopped flying." I've known a few pilots who continued to fly after their skills had eroded to the point of being a menace to themselves and others. I didn't want to be one of them—but then, I almost was!

In May 2013, just barely into the season, I made a serious judgment error that might have ended badly had it not been for the courage of my

Northwestern Michigan College Super Cub heeled up on the shoreline of West Bay in Traverse City, Michigan.

flight student. Chase Mather and I had flown an instructional flight in the morning, and after taking a break for lunch, we took off again on only his fourth flight in a seaplane. We were practicing takeoffs and landings on Lake Dubonnet, a small body of water located twenty-two miles southwest of the Cherry Capital Airport in Traverse City. It was one of my favorite lakes because it was a good spot to perform every type of seaplane landing and takeoff. Chase had just performed a short-field landing over some trees along the eastern shoreline and a few minutes later commenced a short-field takeoff across the narrow axis of the lake. Even though the distance available for takeoff was approximately fifteen hundred feet, it looked much shorter when staring into the tall trees on the far shoreline. But I had taken off on this heading many times and felt comfortable with the conditions—in other words I had my "GO" hat on and aborting the takeoff was not on my radar. Apparently, the wind had shifted to our tail and I didn't recognize that we were now taking off downwind.

The takeoff run seemed a little longer than usual, but I was not concerned, again because I had made this takeoff successfully so many times before. Besides, I liked the realism this path presented to the student—it was a real-life short-field takeoff situation. Chase, on the other hand, did not feel comfortable and, at the last possible second, pulled the throttle to idle and aborted the takeoff. The only problem was we were going too fast to stop before entering a small swamp-like area with tree stumps and downed logs sticking out of the water. Luckily, he was able to frantically steer clear of the obstructions. We came to a sudden stop when the cable running between the two floats in front of the prop hit a stump and parted. Otherwise the propeller would have contacted the stump causing major damage.

It all happened so swiftly. I was absolutely stunned by the sudden turn of events. After he shut down the engine, I started to berate him, "Why did you do that? Why did you abort the takeoff? We could have made it," I said angrily.

I calmed down quickly, however, and we got busy trying to extricate the airplane from the stump-infested swamp, which turned out to be no easy task. I used a Leatherman multi-purpose tool I always carry on my belt when flying seaplanes to cut off the ends of the severed cables to keep them from flying up into the prop.

After replaying the takeoff over and over in my head that night, I came to the realization that Chase probably saved us from crashing. Had he continued the takeoff, we most likely would not have cleared the trees and may well have lost our lives. The next day, I thanked him for his decisive action and his courage in making the call. After all, he was flying with a flight instructor old enough to be his grandfather, a pilot with thousands of hours of flight time. Who was he to question my judgment when I said nothing about aborting the takeoff? It was a very gutsy call on his part.

And, it was a very humbling experience, and one that I readily admitted to Aaron Cook, the Aviation Director, was of my own making. Later that summer, I had two other minor lapses in judgment, but mistakes nonetheless: I took off with one of the fuel caps missing, and I did not comply with the instructions of the Traverse City tower controller who told me to enter the traffic pattern mid-field downwind, instead entering on a base leg.

My track record was heading in the wrong direction. Management didn't quite know what to do with me since I had literally taught all of them to fly and hired many of them to be flight instructors. It was like making the decision to take the car keys away from their father. Do they gently tell me that it's time to quit or do they let me keep flying with the hope that these three occurrences were isolated events? They chose the latter, but I'm sure it wasn't an easy decision.

In May of the following year, I resumed instructing in the NMC yellow Super Cub. The summer was uneventful until September 4, 2014. That afternoon, I was working with a student on Lake Skegemog twenty miles northeast of Cherry Capital Airport. The weather forecast before takeoff indicated that thunderstorms were predicted to move through the area in two to three hours after our planned departure time. In fact, we could see the buildups in the distance on the western horizon. I figured that we could safely conduct an hour of instructional flight and get back well before the storm hit the airport.

The storm cells had a different mind. They swept in early and by the time I realized this and headed for the airport, the thunderstorms were only five or six miles west of the airport. On final approach for Runway 28, the wind gusts were becoming severe. I was moving the stick left and right, stop-to-stop, to keep the wings somewhat level. I had to literally fight the light aircraft all the way to the runway, employing all of my skills. It was easily one of my most difficult landings ever. Somehow, I managed to wrestle the Super Cub to the asphalt. Several mechanics and Aaron Cook, the Director, were watching from the college ramp. From watching the crazy antics on final and just above the runway, they were amazed I didn't damage the airplane.

I was actually quite proud of myself for having pulled off a very difficult landing. But in my hubris, I missed the whole lesson to be learned—why take the chance in the first place? I was getting too complacent and resting on my laurels.

My student didn't want to fly with me again, and I understood. No other students were assigned to me over the next couple weeks. I got the message. It wasn't an overt tap on the shoulder from management to hang it up. It was a subtle and graceful "tap" from the boss saying, "Enough is enough."

I announced that I would officially retire from the college on October 17—a date I chose because it would be fifty years to the day after my first Navy solo in Pensacola. I'm sure the powers that be were elated and relieved that they didn't have to hit me over the head with a chock to get my attention.

My good friend and fellow seaplane instructor, Bill Donberg, suggested that the two of us should go flying one last time in the Super Cub on my retirement date. I smelled a rat. I figured that the staff was up to something, and I didn't want any kind of ceremony or fanfare, so I demurred. As it turned out, the weather was too bad to fly anyway. Bill was persistent, so I agreed to play along and flew with him on October 22. My suspicions were confirmed. As we taxied back to the NMC line, the airport had positioned two firetrucks on each side of the taxiway forming a water arch with their water cannons—just like they do in the airlines when a captain retires. Afterward about thirty current and former students and staff gathered around to shake my hand. It was a fitting end to my NMC flying career.

The bell I purchased and the poem I wrote that started a tradition in 2005. The bell is rung whenever a Northwestern Michigan College flight student reaches the next milestone in his or her piloting career.

Before leaving Northwestern Michigan College, I want the record to reflect my proudest accomplishment during my twenty-year career at the college. Back in 2005, I decided that we needed to somehow immediately recognize the flight accomplishments of our students in the aviation program at NMC. So, I came up with the idea of having a bell that is rung whenever a student reaches a milestone in his or her aviation career, like their first solo or obtaining a new FAA certificate or rating. As soon as the bell sounds everybody within earshot, staff and students alike, immediately stops what they are doing to gather around and congratulate the pilot on his or her accomplishment.

I purchased the bell and plaque with my own funds and wrote the short poem that is affixed to the plaque, thus starting a long-standing tradition which continues to this day; one that will hopefully last long after I am gone. I told my children, "Years from now you may decide to stop by the aviation office to look at the bell and be able to say, 'My dad started this tradition.'"

The poem on the plaque reads:

Ring the bell
Let's all cheer
Salute the pilot
Standing here

Other Part-time Flying Gigs

Ever in a constant state of wanderlust, I always had my eyes peeled for the next grand adventure. Most never got beyond an initial phone call and a mailed résumé, while other employment opportunities actually resulted in a paycheck for a brief period—King Air training in Colorado, helicopter flight instruction in Arizona, and fixed-wing flight instruction in Indiana.

By the summer of 2017, I was slowing down; getting near the end of my "flying road." A fellow pilot for Rust's Flying Service in Alaska, who, like me, was getting up there in years, when asked how he was doing, would often respond, "I'm circling the drain." I guess, in a way I was circling the end of a great flying career that began back in 1964, in the United States Navy at Pensacola. I just wasn't as sharp or as skillful as I once was. However, I had been awarded the prestigious Wright Brothers Master Pilot Award on December 28, 2016, an honor bestowed by the FAA to pilots who have flown fifty years without an accident or violation of the Federal Aviation Regulations. It would not be good for a *Master Pilot* to end up in a "smoking hole." But, before hanging up my leather flight jacket, goggles, and white silk scarf, I had one last mission to complete.

In October 2016, I agreed to teach a bright young man to fly and to facilitate his obtaining a private pilot's license. Sean Harris was a high school senior from southern Indiana, who planned to enroll in the professional flight program at Indiana State University in Terre Haute after graduation. The university agreed to grant full college credit for the private pilot ground school and for the private pilot flight course I would teach him. Over the next ten months, Sean studied hard and diligently applied himself to master the intricacies of private pilot flight. He was a quick study and a joy to fly with. So, on July 10, 2017, I flew with Sean one last time before recommending him to take the FAA Private Pilot checkride, which he passed handily three days later. The flight also marked my retirement from instructing after accumulating 4,813 hours as a flight instructor and 15,319 total flight hours.

Family Update

Most authors don't devote a section in the epilogue to their family but since my family has been an important contributor and facilitator to my aviation career, it is only right that I acknowledge their support and encouragement.

My parents were thrilled when I received my Navy wings in 1965. Making up for three and a half years of lackluster college performance, they were delighted that I finally had some positive direction in my life. To the very end, they followed my aviation career with great interest.

My father, Samuel A. Stock, died in a nursing home in Ocala, Florida on December 22, 2000, three days short of his eighty-sixth birthday. Twelve days before he passed, not knowing the end was so near, I kissed him goodbye and told him that I loved him—sadly, the first time in my life I had done either.

My mother lived to be much older. Alyce M. Stock left this world on April 13, 2017, three months short of her ninety-ninth birthday. She was in a hospital in Dunkirk, New York, fighting an acute infection. She feared she would be forced to leave the pleasant assisted-living facility where she had resided the last three years and have to go into a nursing home. So, rather than fight any longer, she stopped eating and drinking and stopped all medications except for a morphine drip. Right up until the end, she was in full control of her life. She left on her terms. When I kissed her goodbye for last time several days before she died, I leaned down and kissed her on the forehead and whispered in her ear, "I love you, Mom. Bon Voyage." Whether she heard me or not, I don't know, but I thought I detected a slight facial movement. I couldn't have asked for a better mother or father.

As this book goes to press, our three children have grown up to have children of their own. All three are college graduates, smart, hardworking, successful, and model citizens. Barbara and I couldn't be prouder.

Brian, fifty, and his wife, Susan, live in Chicago with their two children, Kayla, fifteen and Devin, twelve. Brian owns a successful engineering and manufacturing company and Susan manages the household after a successful career as an interior architectural designer.

Ashley, forty-three, and her husband, Eric, live in Laveen, a suburb of

Phoenix. They have three children, Samantha, fourteen; Brody, twelve; and Cole, six. Ashley is a stay-at-home mom at present, but for several years held a high-level supervisory position at America West Airlines. Eric is a pilot for American Airlines and a successful realtor on the side.

Our youngest is Julie, thirty-eight, who lives in New Albany, Indiana, with her two children, Peyton, five and Kai, two. Her former husband, Patrick, lives in California. Julie was a successful career U.S. Army officer before she was medically retired at the rank of major after twelve and a half years active duty service, including four combat tours, three in Iraq and one in Afghanistan. She also worked for the FBI for a short time before leaving to have her second child.

Last, but certainly not least, is my faithful back-seater, Barbara, who has "flown" with me for nearly fifty-three years as a loving wife and devoted mother. Without her untiring efforts to hold the family together during my frequent absences—whether during my Navy days and subsequent flying assignments, or when I was locked away in my study preparing ground-school lesson plans during my faculty days at Purdue University and Northwestern Michigan College—I could not have accomplished a fraction of what I did. Because she was so unselfish, she enabled me to

Barbara, my faithful wife and "backseater" during all of my years *Chasing the Four Winds*. Summer 2009

craft the aviation career you have read about in this book. Babe, I love you so much. Thank you!

Our relationship, like that experienced by most married couples, has witnessed tough times and stormy seas. But we always managed to patch things up and move forward. We jokingly tell people that, being the great procrastinators that we are, we never got around to filing for divorce. Actually, our love and respect for each other has gotten stronger with the passage of time.

When she gets under my skin, I remind her who won the war—the war being the Civil War and she being from the Deep South. She, on the other hand, likes to quote the famous Confederate raider, John Singleton Mosby, who jokingly said after the war, "The quickest way for Southern people to get even with the Yankees, is to marry them."

Final Thoughts

After reading about all of the close calls I've had during my fifty-three-year flying career, you will have to agree that I have lived a charmed life; that I've been extraordinarily lucky! A few times skill and experience made the difference, but mostly good old-fashioned luck saved the day. Many of my friends and fellow pilots were not so lucky.

Back in 1984, I was teaching a private pilot ground school two nights a week as part of an adult education program. Throughout the course I would attempt to drive home the seriousness of a particular point by saying, "If you do this, you will kill yourself," or "If you do this, you'll end up in a crash." About half-way through the semester, after I had just made one of these ominous predictions, a middle-aged lady raised her hand and said, "Do you know what your body count is?" I was perplexed. "What do you mean body count?" I asked. She replied, "Every time you said 'you will kill yourself if you do this or that,' I made a notation in my notes. Your body count is 37." Everyone had a good laugh, including me. Because Lady Luck was always smiling on me, I didn't add my carcass to the *body count*.

When my good friend and World War II Marine Corps aviator, Dr. Ted Cline, died in June 2004, his family crafted a simple program that was handed out at his memorial service. On the back cover was a photo of Ted's beloved Cessna 180 flying just above the clouds. The caption said it all: "It's been a great ride." I wish to adopt that same mantra.

As I enter the winter of my life, I am sustained by the great memories I have shared with you in this book. I hope that you have indulged in some vicarious pleasure as you rode along with me and that you will agree that it has indeed been *a great ride*! If you are a pilot (there is no such thing as a former pilot), I salute you. If you are an aspiring pilot, I envy you. As I have said many times, I would not like to relive my life, but, on the other hand, I do not regret for one moment that I became an aviator. As Jimmy Doolittle once said, "I could never be so lucky again."

As I ponder my passing from this life—the day when everyone associated with the photograph I took of my three young, pilot comrades in Vietnam will be gone—I wonder how it will happen. My longtime barber in Traverse City, Mark Beeman, who died at the age of eighty-seven shortly after hanging up his clippers, crossed over the river in grand fashion. A visitor to his hospital room found him sitting in a chair by the window bathed in sunlight, even before the hospital staff knew he was gone. I may not die as peacefully as he did, but I do hope it is a good day for flying!

Appendix

MIKE STOCK

FLIGHT HOURS

Total:	15,319
Command:	11,804
Multiengine:	5,133
Turbojet:	1,918 (1,750 B737)
Turboprop:	1,259 (629 Twin Otter; 459 King Air)
Helicopter:	3,957 (3,263 turbine)
Seaplane:	2,254
Instructor:	4,842

FAA CERTIFICATES AND RATINGS

Airline Transport Pilot:	AMEL, B737
Commercial Privileges:	ASEL, ASES, AMES, Helicopter, Glider, DC-3, SK-58
Instrument Ratings:	Airplane and Helicopter
Flight Instructor:	SE, ME, Helicopter, Glider, Instrument Airplane and Helicopter
Mechanic:	Airframe and Powerplant

EDUCATION

Masters Aviation Management—Embry-Riddle Aeronautical University
Bachelor of Science—University of West Florida
Test Pilot Course—U.S. Naval Test Pilot School

Speaking Engagements

Mike Stock is available to participate in events in a variety of ways—from being the keynote speaker at small, private functions; to participating in a conference on a panel or as a featured speaker; to offering educational and motivational workshops—for businesses, associations, and schools and universities.

Please contact Mike directly at seawolf620@yahoo.com to discuss the needs and requirements of your group or event. Popular presentations include:

- The Crash of the World's Largest Aircraft: A Survivor's Perspective
- Flying Navy Helicopter Gunships in Vietnam
- Flying Floatplanes in Alaska
- Humorous and Bizarre Stories from a 45-Year Professional Flying Career
- The Top Five Priorities to Sustain Life When You Lose Your Binky
- Coping with Engine Failure in Single-Engine Airplanes

Lightning Source UK Ltd.
Milton Keynes UK
UKHW020210171221
395755UK00005B/378